MRT

OECD Reviews of Regulatory Reform

REGULATORY REFORM IN JAPAN

ORGANISATION FOR ECONOMIC CO-OPERATION AND DEVELOPMENT

ORGANISATION FOR ECONOMIC CO-OPERATION AND DEVELOPMENT

Pursuant to Article 1 of the Convention signed in Paris on 14th December 1960, and which came into force on 30th September 1961, the Organisation for Economic Co-operation and Development (OECD) shall promote policies designed:

- to achieve the highest sustainable economic growth and employment and a rising standard of living in Member countries, while maintaining financial stability, and thus to contribute to the development of the world economy;
- to contribute to sound economic expansion in Member as well as non-member countries in the process of economic development; and
- to contribute to the expansion of world trade on a multilateral, non-discriminatory basis in accordance with international obligations.

The original Member countries of the OECD are Austria, Belgium, Canada, Denmark, France, Germany, Greece, Iceland, Ireland, Italy, Luxembourg, the Netherlands, Norway, Portugal, Spain, Sweden, Switzerland, Turkey, the United Kingdom and the United States. The following countries became Members subsequently through accession at the dates indicated hereafter: Japan (28th April 1964), Finland (28th January 1969), Australia (7th June 1971), New Zealand (29th May 1973), Mexico (18th May 1994), the Czech Republic (21st December 1995), Hungary (7th May 1996), Poland (22nd November 1996) and Korea (12th December 1996). The Commission of the European Communities takes part in the work of the OECD (Article 13 of the OECD Convention).

Publié également en français
LA RÉFORME DE LA RÉGLEMENTATION AU JAPON

© OECD 1999

Permission to reproduce a portion of this work for non-commercial purposes or classroom use should be obtained through the Centre français d'exploitation du droit de copie (CFC), 20, rue des Grands-Augustins, 75006 Paris, France, Tel. (33-1) 44 07 47 70, Fax (33-1) 46 34 67 19, for every country except the United States. In the United States permission should be obtained through the Copyright Clearance Center, Customer Service, (508)750-8400, 222 Rosewood Drive, Danvers, MA 01923 USA, or CCC Online: http://www.copyright.com/. All other applications for permission to reproduce or translate all or part of this book should be made to OECD Publications. 2. rue André-Pascal. 75775 Paris Cedex 16. France.

HD
3616
.J33
R448
1999

FOREWORD

The OECD Review of Regulatory Reform in Japan is among the first of a series of country reports carried out under the OECD's Regulatory Reform Programme, launched in 1998 in response to a mandate by OECD Ministers.

The Regulatory Reform Programme is aimed at helping governments improve regulatory quality – that is, reforming regulations which raise unnecessary obstacles to competition, innovation and growth, while ensuring that regulations efficiently serve important social objectives.

The Programme is part of a broader effort at the OECD to support sustained economic development, job creation and good governance. It fits with other initiatives such as our annual country economic surveys; the Jobs Strategy; the OECD Principles of Corporate Governance; and the fight against corruption, hard-core cartels and harmful tax competition.

Drawing on the analysis and recommendations of good regulatory practices contained in the 1997 OECD *Report to Ministers on Regulatory Reform*, the Regulatory Reform Programme is a multi-disciplinary process of in-depth country reviews, based on self-assessment and on peer evaluation by several OECD committees and members of the International Energy Agency (IEA).

The country Reviews are not comprehensive, but, rather, targeted at key reform areas. Each Review has the same structure, including three thematic chapters on the quality of regulatory institutions and government processes; competition policy and enforcement; and the enhancement of market openness through regulatory reform. Each Review also contains chapters on sectors such as electricity and telecommunications, and an assessment of the macroeconomic context for reform in the country under review.

The country Reviews benefited from a process of extensive consultations with a wide range of government officials (including elected officials) from the country reviewed, business and trade union representatives, consumer groups, and academic experts from many backgrounds.

These Reviews demonstrate clearly that in many areas, a well-structured and implemented programme of regulatory reform has brought lower prices and more choice for consumers, helped stimulate innovation, investment, and new industries, and thereby aided in boosting economic growth and overall job creation. Comprehensive regulatory reforms have produced results more quickly than piece-meal approaches; and such reforms over the longer-term helped countries to adjust more quickly and easily to changing circumstances and external shocks. At the same time, a balanced reform programme must take into account important social concerns. Adjustment costs in some sectors have been painful, although experience shows that these costs can be reduced if reform is accompanied by supportive policies, including active labour market policies, to cushion adjustment.

While reducing and reforming regulations is a key element of a broad programme of regulatory reform, country experience also shows that in a more competitive and efficient market, new regulations and institutions are sometimes necessary to assure that private anticompetitive behaviour does not delay or block the benefits of reform and that health, environmental and consumer protection is assured. In countries pursuing reform, which is often difficult and opposed by vested interests, sustained and consistent political leadership is an essential element of successful reform efforts, and transparent and informed public dialogue on the benefits and costs of reform is necessary for building and maintaining broad public support for reform.

OECD 1999

The policy options presented in the Reviews may pose challenges for each country concerned, but they do not ignore wide differences between national cultures, legal and institutional traditions and economic circumstances. The in-depth nature of the Reviews and the efforts made to consult with a wide range of stakeholders reflect the emphasis placed by the OECD on ensuring that the policy options presented are relevant and attainable within the specific context and policy priorities of each country reviewed.

The OECD *Reviews of Regulatory Reform* are published under the responsibility of the Secretary-General of the OECD, but their policy options and accompanying analysis reflect input and commentary provided during peer review by all 29 OECD Member countries and the European Commission and during consultations with other interested parties.

The Secretariat would like to express its gratitude for the support of the Government of Japan for the OECD Regulatory Reform Programme and its consistent co-operation during the review process. It also would like to thank the many OECD committee and country delegates, representatives from the OECD's Trade Union Advisory Committee (TUAC) and Business and Industry Advisory Committee (BIAC), and other experts whose comments and suggestions were essential to this report.

ACKNOWLEDGEMENTS

This series of Reviews of Regulatory Reform in OECD countries was prepared under the direction of Deputy Secretary-General Joanna R. Shelton. The Review of Japan reflects contributions from many sources, including the Government of Japan, Committees of the OECD and the IEA, representatives of member governments, and members of the Business and Industry Advisory Committee (BIAC) and the Trade Union Advisory Committee (TUAC), as well as other groups. This report was peer reviewed in March 1999 in the OECD's Ad hoc Multidisciplinary Group on Regulatory Reform.

In the OECD Secretariat, the following people contributed substantially to the review of Japan: **Head of Programme and lead drafter**: Scott H. Jacobs; **Document preparation**: Jennifer Stein; **Economics Department**: Chapter I was principally prepared by Richard Kohl, and benefited from work by Giuseppe Nicoletti on regulatory indicators; **Public Management Service**: Rex Deighton-Smith; **Trade Directorate**: Akira Kawamoto, DoHoon Kim, Anthony Kleitz; **Directorate for Financial, Fiscal and Enterprise Affairs**: Patricia Heriard-Dubreuil, Patrick Hughes, Bernard J. Phillips, Sally Van Siclen, Michael Wise; **Directorate for Science, Technology, and Industry**: Wonki Min, Dimitri Ypsilanti; **General Secretariat**: Pierre Poret. In the **International Energy Agency**: John Cameron, Peter Fraser.

TABLE OF CONTENTS

Part I

Tables

Figures

Annex Figures

Boxes

Part II

Part I

OECD REVIEW
OF REGULATORY REFORM
IN JAPAN

EXECUTIVE SUMMARY

Regulatory reform has been prominent on Japan's political agenda since the Hosokawa government promoted deregulation as key to economic recovery in 1994, and has been a central element in the broad economic structural reform programme underway since December 1996. The goals of regulatory reform are ambitious: to complete the move from a model of *state-led* growth – in which interventionist styles of regulation were used for decades to manage high economic growth, carry out deep structural reform, and promote producer interests – to a model of *market-led* growth characterized by a more efficient and flexible economy in which the role of the government is diminished. The government has described such a society as one in which personal choice and initiative increase, consumer interests take higher priority, structural change is driven by market pressures, and domestic markets are more open to international competition.

Sustained effort has reduced economic intervention in many sectors, among them, large retail stores, gasoline imports, telecommunications, and financial services, and consumers have already seen significant results. The "Big Bang" proposals in the financial sector are being implemented on schedule, which will assist in restoring the sector to health. Important progress has been made in areas such as increasing the efficiency of pervasive licenses and permits, even though their numbers have increased, by shifting emphasis from *ex ante* approvals to *ex post* monitoring of compliance with general rules. There is slow but steady movement toward more transparent and less discretionary regulatory practices, partly driven by market demands and partly by recognition of the gap between traditional and international practices. The framework for competition policy has been strengthened. Several initiatives underway to promote the use of international standards will help expand trade flows, to the benefit of Japan's consumers. Compared to its predecessors, the 1995-1997 deregulation programme was the most successful yet, capitalising on the strength of a reform-minded prime minister and competitiveness pressures to win commitments to reform in key sectors, and the current 1998-2000 deregulation programme should contribute to the progress achieved.

The challenge today is to deepen and speed up the regulatory transition already underway, while managing its effects on economic and social life so as to sustain and expand political capacities for reform. The need for more rapid progress is urgent. The Japanese economy has stagnated since 1992, and, though the economy rebounded in 1996, it has been in a recession since late 1997 and recovery is still uncertain. Since 1992, in fact, it has had the poorest performance in the G7. While external shocks and cyclical factors have played roles in the current malaise, the most important factor has been structural rigidities resulting from an increasingly outmoded regulatory and institutional framework. In future, the factors that sustained Japanese growth in the past – such as rapid labour force growth – will no longer be present. Without further reform, any economic recovery in Japan will likely be fragile and short-lived, and unemployment will remain high.

This review argues that a sharp break with past regulatory practices is needed. Rapid and forceful action in Japan will help restart growth and contribute to establishing a new basis for sustainable long-term growth. Experiences in other countries show that broad-based regulatory reform, as part of a balanced policy mix, can be effective in stimulating supply and demand. Structural reforms, particularly regulatory reform, stand alongside appropriate fiscal and monetary policy and rapid resolution of the crisis

11

in the financial system as key elements of recovery. Raising Japan's long-term potential growth rate will also help compensate for slower growth of the labour force, and help ameliorate the problems associated with an ageing population.

Building on the cross-cutting reforms included in the current deregulation programme, further reforms are needed on two levels: sectoral reforms and framework conditions.

- Because the benefits of sectoral reform are amplified when competition is vigorous in upstream and downstream sectors, the positive impact to economic performance will be largest when reform is multi-sectoral. Comprehensive, step-by-step sectoral reform plans followed by rapid implementation are needed to open the way for competition in airlines and other transport modes, electricity, telecommunications, land-use, and other areas. Impacts on employment of an ambitious programme are difficult to estimate, since they depend on the larger environment for investment, labour mobility, and other framework conditions, but are likely to be positive over the medium-term.

- Government-wide reforms are needed to improve framework conditions such as administrative transparency, accountability, and adaptability, and competition policy and enforcement. A core problem is lack of adaptability in the public administration. As do some other countries, Japan suffers from a deeply conservative policy process that slows decision-making, discourages open policy debate, encourages clientelism, allows special interests to block needed change, and results in the famous "incrementalism." New incentives, participants, and controls in regulatory reform processes are needed to re-orient old relationships with producer groups, break up information monopolies in the ministries, and reduce wide administrative discretion to regulate "in the public interest".

Chapter 1: *The economic malaise of the 1990s has revealed fundamental structural problems of the Japanese economy and the need for regulatory reform.* From the early 1960s until the early 1990s, Japan experienced the highest growth rates of GDP and exports in the G7, accompanied by very low levels of inflation and unemployment and large external surpluses. By the early 1980s Japan had caught up with other OECD countries in terms of per capita GDP. Despite this strong overall performance, structural problems emerged in the late 1970s, as external conditions changed and the state-led model of economic development became ill suited to the demands of global markets. The economy as a whole and manufacturing exporters in particular began to feel the increasing burden of a highly regulated, high cost and inefficient non-traded goods sector making up a substantial portion of the economy. Around 1990, Japanese asset markets collapsed, and the true costs of underlying structural problems began to emerge. Further buffeted by the crisis in East Asia, the economy fell into a second recession in 1997, with prospects for recovery as yet uncertain. Recognition grew that the problems in the economy are deeply embedded in domestic market structures, and that Japan faces the prospect of prolonged economic stagnation and persistently high unemployment. Structural reform should no longer be delayed.

Chapter 2. *Japan's regulatory governance system has proved to be poorly suited to a modern market economy, and unable to respond quickly enough to the needs of Japanese society.* The capable and powerful Japanese public administration helped lead a process of extraordinary growth, but the lack of a coherent concept of the role of the state in a period of market-led growth has left regulatory intervention fragmented, incoherent, and vulnerable to a host of special interests. Pragmatic incrementalism has tended to become policy rigidity. The top priorities for government reform are improving adaptability, transparency, and accountability. These changes require fundamental reforms in work methods, incentives, and institutions inside the public administration, and in its relations to the market. Current initiatives, such as adoption of public comment procedures and restructuring of the Japanese bureaucracy through the Basic Law on the Administrative Reform of the Central Government, offer good opportunities to build new regulatory capacities and incentives in the public sector.

Chapter 3. *The move to market-led growth implies that competition principles must be at the heart of the emerging new regulatory doctrine in Japan, a sharp break from traditional interventionist practices.* As regulatory reform stimulates structural change, vigorous enforcement of competition policy is needed more than ever to prevent private market abuses from reversing the benefits of reform. Japan's Fair Trade Commission, one of the oldest and largest competition law agencies in the world, wields a wide array of substantive and procedural tools, but it has not always used those tools aggressively enough. Since 1990, the FTC's resources have increased and competition enforcement has intensified. More important, FTC increasingly applies modern concepts of competition. Supplemented with improved administrative transparency and other reforms to further enhance effectiveness, these changes position the FTC to play an indispensable role in the transition to a more dynamic market economy.

Chapter 4. *Japanese consumers are losing substantial wealth, and Japanese businesses are losing competitiveness, because of the higher prices they pay compared to citizens in other OECD countries, which are mainly due to market access problems.* Recognising the benefits from the integration in the open multilateral trading system, Japan has improved market access in border measures to a level equal to or better than many OECD countries. The benefits to Japan of these steps are, however, limited by many "behind the border" regulatory barriers. Regulatory barriers are also contributing to very low levels of foreign investment in Japan, which did not even place among the top 25 countries with respect to FDI inflows, though Japan's economy is the second largest in the world. Lack of transparency in Japan's regulatory and administrative procedures has discouraged foreign traders and investors. Unnecessary trade restrictiveness is a continuing problem due to unsupervised administrative discretion in setting and applying standards and regulations. Complaints persist, but the government is now promoting use of international standards and recognition of foreign regulatory measures. While trade pressures have been helpful in promoting regulatory reform, reform should in future focus on domestic benefits and comprehensive change, rather than on specific trade frictions.

Chapter 5. *The benefits and risks of further competition and consumer choice, and the need to balance multiple economic and social policy goals within a comprehensive policy framework, are illustrated in the reforms currently underway in the electricity sector.* The government has set a target to reduce electricity prices (the highest in the OECD) to internationally comparable levels by 2001, an ambitious target, while balancing energy security, economic growth, and environmental protection in the reform programme. The sector is highly regulated by the Ministry of International Trade and Industry, based on "public interest" and "demand-supply balancing" concepts common in Japan. Opening of tenders for generation revealed the potential for lower costs in generation, and was a good step toward competition. The decision to move forward with partial liberalisation of retail supply is an important and irreversible step for Japan to take towards its goal of international comparability in electricity prices. Many changes in regulation and competition oversight are needed to support a coherent move to market liberalisation. Improved institutions and roles for regulatory and competition policies are needed if investment and competition are to occur. Difficult decisions lie ahead with respect to separation of competitive activities from the transmission grid. A process of change has begun that is a first step toward competition, but after retail liberalisation, performance should be carefully monitored. The government should be prepared to take additional steps if effective competition does not develop.

Chapter 6. *Japan was among the first OECD countries to liberalise the telecommunications sector in the 1980s, but users have not enjoyed full benefits of competition seen in other countries due to too many economic controls, and too few competitive safeguards.* Yet the potential for significant gains to consumers is evident, and Japan has recently taken steps to enhance competition in the sector. Progressive liberalisation of mobile markets has led to significant competition. The rapid growth of cellular mobile services and telephony services based on cable television networks is raising the prospect that these can be an alternative to local fixed voice telephony service. A significant reform is the recent introduction of a tariff notification system, which finally makes price competition possible. While the NTT breakup may bring indirect competition based on quality and price between two regional companies, it is unlikely that there will be facility-based competition because of the holding company structure. In addition, there are outstanding regulatory issues which prevent fair and transparent competition in the marketplace. For example, in reforming the sectoral regulator, it will be important to maintain independence and expertise. Current plans in this respect do not seem adequate.

Conclusions and Policy Options. The major lessons that can be learned from regulatory reform in Japan are:

- *Regulatory reform, if deepened and accelerated, can assist Japan in returning to a sustainable growth path.* Combined with other policy reforms, regulatory reform can help Japan restart growth by boosting consumption and investment and, over the longer-term, enhance the ability of the economy to adapt, grow, and innovate in new sectors.

– A *sharp break with current regulatory practices is needed to construct a state that promotes market-led growth.* Japan's highly-developed state apparatus, created during a more developmental stage of Japanese development, is not functioning well in a mature market economy.

Based on international experience with good regulatory practices, several reforms (further detailed in Chapter 7) are likely to be beneficial to improving regulation in Japan:

– *Sustained strong political support is needed at the highest levels to overcome the vested interests that, in current policy processes, are able to slow or block reform efforts.* One of the strengths of regulatory reform in Japan is that it has enjoyed high levels of political support, but the most difficult reforms lie ahead and require sustained political determination.

– *Regulatory reform should be expanded and accelerated through development of comprehensive sectoral reform plans containing the full set of steps needed to introduce effective competition, followed by rapid implementation and periodic, public evaluation. To maximise positive impacts on economic performance, reforms should proceed simultaneously in key infrastructure and service sectors, and in factor markets.* A multi-sectoral and comprehensive reform programme aimed at introducing full competition will have the greatest and speediest effect in stimulating economic performance and supporting recovery.

– *Investment, market entry, and innovation should be promoted by increasing the transparency and accountability of regulation.* The recent adoption of public comment procedures is a bold and important step forward. A number of other steps would also improve transparency.

– *Current efforts to promote reform by the Deregulation Committee are important to further progress. To accelerate and deepen reform, the Committee's efforts should be strengthened by broadening its mandate beyond regulation, narrowly defined; clarifying its independence from ministries; and boosting its capacities and resources.* The leadership of the Deregulation Committee should be strengthened, as should capacities to safeguard competition principles.

– A *consumer-oriented policy framework of market and competition principles, with efficient regulatory protections, should be strengthened government-wide to guide the use of regulatory powers.* The most important broad-ranging competition-based reform would be the elimination of all remaining "supply-demand balancing" functions that serve to control and prevent pro-competitive entry.

– *More effort is needed to prevent regulatory problems before they occur by strengthening quality control mechanisms for regulatory development inside the administration.*

– *Consumers will benefit from lower prices and more choice, and enterprises will gain from tougher competition and faster innovation, if markets are more fully opened to international trade and investment.*

– *A series of steps are needed in the electricity sector to pave the way for the effective competition that will lower prices.*

– *Much progress is seen in telecommunications, but essential regulatory safeguards – such as number portability, carrier pre-selection, a universal service funding mechanism, an LRIC (Long Run Incremental Cost) accounting system, and a transparent method to select mobile licensees when demand for spectrum resources exceeds supply – should be established to ensure full competition in the marketplace.*

Chapter 1

REGULATORY REFORM IN JAPAN

INTRODUCTION

Regulatory reform has been prominent on Japan's political agenda since the Hosokawa government promoted deregulation as key to economic recovery in 1994, and has been a central element in the broad economic structural reform programme underway since December 1996. The goals of regulatory reform are ambitious: to complete the move from a model of *state-led* growth – in which interventionist styles of regulation were used for decades to manage high economic growth, carry out deep structural reform, and promote producer interests – to a model of *market-led* growth characterized by a more efficient and flexible economy in which the role of the government is diminished. The government has described such a society as one in which personal choice and initiative increase, consumer interests take higher priority, structural change is driven by market pressures, and domestic markets are more open to international competition.[1]

Regulatory reform aims to produce a more competitive and flexible economy in which consumer interests take a higher priority.

Tremendous effort has produced real progress in reducing economic intervention in many sectors, among them, large retail stores, gasoline imports, telecommunications, and financial services. In some cases, consumers have already seen significant results. Less dramatic but important progress has been made in increasing the efficiency of pervasive licenses and permits, though the government has been unable to reduce their numbers. Here, the government is right to shift emphasis from *ex ante* approvals to *ex post* monitoring of compliance with general rules. There is slow but steady movement toward more transparent and less discretionary regulatory practices, partly driven by market demands and partly by recognition of the gap between traditional and international practices. The competition policy framework is stronger. Several initiatives underway to promote the use of international standards will help expand trade flows, to the benefit of Japan's consumers. Compared to its predecessors, the 1995-1997 deregulation program was the most successful yet, capitalizing on the strength of a reform-minded prime minister and competitiveness pressures to win commitments to reform in key sectors and the current 1998-2000 deregulation programme should contribute to the progress achieved.

Tremendous effort has produced real progress in reducing economic intervention in many sectors.

The challenge today is to deepen and speed up reform. Regulatory reform can be a pro-growth strategy to boost investment and demand, and in the longer-term enhance economic flexibility and innovation.

The challenge today is to deepen and speed up the regulatory transition already underway, while managing economic and social effects so as to sustain and expand political capacities for reform. Much is at stake, and the task is urgent. The Japanese economy has stagnated since 1992, and, though the economy rebounded in 1996, it has been in a recession since late 1997 and recovery is still uncertain. Since 1992, in fact, it has had the poorest performance in the G7. Underlying structural problems are a major contributor. Experiences in other countries show that broad-based regulatory reform, as part of a balanced policy mix that includes supportive macroeconomic and labour market policies, can be effective in stimulating both supply and demand. A regulatory framework that encourages efficiency and market-driven restructuring can help Japan to restart growth by boosting consumption and investment, and, over the longer-term, enhance the ability of the economy to adapt, grow, and innovate in new sectors.

A sharp break with past regulatory practices is needed. Recent regulatory reforms are too episodic, slow, and incomplete to contribute significantly to economic recovery.

This review argues that, to establish such a framework, a sharp break with past regulatory practices is needed. The regulatory reforms of the past five years are important steps which led to substantial gains. In aggregate, however, regulatory reform has been too episodic, slow, and incomplete to contribute significantly to economic recovery, much less provide a basis for long-term market-led growth. Excessive state intervention in many forms still distorts and blocks market functioning in important sectors, while insufficient regulation to protect competition and consumer interests is seen in sectors such as telecommunications and electricity. Fundamental and simultaneous reforms to policies, public sector and market institutions, and administrative practices are needed across a range of policies and sectors, accelerating reforms already underway. Strong political leadership will be essential to further progress.

The status quo is not sustainable, since widening gaps between market needs and regulatory rigidities will erode Japan's capacities to recover.

Failure to move decisively from state-led to market-led growth will prolong the slump, reduce long-term potential growth, and erode Japanese competitiveness in global markets, while continuing to damage regional and global performance. The *status quo* is not sustainable. The growing gap between market opportunities and regulatory rigidities will weaken domestic competitive forces, slow healthy restructuring, and contribute to chronic misallocation of resources throughout the Japanese economy. These effects reduce the wealth and choice of Japanese citizens and undercut Japan's long-term capacity to maintain living standards, particularly when the aging of the population requires that resources be put to higher value uses.

Reforms are needed both to sector-specific policies, and to improve framework conditions in the public administration and competition policy.

Deeper reforms are needed on two levels: sectoral reforms and framework conditions:

– Because the benefits of sectoral reform are amplified when competition is vigorous in upstream and downstream sectors, the positive impact to economic performance will be largest when reform is multi-sectoral. Comprehensive, step-by-step sectoral reform plans followed by rapid implementation are needed to open the way for competition in airlines and other transport modes, electricity, telecommunications, land-use,

and other areas. Impacts on employment are difficult to estimate, since they depend on the larger environment for investment, labour mobility, active labour market policies, and other
framework conditions. In other countries, employment effects
have been, on net, positive, with job losses in some areas offset by new jobs in others. Comprehensive reforms to speed
up reallocation of labour will reduce these transition costs.

– Government-wide reforms are needed to improve framework
conditions such as administrative transparency, accountability,
and adaptability, and competition policy and enforcement. A
core problem is lack of adaptability in the public administration. Like some other countries, Japan suffers from a deeply
conservative policy process that slows decision-making, discourages open policy debate, encourages clientelism, allows
special interests to block needed change, and results in the
famous "incrementalism". New incentives, participants, and
controls in regulatory reform processes are needed to re-orient
old relationships with producer groups, break up information
monopolies in the ministries, and reduce wide administrative
discretion to regulate "in the public interest".

Box 1.1.   What is regulation and regulatory reform?

There is no generally accepted definition of regulation applicable to the very different regulatory systems in OECD countries. In the OECD work, **regulation** refers to the diverse set of instruments by which governments set requirements on enterprises and citizens. Regulations include laws, formal and informal
orders and subordinate rules issued by all levels of government, and rules issued by non-governmental or
self-regulatory bodies to whom governments have delegated regulatory powers. Regulations fall into three
categories:

* **Economic regulations** intervene directly in market decisions such as pricing, competition, market entry, or exit. Reform aims to increase economic efficiency by reducing barriers to competition and innovation, often through deregulation and use of efficiency-promoting regulation, and by improving
regulatory frameworks for market functioning and prudential oversight.

* **Social regulations** protect public interests such as health, safety, the environment, and social cohesion. The economic effects of social regulations may be secondary concerns or even unexpected, but
can be substantial. Reform aims to verify that regulation is needed, and to design regulatory and other instruments, such as market incentives and goal-based approaches, that are more flexible, simpler, and more effective at lower cost.

* **Administrative regulations** are paperwork and administrative formalities – so-called "red tape"
– through which governments collect information and intervene in individual economic decisions.
They can have substantial impacts on private sector performance. Reform aims at eliminating those
no longer needed, streamlining and simplifying those that are needed, and improving the transparency of application.

Regulatory reform is used in the OECD work to refer to changes that improve regulatory quality, that
is, enhance the performance, cost-effectiveness, or legal quality of regulations and related government formalities. Reform can mean revision of a single regulation, the scrapping and rebuilding of an entire regulatory regime and its institutions, or improvement of processes for making regulations and managing reform.
Deregulation is a subset of regulatory reform and refers to complete or partial elimination of regulation in
a sector to improve economic performance.

Source: The OECD Report on Regulatory Reform (1997).

A new doctrine for the use of regulation in a market economy is needed to guide reform and development of new regulations in the future

A determined and systematic program to root out regulations that interfere with competition is necessary...

One notion of regulatory reform often heard in Japan is based in the link between deregulation and smaller government. Japan's current administrative reform program aims to streamline ministries and reduce the number of national non-defense public employees by 25 per cent in ten years. It is undeniable that the key to successful regulatory reform lies partly in eliminating many specific regulations and administrative interventions. A determined and systematic program to root out regulations and administrative functions that interfere with competition is necessary as one element of a broader program.

But too much focus on the size of government, rather than its role, can divert reform efforts without addressing underlying problems, and can block creation of new institutions and capacities needed for efficient regulation. Small governments can regulate as badly as large ones. And cost cutting, unless it is based on clear principles of the role of the state, can increase incentives to regulate in order to shift costs from public to private sectors.

... but regulatory reform should also aim to establish the basis for flexible and high-quality regulatory regimes that protect public interests in competitive markets.

Regulatory reform should aim to establish the basis for flexible and high-quality regulatory regimes that protect public interests in competitive markets. Radical and comprehensive deregulation is needed, but this by itself is insufficient because necessary market institutions are not yet in place. In many areas, such as prudential oversight of the financial sector, consumer protection, and environmental protection, cost-effective and market-oriented regulations are also needed, though these kinds of regulations must be both necessary and cost-effective to avoid eroding the benefits of economic reforms. Activist competition institutions are needed to encourage the move from cartels to competition, combined with market openness policies to increase competitive pressures and bring Japanese industries up to world standards. Such a balanced view of regulatory reform needs to be emphasized in current reform efforts in Japan to speed up market-led growth and to reduce risks of painful policy failures.

THE MACROECONOMIC CONTEXT FOR REGULATORY REFORM

From the early 1960s until the early 1990s, Japan experienced the highest growth rates of GDP and exports in the G7.

As is often the case with policy failures, the roots of regulatory failure in Japan lie in past successes. From the early 1960s until the early 1990s, Japan experienced the highest growth rates of GDP and exports in the G7, accompanied by very low levels of inflation and unemployment and large external trade surpluses. This strong performance was based on rapid labour force growth and high levels of public and private sector investment, allowing Japan to steadily improve its competitiveness in existing sectors, gaining world market share and to move into higher value-added sectors. This performance continued through the 1970s and early 1980s as Japan adapted more successfully than most other OECD countries to the oil shocks of the 1970s. By the early 1980s Japan had caught up with other OECD countries as measured by per capita GDP.

Despite this strong overall performance, structural problems emerged in the late 1970s. Fiscal deficits ballooned as the government attempted to sustain growth with large public investment packages. The very success of Japanese exports brought with it increasing difficulties by stimulating increased protectionism by its trading partners, and a tendency for exchange rate appreciation. The economy as a whole and manufacturing exporters in particular began to feel the increasing burden of a highly regulated, high cost and inefficient non-traded goods sector making up a substantial portion of the economy. Japanese exporters were able to overcome these obstacles during the 1980s by high levels of investment, but more and more resorted to transferring production overseas. Between 1985 and 1989 Japanese foreign direct investment totaled nearly $200 billion and the share of Japanese manufacturing output produced overseas doubled, reaching double-digits in key sectors like motor vehicles and consumer electronics, and nearly doubled again between 1991 and 1997 as FDI shifted towards Southeast Asia.[2]

Nonetheless strong investment, spurred by low interest rates, resulted in rapid GDP growth and booming asset prices that dramatically increased Japanese income and wealth. This strong domestic performance restored fiscal balance and undercut motivations to confront structural problems of high domestic costs, stagnating exports, and increasing overinvestment in real and financial assets.

Around 1990, Japanese asset markets collapsed, and the true costs of underlying structural problems began to emerge. Under the weight of asset price deflation and credit contraction, GDP and export growth stagnated and Japan's share of export markets declined further. Unemployment increased steadily in an economy where it had been largely unknown for decades. A series of fiscal stimulus packages and low interest rates failed to rekindle expansion, let alone return the economy to a sustainable long-term growth path. A brief strong recovery in 1996 faltered in part due to fiscal tightening, and, further buffeted by the crisis in East Asia, the economy fell into recession. In early 1999, the situation remains uncertain.

Around 1990, Japanese asset markets collapsed, and the true costs of underlying structural problems began to emerge.

Recognition grew that the problems in the Japanese economy were not purely macroeconomic or a result of external shocks, but were deeply embedded in domestic structures. Structural reform was necessary and could no longer be delayed.

Structural reform was necessary and could no longer be delayed.

To help Japan catch up to more developed OECD countries, post-war industrial policy combined government interventions with targeted competition in traded goods sectors

Following post-war reconstruction, Japanese economic policy focused on catching up to the economic performance levels of wealthier countries. Its strategy was to create an internationally competitive manufacturing sector through high levels of savings and investment capable of moving from low to high value-added sectors.

19

This was believed to require extensive state intervention in the economy.

State intervention during the catch-up phase had several components.

State intervention had several components. Industrial policy aimed at guiding resource allocation ("state-led development") into higher value-added sectors and correcting market failures or solving co-ordination problems in areas such as technology acquisition. Influence over investment decisions was effected through extensive administrative guidance[3] and coordination in areas such as research and development, since direct state ownership was largely confined to infrastructure.[4] Public and highly-regulated private institutions replaced missing market institutions in such areas as finance where they were used to generate high savings rates and allocate savings into investment (see Box 1.3). Government ownership and regulation of key infrastructure sectors were geared to providing world-class supply for export industries.

Non-traded goods sectors were characterized by extensive regulation and limited competition

Unlike manufacturing, where an interventionist policy was complemented by domestic competition and exposure to export markets, competition played little role in non-traded goods. Most infrastructure sectors like transportation, energy, and telecommunications were regulated monopolies and oligopolies with controls on entry and pricing, with some major firms state-owned. Investment by the government was substantial and concentrated in transportation. Government investment was the highest of any G7 country and grew the most rapidly as infrastructure capacities tried to keep pace with rapid economic growth. Cartels were active in many sectors, and were especially widespread in non-traded goods sectors like construction and distribution. Construction, land use and housing were highly regulated by a complex system of zoning restrictions, tenants' rights and technical standards. Zoning, intended to promote rational land use and maintain farmland, in combination with import barriers had the effect of providing strong protection for agriculture, particularly small farmers. Limits on large stores were used to protect small businesses.

Financial institutions mobilized savings to support high levels of investment.

Similarly, financial institutions were created to mobilize savings to support the necessary high levels of investment – price or cost were not relevant. The state set up highly segmented financial institutions, such as long-term credit banks and the main bank system to channel savings at low cost to industrial borrowers in strategic sectors (Box 1.3). This resulted in a special system of corporate finance and governance characterized by minimal reliance on equity investment, extensive cross-ownership, and very high debt ratios, particularly bank debt, which permitted firms to focus on expanding sales and market share instead of maximizing rates of return.[5] This financial structure meant that corporate governance was dominated by managers influenced by administrative guidance from ministries.[6]

Performance was outstanding, with high growth rates of exports and GDP, low unemployment and large current account surpluses.

The causes of Japanese success are widely debated, particularly the role of state intervention and Japanese industrial policy,[7] but the results are clear: economic performance in the 1961-73 period was outstanding by any measure. Real GDP growth was more than double the average of the other G7 countries (see Annex, Figure 1.1) and annual growth in manufacturing export volumes was extremely rapid (Annex, Figure 1.2) so that the Japanese share of G7 exports rose steadily (Annex, Figure 1.3). Unemployment was under two per cent for the entire period.[8] Emphasis on savings and investment, however, meant that consumption levels and growth were suppressed relative to those in other countries.[9]

Sustaining growth became a major concern with the oil crisis, but extraordinary flexibility in traded goods sectors kept Japan in the lead

Japan suffered from a deterioration in economic performance during and after the oil shocks of the 1970s, as did most other OECD countries.[10] Despite the slowdown in performance and substantial yen appreciation (the effective exchange rate appreciated by 47 per cent from 1973-1980), Japan continued to outperform other G7 countries, especially in export performance. By 1980 Japanese per capita GDP and consumption had caught up with most other advanced countries.[11] Its share of G7 exports was double the level of 20 years earlier (Annex, Figure 1.2) and had shifted into higher value-added exports like motor vehicles and consumer electronics.

Growth slowed in the 1970s relative to the 1960s but performance remained the best among the G7 as Japan adjusted faster than most other countries.

Japan's superior performance was largely attributable to greater flexibility in supply response in the traded goods sector. In structurally depressed sectors, capacity was quickly reduced or converted to new uses. In shipbuilding, construction of traditional tankers was replaced with more sophisticated types of ships, and machinery was converted to completely new uses, *e.g.* fabrication of heavy machinery. In many sectors, investments targeted improving energy and raw material efficiency. Continuous casting was rapidly introduced in the steel industry and furnace top generators were installed to recover waste gas. Introduction of automation in production accelerated. In automobiles, body welding, machining and stamping were automated through the introduction of welding robots. Between 1978 and 1979, the number of numerically controlled machine tools in Japan doubled.

Japan's superior performance was largely attributable to greater flexibility in supply response in the traded goods sector.

Japanese manufacturing was able to undertake rapid industrial restructuring, cutting costs and improving productivity within sectors, while shifting production and exports from lower value-added sectors to higher value-added sectors. Lifetime employment in the manufacturing sector facilitated this by allowing substantial flexibility in labour inputs and costs (see Box 1.2). Adjustment was complemented by industry policy initiatives to facilitate the shift out of declining sectors,[12] often through restructuring cartels to reduce capacity in declining sectors. The aluminum smelting industry, for example, lost international competitiveness as energy prices rose. In the ten years to 1988, assisted by a program of incentives for adjustment, output from the industry fell by 97 per cent, and employment by 94 per cent (OECD, 1997a). Japanese firms also globalized, establishing extensive servicing and marketing networks as production shifted into consumer durables. Firms subsequently began to locate productive capacity directly in foreign markets.[13]

These adjustments were facilitated by a system of life-time employment, active industrial policy and substantial private sector initiative.

By the 1980s, exports faced increasing obstacles to further growth while expansionary fiscal and monetary policy was constrained, leading to the first movements towards regulatory reform

Early proposals for regulatory reform were driven by domestic concerns about competitiveness, in the face of constraints on monetary and fiscal policy.

Regulatory reform entered the policy arena for the first time in the early 1980s. Domestically, it was driven by concerns over the ability to sustain growth. Exports were limited by both sluggish growth in Japan's major trading partners, and a proliferation of restrictions on Japanese exports, often in the form of "voluntary export restraints" (VERs)[14] in response to Japan's growing trade surpluses, at the same time that further export growth would have to come through increasing market share. Monetary and fiscal policy also faced constraints. Japan's growing external surpluses inhibited the use of stimulative monetary policy: lower interest rates were likely to cause the yen to depreciate and external surpluses to widen further. Stimulative fiscal policy had been used in the late 1970s, resulting in large public sector deficits[15] and rapid accumulation of public debt.[16]

Reform began moving in the 1980s with privatization in key sectors, lowering of conventional trade barriers and launching of financial reform, but state regulatory intervention did not decline.

Over the same period that the export sector had achieved world class status and was distancing itself from administrative guidance by MITI (discussed below), regulation of the non-traded goods sector was growing more rapidly, further limiting competition.[17] In 1980, 53 per cent of value-added was considered by the Japanese Economic Planning Agency (EPA) to be regulated and 23 per cent highly regulated; by 1990, according to the Fair Trade Commission (FTC), 42.3 per cent of value-added was regulated, but 23.6 per cent was

---

Box 1.2.   **The Japanese labour market**

Japan's unique labour market permits a large degree of flexibility in the use of labour inputs and wage setting. The labour market is characterized, at least for large firms in the manufacturing sector, by three components: an implicit contract of lifetime employment, compensation based on seniority and closely linked to company performance, and a co-operative relationship with management geared toward improving company performance.

Japanese firms achieve flexibility in labour inputs by adjusting overtime, adjusting leads and lags in new recruitment and retirement, and making extensive use of temporary and part-time workers. The relatively flat internal wage structure and the conglomerate nature of many of Japan's largest firms permits flexibility to co-exist with lifetime employment through internal transfers from declining to growing parts of the same firm. It also permits substantial flexibility in labour costs and therefore a close relationship between wages to company performance through heavy reliance on annual bonuses and overtime pay so that changes to workers income occur instead unemployment. Thus, in response to the second oil shock, Japanese wage growth decelerated rapidly, allowing profits, and therefore internally financed investment, to bounce back more quickly than in most countries.

The system has a hidden side. Japan's low recorded unemployment rate, particularly in cyclical downturns, understates the true extent of unemployment as the life-time employment system leads to labour hoarding in the face of slack demand. Much of the burden of labour market adjustment is borne by the relatively large pool of part-time and temporary workers in sectors such as retailing and by the employees of small firms engaged in subcontracting. In periods of recession, large firms demand cost and productivity improvements from their smaller suppliers. Employees in smaller firms – about half of total employment – do not have implicit guarantees of life time employment.

highly regulated. For manufacturers, reform was a way to improve competitiveness by reducing the costs of domestic inputs.

In 1981, the Provisional Commission for Administrative Reform was established and subsequently recommended a program of deregulation, particularly of licensing and approval requirements for businesses, which was largely carried out. However, support for far-reaching reform was muted when yen depreciation after 1982 relieved pressures on manufacturing exports and led to a resumption of strong exports and economic growth. In response to external pressures, tariff and non-tariff barriers were lowered. An important measure taken in the early 1980s was financial deregulation, which was strongly supported by Japanese banks facing increased disintermediation (Box 1.3).

The next step was several large privatizations, but by the late 1980s, the economic boom had eroded willingness to confront structural problems

Interest in regulatory reform increased in the mid 1980s when the yen appreciated after 1985 and economic growth slowed. The 1986 OECD *Economic Survey of Japan* observed (pp. 93-94):

Yen appreciation in the mid-1980s again brought regulatory reform onto the political agenda...

> There is now growing recognition in Japan that the export-led growth pattern of the last few years must be replaced by domestic demand expansion... constraints on macroeconomic policies are such that longer-term reforms of the economic and financial framework will have a key role... There is no doubt that in many cases deregulation could not but enhance market mechanisms, improve economic efficiency and release a significant amount of latent demand...

Despite these concerns, reform was limited, focusing mostly on privatization. Except in the area of telecommunications, the principal motivation for privatization was not to promote competition, but to improve the management of public enterprises, reduce their losses,[18] and bring in revenues. In 1985, the government privatized the Nippon Telephone and Telegraph Public Corporation (NTT) and corporatised the state tobacco monopoly, followed in 1987 by privatization of Japan Air Lines and Japan National Railways. The public aim was "to let the market exert its function to the fullest extent" (Tanaka *et. al.*, 1990, preface), but controls on entry and pricing remained in these sectors, including supply-demand balancing constraints (see Table 1.1).[19] Only in telecommunications markets was sufficient entry allowed to introduce competition.

In the 1985-91 period, Japan enjoyed the highest growth rates in the G7 except for post-reunification Germany (Annex, Figure 1.1). Growth occurred despite a decline in export growth as the exchange rate appreciated sharply beginning in 1985. Exchange appreciation permitted the Bank of Japan to ease interest rates, stimulating a boom in investment and asset prices. Housing, land and stock prices soared. Consumption grew rapidly as yen appreciation caused real incomes to rise, reinforced by increasing consumer wealth. Higher growth rates meant the budget swung into surplus in 1986 and remained there until the 1992 recession.[20] Interest in regulatory

... but the opportunity was missed, and domestic support for reform faded with the boom of 1987-91.

reform evaporated as two major drivers of reform – the need for fiscal consolidation and to shift toward domestic sources of demand – disappeared.

Reforms that did occur were in response to foreign pressures. Progress had been made on lowering tariff barriers (TBs) and eliminating traditional non-tariff barriers (NTBs), and by the end of the decade, Japanese TBs and NTBs were among the lowest in the G7

Box 1.3. Regulatory reform in the financial sector in Japan

The Japanese financial system of the 1960s and 1970s was highly segmented and specialized, with essentially no competition. Competition between different types of institutions was prohibited by strict segmentation and competition from foreign institutions effectively prevented by limits on foreign exchange transactions. Even among similar institutions competition was non-existent: under the so-called "convoy system", policy assured that new products were introduced only after a long lead time and when all institutions in the same category were ready to introduce them. Excess returns were essentially guaranteed thanks to price controls on deposits and other liabilities which provided a stable supply of low cost funds. On the lending side, credit risk was non-existent as many loans benefited from implicit or explicit government guarantees: much bank lending was "guided" by various ministries towards strategic industries or, in the case of the Postal Savings system, transferred directly to public financial institutions to be used for infrastructure investment. As a result, banks did not develop the ability or the information infrastructure to evaluate the creditworthiness of borrowers and projects, relying instead on official guidance, long-term relationships, and the value of collateral. The same was true for the prudential supervisory system; regulators were more concerned with allocating credit through administrative guidance than with evaluating the soundness of bank balance sheets.

Deregulation of the Japanese financial sector began in the early 1980s. Japanese banks had begun losing their major clients, large manufacturers, first to domestic securities markets, and then to foreign firms after the relaxation of foreign exchange controls in 1980 and the increasing globalisation of Japanese manufacturers. Some opening to foreign competition and decontrol of interest rates on some instruments in the 1980s eliminated most restrictions on large denomination instruments.

These partial reforms were unsuccessful in enabling the banking sector to keep pace with global financial innovation and to maintain profits. In the late 1980s, as asset prices rose, banks began financing real estate development, construction projects, and equities investments, as well as previously uncreditworthy small enterprises whose balance sheets had improved with rising asset prices. When asset prices collapsed in 1990-91, the value of collateral on many bank loans declined precipitously as did the value of banks'own substantial securities holdings, leading to a sharp increase in non-performing loans and massive losses. Similar problems arose for most securities firms.

The crisis revealed a number of weaknesses in financial practices and problems in financial sector regulation. Securities firms had employed a number of highly questionable financial practices, including the payment of compensation to large investors for stock market losses. In banking, the consensus-based system of credit allocation, part of the convoy system, and the government's strong directive role in credit decisions, created serious moral hazard problems. Banks assumed that the government would rescue them in the event of serious financial difficulties.

Delays in resolving the crisis illustrated the problems with the use of administrative guidance. Until recently, it was an unstated policy of the government never to allow banks to fail. Regulators kept insolvent institutions afloat by lack of disclosure and delays in the recognition of capital losses, and arranged for healthy institutions to lend to or absorb failing ones (another manifestation of the convoy system). This policy encouraged banks to continue lending without regard to credit risk, and gave banks little incentive to recognize bad loans or pursue problem borrowers. When these policies were abandoned in 1997, allowing several institutions to fail, the lack of disclosure meant that financial markets were unable to distinguish between viable and non-viable banks, increasing the cost of borrowing for all banks (the "Japan premium" charged Japanese banks in international lending). Since then, market confidence has been repeatedly shaken as disclosures reveal the size of bad loans and the widening circle of institutions involved. New sources of worry are the soundness of Postal Savings system investments in the government's infrastructure fund, the *zaito*, which has financed low-value public investment projects as part of the ongoing series of fiscal stimulus packages, and the extent of bad debts among public sector lenders.

Box 1.3. **Regulatory reform in the financial sector in Japan** (*cont.*)

Since the collapse of the asset bubble, financial sector reform has had three goals.

First, creation of an institutional and regulatory framework is aimed at establishing the basis for a sound and dynamic financial system. The segmented and highly regulated financial system contributed heavily to the bad debt problem. Regulatory barriers inhibited competition and prevented financial institutions from keeping up with the rapid pace of world financial innovation and improvements in productivity. It was widely recognized that the financial sector was poorly allocating capital. During the 1990s, reform proceeded in a slow, piecemeal fashion, effectively amplifying these problems. In 1996, the government initiated a comprehensive reform package known as the "Big Bang". Complete implementation by the year 2000 will achieve full deregulation (within prudential limits) of controls on entry, pricing, commissions and the creation of new products. Banks, insurance companies, and securities firms will have complete freedom to enter into each others'line of business.

Second, resolving the bad debt problem was aimed at removing this source of deflationary pressures on the economy. Action was long-delayed by the mistaken belief that asset prices would revive and by close ties between the Finance Ministry and the industry. These delays have substantially raised the cost of any ultimate resolution as the system was kept afloat by continued lending from healthy institutions to weakened ones under implicit government guarantees, while at the same time increasing the potential problem by undermining the solvency of more and more institutions. New legislation adopted in 1998 established a system to deal with failed financial institutions. The most important is the Financial Revitalisation Commission (FRC), which is authorized to deal with failures of financial institutions, either by appointing administrators to manage failed institutions, or through *de facto* nationalization via compulsory acquisition of the shares of the institutions by the Deposit Insurance Corporation (DIC). This has been complemented by government guarantees to the DIC to be used to carry out financial revitalization activities such as equity injections.

The new legislation is comprehensive but questions abound on how it will be implemented. A poor precedent was set in 1998 when full implementation of the plan for tightening accounting and capital standards was delayed for some institutions and banks were allowed to value their equity holdings at historical costs. Debates continue over how big the problem is, who will pay, which institutions will be closed, the terms for financial assistance to weakened institutions, and the transparency.

Estimates of the size of the bad debt problem continue to grow, and is bigger than banks have been forced to provision for. The ¥ 60 trillion fund proposed by the government in autumn 1998 may be inadequate, and questions remain as to whether conditionality will be tough enough to provide incentives for banks to forgive loans, maximize collections or force bankruptcy. Similar questions arise about the willingness of the authorities to rely on market forces in restructuring. In the case of non-viable banks, the current system allows substantial use of direct public administration, *de facto* nationalization. Experience in other countries suggests that insolvent institutions need to be either sold in arms-length transactions or their assets liquidated promptly, whichever is the least cost method. Trying to save non-viable institutions by forcing mergers or placing them under public administration requires managerial capabilities which are lacking in most public administrations. There are concerns that forcing public recognition of the full extent of the problem will further undermine confidence and increase the credit crunch. Experience from other countries has shown that confidence is most rapidly restored by transparency.

Experience has shown that well-functioning capital markets can effectively restructure and recapitalise the industry. This highlights the need for thorough and rapid implementation of the Big Bang reforms, which are currently being implemented on schedule. The authorities should be open to increased foreign presence in the financial sector. Foreign institutions can bring not only capital but valuable management and credit evaluation skills that can greatly reduce the duration of industry restructuring. Parallel regulatory reforms in real estate markets would lead to more liquid asset markets, and reforms in the legal and bankruptcy system would allow for collection of problem loans.

Third, well-functioning capital markets can be sustained only in the context of appropriate prudential supervision. In 1998, a new Financial Supervisory Agency was created as an independent body, removed from control of the Finance Ministry, to regulate the entire financial system. This was an important step and the overall institutional design looks appropriate. The FSA has shown itself willing to condition financial support on management or structural changes. The FSA forcibly nationalised one bank in November and fired the management, and in another case agreed to support the merger of two troubled institutions only after they agreed to substantial downsizing.

Table 1.1. **Sectoral regulatory reforms in Japan by end 1998**

Industry	Key Legislative/ Regulatory Framework	Recent and Outstanding Reforms	Price Regulation	Regulation of Entry and Exit	Other Regulations that Affect Competition	Future Reforms Needed	Mandated Changes in Industry Structure
Air Transport	Aviation Law (1952). Rigid business area restrictions among three domestic airline firms established in 1970 and 1972. Since 1986, Ministry of Transport (MOT) has gradually given licenses to more than one airline in several routes.	The MOT increased since 1986 the number of routes served by two or three airlines and since 1996 has permitted more scope of airfares. Additional relaxation of entry restrictions was recently announced.	Airfares subject to MOT approval. Since 1996, the regulation has been partially relaxed with the introduction of a maximum and minimum tariff. Since 1994, discounts are permitted up to 50 per cent.	New entry and exit on individual routes is subject to MOT approval, based on demand-supply balancing provision. A new airline was awarded entry in 1998, for the first time in 35 years. MOT aims to eliminate demand-supply balancing provision in 2000, and a bill to this effect has been submitted to the Diet.	None, but entry remains restricted by a limited number of airport slots at Tokyo and Osaka.	Major challenges are 1) completing transition to full-fledged competition; 2) transparency in allocation of slots; and 3) services for remote rural areas to be compatible with fuller competition.	None
Road Transport (Trucking)	Trucking Business Law (1990) covers, inter alia, entry, tariffs and definition of business areas.	1990 law eliminated demand-supply balancing, and replaced tariff approval with prior-notification. It relaxed licensing for individual routes.	Advance notification of tariffs is required. MOT can order tariff modification on the ground of, inter alia, unfair competition.	A minimum number of trucks is required for entry. Restriction on business area for trucking is applied in licensing. MOT announced it would expand area for licensing in 1998 and reduce minimum truck number gradually by 2000.	MOT announced it would expand the area for licensing in 1998.	Elimination of regulatory barriers to competition such as business area restriction and tariff notification.	None

Table 1.1. **Sectoral regulatory reforms in Japan by end 1998** (*cont.*)

Industry	Key Legislative/ Regulatory Framework	Recent and Outstanding Reforms	Price Regulation	Regulation of Entry and Exit	Other Regulations that Affect Competition	Future Reforms Needed	Mandated Changes in Industry Structure
Electric Power	Electricity Utility Industry Law, 1964 (most recently amended in 1995). Regulation by Ministry of Industry and Trade (MITI).	1995 amendments required utilities to conduct competitive tenders. Up to 10 per cent of required capacity will be supplied by independent producers (IPPs). In 1999, open tenders to be conducted for all new thermal (fossil fuel) capacity.	Standard retail prices subject to rate of return regulation with a yardstick mechanism for comparing costs between 10 regional utilities. Notification required for optional tariffs and charges for self-wheeling.	Permit required for generation except self-generation and "wholesale supply" (IPP selling to utility). "Special supply" allows a company to set up a new utility within existing utility territory provided there is no adverse effect on existing utility's customers. Self-wheeling (generation of electricity by a company at one site for use at another site of the same firm) is also permitted.	Antimonopoly Act exempts "natural monopoly" services "such as electric power". Subsidies for use of domestic coal. Government financing for part of costs of utility and non-utility generators via Japan Development Bank.	See chapter 5.	Ten vertically integrated utilities retail virtually all electricity. Significant self-generation by industry. New IPPs able to sell power to utility. See Chapter 5.
Telecommunications	Telecommunications Business Law (revised in May 1998). Nippon Telephone and Telegraph (NTT) Law (revised in June 1997). Until mid 1980s NTT had a monopoly on local service and national long-distance, and KDD a monopoly on international long-distance. Entry into direct provision was liberalized in mid-1980s.	In 1997, "supply-demand" balancing was eliminated, foreign entry largely permitted and line-of-business restrictions on NTT and KDD were lifted. Tariff notifications required since November 1998. Price cap to be applied to local service tariffs after reorganization of NTT. Foreign ownership restrictions on KDD lifted in July 1998.	NTT local service tariffs are currently subject to approval.	Individual licensing system is still applied to Type 1 services.	Most problems are due to a lack of regulation to ensure fair and transparent competition.	See chapter 6.	NTT break-up by the revision of NTT Law in 1997.

Table 1.1. **Sectoral regulatory reforms in Japan by end 1998** (*cont.*)

Industry	Key Legislative/ Regulatory Framework	Recent and Outstanding Reforms	Price Regulation	Regulation of Entry and Exit	Other Regulations that Affect Competition	Future Reforms Needed	Mandated Changes in Industry Structure
Retail Distribution (General)	Large Scale Retail Law (1973) required notification prior to opening new stores or expanding existing ones. Reforms in 1990-91 and 1992-93 shortened procedures; abolished local commercial adjustment committees and liberalized establishment of stores less than 1000 m².	New legislation in 1998 will replace 1973 Law, effective as of year 2000. It will eliminate the commercial adjustment provision. Based on guidelines that MITI issues, local governments will make recommendations to those who open large scale stores, and could regulate establishment of large scale retail shops under the City Planning Law to maintain the living environment.	None	Restrictions on entry and expansion of large-scale stores have been gradually reduced since 1990.	1973 Law restricted shop space, opening hours and days. Shop opening times and number of days closed relaxed in 1994.	Monitor and review implementation of the new law by local governments so that it does not restrict free competition in retail markets.	None
Wholesale and Retail Distribution (Specific Products)	Distribution of several products, such as medicine, liquors, tobacco or rice, are regulated by laws.

Copyrighted products (books, journals or CDs) are exempted from Anti-Monopoly Act's prohibition of retail price maintenance. | Gradual relaxation of regulation on liquor retail distribution since 1989.

Retail price maintenance of cosmetics and general medicine was removed as of March 1997. | Prices of tobacco are subject to administrative approval.

Retail price maintenance of cosmetics and general medicine was removed as of March 1997. | Permission from relevant authority is needed to open retail outlets. Competition at retail level is often restricted.
None | Not significant

None | Remaining regulatory restrictions on competition should be abolished. | None |

Table 1.1. **Sectoral regulatory reforms in Japan by end 1998** (*cont.*)

Industry	Key Legislative/ Regulatory Framework	Recent and Outstanding Reforms	Price Regulation	Regulation of Entry and Exit	Other Regulations that Affect Competition	Future Reforms Needed	Mandated Changes in Industry Structure
Housing and Land Use	Construction Standards Law sets standards, inspections for housing construction. Urban Planning Law and others authorize regulations on housing construction and land use, and reserve substantial urban areas for agriculture. Tenants can use land and houses unless owners have "justifiable" reasons.	Some excessive construction restrictions were relaxed. Replacing technical standards with performance based rules is in process. Qualified private agencies will be able to conduct inspections under the CS Law. Tenant protection was relaxed for lands in 1991 and is now being considered for housing.	None	Entry to construction industry is subject to permission by authority under a number of categories.	Land-related tax systems heavily affect use of land and may have the effect of discouraging liquid markets, though progress has been made since 1997 in reducing the cost of land transactions. 1992 reforms raised effective rates on landholding, inheritance of land, strengthened capital gains taxes. 1992 reforms of urban farmland system re-zoned much urban farmland as residential.	Further and more comprehensive review of restrictions on housing constructions. Productivity of construction industry should be improved by more vigorous competition.	None
Wholesale and Retail Distribution (Specific Products: Petroleum)	The Temporary Law on the Import of Specific Oil Products (1986) had prohibited the import of petroleum other than done by refining companies. Up to 1990, construction of gas stations was also restricted by Gasoline Sales Business Law in order to avoid excess competition. There are other regulations of petroleum on quality (for environmental purpose) as well as storage (security).	Construction of gas stations has been liberalized since 1990. The restrictions on petroleum import have been lifted since 1996 as a result of abolishing the 1986 Law.	Implicit co-operative behavior on gasoline prices among oil refining companies appeared to exist before the abolition under the 1986 Law.	Entry to petroleum refining is regulated by MITI. But as the import has been liberalized, the regulations have little impact on market competition.	None	Regular review of regulations for environmental and security purposes.	None

Table 1.1. **Sectoral regulatory reforms in Japan by end 1998** (*cont.*)

Industry	Key Legislative/ Regulatory Framework	Recent and Outstanding Reforms	Price Regulation	Regulation of Entry and Exit	Other Regulations that Affect Competition	Future Reforms Needed	Mandated Changes in Industry Structure
Financial Services	Banking Law, Securities Business Law as well as Insurance Business Law have been the major legal basis of business and prudential regulations in the area.	"Japanese Big Bang" proposals announced in 1996 to reform Japanese financial system based on freedom, fairness and globalism. Following that, various restrictions *e.g.* on foreign exchange transactions have been liberalized. New independent regulator, Financial Supervisory Agency was established in June 1998. Financial Revitalization Commission has been set up since autumn 1998 to oversee bad-loan failure resolution, financial crisis management and other supervisory work, being supported by FAA.	Gradual liberalization of interest rate control has been completed in 1994. Liberalization of commission on equity transactions has started in 1998 and is expected to be completed in 1999. Insurance rates for fire and automobiles have been liberalized since 1998. Rates of life insurance are still regulated by MOF.	New entry has been strictly regulated by relevant business laws, especially in areas of banking and insurance. While cross-entry between incumbent financial firms has been gradually allowed and are expected to continue, restrictions on the entry from non-financial sector has just started to be relaxed.	Various administrative guidance has been often used to control the sector. There have been streamlining efforts of administrative guidance. Approval of new financial products as well as other rule-making procedures by MOF, however, still lack transparency and hence inhibit vigorous competition.	Elimination of remaining regulatory barriers to competition such as entry restrictions. Thorough implementation of prudential regulations through strengthening the capacity of regulator.	Possible acquisition or restructuring of banks under current financial reform scheme.

(see Chapter 4). Yet bilateral trade surpluses did not respond much[21] to these measures, nor to the yen appreciation, nor the increase in domestic demand.[22] External pressures began to focus on structural reforms, leading to the Structural Impediments Initiative with the United States in 1989. In response, Japanese authorities moved to harmonize standards, increase access for foreign exporters to public procurement; promote imports of manufactured goods such as computer chips through quantitative targets; and take other market opening measures in high technology areas.[23]

Lack of attention to structural reform contributed to the creation of a disastrous asset bubble

An asset market bubble emerged. The Japanese authorities had partially liberalized financial markets without installing necessary regulatory oversight.[24] After the loss of major corporate clients Japanese banks turned to commercial real estate lending. The inflow of lending, on top of rising investment due to lower interest rates, caused land and housing prices to rise, followed by other asset prices (Box 1.3). Rising asset prices improved corporate balance sheets. Unrealized capital gains counted towards regulatory capital requirements, generating the illusion that companies were credit-worthy and the banks were well-capitalized. The process became self-sustaining as more lending caused asset prices to rise further. The bubble burst in 1989-90 when the Bank of Japan raised interest rates to cool the economy.

An asset bubble emerged, partly due to regulatory failures in the financial sector.

The economic malaise of the 1990s revealed fundamental structural problems in the Japanese economy and the need for thorough regulatory reform to stimulate market-led growth

Since 1991 Japanese economic performance has been uneven, but on average has seen very slow growth and disinflation.[25] Real GDP growth has averaged around one per cent, largely generated by public investment totaling about 15 per cent of GDP,[26] as well as tax cuts. Export growth was sluggish, and in 1997 key export markets collapsed in Southeast Asia. Private investment contributed negatively to growth, and consumption was weak. Real GDP fell by 2.8 per cent in 1998. As a result, Japan's performance has been the worst in the G7,[27] and prospects for recovery remain uncertain. (The 1998 OECD *Economic Survey of Japan* contains more detail on the outlook.)

Since 1991 Japanese economic performance on average has seen very slow growth and disinflation. Prospects for recovery remain uncertain.

Several factors contributed to poor performance in the Japanese economy in the 1990s. Most immediate was asset deflation. As in the United States and Nordic countries in the late 1980s, a collapse in asset prices caused bank and corporate balance sheets to deteriorate, leading to a credit contraction. In Japan, small and medium sized enterprises were particularly hard hit by the credit crunch. The economy was also hit by negative external shocks that hurt exports – the US recession in 1991-92, yen appreciation, and the crisis in East Asia. Authorities may have moved too aggressively toward fiscal consolidation in 1996 as the economy began to grow, stalling the recovery.

Though the malaise has many causes...

... structural problems, particularly anti-competitive regulation and a distorted financial system, are among the most important. Japan has stood out among the G7 in its inability to adapt to the shocks of the 1990s.

Aggregate demand and supply shocks have been important, but structural problems, particularly anti-competitive regulation and a highly distorted financial system, stand at the heart of the Japanese malaise. In marked contrast to Japan's adaptability to oil shocks in the 1970s, Japan has stood out among the G7 in its inability to adapt to the shocks of the 1990s, which have been common to many OECD countries. Institutional rigidities and a lack of domestic competition resulting from excessive regulation contributed to asset deflation, rising unemployment and difficulties in maintaining competitiveness in domestic manufacturing. These factors also limited the economy's ability to generate and sustain long-term growth, especially growth in total factor productivity, by inhibiting business dynamism – the creation of new products and profit opportunities – in non-traded goods sectors.

The financial system encouraged over-investment, leading to excess capacity, declining enterprise profitability, and rising unemployment in the 1990s...

The financial system and the system of corporate governance also encouraged over-investment, which led to a chronic problem of excess capacity. Japanese growth since the 1960s was built on high rates of savings and capital accumulation, encouraged by institutions created to funnel savings into industrial investment (Box 1.3). This was complimented by subsidies, loan incentives and implicit loan guarantees that permitted industrial firms to be highly leveraged. Under this system, firms maximized sales and market share while earning low rates of return on equity, and responded to increased competition with greater investment (in much the same way that the government's principal response to flagging growth over 25 years has been public investment). This system worked well as long as Japanese firms were small players facing rapidly growing world markets. In the 1990s, it created excess capacity and declining profitability in many sectors. Today, Japanese firms are often market leaders in mature industries characterized by international overcapacity.[28]

... and, combined with other structural problems, contributing to a "hollowing out" of manufacturing, as investments have moved offshore into other parts of Asia.

The "hollowing out" of Japanese manufacturing is closely tied to domestic structural problems. This trend began in the late 1980s as the exchange rate appreciated and accelerated substantially through the 1990s. High domestic input costs led Japanese exporters initially to try and retain market share by cutting profit margins and improving productivity but these measures proved insufficient. The trend toward globalisation of production accelerated. Foreign direct investment increased rapidly and subsequently moved into Southeast Asia to lower labour costs, and then to serve expanding markets. These developments had three impacts. First, increases in demand for Japanese products had less impact on domestic production, weakening the ability of exports to stimulate domestic growth. Second, globalisation of manufacturing increased their access and familiarity with global financial markets and foreign financial firms, compounding the problems of large Japanese commercial banks caused by partial financial reform. Third, exporters became independent of administrative guidance by MITI, and of reliance on loans subsidized, guaranteed or directed by the government. These trends rang alarms in Tokyo. In 1996, the Prime Minister warned that "high-cost structural elements are undermining Japan's attractiveness as a place to do business and there are increasing fears of industrial hollowing... [T] he first structural reform here is thorough-going deregulation..." (Hashimoto, 1996).

Regulatory failures in the financial sector increased and prolonged the costs to Japan of asset deflation (Box 1.3). In other OECD countries, regulatory reform following asset deflation shortened the period of credit contraction by rapidly selling bad debts regardless of the short-term impact on asset prices, minimizing negative impacts on the economy. The Japanese policy response to asset deflation was delayed, which prolonged and increased the negative effects. Until recently the Japanese authorities were reluctant to force institutions to recognize loan and capital losses or to declare weak institutions insolvent, largely in the hope that economy recovery would make difficult measures unnecessary. The persistence of this "business as usual approach", especially the implicit guarantees against institutional bankruptcy inherent in the convoy system and administrative guidance, encouraged problem institutions to continue with imprudent lending policies and for healthy institutions to lend to unhealthy institutions, increasing the risk of systemic collapse. This was compounded by the fact that overdue reforms to the rest of the financial system have been similarly slow, piecemeal and partial.

Improper financial sector reform further contributed by prolonging and deepening the period of asset deflation.

A legacy of regulation inherited from policies of state-led growth stifled competition and innovation in many non-traded goods sectors

It became clear in the 1990s that the scope for regulatory reform was both wider and deeper than previously thought. Structural problems in the financial sector illustrated a greater problem within the economy as a whole – institutional rigidities caused by an outdated and inappropriate regulatory framework stifled competition and innovation. Under an anti-trust policy that was not strong, official policy tolerated vertically or horizontally integrated firms, so-called *keiretsu*, which limited competition in distribution, either through exclusive dealer networks run by a manufacturer or horizontal integration in wholesale distribution.[29] Weakness in competition policy was reinforced by lack of transparency throughout the regulatory system (Chapter 2), giving "insiders", such as organized industry associations or consultative bodies, preferential access to information on regulatory practices or policies.

It became clear in the 1990s that the scope for regulatory reform was both wider and deeper than previously thought.

These policies were compounded in the non-traded goods sector by direct regulatory barriers to entry (Table 1.1). In several sectors, entry was regulated by supply-demand balancing by the ministries. Permission for new entry or the expansion of existing firms into new routes, products or regions was granted only if there was excess demand so that existing producers would not be harmed. Many sectors had other formal barriers to entry such as minimum firm sizes in trucking and limits on opening hours and days in distribution. An extensive network of permits and licenses created barriers to the development of new products as well as entry of new firms: in financial services new products were subject to long delays in regu-

Sectoral regulations limiting entry and competition were pervasive...

latory approval until all institutions in the same category were capable of introducing the product, another aspect of the so-called convoy system discussed above. Finally, substantial barriers to competition in some sectors are due to legally sanctioned self-regulation by industry or professional associations, *e.g.* professional services (OECD, 1997*b*), though an initiative adopted in March 1999 to review qualification requirements for entry into services may help loosen some of these sorts of controls.

... and price controls were widespread.

In many sectors, prices were fixed or subject to controls. In regulated monopolies like telecommunications and electricity, prices were set on the basis of rate of return regulations. In the air transport sector, prices were also set on the basis of rate of return regulations. Resale price maintenance existed in some sectors, such as books, medical products, and cosmetics.[30] Controls on interest rates were applied to loans and deposits by all types of institution from 1954, as well as yields on most bonds, bills and commercial paper, though interest rates on most large accounts were liberalized by 1990.

Sectoral rigidities were reinforced by regulation-induced rigidities in factor markets.

The anti-competitive effects of sectoral regulations were reinforced by regulations in factor markets, particularly capital and land. Land usage was tightly restricted and affected by rigid requirements on construction types and materials, building design and size regulations, and zoning policies targeted towards maintaining small businesses and farmers.[31] Tax policies have favoured long-term holdings of real estate, inhibiting the development of a liquid real estate market, though recent reforms reducing the tax burden on capital gains on land transfers are steps in the right direction. Regulations in capital markets created similar barriers to competition, particularly in the financial services sector. Most important was the ban on foreign exchange transactions in effect until 1980, effectively segmenting domestic financial markets from world markets.

MACROECONOMIC AND SECTORAL SECTORAL IMPACTS OF REGULATION AND REGULATORY REFORM

Highly regulated sectors performed poorly compared to sectors where competition is vigorous.

This pattern of regulatory intervention had both direct and indirect effects on economic performance. Analysis of Japan's economic performance using the OECD's performance database (explained in Box 1.4) shows that sectors characterized by low levels of competition, excessive regulation, or high trade barriers performed poorly. Performance in these sectors, which tended to be non-traded goods and services, stands in marked contrast to traded goods sectors, which faced intense and increasing competition and decreased regulation.[32]

Japanese price levels are higher than in most other countries...

A striking indication of the hidden cost of weak competition is the difference in prices and inflation in the economy, and in key sectors. Results vary depending on the measure used and calculations of PPP (purchasing power parity) exchange rates, but numerous studies confirm that Japanese price levels in 1993[33] were the highest in the OECD, 56 per cent above the OECD average[34] (see Chapter 4 and

---

Box 1.4.   **Estimating the economic impact of regulatory reform**

Regulatory reform can affect both sectoral and macroeconomic performance. Analysis of sectoral impacts draws on the large body of academic research that has developed. Microeconomic effects include benefits to consumers in terms of prices and service, impact on labour markets, changes in industry structure, competition and profits, and changes in costs and productivity, especially from innovations. Where possible, numerical estimates of sectoral effects are based on comparing what actually happened with an estimate of what would have happened without reform; where that is not possible, the observed change is reported. Quantitative measures for features such as service quality and innovation are generally not available, so key changes or anecdotal information are reported. Sectoral impacts are summarized in Table 1.2. The impact of regulatory reform on macroeconomic performance is notoriously difficult to measure, and relies on estimates by other authors and previous estimates by the OECD.

The OECD's Regulation, Structure and Performance Database was also used to generate performance benchmarks of relevance to regulation (see Tables 1.5 – 1.9). Based on information from Member countries and other data sets, macroeconomic and sectoral indicators of economic performance have been developed by the Economics Department. Performance is defined as a multifaceted phenomenon (including static, dynamic and resource mobilization dimensions). Synthetic indicators were constructed using multivariate data analysis techniques such as factor analysis. The database includes indicators for business sector manufacturing and service industries and for six specific service sectors (electricity, telecommunications, rail transport, air passenger transport, road freight and retail distribution).

Annex, Figure 1.5). This was true in both manufacturing and services, and particularly true of prices for non-traded goods in cartelised and highly regulated sectors. Prices for air travel, business service, construction, electricity and rail transport ranked first or second highest among the G7 in the 1990s, and 40 to 60 per cent above average G7 levels,[35] whereas the performance in deregulated telecommunications was relatively good.

Similarly, inflation in sectors characterized by low levels of competition was high. In most countries, service sector inflation tends to be above that in traded goods, but this gap was particularly large in Japan in the 1990s: EPA price comparisons show that between 1990-95 producer prices in manufacturing dropped by 8.1 per cent while they rose 4.9 per cent in non-manufacturing, especially in energy and transportation. High prices for consumer goods were a function of barriers to competition in distribution and also of high land prices which makes large stores, and storage capacity and inventories, expensive.

Efficiency in the Japanese economy is among the lowest in the G7. Static efficiency in both manufacturing and services is the worst in the G7 and the OECD as a whole – reflecting high prices and low levels of labour and total factor productivity (TFP). Dynamic efficiency performance is better in manufacturing because of strong output growth, but, in both manufacturing and services, growth rates of TFP are at the bottom of the G7. Annex, Figures 1.6-1.9 suggest that Japan's static efficiency is negative for both manufacturing and services, and dynamic efficiency is negative for the service sector. These measures reflect the bias towards high levels of capital investment (Annex, Figures 1.1 and 1.4): Japan's capital-output ratio steadily rose

... and efficiency in the Japanese economy is among the lowest in the G7.

35

between the 1960s and 1990s – consistent with negative capital productivity growth – and has now reached the same levels found in most European countries, well above that found in the United States and Canada. Declines in capital productivity have been found in many countries over extended periods, but they have been much larger in Japan than any other G7 country and this gap widened in the 1990s.

These factors contributed to declining corporate profitability and increasing bankruptcy.

As noted, financial and corporate governance systems favored excessive investment and tolerated low rates of return, and these institutions were reinforced by regulatory and institutional barriers that contributed to declining profits and reduced product innovation and restructuring. As a result, profitability for non-financial corporations, measured by return on total assets, declined from an average of 4.3 per cent during 1966-75 to 3.3 per cent in the following decade, and further to 2.9 per cent in 1986-95.[36] As the profitability of non-financial corporations declined, bankruptcies rose.

Initial reforms show encouraging results, but in many areas reform is incomplete and competition is unlikely to develop

A series of regulatory reform packages in the 1990s have addressed a widening reform agenda, and performance has already improved in a few areas.

Regulatory reform efforts have aimed to reduce high domestic costs to improve competitiveness and increase consumer purchasing power, to remove barriers to development of new growth sectors, and to improve Japanese consumers'quality of life. Beginning in 1993, the government announced a series of regulatory reform packages: the *Emergency Economic Package* (September 1993), *The Policy for the Promotion of Administrative Reform* (February 1994), *The Policy for Promoting Regulatory Reform* (July 1994), and *The Deregulation Action Program* (March 1995). By this time, deep cleavages over regulatory reform emerged, as export industries promoted reform in upstream sectors, while service and small producers clung to regulatory protections. The Cabinet adopted in 1996 a broader reform program encompassing public administration, public fiscal structures, social security, financial business systems, and education, and in 1998, it adopted the current *Three-Year Program for the Promotion of Deregulation*, to run from 1998 to 2000. These various packages contained hundreds of reform measures (Chapter 2 discusses critically this incremental approach).

Implementation is ongoing, and visible improvements have been made to the overall transparency and market orientation of regulation (see Chapters 2-6 for details). These changes are complemented by continued progress on market opening. Japan eliminated or tarified quotas on most agricultural products, ended controls on imports of refined energy products, and has agreed with its trading partners to remove administrative barriers to imports.

For example, regulatory reform is showing benefits in two sectors where competition has increased the most – distribution and telecommunications.

Table 1.2 summarizes the impacts of recent regulatory reforms. Regulatory reform is producing benefits in two sectors where competition has increased the most – distribution and telecommunications – whereas transition costs in terms of employment declines have been negligible. Benefits to date of reform in telecommunications

Table 1.2. **Potential impacts of sectoral regulatory reform in Japan**

Industry	Industry Structure and Competition	Industry Profits	Output, Price, and Relative Prices	Service Quality, Reliability and Universal Service	Sectoral Wages and Employment	Efficiency: Productivity and Costs
Wholesale and Retail Distribution	Number of retail shops steadily decreasing since 1990, mostly concentrated among small shops (less than 4 or 10 employees). Since major deregulation in 1994, decline of 5.4% and 8.8% respectively in number of retail and wholesale establishments. Wholesale sector expected to shrink further.	Return on sales has increased in wholesale and retail since 1993. (EPA). Expect profits in industry to fall by 5 per cent (OECD, 1996).	Sales in retail sector is growing, the wholesale sector shrink since 1991, overall sales in distribution declined 1994-97, largely recession effects. (Commercial Statistics, MITI, 1997) Impact of deregulation on consumption and investment 1990-95 estimated at 4.54 trillion yen. (EPA, 1997).	Increased number of stores operating for longer hours and greater number of days per week.	Decline of 9.1% in employment in wholesale distribution since 1994, little change in retail, but composition has shifted. Between 1988-97 the employment share of SM shops declined from 88.0% to 83.7%, employment in large retail stores increased by 46 %. Wages have been rising with improved productivity.	Sales per employee in the retail sector increased by 19.6 % between 1988 and 1997. Drop in input costs through greater use of imported goods by discount stores and more competition in wholesale. Expect further improvement in capital productivity as store size increases.
Air Transport	Up until 1998, there was increased entry by pre-existing 3 airlines on competitor's routes. As of October 1998, routes with 3 and 2 competitors were 9.6% and 14.2% of the total, respectively. New entry of airlines was approved in 1998, but the number of flights is very limited due in part to slot constraints. Competition is largely still restricted to service quality.	Profits have declined due to increased use of discount fares and falling demand because of the recession.	Prices are about 10 per cent above international levels despite long average flight length. Deregulation increased transport volume (measured by passenger-kilometers) by around 6 % of the total transport volume in 1994/5. Discount rates of airfares from approved tariffs have risen from 18.3% in 1992 to 26.7 % in 1996. (EPA, 1997).	Increased flight frequency on major routes.	Wages about 15 per cent above those likely to prevail under competition. Employment cuts of twelve per cent anticipated (OECD, 1996).	Labour productivity is quite low by international standards. As of 1993 average cost per seat kilometer and operating expenses per kilometer were nearly 2x levels in US (though lower than major European countries), despite comparable average stage length and load factors. Some increases in productivity and value-added per employee already (EPA), expected increases of 30% (OECD, 1996).
Road Transport	Number of new entrants increased since reform law of 1990; up 21% from 1994 to 1997.	Profits have tended to increase since the reform of the law.	Prices have been declining since 1993. Home delivery services have grown rapidly.	Introduction of several new transport services, including frozen delivery, guaranteed delivery times, and more rapid deliveries.	Total earnings have decreased since 1995.	Increases in labour productivity and value-added per employee.

Table 1.2. **Potential impact of sectoral regulatory reform in Japan** (cont.)

Industry	Industry Structure and Competition	Industry Profits	Output, Price, and Relative Prices	Service Quality, Reliability and Universal Service	Sectoral Wages and Employment	Efficiency: Productivity and Costs
Electric Power	Ten vertically integrated utilities retail virtually electricity. Significant self-generation by industry. New "wholesale supplier (IPP)" able to sell power to utility.	Appear to be high despite rate of return regulation, should come down with greater entry. No change to date.	Industrial prices are well above long-run marginal costs. Bids in 1997 by IPPs were 25-40% electricity company marginal costs. In 1998 regional monopolies reduced prices by 4.7% on average.		No clear evidence of excess wage premia or employment. No change to date.	Excessive capital investment has resulted in high level of technical service quality and very low levels of capital productivity in OECD. High levels of labour productivity though small gap with US.
Housing Market		Profit to sales ratio declining since 1993.	Prices declined steadily from 1991-95 and rose slightly in 1996-97.		Employment increased since 1990.	Construction costs have decreased since 1992.
Telecommunications	NTT has 98% market share in local fixed voice service and 62% share in the national long distance market. In international long distance KDD has over 63% market share. In mobile, 5 or 6 carriers are competing in each market bloc: NTT DoCoMo has a 57% market share in cellular service and DDI has a 51% market share in PHS.		Long distance and international rates fell (25% since 1997), but still higher than those of most OECD countries. No change in local usage charges. Monthly subscription charges were increased. Mobile charges have been significantly reduced.	Service levels were already very high and have improved: completion of fixed network digitalization. Very high anwer seizure ration (6.2) and very low faults per 100 lines per annum (1.7). Since 1985, 88 new services and discount services have been introduced.	Loss of jobs in components of NTT offset by growth in new entrants, especially in mobile. Total expenditure on wages reduced 24.5 billion dollars to 19.4 billion dollars. Creation of over 300 000 jobs in other industries from increased investment.	Between 1990 and 1997, access lines per employee has been increased from 200.3 to 274.8., i.e. 37 per cent.
Financial Services	Number of financial institutions fell by 8.4% between 1993 and 1998.	Decline in profits since 1990 as implicit subsidies disappeared after liberalization of interest rates.	EPA estimates annual benefits of ¥766 billion from deregulation.		Earnings increased 1990-97.	

are detailed in Chapter 6, but are highlighted by the large declines in long distance rates and explosive growth in mobile phones and various business services.

Reforms in 1990-96 to the Large Scale Retail Store Law[37] established clear deadlines for processing applications, improved transparency, and raised the size threshold for stores needing notification. These changes substantially weakened the ability of local merchants and politicians to block or delay opening or expansion of large stores. Also in the retail sector, the number of hours per day and days per week that stores could be open were expanded, and sector specific measures, such as geographical restrictions on petrol stations, were dropped. The impacts have been positive. Larger stores are expanding both in number and in size; discount stores have emerged as a major force; and more stores are operating for longer hours and greater number of days per week.[38] The net results have been a gain in efficiency, greater consumer benefits, and increasing sales volumes, while employment has not changed.[39] These results more than offset the closing of many smaller stores (which is only partly due to deregulation, see Box 1.5). Japan's Economic Planning Agency estimated the annual average economic gains in 1990-97 at 3.2 trillion yen, and that number has probably increased substantially since.

Box 1.5. Why have traditional small businesses declined in Japan?

Effects of regulatory reform on small and medium-sized enterprises are often given special consideration. SMEs, particularly in distribution, are important in OECD countries: they account for a large share of the total number of businesses and an important share of employment, which also gives them political weight, especially at the local level. They can also represent a traditional way of life and embody social values. These factors are particularly relevant in Japan where regulations on land, zoning, and large stores have resulted in a much smaller average store size than most other countries. In 1991, stores with fewer than 10 employees accounted for 90 per cent of the number of retail stores, 60 per cent of sectoral employment; and 47 per cent of sales.

During the 1990s SMEs, particularly, in distribution, have been difficult, especially the self-employed. Between 1991 and 1994, the number of stores with less than 4 employees declined by over 10 per cent and their sales declined even more. SMEs account for the vast majority of the rapidly growing number of bankruptcies over the last few years. This type of social dislocation has been disturbing in a Japan accustomed to a very stable economy.

Deregulation of distribution is not the most important reason for this development. In the ongoing recession, SMEs, with small workforces, are less able to lower labour costs, in contrast to larger enterprises which can reduce bonuses or overtime, reduce the hiring of new workers, or shift workers from declining to growing market segments. In fact, much of the burden of adjustment by large enterprises to declining demand was shifted onto suppliers, often SMEs, through declining orders and shrinking profit margins. Moreover SMEs, lacking direct access to financial markets, are more affected by cutbacks in lending by commercial banks. Finally, SMEs are more sensitive to structural changes in the economy. Increasing suburbanisation, a result in part of land and housing market liberalization but also of a generational shift in lifestyle preferences, has made many small urban stores unprofitable. Population ageing and a low birth rate mean that many small family-owned businesses have no one to take over the business. Elderly owners have chosen to close shop and retire, a decision reinforced by the generally unfavourable economic climate. In the light of these factors, the contribution of regulatory reform to the problems of small shops is probably small.

Price and entry controls have also been relaxed but some form of control or monitoring still exists in many sectors.

Entry has been partially liberalized in other sectors, but for the most part substantial barriers remain in the form of supply-demand balancing conditions, and registration or licensing requirements.[40]

Reform of price regulation has in most cases paralleled that of barriers to entry. Progress has been most extensive in distribution, where retail price maintenance was ended on a number of products, such as medical products. In telecommunications, the substantial deregulation of entry has been accompanied by heavy regulation on pricing until very recently.[41] In electricity and transportation price controls remain entrenched and inefficient – *e.g.* electricity pricing still does not adequately reflect peak load demand. Price controls in transportation are to be phased out over the next few years in parallel with the phasing out of supply-demand balancing.

Important supporting reforms in the land, labour and capital markets are good steps to reduce factor costs and reallocate resources.

Complementary reforms began in factor markets. Most important was the deregulation of financial markets in 1998 – the "Big Bang" – discussed in Box 1.3. In the land, construction, and housing markets, steps have been taken. Zoning rules such as those regulating business height or earthquake-related requirements have been relaxed, as have discriminatory inspection of imported construction materials, and a number of tax changes have been made to increase the liquidity and depth of real estate markets. In labour markets, initial steps were taken to improve job search and labour flexibility in the face of rising unemployment. The number of sectors and occupations permitted by private job placement agencies has increased.

But reform to date has been too partial, piecemeal and incomplete to provide a basis for market-led recovery and long-term growth

But, overall, reform has not significantly reduced the high costs in the Japanese economy, contributed to restoring consumer confidence, nor created the new investment opportunities necessary for long-term growth.

Despite the substantial number of reforms undertaken, concrete gains from reform are as yet insufficient to significantly reduce the high costs in the Japanese economy, contribute to restoring consumer confidence, and create new investment opportunities necessary for long-term growth. In part, this reflects the fact that, outside of distribution and telecommunications, many reforms have been implemented recently and their impact has yet to be felt. However, as detailed in Chapters 2-6, much regulatory reform in Japan has been slow and piecemeal, rather than a sharp break with uncompetitive practices. More is needed if regulatory reform is to play a substantial role in economic recovery and establish a basis for sustainable market-led growth in future.

ANTICIPATED EFFECTS OF FAILURE TO TACKLE STRUCTURAL PROBLEMS

Hard choices on structural reform lie ahead. Historical sources of growth – exports, high rates of capital accumulation, government spending, and labour force growth – are not sustainable

The engines that drove Japanese growth over the 1960-1990 period are running out of fuel.

The engines that drove Japanese growth over the 1960-1990 period will not provide the same momentum over the next 30-50 years. High export growth is unlikely, given the maturity and hollowing out of Japanese manufacturing. Other forces will make continued export growth more difficult: the end to the "catch-up" phase in many sectors, more intensive competition from other OECD countries following the successful restructuring of their manufacturing sectors; and increased competitiveness from China and East Asia, which, as Chapter 4 shows, enjoy much lower costs for intermediary inputs.

Nor can fiscal stimulus, rapid labour force growth and capital accumulation provide growth as they have in the past. Japanese labour force growth has begun to decline, reversing a major driver of growth, and the decline will accelerate over the next 25 years, becoming a major drag on growth.[42] High rates of capital accumulation and public investment – a traditional solution in Japan – will be inefficient, given a shrinking labour force, and incompatible with the rates of return demanded in liberalised financial markets.[43] Moreover, medium-run fiscal consolidation will be necessary to restore consumer confidence which has been shaken by the prospective burden of high future tax payments to cover the costs of all the fiscal stimulus packages of the 1990s as well as concerns over the long-term viability of the social security system.[44]

Fiscal stimulus, rapid labour force growth and capital accumulation cannot spur growth as they have in the past.

Japan faces the prospect of economic stagnation and persistently high unemployment

The 1997-98 OECD *Economic Survey* estimates Japan's potential growth rate at between 1¼-1½ per cent,[45] and argues that potential growth could decline to around 1 per cent per year in the next few years. It projects that:

Potential growth could decline to around 1 per cent per year in the next few years.

> ... **if total productivity growth does not benefit significantly from structural reforms**, [emphasis added] potential growth would fall to 1 per cent per year on average over the next decade or so and then further to around to ½ to ¾ per cent thereafter. Clearly, in the future realised GDP growth will be increasingly determined by productivity performance...[46]

The implications of these trends for the Japanese economy are sobering. Assuming conservatively that potential GDP growth for the rest of the G7 maintains its current average level, then Japan's per capita GDP, currently about 21 per cent higher than the EU15 average, would be 21 per cent lower in 25 years, completely reversing the relative gains in growth and lifestyle of the last 35 years. While Japan has accumulated an enormous stock of savings and wealth with which it could sustain consumption for many years, the example of other economies that have experienced relative declines and chosen to live on accumulated wealth, such as post war Britain, is not inspiring.

Such low rates of growth could reduce Japan's per capita GDP from 21 per cent higher than the EU average, to 21 per cent lower in 25 years.

Rising unemployment, a result of structural imbalances in the economy, will persist and grow worse

These costs will show up not only in terms of economic growth or material lifestyle but are likely to affect the fabric of Japanese society. Some opposition to reform is based on deep concern over the social costs of restructuring. Yet if reform is not pursued, the social costs will

The social costs of restructuring could be important, but if reform is not pursued, the social costs will occur anyway.

occur anyway, and as reform is delayed, the social costs will increase. Unemployment has risen steadily over the 1990s to nearly five per cent, a post-war high despite a slowdown in the growth rate of the working age population.

To date the lifetime employment system has protected the majority of jobs. Rather than cutting jobs, large firms are reducing hiring, reallocating jobs internally, and cutting bonuses and overtime hours. This approach has concentrated rising unemployment among new entrants to the labour market (18-24), the elderly, and those in sectors not protected, It has reduced the growth rate of personal income through cuts in bonuses and overtime pay, reducing consumption. Layoffs have begun to occur even in the primary sector and this will grow as Japanese manufacturers become increasingly unable to sustain profits in the face of excess capacity, high domestic costs and weak domestic demand. The motor vehicle sector is a case in point. Production has declined steadily, and by 1998 was 75 per cent of capacity. Companies such as Nissan, which has been among the hardest hit, closed a plant south of Tokyo in 1995 without laying off workers, instead imposing layoffs on their suppliers, but this policy cannot be sustained and further shutdowns of production are anticipated.[47] Without reform, unemployment will rise further, affect a broader segment of the population, especially primary male wage earners, and become long-term in nature.

ANTICIPATED EFFECTS OF REGULATORY REFORM

Regulatory reform is essential to create new foundations for long-term growth.

Regulatory reform is essential to create new foundations for long-term growth. The simple mathematics of growth accounting show that if growth in capital and labour are falling, growth can only be sustained by an increase in total factor productivity. This will require improving the efficiency with which the economy uses inputs, organises production, innovates new technology and generates new products and profit opportunities. Achieving this will be difficult for it requires different market institutions and fundamental changes in the roles of ministries and a range of other public and semi-public institutions that have dominated post-war Japan (see Chapter 2).

Recommendations for specific reforms must be directed towards rapid achievement of full competition, with construction of new, pro-competitive regulatory regimes to efficiently protect consumer interests, the environment, and competition itself. A package of reforms is outlined in Chapter 7, and should include rapid action to:

- eliminate the remaining regulation related to large-scale retail stores, as is planned for June 2000, while ensuring that new regulations do not impede competition in the sector;

- eliminate remaining price controls, such as those on petroleum products;

- accelerate the elimination of remaining controls on entry and pricing in transportation, and move to competitive allocation of airport slots to enhance entry of new firms;

- launch additional reforms in land, housing, and construction, including modifying tenant rights, increasing the ratio of building to plot size, promoting suburban construction and eliminating administrative review of prices of large real estate transactions;
- eliminate or simplify most licensing and registration requirements which continue to serve as barriers to entry and surrogate methods of exercising ministerial discretion.

Experience in other OECD countries shows that regulatory reform generates rapid increases in productivity and efficiency. Excessive capital investment in most sectors will be reduced, generating large increases in capital productivity. OECD studies indicate potential gains of 25 per cent or more in electricity, telecommunications, road transport and distribution (see Table 1.2) which are projected to substantially lower costs. Synergistic effects are important, both between sectors and between reforms in individual product markets and labour, land and capital markets,[48] suggesting that broad-based regulatory reform will amplify the gains in individual sectors.

... that can improve long-term growth prospects and reduce the level and duration of unemployment...

Regulatory reform will generate large gains for consumers and exporters as prices levels drop substantially and the variety and quality of services improves. This has already started to occur in Japan due to progress on deregulation: prices for national and international long-distance fell by 77 per cent through 1996 and reforms in distribution have lowered prices by approximately one per cent annually since 1990 (OECD 1996, p. 76). More broadly, a recent EPA study revealed that the gap between Japanese and foreign prices has started to decline due to a substantial improvement in prices in deregulated sectors; prices in these sectors showed a four per cent greater improvement between 1990-95 than in regulated sectors (EPA, 1997).

... lower prices and improve consumer choice...

Price performance will be substantially improved if reforms currently proposed or in process are completed and extended. Electricity prices, a key input for many industries, have fallen by 4.2 per cent thanks to the introduction of yardstick competition, but the introduction of full competition (not yet accepted in Japan) could lead to a price drop of another 15 per cent. OECD studies project declines in other sectors air and road transportation, telecommunications and distribution of around 10 per cent.

The supply-side effects of reform are expected to be substantial. EPA estimates that reforms in distribution raised GDP by 0.67 per cent during 1990-97. Studies by the OECD (1996) show that reform in five sectors could increase GDP by nearly six per cent and a broader study by Japan's EPA which included seven sectors suggested an increase in GDP of ten per cent over the next few years, with the biggest gains coming from reforms to land, housing, and construction markets.

Declining prices should mean greater consumer income and demand. Financial market reform, too, should increase consumer

... and boost consumer demand.

spending by making consumers more liquid and increasing returns on savings. These demand effects, complementing the supply side effects of regulatory reform, can be multiplied by further reducing prices through rapid implementation of reforms, helping to spark a recovery and to sustain growth in the longer run.

Job losses can occur in restructuring sectors, but increases in demand should generate more new jobs than are lost, and in higher-value sectors

Regulatory reform has generated sectoral job losses and wage cuts in some sectors...

In other countries, particularly the United States, regulatory reform generated sectoral job losses and wage cuts as firms adjusted to increased competition through restructuring and weaker firms are forced out. But such job losses in most reformed sectors are reversed in the medium-term as prices fall, demand increases, and innovation creates new products.

– In airlines, large price declines following reform in the United States led to such huge increases in demand that employment grew rapidly after short term declines, both in existing firms (after initial job losses) and in new entrants.

– In transportation, more sophisticated routing and pricing practices and the accelerating use of intermodal transportation stimulated employment in software and logistical firms which specialise in optimal routing software as well as the creation of jobs such ancillary services such as freight brokers.

– In financial services, losses of bookkeeping and customer service employment – generally low wage and low-skilled[49] – were more than offset by high wage jobs in trading and product development due to rapid innovation in new financial products and services.

– In telecommunications, large price drops and product innovation produced substantial net increases in employment and this is likely to be the case in Japan. The OECD Report on Regulatory Reform (1997) projects that an initial decline in employment of six per cent in this sector will be followed by a medium-term employment increase of 8 per cent, due to innovation.

... but a net positive effect on employment is projected for Japan.

Regulatory reform can result in permanent decreases in employment in a few sectors, particularly those characterised by oligopolies or regional monopolies prone to overstaffing, *e.g.* transportation and electricity.[50] In most countries, the net effect on economy-wide employment has been zero or positive, as losses in some sectors are more than offset by gains in others. The size of potential job losses in Japan due to reform is not clear, in part because jobs are being lost today due to lack of reform, but the employment effects of an ambitious, multi-sectoral reform programme are likely to be positive in Japan over the medium-term.

Experience in other countries has shown that the effects of regulatory reform on wages tend to be small and confined to unionised sectors with substantial monopsony power, such as truck drivers in the United States. There is little evidence that this type of phenomenon exists in Japan. The OECD Report on Regulatory Reform (1997) projected negligible changes in wages except in air transport.

While not usually considered a social cost, regulatory reform has been attacked in Japan as creating excessive competition which prohibits firms from earning a "normal" rate of return. Experience in other countries shows that profits generally decline by modest amounts and only in formerly monopolistic sectors. Large declines in profits usually prove temporary, a result of cyclical downswings following previous periods of excessive investment. It can take a reformed industry several years and business cycles to readjust its capital stock to an optimal size. In Japan, profits have been under pressure in most sectors due to economic stagnation, excess capacity and labour hoarding. The only Japanese sectors where profits are expected to fall substantially following reform are construction and electricity, where cartel and monopoly behaviour have led to above average rates of return.

Other social costs, e.g. wage declines, have been minimal elsewhere and unlikely to exist in Japan.

Social costs can be further reduced by simultaneously introducing complementary structural reforms in labour and other factor markets

Complementary structural reforms in factor markets can further reduce these costs. Labour market reforms can facilitate job creation and minimise dislocations, as can active labour market policies such as job training and placement programs. In Japan, such programmes are already necessary as unemployment rises independently of regulatory reform. Internal labour markets work well for those covered by the life-time employment system, but are breaking down in the face of persistent excess capacity and financial losses. Many other workers are not in sectors where the lifetime employment system operates. In both cases, they need help in locating to growth areas, and this will be even more the case if regulatory reform accelerates.

Complementary structural reforms in factor markets can further reduce these costs...

In particular, Japan needs to improve job training and job placement. An important step will be to increase the role of private job placement and temporary work agencies. These are already allowed to fill jobs in a growing number of occupations, but should be completely deregulated. In the longer run, several reforms will facilitate labour mobility as Japan moves away from careers served entirely in one firm. One is greater portability of pensions. Another is educational reform, where schooling is less targeted towards exams and more toward giving employees greater skill set to perform many different jobs.

... by improving job training and job placement...

Improved labour market flexibility and active labour market policies can be complemented by reforms outside the labour market which will encourage entrepreneurialism and job creation. In Japan a greater role for venture capital can be stimulated through more

... and by allowing a greater role for venture capital.

favourable tax and legal treatment of risk capital, improving the marketability of venture company shares, and increasing sources of borrowing for venture firms. Japan is moving toward a tax system more favourable to venture capital, but the OECD has noted the need to move further. More generally, income tax reform is necessary to increase incentives for higher earnings. Japan has proposed useful reforms to lower relatively high marginal personal income tax rates and to eliminate disincentives for elderly workers to stay in the labour force.[51]

In the medium-run, reforms will improve business dynamism, broaden and deepen markets and create dynamic innovations...

Experience in other countries shows that regulatory reform has synergistic effects on the whole economy beyond its effects on specific sectors.

Experience in other countries shows that regulatory reform has synergistic effects on the whole economy beyond its effects on specific sectors. As markets become broader and deeper, products and prices become more tailored to individual customer and business needs. This leads to dynamic innovation with economy-wide effects: transportation deregulation lowered shipping costs for many industries in other countries, improved reliability and allowed for customised service. Innovations in telecommunications and financial services, in part due to deregulation, interacted with rapid changes in information technology, spurring product innovation and employment creation in all three sectors. Development of commodities markets for energy allowed companies to better plan energy expenditures, allowing for reductions in short-term production costs in manufacturing as well as facilitating long-term investments. These developments, along with lower prices, will improve the competitiveness of exporters.

... improving overall economic performance and raising the long-term growth rate

Carried forward boldly, regulatory reform should be able to raise potential and actual Japanese growth rates.

Together with other structural reforms, regulatory reform, if accelerated and broadened, should be able to raise potential and actual Japanese growth rates in the long-term by stimulating supply side gains in efficiency and technology and at the same time increasing consumer demand.

Chapter 2

GOVERNMENT CAPACITY TO ASSURE HIGH QUALITY REGULATION

The debate over economic recovery and regulatory reform has focussed attention on the structure and role of government in Japan's future. During the period of state-led growth, the capable and powerful Japanese public administration helped lead a process of extraordinary growth that made Japan a post-war economic miracle and in which rapid policy shifts and social change were accommodated without major political disruptions.[52] If regulatory reform is to succeed in stimulating market-led growth, while ensuring that social goals are efficiently achieved, the public administration must again administer a rapid shift in policy and structures. This time, the administration must diminish its own influence over market decisions, and build new capacities for flexible and efficient regulatory regimes that protect public interests in competitive markets.

The top priorities for government reform are improving adaptability, transparency, and accountability. The Administrative Reform Council said that it intended to reform a government that had "grown excessively large and rigid" and to create a "streamlined, transparent and efficient" government.[53] These changes require fundamental reforms in work methods, incentives, and institutions inside the public administration, and in its relations to the wider society. Current initiatives, such as adoption of notice and comment consultation procedures and restructuring of the Japanese public administration through the Basic Law on the Administrative Reform of the Central Government, offer good opportunities to build new regulatory capacities and incentives in the public sector.

The top priorities for government reform are improving regulatory adaptability, transparency, and accountability.

After more than a decade of effort, the framework of a potentially effective regulatory reform system is taking shape, piece by piece. Mechanisms are in place to translate political support into action. These include the Deregulation Committee of the Administrative Reform Headquarters; a flexible and expanding reform programme; articulation of a set of market-based principles for regulation to be applied by regulators in their day-to-day activities; movement toward a cross-sectoral approach so that regulatory problems are addressed consistently; building reform expertise and capacities in the administration; oversight processes such as annual reports and a database of permits; adoption of an Adminis-

The framework of a potentially effective regulatory reform system is taking shape, piece by piece.

trative Procedure Act and notice and comment procedures; and efforts to improve accountability, especially with respect to informal regulatory instruments such as administrative guidance.

Japan's administrative system is difficult to change, since it is decentralised, closely linked to interest groups, and incrementalist

The public administration operates through balanced power relations; private negotiations and policy development; and mutual accommodation and consensus, guided by a preference for pragmatic, step-by-step solutions.

Japan's administrative system is characterised by decentralised and independent ministries, by powerful bureaucracies armed with broad administrative discretion, and by close and informal links between public servants, producer groups, and political parties through the *zoku* system. Its operating principles include balanced power relations; private negotiations and policy development; and, if attainable, mutual accommodation and consensus, guided by a cultural preference for pragmatic, step-by-step solutions. Conflict, which is as intense as in any country, is often mediated through consultation and coordination behind closed doors. This governing approach, consistent with wider values, has supported policy consistency during periods of rapid change, encouraged public/private cooperation in reaching mutual aims, spread benefits widely (Japan has a highly equal income distribution compared to other countries), and speeded implementation once agreement is reached.

As "state-led" growth gives way to market-led growth, some of these administrative practices impede adjustment in both public and private sectors.

As "state-led" growth gives way to market-led growth, however, some of these administrative practices impede adjustment in both public and private sectors. The lack of a coherent concept of the role of the state for the current phase of Japanese development has left regulatory intervention fragmented, incoherent, and vulnerable to a host of special interests. Wide discretionary powers of public officials, combined with lack of transparency, result in opaque decision processes and information monopolies. Movement of top officials to jobs in the private sector strengthen incentives for regulators to maintain close ties with regulated bodies, while numerous "satellite" bodies around the ministries – such as public corporations and trade associations – enjoy self-regulatory authority. The central government in Japan operates directly more than 9 000 permissions, registrations, and notifications. These aspects increase uncertainty and risk for market entrants.

Pragmatic incrementalism has become policy rigidity, and in some cases policy obsolescence and paralysis.

The most damaging development is that pragmatic incrementalism has become policy rigidity, and in some cases policy obsolescence and paralysis. "The actual progress of reform has been much slower than the speed of changes of the real world", concluded the Administrative Reform Committee in 1995.[54] Incrementalism in regulatory reform has contributed to an increasingly outmoded regulatory governance system in Japan that is poorly suited to a modern market economy, unable to respond quickly enough to challenges and shocks nor to the evolving needs of Japanese society. It is hindering the transition to sustainable economic growth.

Improving the rapid adaptability of regulation is a top priority...

Technological change and globalisation increasingly reward flexibility and regulatory adaptation. Yet costly regulatory rigidities are common in most OECD countries, as in Japan. Experience suggests that capacities for timely reform depend on building organisational structures, policy, and legislative frameworks to drive and sustain effective reform. Adaptability is improved by 1) contestability and transparency of regulatory policies; 2) comprehensive rather than incremental reform; 3) establishing powerful "motors" of reform that cut across and challenge narrow interests in line ministries; and 4) continuing evaluation of regulation. Contestability means open processes, multiple actors in the policy process, and administrative, political, and judicial channels for challenge. Transparency in regulatory decisions and application helps to cure regulatory failures: capture by special interests, "insider" access to information, policy rigidity, uncertainty, and lack of accountability. These concepts should guide administrative reform in Japan.

Regulatory adaptability is driven by contestability and transparency of regulation, as well as by comprehensive reforms and continuing evaluation.

... and the item-by-item approach should be replaced by more comprehensive sectoral and cross-sectoral reforms aimed at results, *i.e.*, introducing competition

The 1997 OECD Report on Regulatory Reform recommends that countries "adopt at the political level broad programmes of regulatory reform that establish clear objectives and frameworks for implementation" (OECD, 1997*a*). Japan's 1998-2000 deregulation programme takes further useful steps in this direction by clarifying the principles for reform and setting out a cross-sectoral approach based on consistent goals. In the past, in part due to the value placed on pragmatic and concrete action and the administrative styles of consensus and accommodation, Japan's reform programmes tended to be based on the accumulation of many individual reform "items". Oversight consisted of tracking ministerial responses to the "items". This approach can claim credit for almost all reforms that have occurred, and it has improved the transparency of reform.

Japan's reform programmes, while moving toward general policies, have tended to be based on the accumulation of many individual reform "items".

Building on the current programme, Japan should move decisively toward comprehensive approaches aimed at results. The item by item approach is slow and not very effective in producing concrete results in economic performance. One reason is that ministries and businesses can produce an almost infinite number of "items" for action, but their value is quite another matter. A widely-cited fact about the 1995-1997 Deregulation Action Plan is that it contained over 2800 items. The 1998-2000 plan starts with 600 items. This focus on numbers has obscured the fact that the importance of the individual items varies widely. Many of the items require ministries to study features of the regulatory system, to make reports, or even to implement proposals through administrative guidance. The fragmentary nature of the item by item approach has reduced coherence and slowed results (Lincoln, 1998*a*).

This approach has made some progress, but is slow and not very effective in producing concrete results in economic performance.

A notable example is the absence of consistent action to eliminate "supply and demand balancing regulations". The current reform programme has set an overall goal of removing these anti-competitive regulations and considerable progress has been

---

Box 2.1. **Managing regulatory quality in Japan**

Ensuring regulatory transparency:

- Japan's first Administrative Procedure Law, enacted in 1993, required ministries and agencies to publish objective criteria for judging applications for licenses and permissions, to explain why applications are rejected, to reduce delays, to guarantee hearing procedures and disclosure of relevant documents, and to ensure that administrative guidance is within legal mandates and that responsibility for such guidance is clear.

- There has been no standardised procedure for public consultation. Over 200 advisory councils (*shingikai*) are consulted to give policy advice on proposals and regulations.

- In October 1998, the government proposed to adopt a notice and comment procedure ("Public Comment Procedures") to make consultation more systematic and widen access by interested parties. The procedure should be in place for all government regulations from April 1999. A standardised comment period is set at one month.

Promoting regulatory reform and quality within the administration

- The "Three-Year Programme for the Promotion of Deregulation", adopted by the Cabinet in March 1998, will operate from 1998 to 2000 in several areas. Nine areas for cross-sectoral action are identified, including reducing entry regulation, promoting innovation, reviewing the standards system, and so forth. A series of actions to promote deregulation is aimed at enhancing the programme itself and increasing support within Japanese society.

- The current reform policy establishes a Deregulation Committee attached to the Cabinet. The Management and Co-ordination Agency in the Prime Minister's Office is tasked with co-ordination and oversight functions on regulatory reform, and also works as the Committee's secretariat.

- The Basic Law on the Administrative Reform of Central Government adopted in 1998 will, by 2001, reorganise the structure of the administration so that it is smaller and more effective (see Box 2.3). The Headquarters for the Administrative Reform of the Central Government carrying out the process is chaired by the Prime Minister.

Adopting explicit standards for regulatory quality

- The "Guideline for the Promotion of Deregulation" adopted by the Cabinet in 1988 identified as its central principle, "freedom in principle and regulation only as an exception". The 1998 programme adopted several principles for regulation. They include 1) economic regulations shall be lifted and social regulations minimised; 2) Regulatory arrangements shall be rationalised; 3) Regulation shall be simplified and clarified; 4) regulation shall conform to international standards; 5) regulatory procedures shall be speeded up; and 6) transparency shall be increased in the procedures for introducing new regulations; 6) transform a priori regulation and supervision to ex post checking.

Assessing regulatory impacts

- Measures have been introduced to reduce regulatory burdens on the public, but there is no systematic effort to assess regulatory benefits and costs. The revised three-year programme for the promotion of regulation of 30 March 1999 instructed ministries and agencies to "work toward creation of a system" to improve accountability for the effects and burdens of regulations, though no mention was made of regulatory impact analysis.

Regulatory review

- The 1998 deregulation programme identifies many regulatory areas for review, including barriers to entry, "supply and demand balancing regulations", qualification requirements, and product standards.

made. However, for almost half of them the current commitment is not to eliminate them in the near future, but to limit their application pending future legal changes, or further study or review of legal changes. Another example of incomplete reform is the abolition of the domestic shipping cartel, which was agreed after a long discussion. However, transition measures will have the effect of limiting competition for several more years.

Piecemeal approaches in other countries usually address easy reforms first, even if the more difficult have the most impact. The result is delayed or even lost benefits, exhaustion of the political resources needed to sustain the process, and vulnerability to blocking or delaying by vested interests. Some reforms are nearly impossible to introduce gradually without careful and transparent advance planning. For example, it is difficult to manage a gradual evolution to full competition when there is a mix of competitive and monopoly elements during the transition. Private investors are reluctant to enter the market when reform takes a very long time, future steps are uncertain, and there are risks of delays. While recognising the progress that can be made with the item by item approach, it is not an adequate basis for coherent, consistent, and sustained programmes of reform.

Comprehensive reform is based on a complete and transparent package of reforms (aimed at a single policy area, sector or multiple sectors) designed to achieve specific goals on a well-defined timetable. The "Big Bang" in the financial sector is an example of this approach. Comprehensive reform does not mean that all changes occur immediately; rather, it is consistent with sequencing strategies and transitional steps as long as they are temporary and steps and timing are clear. There are several advantages to comprehensive reform: benefits appear faster (which means that pro-reform interests are created sooner); affected parties have more warning of the need to adapt; vested interests have less opportunity to block change; and reform enjoys higher political profile and commitment. Producing an integrated package of reforms also facilitates balancing of multiple policy objectives and interests. Comprehensive reform still requires an effective mechanism for monitoring and implementing reform, because reform may produce unforeseen results that will require adjustment and response

On the other hand, comprehensive reform offers several advantages: benefits appear faster; affected parties have more warning of the need to adapt; vested interests have less opportunity to block change; and reform enjoys higher political profile and commitment.

Japan has developed motors to promote reform, but the Deregulation Committee should be further strengthened to ensure its independence and capacity for action

Reform mechanisms with explicit responsibilities and authorities for managing and tracking reform inside the administration are needed to overcome vested interests and keep reform on schedule. Establishing motors of reform has been more difficult in Japan than in many countries, due to the independent ministries and the relatively weak centre. One of the great strengths of Japan's programme has been the prominent personal role of a series of prime ministers. The success of reform will continue to rest on strong political leadership.

Establishing motors of reform has been more difficult in Japan than in many countries, due to independent ministries and the relatively weak centre.

Yet the Prime Minister must have tools to promote reform. In 1995-1997, a Deregulation Subcommittee was established under the Administrative Reform Committee, a council of the Prime Minister's Office. The Subcommittee pioneered the effective technique of holding its hearings in public, rather than negotiating privately with the ministries. Legislation provided that the Prime Minister respect the Council's opinions, either accepting or refusing its recommendations. This was widely considered to be among the most successful of the reform approaches in Japan, because the ministries had less power to block recommendations. The Cabinet accepted nearly all recommendations.

The Deregulation Committee is the current body overseeing the reform programme in 1998-2000. The Committee should be further strengthened so that it can promote reform as boldly as is necessary.

The Deregulation Committee is the current body overseeing the programme for 1998-2000, and is contributing to progress on regulatory reform. The Deregulation Committee is established under the Administrative Reform Headquarters, a ministerial body. Officials argue that this provides a direct link to the Cabinet and will enhance the Committee's role in providing feasible recommendations that can be quickly implemented, which is an important .consideration. In

---

Box 2.2.   **Elements in the Basic Law on the Administrative Reform of the Central Government of particular importance to regulatory reform (new names of ministries are tentative)**

A Ministry of General Affairs is to be established "to strengthen assistance and support for the Cabinet and the Prime Minister". It would evaluate and oversee government activities.

The Ministry of Justice is to support judicial reforms, including the area of administrative tribunals.

The Ministry of Economy and Industry is to "withdraw from or reduce activities relating to promotion of specific business sectors", switching instead to an emphasis on improving the overall business environment while respecting market principles. This orientation, while consistent in direction with the general pro-market orientation of the reform policies, is equivocal in its tone, falling short of a clear rejection of sectoral promotion. In energy policy, the Ministry is to emphasise energy efficiency and new energy sources while "drastically eliminating and loosening regulations aimed at adjusting demand and supply".

The Ministry of National Land and Transport is to "promote systematic efforts aimed at integrated development and utilisation of national land and related resources" and develop an integrated transport system while "drastically deregulating governmental controls over transportation business". It will implement "a thoroughgoing programme of decentralisation and the utilisation of private sector capabilities in relation to the execution of public works projects".

The Ministry of Environment is to unify jurisdiction over matters including "regulations on air, water and soil pollution, waste management etc.", although it will share jurisdiction over "recycling, CO_2 emissions, etc."

The Headquarters for the Administrative Reform of Central Government is working on "Augmenting and Strengthening Evaluation Capacities". This aims to establish evaluation sections within each Ministry as well as a central evaluation body in the Ministry of General Affairs. In addition, transparency is to be assured by the release of the results of evaluations conducted and the strengthening of the Board of Audit.

The Basic Law provided that the government will reduce the number of non-defense employees by at least ten per cent through a Staff Number Reduction Plan that shall be designed in the future. In addition the Law provided that additional reductions be obtained by measures such as transfer of some functions to independent administrative institutions. More recently, the government adopted a reduction target of 25 per cent. In some quarters – for example among some Keidanren members – a reduction in the number of civil servants is seen as an indirect way to control the ability of regulatory ministries to intervene in the economy.

light of the need to accelerate and deepen comprehensive reforms, however, independence from the interests of the line ministries is likely to be equally important, and this aspect should be strengthened. For example, the Prime Minister's Economic Strategy Council recommended in February 1999 the establishment of a new "regulatory reform commission" reporting to the prime minister, empowered to review not only regulation, but also taxation and subsidies, with a significant increase in personnel. These would be useful steps. Another possible approach could be that the Committee, like its predecessor, operate under an independent legal mandate. As noted, the Committee's mandate is narrowly focussed on regulation, which has limited its ability to consider other possible impediments to competition as part of a comprehensive reform plan. Consistent with the need to move to more comprehensive sectoral plans, the mandate of the Committee should be expanded. Recent decisions by the Prime Minister in March 1999 to this effect are steps in the right direction. In addition, the Committee does not have the analytical resources or staff (currently around 20) to be truly independent of the information and expertise in the ministries. A significant increase is warranted.

Japan ranks high among OECD countries in installing capacities for continuing evaluation in the future

The 1998 deregulation programme also states that "as a rule" regulations (and new laws) shall include clauses requiring them to be subjected to *ex post* review after a fixed period of time. Much regulation has already incorporated such requirements, with review periods ranging from about 3 to 10 years after introduction. Ministries and agencies are required to release review findings "promptly after the closing of each ordinary session of the Diet in a format that can be readily understood by the public", thus providing an element of transparency, although there is no specific requirement to take comment from the public. This is a significant reform. According to MCA officials, a significant and increasing proportion of new regulation already incorporates review requirements. This *ex post* review process is a good practice also used in some other OECD countries, but it should be combined with *ex ante* regulatory impact analysis of regulatory proposals to reduce the risk of poor regulations from the very beginning.

Automatic review processes are a good practice in which Japan is ahead of most countries, but they should be combined with regulatory impact analysis to reduce the risk of poor regulations from the very beginning.

To establish a sound basis for market-led growth while maintaining high levels of regulatory protection, reform should focus on early prevention of regulatory problems. This requires more stringent quality controls and co-ordination inside the administration

It is important to note that reforming existing "items" does not change the quality of the stream of new regulations, which can simply repeat old mistakes. A long-lasting solution to problems of poor regulation requires that principles of good regulation are applied equally to new and old regulations. To this end, the Japanese government has made progress toward establishing market-based principles for the use of its regulatory powers, but there is considerable fragmentation

The current review of existing regulations neglects the "flow" of new regulations, and is not a long-lasting solution to problems of poor regulation.

and incoherence in application of these general principles at the ministry level. The government should develop more explicit and measurable government-wide criteria based on OECD recommendations for making decisions as to whether and how to regulate. Such objective criteria will help the public administration regulate only when necessary, and at lowest cost, to protect health, safety, the environment, and other public goals. As the public administration shifts toward policy instruments such as social regulation and market-driven approaches that are competition neutral, and away from economic regulations that impede competition, such principles become even more important to protect the gains of current reforms.

The OECD recommends as a key principle that regulations should "produce benefits that justify costs, considering the distribution of effects across society". This principle is referred to in various countries as the "proportionality" principle or, in a more rigorous and quantitative form, as the benefit-cost test. This test is the preferred method for considering regulatory impacts because it aims to produce public policy that meets the criterion of being "socially optimal" (i.e., maximising welfare).[55] This key principle is insufficiently developed in Japan. The Japanese principles include neither consideration of proportionality nor a benefit-cost test. Thus, there is no standard by which ministries justify the need for regulations, no public testing of these conclusions, and little basis for challenge.

Regulatory analysis would help officials understand the consequences of their regulatory decisions, improve the transparency of regulation, and identify more flexible and cost-effective policy instruments, such as economic instruments.

The benefit-cost principle should be implemented through regulatory impact analysis. The 1997 OECD Report on Regulatory Reform recommended that governments "integrate regulatory impact analysis (RIA) into the development, review, and reform of regulations". Though 24 OECD countries now use RIA, the use of RIA is currently in its infancy in Japan. Though the majority of OECD countries has formal RIA programmes, in Japan there is no requirement for impact assessment, and the 1998 deregulation programme contains no reference to RIA, though it does have a system for checking some aspects of regulatory quality. Regulatory analysis would help officials understand the consequences of their regulatory decisions, improve the transparency of regulation, and identify more flexible and cost-effective policy instruments, such as economic instruments. Such alternatives are not widely used in Japan. RIA is more effective when it is part of public consultation, and the new public consultation procedures provide Japan an opportunity to improve its use of RIA.

Substantial steps have been taken to improve regulatory transparency, and progress should continue in several areas

If implemented effectively, Japan's recent adoption of a "notice and comment" process for new regulations will at a stroke put Japan in the forefront of OECD countries in the transparency of regulatory development.

Transparency of the regulatory system is essential to establishing a stable and accessible regulatory environment that promotes competition, trade, and investment, and helps ensure against undue influence by special interests. Public consultation has been weak – relying on a network of over 200 advisory councils (*shingikai*) that are criticised for being unrepresentative and closed to outsiders – but a major improvement now underway in Japan is the adoption of a "notice and comment" process (called "Public Comment Procedures" in Japan) for new regulations that is expected take effect in April 1999. If implemented consistently and systematically across ministries, this process will be open to all stakeholders, rather than being based on representative groups, and could at a stroke put Japan in the forefront of OECD countries in the transparency of regulatory processes.

Japan should also consider the benefits to transparency of moving to a central regulatory registry. Information on some regulations (laws, cabinet orders and ministerial orders) is published, and can be found on individual ministries'and agencies'Internet sites. But, other than a list of permits, licenses, and procedural requirements kept by the Management and Coordination Agency, there is no centralised system in Japan for communicating regulations to citizens and firms. Some countries have found that establishment of a central registry with positive security (that is, no regulation can be enforced unless it is included in the registry) has assisted in improving transparency and certainty of the national regulatory system for users.

Japan should also consider the benefits to transparency of moving to a central regulatory registry.

One possible model is the innovative Swedish approach (Jacobs *et. al*, 1997*b*). In the 1980s, Sweden enacted its well-known "guillotine" rule nullifying hundreds of regulations that were not centrally registered. Many other countries have established registries, tracking systems, and codification programmes to support reform.[56] In France, an ambitious codification project to be completed by the year 2000 aims at making the law simpler, clearer, and more accessible to citizens and enterprises. In Finland, the Norms Project of 1986-1992 reduced the total number of norms from 7 500 to 5 500, and was concluded with the establishment of a special registry for subordinate regulations. Mexico has recently established its first comprehensive Federal Register of Business Formalities. In Australia, a Legislative Instruments Bill, currently before the Parliament, will create a Federal Register of Legislative Instruments, in which new regulations must be listed before they can be enforced. In most cases in which such registers are used, listing is a final step in the procedural requirements for making regulations. In other cases, listing is not a formal procedural requirement, but provides a defence to prosecution if non-compliance is due to lack of a reasonable opportunity to know the regulation – including failure to list the rule in the register. Information technologies add new possibilities to this work. In the United States, regulations are indexed and published in the Code of Federal Regulations, which is also available via the Internet. The Code is regularly updated, and regulations not listed in the current edition are unenforceable.

Accountability for regulators will be strengthened by clearer definition of regulatory authority, and more frequent judicial review of administrative actions

Japan will also reduce the number of ministries to 12, and redefine their roles. The Basic Law on the Administrative Reform of the Central Government includes a number of major points in relation to each ministry which are expected to guide the drafting of the "foundation laws" (the broad authorising statutes for the ministries). This is a

Current reforms to reduce the number of ministries provides a good opportunity to specify more clearly the regulatory powers and mandates of each ministry...

matter of considerable importance, given the prominence of administrative discretion among the regulatory problems cited by many commentators. The current foundation laws establishing the ministries appear to describe the ministries'mandates in very broad terms, which may allow wide administrative discretion in the application of foundation or other laws. The Keidanren has strongly supported current administrative reform proposals, taking the view that a rewriting of the foundation laws is an essential step toward limiting the scope of administrative discretion by limiting and better defining their powers.[57] Other major points in the administrative reform programme of importance to regulatory reform are listed in Box 2.2.

Box 2.3. Use of administrative guidance in Japan

Use of "administrative guidance" (*gyosei shido*) by the Japanese administration has received considerable attention. One definition of guidance is "Administrative actions taken by administrative organs, although without legal binding force, that are intended to influence specific actions of other parties... in order to realise an administrative aim".[58] The techniques include recommendations, suggestions, requests and warnings. Administrative guidance works best in a relatively concentrated market. Where regulations restrict competition by entry licensing, administrative guidance is at its most effective. Hence, opening of markets to competition may be incompatible with its use. Conversely, critics fear that the use of guidance may undermine the scope for new competition in reformed sectors.

There is considerable disagreement about whether it continues to be an important regulatory tool. The 1993 Admnistrative Procedure Act forbids the use of coercive guidance, and requires that it be based on the "voluntary co-operation" of the subject. Officials are required, upon request, to provide a written copy of guidance provided "by word of mouth". If guidance contains any standards or items that are also applicable to other persons, the content that is uniformly applied is to be made public in advance. The degree of progress in eliminating guidance as a regulatory tool is not clear. According to MCA, it knows of 33 public disclosures of guidance. This small number may mean either that exemptions for cases of "extraordinary administrative inconvenience" are being widely used, that unwritten administrative guidance is not being written down, or, conversely, that the use of administrative guidance is actually rare. There are various views in Japan on this.

There is no doubt that the tool has been an important regulatory instrument. MITI stated in 1981 that "administrative guidance has played an important role in the development of the Japanese economy and it will continue to be effective in the future". Working through a network of "policy councils" and working groups composed of representatives of private companies and related interests such as banks, MITI has used guidance to guide patterns of investment in industries according to national priorities, request controls on prices, request voluntary controls on exports to avoid trade friction, recommend production increases in conditions of tight supply, encourage the use of certain technologies (*e.g.* robotised production) or direct industry consolidation or mergers. Neary[59] argues that administrative guidance has been "the principal instrument of industrial development" in the post-war period.

Administrative guidance can also be a more rapid substitute for law, as in the case of Environmental Impact Assessment (EIA). Work began on a bill to implement EIA in 1974, but eight years elapsed before Cabinet approved a concrete proposal. A 1983 Cabinet decision to implement EIA through administrative guidance was implemented the following year, while a EIA law has had to wait until 1999-25 years after the original proposal.

In some cases, administrative guidance has been converted into more formal regulatory instruments, a positive step that improves transparency but does not necessarily affect substance. As part of the Big Bang's commitment to fairness, the Ministry of Finance announced in 1998 that it had abolished 400 pieces of *tsutatsu* or internal orders, and *jimu-renraku* or communication notes, following criticism that they were burdensome and limited innovation in the sector. Much of the substance of these instruments were converted into published ministerial ordinances (*shorei/seirei*) or guidelines (*gaidorain*). This example suggests that positive steps toward more transparent regulation should be accompanied by substantive review of policy content.

The role of judicial review of administrative actions is limited in Japan compared to other OECD countries. Japan has an administrative appeals procedure and a process for litigating administrative cases, but these avenues are often criticized as inconvenient and costly. The reasons may be related to lengthy delays and high costs of court action, fear of retribution by the administration, or cultural issues such as avoidance of adversarial resolutions. The Keidanren has called for revision of the APA and other laws on administrative appeals to make the system easier to use by citizens.[60] The government recognises that action is needed. The 1998 deregulation programme commits to develop a greater role for the judiciary in relation to "surveillance of compliance with the rules". An increase in new lawyers admitted to the bar is one measure. Similarly, the Basic Law on the Administrative Reform of the Central Government commits to judiciary reforms, including reforms to administrative tribunals. How these programmes will develop remains as yet undetailed.

... and judicial review of administrative actions should be easier for citizens to use.

Transparency and accountability would be boosted by establishing independent sectoral regulators

There is no general policy on functionally separate regulators, nor any recommendation from the Administrative Reform Committee. Many accountability, transparency, and competition problems in sectoral regulation result from lack of institutional clarity about the source, powers, and purpose of regulation. In addition, key regulatory failures such as the current bad loan banking crises have been blamed in part on inadequate capacities for supervision by the public sector, in this case the Ministry of Finance. The current mix in Japanese ministries of regulatory with policy and industry promotion functions is an outmoded approach that is being rejected in several sectors in many OECD countries (and also in the WTO and the European Union) in favour of institutional designs that functionally separate regulatory from other activities to maintain a competitively neutral regulatory regime.[61]

The current mix in Japanese ministries of regulatory with policy and industry promotion functions is an outmoded regulatory approach that is being rejected in several sectors in many OECD countries.

The Financial Supervisory Agency set up alongside the Ministry of Finance is the clearest example of how Japanese institutions are evolving in the direction of international best practices, though the independence and enforcement capacities of the new regulator are as yet unproven. A more general approach is needed to provoke change across a broader front, and to ensure that institutions are designed on consistent principles of competition, transparency, and accountability for results. The current administrative reform programme of the central government aims to separate policy-making from implementation, as has been done in several countries such as the United Kingdom, but there is little discussion in the current reform of the need to separate policy-making from regulatory functions. It is also necessary to strengthen the role of the Japanese Fair Trade Commission in those aspects of sectoral regulation that affect competition policy issues. This is discussed in more detail in Chapter 3.

Chapter 3

THE ROLE OF COMPETITION POLICY IN REGULATORY REFORM

The move to market-led growth implies that competition principles must be at the heart of the emerging new regulatory doctrine in Japan, a sharp break from traditional interventionist practices. Efficiency, investment, and innovation – and, ultimately, consumer welfare – will be greatly boosted by measures that make competition principles operational economy-wide and across the public administration. Cross-country comparisons show that high productivity is best explained by the strength of competition.[62]

As regulatory reform stimulates structural change, vigorous enforcement of competition policy is needed more than ever to prevent private market abuses from reversing the benefits of reform. Japan's Fair Trade Commission, one of the oldest and largest competition law agencies in the world, wields a wide array of substantive and procedural tools, but it has not always used those tools aggressively enough. Since 1990, the FTC's resources have increased and competition enforcement has intensified. More important, FTC increasingly applies modern concepts of competition that are radical changes from the managed, orderly accommodation that characterises much of Japanese business relations and traditional government-business relationship. Supplemented with improved administrative transparency discussed in Chapter 2, these changes position the FTC to play an indispensable role in the transition to a more dynamic market economy.

The need for strong competition policy will be even greater in future.

The historical roots of modern competition policy are shallow

For most of the post-war era, Japan's principal economic policy goal was development and growth through managed competition. Competition policy was assigned to a separate agency, independent of the government but politically not strong enough to promote its policies effectively, while the ministries that regulate industry and investment were more powerful. In many sectors, competition and growth were treated as inconsistent through much of that period.[63] Because of concerns about growth and fairness of market outcomes, competition policy yielded to policies for ensuring stable supply or promoting specific industries.

Japan's pre-war experience provided no foundation for an anti-cartel competition policy. Social values of harmony (*wa*) contributed

Historically, competition policy took second place to managed development and strong government intervention...

to a scepticism of the value of competition. Bureaucratic anxieties of "excess competition" or "confusion in the market" (Lincoln, 1998b) led to regulatory policies such as tolerance or promotion of cartels, and to contemporary "supply and demand balancing" by the administration.[64] In the post-war US occupation, cartel policy reversed, and a new antimonopoly act and enforcement agency were established based on US models. But the imported policy did not enjoy support in the business community, and it was politically vulnerable. When the occupation ended, the AMA was cut back. Through most of the 1950s and 1960s, the competition law went essentially unenforced.[65] "Competition" policy in many sectors became centrally guided investment, explicit exemptions, and implicit guidance. Rivalry and entry were controlled in key sectors.

The FTC continued to hold to the idea of promoting the competitive process. In the 1970s, the FTC used the law's criminal sanctions against price fixing for the first time, in response to the oil shocks. The FTC followed increased enforcement efforts with proposals for major amendments to strengthen the law. But other ministries also received new powers to guide industries through restructuring, and in the early 1980s the FTC's efforts to attack cartels were blunted (Sanekata and Wilks, 1996). Despite the stronger competition law, FTC enforcement activity dropped.

... but competition enforcement revived in the 1990s in response to globalisation and trade pressures.

Competition enforcement revived again in the 1990s in response to globalisation. Claims that lax competition law enforcement gave Japanese firms unfair trading advantages in world markets led the Japanese government to commit to increasing enforcement against exclusionary cartels, to greater reliance on more formal and public enforcement and prosecutions, and to boosting attention to competition issues in the distribution system and in inter-corporate *keiretsu* groups. Many of these commitments represented changes that the FTC had long advocated. The FTC increased its formal enforcement activity, strengthened its guidelines on horizontal and vertical issues, modernised its merger standards, added to its staff and budget, and raised its profile in advocating competition issues at other ministries.

One reason why the government has done so much to manage risk and suppress supposedly "excessive" competition is a deep concern that more competition could lead to job losses. Not only Japanese businesses, but Japanese consumers, are reportedly willing to pay higher prices, believing that the non-competitive system that produces them is more stable, secure, and fair than a competitive market would be. Recognising Japanese cultural attitudes toward competition policy is important in assessing what direction policy and reform may take.

Japan's economic success now makes it imperative to shift policy goals from "catch-up" development to consumer welfare. Competition policy is the key to that shift.

Still, Japan's economic success now makes it possible, indeed imperative, to shift policy goals from "catch-up" development to consumer welfare. The competition agency is responding to this change by redirecting its efforts to practices that impair efficient markets. The current deregulation programme recognises that growth can no longer come through direction from the centre, but must result from the self-reliant risk-taking of competitive enterprises. For that to happen, competition policy must take a larger role than it has to date.

The basic tools of Japan's competition policy are becoming stronger, more deterring, and more oriented to market competition

The basic competition law is the Antimonopoly Act ("AMA"), which prohibits unreasonable restraints of trade, "private monopolisation", and monopoly, as well as unfair practices and anti-competitive mergers. Competition policy in the broader sense has also been shaped by special laws and exemptions, formal and informal, that have encouraged or tolerated cartels, mergers, and distribution controls. In the last few years, steps have been taken to clear these away, and to move toward a generally applicable, consistent policy of competition as the rule for business behaviour.

The Antimonopoly Act provides a solid basis for competition policy enforcement.

Among the most important steps is stepped-up enforcement of the prohibition of anti-competitive agreements among competitors as "unreasonable restraints of trade".[66] The FTC applies a presumption that agreements affecting price are unreasonable. In its Guidelines, such as those for trade associations, agreements that affect price or restrict entry, quantities, customers, sales channels, facilities or technology are described as violations "in principle", and are contrasted with other kinds of conduct that might be defended on the grounds that there is no anti-competitive effect. For violations related to prices, the most important sanction is a pecuniary surcharge, conceived as a confiscation of improper profits. Criminal penalties are also available, both under the AMA[67] and under Criminal Code prohibitions against bid-rigging involving public projects[68] (see Box 3.1). The FTC has announced a policy of criminal enforcement in the most egregious cases of price and output cartels, market allocation agreements, bid-rigging, boycotts, and other AMA violations that affect important national interests.

Agreements that affect price or restrict entry are described as violations "in principle".

In Japan's traditional approach to market competition, fair treatment has been as important as free processes. But concern about fairness among competitors makes it hard to develop clear rules against anti-competitive co-operation. Government guidance of industry to consensus about common industry practices is a point of reference for identifying what is unfair. Thus, a pervasive competition policy problem has been government sponsorship or toleration of horizontal industry co-ordination.

Trade associations have facilitated long-standing anti-competitive relationships, both within and among industries. Correcting their behaviour is more difficult where, as in Japan, associations have close relationships with related ministries, which use the associations to achieve administrative objectives. Thus an association may try to defend its action by claiming that it was doing what a ministry told it to do. The FTC has found that a high proportion of violations by trade associations have some connection with government regulations or

Trade associations present recurring competition problems, particularly when their actions are linked to instructions from a ministry.

administrative actions.[69] In dealing with trade association problems, the FTC has relied strongly on guidelines and education as well as enforcement, and has given trade associations the opportunity to consult with the FTC in advance about whether their plans comply with the law. About 30 per cent of these applications disclose potential violations.

Rules about anti-competitive administrative guidanceseem clear...

Ministries' reliance on administrative guidance to help industries control or prevent competition has been a contentious and difficult problem. Informal guidance is officially banned (see Chapter 2). The FTC's 1994 Guideline says that even formally proper administrative guidance may not be a complete defence against competition law enforcement, and an agreement among competitors to facilitate compliance could violate the AMA. Following guidance that is not based on specific law or regulation exposes a firm to liability that depends on the purpose, content and method of the guidance.

... but little action seems to have been taken to enforce them.

These efforts to control anti-competitive administrative guidance point in the right direction, but it is not clear how much effect they are having. In four years, only two cases have found violations of the AMA where firms were evidently following informal administrative guidance. The 1998 deregulation programme instructs ministries to consult with the FTC so that anti-competitive regulations are not simply replaced by the equivalent in the form of administrative guidance. But this instruction would only deal with overt guidance. Covert, implicit guidance is also a serious concern.

Box 3.1. Government-sponsored collusion: the problem of bid rigging

For a century, it was common for a ministry to designate which firms it would accept bids from, and for those firms then to agree among themselves which one would win it. Consumer groups have protested the high taxes that pay for this system, but the high profits have also underwritten support from powerful politicians.

A consensus for reform, which developed after the Shin Kanemaru scandals in the early 1990s brought down the LDP government, now supports the FTC's concentration on bid rigging as its top enforcement priority. The 1984 guidelines were replaced in 1994. In the current guidelines, agreements about who will win a bid, what the minimum bid will be, or how to divide bids all violate the AMA "in principle", that is, the parties cannot defend by claiming their conduct did not impair competition. Other kinds of conduct, including exchanges of information, are treated as "highly suspect" if they have a high probability of leading to a tacit understanding or common intent about who will win a bid.

Criminal actions against bid rigging are increasing. A 1997 AMA case against the 25 designated vendors of water supply meters, for rigging bids to the Tokyo Metropolitan Government, led to convictions of 25 companies and 34 employees. Fines totalled ¥ 155 million, and the employees received prison sentences of six to nine months (FTC, 1998). A 1995 FTC accusation led to a 1996 conviction against nine electrical equipment manufacturers for rigging bids to the Japan Sewage Works Agency, with fines totalling ¥ 460 million and (suspended) prison sentences. In addition, the FTC assessed surcharges of ¥ 1 036 million (FTC, 1997). The FTC has also educated the agencies that solicit bids about what they can do to protect themselves. Some successes are reported: the city of Zama adopted a policy to discipline suspected bid-riggers, and applied that policy in its latest tender to save ¥ 700 million on a road project.[70]

Vertical agreements and constraints, among suppliers and distributors, are also subject to AMA prohibition of "unfair trade practices". This is particularly important, as competition problems in Japan's distribution sector are widely recognized.[71] One aspect of the law about vertical relationships is being re-examined. The law prohibits resale price maintenance, but permits exceptions. The FTC has moved to abolish nearly all of the exemptions except, as do other OECD countries, Japan is considering whether to treat copyrighted works differently. An FTC study group has recommended moving toward repealing the exemption for these, too (FTC, 1998).

The law can deal thoroughly with distribution constraints.

The AMA prohibits "private monopolisation",[72] that is, substantial restraints of competition accomplished by a single firm (or by firms acting together) through overtly exclusionary or controlling conduct. The law also empowers the FTC to break up monopolies.[73] That power is subject to demanding requirements, though, and has never been used. Because the evidentiary requirements are so difficult to meet, the AMA power to break up monopolies has not been applied effectively to restructuring network monopolies, nor to other commonly encountered competition problems that arise in the course of restructuring.

But the law about "monopolistic situations" has not been used.

If cartel co-operation were to be prohibited more effectively, then even more mergers are likely. Thus, the rules applied to mergers must be up-to-date and transparent, and they must be applied sensitively yet firmly. Economically sensitive merger policy could facilitate larger-scale reforms. Permitting mergers rather than cartels, especially when they involve financially weak firms, might be a faster and more efficient way to shift assets to more productive uses as economic and technical conditions change. Of course, these mergers, which are harder to undo than cartels, must not be allowed to create monopolies or erect barriers to new entry after conditions improve.

Merger enforcement may become a very important tool as reform proceeds.

The law prohibits mergers (and other complete or partial combinations among businesses) whose effect may be to restrain competition. Because merger cases have commonly been resolved through informal and voluntary consultations between the FTC and the merging parties, for a long time there were few cases or public explanations of how decisions had been reached. The FTC has undertaken reforms to improve merger enforcement such as new merger guidelines, which put less emphasis on structural measures than did its previous guidelines and more on other elements of the analysis, and publication of summaries of leading merger matters.

Until recently, lack of transparency has impaired the credibility and effectiveness of FTC merger enforcement.

Several merger issues relevant to regulation would benefit from clearer rules. A good explanation of how financial difficulties are considered would encourage substitution of merger controls for the recession cartels that are soon to be eliminated, and for ministry-directed restructuring programs. A continuing uncertainty is the relationship between competition analysis and related policies and decisions of sectoral regulators.

63

Eliminating the ban on holding companies signaled reform in the AMA itself.

Historically, the most important law about structure was the AMA's prohibition of holding companies. This was eliminated at the end of 1997 (FTC, 1998). This reform, with other changes to modernise Japan's merger enforcement processes, have been promoted as necessary for Japanese corporations to be able to restructure themselves flexibly and quickly and move into new businesses. The changes are seen as "deregulation" of the AMA itself. The FTC endorsed repealing the holding company ban, after decades of bitter resistance, signaling that it was willing to change its traditional position in the interest of reform.

Competition policy is not tied well enough to consumer policies, though.

Policy linkages between competition and consumer protection, though consistent and appropriate, are not institutionalised and are less effective than they could be as tools for reform. There seems to be no systematic co-ordination between consumer and competition issues and policies. The lack of clear co-ordination and mutual support mechanisms represents a missed opportunity to promote an effective reform agenda. Consumer groups, although sometimes wary about how businesses might take advantage of consumers and thus wary of regulatory reform, nonetheless can be allies if they are persuaded of the benefits of greater choice and lower prices that come from more competition and market openness.

In the 1990s, the FTC emerged as an ambitious enforcer of competition-based policies

The FTC's institutional independence is a strength...

The FTC was designed to act independently of the government or any ministry. Independence is reinforced by the Commissioners'tenure protections, though appointment of personnel from other ministries sustained long-term ties with the rest of the government. These historic patterns of appointment are changing, though, and these changes may portend greater independence and activity. The final report of the Administrative Reform Committee in December 1997, which proposed to make the FTC an external bureau of a newly-created Ministry of General Affairs, emphasised the importance of maintaining its investigational and decisional independence, noting that because competition policy under the AMA sometimes works at cross purposes to industrial policy, the two should be kept clearly separate (FTC, 1998).

... and a weakness, if it makes it more difficult for the FTC to promote competition policy in other regulatory areas.

The FTC is one of the few independent agencies in the Japanese government structure to survive from the occupation era. Now, as controversy grows over government economic policies, the FTC's separation from other government structures, once seen as a sign of weakness, may be seen as a strength. But a problem of institutional independence is that it can cut off access to policy processes within the government. To counteract this risk, the FTC has statutory responsibilities[74] for co-ordinating laws and orders that relate to the substantive concerns of the AMA, and has also informally offered views of its study groups to other ministries. The FTC can veto proposals for legislation that contradict the AMA, but in practice it has never done so. Instead, compromises have been reached. But FTC views have sometimes been effective. For example, on several occasions MITI has withheld administrative guidance at the FTC's request, particularly concerning the formation of joint sales agencies.

Although policy is technically applied through law enforcement, the FTC's methods are more administrative and regulatory than litigious, and the agency has been criticised for concluding too many cases with statements of "caution" or "warning". In the 1990s, the FTC greatly increased its reliance on stronger, more formal measures. The FTC responded to criticism about the transparency of its processes by issuing detailed guidelines, usually developed through a public consultation process, and by regular publicity about its consultations and actions.

The FTC has improved its enforcement processes...

Criminal enforcement has also revived in the 1990s, but is still rare. The most significant use is in public procurement, where prosecution may be the most effective weapon against pervasive bid-rigging. Despite calls for increased action, FTC referrals for prosecution average only about one cartel case per year.[75] A liaison arrangement has been set up with the Ministry of Justice to coordinate criminal actions. Now that the FTC and the prosecutor have brought exemplary actions to establish the principle, and the FTC leadership is better connected to the prosecutor's office, the use of criminal sanctions might increase.

... but its approach to criminal enforcement is still tentative.

Box 3.2. **Private suits as a supplement to public enforcement**

Stronger and more effective private relief has been a subject of trade negotiations and of study by the FTC and others. US and EU negotiators urged that Japanese law and procedure make it easier for alleged victims to challenge anti-competitive conduct in court, without having to rely first on the FTC. Demands have concentrated on two issues: authorizing private parties to obtain injunctions under the AMA's substantive rules, and changing rules about proof of damages so plaintiffs could win more easily. A recent report by a MITI-sponsored study group on a related subject encouraged changes like these. The FTC's own views on this are guarded, neither endorsing nor rejecting the expansion of private rights of action. An FTC study group prepared a partial interim report which the FTC publicized in late 1998, and continues to review whether new legislation should be introduced.

If reliance on the courts is to increase, though, other problems need attention. The court system is relatively small, so there are few judges. The greater practical impediment is that there are not enough lawyers, since the legal profession is, in practical terms, equivalent to a cartel that has effectively protected itself against competitive new entry. The current deregulation programme calls for expanding the number of new lawyers. Even at the highest rate of expansion being considered, though, it will take 50 years for the number of lawyers per capita in Japan to equal that in the EU.

Suits by consumers have been rare, but suits by businesses have increased and some have succeeded. Despite the practical problems, expanding rights of private action could be valuable. It would bring in additional resources to competition policy enforcement. It would offer the prospect of tangible recoveries for victims of illegal practices. And it would galvanise the FTC by indirectly pressuring it to continue producing a high-quality product, namely effective, independent law enforcement. For if it did not, "customers" could shift their business to the courts.

The reach of competition policy, however, remains constrained by exemptions and regulations, though some progress has been made. This limits its contribution to economic recovery

Exemptions from the law have been a serious impediment...

The problem of government-sponsored anti-competitive behaviour is unusually great in Japan. Even where national government regulation has been reformed to promote competition, local government levels have sometimes interfered.

... but recent reform efforts have sharply reduced the number of exemptions...

At one time, there were more than a thousand explicit exemptions from the AMA. That number was cut about 90 per cent, and steps are underway to reduce or eliminate still more. Of the approximately 90 exemptions that remained in March 1996, about one-third have now been eliminated, there are plans to eliminate about another third, and current plans show that about a third will be retained, in many cases with modifications to reduce their scope. Those that remain are significant, although many appear in areas where other OECD countries also have a history of exemption or special treatment. The fact that most items discussed in the current plans will be retained indicates that the remaining exemptions will be harder to eliminate.

But, after formal exemptions are removed, continuing attention is needed to ensure that other laws do not provide special competition-policy treatment for particular industries. For example, although depression and rationalisation cartels will no longer be provided in the AMA itself, other industry-specific laws should be monitored to ensure that they do not provide protection against competition law liability for firms that co-operate in restructuring under ministry guidance.

... and controlling entry by supply-demand balancing should be eliminated as a high priority.

Government bodies are deeply involved in managing a critical competitive strategy variable – entry – by using judgements about an appropriate supply-demand balance as a criterion for issuing licenses or other necessary permits, or for informal or even indirect administrative guidance to the same effect. The 1998 deregulation programme set out principles for the next stage of reform, which if implemented could help eliminate some of these problems. It calls for the FTC to survey and make proposals about fields where entry is restricted, by supply-demand balancing or other regulations. The FTC is to study fields where there has already been relaxation to report on the results and recommend further steps. The programme states that the eventual goal is to ease or abolish such regulations. Reaching that goal is critical to the success of reform based on competition principles. It is unfortunate that the programme calls only for further study and does not set clear, specific targets for eliminating important and well-known constraints by a date certain.

The FTC is becoming an effective advocate in embedding competition principles into administrative actions at national and local levels

FTC study groups have contributed to reform, but more could be done.

The FTC has a statutory responsibility to advise about laws and regulations that could affect competition.[76] It has fulfilled this function principally through the products of academic study groups. The

FTC study group's projects have included trucking, airlines, electricity, gas, telecommunications, broadcasting, and resale price maintenance of copyright works. Recommendations by FTC study groups are credited with helping accomplish several major goals. The group played a role in changing the policy and the law about large scale retail stores. The FTC is undertaking surveys about anti-competitive entry barriers erected by local governments.

More could be done to demonstrate the FTC's seriousness. In the current deregulation programme, the FTC may have an important avenue for access and advocacy as part of the Secretariat to the Deregulation Committee. And the FTC's views would be taken even more seriously if the study group work was connected clearly to the FTC's main law enforcement responsibilities. The FTC staff who are doing the background research for the study group could be a nucleus of expertise for bringing enforcement actions in these industries.

Regulatory reform will not succeed without effective competition policies, but competition enforcement is not yet strong enough

The substantive legal basis for competition policy in Japan is sound. Resources applied to enforcement, in budget and personnel, are increasing despite belt-tightening elsewhere in the government. The FTC has a record of more vigorous action over the last several years. A growing number in the government recognise the need for reform of regulatory systems that affect business initiative, for more competitive, self-reliant industry, and for less central direction.

The recent revival of competition enforcement is promising...

But countervailing weaknesses are troubling. There is pervasive scepticism, in the public and the government, about the process and benefits of competition. Support for, or even interest in, competition policy has been rare at the highest levels of the government. Even those who accept the need to move toward more competitive markets tend to see opportunities and needs for government intervention to facilitate the flow of capital and talent into new industries. That tendency undermines the more fundamental issue of ensuring that competitive decisions are made freely and independently in the market, by actors who assume the risks, as the basis for sustainable growth. Calls for stronger antitrust enforcement have traditionally come from labour and consumer groups worried about market abuses, rather than from reformers.

... but the breadth of support for reliance on markets rather than central direction is uncertain.

The present deregulation programme continues in the right direction, but the pace is slow. Gradual introduction of competitive institutions permits inefficiency to survive and delays potential gains in investment, innovation, and growth. Competition enforcement, though intensified, is not yet strong enough to take a leading role. The objectives of the 1998 programme cannot be achieved without stronger competition policy enforcement, which can energise the process of regulatory reform by challenging existing structures that are no longer working.

The objectives of regulatory reform cannot be achieved without stronger competition policy enforcement.

67

Chapter 4

ENHANCING MARKET OPENNESS THROUGH REGULATORY REFORM

Market openness further increases the benefits of regulatory reform for consumers and national economic performance. Reducing regulatory barriers to trade and investment enables countries in a global economy to benefit more from comparative advantage and innovation. This also means the costs to Japan of poor regulations increase in global markets. As traditional barriers to trade have been progressively dismantled, "behind the border" measures have become more relevant to effective market access, and national regulations are exposed to unprecedented international scrutiny by trade and investment partners. Regulatory quality is no longer (if ever it was) a purely "domestic" affair.

Japan's achievement in reducing barriers at the border is impressive among OECD countries...

Recognising the benefits from the integration in the open multilateral trading system, Japan has improved market access in border measures to a level equal to or better than many OECD countries. Japan reduced general tariff rates to one of the lowest average tariff rates in the OECD: 4.8 per cent for all products and 2.5 per cent for manufactured products.[77] Good progress on formal non-tariff border measures in Japan is also notable.[78] These measures helped bring down consumer prices in Japan, reduce the cost structure of exporting firms, and bring in new technologies and innovations that supported dynamic adjustment.

Japan has improved market access in border measures to a level equal to or better than many OECD countries...

... yet Japan's consumers and industries continue to face high prices due to behind-the-border regulatory barriers.

The benefits to Japan of these steps are, however, limited by many "behind the border" regulatory barriers. Japan's government has stated that it will further open its economy to global competition through deregulation. In its 1998 "Three-Year Programme for the Promotion of Deregulation", the government said it would achieve "an open and fair socio-economic system which is internationally open and based on principles of self-responsibility and market mechanism". Broad-based regulatory reform will indeed make an important contribution to opening Japan's markets. Major reforms, such as oil import deregulation, the Big Bang in financial services, and abolishment of the Large Scale Retail Store Law, have already improved market openness.

... yet continuing regulatory barriers reduce the benefits to Japanese consumers of international trade.

These steps are necessary. Japanese consumers are losing substantial wealth, and Japanese businesses are losing competitiveness, because of the higher prices they pay compared to citizens in other OECD countries. Higher prices are mainly due to market access problems. Price differences between Japan's domestic markets and comparable foreign markets[79] are persistently wide, perhaps due to high trade protection for agriculture and some manufacturing sectors (according to Sazanami), or to the inefficiency of highly regulated service sectors and utilities (according to Daiwa Economic Research Institute), or a combination of factors. As a result, Japanese consumers are losing major sources of welfare increases, that is, foreign sources.

One consequence is that consumers and industries pay higher prices for many goods and services.

Government surveys of price differences (EPA, 1997a and MITI, 1996) show that citizens of Tokyo pay 8-30 per cent more for purchases than do citizens in other major international cities. Japanese industries pay almost twice as much for non-manufacturing intermediary inputs compared to their competitors, and three or four times as much as those in Asian emerging economies[80] (Table 4.1). Price differences appear to be lower for manufacturing inputs. Sazanami (1995) estimated that Japanese tariff and non-tariff barriers cost Japanese consumers 10 to 15 trillion yen in 1989 (75 to 110 billion 1989 US dollars). At the expense of consumers, Japanese producers gained 7 to 9.6 trillion yen.[81]

Table 4.1.　**International price differences for intermediary inputs**

	Japan	US	Germany	Korea	Taiwan	Hong Kong	Singapore	China
Total inputs	100	88	70	39	33	53	46	20
Manufacturing	100	91	101	55	65	67	66	45
Non-manufacturing	100	85	51	28	21	43	33	12

Source:　MITI, *Survey on Price Differentials between Domestic and International Markets for Intermediary Inputs*, 1998.

Alarmingly, regulatory barriers are also contributing to very low levels of foreign investment in Japan

Japan does not even place in the top 25 countries in attracting foreign investment, although it is the world's second largest economy.

Compared to other OECD countries, Japan has been far below average in attracting foreign direct investment, despite the government's expressed policy stance to welcome it (Figure 4.1). This is seen by trading partners as a sign of the restrictive nature of the Japanese business environment, notably from domestic regulations. Figures for 1997 suggest that FDI (foreign direct investment) inflows to Japan amounted to only US$ 3 224 million. It did not even place among the top 25 countries with respect to FDI inflows (OECD, 1998b), though Japan's economy is the second largest in the world.

Current policies to promote imports and investment are not a substitute for freeing market forces through regulatory reform.

Recognising the high costs of structural barriers to investment, the Japanese government has shifted from export promotion policies to focus on promoting imports and inward investment. Incentives to inward investments were introduced to supplement financial and fiscal incentives for domestic activities. Japan has strengthened policy efforts on infrastructure for imports and inward

Figure 4.1. **Share of stocks of inward and outward direct investment in GDP in OECD countries (1995)**

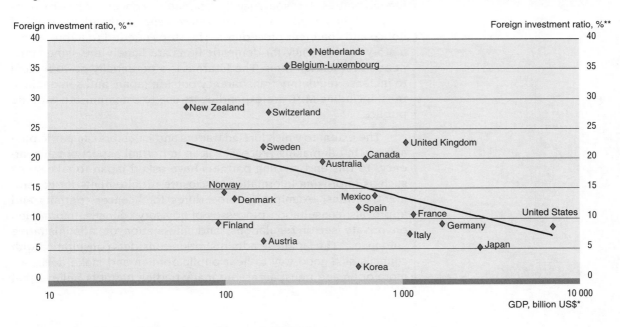

* GDP measured at current prices and current PPPs in billion US dollars.
** Average of inward investment and outward investment relative to GDP (except for Mexico, inward only).
Source: OECD, *Regulatory Reform: Netherlands Review,* TD/TC/WP(98)41, calculated from AFA databases and OECD's Foreign Investment Database.

investments, especially by expanding Foreign Access Zones.[82] Removing barriers to market-driven decisions on trade and investment could, however, be a more effective approach to stimulate imports and inward investment.

Japan has not sufficiently integrated the OECD efficient regulation principles into its domestic regulatory regimes

An important step in ensuring that regulations do not unnecessarily reduce market openness is to build the OECD "efficient regulation" principles (see Box 4.1) into domestic regulatory process for social and economic regulations, and administrative practices. Despite some progress, the Japanese regulatory system in many respects is still perceived as unfriendly to new competition, especially foreign competition. This reflects the relatively poor extent to which six efficient regulation principles related to market openness are integrated into the Japanese regulatory system.

Lack of transparency in Japan's regulatory and administrative procedures have discouraged foreign traders and investors

Lack of transparency in regulatory and administrative processes is a major weakness of Japan's domestic regulatory system. Non-transparency affects all potential market entrants and competitors, who must have adequate information on regulations so that they can base their decisions on accurate assessments of potential costs,

Transparency is a continuing concern of Japan's trading partners, who have welcomed reforms such as the planned use of notice and comment procedures.

71

risks, and market opportunities, but has disproportionate costs for foreign parties. Transparency is a continuing concern of Japan's trading partners, who have welcomed reforms such as the planned use of notice and comment procedures. The steps needed to improve regulatory transparency for domestic firms are largely the same steps needed for foreign firms. The Internet is a potentially powerful tool to increase regulatory transparency outside Japan, and some ministries, including MPT, are expanding its use to communicate with the public.

The extent to which foreign traders and investors can participate actively in rulemaking processes is an important aspect of transparency. To this end, trading partners have asked Japan to take steps such as improving information disclosure requirements for government entities; examination procedures for licences, permits and approvals; consultation processes of advisory councils; information on private sector regulations; and information on administrative guidance.[83] The Japanese administration considers consultation with councils as a good way to hear public opinion and make decisions more open and transparent, but many trading partners believe that

---

Box 4.1. **The OECD efficient regulation principles for market openness**

To ensure that regulations do not unnecessarily reduce market openness, "efficient regulation" principles should be built into domestic regulatory processes for social and economic regulations, and for administrative formalities. These principles, described in The OECD *Report on Regulatory Reform* and developed in the OECD's Trade Committee, have been identified by trade policy makers as key to market-oriented, trade and investment-friendly regulation. This review does not judge the extent to which Japan has complied with international commitments, but assesses whether and how domestic regulations and procedures are consistent with these substantive principles.

- *Transparency and openness of decision-making.* Foreign firms, individuals, and investors seeking access to a market must have adequate information on new or revised regulations so they can base decisions on accurate assessments of potential costs, risks, and market opportunities.

- *Non-discrimination.* Non-discrimination means equality of competitive opportunities between like products and services irrespective of country of origin.

- *Avoidance of unnecessary trade restrictiveness.* Governments should use regulations that are not more trade restrictive than necessary to fulfil legitimate objectives. Performance-based rather than design standards should be used as the basis of technical regulation; taxes or tradable permits should be used in lieu of regulations.

- *Use of internationally harmonised measures.* Compliance with different standards and regulations for like products can burden firms engaged in international trade with significant costs. When appropriate and feasible, internationally harmonised measures should be used as the basis of domestic regulations.

- *Recognition of equivalence of other countries' regulatory measures.* When internationally harmonised measures are not possible, necessary or desirable, the negative trade effects of cross-country disparities in regulation and duplicative conformity assessment systems can be reduced by recognising the equivalence of trading partners' regulatory measures or the results of conformity assessment performed in other countries.

- *Application of competition principles.* Market access can be reduced by regulatory action condoning anticompetitive conduct or by failure to correct anticompetitive private actions. Competition institutions should enable domestic and foreign firms affected by anti-competitive practices to present their positions.

the councils make decision making more closed (because vested interests are included, not potential competitors) and very slow.

Another aspect of transparency is the extent to which the basis for administration actions is clear to market participants so that they can compete fairly. Trading partners[84] have identified numerous transparency problems at sectoral levels, such as implementation of the Building Standards Law in the housing sector; approval processes for new products and regulation of private organisations in the financial services sector; procurement processes in the energy sector; consideration of a more cost-oriented interconnection accounting system for telecommunications; and approval procedures for medical machines. Transparency of slot allocations for international airports was noted as a problem by the EU.

Complaints persist, but the government is promoting use of international standards and recognition of foreign regulatory measures

Reliance on internationally harmonised measures (such as global standards) as the basis of domestic regulations can expand trade flows. Japan has announced several initiatives in this area. A 1997 ministerial directive encourages ministries and agencies to use international standards and certification procedures and to use foreign conformity assessment bodies, to promote mutual recognition and to simplify and speed up conformity assessment procedures. The

Japan has announced several initiatives to harmonise with international standards, which should improve market openness.

Box 4.2. OTO: Ombudsman for Foreign Traders and Investors

In some cases, procedures have been created expressly to improve access to the regulatory system by foreign parties. An important step in favour of market openness in Japan was the establishment of the Office of Trade and Investment Ombudsman (OTO) in 1982. The OTO, a unique organisation among OECD countries, aims to reduce obstacles to market openness by receiving complaints on market access relating to imports or inward investment,[85] and by organising inter-ministerial co-ordinating efforts to deal with those complaints.

Foreign firms have often chosen to appeal adverse decisions by the administration to the OTO. Issues can be resolved at the OTO Co-ordination Meeting by bureau directors, or at the OTO Executive Meeting, whose members are vice-ministers of ministries and agencies. In extraordinary cases, the Office of Market Access, chaired by the Prime Minister, will decide. By October 1998, the OTO had received 584 complaints. In 189 cases, Japanese procedures were modified to facilitate imports, and 212 complaints were judged to be based on misunderstandings.[86]

OTO cases have declined recently, possibly reflecting disappointment by foreign parties about the limitation of its authority.[87] Foreign firms point out the risks arising from appealing issues publicly, because of the discretionary power of regulatory agencies and possible retaliation.[88] According to those trading partners,[89] the OTO has focussed increasingly on border measures, shying away from barriers behind the border. Those trading partners evaluate the strengths of the OTO as its policy objectives and its composition, which includes foreign representatives. Its weaknesses are judged as its lack of authority *vis-à-vis* ministries and agencies and the fact that most issues handled lead to minor improvements in implementation of regulations rather than more fundamental change in regimes. They claim that even the OTO solves minor market access problems, those are insufficient to effectively enhance market openness in Japan and contribute to structural reforms of the Japanese economy.

new deregulation programme stresses international harmonisation. MITI introduced 237 international standards under the Electrical Appliance and Material Control Law. Japan introduced the OECD principle of Good Laboratory Practice (GLP) for chemical substances. Recent moves toward performance-based standards are notable in building materials and electricity equipment.

Yet the potential gains of further action are very large. Trading partners are requesting the alignment of Japanese standards and certifications to international norms in numerous fields such as International Electrotechnical Committee standards for many electrical products; ISO standards and performance-based standards for various building materials and tank containers specifications; and global standards of financial disclosure, supervision, accountancy rules and asset valuation.

Recognising the equivalence of trading partners' regulatory measures or the results of conformity assessment performed in other countries are two promising avenues being pursued in Japan. Trading partners and Japan's domestic businesses are supporting progress in many fields, such as acceptance of foreign standards, foreign test data, foreign testing organisations and test laboratories for construction and building materials; acceptance of foreign clinical data for medical devices and pharmaceuticals; and generalised recognition by Japanese standards related laws of European wide accreditation bodies or equivalent international bodies.

Progress has been made through cross-cutting initiatives such as the 1997 Social and Economic Action Plan, which directs that Japanese standards bodies should accept foreign data, introduce mutual recognition systems, and move toward self-certification for appropriate items. Concrete progress was made in telecommunication equipment in 1998, the first time that foreign bodies are allowed to conduct certifications in the Japanese system for mandatory standards. Another important step was introduction of an accreditation system for testing laboratories in 1997, based on internationally accepted guidelines.

The picture is mixed. The question now is speed and momentum in these critical areas. A fundamental problem not unique to Japan lies in the lack of data in assessing progress in harmonisation. Data collection and assessment would be a useful step in assessing the scope for further progress. A government-wide initiative to promote, wherever possible and appropriate, acceptance of foreign certifications and to introduce less burdensome conformity assessment procedures such as manufacturer's declaration of conformity could also speed up progress.

Unnecessary trade restrictiveness is a greater problem, due to unsupervised administrative discretion in setting and applying standards and regulations

Policies are sometimes applied in unnecessarily restrictive ways...

The Japanese administration has constructed mechanisms to ensure that regulations are not more trade restrictive than necessary to fulfil a legitimate objective. In 1997, the Office of Market Access (a cabinet level group) directed that government bodies avoid the use of standards, technical regulations and conformity assessment procedures that are unnecessary obstacles to trade (EPA, 1997b). MITI and MOFA review some regulations to check this aspect. Yet there are wide gaps in these quality controls. Japan does not have a system of regulatory impact assessment for proposed regulations (see Chapter 2), nor do MITI and MOFA see other regulations than those submitted to cabinet discussions.

As a result, policies are sometimes applied in unnecessarily restrictive ways, often justified by policy objectives such as safety. Such measures function as protections for domestic firms.[90] Regulations on construction and building materials have frequently been criticised by trading partners as burdensome and complicated,[91] resulting in major obstacles to trade, though the adoption of performance-based standards in June 1998 may improve matters. Quarantine and inspection procedures for fresh fruits and vegetables, flowers, frozen foods, and food supplements are frequently criticised as trade restrictive. Other complaints focus on burdensome regulations in other areas, including electricity equipment, telecommunications services and equipment, custom procedures, medical products, and vehicle inspection.

Burdensome regulations have hampered inward investment as well. Complex legal provisions related to mergers and acquisitions have been pointed out as an important obstacle to investment in Japan, though other cultural and institutional barriers such as a high level of cross-shareholding between allied companies; a low percentage of publicly-traded common stock; widespread mistrust of foreign ownership; reluctance of keiretsu members to see fellow members under foreign control; and non-transparent accountancy regulations are also noted.[92]

Japan has a good record of formal adherence to non-discrimination, but practices by ministries and self-regulated bodies are problematic

In trade and investment agreements and most laws, Japan has consistently adhered to the principle of non-discrimination although, as in all countries, there are exceptions. Important exceptions to the national treatment principle include prohibitions on partnerships between Japanese lawyers and foreign legal consultants and against employment of Japanese lawyers by foreign legal consultants; discrimination between foreign and domestic banks in funding mechanisms by the Bank of Japan; and special notification procedures on foreign investment in some sectors. In the latter case, for example, the new Foreign Exchange and Foreign Trade Law provides for waiting periods – of 30 days or 5 months depending on the sector concerned – before the execution of a foreign direct investment, in order for the Minister of Finance and the regulating minister to determine if the investment could be detrimental to national security, hinder the maintenance of public order, obstruct the protection of public safety; or cause "a notable adverse effect on the smooth operation of the national economy".[93]

... though Japan has consistently adhered to the principle of non-discrimination, with a few exceptions.

75

More frequent problems seem to arise during the application of regulations at ministerial level. Trading partners have raised numerous examples. Other concerns are expressed about discriminatory self-regulation by industry associations and professional services associations such as legal and accounting services.[94] Exclusionary self-regulations by the professional associations do not allow foreigners the same opportunities to practice in Japan as have their own members.

Competition policy enforcement in Japan has attracted acute concerns of trading partners and its significance will increase

The role of competition policy as a tool in addressing market access concerns will increase in importance.

A key problem with current efforts is that reforms have concentrated on procedures rather than on market structures, often the major obstacle to market access when weak enforcement of competition policy permits anti-competitive practices by private firms or semi-public organisations. Too, demand supply adjustment clauses in individual sectors give regulatory authorities the right control the number of firms and limit the entry of new competitors, domestic and foreign.[95] As more sectors of the Japanese economy are subject to regulatory reform, the role of competition policy as a tool in addressing market access concerns will increase in importance.

Chapter 3 discusses how the enforcement and advocacy of competition laws and policy can be strengthened with respect to private abuses of the market, anti-competitive government regulation, and actions by trade associations or others with regulatory powers. The nature of procedures for hearing and deciding complaints about actions that impair market access and effective competition by foreign firms, the nature of the institutions that hear such complaints, and adherence to deadlines (if they exist) are key issues for market openness. There are no overt differences in access to competition complaint processes for domestic and foreign firms in Japan. Nonetheless, restrictions on the legal profession could hamper foreign firms in particular in gaining legal expertise.

Increased competition surveillance would be particularly valuable for market openness in the distribution sector. Traditions of long-term close relationships between manufacturers and distributors remains a major obstacle to foreign access to the Japanese market. The JFTC might consider reviewing antitrust compliance programs of influential firms in these and other "highly-oligopolistic industries" to confirm that dominant firms are complying with the Anti-Monopoly Law and the JFTC's Distribution Guidelines. The JFTC might also consider initiating a survey on the relationship between vertical keiretsu and certain perceived market access problems with respect to distribution.

Trade pressures have been helpful in promoting regulatory reform, but reform should in future focus on domestic benefits and comprehensive change, rather than on specific trade frictions

Trade pressures revealed weaknesses in Japan's regulations that were useful in supporting reform...

The main value of complaints by other countries and foreign firms is that they underscore systemic regulatory weaknesses that impose costs on domestic economic development. Complaints from foreign parties about the Japanese regulatory system demonstrate that serious regulatory problems in Japan also have important effects in other countries. Hence, there is a shared interest in reform, and foreign pressures will continue to be valuable. Deregulation became a major part of trade debates in 1990 under the Japan-US Structural Impediment Initiative Talks, and were carried forward in the 1993 Japan-US Framework for a New Economic Partnership. With the EU, Japan reached an agreement in 1995 on deregulatory measures for autos and components.

Helped by political support in resolving trade debate, foreign pressure undeniably promoted reform in Japan against strong domestic opposition. Yet trade and investment-related complaints have weaknesses. They have tended to support incremental and item-by-item strategies rather than comprehensive reform plans, because of priorities arising from specific trade interests. Worse, bilateral trade discussions may have given the Japanese public the impression that regulatory reform has been imposed from the outside. They did not help the public to understand how reform is in its own interests and may have prevented the support for reform from expanding to a broader basis.

... but foreign pressure also helped to shift the reform priority to incremental and item-by-item changes and may have given the Japanese public the impression that regulatory reform has been imposed from the outside.

If reform is to successfully address deeper changes to regulatory institutions, habits, and long-held practices, reform must be understood, not as only reacting to foreign pressures, but as promoting the welfare of Japan. In particular, better recognition is needed of the domestic benefits of greater market openness. More attention to fundamental issues and reforms to domestic regulatory systems will, in turn, help to resolve trade tensions more effectively.

Regulatory reform must be understood by the public as promoting the welfare of Japan. This will in turn resolve trade problems more effectively.

Chapter 5

REGULATORY REFORM IN THE ELECTRICITY INDUSTRY

Major reforms of the power sector are being launched in Japan, with long-term consequences for the development of the sector. The benefits and risks of further competition and consumer choice, and the need to balance multiple economic and social policy goals within a comprehensive policy framework are illustrated in these reforms.

Reforms in the electricity sector must balance multiple policy goals.

Reform must balance the 3Es of Japanese energy policy

The key policy goals in the sector are known as the 3Es of Japanese energy policy: energy security, economic growth, and environmental protection:

- **Energy security**, or security of supply, has been a fundamental aim of electricity policy for 25 years, since the oil crises of the 1970s illustrated the risks of over-dependence on imported oil. Japan has no natural energy resources of significance. Policies have included government support for nuclear power, bans on oil-fired power baseload capacity generation, low interest loans from the Japan Development Bank for utilities to invest in other power sources, and research and development funding by government and utilities. As a result, the generation sector is more diversified. Today, companies use more nuclear, coal and natural gas-fired power generation and some renewable sources, although Japan's dependency on oil fired power generation remains among the highest in OECD countries.

Energy security goals have shaped electricity policy since the oil shocks of the 1970s, and diversity of fuel supply remains a high priority.

- **Economic growth** should be stimulated by improving the efficiency of the energy industry. Concerns about high electricity prices (the highest in the OECD, see Figure 5.1) have led to reforms based on the introduction of competition. Although the electricity sector accounts for a small fraction of employment and GDP, the sector is strategically important as a key input to other sectors of the Japanese economy. Liberalising the electricity market could improve capital and labour productivity, reduce electricity prices and boost output. Explicit targets have been set for economic performance in the sector.

Japan has the highest electricity prices in the OECD, which is a drag on economy-wide performance.

79

Figure 5.1. **Electricity prices in IEA countries, 1997**
Industry sector*

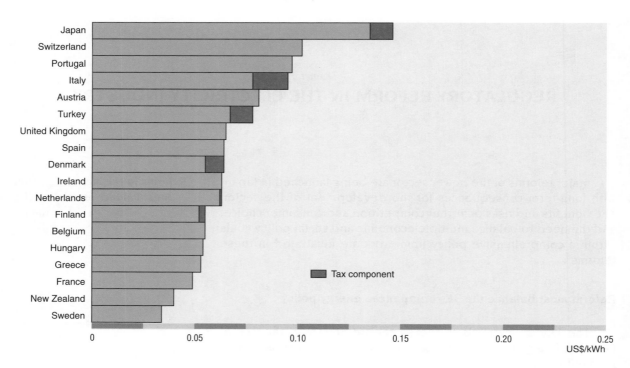

Figure 5.2. **Household sector****

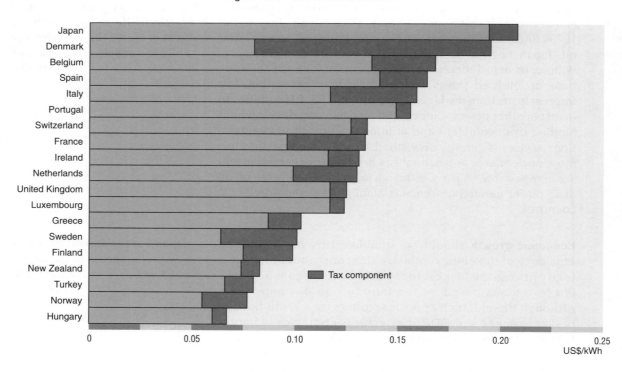

*   Data not available for Australia, Canada, Germany, Luxembourg, Norway and the United States.
**   Data not available for Australia, Austria, Canada, Germany and the United States.
Source: Energy Prices and Taxes, IEA/OECD Paris, 1997.

– **Environmental protection** goals focus on greenhouse gas emissions from the energy sector, particularly the government's commitments to stabilise carbon dioxide emissions at 1990 levels by the year 2000 and, with the Kyoto agreement, to cut emissions of greenhouse gases by 6 per cent below this level over the period 2008-2012. Emissions of sulfur and nitrogen oxides from Japan's electric utilities are extremely low due to strict environmental standards. Emissions control investments in coal- and oil-fired generation brought emissions intensity in 1996 from all plants to 0.17 g/kWh for sulfur oxides and 0.21g/kWh for nitrogen oxides. This is bettered only by countries relying almost entirely on non-fossil generation. Carbon dioxide emissions intensity fell to 0.1 kg-C/kWh with the substantial rise in nuclear generation and combined cycle gas power generation.

Today, environmental protection goals are focussed on greenhouse gas emissions. Environmental performance for other emissions is very good due to strict standards.

Japan's electricity sector is structured around ten private, regional, vertically integrated utilities...

Ten heavily regulated, investor-owned, regional, and vertically integrated utilities dominate the sector. While not monopolies in law, no new general electric utilities have been created since 1951, with the exception of Okinawa. The utilities are vertically integrated and responsible for generation, transmission, distribution and retail supply. Three (Tokyo, Kansai and Chubu) are large by world standards, with Tokyo second in size only to Electricité de France. Inter-utility trade amounts to about 46 TWh, or 5 per cent of the total generated. There is no grid connection with other countries.

Ten investor-owned vertically integrated utilities are responsible for generation, transmission, distribution and retail supply.

In addition, the Electric Power Development Corporation (EPDC) owns 6 per cent of total generating capacity, and sells power at cost to the utilities through long-term contracts. The government owns two-thirds of EPDC, but has announced plans to privatise it by 2003. Japan Atomic Power Corporation (JAPC) was established by the utilities, EPDC and other nuclear enterprises to commercialise nuclear power development in Japan. It sells power at cost to the utilities. Concluding that additional nuclear energy is necessary to balance the 3Es, the government intends to promote nuclear power and, more specifically, the construction of 16-20 additional nuclear reactors by 2010.

... whose commercial decisions are heavily regulated by MITI

The sector is regulated by the Ministry of International Trade and Industry. Under the Electric Utilities Industry Law, MITI has a central role in developing the structure of the industry (entry, exit and expansion), co-ordinating utilities, and regulating tariffs. MITI is also responsible for technical and safety regulations.

MITI has a central role in developing the structure of the industry (entry, exit and expansion)...

Regulation is based on "public interest" and "demand-supply balancing" concepts common in Japan (see Chapter 3). MITI issues permits for various types of utilities, but for MITI to issue a permit,

... based on concepts of "public interest" and "demand-supply balancing".

there must be demand for the service. For the most common types of utilities, a new business "must be necessary and appropriate for the comprehensive and rational development of the electric utility supply business or otherwise for the promotion of the public interests". Permission of MITI is also needed to exit; permission is granted if the exit does not impair public interests. If a utility wishes to supply outside its service area, it needs the permission of MITI. MITI will not grant permission unless supply would "be not easy to accomplish and not apposite to undertake" for the general utility in whose area the supply is to be made.

Electricity prices are to be reduced to international levels by 2001. This requires substantial increases in efficiency, driven by competition.

Reducing electricity prices to international levels by 2001 will require rapid and large efficiency increases, which are achievable only through vigorous competition.

The government has set a target to reduce electricity prices to internationally comparable levels by 2001, an ambitious target in light of the exogenous factors which contribute to high costs in Japan (*e.g.*, high fuel and siting costs). This target will be achieved only through substantial increases in economic efficiency. The government's 1997 Action Plan for Economic Structure Reform identified efficiency through competition as a basic principle for reform in the electric power sector.

High costs are the main reason for high electricity prices (see Box 5.1). A consequence of high prices has been the development of significant in-house generation of electricity in the industrial sector, amounting to 28 per cent of all industrial demand.

Opening of tenders for generation revealed the potential for lower costs in generation, and was a good step toward competition

Competitive tenders for power generation showed that competition can significantly reduce costs of new generation, due to better economic use of valuable resources such as land.

Amendments in 1995 to the Electric Utilities Industry Law liberalised entry rules for independent power producers (IPPs), that is, generators independent of the utilities and that sell power to the utilities. Utilities are now required to conduct tenders to meet additional thermal power needs that would arise within a seven-year period. Two sets of tenders have been conducted, and the average quantity of capacity bid exceeded the average quantity tendered by at least fourfold. Prices of successful bidders averaged almost 30 per cent lower than the "upper limit prices" calculated by the utilities. Successful IPP bids total about 3 per cent of installed capacity, but MITI estimates that up to 50 GW may be available, or about 25 per cent of the existing capacity of the utilities. This is large enough to account for most of the entire forecast increase in power demand between 1998 and 2010.

The majority of capacity bid and potential for new IPP capacity came from steel and petroleum refining firms that have idle industrial land and relatively easy access to fuel sources. This allows them to overcome two major hurdles in building generating plants and bringing them online quickly.

Box 5.1. Why are electricity prices in Japan the highest in the OECD?

High capital costs: Japan has the highest investment costs for nuclear, gas and coal fired power in the OECD. High land costs, compensation payments to communities, and high safety standards (*e.g.*, earthquake resistance) contribute to high costs. Too, Japan's utilities historically relied on a small number of suppliers and only recently have encouraged foreign participation in equipment procurement tenders. Stringent standards for equipment compared to other countries force prices up and limit the number of competitors.

High fuel costs: Japanese power utilities pay 20 per cent more for oil than the OECD average and 80 per cent more for coal. Oil costs are increased by customs duties on petroleum – the revenues go toward restructuring the coal industry. High coal costs are partly attributable to use of the lowest sulfur coal to meet environmental standards, technical requirements for utility boilers and use of long term contracts with price premia for security of supply. Natural gas costs are much higher due the need to import liquefied natural gas and due to taxes.

High transmission and distribution costs: Costs for transmission and distribution infrastructure are high because of land costs, mountainous terrain, remote siting of new power stations, very high construction standards to withstand earthquakes and typhoons, and very high operating standards.

High regulatory costs: Japanese environmental regulations are strict. Most coal-fired and oil-fired power stations have equipment to greatly reduce SOx emissions. Most coal-fired plants also have advanced NOx removal technologies. The Air Pollution Control Law allows local governments to set stricter limits, resulting in additional expenses. Regulations on maintenance of power plants are highly prescriptive. Nuclear plants must have a refueling outage every 13 months though longer fuel cycles have proven elsewhere to be safe and feasible. Regulations require natural gas turbines to be completely disassembled for inspection every 30 months, a requirement not duplicated elsewhere and not recommended by the manufacturer.

Low load factors: The load factor in Japan (the ratio of the average electricity demand to the annual peak demand) is extremely low in comparison with other OECD countries, largely because of air conditioning.

Taxes and obligatory purchases of domestic coal: Subsidies for power development, primarily payments to communities near power plants for regional development, are recovered through an electricity power development tax. The 1998 budget for subsidies was 224 billion yen. Remaining revenues (238 billion yen) raised by this tax go to develop alternative energies to oil. Electric utilities are also committed to purchasing domestic coal (about 10 per cent of total utility requirements) at a price about three times higher than imported coal. Utilities also purchase power above cost from renewable sources, although the amounts involved are quite small.

Due to the success of coal and oil-fired capacity in the bidding the IPP policy could raise Japan's CO_2 emissions by 1 per cent, according to the Environment Agency. MITI plans to ask utilities to treat lower CO_2 emitting plant more favourably by limiting the tender to certain kinds of fuels or requiring them to consider fuels in evaluating future bids.

But competition could increase emissions, perhaps requiring offsetting measures in the market.

MITI plans to further open the bidding system in 1999 to allow both utilities themselves and IPPs to bid for thermal power plants coming on stream in 2008 and beyond. This is a logical step forward. The bidding process will be overseen by a neutral party, and utilities will be required to separate accounting for bidding on new plants. Care will be needed to ensure adequate protection against utilities subsidising this activity from regulated activities. Access to fuel, particularly natural gas, is a vital factor in establishing IPPs. Third party access to LNG terminals may be one way of introducing competition,

Bidding will be further opened to utilities and IPPs. This is a logical step, but care is needed to protect against utilities subsidising this activity from regulated activities.

lowering costs of natural gas, and increasing the number of IPP using natural gas.

Partial retail liberalisation is necessary to reduce electricity prices, while supporting energy security and environmental protection

Tendering will not sufficiently reduce prices – partial retail liberalisation is a necessary step.

Japan is expected to broaden tendering to encompass all thermal generation by both IPPs and utilities, but the contracted IPP capacity represents only 10 per cent of new capacity scheduled to come into service over the next several years. Tendering will not be enough to meet the objective of reducing power costs to internationally competitive levels by 2001. Moving to partial retail liberalisation is a necessary step.

Full liberalisation and introduction of a pool market are judged by the EUIC to be premature, but partial liberalisation of retail supply is under consideration.

An interim report of May 1998 produced by the Committee on Basic Policy of the Electric Utility Industry Council recommended partial liberalisation of retail supply. The report ruled out full liberalisation and introduction of a pool market as premature. Partial liberalisation of retail supply would allow some customers to choose suppliers, but the rest would remain exclusive customers of their utilities (captive customers). This means that prices will no longer be set by regulated tariffs, that these customers will choose their suppliers, that these customers would be able to contract for a variety of terms, and that the customers would manage their own energy risks.

This would be an important step in reducing prices, and setting a basis for future liberalisation.

A decision to move forward with partial liberalisation of retail supply would be an important step for Japan in reducing electricity prices, and would be consistent with other major goals of energy security and environmental protection. It could substantially lower generating costs to industrial consumers and provide a sound basis for further liberalisation.

The core issue is deciding which customers will benefit from this programme.

The key issue for partial retail liberalisation is which customers are eligible. In Japan, it would be administratively convenient to limit, at the first stage, liberalised customers to "extra high voltage" industrial and commercial customers taking power at 20 kV or above. This would liberalise 28 per cent of energy sales, a significant step. Alternatively, eligibility could be based on an equivalent annual consumption level, which can include groups of small and medium companies if they decide to jointly purchase electricity. The government should encourage utilities to implement, on a voluntary basis, a program for such aggregation.

Many regulatory changes are needed to make retail liberalisation work

The move to market requires far-reaching reforms...

Many changes in regulation and competition oversight are needed to support a coherent move to market liberalisation:

– ensure that access to transmission and system ancillary services (including backup) is cost-reflective, economically efficient, and non-discriminatory in tariffs, terms and conditions;

- boost vigilance to avoid subsidy of competitive activities from regulated activities, and encourage efficient use of system services;
- protect against anti-competitive behaviour;
- liberalise generation so that generators, including utilities, IPPs and new entrants, are free to compete for customers.

Price regulation: The present rate-of-return based mechanism, even with a yardstick approach for setting the rate, gives utilities very limited incentives to reduce costs, as they must pass on nearly all cost savings to customers. Other forms of yardstick regulation make a more direct link between one utility's regulated maximum price and other utilities'costs and allow more costs savings to be retained as profits. This provides much greater incentives for a utility to be cost efficient.

... in establishing price regulations with efficiency incentives...

Time of use tariffs: Although the load factor (ratio of maximum demand to average demand) continues to deteriorate, the high cost of producing electricity at peak periods is not reflected in prices except through a variety of optional programs. Changing standard tariffs to reflect costs by time of use could reduce peak load significantly, saving Japanese consumers billions of yen, and reducing the need for additional peak capacity.

... in pricing energy by time of use to reduce peak load...

Transmission and ancillary services: Transmission and ancillary services must be accessible at tariffs that reflect costs and are non-discriminatory to ensure that independent generators can compete with utilities to supply to end-users. For liberalised customers and IPPs, efficient pricing of the use of network services is the key to ensuring efficient use and augmentation of the transmission network.

... in ensuring that transmission and ancillary services are accessible and priced efficiently...

Investment in nuclear plants: The government has identified increased investment in nuclear power as important to meeting energy security and greenhouse gas emission goals. Hence, utilities will continue to require assurances that they will be able to recover costs from investments in new nuclear plants. If economic incentives are expected to be insufficient, one option would be to guarantee that a share of demand will be met by nuclear-generated electricity. Creating a market for nuclear-generated power would give utilities greater assurance for cost-recovery, and, with liberalisation of retail supply, would encourage utilities to compete to supply this power in the most cost efficient way.

... in creating market incentives to invest in nuclear power...

Electricity markets: Open transparent markets for trading electricity, combined with a legal framework that facilitates bilateral contracts between customers and suppliers, forges a critical link between generation competition, competition in supply and end user choice A limited spot "balancing" market could also provide a practical means of managing supply and demand imbalances.

... in deepening markets for trading electricity...

Competitive rivalry in generation: In addition to some degree of vertical separation, competitive rivalry among generators is necessary

... and in intensifying rivalry among generators.

for effective competition. Competitive rivalry is enhanced by entry by IPPs selling to liberalised customers, and by installation of private generating capacity that might generate surpluses for sale to other customers. Another, complementary means of increasing competitive rivalry is to enlarge the geographic scope of the electricity market to include several utilities. To this end, strengthening interconnections between utilities should be encouraged.

... in consumer protection...

Consumer protection: Consumers will be faced with more choices in a liberalised electricity sector. Effective consumer protection may require more information and confidence- building measures. Here, market liberalisation may require more regulation. Cooperation with consumer authorities in the course of planning is essential.

Improved institutions and roles for regulatory and competition policies are needed if investment and competition are to occur

A market environment requires regulatory institutions whose decisions are competitively neutral, transparent, and not subject to day-to-day political pressures.

Changing the structure of a network based industry such as electricity from monopoly to competitive markets requires a sophisticated regulatory structure. A market environment requires regulatory institutions whose decisions are competitively neutral, transparent, and not subject to day-to-day political pressures. The new environment will increase the responsibilities of the regulator, particularly to ensure non-discriminatory access and economically rational pricing for those system services used by IPPs and large users. The competition authority and the regulator will need to prevent anti-competitive behaviour.

Transparency of objectives, powers, processes, decisions, and information strengthens the regulator's role as a neutral arbiter of market competition.

To provide a solid basis for market regulation, many countries have established or are examining the establishment of "independent" regulatory bodies to regulate electricity after reform. Australia, Finland, Norway, Netherlands, Spain, Sweden, the United Kingdom, and the United States use independent electricity regulators. Germany and New Zealand use the competition authority to regulate electricity. Arrangements differ in each country, but the essential features include complete independence from the regulated companies, a legal mandate that provides for separation of the regulators and the regulatory body from political control, a degree of organisational autonomy, well-defined obligations for transparency (*e.g.* publishing decisions) and for accountability (*e.g.* appealable decisions, public scrutiny of expenditures). The combination of transparencies – of objectives, powers, processes, decisions, and information – enables the public to evaluate how the regulator is fulfilling its role as a neutral arbiter of market competition and enforcer of regulation.

Liberalised aspects of the sector should be subject to the Anti-monopoly Act.

In a partially liberalised market, the utilities'behaviour with respect to liberalised aspects of the sector should be subject to the Anti-monopoly Act. The Anti-monopoly Act should be amended to clarify that it also applies to the electricity sector. Areas of joint and primary responsibility of the sector regulator and the FTC should be specified, and each institution should act in consultation with the other.

The Japanese government plans for MITI to remain the electricity sector regulator but to separate regulatory activities from policy-making. However, at present there are few safeguards from political pressures that give confidence to the market. Transparency needs to be ensured to regulate a competitive market in an open and fair manner. Significant reform of the institutional arrangements is needed to support partial liberalisation of retail supply.

Significant reform of the institutional arrangements in Japan is needed to support partial liberalisation of retail supply.

Difficult decisions lie ahead with respect to separation of competitive activities from the transmission grid

A major challenge lies in ensuring equal access to the transmission grid. Effective competition in generation requires non-discriminatory access, including economically rational pricing, to the transmission grid and provision of ancillary services.

Current proposals would make discrimination illegal in Japan, and use accounting separation to ensure equal access to the grid.

Current proposals would make discrimination illegal in Japan under the Electric Utilities Industry Law. Beyond keeping separate accounts, no changes in the structure or operation of the electric utilities would be mandated. Accounting separation does not require large changes in the structure of companies. It can be implemented relatively quickly and, for private firms, without intruding into private property issues. To be successful, accounting separation needs to be accompanied by regulation to ensure nondiscrimination and cost-reflective pricing. Accounting information made available to the regulator must reliably detect anticompetitive or discriminatory behaviour that might occur.

A combination of regulation and vertical separation of utilities is used in OECD countries to counter discrimination in transmission access (see Box 5.2). There are tradeoffs between regulation and degree of vertical separation: Where there is less vertical separation, there is a need for greater regulation, and vice versa. These two policy tools are used to reduce the incentives and the ability to discriminate.

A process of change has begun that is a first step toward competition

The 1995 amendments to the Electric Utility Industry Law have begun a process of change in the Japanese electricity sector. The tendering for new capacity by independent power producers, which the amendments enabled, revealed significant scope for cost savings in generation. A revised regulatory process has put greater emphasis on improving efficiency at the utilities.

Tendering for new capacity by independent power producers revealed significant scope for cost-savings.

The principles guiding the discussion appear to be soundly based. In particular, the recognition of the need for equal conditions for competition between the utilities and new entrants, the need for fair and transparent rules on the use of power transmission lines, and the commitment to set a timetable for liberalisation highlight essential points of any successful market liberalisation in electricity. Furthermore, the Committee's recent decision to recommend that all

The decision to move forward with partial liberalisation is an important step toward the goal of international comparability in electricity prices.

87

Box 5.2. Vertical separation between transmission and generation

Discriminatory access to the transmission grid creates two types of inefficiencies: 1) higher-cost generators may be used in preference to lower-cost generators; and 2) efficient entry by generators may be discouraged. Both of these effects increase costs. A vertically integrated utility has strong incentives to discriminate in favour of its own generating assets to provide them with preferential access to its transmission grid. OECD countries are trying various approaches to separate generation and transmission, including (ordered from weaker to stronger types):

- *Accounting separation*: keeping separate accounts of the generation from the transmission activities within the same vertically integrated entity. This includes a vertically integrated entity charging itself the same prices for transmission services, including ancillary services, as it does others and stating separate prices for generation, transmission, and ancillary services.

- *Functional separation*: accounting separation, plus 1) relying on the same information about its transmission system as its customers when buying and selling power and 2) separating employees involved in transmission from those involved in power sales.

- *Operational separation*: operation of and decisions about investment in the transmission grid are the responsibility of an entity that is fully independent of the owner(s) of generation; ownership of the transmission grid remains with the owner(s) of generation.

- *Divestiture or ownership separation*: generation and transmission are separated into distinct legal entities without significant common ownership, management, control, or operations. Divestiture eliminates incentives to discriminate.

Different strategies for vertical separation of generation and transmission are employed in different countries. Japan has decided to implement accounting separation. In many OECD countries who restructured publicly-owned electricity systems, the transmission business is placed as a separate company (United Kingdom (England and Wales), Norway, Sweden, Spain, Hungary, Finland, most states of Australia). Other countries with publicly-owned utilities, such as France, Italy, and Austria, opted for accounting separation with an independent network manager as required by the EU Electricity Directive.

There are fewer examples of electricity reform in countries where utilities are predominantly privately owned, as in Japan. Accounting separation is used in Germany and Scotland (United Kingdom). In the United States, federal regulators require functional separation of transmission and encourage operational separation. In some US states that have fully liberalised retail supply, utilities are encouraged (in Connecticut and Maine are legally required) to divest much or all generating capacity. Utilities in Japan are privately owned, and the government considers that it has no legal authority to require electric utilities operating in ordinary circumstances to divest their property and assets.

---

extra high voltage industrial and commercial customers, representing 28% of total utilities'sales, is an important milestone.

Careful monitoring is needed to assess whether partial liberalisation of retail supply meets the energy policy goals of the Japanese government. It is likely that further liberalisation will be needed.

However, this first step under consideration will need to be carefully monitored to assess whether partial liberalisation of retail supply meets all the energy policy goals of the Japanese government. To establish the foundation for reducing Japan's electricity costs on a medium- to long-term basis, and to meet all of Japan's policy goals, further liberalisation will be needed. Further liberalisation will enable markets to become established and to expand, which will induce more efficient ways of organising the sector, and ways of using existing assets in the sector. It is important that access to the transmission grid and ancillary services be non-discriminatory and cost-reflective. Both the demand and the supply sides of the markets for electricity should be sufficiently unconcentrated, and those parts of the sector remaining under economic regulation should be subject to credible, transparent regulation. Each of these conditions are part of the foundation upon which an efficient electricity sector is built. A more robust foundation would require additional conditions.

After retail liberalisation, performance should be carefully monitored. The government should be prepared to take additional steps if effective competition does not develop

The government should develop a comprehensive reform plan for the industry that lays out the options for reform steps which might be taken, and the timing and criteria for evaluating progress towards its major policy goals and objectives for the electricity sector. As part of this plan, the government should monitor progress against measurable indicators, and take further steps if problems emerge. Several indicators would probably show that further steps are needed:

- limited switching by liberalised customers;
- limited entry by IPPs;
- complaints by IPPs about discriminatory activity by utilities with respect to network services;
- complaints by IPPs about abuse of market dominance;
- limited activities by utilities to compete with one another for customers;
- regulatory difficulties with accounting separation.

If these difficulties emerge, the government should be prepared to move quickly with other measures, taking into consideration policy goals such as economic growth, energy security, environmental protection, universal service and supply reliability: further steps include:

- Additional liberalisation of supply by enlarging the number of eligible customers. If possible, all customers should be eligible.
- Strengthening protection against cross subsidy of liberalised activity by strengthening regulatory enforcement, more strictly applying accounting separation, or adopting other combinations of vertical separation and regulation. Functional separation or, if possible, operational separation of network services (transmission, distribution, and system operations) with appropriate regulation may bring more benefits of competition. All feasible forms of separation should be considered. Circumstances may arise where divestiture becomes feasible, for example, and this should remain open for consideration.
- Regulation, independent of policy-making functions, designed to enhance transparency and credibility of the regulator.
- Promoting electric power trading by introducing, at least on a limited basis, a wholesale market, expanding interconnections and requiring utilities to purchase power for captive consumers from the most economic source.
- Ancillary services by requiring the utility to offer, and the customer to purchase backup power and other system services.
- Nuclear power and renewables should continue to be supported by all customers.

The government should develop a comprehensive reform plan for the industry.

Further liberalisation will enable markets to expand, which will induce more efficient ways of organising the sector, and of using existing assets.

Chapter 6

REGULATORY REFORM IN THE TELECOMMUNICATIONS INDUSTRY

The telecommunications industry is extraordinarily dynamic. Rapid evolution of technologies has shaken up industries and regulatory regimes long based on older technologies and market theories. Twenty-three OECD countries have unrestricted market access to all forms of telecommunications, including voice telephony, infrastructure investment and investment by foreign enterprises, compared to only a handful a few years ago. The industry's boundaries are blurring and merging with other industries such as broadcasting and information services.

Regulatory regimes must simultaneously promote competition and protect other social policies in dynamic markets

The role of regulatory reform in launching and shaping the rapid evolution of the industry has been described by some as pivotal, and by others as at best supportive. Whatever the truth, strong competition policies and efficiency-promoting regulatory regimes that work well in dynamic and global markets are crucial to the performance and future development of the industry.

Strong competition policies and efficiency-promoting regulatory regimes are crucial to the performance and future development of the industry.

The central regulatory task is to enable the development of competition in local markets, while protecting other public interests such as reliability, universal service and consumer interests. Entry must be actively promoted in markets where formerly regulated monopolists remain dominant, and consideration must be given to convergence of separate regulatory frameworks applicable to telecommunications and broadcasting infrastructures and services.

Japan was among the first OECD countries to liberalise the sector in the 1980s, but users have not enjoyed full benefits of competition due to too many economic controls, and too few competitive safeguards

Along with the United States and the United Kingdom, Japan is one of the few countries to have introduced competition in the 1980s. Since market liberalisation began in 1985, Japan has introduced many liberalisation measures to encourage competition. In 1993, MPT allowed CATV companies to offer telecommunications services using CATV networks. In 1996, MPT announced "the second reform of the info-communications system in Japan"[96] which included many impor-

*Along with the **United States** and the **United Kingdom**, Japan is one of the few countries to have introduced competition in the 1980s.*

tant policy changes, notably the break-up of NTT, the establishment of interconnection rules and further deregulation measures such as the introduction of a tariff notification system for mobile companies. Following the February 1997 WTO agreement on basic telecommunications services, Japan made significant changes to its regulatory regime such as elimination of the "supply-demand" standard for market entry and foreign ownership restrictions on Type 1 carriers, except NTT.

Box 6.1. **Major drivers of Japanese regulatory development
in the telecommunications sector**

Five major elements have led Japanese regulatory developments in the telecommunications sector.

Catch-up: While Japan is one of the three countries that initiated liberalisation of the telecommunications market in the 1980s, it never took a leading role but followed developments or positions elsewhere on important regulatory issues. In certain cases, Japan tried to follow the US model, for example in the original proposals for divestiture of the incumbent. In other cases, such as market entry regulation, it followed the UK model. The catch-up policy tended to result in an incremental approach to the liberalisation of telecommunications market through individual deregulation measures rather than a single comprehensive deregulation package underpinned by a clear goal of creating effective competition.

MPT vs. NTT: After 1985, one of the MPT's main policy goals was the weakening of NTT's power by divestiture to promote competition in the telecommunications market. However, because of NTT's political strength, due to its more than 220 000 employees, and its economic power, NTT was able to resist MPT's attempt to break it up for 12 years. In place of divestiture, MPT used regulatory safeguards as an alternative, and perhaps more effective, tool.

Unique market structures: Japan had a unique telecommunications market structure which was based on the line-of-business restrictions on NTT and KDD. From the outset, NTT could not enter the international market and KDD was limited to providing international telecommunication services. Therefore, unlike many other OECD countries, there have been two incumbents in the Japanese telecommunications market, one for domestic and one for international. Furthermore, for long time there had been no cross-competition between domestic long distance carriers and international carriers. In fact, there had been no company operating both domestic and international services until 1997. In addition, because of the way that competition has developed, new entry is easier in international than in long distance markets. This is because, in the long distance market, new common carriers (NCCs) have used least-cost routing chips (LCR) to entice customers from NTT, which makes it more inconvenient for customers to switch carriers, but in the international market, NCCs are competing with KDD through carrier identification codes, and hence customers are readier to switch to new carriers.

Consumer protection vs. industry promotion: MPT has authority both as a regulator and a policy maker in the telecommunications sector. As a result, unlike many other regulatory bodies in the OECD member countries with the sole legal mandate to protect consumer benefits, MPT is responsible for consumer protection as well as industry promotion in the telecommunications sector. For instance, the "second info-communications reform" in 1995 had two goals: promotion of users'benefits and revitalisation of industry. Since the regulatory body's independence can be effectively ensured only when it distances itself from interested parties, there is concern that MPT's industry promotion function may have negative impacts on its regulatory function. In fact, it seems that previously MPT put more emphasis on the role of industry promotion by protecting carriers'interest through the recently abolished "supply-demand" provision and "tariff approval system".

Foreign pressure: Since the early 1980s, Japan's trading partners, mainly the United States, but also the EU, made the telecommunications sector the major target of pressure for open markets.[97] Annual Japan-US bilateral exchanges increased pressure to liberalise Japan's telecommunications market. Some significant changes in Japan's telecommunications regulatory regime resulted from WTO commitments in the agreement on basic telecommunications services. The role of multilateral negotiation in pushing further reform in the Japanese telecommunications market will be strengthened as increased globalisation of telecommunications services occurs.

While "the first reform of the telecommunications system" in 1985 opened up Japan's telecommunications market, competition was far from effective. Since market entry and tariffs were subject to individual licensing or approval from the Minister, carriers were not able to make important business decisions without first obtaining permission from the Minister. Moreover, there was no competition in the local market, and competition between NTT (or KDD) and the new entrants in long distance and international telecommunications markets was managed by MPT through the tariff approval system. As a result, Japanese users have not seen the rate reductions enjoyed in the United Kingdom and the United States (see Figure 6.1).

Yet, compared to other countries, competition has been far from effective due to continuing intervention by the Ministry.

Price is arguably the most important indicator in evaluating the success of liberalisation for users. According to MPT's "1998 White Paper Communications in Japan", in contrast to an average price rise of 4.7 per cent in Japanese industry as a whole between 1990 and 1996, the telecommunications sector delivered reduced prices to consumers by an average 16.1 per cent.

Initial steps delivered some promising results: prices in the telecommunications sector fell by an average 16.1 per cent.

Since NTT's usage charges (10 yen for three minutes) for local fixed voice telephony service have not changed for decades, most reductions have occurred in national long distance and international fixed voice telephony services. The drop in long distance call charges between Tokyo and Osaka is often mentioned as an example of rapid

Figure 6.1. **Comparison of long distance call charges**

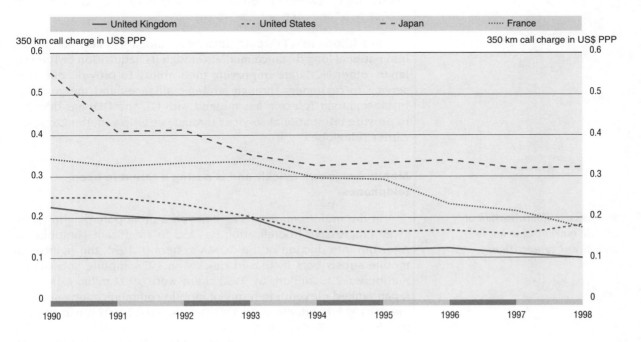

Note: Price of one minute, based on 4.5 minute call.
Source: OECD and EURODATA.

OECD 1999

rate reduction in Japan; it declined by 77.5 per cent from 400 yen to 90 yen between April 1985 and February 1998.

Nevertheless, the benefits of competition have not been fully felt owing to heavy price regulation.

Nevertheless, the benefits of competition have not been fully felt owing to heavy price regulation. Figure 6.1 compares Japan's long distance charges with those of selected OECD countries. In spite of the massive price reductions in long distance call charges in Japan, Figure 6.1 shows that even France, which introduced competition only in 1998, has performed better than Japan over the period.

The structure of Japan's telecommunications industry is unique in OECD countries, and, consequently, so are the regulatory challenges

With telecommunication revenues of $110.0 billion, Japan has the second largest telecommunications market in the world.[98] Its market size is less than half that of the United States ($256.8 billion) but twice that of Germany ($43.6 billion). The incumbent operator, NTT, is the world's largest telecommunications operator with $78.1 billion in revenues.[99]

The most significant change in the Japanese telecommunications market is the possibility for carriers to provide an integrated telecommunication service or a "one-stop service" to customers.

Until recently, Japan had a very distinctive telecommunications market structure based on line-of-business restrictions on NTT and KDD. However, abandoning line-of-business restrictions not only allows NTT and KDD to expand their business coverage, but also fundamentally changes the competitive environment. In terms of competition, the separation between national long distance and international markets is not significant any longer. In fact, the most significant change in the Japanese telecommunications market is the possibility for carriers to provide an integrated telecommunication service or a "one-stop service" to customers.

In addition to NTT's entry into international markets and KDD's into national long distance market through its acquisition of Teleway Japan, other NCCs are improving their ability to provide one-stop service to customers through strategic alliances and mergers. For instance, Japan Telecom has merged with ITJ, and DDI has decided to provide international services through a tie-up with the Canadian carrier Teleglobe.

Mobile has grown quickly and is posing a threat to fixed telephones

Progressive liberalisation of mobile markets has led to significant competition.

In the mobile market, NTT enjoyed a monopoly position until 1988. Progressive liberalisation has led to significant competition. After the introduction of the COMA system in 1994, the number of mobile subscribers increased quickly. In 1993, mobile subscribers numbered 2.13 million; by 1998 there were 39.21 million. In 1995, Japan ranked eleventh in terms of mobile communication subscribers per 100 inhabitants in the OECD area, but by 1997 it had risen to fourth place. Today, in the mobile market, in addition to NTT DoCoMo, there are several cellular and PHS (Personal Handy-phone System) carriers in each market block.[100]

The explosive growth of mobile communication in Japan has had implications for fixed telecommunication services through substitution effects. The relatively high cost of joining the fixed network as compared to a mobile subscription seems to be attracting a growing number of users who only subscribe to mobile services. As a result of this high initial connection charge, the very low initial fee to join a mobile communication network, together with low user packages, is very attractive for users such as university students and new entrants to the labour market.[101] Since 1994, growth of numbers of mobile subscribers has surpassed that of PSTN (public switched telephone network) subscribers. More importantly, in 1997 the number of PSTN subscribers started to decrease.

The explosive growth of mobile communication in Japan has had implications for fixed telecommunication services through substitution effects.

There are concerns about the NTT break-up plan because of the holding company structure

The proposed NTT break-up is not likely to promote infrastructure competition because of the holding company structure. Efforts to restructure NTT have been at the heart of Japanese telecommunications reform for a long time. The NTT divestiture debate began as early as 1981 when an MPT internal study group proposed the divestiture of NTT together with privatisation. Ever since, this issue has been under debate. A 1990 recommendation to break-up of NTT into one long distance company and a local company faced strong opposition from many parties. Many argued that it was too early to decide and the Ministry of Finance was afraid that a divestiture would adversely affect NTT's share price.

The proposed NTT break-up is not likely to promote local competition because of the holding company structure.

In 1995, the debate was reopened. NTT's argument against break-up stressed the importance of an integrated company to ensure NTT's R&D function, which was highly regarded as a national asset. The final report of the Telecommunications Council, in 1996, proposed to split NTT into one long distance company and two regional companies. The government announced its final decision in March 1997: it maintained the idea of dividing NTT into one long distance company and two regional companies, but also proposed a holding company to ensure unified R&D and manage the shares of the two regional companies.

The break-up will be much less effective in promoting local loop competition because of the holding company structure. It is unlikely that NTT East and West will be involved in infrastructure competition, given that it is not in the shareholders' interests for the holding company to allow NTT East and NTT West to enter each other's market. In addition, under the NTT Law, NTT East or NTT West cannot enter long distance markets.

Local telephony service is monopolized by NTT but there are signs of potential competition from CATV companies and utility based companies

The rapid growth of cellular mobile services and telephony services based on cable television networks is raising the prospect that these can be an alternative to local fixed voice telephony service...

In the market for local fixed telephony services, as of 31 March 1998, NTT had a 99.5 per cent market share, as measured by the percentage of access lines (and 98 per cent in terms of revenue). But the rapid growth of cellular mobile services and telephony services based on cable television (CATV) networks is raising the prospect that these can be an alternative to local fixed voice telephony service. As a result of earlier regulatory constraints on CATV, Japan's penetration rate for CATV service is very low (11.32 per cent of households at the end of 1996) as compared with other OECD countries. However, the growth rate of CATV penetration (37.5 per cent between 1995 and 1996) is much higher than the OECD average (7.8 per cent).[102] By October 1998, there were 48 CATV companies with a Type 1 carrier license. Yet only five companies currently have interconnection agreements with NTT and only two provide voice telephony services using their CATV networks.

... and the emergence of utility-based Type 1 carriers could also facilitate competition in the local voice telephony market.

The emergence of utility-based Type 1 carriers could also facilitate competition in the local voice telephony market. Local fixed optical fibre networks are being constructed by new entrants, such as electrical power companies, which can use their power cables as rights of way for optical fibre cables. Currently, ten electric utility company NCCs are providing telecommunications services such as leased lines and integrated services digital network (ISDN). TTNet is one of the first local companies offering cheaper local calls than NTT. Owing to its relatively cheaper price for local calls (9 yen for three minutes, or 1 yen cheaper than NTT), TTNet obtained 1.4 million subscribers in just six months after launching its business in January 1998.

Japan made significant reforms including the introduction of a tariff notification system in favor of further liberalisation of the telecommunications market

In November 1998, a tariff notification system was adopted to allow companies to determine prices without approval from MPT. This decision finally makes price competition possible.

In November 1998, the Ministry of Post and Telecommunications (MPT) introduced a tariff notification system which allows companies to determine their own prices without obtaining approval from MPT except for NTT's local basic services. This decision is a milestone for the liberalisation of the telecommunications market since it finally makes effective price competition possible.

Yet, there are still outstanding regulatory issues which prevent fair and transparent competition in the marketplace

Many outstanding regulatory issues need to be addressed in order to ensure a fair and transparent competitive environment for all market players.

However, there are still outstanding regulatory issues that need to be addressed properly and promptly in order to ensure a fair and transparent competitive environment for all market players. MPT should take steps to eliminate remaining regulatory barriers and to establish effective regulatory safeguards in order to promote effective competition, increase consumer benefits and allow market-oriented business activities to develop.

Box 6.2. 1997 Changes in the NTT Law

- NTT will be restructured into one long distance company and two regional companies under a holding company which is not allowed to enter into any communications business.
- The holding company (Nippon Telegraph and Telephone Corp.) will be a special corporation which manages all shares of the two regional companies.
- The holding company is responsible for fundamental research.
- The regional companies (NTT East and NTT West) will be special corporations providing only regional communications services and obliged to provide universal service in their business areas.
- The long distance company will be a private company which can enter the international telecommunications market.
- The holding company and the two regional companies will be regulated as special companies like the present NTT.
- NTT is allowed to enter the international telecommunications market through its affiliates even before the establishment of the long distance company.
- The changes should be implemented within two and a half years from the date of promulgation (that is, before the end of 1999).

- MPT uses examination standards based on public interest provisions when it determines whether Type 1 business applicants meet the entry requirement standards in the Telecommunications Business Law. These examination standards do not provide clear-cut information to applicants on the minimum requirements to receive licenses. This results in an informal consultation process whereby new entrants understand whether or not an application, once made, would be approved by MPT. This can cause lengthy delays in launching a new business in spite of the standard processing period of 1-2 months guaranteed under the Administrative Procedure Law for handling applications. It also tends to reduce transparency further. To avoid such problems, except in the case of spectrum allocation, which requires an individual licensing system due to its scarcity, many OECD countries are lowering entry barriers to the telecommunications market. For example, the Netherlands has introduced a class licensing system whereby all applicants that meet clearly stated criteria attain market entry. Denmark requires no official procedure to enter the market.

- Due to fragmented regulations on rights-of-way, new carriers have experienced difficulties in establishing their own networks even after receiving Type 1 licenses. Effective implementation of regulations on facility sharing (such as sharing of ducts) become even more important for ensuring that new entrants have fair access to end users. If facility sharing is effective, new entrants can construct new networks relatively cheaply and rapidly.

- The most important regulatory safeguard to ensure fair competition is the establishment of a fair and transparent interconnection framework. Access to NTT's local loop is a cornerstone for

97

the promotion of market competition. Although a new interconnection scheme, including accounting separation and non-discriminatory interconnection for "designated facilities", was introduced in 1997 to ensure transparent and fair interconnection conditions between the incumbent and new entrants, NTT's interconnection charge is still high compared with other major carriers in the OECD region.

– Regarding spectrum allocation, there is no legal provision on how to select licensees when there are many applicants for a limited number of licenses. The lack of a transparent and fair method to select mobile licensees when applicants outnumber licenses is a significant weakness of the Japanese telecommunications regulatory regime.

– Foreign ownership restriction on NTT still exists. In addition, mandatory minimum one-third government ownership of NTT raises a problem of conflict of interest, given that the government is both shareholder and regulator.

– The lack of essential regulatory safeguards such as number portability and carrier pre-selection gives an unfair advantage to the incumbents and the early NCCs.

– The lack of a universal service funding mechanism makes it difficult to prevent cross-subsidisation of NTT's services.

In reforming the sectoral regulator, it will be important to maintain independence and expertise. Current plans do not seem adequate

In Japan, the Ministry of Posts and Telecommunications is responsible for telecommunications policy and regulation. It is also responsible for broadcasting policy and for operating postal services, postal savings services and postal life insurance services. Unlike the situation in most other OECD countries, the same ministry has both a policy and a regulatory role. MPT is one of the few regulators in OECD Member countries with the authority to supervise both the broadcasting (including content regulation) and telecommunications markets.

In Japan, the MPT is one of the leading ministries in the use of the so-called "green paper" approach to solicit public comment when establishing new regulations. MPT's approach has been highly appreciated by many interested parties and clearly increases the transparency of the policy-making process.

In addition to MPT, the Fair Trade Commission (the FTC) has jurisdiction in the telecommunications sector. The FTC's authority is based on the Anti-monopoly Act (AMA). In telecommunications, there is no formal exemption from the AMA, so the FTC and the Ministry share jurisdiction. However, the FTC's involvement has been very limited. In June 1998, 'the Basic Law for the Reorganisation of the Central Government Ministries and Agencies'was enacted. According to this law, MPT is to be integrated into a new Ministry of General Affairs by 2003 (the target year for restructuring is, however, 2001). After the restructuring, MPT will retain all of its functions as regards telecommunications and broadcasting policy and regulation.

The restructuring plan has raised concerns relating to telecommunication policy and regulation. First, the number of different functions of the new Ministry of General Affairs will arguably be too large for a single ministry. Second, it does not seem that the integration of three ministries will facilitate the government's objective of building professional expertise within the Ministry, particularly in light of the fact that, in Japan, ministry personnel are shifted regularly every two years. Third, although the FTC is to implement the AMA independently regardless of the restructuring, the appearance of lack of independence because the FTC and MPT will be under the same Minister could introduce uncertainty in the market. To ensure fair market competition, the regulator must be separated from all interested parties. The suggested institutional changes do not take account of this requirement for the communications sector. The restructuring plan should ensure an institutional structure which can provide an effective and transparent regulatory and policy regime for the Japanese communications market.

In sum, in spite of recent regulatory developments, Japan has yet to complete the reforms in its regulatory framework that would facilitate the transition from a monopoly to a competitive telecommunications market. While Japan took a big step by abolishing the tariff approval system in favour of free price competition, essential regulatory safeguards are not in place. Unless MPT acts to implement safeguards, competition will develop slowly. However, if MPT makes the necessary changes, the impact could be rapid and significant, thanks to the developed market structure.

Chapter 7

CONCLUSIONS AND POLICY OPTIONS FOR REGULATORY REFORM IN JAPAN

The shift to market-led growth through regulatory reform is only one of many profound policy shifts that Japan has faced in its remarkable post-war ascendancy, and it is likely that, in the end, the Japanese government will succeed. Since the early 1990s, the pace of regulatory reform has accelerated. Much has been accomplished, building on and continuing the market openness measures taken in the 1980s. Comprehensive liberalisation of financial services is being implemented and progress has been made in key sectors like distribution and telecommunications. These sectors are showing the predicted positive results of lower prices, a greater variety of services and products and more rapid demand growth. The legal basis for competition policy in Japan is sound, and enforcement action has become more vigorous over the last several years. Substantial steps to improve regulatory transparency have been taken.

Since the early 1990s, the pace of regulatory reform has accelerated. Much has been accomplished.

Yet, as Japan started later than many OECD countries and is moving more slowly, it is falling further behind OECD good regulatory practices and this is reflected in its poor economic performance in the 1990s. For example, the single market and single currency in Europe are driving major reforms across many sectors, and European countries are moving faster than Japan. In telecommunications, for example, Japan started earlier in liberalising, and made progress recently, but still has not completed the regulatory framework for ensuring full competition in the marketplace. Economy-wide, the task of establishing a regulatory environment that promotes efficiency, innovation, and adjustment, while cost-effectively protecting health, consumers, and the environment, is only begun.

The need for progress is more urgent than ever. The Japanese economy has stagnated since 1992. In the long-run, the factors which sustained Japanese growth in the past – particularly rapid labour force growth – will no longer be present. While both adverse external shocks and cyclical factors have played a role in the multi year slump, the most important factor has been structural rigidities resulting from an increasingly outmoded regulatory and institutional framework. Rapid and forceful action is needed to restart expansion, and to re-establish a path of sustainable long-term growth. Structural reforms, particularly regulatory reform, stand alongside appropriate fiscal and monetary policy and rapid resolu-

Yet the need for progress is more urgent than ever. Regulatory reform is essential to avoid long-term economic stagnation and decline.

tion of the crisis in the financial system as key elements of such action.

Regulatory reform, if deepened and accelerated, can assist Japan in returning to a sustainable growth path

The current malaise presents both a great challenge, and a great opportunity. Structural reforms can remove the institutional biases which have, by inhibiting competition and misallocating resources, resulted in higher prices, low levels of efficiency and favour existing firms, and excess capital investment, and instead lower costs, encourage greater efficiency and stimulate business dynamism and entrepreneurial activity. A multi-sectoral and comprehensive reform programme aimed at introducing full competition will have the greatest and speediest effect in stimulating economic performance and supporting recovery. The benefits of sectoral reform are amplified when competition is vigorous in upstream and downstream sectors. Already, in Japan, simultaneous implementation of reforms in different sectors is beginning to generate the synergistic effects seen in other countries: deregulation in retail distribution and increased openness to imports have fed back into improvements in the costly and inefficient wholesaling system. Such a programme can contribute to:

A multi-sectoral and comprehensive reform programme aimed at introducing full competition will have the greatest and speediest effect in stimulating economic performance and supporting recovery.

Such a programme can boost consumer demand...

– boosting consumer demand and welfare through lower prices, better service quality, and a greater variety of goods and services. Consumers have welcomed, for example, larger stores built after liberalisation of the retail sector;

... reduce costs in exporting sectors...

– reducing the domestic cost structure of exporting sectors to improve their competitiveness in regional and global markets, while reducing the risk of trade tensions due to possible regulatory barriers;

... improve innovation and flexibility, raising the long-term potential growth rate...

– improving the flexibility of the supply-side of the economy by stimulating investment, by increasing the efficiency of the allocation of capital, currently a major constraint to growth, and by lowering barriers to the creation of new firms, products and services, which will increase Japan's long-term potential growth rate and help ameliorate the problems associated with an ageing population;

... increase employment through new job opportunities...

– helping to increase employment by creating new job opportunities. Positive employment effects will be limited, however, unless reforms are complete and comprehensive and are accompanied by further reforms to the labour market and positive labour market policies;

... and maintain high levels of regulatory protections.

– maintaining and increasing high levels of regulatory protections in areas such as health and safety, the environment, and consumer interests by introducing more flexible and efficient regulatory and non-regulatory instruments, such as market approaches. Reforms that enhance policy responsiveness allow the administration to react to rapidly changing environments and new policy problems.

A sharp break with current regulatory practices is needed by constructing a different kind of state

Japan's highly-developed state apparatus, created during a more developmental stage of Japanese development, is not functioning well in a mature market economy. Interventions by the administration into economic decisions are no longer based on any coherent view of the role of regulation in globalised market economies. Practices such as demand-supply balancing and administrative guidance are based on outdated concepts of managed competition and immature market institutions; in a mature economy they stifle innovation and inhibit efficiency. A new philosophy of regulation is needed, based on market principles, consumer choice, adaptability, and transparency. The role of government should shift from economic management to safeguarding competition and providing social services that the market cannot provide. In some cases, such as consumer protection and dispute resolution, state action will need to increase as markets expand. With these kinds of reforms, the Japanese government will establish the basis for a dynamic regulatory system that will continue to adapt and meet new challenges into the future.

The role of government should shift from economic management to safeguarding competition and providing social services that the market cannot provide.

The need to rebalance the reform programme between deregulation and good regulation, particularly sectoral governance and consumer protection, is urgent. The focus of the current programme is deregulation, a considerable and necessary task. Yet good regulation is also needed to address public policy concerns. Reform of the financial sector vividly demonstrated that good regulatory governance is vital. Changing the structure of a network based industry such as electricity from monopoly to competitive markets requires a sophisticated regulatory structure. Market liberalisation does not mean less of all kinds of regulation. On the contrary, in some areas it may mean more, although any regulation should be efficient and flexible. Consumers faced with more choices may require more information and confidence-building measures.

POLICY OPTIONS FOR REGULATORY REFORM

This report is not a comprehensive review of regulation in Japan, but the areas reviewed show recurring weaknesses in Japan's regulatory regimes. This section identifies actions that, based on international consensus on good regulatory practices and on concrete experiences in OECD countries, are likely to be beneficial to improving regulation in Japan. The summary recommendations presented here are discussed in more detail in the background reports to Chapters 2-6, published in this volume. They are based on the recommendations and policy framework in The OECD Report to Ministers on Regulatory Reform.

Recurring patterns in Japanese regulatory regimes reduce consumer welfare and policy effectiveness.

Sustained strong political support is needed at the highest levels to overcome the vested interests that, in current policy processes, are able to slow or block reform efforts

Japan has enjoyed good political support for reform, and this is the most essential ingredient for success.

Good advice on regulatory reform is plentiful in Japan. Reports from advisory bodies, the private sector, foreign governments and government bodies have contributed to a growing consensus on the reform agenda. The reform task is largely a political one. No OECD country has been able to carry out similar structural reforms without sustained, intensive political support over a multi-year period. Broad political consensus adds value to reform by increasing its credibility and reducing the risk of policy reversals.

One of the strengths of regulatory reform in Japan is that it has enjoyed high levels of political support. Political support may have suffered from the tendency to support reform in general but not in specifics, but the extent of personal involvement of a succession of prime ministers has been rarely equalled in other countries.

Regulatory reform should be expanded and accelerated through development of comprehensive sectoral reform plans containing the full set of steps needed to introduce effective competition, followed by rapid implementation and periodic, public evaluation. To maximise positive impacts on economic performance, reforms should proceed simultaneously in key infrastructure and service sectors, and in factor markets

The need to take bold and comprehensive action justifies examining a different approach than the item by item strategy.

The need to take bold and comprehensive action in Japan justifies exploration of different strategies with faster impacts in promoting market competition and adjustment. The OECD Report on Regulatory Reform stated, "Regulatory reform should be guided by coherent and transparent policy frameworks that establish concrete objectives and the path for reaching them..." As noted, the Three-Year Programme for Promoting Deregulation moves in this direction, but should be more rapid, comprehensive and results-oriented in sectors under reform. To this end, the Programme should be based on an even clearer commitment to market competition as the central objective of reform. In this regard, as part of the overall programme, the Fair Trade Commission should evaluate at least annually the extent to which barriers to competition still exist in each sector under reform, and how competition is developing in response to reform efforts. These evaluations should be made public. This market evaluation would complement the surveillance of ministry actions carried out by the Deregulation Committee and extend the current expert role of the FTC in assessing barriers to competition as part of programme evaluation and correction.

Success is increased by including at the outset the full mix of policies needed to gain full benefits of reform.

The emphasis on broad programmes is deliberate, since the likelihood of success is increased by including at the outset the full mix of policies needed to gain full benefits of reform.[103] Japan's "Big Bang" in the financial sector demonstrates the effectiveness of sectoral plans that include not only regulations but other forms of intervention such as subsidies, procurement policies, and tax policies.

Stable macroeconomic policy, flexible labour markets, and complementary structural reforms facilitate the adjustments that follow from regulatory reform. Strong competition authorities help prevent consolidation in new markets from going too far and undermining the benefits of reform. Positive effects of regulatory reform on employment are amplified and negative effects minimised if labour markets are flexible. Positive effects on competition of new entrants and the ability to innovate new products are stimulated by the efficiency of capital markets. Pro-competitive regulation allows entrepreneurship to flourish in combination with other institutions such as private financing and well developed stock markets, corporate governance such as bankruptcy laws, patent laws, and, again, flexible labour markets.

Sectoral reforms must be accompanied by other structural reforms. Reforms affecting factor markets – land, labour and capital – are essential. Experience in other OECD countries shows that greater labour market flexibility, combined with active labour market policies, can minimise the short-run adjustment costs of sectoral reform and multiply the effects on new employment creation. Efficient land and capital markets can allow more rapid introduction of new products and enterprises and accelerate the reallocation of resources, the pace of efficiency increase, and reduction in prices. Progress has been made in improving labour and real estate market flexibility, but additional reforms liberalising job placement agencies are necessary, with reforms to land use and construction regulations. In the financial sector reforms should substantially improve the allocation of investment. Additional steps need to be taken to encourage risk capital and entrepreneurialism.

Reforms affecting factor markets – land, labour and capital – are essential.

A comprehensive reform strategy will raise trade-offs and additional difficulties, however. Moving forward quickly on a broader front may require attention to design of transitional programmes that reduce opposition to change. A comprehensive plan will require reformers to cut across a partitioned and segmented government structure, which will increase transaction costs and upfront delays.

Investment, market entry, and innovation should be promoted by increasing the transparency and accountability of regulation

Transparency in regulatory decisions and application helps to cure many reasons for regulatory failures: capture and bias toward concentrated benefits, inadequate information in the public sector, policy rigidity, market uncertainty and inability to understand policy risks, and lack of accountability. Moreover, transparency helps create a virtuous circle – consumers trust competition more because special interests have less power to manipulate governments and markets. Also, the administration should be accountable for its use of regulatory discretion and for the policy performance of regulation. The current administrative reform programme of the central government provides a valuable opportunity to address legal, institutional and cross-cutting regulatory issues not addressed elsewhere.

Adoption of notice and comment procedures is a bold and important step forward. A number of other steps would also improve transparency:

... a single authoritative source for regulations...

– *Improve transparency by establishing a centralised registry of all regulatory requirements.* Many OECD countries are adopting new registry requirements to improve transparency and quality control of new regulations. A single authoritative source for all regulations – including permissions and approvals but also including other forms of regulation – would significantly enhance transparency and certainty for enterprises and the public. Such a registry could build from the registry of permits and licenses already used by the Management and Coordination Agency, but should also include regulations of general applicability. This will be increasingly important as Japan moves away from permits and licenses to general rules and *ex post* monitoring. Some countries have found that "positive security" can increase certainty and confidence for market players ("positive security" means that penalties cannot be enforced against non-compliance with regulations not included in the registry). One option to get full value from the registration process may be to expand and strengthen the office of the prime minister or another appropriate office to manage a single, authoritative, government-wide registry.

... standardised procedures for openness for the advisory councils...

– *Ensure the effective implementation of public comment procedures, and standardise procedures for openness for the advisory councils.* Japan has made significant efforts to include a wide range of parties in consultations on regulatory and policy decisions. The public comment procedures announced in October 1998, and that have become effective from April 1999, represent a major step forward. The new procedures should open regulatory decision-making to a broad range of interests for all significant regulation, including foreign interests. Transparency is supported by the opening of advisory council deliberations now underway. New policies in these areas should include the provision of better information, based on a regulatory impact analysis requirement, during the consultation process and the adoption of standard openness procedures for advisory council deliberations. Adoption of notice and comment procedures could also permit a central unit to review new ministerial regulations against the principles of good regulation and to advise the responsible ministries on how to improve the regulations, as is done in other OECD countries where the responsible ministries retain legal authority to issue regulations.

... clear governmental guidelines on the use of regulatory powers by non-governmental bodies...

– *Improve transparency by extending requirements for transparency to non-governmental bodies with delegated regulatory authorities.* A form of regulation widely used in Japan is that of "co-regulation", or sharing of regulatory functions between government and industry or other bodies. This has been implemented predominantly through trade associations, public corporations, and non-profit organisations. Such industry based regulatory and enforcement systems can have major benefits in terms of cost and effectiveness, but in many countries such bodies have used this role to limit competition and increase incomes and, hence, consumer prices. The incentives that exist for rent-seeking require that governments carefully supervise the use of such delegated regulatory powers. It is useful that the APA applies to non-governmental bodies with regulatory powers. As part of the 1998 programme's review of "non-governmental restrictions in the private sector", it would be useful to further develop clear governmental guidelines on the use of regulatory powers by non-governmental bodies. Issues include the representation of independent "public interest" advocates, the review role of competition authorities, and the need for specific legislative authorisation of regulatory powers, as well as transparency standards.

– *Expand the dissemination of detailed and updated regulatory information such as all the lower level regulations, ongoing proposals put for comment procedures, and business formalities to ensure its maximum public availability, such as via the Internet.* Considering the persistent concerns from abroad about lack of openness of regulatory procedures, the use of the Internet for dissemination of detailed and updated information has great potential. Although such use has started in Japan, it remains under-exploited when compared to practices in some other countries. Expansion of the Internet for this purpose will benefit new or potential entrants for markets, especially foreign firms.

... expanded use of the Internet to disseminate regulatory information.

– *Improve regulatory accountability by defining the limits of ministry action in the foundation laws and laws delegating regulatory authorities to the public administration.* Ministerial mandates and regulatory powers should be more closely defined in law to avoid abstract powers such as protecting the "public interest". There are two complementary approaches. First, the foundation law of each of the new ministries is being revised as part of a reduction in the number of ministries. Clearer definitions of the responsibilities and missions of the ministries in the Foundation Laws, including the requirement that the ministries avoid unnecessary constraints on competition, would improve political oversight by the Cabinet and the Diet and provide the basis for a more consistent approach across the government to the balance between consumer and producer interests. Second, clear definition of policy objectives and regulatory authorities should be included in each law delegating regulatory power.

Accountability would be improved by defining regulatory authorities more clearly...

– *Improve regulatory accountability by separating regulatory from policy and industry promotion functions in key infrastructure sectors.* Many accountability, transparency, and competition problems in sectoral regulation result from lack of institutional clarity about the source, powers, and purpose of regulation. There is no single organisational model that can be recommended across countries – and it is not yet clear that the new Financial Supervisory Agency offers a model for other sectors in Japan – but functional separation should aim at boosting the expertise of regulators; establishing clear performance criteria for the regulator based on maximising consumer welfare in the sector; improving the transparency of regulatory ac-

... and by separating regulatory from policy and industry promotion functions in key infrastructure sectors.

tions; and putting at arms-length any intervention by political officials and policy bureaus into specific regulatory decisions. The expertise and permanence of the staff is of paramount importance, since one of the purposes of this reform is to improve policy stability and reduce reliance on the regulated industry for expertise. Care should be taken to avoid "colonization" of new regulatory bodies by existing ministries, such as through the practice of rotating staff through short-term assignments.

The capacity of the judiciary to review actions by the public administration is important in the structure of interlocking institutions that establish the incentives and pressures for high-quality administrative action. In most OECD countries, the ultimate check on administrative abuses is the potential for review and reversal by the courts under principles of administrative law. Such deterrence must be credible to be effective. It is particularly important in Japan for the government and courts to provide an effective and practical judicial infrastructure for dispute settlement, since the government's role as mediator or arbitrator among interests should be eliminated as economic intervention is reduced. Reform to the judicial system to expand its capacities for review and reduce the costs and delays of private actions is essential if the policy reforms are to have their full effect.

Current efforts to promote reform by the Deregulation Committee are important to further progress. To accelerate and deepen reform, the Committee's efforts should be strengthened by broadening its mandate beyond regulation, clarifying its independence from ministries, and boosting its capacities and resources

The work of the Deregulation Committee is central to the future of regulatory reform, and it should be strengthened.

– *Further strengthen the leadership of the Deregulation Committee by i) enhancing its capacity for independent and comprehensive reform recommendations through such means as putting it under the direct control of the Prime Minister or by giving it legal authority to make recommendations; ii) broadening its mandate to consider the full range of government policies – beyond a narrow definition of regulation – that impede competition in the sector under reform; and iii) expanding and strengthening the analytical expertise of the Committee's Secretariat as an interim step to creating a permanent office on regulatory reform responsible to the Prime Minister.* The work of the Deregulation Committee is central to regulatory reform and should continue while ways of strengthening it are considered. First, the need for enhanced independence from the ministries is paramount to enable the Committee to play a leadership role in making decisive and bold recommendations. There are various ways to strengthen the independence of the Committee. Second, the Committee should be given a broader mandate to examine all government policies and instruments that have the effect of impeding competition in the sector under reform, as recommended by the Prime Minister's Economic Strategy Council in February 1999. Third, the Deregulation Committee requires expert advice in developing recommendations, and a stronger role in overseeing implementation of recommendations as Japan moves to more comprehensive reforms. This requires an expert secretariat with cross-government views. Rather than creating a permanent unit in the short-term to advise the prime minister, we suggest as an interim step significantly strengthening the size and analytical expertise of the Secretariat of the Deregulation Committee, which already has representation from major centre of government ministries. Its personnel should be drawn largely from non-regulatory ministries to enhance its "challenge" function; it should have sufficient financial resources to collect and assess information and buy the expertise of private think-tanks and scholars; and its role in the government's legislative and regulatory procedures should be formalised. Inclusion of personnel from the FTC is important to ensure that competition principles are kept foremost in the reform programme. In the longer-term, the government should consider creating a permanent advisory and analysis body on regulatory reform that is responsible to the prime minister.

— *Improve the FTC's economic and legal resources to enable it to undertake more sophisticated merger and monopoly enforcement, prepare more successful cartel cases, and resolve market access problems.* To demonstrate its credibility in expanding markets, the FTC should maintain and increase its attention to cartels and bid-rigging, and to mergers. Strengthened anti-cartel enforcement (particularly with respect to bid-rigging and other "hard core" cartels) and monitoring of potential anti-competitive abuses with respect to distribution channels are also important tools in redressing the market access concerns. As more effective enforcement against cartels leads to restructuring, particular attention to mergers is needed. This will call for continuing to deepen its expertise and improve the mix of skills, with greater emphasis on both economic analysis and on investigative and legal techniques.

The capacities of the FTC to take more enforcement actions should be boosted.

— *Increase the visibility and impact of* FTC *participation in policy-making.* Establishing a forum for discussing and clearly deciding about matters that affect competition in the context of overall economic policy is critical for reform to succeed. The FTC should become in fact what it is in theory, the principal "horizontal" authority responsible for assessing as well as applying competition policy. This will require preserving the FTC's independence from political direction while permitting it to take a more central role in policy formation. The FTC already has statutory responsibilities and opportunities for consultation, which it could and should exercise more vigorously. The plan for a Ministry of General Affairs, to which the FTC will be attached, may also promote a more visible and central policy role, though care is needed to avoid compromising the FTC's mission against competing mandates in the giant ministry.

The FTC should advocate for regulatory reform within the administration.

OECD 1999

To strengthen rights of private action, the quota on new lawyers should be eliminated, among other reforms.

– *Strengthen rights of private action by providing for injunctions in independent private suits, easing the proof of damages in competition cases, and facilitating consumer and customer recoveries in price-fixing cases. The quota on new lawyers should be eliminated.* These steps would apply more resources to competition policy issues, expand the base of support for it, and enlist other institutions in developing important policy principles. Broader rights of private action, more effectively vindicated, would signify that competition policy creates basic legal rights for market actors and is not just a technical regulatory speciality. In addition to the obvious need to end the limit on the number of lawyers, it may also be necessary to add judges or establish a special court division, similar to the one that handles patent issues, to hear complex economic matters such as competition cases.

Systematic improvements to regulations on market openness principles would be valuable.

– *Promote market openness in regulatory reform by creating a capacity, in co-ordination with the economy-wide regulatory reform programme 1) to recommend reform measures from a market openness perspective and 2) to monitor vigorously implementation of those reform measures through strengthened power vis-à-vis other ministries and agencies.* Domestic regulations will continue to be a focus of trade discussions concerning Japan, yet there is no governmental function to work with regulators to systematically improve regulations for market openness. To better achieve the Japanese policy stance in favour of international harmonisation of regulations, a more effective mechanism to plan and implement reform from a market openness perspective is needed. The capacity of government officials to cope with the market openness issues could be improved by creating a training programme on international rules for all regulatory officials.

A consumer-oriented policy framework of market and competition principles, with efficient regulatory protections, should be strengthened government-wide to guide the use of regulatory powers

The most important broad-ranging competition-based reform would be the elimination of all "supply-demand balancing" functions.

– *Eliminate all "supply-demand balancing" aspects of permitting, licensing, and other forms of advice or intervention, formal or informal, within a fixed period, such as one year. Fix sunset dates of preferably less than two years on all such requirements that remain.* The most important broad-ranging competition-based reform would be the rapid elimination of all remaining "supply-demand balancing" functions that serve to control and prevent pro-competitive entry. In addition to the 11 such provisions included in the current deregulation programme, there are 17 other provisions in various sectors. The current programme promises to move in the right direction, and bills are pending before the Diet to eliminate several provisions, but in several areas the concrete actions and target dates are imprecise. The action needed now is a firm, short deadline for the repeal of these provisions.

Exemptions to the AMA should be closed...

– *Eliminate or narrow sectoral and other exemptions from the AMA.* Plans to eliminate, narrow, and simplify exemptions from the AMA have been underway for several years, in several stages. It is imperative to follow through on the plans already announced for legislative action. For those items calling for further study, that process should be completed and legislation drafted to narrow any remaining exemptions as much as possible.

– *Establish a clear, effective relationship between consumer policy and competition policy.* Competition policy should be coordinated with consumer policy. In the short term, a clearer institutional relationship should be developed between competition policy in the FTC and consumer protection in the Economic Planning Agency and other responsible bodies. Over the longer term, the government should examine the establishment of a stronger authority for consumer protection.

... and competition policy should be coordinated more clearly with consumer policy.

– *Explicitly include in the mandates of sectoral ministries and regulators the responsibility to support competition principles and enforcement.* All ministries should be responsible for eliminating constraints on competition within their own jurisdiction to extend the scope of competition principles and reduce the risk of anti-competitive state actions. To maintain the FTC's central role, ministries should be held responsible for co-ordinating with the FTC so that enforcement issues are referred there quickly. Major ministries might have antitrust bureaux (similar to MITI's Industrial Organisation section) to work with the FTC and to advise industries about compliance obligations.

All ministries should be responsible for eliminating constraints on competition.

– *Target competition enforcement on practices that have been tolerated or promoted by informal administrative guidance, to reinforce the shift in regulatory philosophy away from central direction.* Exemplary enforcement actions should vigorously implement the principles set out in the 1994 FTC guidelines about administrative guidance. Steps against co-ordination sponsored by other ministries are at the heart of the regulatory reform agenda. It will not be enough to consult with other ministries and ask them to stop encouraging or tolerating non-competitive behaviour. Rather, effective and visible sanctions must be applied to the private parties who use the cover of ministerial acceptance or instruction to prevent competition. The FTC faced up to some anti-competitive actions by other ministries even in the 1950s and 1960s. The FTC appears stronger now, and thus it should be able to do so with more confidence. FTC oversight of trade associations activities, where much of the impact of administrative guidance is felt, must be maintained and even intensified. The trend toward seeking stronger sanctions in trade association cases is right and should continue.

Practices encouraged by administrative guidance should be a particular target of enforcement.

More effort is needed to prevent regulatory problems before they occur by strengthening quality control mechanisms for regulatory development inside the administration

A sustained effort is needed to embed good regulatory practices into the "culture" of the public administration. Some of the reforms in the Basic Law for the Administrative Reform of the Central Government, such as strengthening the policy capacities of the Cabinet, will greatly boost regulatory reform capacities in the government and reduce the risks of regulatory failures. A great opportunity for change lies in expanding the Basic Law for Administrative Reform of Central Government, and linking it more explicitly to regulatory reform. Professional and cultural change in the administration will not come easily. The policy reforms suggested will require new training programmes, new skill mixes, and new funding in some cases.

– *Adopt principles of* good *regulation based on those accepted by Ministers in the* 1997 OECD *Report on Regulatory Reform.* The regulatory principles in the current deregulation programme are clearer and closer to international best practices than those in previous programmes. The explicit use of market principles is a good step. Yet significant gaps remain in defining the dimensions of regulatory quality, such as the principle that all regulations shall have a sound legal basis, and that regulations shall be adopted only if costs are justified by benefits. The benefit-cost principle should be implemented through regulatory impact analysis. Competition principles should be strengthened in the overall policy framework.

Regulatory impact analysis would help assess, in advance, economic impacts of new proposals.

– *Implement across the administration a step-by-step programme for regulatory impact assessment, based on OECD best practice recommendations, for all new and revised regulations. The analysis should begin with feasible steps such as costing of direct impacts and qualitative assessment of benefits, and move progressively over a multi-year period to more rigorous and quantitative forms of analysis as skills are built in the administration, and should be made public as part of public comment procedures.* There is no explicit commitment to the use of regulatory impact assessment in the current reform programme, though the revised programme of 30 March 1999 calls for ministries to "work toward" improving their accountability for the impacts of regulations. This is a useful step that should pave the way for a decision to implement RIA as soon as possible to bring Japan up to international good practices. Three-quarters of OECD countries now use RIA and the direction of change is universally toward refining, strengthening and extending the use of RIA disciplines. RIA can be a powerful tool, especially if integrated with notice and comment procedures, to boost regulatory quality by giving policy officials better information on the impacts of regulation on the economy. While benefit-cost analysis may be a long-term goal, interim steps feasible with current administrative skills, such as user panels and surveys, could be implemented quickly. OECD's best practice principles should be the basis for a RIA programme, overseen by an appropriate quality control body with analytical expertise at the centre of government.

Market-oriented instruments would reduce the cost of government action.

– *Use of flexible and market-oriented policy instruments should be expanded.* A significant omission in the current programme is its failure to promote the use of market based alternatives to regulation in those areas where government action is justified. The OECD Report on Regulatory Reform[104] documented movement toward a range of alternative instruments in numerous Member countries and pointed to evidence on gains in policy effectiveness. Consideration of alternatives should be an integral part of the RIA programme, with the range of alternatives considered expanding over time as familiarity, and expertise, with the use of a wider range of policy tools grows.

Consumers will benefit from lower prices and more choice, and enterprises will gain from tougher competition and faster innovation, if markets are more fully opened to international trade and investment

– *Enhance regulatory co-operation with other countries. Engage more vigorously in work with trading partners to promote harmonisation and recognition of foreign conformity assessment.* Considering the weight it represents for the global economy, Japan's actions to harmonise regulations and promote recognition of conformity assessment across countries are increasingly crucial for the success of international co-operation. Japan's recent accession to international harmonisation agreement in the automobile sector and its leadership in APEC standards are promising examples. Recent progress toward MRAs with the EU in several sectors is also a positive. Current efforts should be strengthened and accelerated.

Promoting harmonisation and co-operation will bring benefits to Japan's consumers...

– *Improve capacities to address international competition problems by reaching agreements with other countries on co-operation and enforcement.* The FTC should enter bilateral co-operation agreements with other national competition agencies. As the scope of its international jurisdiction expands, and as the market in Japan continues to open to more foreign trade and investment, the proportion of enforcement matters with significant international dimensions will only increase. Without clear arrangements with the enforcement authorities of its major trading partners, the FTC will be at an increasing disadvantage in taking accurate, timely action in these matters.

... as will international co-operation on competition problems.

– *Launch government-wide measures to accept the equivalence of foreign conformity assessment, and establish sectoral programmes of reviewing and harmonising technical regulations and standards.*

A series of steps are needed in the electricity sector to pave the way for the effective competition that will lower prices

The decision to move forward with partial liberalisation of retail supply is an important and irreversible step for Japan to take towards its goal of international comparability in electricity prices. The first step of partial liberalisation may bring benefits to both liberalised and non-liberalised customers, since it may bring the significant benefit of information about potential efficiency gains, and make clearer the way forward.

113

Reform in the electricity sector should proceed on a step by step basis.

– *The government should adopt a comprehensive reform plan for the industry that lays out the timing and criteria for evaluating progress with reform, taking into account the three major energy policy goals.* Development of a comprehensive plan is consistent with the OECD report of Ministers on Regulatory Reform, which recommends a complete and transparent package of reforms designed to achieve specific goals on a well-defined timetable.

– *As part of this reform plan, the government should define measurable indicators of these reforms* so that progress toward their achievement can be monitored and, if there are problems with this progress, the government can make a timely adjustment toward other policies.

– *Competition principles should be strengthened in the overall policy framework.*

The following recommendations would apply particularly to the first step of reform:

– Regulatory independence from day to day political pressures is essential to build confidence of all electricity market participants that government intervention in the electricity market will be neutral and transparent. Further, independence from the regulated companies, including but not limited to utilities, is needed to ensure transparent, fair, and reasonably predictable decisions. Therefore, *the regulation of the electricity sector should be independent from policy-making functions and electricity industry promotion functions, with transparent procedures and due process for the review of decisions.* Transparency, expertise, independence and adequate legal powers are particularly important. *Co-ordination with the Fair Trade Commission should be clearly defined.*

– Non-discriminatory tariffs and terms of access to the networks and system services are cornerstones of electricity reform. *The first step of reform should include the requirement for regulated terms and conditions of access to the network and provision of ancillary services.* Separate accounts for natural monopoly activities and supply of electricity to captive customers are needed from the potentially competitive activities. Prices should reflect, to the extent possible, underlying costs to encourage efficient development and use of the networks.

– Standard customer tariffs do not reflect the high cost of peak power. Cost reflective pricing of energy would encourage those customers able to manage their load to use less energy on peak, thus reducing total electricity costs. Therefore, *standard electricity tariffs for captive customers, and network/ancillary service tariffs for liberalised customers, should reflect costs by time of use.* Implementation of the time of use tariffs should be phased in, beginning with liberalised customers and the larger (power) captive customers.

– The current application of yardstick assessment to economic regulation provides only diffuse incentives for utilities to improve their efficiency. Therefore, *the yardstick assessment scheme should be revised to provide a greater incentive for utilities to improve their efficiency by providing a less direct link between prices a utility can charge and the corresponding cost, and providing a more direct link with the cost efficiency of other electric utilities,* making suitable adjustments for utilities'unique physical situations.

– Competition law needs to be enforced vigorously where collusive behaviour, abuse of dominant position, or anti-competitive mergers risks frustrating reform. *The Anti-monopoly Act should be amended to clarify that it also applies to the electricity sector.*

If after a reasonable period, such as 2003, there continues to be evidence of discriminatory behaviour, and the market is not sufficiently competitive, despite accounting separation, further changes will be necessary:

– The Government should expand the set of eligible customers. If possible, make all customers eligible.

– If difficulties with accounting separation are found, and if measures to strengthen accounting separation appear unlikely to improve matters, then utilities should be required to functionally separate their regulated activities from unregulated activities and the regulatory regime may need to be strengthened. The government should consider the full range of feasible separation options to promote competition in the industry.

– Increased activity in the trading of electricity will increase the need and the opportunity for a short- term electricity market to deal with imbalances between generation and loads. Therefore, a *short-term market for electricity sales should be created to optimise use of generating resources.*

Following the second step in the regulatory reform in the electricity sector, the Government of Japan should undertake a review of the operation of the competitive electricity market in each utility service area in Japan. Depending on the outcome of such an evaluation, the Government should consider what further practical regulatory and/or structural reforms might be introduced, consistent with Japan's overall energy policy goals and objectives. Among the options to be considered are:

– Measures to encourage entry of new generating companies.

– The expansion of interconnections between regions in a way that supports greater competition as well as reliability of supply

– Modification of economic regulation applied to the utilities to provide them with greater incentives to operate and invest efficiently in monopoly activities of the sector, as well as to compete for customers in the competitive activities of the sector.

– Measures to encourage the voluntary sale of utilities'generating capacity to multiple buyers.

– The full range of feasible horizontal and vertical separation options to promote further competition in the industry.

115

Much progress is seen in telecommunications, but essential regulatory safeguards should be established to ensure full competition in the marketplace

In telecommunications, regulatory safeguards are needed to protect and encourage competition and market entry.

– *Establish effective government-wide measures which resolve access to rights of way problems for new entrants in order to promote facility-based competition.* The Japanese government should provide effective measures for resolving carriers'difficulties related to access to rights of way due to the fragmented responsibilities for rights of way. In particular, the transparency of rights of way regulation should be enhanced by publishing guidelines for rights of way, as was done for market access.

– *Implement the* LRIC *methodology as soon as possible as a means of ensuring more cost-oriented interconnection pricing.* Since the ABC accounting system is based on historical cost, new entrants face high interconnection charges. This prevents them from offering low-cost services to customers. Although MPT has already decided to submit the bill to the Diet in 2000 to introduce the LRIC method, the implementation timetable should be accelerated to ensure more cost-oriented pricing.

– MPT *should establish as rapidly as possible a transparent and fair spectrum allocation method to select mobile licensees when applicants outnumber licenses in order to ensure that all applicants can compete fairly when applying for a mobile license.* The lack of a transparent spectrum allocation method is a significant weakness of the Japanese telecommunications regulatory regime. Although MPT is considering introducing a new spectrum allocation method, it is not decided which method will be adopted and what the criteria will be for selecting new licensees. To ensure a fair chance to all potential entrants, the new spectrum allocation method should be in place in time for the allocation of spectrum for IMT 2000 services.

– MPT *should rapidly implement number portability and carrier preselection to ensure fair competition between current players and new entrants.* The lack of number portability and carrier preselection gives an unfair advantage to the incumbent and to some extent to the early NCCs. MPT should promptly introduce these regulatory safeguards, which are essential to fair competition. Mobile services should be included in the number portability plan, and consumers should have sufficient carrier pre-selection choices to ensure fair competition between new entrants and current players.

– *To promote competition, the present carrier market entry requirements should be made simpler and more transparent.* Under the TBL, the Minister has authority to grant Type 1 and to refuse Special Type 2 licenses using -examination standards based on the public interest provisions in the telecommunications law. Furthermore, carriers are not allowed to combine Type 1 and Type 2 services. These regulations impose unnecessary economic burdens on carriers. MPT should abolish the current market entry scheme and establish a simple and transparent scheme such as 'class license'system for all carriers.

- *The requirement of partial government ownership on NTT should be lifted so as to eliminate any conflict of interest by having the government as both a regulator and a shareholder.* The NTT Law requires the government to hold at least one-third of NTT shares. As competition develops, the basis of regulation for NTT should move from treating it as a special company to using market power criteria and treating the company as a dominant player which controls essential facilities. In this regard, ownership restrictions on NTT should be removed and it is also recommended that the Japanese government move faster towards full privatisation of NTT. In addition, current foreign ownership restriction also should be lifted.

- A *transparent universal service funding mechanism, that is also competitively and technologically neutral, should be established.* Current universal service obligations on NTT are implicitly funded through cross-subsidisation of NTT's services and make it difficult for NTT to establish cost-based charges for its services. Universal service cost should be transparent and clearly separated from interconnection charges. In this context, it is essential to establish a transparent and competitively and technologically neutral universal service funding mechanism in line with the break-up of NTT and the introduction of the LRIC system.

- As *competition develops, the role of competition law in the telecommunications market should be strengthened, and sector specific regulation should be reviewed periodically in order to streamline the regulation.* MPT should forebear from regulation in areas or for activities where sufficient competition has emerged and conditions will allow the development of effective and sustainable competition between carriers. Excessive sector-specific regulation on carriers may hamper development of the full benefits of competition. Periodic reviews of regulation to determine where streamlining can take place should be undertaken.

- *Options for making the NTT regional companies fully independent should be reviewed, because infrastructure competition between NTT regional companies appears unlikely develop under common ownership.* The break-up of NTT is consistent with competition in the local market to the extent that other competitors enter the market, but the holding company structure means that the NTT companies do not have strong incentives to compete against each other, and have no incentive to enter into infrastructure competition. Thus, the benefits of divestiture may not be realised. The Japanese government should review the current holding company structure, making the NTT regional companies fully independent of each other, in order to realise the benefits of divestiture.

- *Regulatory functions should be independent from industry promotion functions, with transparent procedures and the process for the review of decisions.* Both as a regulator and a policy maker, MPT is responsible for consumer protection as well as industry promotion in the telecommunications sector. Since the regulatory body's independence can be effectively ensured only when it

117

is separated from interested parties, the Japanese government needs to ensure greater separation of regulatory functions from industry promotion functions.

MANAGING REGULATORY REFORM

Transition measures should be a means of supporting timely change.

An issue important in many OECD countries, but perhaps even more vital to structural change in Japan is the management of transition periods. There will certainly be tangible costs of restructuring, to move assets into more productive uses, and this risk should not be minimised. Fears about the effect of regulatory reform on employment, on small businesses, on local economies, and on traditional producers have necessitated government transitional initiatives during periods of adjustment, along with other reforms such as active labour market policies and more flexible labour markets. The Administrative Reform Committee's 1995 report addressed this issue in a section titled, "On suffering" that called for "more effective means to overcome the pain while promoting reform". The current issue is how to ensure that transition is not a means of delaying reform, but of supporting timely structural change by adjusting benefits and costs across society.

The length and depth of the current crisis offers an unprecedented opportunity to get on with long delayed reforms, but a broader constitency is essential.

The Japanese government has put into place processes for assessing and communicating the results of reform, which recognises that an important determinant of the scope and pace of further reform is the attitude of the general public. The length and depth of the current recession offers an unprecedented opportunity to get on with long delayed reforms, but a broader constituency is essential. A high priority to motivate support for reform is to deliver visible benefits to consumers, as reform of the large-scale retail store law did when discount stores began opening in greater numbers. In the business community, deep cleavages over regulatory reform provide an opportunity to build a constituency for reform. This suggests that urban consumers and export-oriented industries will be the two major reform allies. Evaluation of the impacts of reform and communication with the public and all major stakeholders with respect to the short and long-term effects of action and non-action, and on the distribution of costs and benefits, is increasingly important to further progress. Here, the white paper on regulatory reform to be prepared by the Management and Coordination Agency under the current programme and the evaluation mandate for the Economic Planning Agency could be important, as will other efforts to communicate the importance of reform.

Reformers will need to take concrete steps to demonstrate that regulatory protections have been maintained.

Equally important is a balanced reform programme emphasizing both deregulation to allow market forces more space, and better regulation to protect consumers, health and safety, and the environment. At this juncture, it seems that fears about the effects of reform on levels of protection have not been borne out, but continued reform will proceed faster and more deeply if reformers take concrete steps to demonstrate that protection has been maintained.

NOTES

1. In 1995, the Commission on Administrative Reform described the issue as one of turning Japanese values from "Japanese-ness" – uniformity, dependence on government, and controls – to those of small government, individuality, coexistence of diverse values, and freedom. "Such a sharp turn in the nation's path is exactly what we seek through deregulation". Commission on Administrative Reform (1995).

2. The share of foreign production in manufacturing overall went from 3 to 6 to 13 per cent from 1985 to 1991 to 1997, respectively. For firms with any overseas production the comparable figures were 8.7, 16.7 and 31.0 per cent, respectively. In motor vehicles, overseas production reached nearly 25 per cent in 1997. *Source*: MITI. See also Table 5 "Indicators of globalisation" in the 1998 OECD *Survey of Japan*.

3. Sectoral ministries influenced enterprises through their control of regulatory process such as granting permits and licences, permission to enter new markets or change prices, as well as access to low-interest loans, subsidies, loan guarantees, tax incentives, as well as concrete tools broad discretionary powers The state provided grants and concessional loans for investment, tax incentives for research and development (R&D), helped set up joint ventures and industry associations to pool R&D and technological improvements, often with active public sector participation, facilitated the acquisition of technology from abroad (the government discouraged FDI in favour of licensing). As part of this, the state fostered R&D in applications and industrial processes and helped firms acquire basic technology from abroad. Both administrative guidance and R&D co-ordination were effected in a number of ways including sectoral co-ordinating bodies (see also Box 2.3).

4. The state often did take equity positions in startup firms in new industriese where risks were high and in R&D associations.

5. The government itself maintained a primary budget surplus between 1961-73 (0.7 per cent of GDP) and created various institutional structures such as the postal savings system to encourage household savings, which averaged 16 per cent for the period.

6. Japanese unions have traditionally been weak in most manufacturing sectors and labour has played little role in corporate governance.

7. Some observers have credited the "Japanese miracle" to state-led industrial policy while others have focused largely on stable macroeconomic policy, the external orientation of the economy (in contrast to the Latin American import substitution model prevalent at the time), high levels of savings and the rapid rates of factor accumulation (see Figure 1.4). See the World Bank volume, *The East Asian Miracle* (1996) for a summary and evaluation of this debate. The seminal work favouring the importance of industrial policy was Chalmers Johnson (1982) MITI *and the Japanese Miracle: The Growth of Industrial Policy, 1925-1975* (Stanford University Press).

8. *vs.* the non-Japan average of 4.4 per cent.

9. Consumers were compensated by the high rate of consumption of growth overall, nearly eight per cent, approximately double that of any other G7 country.

10. Over the 1973-84 period, average GDP growth was half that of the 1961-73 period and average unemployment rose slightly from 1 to 2 per cent. Consumer inflation was stable as a very large exchange rate appreciation and successful macroeconomic adjustment offset the rise in energy prices. Japan's nominal effective exchange rate appreciated by 47 per cent from 1973-80 and 125 per cent from 1980-90. The unweighted average for the rest of the G7 was −9 and +12 per cent for the same periods, respectively.

11.

Japanese as per cent of	Per capita GDP					Per capita consumption				
	1970	1980	1986	1990	1996	1970	1980	1986	1990	1996
United States	58.4	67.6	71.8	80.2	84.6	48.3	62.6	64.1	69.4	73.6
EU 15	94.8	101.4	107.9	115.4	121.7	84.7	100.3	105.7	112.3	119.0
Note: EU 15/US	61.6	66.6	66.5	69.5	69.5	57.1	62.4	60.6	61.8	61.8

Measured at Current PPP in US$.

12. Beginning in the mid-1970s the Ministry of International Trade and Industry (MITI), facilitated a shift away from energy-intensive products (fertilisers, synthetics, petrochemicals), semi-processed industrial goods (natural fibres) and heavy industries (shipbuilding, iron and steel) towards machinery and industrial applications (numerically-controlled machine tools), particularly in electrical machinery, electronics (colour Tvs, VCRs and semi-conductors) and other consumer goods (motor vehicles).

13. As part of this process, the government provided support for rationalisation of small and medium-sized enterprises (SMEs) and in 1978 a law was passed on the restructuring of industries in structural decline (especially those facing competition from lower wage countries) which included the use of so-called restructuring cartels to manage reductions in capacity while avoiding "destructive" competition. By the time it expired, capacity had been reduced by 33% in 14 sectors. This law was renewed again in 1983 for another five years.

14. VERS were found in key sectors like motor vehicles, machine tools and colour televisions. Because of VERs Japanese passenger cars exports to the US between 1981-84 remained below the the 1980 level of 1.9 million units. Other sectors subject to some sort of VER included video cassette recorders, motorcycles, watches, and various types of steel. While constraining Japanese export growth, these developments resulted in higher export unit values and larger profit margins.

15. While Japanese fiscal deficits were not much higher than that of other OECD countries, a much larger component was seen to be structural. The OECD Survey (1982/83, p. 64) estimated that about ¾ of the deficit was structural. Much of this was attributable to the continuing high levels of public infrastructure investment in order to catch up with the previous rapid growth in the economy. As was noted in the 1982/83 OECD Survey, social capital investment accounted for 9 per cent of GDP in the 1960s and 1970s but was insufficient to keep up with rapid growth.

16. By 1984, real debt service was 18.1 per cent of expenditures, greater than spending on public works (12.9 per cent) and roughly equivalent to spending on social security (18.4 per cent).

17. See Chapter 2 for more details.

18. Current losses for public enterprises in 1984 were ¥ 2.2 trillion (0.8 per cent of GDP) compared with general government net lending of ¥ 6.4 trillion (2.4 per cent of GDP). This does not include over ¥ 7 trillion in investment expenditures.

19. For example, some entry onto new routes was permitted in air traffic between the three carriers, but this replaced existing monopolies with duopolies with prices still regulated by the Ministry of Transport. Despite privatisation JR was still required to expand bullet train service into less populated areas where existing service were already making losses.

20. The consolidated surplus reached a peak of just under 3.0 per cent of GDP in 1990-91.

21. The current account surplus did fall by 2.7 percentage points from the 1986 peak.

22. In part this was because exports surged once quantitative restraints – VERs – were removed. During the period 1981-84 – while VERs were in place – Japanese passenger cars exports to the US remained below the 1980 level of 1.9 million units. (Other sectors which had been subject to some sort of VER included video cassette recorders, motorcycles, watches, and various types of steel.) When VERs were removed, car exports to the U.S. surged to over 2.5 million units in 1985 and 1986 and only declined gradually in the face of a depreciating dollar as Japanese producers attempted to maintain prices and market share by reducing profit margins and improving productivity. Exports to the US did not dip below 2 million units again until 1990, and a similar process unfolded in other key sensitive sectors like computers, semiconductors and consumer electronics.

23. Privatisation of telecommunications, discussed above, included permitting the entry of foreign firms and was one of a number of measures taken in response to foreign pressures.

24. This situation was similar to that which occurred in the United States in the case of savings and loans and commercial banks. In the US case, deregulation of interest rates and lending occurred as traditional financial institutions lost major corporate clients to financial markets, or, in the case of S&Ls, simply lost money. In both cases, new freedoms were not accompanied by increased regulatory oversight, so that commercial banks vigorously pursued Third World lending to replace lost corporate clients while S&Ls made loans to real estate developers, especially in areas booming due to higher oil prices. In both cases these institutions became overextended, resulting in a credit contraction and, in the case of S&Ls, the need for a Federal bailout (see The OECD Review of Regulatory Reform in the United States (1999), Chapter 1).

25. Consumer inflation has been near zero and several other inflation measures have been negative for extended periods, signalling the risk of actual price deflation.

26. Cumulative fiscal stiumulus was equivalent to fifteen per cent of GDP and public investment alone grew at an annual real rate of over 8 per cent.

27. Japanese economic performance has gone from the best to the worst in the G7. GDP growth has been the lowest of any country and Japan's share of G7 manufacturing exports has declined precipitously, returning to levels not seen since the early 1970s (see Figure 1.3). Labour productivity growth has been also at the bottom of the G7 – near zero – even as growth in the capital stock remains nearly the highest despite the collapse in investment, indicative of how heavily the economy has been biased towards investment.

28. A clear example of this problem is in the motor vehicles industry. Japanese domestic production capacity is 14 million cars, while production in 1998 was 10.4 million. The excess capacity is 25%.

29. Japan's trading partners have frequently complained that keiretsu, in addition to inhibiting new entry because of limiting access to distribution, also discouraged competition in industry. Keiretsu members tended to turn to other members as suppliers rather than purchasing inputs based on market criteria of price and quality, further discouraging competition and making market penetration by foreign firms particularly difficult.

30. Since 1997, this exemption has been limited to copyright works. See Chapter 3.

31. As in most countries many of these regulations were targeted in principal towards addressing issues like safety concerns, *e.g.* earthquake survivability or environmental concerns such as maintaining open spaces.

32. This differential treatment widened over the 1980s as Japanese industrial policy began to wither away while heavy regulation of non-traded goods continue. In terms of the competitive environment, as noted above, the traded goods sector, while shielded from import competition and foreign investment was nonetheless forced to compete in world export markets and faced intense domestic competition between Japanese firms. Moreover slow but steady progress on market opening measures in the 1980s increased competition from imports. On the regulatory side, the very success and globalisation of Japanese manufacturing undermined both the justification for administrative guidance and regulation and the ability of ministries to engage in it. Ministries'ability to influence enterprise behaviour weakened steadily as exporters developed global production networks and gained access to world financial markets. As a result, by the 1990s, administrative guidance, restructuring cartels and the state's overall influence on private investment through financial incentives had largely dwindled away.

33. Data on comparative price performance is for the benchmark year 1993 for OECD-wide comparable PPPs have been calculated.

34. The 1993 OECD *Survey* cites evidence that Japanese prices at the time were on average 20 per cent above the OECD average, particularly in food and beverages, fuel and power, transportation, communications and services. A recent study by the Japanese EPA – see also Chapter 4 – found prices in a medium-sized Japanese city (Kanazawa) to be 57 per cent higher than a comparable American city (St. Louis), with the largest differentials found in food, energy, housing rents, clothing and footwear.

35. Are well above the OECD average and twice US prices despite comparable average flight length.

36. OECD (1997-98), p. 153.

37. There are no longer any line-of-business restrictions and there is strong competition in the national and international long distance markets, as well as cellular mobile services and CATV (cable) telephony. However, as in many countries, lack of adequate interconnection services has hampered full development of competition, particularly in local telephony (see Chapter 6 for details), and as in other public and quasi-public sectors (*e.g.* electricity, the postal system) the Japanese authorities have favoured accounting separation rather than divestiture so that NTT's was separated into one long-distance company and two regional companies within a holding company structure.

38. This has been strengthened by easier access to low-cost imports from Southeast Asia and China thanks to market openness measures and by the elimination of retail price maintenance in many sectors so that price increases have slowed substantially in many products.

39. They have shrunk in the highly inefficient and previously cartelised wholesale sector.

40. In electric power, reform has been quite partial. On the one hand, utilities can now tender for some of their power from independent power producers, and they may soon be permitted compete to sell power to extra high voltage customers. On the other hand full competition in generation, full wholesale or retail wheeling, and the separation of generation and transmission have been rejected (see Chapter 5 for details). In transportation there remain minimum size requirements for trucking firms and notice for new routes or regions is still required while in air, reforms have been largely confined to allowing the three existing firms to fly on

some of each others routes, at the regulator's discretion. Until recently no new firms have entered in large part because of shortages of airport landing slots.

41. In November 1998 the MPT introduced a new system allowing companies to determine their own prices without approval except for NTT's local services, which should all for effective price competition to emerge. See Chapter 6 for details.

42. Inflation was the highest in the G7 at six per cent though relatively modest compared to other very rapidly growing countries during that period, such as those of Latin America. As noted in the 1997 OECD Economic Survey: "Over the period 1995-2025, the working-age population will fall at an annual rate of 0.7 per cent, with the decline accelerating to 1.0 per cent in the following 25 years". (p. 113). While trend labour force participation (LFP) is rising, particularly amongst men over 60 and women, Japanese LFP is already amongst the highest in the OECD and not likely to be sufficient to offset the decline in the labour force, so that labour supply is in fact likely to become a drag on economic growth. OECD projections indicate that between 2000-2025 hours worked and employment are likely to both decline at an annual rate of 0.3 per cent.

43. Between 1961 and 1973, Japanese consumption grew by 0.4 percentage points less than the rate of GDP growth, the highest differential among the G7 (Figure 7A), and this pattern continued through the 1980s. As noted above, historically, rapid rates of capital accumulation were based on a financial and corporate governance system which made large amounts of capital for private and goverment investment available at very low cost, allowing for highly negative growth rates of capital productivity accompanied by declining profitability and excessive levels of capital stock, especially in public infrastructure.

44. See the 1997-98 OECD Survey for a more detailed discussion of these points.

45. As noted above, Japanese GDP growth averaged 3.7 per cent from 1973 to 1990 fifty per cent higher than the other G7 average; in the 1990s Japanese GDP growth has averaged 1.2 per cent, roughly half that of the other G7. Given the factors described above, this relative stagnation is likely to persist if nothing is done.

46. These projections are largely based solely on the long-term effects of population ageing on the labour force and savings and investment rates discussed above OECD *Economic Survey of Japan*, 1997-98, p. 119, and see also Box 3.

47. As reported in the New York Times, 6 January 1999, p. C4.

48. There are already examples of this from Japan's own experience: the elimination of limits on the geographic expansion of petrol stations and controls on petroleum imports will mean that supermarkets will now open petrol stations, with substantially lower prices.

49. Financial sector reform in Japan is expected to result in short-term job losses due to substantial overstaffing by large banks.

50. For Japan, the OECD Regulatory Reform study projects initial declines in employment of around 11-12 cent in air and road transport and electricity.

51. OECD (1997-98), p. 85.

52. Among the many examinations of the role of the State in Japanese economic, social and political development see, for example, Calder, Kent E (1988) and Richardson, Bradley (1997).

53. Final Report of the Administrative Reform Council (Executive Summary), December 3, 1997.

54. Commission on Administrative Reform (1995), p. 4.

55. Deighton-Smith (1997), p. 221.

56. Jacobs (1997a), pp. 291-297.

57. "For the Promotion of Deregulation Aimed at Economic Revival and the Establishment of a Transparent System of Governmental Management" Keidanren submission to Government of Japan, 20 October 1998.

58. See Shiono, Hiroshi, "Administrative Guidance" in Public Administration in Japan, pp. 221-235, from which much of the material for this section is drawn.

59. "Power and Policy", p. 63.

60. "For the Promotion of Deregulation Aimed at Economic Revival and the Establishment of a Transparent System of Governmental Management" Keidanren submission to Government of Japan, 20 October, 1998.

61. Jacobs (1995), pp. 291-297.

62. OECD (1997).

63. Iyori and Uesugi (1994), pp. 41-48.

64. Iyori and Uesugi (1994), pp. 1-11.

65. Sanekata and Wilks, 1996, pp. 102-138.

66. The statutory definition of this term includes all forms of horizontal contract, agreement, or concerted action that control price or limit production, technology, products, facilities, or customers or suppliers. AMA, Sec. 2 (6).

67. AMA, Secs. 89-100.

68. Criminal Code, Art. 96-3.

69. Fair Trade Commission (1997).

70. Asahi News (Internet), 9 September 1998.

71. See OECD (1997c), pp. 108-109; Iyori and Uesugi (1994), p. 293.

72. AMA, Sec. 3.

73. AMA, Sec. 8-4 (1).

74. AMA, Sec. 27-2.

75. First (1995), pp. 167-68; Fair Trade Commission (1998).

76. AMA, Sec. 27-2 (v).

77. Simple mean of post Uruguay Round Bound Tariffs. See OECD (1998).

78. For example, Japan currently does not apply any kind of quantitative trade restriction measures, except the import licencings applied to Chinese and Korean silk and silk products and MFA quotas for some textile products.

79. See among others Sazanami, Yoko and others (1995), *Measuring Costs of Protection in Japan*, Institute for International Economics, January 1995; Daiwa Economic Research Institute (1994), *Deregulation Impact on Business*, (in Japanese) January 1994; and Kato, Masashi (ed. 1995), *Economics of Deregulation*, (in Japanese) Toyokeizaishimbunsha, July 1995.

80. As Kato (1995) said, "Japanese consumers are living miserably in spite of the abundant wealth they are creating".

81. Sazanami and others (1995), p. 2. Because they compared the level of cif price of imported goods and the level of producer prices for similar goods, the welfare loss might have been underestimated. In fact, in their studies, the supplementary adverse effect of inefficient distribution system was ignored.

82. As one of the special measures to promote imports and inward investment, the Japanese government has established several special zones in the vicinity of main ports and airports. Those who want to establish infrastructure for the purpose of import facilitation in these zones can get various financial and tax incentives from the government.

83. US (1998), *Submission by the Government of the United States to the Government of Japan regarding Deregulation, Competition Policy, and Transparency and Other Government Practices in Japan*, October 7 1998; European Union (1998: Commission of the European Communities), *Indicative list of EU Deregulation Proposals for Japan*, October 12 1998.

84. US (1998), EU (1998), and Australian Government, *Submission of the Australian Government to the Japanese Government on the Deregulation Promotion Program*, November 6 1998.

85. The Japanese government gave priority to resolving trade obstacles over investment obstacles at the outset of the OTO. At that time, the OTO was called the Office of Trade Ombudsman. That is why the OTO omits the letter "I" even after it changed its name to include investment as well.

86. The remaining 158 cases are in a group for which the situation remains unchanged. In these cases, related ministries explained the reason why they do not change the current situation, and complainants understood the reason.

87. It seems that the OTO is recently receiving some collected packages of complaints directly from foreign chambers of commerce in Japan and foreign embassies, apart from the complaints directly addressed to the OTO at the individual company level. However, the fact that foreign companies are taking the option to pass through their representatives and not to lodge them directly to the OTO may show the disappointment of foreign companies on the effectiveness of the OTO.

88. The remaining 161 cases are classified in the group for which the situation remains unchanged. In these cases, related ministries explained the reason why they do not change the current situation, and complainants understood the reason.

89. Meetings with the American Chamber of Commerce in Japan (ACCJ) and the European Business Council (EBC), July 23, 1998.

90. Gibney (1998), pp. 2-3.

91. US (1998), EU (1998), and Web Site of Canadian Ministry of Foreign Affairs and Trade.

92. EU (1998).

93. Article 27 of the Foreign Exchange and Foreign Trade Law. The Japanese authorities are committed to use these provisions only in accordance with Japan's rights and obligations under the OECD Codes of Liberalisation.

94. EU (1998).

95. The current three-year deregulation programme plans to lift the demand supply adjustment clauses.

96. Deregulation, promotion of network interconnection and NTT's reorganization are the three main goals of the "second info-communications reform".

97. In December 1980, the United States and Japan signed the first NTT Procurement Agreement.

98. OECD, *Communications Outlook* 1999.

99. NTT's revenue includes NTT DoCoMo's revenue.

100. There are ten market blocks.

101. Age distribution of cellular and PHS users.

	Percentage, as of March 1997								
	-9	10-14	15-19	20-29	30-39	40-49	50-59	60	No response
Cellular	0.9	0.5	4.1	30.5	21.0	21.2	11.8	4.6	5.3
PHS	0.3	1.2	18.3	28.7	16.7	13.7	8.0	7.1	5.9

Source: MPT.

102. *Communications Outlook* 1999.

103. OECD (1997*a*), p. 38.

104. OECD (1997*c*), pp. 220-222.

Annex

OTHER FIGURES

Figure 1.1. **Japanese macroeconomic performance**
In per cent

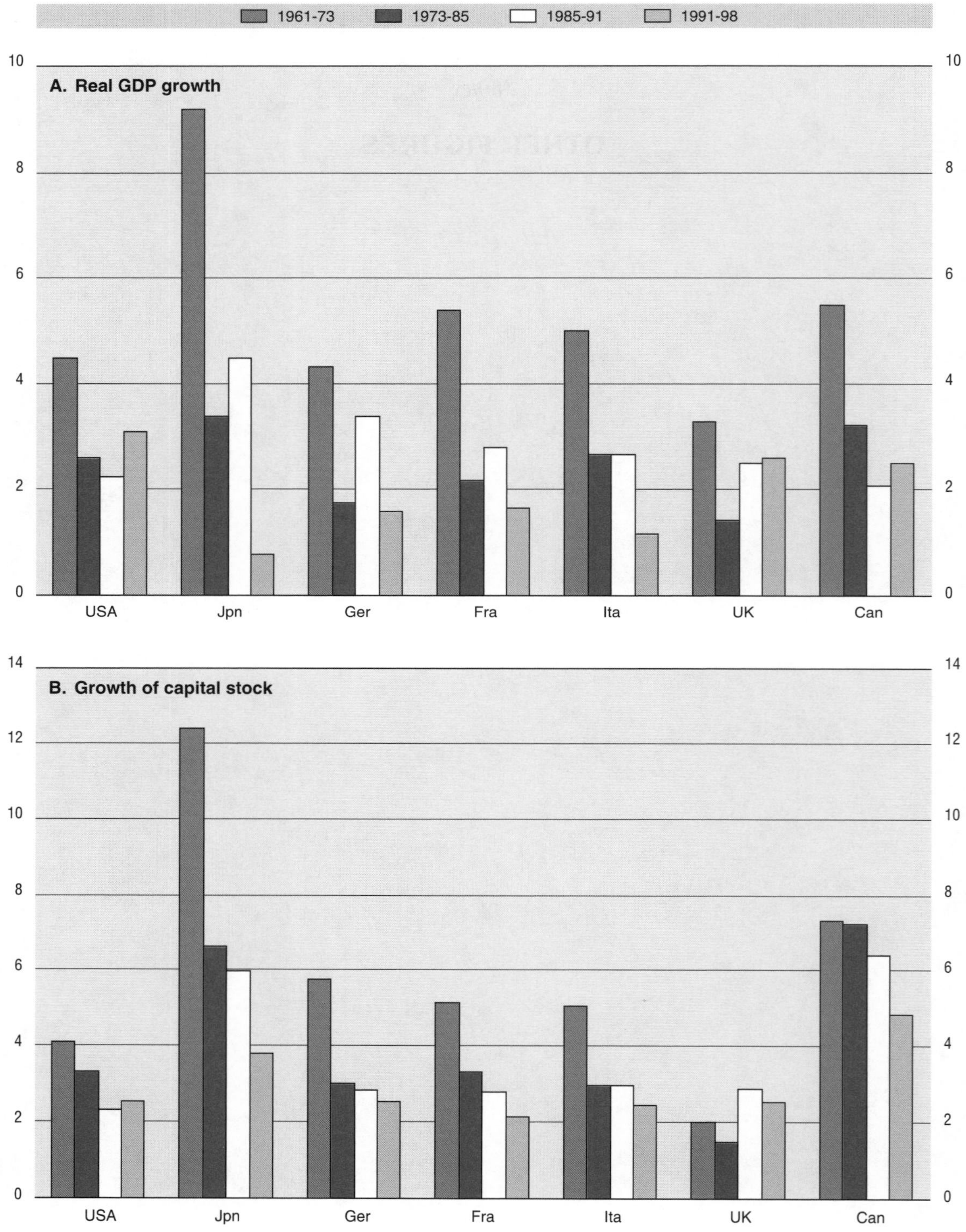
1961-73
1973-85
1985-91
1991-98
A. Real GDP growth
B. Growth of capital stock
0
2
4
6
8
10
12
14
USA
Jpn
Ger
Fra
Ita
UK
Can

Note: For Germany, 1985-90.
Source: OECD Secretariat.

Figure 1.2. **Japanese macroeconomic indicators, 1991-1998**

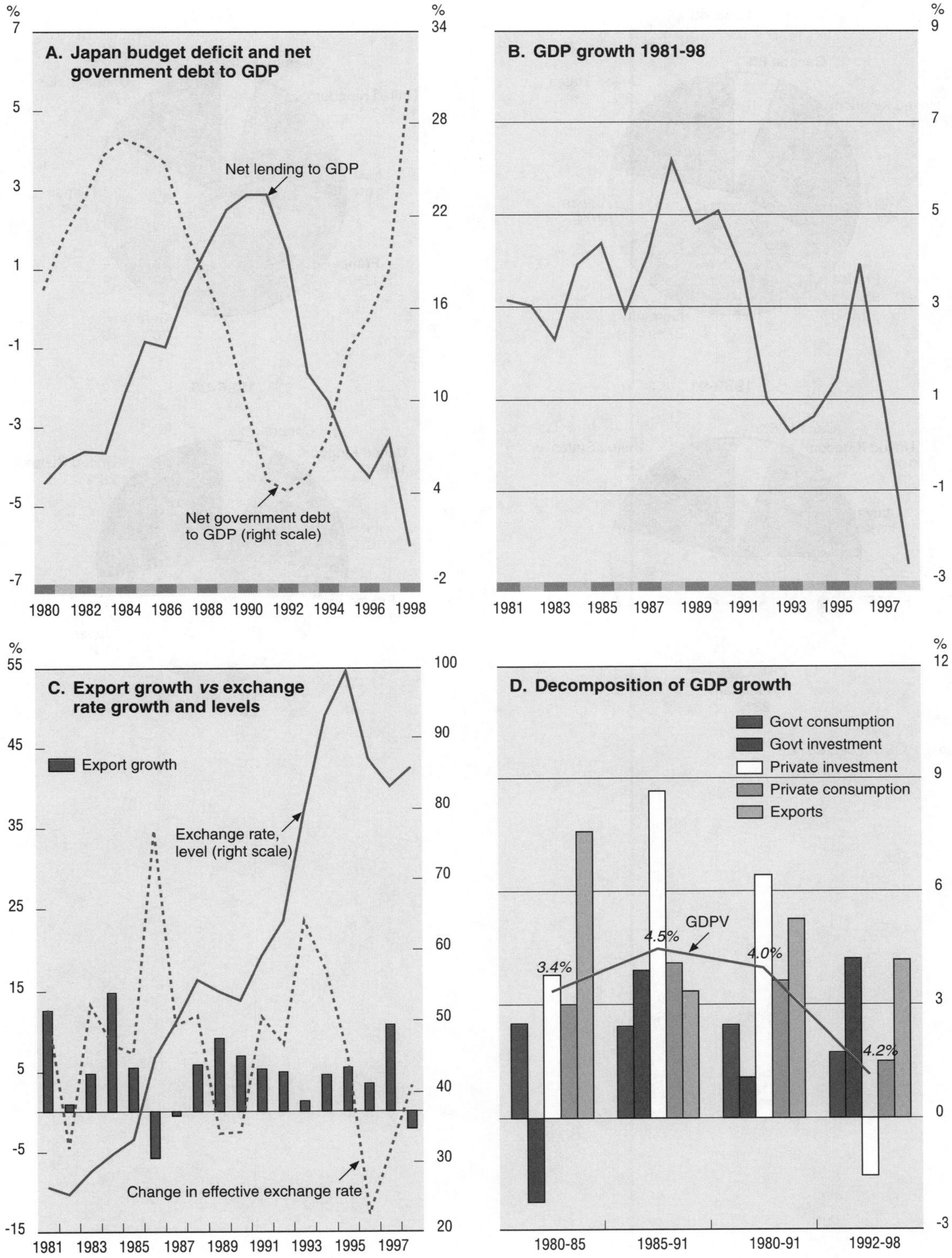
A. Japan budget deficit and net government debt to GDP
Net lending to GDP
Net government debt to GDP (right scale)
%
7
5
3
1
-1
-3
-5
-7
%
34
28
22
16
10
4
-2
1980 1982 1984 1986 1988 1990 1992 1994 1996 1998
B. GDP growth 1981-98
%
9
7
5
3
1
-1
-3
1981 1983 1985 1987 1989 1991 1993 1995 1997
C. Export growth vs exchange rate growth and levels
Export growth
Exchange rate, level (right scale)
Change in effective exchange rate
%
55
45
35
25
15
5
-5
-15
100
90
80
70
60
50
40
30
20
1981 1983 1985 1987 1989 1991 1993 1995 1997
D. Decomposition of GDP growth
Govt consumption
Govt investment
Private investment
Private consumption
Exports
GDPV
3.4%
4.5%
4.0%
4.2%
%
12
9
6
3
0
-3
1980-85 1985-91 1980-91 1992-98

Source: OECD Secretariat.

OECD 1999

Figure 1.3. **Japan share of G7 exports**

1963-65

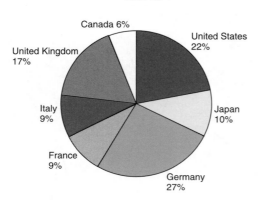

1971-73

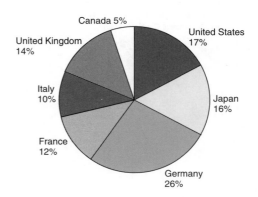

1989-91

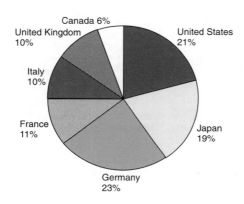

1996-98

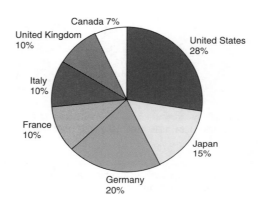

Source: OECD Secretariat.

Figure 1.4. **Sources of growth**

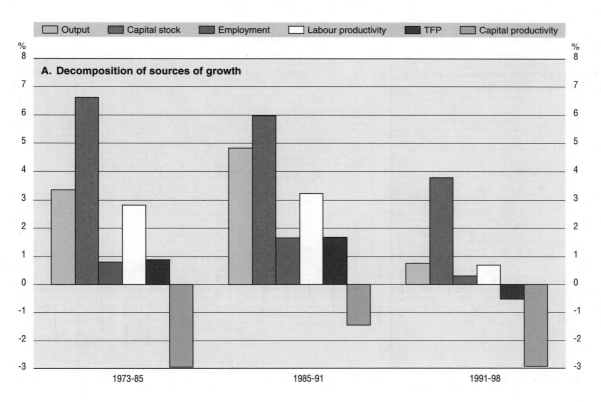

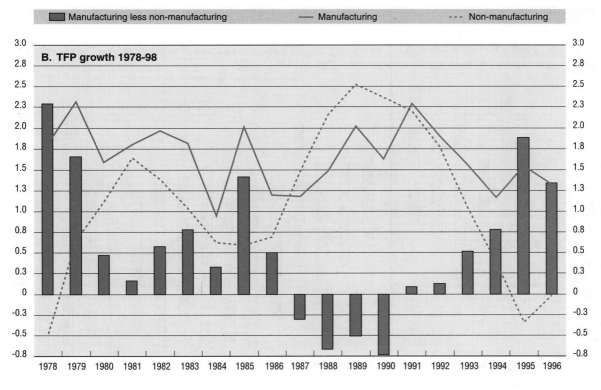

Source: OECD, Estimates for total business sector.

Figure 1.5. **Comparative price performance in manufacturing and service industries**
1993 PPP's, OECD = 100

A. Manufacturing

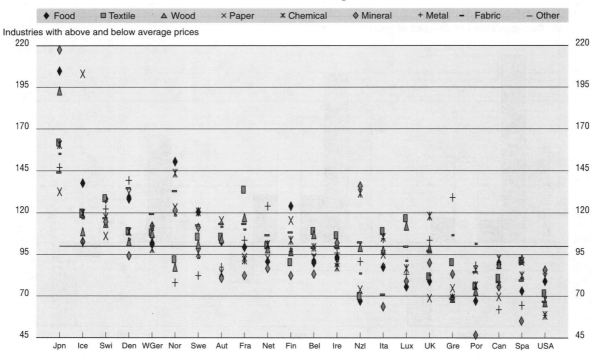

Source: OECD *projection, structure, and performance database,* 1999.

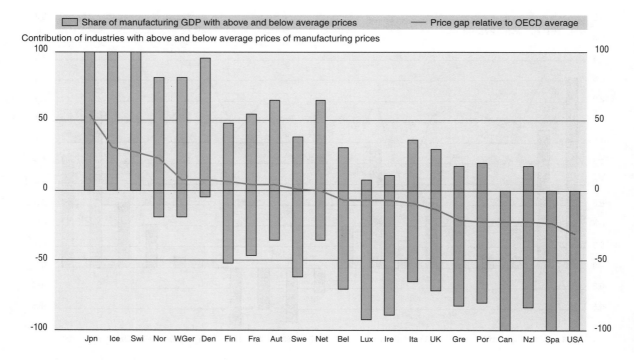

Source: OECD (1996), *Purchasing Power Parities and Real Expenditures 1993: EKS and GK results.*

Figure 1.5. **Comparative price performance in manufacturing and service industries (cont.)**
1993 PPP's, OECD = 100

B. Services

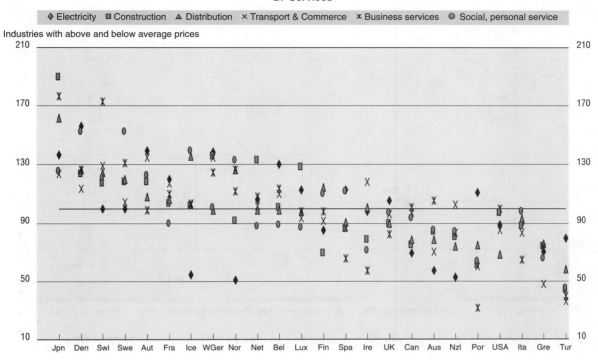

Source: OECD, *Regulation, Structure, and Performance database, 1999.*

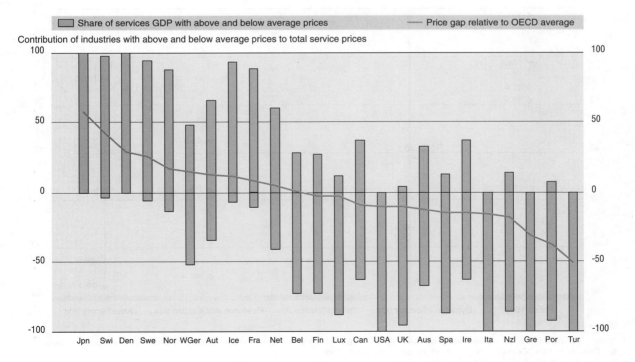

Source: OECD (1996), *Purchasing Power Parities and Real Expenditures 1993: EKS and GK results.*

Figure 1.6*a*. **Japan growth performance in manufacturing *vs* G7 countries**[1]

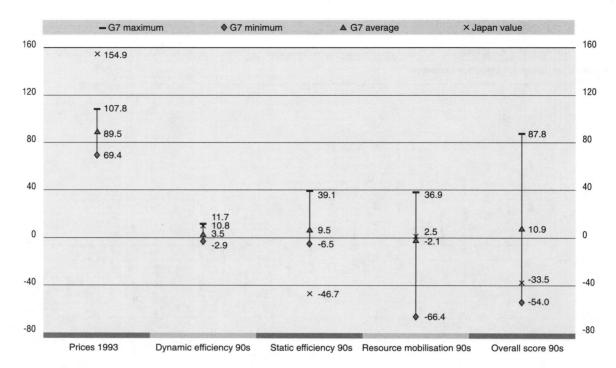

Figure 1.6*b*. **Japan growth performance in services *vs* G7 countries**[2] **(OECD = 100)**

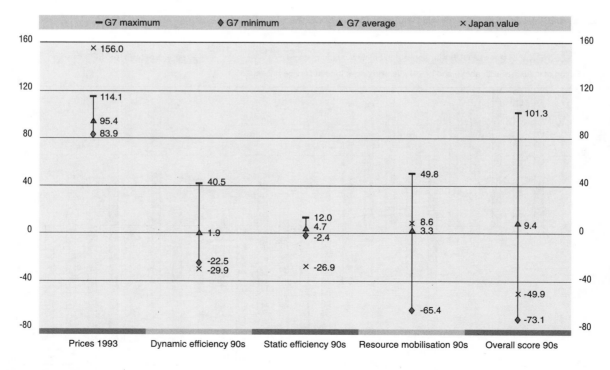

Notes: For each figure the vertical line covers the range of all values from the maximum to the minimum of the relevant group of countries.
1.   Canada, France, Germany, Italy, United Kingdom and United States.
2.   Same countries as note 1 except Germany.
Source: Secretariat estimates.

Figure 1.7*a*. **Japan growth performance in electric power *vs* G7 countries**

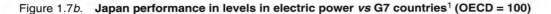

| — G7 maximum | ◆ G7 minimum | ▲ G7 average | × Japan value |

Output growth 90s[1]

Employment 90s[2]

Figure 1.7*b*. **Japan performance in levels in electric power *vs* G7 countries[1] (OECD = 100)**

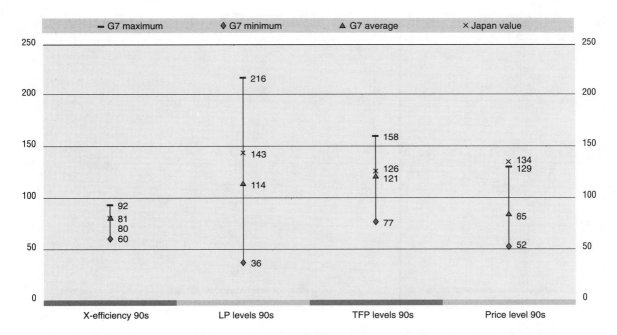

Notes: For each figure the vertical line covers the range of all values from the maximum to the minimum of the relevant group of countries.
Output = net electricity production.
Employment = total employment.
Labour productivity (LP) = net electricity production/employment.
Total factor productivity (TFP) = output is net electricity production, inputs are employees and total installed capacity (the labour share is set to 0.25
    which is the OECD average for electricity, gas and water).
DEA = data envelope analysis with net electricity production as output and labour and installed capacity as inputs.
Price level = business electricity price, converted with GDP-PPP.
1.   Canada, France, Germany, Italy, United Kingdom and United States.
2.   Canada, France, United Kingdom.
Source: International Energy Agency.

Figure 1.8*a*. **Japan growth performance in telecommunications *vs* G7 countries**[1]

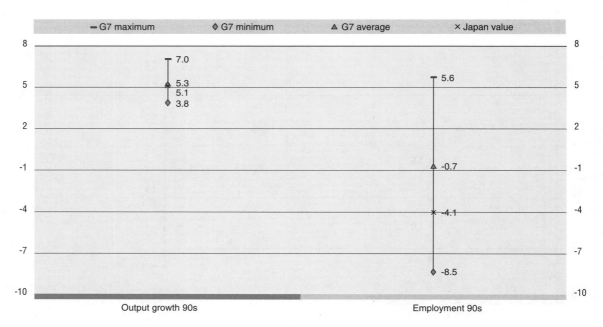

Figure 1.8*b*. **Japan performance in levels in telecommunications *vs* G7 countries**[1] **(OECD = 100)**

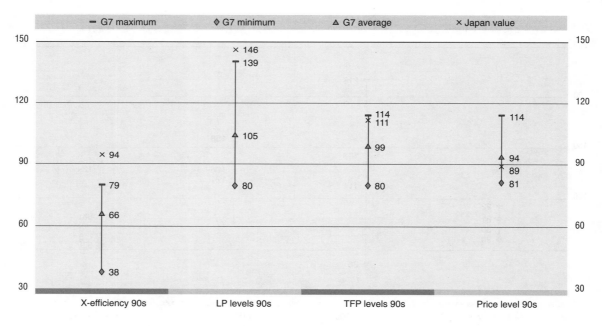

Notes: For each figure the vertical line covers the range of all values from the maximum to the minimum of the relevant group of countries.
Output = mainlines + cellular subscribers.
Employment = total employment.
Labour productivity (LP) = mainlines + cellular subscribers/employment.
Total factor productivity (TFP) = capital is calculated using the perpetual inventory method and the investment PPP (the labour share is set to 0.54 which is the OECD average for communications).
DEA = results of data envelope analysis with revenue (converted with sectoral PPP), mainlines + cellular subscribers and numbers of pay phone as output concepts and employment and capital (as in TFP) as inputs.
Price level = simple average of a basket of services (including business and residential prices of local, trunk and international fixed voice telephony, mobile telephony, leased lines and internet).
1.   Canada, France, Germany, Italy, United Kingdom and United States.
Source: ECD Telecommunications database 1997, *OECD Communications Outlook 1997.*

Figure 1.9*a*. **Japan growth performance in air passenger *vs* G7 countries[1]**

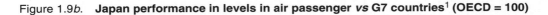

Figure 1.9*b*. **Japan performance in levels in air passenger *vs* G7 countries[1] (OECD = 100)**

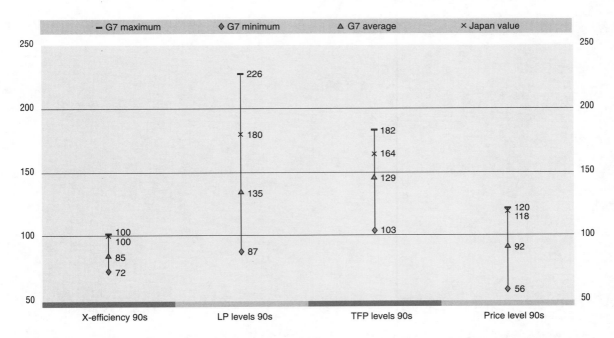

Notes: For each figure the vertical line covers the range of all values from the maximum to the minimum of the relevant group of countries.
Output = transported passenger-km (TPK).
Employment = total employment.
Labour productivity (LP) = TPK/employment.
Total factor productivity (TFP) = output is TPK and capital is total seating capacity (the labour share is set to 0.6, which is the OECD average for transport).
DEA = data envelope analysis using passengers transported and TPK as output and total personnel, numbers of planes, km flown and total seat capacity as inputs.
Price level = operating revenue per TPK.
1.   Canada, France, Germany, Italy, United Kingdom and United States.
Source: Institut du transport aérien (ITA) and OECD.

OECD 1999

REFERENCES

Calder, Kent E. (1988),
   Crisis and Compensation: Public Policy and Political Stability in Japan, Princeton University Press.

Carlile, Lonny E. and Mark C. Tilton, ed. (1998),
   Is Japan Really Changing its Ways – Regulatory Reform and the Japanese Economy, Brookings Institution Press, Washington, DC.

Commission on Administrative Reform (1995),
   "Opinions Concerning the Promotion of Deregulation – Towards a Resplendent Country", Tokyo, 14 December (provisional translation in mimeo).

Deighton-Smith, Rex, ed. (1997),
   Regulatory Impact Analysis: Best Practices in OECD Countries, OECD, Paris.

EPA (1997a),
   1997 Price Report, October 1997.

EPA (1997b),
   Policy Actions on Market Access Issues as Concerns Standards, Certification and Others, July 1997.

Fair Trade Commission (1997),
   Annual Report on Competition Policy Developments in Japan, Jan.-Dec. 1996.

Fair Trade Commission (1998),
   Annual Report on Competition Policy in Japan, January – December 1997.

Gibney, Frank, ed. (1998),
   Unlocking the Bureaucrat's Kingdom: Deregulation and the Japanese Economy, The Brookings Institution, Washington, DC.

Hashimoto, Ryutaro, Prime Minister (1996),
   "Policy Speech to the 136th Session of the National Diet", 22 January, Tokyo, unofficial translation, Ministry of Foreign Affairs.

Iyori, H. and A. Uesugi (1994),
   The Antimonopoly Laws and Policies of Japan, New York.

Jacobs, Scott H. (1995),
   "Building Regulatory Institutions in Central and Eastern Europe", Proceedings of the OECD/World Bank Conference on Competition and Regulation in Network Infrastructure Industries, Budapest, 28 June-1 July 1994, OECD, Paris.

Jacobs, Scott H. (1997a),
   "La codification, facteur de croissance économique", Revue française d'administration publique, No. 82, April-June.

Jacobs, Scott H., et al. (1997b),
   "Regulatory Quality and the Public Sector Reform", in The OECD Report on Regulatory Reform, Volume 2: Thematic Studies, OECD, Paris.

Lincoln, Ed. (1998a),
   "Deregulation in Japan and the United States: A Study in Contrasts" in Unlocking the Bureaucrat's Kingdom: Deregulation and the Japanese Economy, ed. Frank Gibney, The Brookings Institution, Washington, DC.

MITI (1996),
   Survey on Price Differentials between Domestic and International Markets for Intermediate Inputs.

OECD (1982/83),
   Economic Survey of Japan, OECD, Paris.

OECD (1993),
   Economic Survey of Japan, OECD, Paris.

OECD (1997-98),
   Economic Survey of Japan, OECD, Paris.

OECD (1997*a*),
   The OECD Report on Regulatory Reform: Synthesis, Paris.

OECD (1997*b*),
   The OECD Report on Regulatory Reform, Volume 1: *Sectoral Studies*, Paris.

OECD (1997*c*),
   The OECD Report on Regulatory Reform, Volume 2: *Thematic Studies*, Paris.

OECD (1998*a*),
   "Review of Tariffs and Non-Tariff Barriers, Tariff Regimes of the Quad Countries", February, TD/TC (97) 11/REV1.

OECD (1998*b*),
   Financial Market Trends – 70, OECD, Paris, June.

Richardson, Bradley (1997),
   Japanese Democracy: Power, Coordination, and Performance, Yale University Press, F.

Sanekata, K. and S. Wilks, (1996),
   "The Fair Trade Commission and the Enforcement of Competition Policy in Japan", in *Comparative Competition Policy: National Institutions in a Global Market*, G. B. Doern and S. Wilks, ed., Oxford.

Tanaka, Kazuaki and Masahiro Horie (1990),
   "Privatization and Deregulation: The Japanese Experience" (mimeo) by Administrative Inspection Bureau, Management and Coordination Agency.

Part II

BACKGROUND REPORTS

BACKGROUND REPORT
ON GOVERNMENT CAPACITY TO ASSURE
HIGH QUALITY REGULATION*

---

* This report was principally prepared by **Scott H. Jacobs**, Head of Programme on Regulatory Reform, OECD, and **Rex Deighton-Smith**, Administrator for Regulatory Management and Reform in the Public Management Service. It has benefited from extensive comments provided by colleagues throughout the OECD Secretariat, by the Government of Japan, by Member countries as part of the peer review process, and by the OECD's Trade Union Advisory Committee and the Business Industry Advisory Committee. This report was peer reviewed in October 1998 in the OECD's Working Party on Regulatory Management and Reform of the Public Management Committee.

OECD 1999

TABLE OF CONTENTS

OECD 1999

Executive Summary

Background Report on Government Capacity to Assure High Quality Regulation

Is the national administration able to produce and apply social and economic regulations that are based on the core principles of good regulation? Regulatory reform requires the development of administrative capacities within the public sector to judge when and how to regulate in a highly complex world. Administrative transparency, flexibility, policy co-ordination, understanding of markets, and responsiveness to changing conditions are increasingly important to achieve results that are both effective and efficient.

Since the early 1980s, and particularly since the Hosokawa government promoted deregulation as key to economic recovery in 1993, regulatory reform has been prominent on Japan's political agenda. It has been a central element in the broad economic structural reform programme underway since December 1996. Indeed, it has become a symbol of a broader economic and social transformation.

Sustained effort has reduced economic intervention in many sectors, among them, large retail stores, gasoline imports, telecommunications, and financial services, and consumers have already seen significant results. Important progress has been made in areas such as increasing the efficiency of pervasive licenses and permits, even though their numbers have increased, by shifting emphasis from ex ante approvals to *ex post* monitoring of compliance with general rules. There is slow but steady movement toward more transparent and less discretionary regulatory practices, partly driven by market demands and partly by recognition of the gap between traditional and international practices. The framework for competition policy has been strengthened. Several initiatives underway to promote the use of international standards will help expand trade flows, to the benefit of Japan's consumers. Compared to its predecessors, the 1995-1997 deregulation programme was the most successful yet, capitalising on the strength of a reform-minded prime minister and competitiveness pressures to win commitments to reform in key sectors, and the current 1998-2000 deregulation programme should contribute to the progress achieved. The debate over strategies for change has stimulated a continuing examination of the structure and role of government, and of the uses and processes of regulation, in Japan's future. The restructuring of the Japanese bureaucracy currently underway through the Basic Law on the Administrative Reform of the Central Government offers a rare opportunity to build new regulatory capacities and incentives in the public sector.

While recognising the importance of the gains that have been made, this report argues that the size and nature of the problem has been consistently underestimated. Regulatory reform in Japan has struggled against long-standing administrative traditions of economic interventionism, clientelism, relatively uncontrolled administrative discretion, and nontransparent policy processes. These characteristics have meant that regulatory reform has often been episodic, reactive, slow, and incomplete. Intervention by the administration into economic decisions continues on a scale rare in OECD countries, and these interventions are no longer based on any coherent view of the role of regulation in modern government or market economies. As the gap between market needs and regulatory rigidities grows wider, the regulatory system is weakening domestic and international competitive forces, slowing healthy structural change, and contributing to a chronic misallocation of resources throughout the Japanese economy.

A more encompassing view of the nature of reform – to include not only deregulation, but also restructuring outdated institutions, changing incentives in public sector cultures, and moving the state toward service provision and away from economic management – is a precondition to progress of the kind needed to adapt Japanese regulation to the needs of modern society. The emphasis should be on organising decision-making systems that are transparent, accountable, and adaptable, in which those who benefit from the current regulatory system do not have the power to block change. With those kinds of reforms, the Japanese government will establish the basis for a dynamic regulatory system that will continue to adapt and meet new challenges into the future.

1. THE INSTITUTIONAL FRAMEWORK FOR REGULATORY REFORM IN JAPAN

1.1. The administrative and legal environment in Japan

Since the early 1980s, and particularly since the Hosokawa government promoted deregulation as key to economic recovery in 1993, regulatory reform has been prominent on Japan's political agenda. Indeed, it has become a symbol of a broader economic and social transformation. Since December 1996, regulatory reform has been a central element in the broad economic structural reform programme. The goals of regulatory reform are ambitious: to move a deeply entrenched system, in which regulation has been used for decades as an instrument to manage high economic growth, carry out periods of deep structural reform, and promote producer interests, toward a more competitive and flexible economy in which the role of the state is diminished, personal choice and initiative is increased, structural change is driven by market pressures, consumer interests take higher priority, and Japan's markets are more open to international competition.

Such changes threaten many interests. Japan's administrative system is characterised more than those in most OECD countries by decentralised and independent ministries, by powerful bureaucracies armed with broad administrative discretion, and by close and informal links between public servants, producer groups, and political parties. The dominance of a single political party for four decades (the so-called "1955 system" of the LDP) helped to further solidify relations between political and bureaucratic actors through the *zoku* system. This combination, while responsive to social and economic needs that fall within the paradigm of state management, has proven highly resistant to reforms that diminish state control.

The operating principles of Japanese administration are balanced power relations; private negotiations, policy development, and conflict mediation; and, if they are attainable, mutual accommodation and consensus, guided by a cultural preference for pragmatic, non-ideological solutions. Conflict between interests, which is as intense as in any other country, is usually managed through consultation and coordination. This governing approach had advantages: it has supported policy stability through periods of rapid change, encouraged public/private cooperation in reaching mutual aims, spread benefits widely (Japan has highly equal income distribution compared to other OECD countries), sustained legitimacy, and speeded implementation once agreement is reached. The World Bank has found that "(economic) intervention has taken place in an unusually disciplined and performance-based manner", based on the concept of "shared growth", carried out by dedicated, expert technocrats in consultation with business leaders.[1]

Either aided by or hindered by these administrative styles (there is little solid evidence in either direction), the capable and powerful Japanese public administration helped lead a process of extraordinary growth (from 1955 to 1973, Japanese economic growth averaged 10 per cent annually) that made Japan a post-war economic miracle and in which rapid social change was accommodated without major political disruptions.[2]

Yet the dangers today are complacency and obsolescence. This governing approach has produced a deeply conservative policy process that slows decision-making, discourages policy debate, encourages clientelism, allows special interests to block needed change, and results in the famous Japanese "incrementalism". These tendencies are amplified by numerous institutional and procedural characteristics of the Japanese administration. Wide discretionary power of public officials has led to opaque decision processes and information monopolies. A life-long career system implemented by official personnel policy strengthens incentives for regulators to maintain close ties with regulated bodies. Numerous "satellite" semi-public bodies surrounding the ministries – such as the public corporations and trade associations – work to maintain special interests, or even to share regulatory authority. Importantly, the disappearance of a coherent and long-term concept for economic management for this phase of Japanese development has left economic interventions more arbitrary, incoherent, and vulnerable to a host of special interests. For this last reason, it is possible that regulation is in general becoming less efficient rather than more efficient.

These characteristics have meant that regulatory reform, while it has produced some results in some sectors and improved administrative transparency (see below) has often been episodic, reactive, slow, and incomplete. Incrementalism in regulatory reform has contributed to a regulatory governance system in Japan that has proved to be in many ways poorly suited to a modern market economy, that is unable to respond quickly enough to the challenges and shocks facing it, that is not responding to evolving needs of Japanese society, and that is hindering the current transition to a sustainable economic growth path. Historical and social context is important: regulatory reform is seen by some Japanese and Western analysts as "essential" to an "historical turning point" in a national modernization process that began over a century ago.[3] This is not yet the public view in Japan. Pervasive regulation has during the post-war period been widely accepted by the public. Social consensus around the need to rebuild the economy and "catch up" with the West in post-war years was reflected in a set of close relationships between government and industry, and among industry players (for example through *keiretsu* structures).

This development strategy grew in part on long-standing economic structures extending into pre-war years, and in part from the legacy of US occupation which imposed comprehensive economic controls on Japan.[4] Importantly, it was also based on social values of harmony (*wa*) that contributed to a scepticism of the value of competition. Bureaucratic anxieties of "excess competition" or "confusion in the market"[5] led to regulatory policies such as tolerance or promotion of cartels, and to contemporary "supply and demand balancing" by the administration. The regulatory system has been shaped as much by these broader social values and historical relationships as by special interests in the public and private sectors, though the latter are probably the dominant factor today in preserving regulations.

An important debate today concerns the implications for governing traditions and public institutions of the possible emergence of new values and interests among Japanese enterprises, consumers, and other interests. Analyses of eroding social consensus, changing values in younger voters, and diminishing trust in government leadership, due in part to recent scandals, suggest that stress is mounting on the capacities of the administration to mediate conflict through traditional tools. There are, for example, more expectations of transparency in decision-making and policy application, and the continuing development of opposition parties in Diet has supported policy debates that are more open and issues-oriented.

In the medium-term, regulatory reform in Japan will require basic changes in structures and policies in public and private sectors to allow more room for market based decisions. The assets for reform include a bureaucracy that is widely recognised as highly talented and educated, which was often able in the past to exploit its broad administrative discretion to national benefit. But the government has noted that changing domestic and world conditions require a more flexible and efficient public administration that is less centralised in Tokyo and less interventionist inside Japan and more open to the international community. The key management challenges to be faced are those of organising a decision-making system that is transparent, accountable, and adaptable, based on concepts of new public management that are being adopted throughout the OECD area. Such a system will reduce the power of those who benefit from the current regulatory system to block change.

The debate over strategies for change has stimulated a continuing examination of the structure and role of government, and of the uses and processes of regulation, in Japan's future. The restructuring of the Japanese bureaucracy currently underway offers a rare opportunity, as yet unexploited, to build new regulatory capacities and incentives in the public sector.

An issue important in many OECD countries, but perhaps even more vital to structural change in Japan is the management of transition periods. Fears about the effect of regulatory reform on employment, on small businesses, on local economies, and on traditional producers have necessitated government transitional initiatives during periods of adjustment. The Administrative Reform Committee's 1995 report addressed this issue in a section titled, "On suffering" that called for "more effective means to overcome the pain while promoting reform". The current issue is how to ensure that transition is not a means of delaying reform, but of supporting timely change.

The Japanese notion of regulatory reform has been narrowly based in ideas of deregulation and smaller government, rather than of establishing the basis for high-quality regulatory regimes that protect public interests in competitive markets. But current calls in Japan for smaller government, while perhaps desirable for other reasons, are insufficient as a regulatory reform philosophy. In part because it has shared social policies (such as employment protection) with the private sector, Japan has a small government by OECD standards (measured in contribution of government to GDP and by government employment as a ratio of total employment). Its role in important areas, such as building social security for an ageing population and labour policies for a society where lifetime employment is becoming less prevalent, may need to increase. Regulations in other areas, such as prudential oversight of the financial sector, consumer protection, and environmental protection, may also need reinforcement – in terms of either enhanced policy effectiveness or new policies – rather than reduction.

The key to successful regulatory reform lies partly in eliminating some fraction of Japan's current regulatory stock – a determined and systematic programme to root out many regulations that interfere with competition is necessary as one element of a broader programme. To sustain real change, however, the key lies in 1) fundamentally changing the role of government toward providing social services not provided by the market and away from economic intervention, and 2) in those cases where regulation is justified, changing the style of regulation from anti- to pro-competitive. Destructive habits of economic control in the public administration will change only if incentives and cultures change, which is why this report places so much emphasis on administrative reform and the opportunities it presents for regulatory reform.

Box 1.   **Good practices for improving the capacities of national administrations to assure high-quality regulation**

The OECD Report on Regulatory Reform, welcomed by Ministers in May 1997, includes a co-ordinated set of strategies for improving regulatory quality, many of which were based on the 1995 Recommendation of the OECD Council on Improving the Quality of Government Regulation. These form the basis of the analysis undertaken in this report, and are reproduced below:

A. BUILDING A REGULATORY MANAGEMENT SYSTEM

  1. Adopt regulatory reform policy at the highest political levels
  2. Establish explicit standards for regulatory quality and principles of regulatory decision-making
  3. Build regulatory management capacities

B. IMPROVING THE QUALITY OF NEW REGULATIONS

  1. Regulatory Impact Analysis
  2. Systematic public consultation procedures with affected interests
  3. Using alternatives to regulation
  4. Improving regulatory co-ordination

C. UPGRADING THE QUALITY OF EXISTING REGULATIONS

  (In addition to the strategies listed above)
  1. Reviewing and updating existing regulations
  2. Reducing red tape and government formalities

The task ahead is difficult. More so than in many OECD countries, it is difficult to assess the use, quality, and effects of regulation in Japan. The Japanese regulatory system is often characterised by informality in procedures, in instruments, and in relationships between interested parties that increases the difficulty of understanding the scope and structure of the regulatory system, and in designing systematic reform. The Japanese term "regulation" itself is not simple. The Japanese language offers more than a hundred separate terms for regulation depending on its basis, its generality (or specificity), and the degree to which it constrains behaviour. Moreover, administration discretion as to the form of government intervention is virtually uncontrolled. For example, a widely-remarked feature of the Japanese regulatory system is the use of informal "administrative guidance" with regulatory effect, though the frequency of its use today is very hard to determine (see Box 5). The range of administrative instruments that could be considered "regulatory" suggests that it would, perhaps, be more useful in the Japanese context to define regulations as "administrative decisions with regulatory effects".

1.2. Recent regulatory reform initiatives to improve public administration capacities

Japanese approaches to regulatory reform have become progressively structured and formalised since the early 1980s as reformers grappled with the difficulties of changing a system that gives bureaucrats substantial control over the scope and pace of reform. The objectives of regulatory reform over the years, as expressed by various government offices, included stimulation of economic growth; preservation of international trading relationships; improvement of quality of life for consumers; strengthening of individual liberties and self-reliance; and better government efficiency and openness at national and local levels.

The current "Three-Year Programme for the Promotion of Deregulation" was adopted by the Cabinet on 31 March 1998 to run for three years, from 1998 to 2000. On 30 March 1999, the Cabinet adopted a revised programme that expanded the range of areas under review. The activities in the Programme fall into four broad areas for reform:

Promoting Comprehensive Examination and Review. Several areas for action were identified in 1998, and expanded in 1999. This part of the programme is discussed in Section 4 below.

Measures Relevant to Specific Fields. Annexes to the Programme list measures to be taken across a wide range of fields. The choice of deregulatory measures reflects, in large part, the wider policy priorities of the Government's Action Plan for Economic Structural Reform. See Section 4 below.

Methods Related to the Promotion of Deregulation. Several measures aimed at enhancing the programme itself and increasing the level of support within Japanese society are presented under this heading. See Section 2 below.

Measures Related to the Promotion of Deregulation. The final category of measures is composed of broader, framework reforms that support reform initiatives at all levels, including local government (see Section 2.3 below). One such measure is the promotion of "fair and free" competition through improved enforcement of the anti-monopoly law by a strengthened Japanese Fair Trade Commission (FTC) as well as the presentation of positive sector-specific recommendations for further reforms by the FTC. Such emphasis on compliance and enforcement is relatively unusual in regulatory reform programmes and indicates an explicit recognition of the connection between regulatory reform and competition principles (The following report discusses competition policy and enforcement in detail).

The 1998-2000 programme builds on a Deregulation Action Programme (DAP) that was in place from 1995 to 1997, under the supervision of a high-level Administrative Reform Committee. The 1995 DAP included over 2 800 actions during its three-year life. One third of these were identified from the start, while the remainder were added during annual programme reviews. This process of revising and expanding will be continued in the current programme. 174 actions were unfinished when the DAP was wound up. They were elaborated and carried over into the new three year programme, forming about half of its initial 624 items.

The Administrative Reform Programme (ARP), adopted in 1996, is potentially a far-reaching complement to the Programme for the Promotion of Deregulation. Through the Basic Law on the Administrative Reform of the Central Government, Japan expects to complete, by 2001, a reorganisation of the structure of the government administration that is billed as the most fundamental in the post-1945 period and is expected to result in a smaller and more effective administration.

The Administrative Reform Headquarters established to carry out this process is chaired by the Prime Minister. The reforms envisaged by the final report of the Administrative Reform Council[6] (ARC) are intended to reform a government that has "grown excessively large and rigid" and to create a "streamlined, transparent and efficient" government. The ARC argues that the administrative reform process should "initiate comprehensive changes in social and economic systems". The steps recommended by the ARC include reinforcement of Cabinet functions (including adoption of majority voting, appointment of Ministers of State with responsibility for specific issues and Cabinet authorisation of key bureaucratic appointments), and strengthening the powers and policy capacities of the Prime Minister, including the Cabinet Office and Cabinet Secretariat support functions.

The conceptual framework underlying the ARC proposals includes:

– Deregulation, decentralisation and role sharing between public and private sectors, along with streamlining of government and resource allocation better reflecting policy priorities.

– Enhancing policy development capabilities, particularly through functionally separating policy making and implementation, similar to the UK Next Steps reforms.

– Close collaboration between policy-making and implementation arms, with both establishing a framework for policy evaluation.

The Basic Law on the Administrative Reform of the Central Government that implements the ARC recommendations will also reduce the number of ministries to 12, and redefine their roles. It includes a number of major points in relation to each ministry, which would be expected to guide the drafting of the "foundation law" for each Ministry. This is a matter of considerable importance given the prominence of the issue of administrative discretion among the regulatory problems cited by many commentators. The foundation laws establishing the Ministries appear to allow administrative discretion, as they are currently written in very broad terms. A rewriting in more specific terms would clarify how the actions of the ministry serve public interests. Other major points in the Basic Law for Administrative Reform of particular importance to regulatory reform are included in Box 2. The ARC report and the links drawn between administrative and regulatory reform indicate a recognition that fundamental reforms require a cultural shift and that this can be brought about by a major reorganisation of the structures of government and the objectives given to the ministries.

An important but disappointing legislative initiative is the Administrative Procedure Act of 1993, discussed in Section 2.1. below. The Act sought to limit the uses of administrative discretion by defining and limiting the uses of particular mechanisms (notably administrative guidance) and enhancing the transparency of their use and the ability to appeal against adverse uses of discretion. However, there are concerns with the design and implementation of the Act and little evidence that it has significantly improved transparency or reduced administrative discretion.

History of regulatory reform. A prominent analyst of regulatory reform in Japan has traced the use of regulation through three phases: 1) the first structural reforms of 1955-1972, when the government used regulation and many other policy instruments to carry out top-down economic planning based on domestic investment and expert promotion and when the policy of restricting consumption to allocate a maximum of resources to producers was formulated; 2) the second structural reform of 1973-1985, when high-tech industries took control of industrial policy, private regulation replaced much public regulation, and industrial concentration increased; 3) the third structural reform of 1986 to the present, in which special industry, agricultural, and financial interests took more prominence, and in which, according to the analyst, industrial policy became fragmented.[7]

As Chapter 1 details, current regulatory reform programmes have their roots in the shocks of the 1970s and policies aimed at boosting growth levels, which had slowed significantly in the late 1970s. There was a view, particularly among exporter industries exposed to global competition, that the need for extensive economic planning and support by government was a feature of the "catch up economy" and

---

Box 2.   Elements in the Basic Law on the Administrative Reform of the Central
Government of particular importance to regulatory reform
(new names of ministries are tentative)

A Ministry of General Affairs is to be established "to strengthen assistance and support for the Cabinet and the Prime Minister". It would evaluate and oversee government activities.

The Ministry of Justice is to support judicial reforms, including the area of administrative tribunals.

The Ministry of Economy and Industry is to "withdraw from or reduce activities relating to promotion of specific business sectors", switching instead to an emphasis on improving the overall business environment while respecting market principles. This orientation, while consistent in direction with the general pro-market orientation of the reform policies, is equivocal in its tone, falling short of a clear rejection of sectoral promotion. In energy policy, the Ministry is to emphasise energy efficiency and new energy sources while "drastically eliminating and loosening regulations aimed at adjusting demand and supply".

The Ministry of National Land and Transport is to "promote systematic efforts aimed at integrated development and utilisation of national land and related resources" and develop an integrated transport system while "drastically deregulating governmental controls over transportation business". It will implement "a thoroughgoing programme of decentralisation and the utilisation of private sector capabilities in relation to the execution of public works projects".

The Ministry of Environment is to unify jurisdiction over matters including "regulations on air, water and soil pollution, waste management etc.", although it will share jurisdiction over "recycling, CO_2 emissions, etc.".

The Headquarters for the Administrative Reform of Central Government is working on "Augmenting and Strengthening Evaluation Capacities". This aims to establish evaluation sections within each Ministry as well as a central evaluation body in the Ministry of General Affairs. In addition, transparency is to be assured by the release of the results of evaluations conducted and the strengthening of the Board of Audit.

The Basic Law provided that the government will reduce the number of non-defense employees by at least ten per cent through a Staff Number Reduction Plan that shall be designed in the future. In addition the Law provided that additional reductions be obtained by measures such as transfer of some functions to independent administrative institutions. More recently, the government adopted a reduction target of 25 per cent. In some quarters – for example among some Keidanren members – a reduction in the number of civil servants is seen as an indirect way to control the ability of regulatory ministries to intervene in the economy.

---

that the Japanese economy had now matured to a point where these interventions were no longer necessary – indeed were likely, on balance, to be harmful. Reduction of government intervention in the economy "to let the market exert its function to the fullest extent" was at the core of the 1980s-era transition policies.[8] The most dramatic and visible steps were the privatisation of three major public corporations, include Japanese National Railways (JNR) and Nippon Telegraph and Telephone Public Corporation, carried out through the 1980s against stiff opposition. These privatisations, "the biggest reform undertaken in [Japan's] history", became the "symbol of reform" because of their size and importance.[9] As in other countries, privatisation has given rise to new regulatory issues. There is considerable debate over the quality of the regulatory regime for some of these sectors where competition is weak due to lingering dominance and cartel problems (see the background reports on The role of competition policy and Enforcement in regulatory reform and on Regulatory reform in the telecommunications industry).

Substantive deregulation programmes began in 1981, directed by the Provisional Commission for Administrative Reform. Concerned that regulation was growing rapidly without any control mechanism, the Provisional Commission recommended initiation of a full-fledged programme of deregulation, and specifically targeted licensing and approval requirements for businesses. The new thinking on a diminished role for regulation was reflected in the "Guideline for the Promotion of Deregulation" adopted by the Cabinet in 1988. The Guideline identified as its central principle that of *freedom in principle and regulation only as an exception*.

Emphasis on regulatory reform as a precondition to necessary economic restructuring became more pronounced in the 1990s as barriers to international trade and investment fell, and as anxieties grew about the effects on Japanese producers of competition, particularly from dynamic Asian economies. Numerous deregulation packages were announced by the government in 1993, 1994, and 1995. By this time, deep cleavages over regulatory reform became obvious, as export-oriented industries promoted reform in upstream sectors, while small producers and services clung to their regulatory protections.

Despite the rolling programmes of reform, concrete progress through 1995 was patchy. Critics continued to call for wider and faster regulatory reform to bring about economic structural reform. "The actual progress of reform has been much slower than the speed of changes of the real world" concluded the Administrative Reform Committee in December 1995.[10] The Keidanren called in October 1995 for "a bold step [in regulatory reform] to achieve drastic reform of the economic structure... in order to wipe out the sense of'suffocation'that permeates the Japanese economy."[11] In January 1996, the Prime Minister warned that:

"... high-cost structural elements are undermining Japan's attractiveness as a place to do business and there are increasing fears of industrial hollowing... [T]he first structural reform here is that of thorough-going deregulation... we will... weed out any that may have become ends in their own right and any that have been perverted into citadels of protection for vest interests. As well as working to rectify the high-cost structure, we will, seeking to eliminate barriers impeding the development of new growth sectors and to promote the revitalisation of the economy, move resolutely to deregulate..."[12]

Another principle underlying reform is that of improving the quality of life. This policy is rooted in public expectations, dating from the 1970s, that economic success would be rewarded by construction of a "welfare state", and in the belief that even today the affluence of Japan has not been felt in private life. Japan is "often referred to 'as an economic and regulatory superpower with unimpressive living standards'", the Administrative Reform Committee noted in December 1995.[13]

Japanese consumers have long accepted the costs to them imposed by producer oriented policies in terms of higher prices and less choice, and consumer movements continue today to be focused on quality and consumer protection rather than consumer sovereignty. Yet consumer interests have often been cited by reformers as a primary justification for regulatory reform. In 1991, the Prime Minister's Office argued that the economic goal of overtaking" more economically advanced countries should be reconsidered in light of the need to "respect a variety of consumers' values". For example, deregulation could "narrow the disparities between internal and external prices".[14] This point was also made in the 1991/2 OECD *Economic Survey of Japan*, which noted that the prices of goods not subject to regulation had fallen considerably more than their regulated counterparts following the mid-1980s yen appreciation. In 1991, a "Sub-Council for Better Quality of Life" was created by an advisory council to the Prime Minister. Its mandate stated, in part, "Public administration which has basically been on the side of producers and industries has induced a large discrepancy between economic power and quality of life".[15]

External pressures for regulatory reform have been sustained and significant, largely due to large trade deficits with the United States, and charges from Americans and Europeans that the style and content of Japanese regulation created non-tariff barriers to trade and foreign investment. Trade pressures in specific product and service markets have in general tended to support the larger goals of economic structural change (see the background report on Enhancing market openness through regulatory reform).

As detailed in Chapter 1, the key domestic factor recently leading to calls for regulatory reform from within Japan has been the prolonged slowdown of the Japanese economy, evident through the 1990s. Microeconomic supply-side reforms – and in large part regulatory ones – are seen to have a major role in restoring Japanese economic growth. Japanese businesses have increasingly focused on the role of regulation in increasing the costs of productive inputs and reducing international competitiveness. The Keidanren (Japanese Federation of Economic Organisations) has supported deregulation as a general concept and has suggested a wide range of specific initiatives. However, the extensive benefits gleaned by business from some regulations means that business support for reform in Japan, as in most countries, remains uneven and at times inconsistent. Generally strong support for deregulation of markets for business inputs is not matched by a similarly liberal view of output markets.

As noted above, the focus on restoring economic dynamism was also a key driver of the earliest Japanese regulatory reform policies almost two decades ago. This is evidence that there is no quick fix to regulatory reform issues in Japan. For the foreseeable future, regulatory reform will be an important element of the policy mix underlying the transition to sustainable growth.

2. DRIVERS OF REGULATORY REFORM: NATIONAL POLICIES AND INSTITUTIONS

2.1. Regulatory reform policies and core principles

The 1997 OECD *Report on Regulatory Reform* recommends that countries "adopt at the political level broad programmes of regulatory reform that establish clear objectives and frameworks for implementation".[16] The 1995 OECD *Council Recommendation on Improving the Quality of Government Regulation* contain a set of best practice principles against which reform policies can be measured.[17] Recent Japanese regulatory reform programmes, particularly the most recent programme adopted in March 1998 and revised in March 1999, have moved in the direction of embracing these principles. This and the next section consider whether the goals and strategies set out in this programme meet Japan's regulatory needs and priorities, and whether the mechanisms proposed are likely to allow them to be put into practice. The conclusion is that, while progress has been made toward establishing market-based principles for the use of regulatory powers, there is still considerable fragmentation and incoherence in application of these general principles at the ministry level.

One of the great strengths of Japan's regulatory reform programme relative to other OECD countries has been the prominent personal role in both the 1980s and 1990s of a series of Prime Ministers. Given the great difficulty in driving reform forward against entrenched interests, the degree of personal involvement and accountability of the Prime Minister has, and will continue to, determine the degree of success of any programme. Supporting actions at the political level include the work of an LDP study group on reform to advise Diet members on proposals.

In addition, in the 1995-1997 Deregulation Action Plan, the Deregulation Subcommittee was established under the Administrative Reform Committee, a council of the Prime Minister's Office. Legislation provided that the Prime Minister must respect the Council's opinions, either accepting or refusing recommendations made by it. This was widely considered to be among the most successful of the reform approaches developed in Japan, because interests in the ministries had less power to block recommendations. The Cabinet accepted nearly all recommendations. The Subcommittee also pioneered the effective technique of holding its hearings in public, rather than negotiating privately with the ministries.

The Deregulation Committee is the current body overseeing the programme for 1998-2000, and is contributing to progress on regulatory reform. The Deregulation Committee is established under the Administrative Reform Headquarters, a ministerial body. Officials argue that this provides a direct link to the Cabinet and will enhance the Committee's role in providing feasible recommendations that can be quickly implemented, which is an important consideration. In light of the need to accelerate and deepen comprehensive reforms, however, independence from the interests of the line ministries is likely to be equally important, and this aspect should be strengthened. For example, the Keidanren recently stated that "… based on the final opinion of the Administrative Reform Council issued last December, there is a need to reorganize the current Committee on Deregulation into a more significant third party body with statutory responsibility for drafting plans and monitoring the process of deregulation and of reviews of related systems".[18] The Prime Minister's Economic Strategy Council recommended in February 1999 the establishment of a new "regulatory reform commission" reporting to the prime minister, empowered to review not only regulation, but also taxation and subsidies, with a significant increase in personnel. These would be useful steps. Another possible approach could be that the Committee, like its predecessor, operate under an independent legal mandate. As noted, the Committee's mandate is narrowly focussed on regulation, which has limited its ability to consider other possible impediments to competition as part of a comprehensive reform plan. Consistent with the need to move to more comprehensive sectoral plans, the mandate of the Committee should be expanded. Recent decisions by the Prime Minister in March 1999 to this effect are steps in the right direction. In addition, the Committee does not have the analytical resources or staff (currently around 20) to be truly independent of the information and expertise in the ministries.

The "Three year Programme for the Promotion of Deregulation" adopted by the Cabinet in March 1998 and revised in March 1999 is more far reaching in its objectives than previous programmes. The Programme sets out explicit objectives and a set of core strategic goals aimed at achieving them. The objectives are to:

- implement fundamental reforms in Japan's socio-economic structures;
- create a free and fair socio-economic system which is fully opened to the world and based on rules of accountability and market principles; and
- transform administrative stance from *a priori* regulation and supervision to *ex post facto* checking and scrutiny.

These objectives are a mix of the abstract ("free and fair") and the concrete (the intent to move from approvals to "checking"). The policy direction is explicitly market-based. Consistent with the OECD recommendation that "governments establish principles of 'good regulation' to guide reform" the guiding principles for the pursuit of these objectives provide more operational indications of what is meant by regulatory reform. They are:

- as a rule, economic regulations shall be lifted and social regulations minimised as regulations are abolished or otherwise relaxed;
- regulatory arrangements shall be rationalised, such as by the transfer of inspection functions to the private sector;
- regulation shall be simplified and rendered more specific;
- regulation shall be modified so as to conform to international standards;
- regulatory procedures shall be speeded up; and
- transparency shall be increased in the procedures for introducing new regulations.

This set of principles is intended to provide operational guidance to the ministries, but is less concrete than principles used in other countries or the OECD principles accepted by Ministers in 1997, which read:

Establish principles of "good regulation" to guide reform, drawing on the 1995 OECD Recommendation on Improving the Quality of Government Regulation. Good regulation should: *i*) be needed to serve clearly identified policy goals, and effective in achieving those goals; *ii*) have a sound legal basis; *iii*) produce benefits that justify costs, considering the distribution of effects across society; *iv*) minimise costs and market distortions; *v*) promote innovation through market incentives and goal-based approaches; *vi*) be clear, simple, and practical for users; *vii*) be consistent with other regulations and policies; and *viii*) be compatible as far as possible with competition, trade and investment-facilitating principles at domestic and international levels.

To provide a firmer basis for efforts in the ministries and to hold ministries more accountable for performance, a clearer statement of principles for good regulation, based on the OECD recommendation, would be useful. The problem of making these core principles operational in the ministries is a real one. In part due to the high value placed on pragmatic and concrete action, Japan's reform programmes tend to be based on the accumulation of many individual reform "items", some of which are very significant in economic terms and others which are trivial or recommendations for more study. Oversight consists of tracking ministerial responses to the "items". This system can claim credit for almost all of the reforms that have occurred in Japan, and it has in general improved the transparency of reform and the attention to the programme by ministries.

Yet it is not the model for future reform. The item by item approach has proven slow and not very effective in producing concrete results in economic and policy performance. It is not an adequate basis for coherent, consistent, and sustained programmes of reform, nor for changing deep-seated habits and cultures in the public administration. One reason for this is that ministries and businesses can produce an almost infinite number of "items" for action. The value of these items is quite another matter. The most widely cited fact about the 1995-1997 Deregulation Action Plan is that it contained over 2800 items, and about the 1998-2000 plan is that it starts with 600 items. This focus on numbers has obscured the fact that the importance of the individual items varies widely. There has, as a result, been little in the way of a strategic focus in these deregulation plans to date.[19]

Reliance on ministerial and business proposals to identify items adds other distortions. Ministries tend to propose "items" in areas that do not threaten their authority, or that can be compensated by other ministerial actions or where they have discretion. As a result, many of the items in the 1995-1997 and 1998-2000 reform programmes are unspecific. They require ministries to study particular areas or features of the regulatory system, to report and to propose solutions, or even to implement these proposals directly through administrative guidance. The principles guiding this bureaucratic activity allow very wide latitude in interpretation and action that often frustrates reform.

A notable example is the absence of consistent action to eliminate "supply and demand balancing regulations". The current reform programme has set an overall goal of removing these anti-competitive regulations and considerable progress has been made, but for almost half of them the current commitment is not to elimination in the near future, but to limit their application pending future legal changes, or for further study or review of legal changes. Current plans for such regulations are as follows:

– The current programme aims to eliminate supply-demand balancing regulations in eleven areas: liquor retailing, chartered busing, ordinary busing, taxiing, passenger railways, domestic passenger boats, cargo ferries, harbour transportation, domestic airways, waste-oil disposal (for shipping), customs clearance services. The Government of Japan has stated that these are already eliminated or will be eliminated in the near future. Three other supply and demand balancing provisions – affecting wholesale dealers, credit card companies, and public bathhouses – are nearing elimination and bills are pending before the Diet.

– For seven other provisions in various sectors, the relevant ministry has said that it will not apply the provision pending legal reforms not yet scheduled, or has committed only to future legal reforms that are not scheduled. In addition, seven regulations similar to supply and demand balancing were identified in areas that were considered to be natural monopolies. Among these, one has been eliminated. The others are subject to future review.

Incomplete reform can be seen in other areas. For example, the abolition of the domestic shipping cartel was agreed after long discussion at the Deregulation Committee of the Administrative Reform Council, but "temporary" measures which limit competition were put into place for 15 years.

Businesses, on the other hand, tend to identify "items" that affect their operating costs or expansion plans, not those that open up competition. This tends to bias results toward increasing profits, rather than stimulating competitive pressures that benefit consumers and promote economic growth.

Finally, it is important to note that reforming *existing* "items" does not change the quality of the stream of *new* administrative actions, which can simply repeat old mistakes. That is, the current approach neglects the "flow" of new regulations because it focuses on the "stock" of existing regulations. Therefore, it cannot be seen as a long-lasting solution to problems of poor regulation.

The Japanese government has made progress toward establishing market-based principles for the use of its regulatory powers, but there is considerable fragmentation and incoherence in application of these general principles at the ministry level. To improve the coherence of the item by item approach and to ensure that reform principles are applied equally to new and old regulations, the Japanese government should develop more explicit and measurable government-wide criteria for making decisions as to whether and how to regulate, and support those principle with written guidance to ministries. The OECD recommends as a key principle that regulations should "produce benefits that justify costs, considering the distribution of effects across society." This principle is referred to in various countries as the "proportionality" principle or, in a more rigorous and quantitative form, as the benefit-cost test. This test is the preferred method for considering regulatory impacts because it aims to produce public policy that meets the criterion of being "socially optimal" (*i.e.*, maximising welfare).[20] This key principle is insufficiently developed in Japan. The Japanese principles include neither consideration of proportionality nor a benefit-cost test. Thus, there is no standard by which ministries justify the need for regulations, no public testing of these conclusions, and little basis for challenge.

The OECD Report also recommends that governments "ensure that reform goals and strategies are articulated clearly to the public". Engaging the public in a dialogue on the aims, benefits, and costs of regulatory reform has received, and will continue to need, attention in Japan, given opposition from entrenched market interests, and others anxious that "excessive competition" will produce painful change. The current Japanese programme scores high on this recommendation, since it includes several measures aimed at enhancing the Programme and increasing the level of support within Japanese society. The focus of these measures is on monitoring and reporting of progress made, both within government and publicly, and on continuing to revise and update the programme to maintain relevance.

In relation to monitoring, the Economic Planning Agency is required to report on the economic impact of the programme and specifically the impact on demand, productivity and prices. Effective communication with consumers and other interests in society is an important means of building the constituency for reform – a consideration which may be increasingly important in the longer term as the current strong pressure for reform deriving from poor economic circumstances dissipates. To further develop the programme, MCA was required to produce and publish a white paper on deregulation, and did so in August 1998. Through this mechanism, the authors of the programme seek to provide a means for major domestic and international interests to influence the future process of the deregulation initiative.

The OECD principle that regulation "have a sound legal basis" merits examination in Japan, given the extent to which laws empower the administration to apply discretion in interpreting and applying regulation, and the fact that the exercise of this discretion is not widely challenged through administrative law processes. Relative to some other OECD countries, lower level rules and administrative guidance and directions in Japan are prominent. Addressing problems of transparency constitutes a major theme of reform, as indicated by the passage of the Administrative Procedure Act of 1993 to improve transparency in the use of administrative guidance (see below) and the recent introduction of public notice and comment procedures to the regulation-making process.

2.2. Mechanisms to promote regulatory reform within the public administration

Reform mechanisms with explicit responsibilities and authorities for managing and tracking reform inside the administration are needed to keep reform on schedule, and to avoid a recurrence of over-regulation. As in all OECD countries, Japan emphasizes the responsibility of individual Ministries for reform performance within their areas of responsibility. But it is often difficult for ministries to reform themselves, given countervailing pressures, and maintaining consistency and systematic approaches across the entire administration is necessary if reform is to be broad-based.

Establishing central drivers of reform has been more difficult in Japan than in most other countries, due to the traditional strong independence of the ministries and the relatively weak centre. In this environment, regulatory management in the form of day-to-day oversight of regulatory activities has not developed as a routine function independent of the ministries, although this may be changing. In the late 1980s, the ministries agreed to periodically review certain kinds of existing regulations, and to allow central agencies an opportunity to review some new regulations. Independent review of new regulations outside of regulatory ministries and agencies was increased with respect to Cabinet orders and proposed laws, but not with respect to ministerial ordinances and lower-level rules.

In 1990, after surveying the experience of deregulation, officials of the MCA concluded that it was necessary to "enrich and strengthen the review of existing regulations and examination of newly proposed regulations". In particular, "to promote deregulation forcefully", third parties such as the MCA and independent deliberative parties such as the series of Provisional Councils for the Promotion of Administrative Reform (the PCPARs)[21] should have a greater reviewing role. Following concerns expressed by the Second PCPAR in 1987 about "the expansion of regulatory programs and lack of a built-in mechanism to curb and rationalise regulations" review of proposed and existing regulations received more attention. Most notably, the November 1987 agreement among ministries and agencies "On the Examination and Periodic Review of New and Existing Permissions, Authorizations, etc." committed the ministries and agencies to vigorously review both new and existing permission/authorisation regulations, to involve internal central units such as ministers'offices, and to give three outside agencies an opportunity to comment as needed. This agreement was later adopted by the full Cabinet.

Under the Agreement, the Administrative Management Bureau in the MCA, the Cabinet Legislation Bureau in the Cabinet, and the Budget Bureau in the Ministry of Finance were to independently review new regulatory proposals "on the basis of their respective functions" to ensure "the appropriateness and rationality" of the requirements. These reviewers were to submit their comments – orally or in writing – directly to the regulatory body concerned. The Agreement did not include any formal enforcement mechanism. It is difficult to determine the effect of this review process, since a formal assessment has not been carried out. Most regulatory decisions in ministers'ordinances and lower-level rules continue to be wholly the province of the regulatory ministries and agencies themselves.

Rather than interministerial pressures, regulatory reform has depended on high-level pressure brought by a series of short-term advisory councils reporting directly to the Prime Minister. This has had certain advantages: the expert advisory council model has a long and respected tradition in Japanese administration; the council is independent of the ministries and existing administrative structures and has more freedom to examine unpopular options; and, except for the current Deregulation Committee, opinions of the councils were required by law to be "respected" by the Prime Minister. The councils were charged with investigating and making recommendations for administrative reform from a comprehensive and long-term perspective, and with responding to specific requests from the Prime Minister.

The councils – called the "locomotives of administrative reform"[22] – have worked at a high and visible level. Their members are approved by the Diet, and they report directly to the Prime Minister, who is required by law to "respect" their opinions and recommendations. The Cabinet has also repeatedly and formally announced its intentions to "pay maximum respect" to their opinions, and has proceeded with most major reforms recommended in key policy areas. Under their mandating laws, the councils have had wide investigative authority. They may, for example, request the submission of information and materials from administrative agencies, hold public meetings and local hearings, or hire experts to study particular issues.

The Deregulation Committee of the Administrative Reform Committee Headquarters is the current body providing independent oversight and direction under the new Programme for 1998-2000. It replaced the Administrative Reform Committee, which worked from 1995-1997. The ARC had a high level of private sector involvement and operated in a relatively transparent fashion, being required to respond formally to inputs received. The current Committee continues a broadly similar function to the ARC, but has new responsibilities based on the development of the deregulation programme. Importantly, the Committee is playing a role in relation to new "horizontal projects" pursued under the deregulation programme (*e.g.* the requirement to report on public comment procedures) by soliciting input from regulating Ministries and investigating public opinion.

An important mechanism within the responsibility of the Committee is the preparation of annual progress reports on the deregulatory programme for the consideration of the Cabinet. This annual reporting mechanism, which was also followed under the 1995-1997 programme, provides a dynamic element, with additional initiatives being announced (for example, more than half of the initiatives finally included in the 1995-97 programme (over 1800 of a total of 2800) were added after the release of the initial programme. In addition, the annual reports provide a means of ensuring responsiveness to external inputs on regulatory reform. Both domestic and foreign opinions and proposals are expected to be taken into account in the preparation of the progress report. The progress report is also a mechanism for making known the results of the Deregulation Committee's monitoring of the work.

The *Management and Co-ordination Agency* (MCA) in the Prime Minister's Office is tasked with co-ordination and oversight functions on regulatory reform as the Committee's secretariat. The MCA, created in 1984, is responsible for general oversight and evaluation of administration and has two bureaux for this role. One is the Administrative Management Bureau, which is responsible for the promotion of administrative reform as a whole. The Secretariat of the Deregulation Committee is established within this bureau and its staff includes bureaucrats from other Ministries as well as secondees from the private sector. The other bureau is the Administrative Inspection Bureau, which is the only specialised and comprehensive body for policy and administrative evaluation.

The MCA monitors agency performance, administering questionnaires on reform progress and publishing the results through an annual white paper. Ministries are required to report progress on implementation to the Deregulation Committee of the Administrative Reform Promotion Headquarters. The Deregulation Committee is also required to "promote the process of deregulation" through its surveillance activities and by "addressing new issues and challenges" in co-operation with the "responsible administrative offices". This emphasis on performance monitoring is unusual in regulatory reform programmes and constitutes a potential strength of the Japanese programme.

The Administrative Inspection Bureau has for several years used its inspection activities as an opportunity to examine regulation. In response to the request of the Sub-Committee on Public Regulation of the Second PCPAR, the Bureau carried out in the late 1980s a series of inspections on regulations in the transportation, distribution, financing, and energy sectors. It also examined regulatory requirements on new businesses. A 1989 report from the subcommittee on desirable public regulation of Second PCPAR recommended that the MCA go further by developing a medium-term inspection programme to review the use of regulation by ministries and agencies. The MCA responded that it would begin to use its inspection authority in 1990 to conduct "planned and continuous" surveys on regulatory administration.[23] Since then, the MCA has conducted a series of inspections on deregulatory initiatives such as simplification of permission/authorisation requirements, and simplification of requirements for testing of goods.

The *Ministry of International Trade and Industry* (MITI) promotes regulatory reform as part of national economic policy. Its priorities in regulatory reform include changing economic structures, and encouraging more open and competitive industries.

In addition, the *Economic Planning Agency* is required to undertake and publish quantitative analyses of the economic impact of the deregulation programme, addressing effects on demand, productivity and price levels. The purpose of this is "to enhance people's interest in and understanding of the mitigation and abolition of regulation".[24]

In sum, regulatory reform mechanisms in Japan, faced with the difficulty of governing from the centre, compare favourably with mechanisms in other OECD countries that have not yet established a permanent body responsible for regulatory reform. The independent committees and councils enjoyed a combination of authority, analytical capacity, public credibility, and linkage to political officials that enabled them to animate many important reforms that ministries had not carried out on their own. In fact, almost all significant regulatory reforms since 1981 originated with these councils. Approaches that should be considered by other countries as good practices include:

– Direct links to the Prime Minister and Cabinet, combined with legal mandates.

– Independence from the regulatory ministries and a horizontal perspective across the entire range of administrative activity. This should not be taken too far. A great deal of coordination and discussion with affected parties ensures that the opinions of the councils have been, as far as possible, palatable to the ministries and political parties. The councils' final opinions have usually been "fea-

157

sible" rather than "ideal", and represent a compromise position. Hence, the advisory councils are not academic bodies, but are the focal point of a consensus process that integrates political and practical considerations with efficiency objectives. Managing this relationship with the ministries is key to the council's effectiveness: if regulatory ministries have *de facto* veto rights, the contents of reform will be timid, and the pace slow. The relative success of the 1995-1997 ARC is due in part to its relative independence.

– Well-known and respected members who present a credible alternative to ministry views. "The fact that the members of the PCAR, selected from a broad range of candidates, [had] backgrounds in industry, trade unions, academia, government service and journalism, was persuasive enough to secure the trust of the public in the results of the deliberations" noted the MCA.[25]

– Investigative authorities and information collection capacities to pierce the information monopolies of the ministries. The 1995-1997 Administrative Reform Committee strengthened its capacity to initiate reform by pioneering an innovative method in Japan: it met with ministries to examine reform proposals in public, before the media, rather than behind closed doors, as was previously done. Many observers credit the successes of the Committee largely to the openness of discussions with ministries.

– Support from a permanent central administrative agency responsible for inspection and evaluation, and capable of long-term follow-up. A possible weakness is that perspectives of the MCA and the MITI are different and not well coordinated: MCA is concerned primarily with administrative efficiency and effectiveness, while MITI is concerned with economic performance. A more integrated structure for coordinating these concerns could be useful in improving the coherence of the reform programme.

– Public support, considered the key to reform. Public support was reinforced by wide coverage through the media of the councils'hearings and recommendations.

– A three-year sequential mandate, which allowed each succeeding council to follow up on implementation of earlier recommendations.

2.3. Co-ordination between levels of government

The 1997 OECD Report advises governments to "encourage reform at all levels of government". This difficult task is increasingly important as regulatory responsibilities are shared among many levels of government, including supranational, international, national, and subnational levels. High quality regulation at one level can be undermined or reversed by poor regulatory policies and practices at other levels, while, conversely, co-ordination can vastly expand the benefits of reform.

At the subnational level in Japan, there are 47 prefectures and over 3 000 municipal governments. Most of these bodies have regulatory powers of one type or another. In the deregulation programme of March 1998, the Japanese government encourages local government to play a supporting role in deregulation by investigating and reviewing both those regulations independently enforced by local government and those based on national laws and ordinances. However, the policy implicitly recognises the difficulty in doing this "while paying due respect to local autonomy and the principles of administrative decentralisation". Despite the principle of local autonomy, expansion of mandates and "delegated" functions from national ministries to local governments has created a "highly centralised" regulatory system.[26]

The government has recently renewed policies to promote decentralisation and enhance the administrative autonomy and independence of local public entities. In May 1998 the Cabinet adopted the "Decentralisation Action Plan", based on four reports submitted by the Committee for the Promotion of Decentralisation, which was established in July 1995. No detail on how conflicting government policies – that is, to both decentralise decision-making and harmonize regulatory reform policies – will be reconciled are given. This is an area for further attention, particularly since there are concerns that local government actions could frustrate some important reforms underway, such as deregulation of siting of large scale retail stores.

3.   ADMINISTRATIVE CAPACITIES FOR MAKING NEW REGULATION OF HIGH QUALITY

3.1. Administrative transparency and predictability

Transparency of the regulatory system is essential to establishing a stable and accessible regulatory environment that promotes competition, trade, and investment, and helps ensure against undue influence by special interests. Transparency also reinforces legitimacy and fairness of regulatory processes. Transparency is a multi-faceted concept that is not easy to change in practice. It involves a wide range of practices, including standardised processes for making and changing regulations; consultation with interested parties; plain language in drafting; publication, codification, and other ways of making rules easy to find and understand; controls on administrative discretion; and implementation and appeals processes that are predictable and consistent.

Transparency and predictability are major regulatory reform issues in most countries, but in Japan, they are especially prominent. Concern over lack of transparency and predictability is a central theme for critics of the Japanese regulatory system. A recent US Government submission to the Japanese government on regulatory reform[27] identified enhancement of transparency and accountability as one of seven basic principles for an extended commitment to deregulation. Within Japan, important voices have taken a similar view. Keidanren has strongly supported the current administrative reform proposals, taking the view that a rewriting of the "foundation laws", which are the broad authorising statutes for the Ministries, is an essential step toward limiting the scope of bureaucratic discretion by limiting and better defining their powers.[28]

3.1.1. *Transparency of procedures*

Three characteristics of regulatory processes in Japan reduce transparency: imprecision in the form of basic regulatory instruments, opaque decision-making, and limited judicial review. As mentioned earlier, there is no authoritative definition of permissible administrative action. In most cases there are neither open hearings nor published criteria on which decisions are based. The US government has charged that "Decision-making on regulatory matters is arbitrary and depends on the integrity and common sense of the individual bureaucrats responsible".[29] These issues are handled in most countries by administrative law, and hence the focus of this section is on the 1993 Administrative Procedure Act (APA), an important instrument. This section also discusses three other issues related to regulatory transparency: the use of administrative guidance, the benefits of moving to a central regulatory registry, and judicial review of administrative actions. Recommendations for improvement are made in each of these areas

Administrative Procedure Act. Japan does not have a general law governing the process of rule-making by the ministries, although the APA establishes requirements for making the existence of rules more transparent, and for explanations by the responsible administrators of the reasons for their actions. For many years, observers noted the need for a general administrative procedure law on decision-making processes within the ministries. Two professors noted in 1974 that Japan uses "administration through law interpreted by bureaucrats (horitsu ni yoru gyosei)" rather than "rule of law (hochishugi)".[30] A group of professors of public administration concluded in 1982 that, "Legal control of administrative procedures... is still far from adequate. In this sense, establishment of the general administrative procedure law is an urgent task...".[31] In the early 1980s, the PCAR also pointed out the need for a unified system of administrative procedure.

Work on a draft law began soon after. In October 1988, a preliminary report and draft guidelines were produced by the Second Study Group on Administrative Procedures. The Second PCPAR recommended in 1990 that a "special organ" be established to deliberate on the matter and that its recommendations be implemented as soon as possible. In response, the Prime Minister asked the Third PCPAR to "examine promptly the measures to introduce uniform legislation to improve transparency and to ensure fairness in administrative procedure...".[32] In December 1991, the Subcouncil on Fair and Transparent Administrative Procedure produced a draft bill that would introduce a uniform legal system of administrative procedure.

Box 3.   **Transparency of regulatory systems in selected OECD countries**

Based on self-assessment, this broad synthetic indicator is a relative measure of the openness of the regulation-making and regulatory review system. It ranks more highly national regulatory systems that provide for unrestricted public access to consultation processes, access to regulation through electronic and other publication requirements, access to RIAs, and participation in reviews of existing regulation. It also ranks more highly those programmes with easy access to licence information, which tends to favour unitary over federal states. Japan has a score of about 30 out of 100 on these criteria, although it would be expected to improve somewhat following implementation of the recently announced public notice and comment process. Some of the recommendations made to improve transparency are based on practices in high scoring countries, such as notice and comment in the United States and Canada, and the central registry in Sweden.

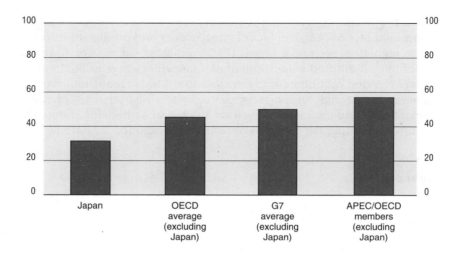

Source: Public Management Service, OECD, 1999.

In 1993, the Diet adopted the Administrative Procedure Act. The law, intended to "secure fairness" "increase transparency" and "protect the rights and interests of the population" covered "dispositions, administrative guidance and notifications". Notably, the purpose clauses specifically limit the scope of the law to those activities not subject to provisions in other laws; in other words, it does not cover all government activities. The Act deals separately with Dispositions, Administrative Guidance and Notifications, defined in Article 2 of the Act. Dispositions are defined as "involving the exercise of public authority by administrative agencies" while administrative guidance is "guidance, recommendations, advice or other acts by which an Administrative Organ may seek... [certain behaviour in pursuit of administrative aims]". Thus, guidance is seen as having a voluntary element, in contrast with dispositions.

Most of the protections of the APA relate to two kinds of administrative actions: permits and licenses, and administrative guidance. The APA requires ministries and agencies to publish objective criteria for judging applications for licenses and permissions, to explain why applications are rejected, to reduce delays, to guarantee hearing procedures and disclosure of relevant documents, and to ensure that administrative guidance is within legal mandates and that responsibility for such guidance is clear. Key provisions of the Act relating to Dispositions include:

– **Article 5** which requires agencies to develop explicit standards to guide decision making which are "as concrete as possible" and which are (with limited exceptions) available for public inspection.

– **Article 6** which requires agencies to develop and inform applicants of, indicative timeframes for decision-making.

- **Article 8** which requires that reasons for adverse decisions be provided.

- **Article 10** providing that, where Acts require the interests of third parties be taken into account, agencies should establish public hearings or other mechanisms for determining their views.

- **Article 13** providing that the subject of an adverse disposition must be given the right to be heard.

- **Article 24** requiring that a record and report be drawn up in cases of formal hearings, and that they can be inspected by the parties.

The definition of "dispositions" provided in the Act is vague and, in part, circular. However, the above provisions seem to include the key elements necessary to an improved level of transparency and predictability in decision-making in this area. Lacking, however, is detail or institutional arrangements for implementing the key requirements: What rules govern public hearings? What mechanisms are acceptable as alternatives? What rules govern the "right to be heard"? There is little information on how the APA is being implemented in practice, though the MCA has issued a positive report annually on its performance. The 1998 deregulation programme commits the government to "strict enforcement and public education with respect to the Administrative Procedure Law".

Use of "Administrative Guidance" in Japan. The use of "administrative guidance" (*gyosei shido*) in all areas of Japanese administration has received considerable domestic and international attention. This type of regulatory instrument has been called "the most informal type of political rulemaking"[33] and as a result there is considerable disagreement about whether it continues to be an important regulatory tool of the administration.

What is administrative guidance? One definition, by a Japanese professor of public administration[34] is "Administrative actions taken by administrative organs, although without legal binding force, that are intended to influence specific actions of other parties… in order to realise an administrative aim". An American scholar has called it "a varied and ill defined combination of informal techniques by which a ministry carries out its responsibilities and gets what it wants"[35]. The techniques of administrative guidance include recommendations, suggestions, requests and warnings.

Administrative guidance may also be routed through third parties, such as trade associations (as when export "self restraint" is needed) (see the background report on Enhancing market openness through regulatory reform). It may affect individual transactions (as when the Ministry of Finance advises against a big loan by a particular bank or a local office suggests that a supermarket reduce its floorspace to resolve its conflict with smaller stores), entire industries or local governments. As these examples suggest, guidance makes possible a network of informal and often invisible influence by the Japanese government on private and public sector entities.

The 1993 APA attempts to reduce the coercive nature of guidance and increase its transparency, very difficult tasks given the inherent ambiguity in distinguishing between "bad" guidance and "good" guidance that helps the public understand its regulatory obligations. Two general principles on administrative guidance are given in Article 32 of the Act:

- use of guidance should be strictly confined to matters within the duties and functions of the administrative agency as well as based "solely on the voluntary co-operation of the subject party", and

- subjects of administrative guidance should not be treated adversely owing to their non-compliance with the guidance in question.

Articles 33-36 deal with substantive requirements. The first three articles clarify the status of guidance and administrative behaviour. Officials are instructed not to continue with attempts at guidance when applicants have indicated they do not intend to follow it. They are instructed not to try to compel compliance with guidance by misleadingly claiming to be able to exercise other, more formal, authority as a means of coercing compliance. They are instructed to make clear to affected parties the purpose and content of the guidance in question and, upon request, provide a written copy of any guidance provided "by word of mouth". Perhaps most importantly, Article 36 requires that, if guidance contains any standards or items that are also applicable to other persons, the content that is uniformly applied is to be made public in advance.

Compliance with administrative guidance has traditionally been high, even where those required to comply do not agree with its contents. Three reasons for the compliance of private businesses have been suggested. Firstly, such an approach is preferred to formal regulation because there is more scope for flexibility in individual responses and more co-operation in the development of the guidance. Secondly, the Japanese state has traditionally intervened in many private activities, leading to state paternalism and "excessive dependence" by businesses (exemplified by their requests to government bodies to mediate disputes between them). The habit of "listening closely" to government seems, however, to be weakening over time. Third, Ministries have at hand "a range of inducements and covert blackmail techniques"[36] including subsidies, loans, loan guarantees, tax advantages, licensing powers and public announcements. Businesses may fear that relationships with the authorities will be strained. Officials have delayed the issue of licences to "non-compliers" – a sanction which has been upheld by the courts – while ministries may also threaten to public announce the names of non-compliers.[37]

The use of administrative guidance can have benefits *vis-à-vis* formal regulatory standards. Guidance is more flexible and quicker to implement. It is better suited to dealing with localised problems than regulations, which generally have more widespread impact and are less able to distinguish different circumstances. Moreover, guidance encourages co-operative and consultative relationships and avoids the adversarial aspects of formal regulatory proceedings.

Nonetheless, critics of administrative guidance raise several concerns. Accountability is not yet clear. Laws do not designate who can issue guidance or what are its limits. In the financial industry, for example, it has been given both explicitly in the form of a bulletin or notice to banks and as a verbal or implicit message.[38] Administrative guidance works best in a relatively concentrated market. Such an environment is often created and maintained by regulations. Where regulations authorise restriction of competition by entry licensing, administrative guidance is at its most effective. Administrative guidance has been most prevalent, therefore, in those industries that are most highly regulated. Hence, the opening of markets to competition may be incompatible with its use. Conversely, critics fear that the use of guidance may tend to undermine, in a hidden fashion, the greater scope for new competition apparently provided by new, more flexible, laws.

The thrust of the 1993 APA is toward increasing transparency and public consultation, reducing the use of guidance as a substitute for formal action and providing a means of redress for aggrieved parties. These are positive steps, but the degree of progress in eliminating guidance as a regulatory tool is not clear. According to MCA, it knows of 33 public disclosures of guidance. This small number may mean either that exemptions for cases of "extraordinary administrative inconvenience" are being widely used, that unwritten administrative guidance is not being written down, or, conversely, that the use of administrative guidance is actually rare. There are various views in Japan on this. One possible difficulty in making the APA effective is that an outright challenge to regulatory agencies can look risky to market players, and some private firms have expressed concern about possible retaliatory action from regulators. This is a disincentive to take cases through APA legal procedures. Some stakeholders believe that the use of administrative guidance is likely to continue to be a source of regulatory uncertainty, lack of transparency and fears of unequal treatment, especially if misused. Given the long history of the use of guidance, it seems likely that a robust process to monitor compliance with the APA by administrators will be necessary.

Registration and codification processes are often a necessary first step to understanding what actually exists in the regulatory system so that systematic reform can commence. Surprisingly, many OECD countries have no registry of existing regulations, or any system to track regulations. Yet it is difficult to see how one can understand or reform regulations without knowing what regulations exist, or who is regulating what. As the French *Conseil d'État* observed in 1992, "it will be impossible to stem the tide without first establishing ways of measuring it".

Box 4.   Some examples: administrative guidance in Japan

MITI stated in 1981 that "administrative guidance has played an important role in the development of the Japanese economy and it will continue to be effective in the future". Working through a network of "policy councils" and working groups composed of representatives of private companies and related interests such as banks, MITI has used guidance to guide patterns of investment in industries according to national priorities, request controls on prices, request voluntary controls on exports to avoid trade friction, recommend production increases in conditions of tight supply, encourage the use of certain technologies (*e.g.* robotised production) or direct industry consolidation or mergers. In some cases, MITI's guidance has amounted to "micro-economic programmes for the development of specific industries" (see Neary[39], who argues that administrative guidance has been "the principal instrument of industrial development" in the post-war period).

Administrative guidance can also be a more rapid substitute for law, as in the case of Environmental Impact Assessment (EIA). The concept of EIA was introduced in Japan in 1972, when the Cabinet approved guidelines "On the Environmental Conservation Measures Relating to Public Works". However, the guidelines did not describe specific EIA procedures. In 1974, the Environment Agency began to prepare a bill to establish a common EIA procedure. The process of studying systems of EIA, conducting discussions within government, and securing Cabinet approval lasted eight years. When the Diet went out of session in November 1983 without passing the bill, the Cabinet decided to implement EIA processes via administrative guidance. The guidelines "On the Implementation of EIA" were approved in August 1984. Other administrative guidelines were issued by MITI to govern EIA for power plant construction projects. Finally, 45 of 47 prefectural governments have issued their own EIA regulations or guidelines. A new EIA law does not come into effect until 1999-25 years after the first attempts to produce a law began.

In some cases, administrative guidance has been converted into more formal regulatory instruments, a positive step that improves transparency but does not necessarily affect substance. As part of the commitment to "fairness" in the Big Bang, the Ministry of Finance announced in June 1998 that it had abolished 400 pieces of administrative guidance (tsutatsu and jimu-renraku) pertaining to business practices in financial services.[40] This action followed criticism that administrative guidance on business activities and financial products was burdensome and limited innovation in the sector. MOF codified some of the guidance into published ministerial ordinances (shorei/seirei) (and reconstituted others as "guidelines" (gaidorain), another form of guidance. The latter were compiled in four thick books, one for each major sector of the financial industry – banking, non-banking, insurance, and securities). In many cases, the substance of the rules were not changed very much. For example, asset allocation guidelines imposed on life insurance companies (so-called 5-3-3-2 rules) were revised to eliminate duplication and make other adjustments, but the basic thrust of the guidelines remains intact – *i.e.*, insurance companies are subject to quantitative limits on the amount of funds they can invest in certain classes of assets (*e.g.*, stocks, real estate, etc.). This example suggests that positive steps toward more transparent regulation should be accompanied by substantive review of policy content.

Japan has publication requirements for regulations. Regulations in the forms of parliamentary laws, cabinet orders (currently numbering around 1 800), ministerial or Prime Minister's Office ordinances (currently numbering around 2 600), commission and agency rules and special orders and notices are published in the Official Gazette (Kanpo), under a 1947 agreement between the ministries. Local bylaws are published in the official bulletin of the issuing local government.

The MCA has compiled a registry of over 9 000 permission, registration, and notification requirements that is a useful management tool for the reform programme, but this registry has no legal status, and other kinds of regulations are not included. Hence, there is no centralised system in Japan for communicating regulations to citizens and firms. Establishment of a central registry would assist the Japanese government in improving transparency and certainty of the national regulatory system for users. The OECD has found that efforts to count, register, and codify regulations are useful management and oversight tools. Their visibility engenders a new sense of responsibility and discipline by making apparent the size and scope of the regulatory system and the rate of growth, which in some OECD countries has become a symbol of over-bureaucratisation and red tape. Codification, therefore, can improve both juridical and substantive regulatory quality. In Spain, for example, codification aims to update existing regulations in accord with modern principles and criteria more fitted to society.[41] Establishing a central registry will also assist the government in making one-stop shops available to businesses, a goal of the current reform programme.

One possible model for Japan is the innovative Swedish approach[42] (other approaches are discussed in Box 5). In the 1980s, Sweden enacted its well-known "guillotine" rule nullifying hundreds of regulations that were not centrally registered. In 1984, the government found that it was unable to compile a list of regulations in force. The accumulation of laws and rules from a large and poorly-monitored network of regulators meant that the government could not itself determine what it required of private citizens. To establish a clear and accountable legal structure, it was decided to compile a comprehensive list of all agency rules in effect. The approach proposed by the Government and adopted by the Riksdag was simple. The Government instructed all government agencies to establish registries of their ordinances by July 1, 1986. As these agencies prepared their lists (over the course of a year), they culled out unnecessary rules. Ministry officials also commented on rules that they thought were unnecessary or outdated, in effect reversing the burden of proof for maintaining old regulations. When the "guillotine rule" went into effect, "hundreds of regulations not registered... were automatically cancelled" without further legal action. All new regulations and changes to existing ones were henceforth to be entered in the registry within one day of adoption.

Box 5. "Positive Security" and regulatory registers

Positive security means that a regulation not listed in a central register is not enforceable. Some countries have found it useful as a way to ensure that registers provide comprehensive coverage of all regulations. This maximises access to regulation and certainty in the market: citizens and businesses can have confidence that they are aware of all relevant regulations.

Many other countries have established registries, tracking systems, and codification programmes to support reform (Jacobs, 1997a, pp. 291-297). In France, an ambitious codification project to be completed by the year 2000 aims at making the law simpler, clearer, and more accessible to citizens and enterprises. In Finland, the Norms Project of 1986-1992 reduced the total number of norms from 7 500 to 5 500, and was concluded with the establishment of a special registry for subordinate regulations. Mexico recently established its first comprehensive Federal Register of Business Formalities. In the United States, regulations are indexed and published in the Code of Federal Regulations. The Code is regularly updated, and regulations not listed in the current edition are unenforceable. In Australia, a Legislative Instruments Bill, currently before the Parliament, will create a Federal Register of Legislative Instruments, in which new regulations must be listed before they can be enforced. "The Register will help reveal outdated or unnecessary regulations, assisting programs of review" stated the Prime Minister.[43]

Information technologies add new possibilities to this work. In 1995, Sweden was building a comprehensive electronic listing of regulations, with text on issues such as motives, magnitude of costs and effects. Many of the federal regulations in the United States are now available to affected parties over the Internet.

In most cases in which such registers are used, listing is a final step in the procedural requirements for making regulations. In other cases, listing is not a formal procedural requirement, but provides a defence to prosecution if non-compliance is due to lack of a reasonable opportunity to know the regulation – including failure to list the rule in the register.

This approach was considered a great success. In the education field, for example, 90 per cent of rules was eliminated. The government had for the first time a comprehensive picture of the Swedish regulatory structure that could be used to organise and target a reform programme. The registry may also have had the indirect effect of slowing the rate of growth of new regulations, and by 1996 the net number of regulations had indeed dropped substantially.

The role of judicial review of administrative actions is very limited in Japan compared to other OECD countries. Japan's "ministries are... unique in one way: they are remarkably free from external judicial accountability" a recent report concluded.[44] Ministries in other countries are subject to various kinds of administrative courts and other forms of judicial review. In France, for example, there is a "barrage" of control mechanisms, such as a network of Administrative Tribunals headed by the Council of State and the Mediator's Office, which are judicial bodies with the task of judging alleged administrative abuses against citizens.[45]

Japan has an active administrative appeals procedure, and a little-used process for litigating administrative cases. About 36 000 administrative appeals were filed in 1994 under the Administrative Appeals Law, but review by the judiciary is not often used in practice. The reasons for lack of judicial review are unclear, but may be related to high costs of court action, fear of retribution by the administration, or cultural issues such as avoidance of adversarial resolutions. The Keidanren has called on the Government to revise the APA and to amend the Law on Suits Relating to Governmental Incidents and the Administrative Appeal Law to make the system easier to use by citizens.[46] A process of review carried out by the Administrative Inspection Bureau in the MCA is much more frequently used than the two means of redress mentioned above. The MCA accepts complaints, opinions and demands concerning public administration from the public, examines them, and makes recommendations for resolution of the issues. The MCA receives almost 230 000 cases every year. The MCA also inspects administrative operations by the national government and makes recommendations for procedural reform to the administrative bodies concerned. According to the MCA, the aims are to 1) ensure appropriate execution of laws, government ordinances and the budget; and 2) deal with change, ensure comprehensiveness, simplicity and efficiency, and keep the trust of the citizen.

The government has recognised that action is needed to improve access by citizens to judicial oversight of administrative action. There is a commitment in the 1998 regulatory reform programme to develop a greater role for the judiciary in relation to the development of "clear rules of surveillance of compliance with the rules". An increase in the number of new lawyers admitted to the bar is one of the measures. Similarly, the Basic Law on the Administrative Reform of the Central Government commits to judiciary reforms, including reforms to administrative tribunals. How these programmes will develop remains as yet undetailed.

3.1.2. *Transparency as dialogue with affected groups: use of public consultation*

A strong trend toward renewal and expansion of public consultation in regulatory development is underway in OECD countries. Much has been invested in efforts to make more information available to the public, to listen to a wider range of interests, to obtain more and better information from affected parties, and to be more responsive to what is heard. A well-designed and implemented consultation programme can contribute to higher-quality regulations, identification of more effective alternatives, lower costs to businesses and administration, better compliance, and faster regulatory responses to changing conditions. It can also reduce the risk of capture and undue influence from special interests.

Japan took a major step forward when public comment procedures for new regulations and revisions to existing regulations went into effect in April 1999. Until then, Japan did not have a general law or government policy on the use of consultation in making or modifying regulation. Individual laws and government policies requiring the use of consultation existed in certain areas and a wide variety of forms of consultation (including notice and comment, circulation for comment, information consultation, advisory groups and public hearings) were used. It will be important to ensure that ministries carry out the new procedures systematically and consistently, that draft regulations are published early enough to allow meaningful public review, and that ministries actually respond to public comments, even if only to explain why the comments were not accepted.

Advisory councils, whose views are sought during the drafting process, are particularly important. Each ministry has two to 33 such councils (numbering 212 in all as of 1 October 1998), organised around specific fields and composed of experts, professors and representatives of trade unions, businesses, and consumer interests. The councils are established by law or cabinet order to consider and give recommendations on issues within their expertise. Highly respected and influential with the ministries, they are said to "play an important role in guaranteeing the fairness and appropriateness or neutrality... of

Box 6.   Best practices in consultation: "notice and comment" in the United States

The 1946 Administrative Procedure Act (APA) established a legal right for citizens to participate in rule-making activities of the federal government on the principle of open access to all. It sets out the basic rule-making process to be followed by all agencies of the US Government. The path from proposed to final rule affords ample opportunity for participation by affected parties. At a minimum, the APA requires that in issuing a substantive rule (as distinguished from a procedural rule or statement of policy), an agency must:

i)   Publish a notice of proposed rulemaking in the Federal Register. This notice must set forth the text or the substance of the proposed rule, the legal authority for the rulemaking proceeding, and applicable times and places for public participation. Published proposals also routinely include information on appropriate contacts within regulatory agencies.

ii) Provide all interested persons – nationals and non-nationals alike – an opportunity to participate in the rulemaking by providing written data, views, or arguments on a proposed rule. This public comment process serves a number of purposes, including giving interested persons an opportunity to provide the agency with information that will enhance the agency's knowledge of the subject matter of the rulemaking. The public comment process also provides interested persons with the opportunity to challenge the factual assumptions on which the agency is proceeding, and to show in what respect such assumptions may be in error.

iii) Publish a notice of final rulemaking at least thirty days before the effective date of the rule. This notice must include a statement of the basis and purpose of the rule and respond to all substantive comments received. Exceptions to the thirty-day rule are provided for in the APA if the rule makes an exemption or relieves a restriction, or if the agency concerned makes and publishes a finding that an earlier effective date is required "for good cause". In general, however, exceptions to the APA are limited and must be justified.

The American system of notice and comment has resulted in an extremely open and accessible regulatory process at the federal level that is consistent with international good practices for transparency. The theory of this process is that it is open to all citizens, rather than being based on representative groups. This distinguishes the method from those used in more corporatist models of consultation, and also from informal methods that leave regulators considerable discretion in who to consult. Its effect is to increase the quality and legitimacy of policy by ensuring that special interests do not have undue influence.

administration and the adjustment of policy to the interests of the concerned parties".[47] When a relevant council does not exist, a ministry may hold meetings of an ad hoc study group to perform similar independent advisory functions. While the councils have traditionally worked in private, a Cabinet decision of September 1995 requires that their meetings be open to the public or, at a minimum, that outlines of the proceedings of these meetings be made available.

These arrangements are similar to those used in many OECD countries, and their usefulness in improving policy quality has been repeatedly demonstrated. Yet they fall short of best practice because of the differing degree of access for "insiders" and special interests compared to "outsiders". For example, ministries themselves decide when and how much to consult. Other problems that have been identified are the slowness of advisory bodies, and their lack of accountability for recommendations. For those reasons, complaints about consultation in Japan resemble complaints in corporatist European countries about highly organised but exclusive "social partner" consultation bodies.

The Japanese Government includes reforms to consultation arrangements as a major element of the current deregulation programme. The programme required the MCA, in co-operation with responsible ministries and agencies, to "promptly undertake" a study of public comment procedures and of "current procedures related to the introduction, amendment and abolition of regulations". The study is to draw up its conclusions "as an administrative measure" prior to the scheduled 1999 revision of the programme. Thus, a significant move in the direction of creating consistent and transparent consultative requirements is expected in the short term.

An area where consultation is extensively developed is the regulatory reform programme itself. The previous three year programme was substantially revised and amended on an annual basis. The current programme is intended to be updated in a similar fashion and, as part of this process, the MCA will publish an annual "white paper on deregulation" describing the initiatives being undertaken and their effect on the community. The purposes of publishing the white papers are to inform the public of progress on deregulation and to encourage comment and suggestions on future reform initiatives from both domestic and international sources. In fact, dialogue with major trading partners (notably the United States and the European Union) has contributed to Japanese reform programmes since 1995 and constitutes one of the more open aspects of Japanese regulatory arrangements.

3.1.3. The changing institutional basis for regulation

A positive trend in Japan is the emergence of new kinds of regulatory bodies in the direction of functionally separate regulators, though there is no general policy on this, nor any recommendation from the Administrative Reform Committee. Many accountability, transparency, and competition problems in sectoral regulation result from lack of institutional clarity about the source, powers, and purpose of regulation. In addition, key regulatory failures such as the current bad loan banking crises have been blamed in part on inadequate capacities for supervision by the public sector, in this case the Ministry of Finance. The current mix in Japanese ministries of regulatory with policy and industry promotion functions is an outmoded approach that is being rejected in several sectors in many OECD countries (and also in the WTO and the European Union) in favour of institutional designs that functionally separate regulatory from other activities to maintain a competitively neutral regulatory regime.[48] This will be particularly important if Japan wishes at some point to replace public works spending on social infrastructure with private investment in infrastructure.

The financial sector supervisory board set up alongside the Ministry of Finance is the clearest example of how Japanese institutions are evolving in the direction of international best practices, though the independence and enforcement capacities of the new regulator are as yet unproven. A more general approach is needed to provoke change across a broader front, and to ensure that institutions are designed on consistent principles of competition, transparency, and accountability for results. The current Administrative Reform Programme aims to separate policy-making from implementation, as has been done in several countries such as the United Kingdom, but there is little discussion in the ARP of the need to separate policy-making from regulatory functions. It is also necessary to strengthen the role of the Fair Trade Commission in those aspects of sectoral regulation that affect competition policy issues, meaning that institutionalised cooperation between sectoral regulators and the FTC should be designed from the very beginning. This is discussed in more detail in the background report on The role of competition policy and enforcement in regulatory reform.

3.2. Choice of policy instruments: regulation and alternatives

A core administrative capacity for good regulation is the ability to choose the most efficient and effective policy tool, whether regulatory or non-regulatory, while respecting principles of transparency and accountability. The range of policy tools and their uses is expanding in OECD countries as experimentation occurs, learning is diffused, and understanding of the markets increases. At the same time, administrators often face risks in using relatively untried tools, bureaucracies are highly conservative, and there are typically strong disincentives for public servants to be innovative. A leading role-supportive of innovation and policy learning-must be taken by reform authorities if alternatives to traditional regulation are to make serious headway into the policy system.

The use of alternatives to traditional regulation is, in many countries such as the United States and the Netherlands, most highly developed in the area of environmental protection. The same situation is seen in Japan, where the Basic Environment Law of 1993 and its predecessor, the Basic Law for Environmental Pollution Control of 1967, provide for the use of a range of policy instruments. Instruments used under these laws, in addition to regulation, include voluntary agreements with industry and a range of

167

economic instruments such as financial incentives, subsidies and user charges. Discussion of the environmental field should be seen as best practice in Japan, since the use of alternatives is not widely spread through other regulatory fields where command and control styles are dominant.

Voluntary agreements are generally concluded between firms and municipal or prefectural authorities. According to the Environment Agency.[49] The promotion of voluntary environment management efforts by private enterprises is defined as part of the most important protection measures in the country's "Basic Environment Plan". While voluntary approaches are innovative in many OECD countries, this approach is not new in Japan. "Pollution agreements" started in Japan in 1964 (in Yokohama city) as local government initiatives. The purpose of these agreements was to compensate for the lack of environmental regulations in the early 1960s. Hence, these initiatives were a precursor of regulations, designed to fill regulatory gaps and resolve local conflicts. About 1 000-2 000 voluntary agreements are concluded every year, and in March 1998, 32 000 agreements were in force. Agreements can relate to pollution control in general or be confined to (or focused on) specific concerns, such as waste water, noise, offensive odours or soot. Authorities may ask enterprises to formulate plans to reduce waste and emissions beyond the legal standards. In many cases, industry associations have adopted sector-wide plans or standards, such as the chemical industry's Responsible Care plan. In addition, the Keidanren adopted a Global Environmental Charter in 1991 which proposed the creation of environmental management systems by its members.

While there has been some public involvement in making these agreements (7 per cent of agreements concluded in 1991/92) the majority are negotiated solely between government and industry and are not available for public scrutiny. On the other hand, about 9 per cent of agreements signed in 1991/92 were concluded directly between companies and the local citizens. Thus, the transparency aspect of voluntary agreements shows a slightly mixed picture, though one which indicate a generally low level of openness. This lack of openness may be problematic in terms of ensuring public confidence in, and hence support for, the use of such voluntary agreements in place of traditional regulation. Mechanisms to ensure that the public has access to information on voluntary agreements should be investigated.

The OECD concluded in 1994 that voluntary agreements have played an important role in improving environmental performance in Japan, to a much greater extent than in most Member countries. Key advantages identified were lower implementation costs and enhanced economic and environmental effectiveness – partly through helping stimulate the use of preventive, rather than remedial, technology.[50]

Economic Instruments are relatively less widely used in Japan. To the extent that they have been used, the focus has been on financial and fiscal incentives, with instruments such as effluent and emissions charges playing little role in Japanese environmental policy. For 25 years, the Government has made low interest loans and tax incentives available to companies for both research and development on pollution control and for actual pollution control investments. But this kind of instrument is not necessarily environmentally sound. Some low interest loans and especially tax breaks are in fact subsidies, in contradiction with the polluter-pays principle. Another mechanism has been to encourage the relocation of existing polluting activities away from residential areas by financing the construction of new plant on a long-term low interest loan basis. Almost 600 billion yen were provided under this latter scheme between 1972 and 1989.

In reviewing the use of economic instruments in Japan in 1994, the OECD noted that there was insufficient information from which to draw conclusions about their economic efficiency. It concluded that "from an economic point of view, a review of the cost-effectiveness of current approaches to achieve standards and the development of cost-benefit analysis, particularly for public projects, would be of benefit, as would be the greater use of economic instruments, such as fees, taxes, charges and deposit refund systems."[51] The situation appears to have changed little since this time, with cost-benefit analysis still being relatively little used in the Japanese government and the new environmental impact assessment processes yet to take effect.

User charging constitutes a particular form of economic instrument, in that the absence of proper pricing arrangements for government provided pollution control services implies a "pollution subsidy". Japan has made some use of user charging, though its extent seems to vary widely in different areas. For example, it is relatively well developed in the waste water area, with industry estimated to be paying up to $^1/_3$ of the construction costs and $^1/_4$ of the operating costs of sewerage systems in some areas. However, municipal waste charges are generally absent, the cost being met from local government budgets. Special landing charges have been levied at airports as a noise control initiative.

Performance has been extremely good in the environmental area in Japan. Between 1970 and 1990, while GDP increased by 122 per cent, sulphur dioxide emissions fell 82 per cent and emissions of oxides of nitrogen fell 21 per cent. This was the best performance of all OECD countries.[52] Nonetheless, the lack of use of cost/benefit analysis to weigh the effectiveness of different policy instruments and the lack of use of potentially effective instruments such as pollution charges suggests that their remains considerable room for improvement. The adoption of government-wide policies to encourage the use of alternative instruments, together with guidance and assistance for regulating ministries in the use of specific instruments in specific circumstances, is necessary to maximise the use of new and unfamiliar instruments in place of "tried and true" – but often less effective – command and control regulation.

3.3. Understanding regulatory effects: the use of Regulatory Impact Analysis (RIA)

The 1995 *Recommendation of the Council of the* OECD *on Improving the Quality of Government Regulation* emphasised the role of RIA in systematically ensuring that the most efficient and effective policy options were chosen. The 1997 OECD R*eport on Regulatory Reform* recommended that governments "integrate regulatory impact analysis into the development, review, and reform of regulations". A list of RIA best practices is discussed in detail in R*egulatory Impact Analysis: Best Practices in* OECD *Countries.*[53]

The use of RIA is currently in its infancy in Japan. There is no requirement for regulatory impact assessment. While the Japanese government uses quality controls, such as checking by the Ministries of Justice and Finance, that it considers as functionally equivalent to RIA, no economic impact assessment programme exists. The revised regulatory reform programme of March 1999 took a positive step by directing regulators to examine the need for new regulations, their projected effects, and their burdens on the public. The programme also directed that ministries and agencies "work toward the creation of a system" to increase accountability for the effects and burdens of regulations. These directives could well open the door to RIA in future, but no decision has been made to use RIA to implement them. This is a major gap in Japan's quality control procedures, because policy officials are unable to base decisions on a clear assessment of the costs and benefits of proposed government actions, such as impacts on economic activity. In moving to a market-led growth strategy, such impact assessments become all the more important in ensuring that government actions are consistent with market-oriented principles of quality regulation. The following section assesses existing quality control practices against OECD best practice recommendations.

Maximise political commitment to RIA. Use of RIA to support reform should be endorsed at the highest levels of government. The Japanese system does not rate highly on this criterion since the current deregulation programme contains no commitment to RIA.

Allocate responsibilities for RIA *programme elements carefully.* To ensure "ownership" by regulators, while at the same time establishing quality control and consistency, responsibilities for RIA should be shared between regulators and a central quality control unit. The Japanese system rates poorly in this respect. To the extent that economic assessment is conducted for lower-level rules it is the sole responsibility of the regulatory ministry, although more general checking on legislative quality is conducted by MCA, MoF and the Cabinet Legislation Bureau, from their various perspectives. Moreover, MCA does not provide training and guidance on economic assessments to Ministries, or otherwise oversee quality.

A significantly enhanced role for MCA in overseeing quality would improve the value of current quality controls in informing policy officials about the impacts of regulations. Other positive steps can be prepared, considering other on-going administrative reform activities. The recommendation of the Administrative Reform Council that ministries set up evaluation bodies could support good RIA if these bodies have the expertise and resources to act as internal RIA consultants to ministerial regulators.

Train the regulators. Regulators must have the skills to do high quality economic assessments, including an understanding of the role of impact assessment in assuring regulatory quality, and an understanding of

169

methodological requirements and data collection strategies. There are currently no formal training programmes in place in Japan in relation to impact assessment. Nor are there formal guidelines on impact assessment. Given the fact that impact assessment is at an early stage in Japan, training should be a high priority, both to develop specific skills and to contribute to longer term cultural changes among regulators. Training and guidance are also essential to ensure methodological consistency between assessments.

Use a consistent but flexible analytical method. Japanese requirements do not include specific methodological standards or guidance. MCA officials have stated that the impact assessments conducted are essentially qualitative in nature.

The absence of a requirement to use quantitative methodologies, combined with lack of guidance and training means that consistency in assessments cannot be assured. Attention to developing detailed methodological requirements for impact assessments, and supporting them with relevant training, guidance and expert assistance, is key if impact assessment is to achieve its potential in improving the quality of Japanese regulation. This report has elsewhere recommended adoption of the benefit-cost principle, and, if Japan adopts RIA, its RIA system should aim in the longer-term to establish benefit-cost analysis as the primary method for assessing regulations.

Box 7.   Good practices: use of Environmental Impact Assessment (EIA) in Japan

A high-quality system for EIA recently adopted in Japan provides important precedents for improving regulatory impact analysis. EIA is a widely used process in OECD countries that is closely related to RIA. The two mechanisms are intended to assess and quantify the impacts of projects to guide policy choice. Both methods focus on the identification and weighing of the consequences of alternative options.

Japan's new EIA law,[54] to take effect in June 1999, establishes procedures for applying EIA to large scale projects with significant environmental impacts. Three basic principles are identified; careful examination of whether the project meets existing environmental standards, comparison of the project with other, similar, projects to encourage reduction in environmental impacts through identification of better technologies and an obligation on project planners to propose means of reducing the environmental impacts of project proposals.

The EIA law replaces a set of administrative guidelines adopted by the Cabinet in 1984. The key changes include: adopting a screening mechanism to ensure that major projects are subject to EIA, while smaller projects are assessed only as justified; requiring project planners to produce documents describing how EIA will be conducted and to seek public comment on that process; wider opportunities for public hearings on draft EIS; increasing the comprehensiveness of EIS to include the results of surveys, predictions, assessments; follow-up surveys after completing EIA through continuous monitoring arrangements; opinions expressed by the environmental agency; and conducting of additional assessments where new information or circumstances arise.

The changes to EIA are consistent with RIA best practices. Wider opportunities for public hearing are consistent with RIA best practice principles of involving the public extensively. Provision for the Environment Agency to express opinions on EIA to responsible authorities is consistent with the principle of independent oversight to ensure the quality of RIA. The requirement for project planners to take account of opinions by the Environment Agency and competent authority is consistent with the principle of integrating RIA into the policy process.

However, commenters have pointed to weaknesses. The law does not clearly define which bodies will make final EIA decisions. Project documents are submitted in accord with Ministry ordinances on which the Environment Agency has only "consultative" input. This implies that ministries involved will have a larger say in EIA assessment and approval than the Environment Agency and may adopt differing approaches.[55] To this extent, the principles of carefully allocating responsibility and ensuring consistency are not well served by the new law.

The principles followed in the new environmental impact assessment are largely consistent with those adopted by the OECD as best practices in regulatory impact assessment. The law has undergone an extremely long gestation, perhaps indicating the difficulty of achieving acceptance of these principles. Emphasis on consistency of principles between the two impact assessment systems may point the way forward for Japanese RIA.

Develop and implement data collection strategies. As RIA has, to date, been confined to qualitative analysis, data collection strategies have not been developed. Since data issues are among the most consistently problematic aspects in conducting quantitative RIA, the development of strategies and guidance for ministries is essential if a successful programme of quantitative RIA is to be developed.

Integrate RIA with the policy making process, beginning as early as possible. Integrating RIA with the policy making process is meant to ensure that the disciplines of weighing costs and benefits, identifying and considering alternatives and choosing policy in accordance with its ability to meet objectives are a routine part of policy development. In some countries where RIA has not been integrated into policymaking, impact assessment has become merely an *ex post* justification of decisions or meaningless paperwork. Integration is a long-term process which often implies significant cultural changes within regulatory ministries. Given the early stage of implementation of economic assessment in Japan, it is too early to assess progress in this area.

Involve the public extensively. Public involvement in RIA has several significant benefits. The public, and especially those affected by regulations, can provide the data necessary to complete RIA. Consultation can also provide important checks on the feasibility of proposals, on the range of alternatives considered, and on the degree of acceptance of the proposed regulation by affected parties. Japanese quality control procedures have not previously contained any provisions for public consultation. However, the newly adopted public comment procedures for regulation provide the opportunity to integrate regulatory impact assessments into public consultation. As the new consultation programme is implemented, attention to links between the two quality control procedures should be developed as a matter of priority.

4. DYNAMIC CHANGE: KEEPING REGULATIONS UP-TO-DATE

Regulations that are efficient today may become inefficient tomorrow, due to social, economic, or technological change. Most OECD countries have enormous stocks of regulation and administrative formalities that have accumulated over years or decades without adequate review and revision. The OECD Report on Regulatory Reform recommends that governments "review regulations systematically to ensure that they continue to meet their intended objectives efficiently and effectively".

Japan ranks high among OECD countries in terms of the scope and ambition of regulatory review programmes. Review of existing regulations has been the centrepiece of its reform programmes for almost 20 years, and the revolving programme backed up by a series of 3-year independent councils has stimulated most of the major reforms that have taken place, as explained in section 2 above. The 1998 deregulation programme continues the focus on review of existing regulations. An innovative step that is continued in the 1998 programme is the inclusion in new regulations of a fixed schedule for future review, which, if rigorous, should make more systematic the future review of regulations.

The 1998 programme, as revised in March 1999, in "Promoting Comprehensive Examination and Review" identifies several areas for action. The first is review of barriers to entry, and includes commitments to remove barriers to foreign firms and products, and removal of "supply and demand balancing regulations". For the latter, an attachment to the policy details a number of reform areas and makes commitments to remove such regulations by given dates (between 1998 and 2001). In other areas, however, the commitment is to "review" such regulations. The policy falls short of general action to abandon the use of this anti-competitive instrument.

Several review commitments relate to various aspects of government formalities: reviews of government approval and notification requirements; qualifications procedures and systems; standards, specifications, inspection and certification systems; and licensing and permitting. In each case, the goal is to abolish approvals wherever possible and to simplify and rationalise the remainder. A major addition to the March 1999 programme is a review of qualification systems for service activities to stimulate entry and competition in those services.

171

The programme also states that "as a rule" regulations (and new laws) shall include clauses requiring them to be subjected to *ex post* review after a fixed period of time. Much regulation has already incorporated such requirements, with review periods ranging from about 3 to 10 years after introduction. Ministries and agencies are required to release review findings "promptly after the closing of each ordinary session of the Diet in a format that can be readily understood by the public", thus providing an element of transparency, although there is no specific requirement to take comment from the public. This is a significant reform. According to MCA officials, a significant and increasing proportion of new regulation already incorporates review requirements. This *ex post* review process is a good practice also used in some other OECD countries, but it should be combined with *ex ante* regulatory impact analysis of regulatory proposals to reduce the risk of poor regulations from the very beginning.

The current programme also lists "Measures Relevant to Specific Fields". In many cases, specific commitments are made and implementation timetables given. In other cases, commitments are to review issues without timetables. However, a general instruction under this heading requires all "deliberative councils" to submit their conclusions by September 1999 or, where necessary, to provide an interim report by this date and a final report by end-February 2000. The choice of specific deregulatory measures reflects, in large part, the wider policy priorities of the Government's Action Plan for Economic Structural Reform. This plan identifies 15 "New and Growth Fields" (see footnote[56]) and sets out to develop a more favourable business environment particularly in these fields through means including "deregulation, development of key technologies, resources and other measures".

These review mechanisms and plans rank in some aspects positively against international best practices. Against stubborn opposition, the Japanese government has organised the machinery to identify regulatory problems, include them in structured programmes, and monitor outcomes. The review programmes have become progressively more ambitious, moving toward more comprehensive sectoral reviews based on consistent principles of good regulation. Methods of review have improved, particularly the move by the 1995-1997 Administrative Reform Committee to conduct its discussions with ministries in public, short-circuiting the private negotiations that have slowed and undercut reform in the past. The inclusion in new regulations of fixed review schedules is a positive step that will place future reviews on a more systematic basis, and improve the adaptability of Japanese regulatory regimes.

There are also important weaknesses in the Japanese approach to reviewing existing regulations that should be corrected to permit reform to move forward more quickly, coherently, and transparently. The critical problem of the "item by item" approach based on incrementalism was discussed earlier in this paper, and the suggestion was made to develop a clearer set of principles to guide reform measures, including particularly competition principles. As a further step to support the reviews, general principles should be complemented by standardised evaluation techniques and decision criteria. Cost savings or enhanced benefits likely to flow from reform proposals are frequently quantified, but regulatory impact analysis is not widely used.

Another step already foreshadowed in the 1998 programme and its focus on 15 growth fields, is the development of comprehensive sectoral and cross-sectoral review plans aimed at introducing competition while crafting transition programmes and protecting important public interests through efficient regulation.

As noted in the OECD Report on Regulatory Reform, comprehensive reform is based on a complete and transparent package of reforms (aimed at a single policy area, sector or multiple sectors) designed to achieve specific goals on a well-defined timetable. Comprehensive reform does not mean that all changes occur immediately; rather, it is consistent with sequencing strategies and transitional steps as long as they are temporary and steps and timing are clear. There are several advantages to comprehensive reform: benefits appear faster (which means that pro-reform interests are created sooner); affected parties have more warning of the need to adapt; vested interests have less opportunity to block change; and reform enjoys higher political profile and commitment. Producing an integrated package of reforms also facilitates balancing of multiple policy objectives and interests. Comprehensive reform still requires an effective mechanism for monitoring and implementing reform, because reform may produce unforeseen results that will require adjustment and response.

In contrast, experience in other countries suggests that piecemeal approaches tend to be unplanned and unpredictable. They usually address easy reforms first, even if the more difficult have the most impact. Hence, benefits are delayed. The result is delayed or even lost benefits, a rapid exhaustion of the political resources needed to sustain the process, and vulnerability to blocking or delaying by vested interests. Moreover, some reforms are nearly impossible to introduce gradually without careful and transparent advance planning. For example, it is difficult to manage a gradual evolution to full competition because that generally means there will be a mix of competitive and monopoly elements during the transition. Large investments in regulatory oversight and information will be needed. And private investors are usually reluctant to enter the market when reform is unpredictable and there are risks of reversals and delays. The move to comprehensive reform plans will reduce the risks of these kinds of failures.

Review of permitting and licensing requirements. One of the more damaging forms of regulation is the *ex ante* licensing or permitting requirement. These kinds of regulations increase investment delays and uncertainties, have disproportionate effects on SME start-up, and are very costly for public administrations to apply. Yet they are pervasive in OECD countries. Recent information from Member countries, though not checked for comparability, indicates that national governments implement the following numbers of permits and licenses:

Country	Number of *ex ante* permits and licenses required at national level (Notifications not included)
United Kingdom	312
Norway	348
Mexico	834
Hungary	1600
Finland	1 700-1 800
Portugal	2 225
Japan*	5 737

* Response for Japan does not include "weak" requirements such as notifications or reports.
Source: Responses to OECD survey on regulatory indicators, March 1998.

The 1998 deregulation programme continues the policy of moving away from licensing and permitting procedures in favour of *ex post* checking and this policy could lead to substantial change in the future in the market orientation of Japanese regulation.

The MCA has divided regulations into three varieties: 1) regulations of general effect that impose obligations or limit rights; 2) regulations that impose obligations or restrict rights through administrative decisions on specific cases; 3) regulatory administrative guidance. Regulation in category two – which includes a vast range of regulatory requirements, including licensing, permission, approval, tests, examinations, registration, reporting, attestation, certification, confirmation, retraction, supervision, and so forth – "represents the core part of public regulation" according to the MCA.[57]

Hence, this category has received considerable attention. In 1985, the Cabinet directed that the MCA should conduct an annual survey of such requirements; the first survey discovered 10,054. In 1987, following concerns expressed by the Second PCPAR about "the expansion of regulatory programs and lack of a built-in mechanism to curb and rationalise regulations"[58] ministries and agencies agreed to conduct internal regulatory reviews to reduce the burden of permission/authorisation and reporting systems.[59] Principles to be considered in the reviews included a check that new requirements are necessary for public welfare; that requirements have benefits, and burdens on applicants and government agencies are smaller than positive effects; coverage and requirements are the minimum possible to achieve objectives; and administration of permission/authorisation requirements are performed as much as possible by local entities or local branch offices of the national government. The 1988 "Guideline for Promotion of

Deregulation" also targeted these sorts of rules, and mandated that the MCA begin to publish in 1989 the results of the ministries'internal reviews. In 1990, a tougher stand was taken. The Second PCPAR recommended that permits and authorisations should be reduced "to essentially half their present level."[60]

Despite these reform efforts, the MCA survey of March 1990 found 10 581 permission/authorisation-type requirements, or a net increase of over 500 since 1986. The number of permissions and authorisations increased each year to 1993, declined in 1994 and 1995, but rose again in 1996 and 1997. According to MCA, the main reason for the increase was deregulation. Activities that had previously been forbidden or restricted were, after deregulation, permitted under certain conditions. These included relaxation of limits and prohibitions; and shifting activities from public to private ownership. Welding tests in nuclear facilities, for example, were shifted to private institutions that had to be certified.

Two other reasons put forward to explain the increase are: 1) New health, safety, environment and business laws required new permissions/authorisations. 2) The numbers do not reveal qualitative improvements, whereas progress has been made in reducing the burden of requirements. By 1990, ministries had reduced the burdens of most of the 500 requirements originally targeted. Some certification periods were extended, reducing the frequency of reporting. More importantly, the MCA noted, "the trend… as a whole can be said to be shifting from strong regulation to weak regulation".[61] Certain varieties of these regulations, particularly permission, approval, and licensing, have very restrictive effects, while "weaker" rules, such as reporting, are less restrictive. Increases have generally occurred in less restrictive requirements, while decreases occurred in the most restrictive. On net, then, these requirements became less restrictive, although the effect on the costs of compliance has not been quantified. An MCA official concluded that, although need and effectiveness were the focus of reform, the "emphasis on numbers has derailed the main point of interest".[62]

5. CONCLUSIONS AND POLICY OPTIONS FOR REFORM

5.1. General assessment of current strengths and weaknesses

Regulation in Japan has for decades been part of an economic management policy that had its high point in the 1960s, and that may have helped elevate Japan to the ranks of the richest and most equitable countries in the world. Regulatory reform is only the latest of many profound policy shifts that the Japanese have faced in their remarkable ascendancy, and it is likely that, in the end, the Japanese government will seize the nettle and succeed with regulatory reform.

Tremendous effort has produced real progress in reducing economic intervention in many sectors where consumers have seen results – among them, large retail stores, gasoline imports, telecommunications, and financial services. Less dramatic but important progress has been made in areas such as increasing the efficiency of pervasive licenses and permits. There is slow but steady movement on many fronts toward more transparent and less discretionary regulatory practices, partly driven by market demands and partly by recognition of the gap between traditional and international practices. Compared to its predecessors, the 1995-1997 deregulation programme was the most successful yet, capitalising on the strength of a reform-minded PM and competitiveness pressures to win commitments to reform in key sectors. The 1998 programme is as yet untested.

While recognising the importance of the gains that have been made, the main point of this report is that the size and nature of the problem has been consistently underestimated. A far more encompassing view of the nature of reform – to include not only eliminating poor regulations, but also restructuring outdated institutions, changing incentives in public sector cultures, and moving the state toward service provision and away from economic management – is a precondition to progress of the kind needed to adapt Japanese regulation to the needs of modern society. The emphasis should be on improving transparency, accountability, and adaptability. With those kinds of reforms, the Japanese government will establish the basis for a dynamic regulatory system that will continue to adapt and meet new challenges into the future.

Experiences in Japan offer positive lessons for other OECD countries. One of the strengths of regulatory reform in Japan is that it has enjoyed high levels of political support, an essential condition for success. Political support may have suffered from the tendency to support reform in general but not in specifics, but the extent of personal involvement of a succession of prime ministers has been rarely equalled in other countries.

A second strength is that the framework of a potentially effective regulatory reform system is taking shape, piece by piece. Numerous mechanisms are in place to translate political support into action. These include the independent council system (currently, the Deregulation Committee of the Administrative Reform Headquarters); a flexible and expanding reform programme; articulation of a set of market-based principles for regulation to be applied by regulators in their day-to-day activities; building of reform expertise and capacities in the administration (particularly in MCA, MITI, and the EPA); oversight processes such as annual reports and a database of permits; adoption of an Administrative Procedure Act; and efforts to improve openness, especially with respect to informal regulatory instruments such as administrative guidance.

As one of the main points of regulatory reform, the reduction of unnecessary regulatory burden is essential. The capacities of the private sector freed from such burdens can be used for more constructive activities. Japan has long taken efforts to minimise the regulatory burden (including activities to eliminate unnecessary "sealing" for identification, to extend terms of validity of various licences or permissions, and to admit digital applications and reports). There is, however, still scope for improvement. Making more use of computers in administration, especially in providing information, would open new possibilities to minimise burden on citizens and would simultaneously contribute to enhancing transparency.

This progress is genuine, but it is too slow and reactive. The past 20 years have seen important shifts toward market-based decisions and integration with global markets, but the anti-competitive styles of regulation and the interventionist tendencies of the public administration have changed only marginally. Reform is still hesitant, piecemeal, and reactive, reflecting the "incrementalism" discussed in section I. Intervention by the administration into economic decisions continues on a scale rare in OECD countries, and these interventions are no longer based on any coherent view of the role of regulation in modern government or globalised market economies. There are still difficulties in persuading ministries of the benefits of reform. As the gap between market needs and regulatory rigidities grows wider, the regulatory system is weakening domestic and international competitive forces and contributing to a chronic misallocation of resources throughout the Japanese economy.

Importantly, the opportunity costs to good government of Japan's pervasive regulatory regimes should be understood. A number of public policy issues – from ageing populations to environmental protection – will require more attention from the government in coming years, yet costly regulatory functions are crowding out the capacities of the public sector to take action in other areas.

To improve public sector capacities for good regulation, three major challenges face Japanese reformers today. First, *the need to take bold and comprehensive action* justifies exploration of different strategies and reform institutions.

Second, the *need to rebalance the reform programme* between deregulation and good regulation, particularly sectoral governance and consumer protection, is urgent. The focus of the current programme is deregulation, which is indeed a considerable and necessary task. Yet good regulation based on market principles is also needed to address public policy concerns. Reform of the financial sector has vividly demonstrated that good regulatory governance is a vital component of the regulatory reform programme. Changing the structure of a network based industry such as electricity from monopoly to competitive markets requires a sophisticated regulatory structure. Consumer protection is another important concern. Many countries have neglected to install consumer protection regimes that work well in new market conditions, in areas ranging from taxis to health care to pension plans to food labelling. In some countries, abuses against consumers have caused backlashes against reform itself. This failure stems from the mistaken notion that market liberalisation means less of all kinds of regulation. On the contrary, in some areas it may mean more. For example, consumers faced with more choices may require more information and confidence-building measures. As in Section 1, we note that "small government" is an insufficient principle to guide regulatory reform.

Third, a sustained and multifaceted effort is needed to *embed good regulatory practices into the "culture" of the public administration*. Some of the reforms in the Basic Law for Administrative Reform of Central Government such as strengthening the policy capacities of the Cabinet, will greatly boost regulatory reform capacities in the government and reduce the risks of regulatory failures. A great opportunity for change lies in expanding the Basic Law for Administrative Reform of Central Government, and linking it more explicitly to regulatory reform. Professional and cultural change in the administration will not come easily. The policy reforms suggested below will require new training programmes, new skill mixes, and new funding in some cases. Leadership at the top will be essential to encourage risk-taking and innovation in the bureaucracy.

5.2. Policy options for consideration

The policy options below fall into three areas which are the most urgent priorities for improving the capacity of the Japanese government to produce high-quality national regulatory regimes:

105. *Capacities for reform* focus on building the organisational structures, policy, and legislative frameworks that are needed to drive and sustain effective reform. These include establishing institutions inside and outside the administration that cut across and challenge narrow interests in line ministries.

106. *Accountability* reforms work to make the administration accountable for its use of regulatory discretion and for the policy performance of regulation, measured against the objectives of regulation. They include clear definitions in policy and law of instruments and procedures that are permissible for government action.

107. *Transparency* reforms seek to improve the openness and accessibility of regulatory decisions by enhancing the public's participation in the regulatory process and, thereby, to also help strengthen accountability and regulatory quality

These policy reforms represent a balanced but far-reaching reform agenda that are intended to work together to produce a national regulatory environment that is, from cradle to grave, more transparent, accountable, and user-friendly for enterprises and citizens. The strategies recommended are in accord with basic good practices in other countries such as the United States and the Netherlands. If implemented, these reforms will change significantly the style and culture of Japan's public administration, and its relations with society at large. Some of the recommendations can be carried out quickly, while others would take some years to complete.

Included only marginally in these recommendations is the crucial dimension of the capacity of the judiciary to review administrative actions by the public administration. This is the missing link in the overall structure of interlocking institutions that together establish the incentives and pressures for high-quality administrative action. In most OECD countries, the ultimate check on administrative abuses is the potential for review and reversal by the courts under principles of administrative law. Such deterrence must be credible to be effective. Long-standing traditions of administrative discretion by public officials in Japan suggest that the courts will only gradually assume the oversight role needed to improve certainty and due process for the public. It is particularly important in Japan for the government and courts to provide an effective and practical judicial infrastructure for dispute settlement, since the government's role as mediator or arbitrator among interests should be eliminated as economic intervention is reduced.

For these reasons, serious reform to the judicial system to expand its capacities for review and reduce the costs and delays of private actions is essential if the policy reforms are to have their full effect The judiciary is, however, largely outside of the scope of this review, and hence we suggest only preliminary actions pending the actions underway in the current deregulation programme and the Basic Law for Administrative Reform of Central Government.

Strengthening capacities for reform

- *Current efforts to promote reform by the Deregulation Committee are important to further progress. Further strengthen the leadership of the Deregulation Committee by i) enhancing its capacity for independent and comprehensive reform recommendations through such means as putting it under the direct control of the Prime Minister or by giving it legal authority to make recommendations; ii) broadening its mandate to consider the full range of government policies – beyond a narrow definition of regulation – that impede competition in the sector under reform; and iii) expanding and strengthening the analytical expertise of the Committee's Secretariat as an interim step to creating a permanent office on regulatory reform responsible to the prime minister...*

The work of the Deregulation Committee is central to regulatory reform and should continue while ways of strengthening it are considered. First, the need for enhanced independence from the ministries is paramount to enable the Committee to play a leadership role in making decisive and bold recommendations. There are various ways to strengthen the independence of the Committee. Such independence will help offset sluggishness, delay, and inefficiencies in regulatory reform, which will increasingly penalise Japan as the pace of globalisation and innovation steps up. It is interesting that lack of policy responsiveness and flexibility is also a problem in the United States, although there it is due, not to the search for consensus and mutual accommodation as in Japan, but to excessively adversarial and procedural policy styles. In both countries, however, the role of the central reform unit is critical to driving change.

Second, the Committee should be given a broader mandate to examine all government policies and instruments that have the effect of impeding competition in the sector under reform, as recommended by the Prime Minister's Economic Strategy Council in February 1999. Third, the Deregulation Committee requires expert advice in developing recommendations, and a stronger role in overseeing implementation of recommendations. This requires an expert secretariat with cross-government views. Rather than creating in the short-term a permanent unit to advise the prime minister, such as exists in the United Kingdom (the Better Regulation Unit) and the United States (the Office of Information and Regulatory Affairs), we suggest as an interim step strengthening the independence, policy authority, and analytical expertise of the Secretariat for the Deregulation Committee, which already has representation from major centre of government ministries. Its personnel should be drawn largely from non-regulatory ministries to enhance its "challenge" function; it should have sufficient financial resources to collect and assess information and buy the expertise of private think-tanks and scholars; and its role in the government's legislative and regulatory procedures should be formalised. In the longer-term, the government should consider creating a permanent advisory and analysis body on regulatory reform that is responsible to the prime minister.

The Secretariat would assist the Committee in designing thematic and sectoral programmes of reforms, coordinated across all relevant policy areas. The Secretariat would incorporate performance targets, timelines and evaluation requirements, and would advise the Committee on the likely impact of reform proposals made by regulating Ministries. Representation by the Ministry of Finance would improve coordination of regulatory reform and budget proposals (see below). Inclusion of economic policy and analysis agencies is intended to establish an independent centre of economic analysis to support the Committee's policy advice, and analytical expertise to oversee greater use of regulatory impact analysis in decision-making. Inclusion of the FTC is intended to ensure that competition principles are kept foremost in the reform programme.

- *Adopt principles of good regulation based on those accepted by Ministers in the 1997 OECD Report on Regulatory Reform. Eliminate all "supply and demand adjustment regulations" by a specified date.*

The regulatory principles in the current deregulation programme are clearer and closer to international best practices than those in previous programmes. The explicit use of market principles is a good step. Yet significant gaps remain in defining the dimensions of regulatory quality, such as the principle that all regulations shall have a sound legal basis, and that regulations shall only be adopted if costs are justified by benefits. Competition principles should be strengthened in the overall policy framework. For example, an overarching principle that "supply and demand adjustment regulations" should be phased out government-wide by a specified date could greatly speed up action in eliminating these anti-competitive policies, as compared to case by case study and recommendations.

- *Follow up regulatory reform decisions with implementing budget and organisational decisions.*

Regulatory reform in some OECD countries operates hand-in-hand with budget offices because many reforms require changes to institutions, personnel, and budgets in the public sector. It is important that reform decisions are coordinated with and reflected in subsequent budget decisions. The cabinet, with the advice of the Deregulation Committee, should advise MOF, MCA and the National Personnel Authority on budget and personnel changes whether reductions or increases are needed to carry out regulatory reform plans in the relevant areas.

- *Regulatory reform should be expanded and accelerated through development of comprehensive sectoral reform plans containing the full set of steps needed to introduce effective competition, followed by rapid implementation and periodic, public evaluation.*

The OECD Report reads, "Regulatory reform should be guided by coherent and transparent policy frameworks that establish concrete objectives and the path for reaching them… Such programmes will both enhance the credibility of reform, and reduce the costs of reform by signalling to the wide range of potentially affected interests what is to come. The emphasis on broad programmes is deliberate, since the likelihood of success is increased by including at the outset the full mix of policies needed to gain full benefits of reform".[63] Japan's traditional "item by item" approach to regulatory reform – based on a series of actions that aim to remove regulatory restrictions one by one, but with no clear strategy or end-point for introducing competition into the sector – has resulted in partial and delayed benefits to consumers. Such review processes work better in analysing individual regulations than in understanding interactions between a group of regulations affecting an economic or social sector, having a cumulative and overlapping impact, originating from different agencies or even different levels of government. These linkages are often not analysed. At the end, this seems a review process focused on pruning each tree rather than improving the health of the forest.

Japan's Big Bang approach in the financial sector demonstrates the effectiveness and speed of more comprehensive sectoral plans based on all policy measures needed for results, including regulations but also other forms of intervention such as subsidies, procurement policies, and tax policies. The "reinvention" of sectoral regimes – based in part on international benchmarks – allows reformers to consider policy linkages and related measures needed to make reform effective, to package related reforms into a coherent programme, and to reassure market entrants that reform is credible and predictable. Adopting reform steps in law, as opposed to leaving the timing or steps to the ministries, will further strengthen the accountability, credibility, and sustainability of reform.

The comprehensive reform strategy will raise some trade-offs and additional difficulties, however. Moving forward quickly on a broader front may require more attention to design of transitional programmes that reduce opposition to change. And a comprehensive plan will require reformers to cut across a partitioned and segmented government structure, which will increase transactions costs and upfront delays.

- *Implement across the administration a step-by-step programme for regulatory impact assessment, based on OECD best practice recommendations, for all new and revised regulations. The analysis should begin with feasible steps such as costing of direct impacts and qualitative assessment of benefits, and move progressively over a multi-year period to more rigorous and quantitative forms of analysis as skills are built in the administration, and should be made public as part of notice and comment procedures.*

There is no explicit commitment to the use of regulatory impact assessment in the current reform programme, though the revised programme of 30 March 1999 calls for ministries to "work toward" improving their accountability for the impacts of regulations. This is a useful step that should pave the way for a decision to implement RIA as soon as possible to bring Japan up to international good practices. Two thirds of OECD Member countries now use RIA and the direction of change is universally toward refining, strengthening and extending the use of RIA disciplines. RIA can be a powerful tool to boost regulatory quality by giving policy officials information on which to judge if a regulation is necessary, or if there are better alternatives. Lack of information on impacts means that regulations are vulnerable to influence from special interests and less transparent to outside parties. OECD's best practice principles, in part already reflected in the new Environmental Impact Assessment law, should be the basis for a RIA programme, overseen by an appropriate quality control body with analytical expertise at the centre of government, to ensure that a minimum and consistent level of analysis is applied to new regulatory proposals. While benefit-cost analysis may be a long-term goal, interim steps feasible with current administrative skills, such as user panels and surveys, could be implemented quickly.

Another significant omission from the current programme is its failure to promote the use of market based alternatives to regulation in those areas where regulation is justified. Mention of alternative mechanism is largely restricted to the enunciation of a principle of moving away from prior authorisation procedures in favour of *"ex post facto* checking". The OECD Report on Regulatory Reform[64] documented significant movement toward a range of alternative instruments in numerous Member countries and pointed to evidence on gains in policy effectiveness being achieved. Consideration of alternatives could be gradually built into a RIA programme as the public sector gained familiarity with alternative policy tools.

Enhancing accountability

- *Improve regulatory accountability by* i) *defining in a revised Administrative Procedure Act permissible regulatory activities and providing standardised administrative and legal remedies for those aggrieved by administrative action;* ii) *establishing further checks on non-permitted forms of administrative guidance by standardising legal due processes for those abused;* iii) *defining the limits of ministry action in the foundation laws and laws delegating regulatory authorities to the public administration, and* iv) *separating regulatory from policy and industry promotion functions in key infrastructure sectors.*

The current reorganisation of the national government provides a valuable opportunity to address fundamental legal, institutional and cross-cutting regulatory issues not addressed elsewhere.

First, it should be a high priority to define by law a limited set of administrative actions with regulatory effects that are permissible and a minimal set of procedures by which they are to be used, including the rules for delegating regulatory powers to other levels of administration or to non-governmental bodies public consultation, registration, review, and impact assessment. It is also necessary to ensure that aggrieved parties have effective access to a standard set of administrative remedies, through standardised dispute settlement mechanisms, and legal remedies, through judicial review, for parties wishing to appeal administrative actions. While a range of formal procedures exist in Japan, they should be used more effectively. Bringing the backlog of existing administrative actions into conformity with any new quality standards – potentially a tremendous task – can be done over time in a phased approach during the establishment of the central regulatory registry recommended below, and during the comprehensive sectoral reviews recommended below.

Second, "administrative guidance", already abolished by law in certain forms as incompatible with transparent regulation, is not consistent with a market-led growth strategy in Japan. While some progress may have been made in curtailing the use of the coercive forms of guidance, the difficulty of monitoring the use of administrative guidance suggests that strong deterrence is needed, and standardised appeals processes through tribunals or the courts – if their capacity review administrative actions is enhanced – seem to offer the most credible approach.

Third, ministerial mandates and regulatory powers should be more closely defined in law to avoid abstract powers such as protecting the "public interest".[65] There are two complementary approaches. First, the foundation law of each of the new ministries is being revised as part of a reduction in the number of ministries. Clearer definitions of the responsibilities and missions of the ministries in the Foundation Laws, including the requirement that the ministries avoid unnecessary constraints on competition, would improve political oversight by the Cabinet and the Diet and provide the basis for a more consistent approach across the government to the balance between consumer and producer interests. Second, clear definition of policy objectives and regulatory authorities should be included in each law delegating regulatory power.

Fourth, as noted in Section 3.1.3 above, many accountability, transparency, and competition problems in sectoral regulation result from lack of institutional clarity about the source, powers, and purpose of regulation. There is no single organisational model that can be recommended across countries – and it is not yet clear that the new Financial Supervisory Agency offers a model for other sectors in Japan – but functional separation should aim at boosting the expertise of regulators; establishing clear performance criteria for the regulator based on maximising consumer welfare in the sector; improving the transparency of regulatory actions; and putting at arms-length any intervention by political officials and policy bureaus into specific regulatory decisions. The expertise and permanence of the staff is of paramount importance, since one of the purposes of this reform is to improve policy stability and reduce reliance on the regulated industry for expertise. Care should be taken to avoid "colonization" of new regulatory bodies by existing ministries, such as through the practice of rotating staff through short-term assignments. This will require attention to personnel and recruiting policies for the new bodies.

Improving regulatory transparency

- *Ensure the effective implementation of public comment procedures, and standardise procedures for openness for the advisory councils.*

Japan has made significant efforts to include a wide range of parties in consultations on regulatory reform. The public notice and comment procedures announced in October 1998, and expected to become effective from April 1999, represent a major step forward. In the procedures, the government is required to make public information on regulations under consideration and give the public an opportunity to comment on it. The new procedures should open regulatory decision-making to a broad range of interests for all significant regulation. It will be supported by the opening of advisory council deliberations which is now underway, with 73% of councils having adopted opening measures. New policies in these areas should include the provision of better information, based on a robust RIA requirement, during the consultation process and the adoption of standard openness procedures for advisory council deliberations. Adoption of notice and comment procedures will also permit a central unit, such as the secretariat of the Deregulation Committee, to review new ministerial regulations against the principles of good regulation.

- *Establish a centralised registry of all regulatory requirements.*

A single authoritative source for regulations would significantly enhance transparency for users in terms of the content and form of permissible regulatory actions, and force a rationalisation of ministry rules. Many OECD countries are adopting new registry requirements, and are using the opportunity to review existing regulations against quality standards before including them in the registry. Some countries have found that "positive security" further increases confidence in the market and reduces search costs for businesses and citizens ("positive security" means that regulations must be included in the registry to have legal effect, which ensures against non-compliance by ministries). *Improve transparency by extending requirements for transparency to non-governmental bodies with delegated regulatory authorities.*

A form of regulation widely used in Japan is that of "co-regulation", or sharing of regulatory functions between government and industry or other bodies. This has been implemented predominantly through trade associations, public corporations, and non-profit organisations. Such industry based regulatory and enforcement systems can have major benefits in terms of cost and effectiveness, but in many countries such bodies have used this role to limit competition and increase incomes and, hence, consumer prices. The incentives that exist for rent-seeking require that governments carefully supervise the use of such delegated regulatory powers.

It is useful that the APA applies to non-governmental bodies with regulatory powers. As part of the 1998 programme's review of "non-governmental restrictions in the private sector", it would be useful to further develop clear governmental guidelines on the use of regulatory powers by non-governmental bodies. A similar recommendation has been made for the Netherlands. Issues include the representation of independent "public interest" advocates, the review role of competition authorities, and the need for specific legislative authorisation of regulatory powers, as well as transparency standards. This is especially important as international market openness develops. Guidelines would improve the transparency of these non-government bodies, enhance their accountability to government and the public, including consumers, and maintain market openness.

5.3. Managing regulatory reform

In some cases, the success of regulatory reform will depend not only on the policy content of the reform, but also on the strategy, pace, sequencing, accompanying targeted policies, and transitional arrangements for reform.

The Japanese experience suggests communication strategies should accompany the policy reforms suggested above. An important determinant of the scope and pace of further reform is the attitude of the general public, and here priority-setting and balance are important. A high priority to motivate support for reform is to deliver visible benefits to consumers, as reform of the Large Scale Retail Store Law did when discount stores began opening in greater numbers. In the business community, deep cleavages over regulatory reform provide an opportunity to build a constituency for reform. This suggests that urban consumers and export-oriented industries will be the two major reform allies. Reforms aimed at their interests – such as in important upstream industries, and areas where consumers can quickly see large price reductions – should come first. Evaluation of the impacts of reform and communication with the public and all major stakeholders with respect to the short and long-term effects of action and non-action, and on the distribution of costs and benefits, will be increasingly important to further progress. Here, the evaluation mandate for the Economic Planning Agency will be important.

Equally important is a balanced reform programme emphasizing both deregulation to allow market forces more space, and better regulation to protect consumers, health and safety, and the environment. At this juncture, it seems that fears about the effects of reform on levels of protection have not been borne out, but continued reform will proceed faster and more deeply if reformers take concrete steps to demonstrate that protection has been maintained.

NOTES

1. World Bank (1993), pp. 157-188.

2. Among the many examinations of the role of the State in Japanese economic, social and political development see, for example, Calder, Kent E (1988), and Richardson, Bradley (1997).

3. Commission on Administrative Reform (1995).

4. Hollerman, p. 243.

5. Lincoln, Edward (1998), Chapter 4 in Gibney, p. 61.

6. Final Report of the Administrative Reform Council (Executive Summary), December 3, 1997.

7. Hollerman (1988a), p. 245.

8. Tanaka, Kazuaki and Masahiro Horie (1990), preface.

9. Tanaka, Kazuaki and Masahiro Horie (1990), p. 1.

10. Commission on Administrative Reform (1995), p. 4.

11. Keidanren (1995).

12. Hashimoto, Ryutaro (Prime Minister) (1996), "Policy Speech to the 136th Session of the National Diet," 22 January, Tokyo (unofficial translation, Ministry of Foreign Affairs).

13. Commission on Administrative Reform (1995), p. 1.

14. Administrative Management and Reform in Japan, MCA, (1991), pp. 21-22.

15. Attachment 1 to a decision by the Provisional Council of the Promotion of Administrative Reform, 23 January 1991.

16. OECD (1997), p. 37.

17. OECD (1995).

18. "For the Promotion of Deregulation Aimed at Economic Revival and the Establishment of a Transparent System of Governmental Management" Keidanren submission to Government of Japan, 20 October 1998.

19. Lincoln, Edward (1998).

20. Deighton-Smith, Rex (1997), p. 221.

21. From 1981 to the present, six successive councils have been created in the Prime Minister's Office: the Provisional Commission for Administrative Reform (PCAR), which worked from 1981-1983, followed by three Provisional Councils for the Promotion of Administrative Reform, which worked from 1983-1986, 1987-1990, and 1990-1993 (referred to as First PCPAR, and so forth). The Administrative Reform Committee worked from 1995-1997. The current council is called the Deregulation Committee.

22. Interview with officials of the MCA by the OECD Secretariat, February 1992.

23. Administrative Management and Reform in Japan (1991), p. 123.

24. Written response to OECD from Government of Japan, June 1998.

25. Tanaka, Kazuaki and Masahiro Horie (1990), p. 9.

26. Shindo, Muneyuki (1982), p. 130 and Sato, Isao. (1982), p. 38.

27. "Submission by the Government of the United States to the Government of Japan Regarding Deregulation, Competition Policy and Transparency and Other Government Practices" Office of the United States Trade Representative, Executive Office of the President, November 7, 1997.

28. "For the Promotion of Deregulation Aimed at Economic Revival and the Establishment of a Transparent System of Governmental Management", Keidanren submission to Government of Japan, 20 October 1998.

29. Lincoln, *op.cit.*

30. Isomaru, E. and M. Kuronuma (1974), "Gendai Nihon no Gyosei", Teikoku Chiho Gyosei Gakkai, Tokyo, as quoted in Terasawa, Katsuaki and William R. Gates (1997), "Better government versus less government: Relationships

between government and economic growth in Japan and other nations", *International Public Management Journal*, Vol. 1, No. 2, published on the Internet.

31. IIAS Tokyo Round Table Organizing Committee (1982), p. 23.

32. Speech by the Prime Minister, at the first meeting of the Third Provisional Council for the Promotion of Administrative Reform, 31 October 1990.

33. Harrop, Martin (1992), p. 236.

34. See Shiono, Hiroshi (1982), pp. 221-235, from which much of the material for this section is drawn.

35. Bingman, Charles (1989), p 82.

36. Neary, *op. cit.*, p. 127.

37. Shiono, *op. cit.*, p. 229.

38. Hollerman, Leon (1988*b*), p. 131.

39. Harrop, Martin (1992), p. 63.

40. Press release from the Japanese Ministry of Finance, 8 June 1998.

41. Institut International d'Administration Publique (1997).

42. Reported in Jacobs, Scott, *et al.* (1997).

43. Prime Minister P.J. Keating (1994), "Working Nation: Policies and Programs", 4 May, Canberra, p. 37.

44. See Richardson, p. 124, and Upham, Frank (1991), pp. 323-34.

45. Wright, Vincent (1989).

46. "For the Promotion of Deregulation Aimed at Economic Revival and the Establishment of a Transparent System of Governmental Management", Keidanren submission to Government of Japan, 20 October, 1998.

47. OECD (1992): The councils have the discretion to operate in either public or closed session.

48. Jacobs, Scott (1995), "Building Regulatory Institutions in Central and Eastern Europe", Proceedings of the OECD/World Bank Conference on Competition and Regulation in Network Infrastructure Industries, Budapest, 28 June 1 July 1994, Paris, OECD, pp. 301-317. See also Majone, Giandomenico (1996), *Regulating Europe*, Routledge, London.

49. Japan's Environmental Protection Policy, Environment Agency, Government of Japan, 1997, p. 7.

50. OECD (1994), p. 104.

51. *Op. cit.* p. 113.

52. *Op. cit.* p. 95.

53. OECD (1997), Paris.

54. This discussion is drawn from "Recent Progress on Environmental Impact Assessment in Japan" (English version), Ministry of Foreign Affairs, 1998.

55. Prof. Junko Nakanishi, Professor of Environment, Yokohama University, quoted in International Environmental Reporter, Vol. 20, No. 13, June 25, 1997.

56. The 15 new and growth fields targeted in Japan's 1996 Action Plan for Economic Structure Reform are: Medical care and welfare; Quality of life and culture; Information and telecommunications; New manufacturing technology; Distribution and logistics; Environment; Business support; Ocean; Biotechnology; Improvement or urban surroundings; Aviation and space; New energy sources and energy conservation; Human resources; Economic globalisation; and Housing.

57. Administrative Management and Reform in Japan (1992), p. 131.

58. OECD (1989), p. 48.

59. The November 1987 agreement "On the Examination and Periodic Review of New and Existing Permissions, Authorizations, Etc." committed the ministries and agencies to vigorously review both new and existing permission/authorisation regulations. This agreement was later adopted by the full Cabinet.

60. Final Recommendation, supra fn 11. This goal was reiterated by the Third PCPAR in its 1992 recommendations.

61. Administrative Management and Reform in Japan (1992), p. 136.

62. Interviews with the OECD Secretariat, February 1992.

63. OECD (1997), p. 38.

64. Jacobs, Scott *et al.* (1997), pp. 220-222.

65. See, for example, telecommunications regulation as discussed in Takigawa, Toshiaki (1998).

REFERENCES

Bingman, Charles (1989),
Japanese Government Leadership and Management, St Martin's Press.

Calder, Kent E. (1988),
Crisis and Compensation: Public Policy and Political Stability in Japan, Princeton University Press.

Commission on Administrative Reform (1995),
"Opinions Concerning the Promotion of Deregulation – Towards a Resplendent Country", 14 December, Tokyo (provisional translation in mimeo).

Deighton-Smith, Rex (1997),
Regulatory Impact Analysis: Best Practices in OECD Countries, OECD, Paris.

Hashimoto, Ryutaro (Prime Minister) (1996),
"Policy Speech to the 136th Session of the National Diet" 22 January, Tokyo, (unofficial translation, Ministry of Foreign Affairs).

Harrop, Martin (1992),
Power and Policy in Liberal Democracies, Cambridge University Press.

Hollerman, Leon (1988a),
"Whither Deregulation? An Epilogue to Japan's Industrial Policy" in *Unlocking the Bureaucrat's Kingdom: Deregulation and the Japanese Economy*, ed. Frank Gibney, The Brookings Institution, Washington DC.

Hollerman, Leon (1988b),
"Japan Disincorporated: The Economic Liberalisation Process", Hoover Institutional Press.

IIAS Tokyo Round Table Organizing Committee (editor) (1982),
Public Administration in Japan, Tokyo.

Institut International d'Administration Publique (1997),
Faut-il codifier le Droit ? Expériences comparées, June, Paris.

Jacobs, Scott, *et al.* (1997),
"Regulatory Quality and Public Sector Reform" in *The OECD Report on Regulatory Reform: Sectoral and Thematic Studies*, Vol. 2, Paris.

Keidanren (1995),
"Proposals for the Annual Revision of the Regulatory Reform Action Program", 12 October, Tokyo.

Lincoln, Edward (1998),
"Deregulation in Japan and the United States: A Study in Contrasts" in *Unlocking the Bureaucrat's Kingdom: Deregulation and the Japanese Economy*, ed. Frank Gibney, Chapter 4, The Brookings Institution, Washington DC.

OECD (1989),
Directory of Regulatory Review and Reform Organisations in OECD Member Countries, Paris.

OECD (1992),
OECD Country Profiles: Japan, Paris.

OECD (1994),
OECD Environmental Performance Reviews: Japan, Paris.

OECD (1995),
"Recommendation of the Council of the OECD on Improving the Quality of Government Regulation", OCDE/GD(95)95, Paris.

OECD (1997),
The OECD Report on Regulatory Reform: Synthesis, Paris.

Richardson, Bradley (1997),
Japanese Democracy: Power, Coordination, and Performance, Yale University Press, New Haven and London.

Sato, Isao (1982),
"Cabinet and Administrative Organization" in *Public Administration in Japan*, edited by Tokyo Round Table Organizing Committee, International Institute of Administrative Sciences.

Shindo, Muneyuki (1982),
"Relations between National Government and Local Government" in *Public Administration in Japan*, edited by Tokyo Round Table Organizing Committee, International Institute of Administrative Sciences.

Shiono, Hiroshi, (1982),
"Administrative Guidance" in *Public Administration in Japan*, edited by Tokyo Round Table Organizing Committee, International Institute of Administrative Sciences.

Takigawa, Toshiaki (1998),
"Impact of the WTO Telecom Agreement on US and Japanese Telecommunications Regulations" forthcoming in the *Journal of World Trade*.

Tanaka, Kazuaki and Masahiro Horie (1990),
"Privatization and Deregulation: The Japanese Experience", *mimeo* by Administrative Inspection Bureau, Management and Coordination Agency.

Upham, Frank (1991),
"The Man Who Would Import: A Cautionary Tale about Bucking the System in Japan", *Journal of Japanese Studies* 17.

World Bank (1993),
The East Asian Miracle: Economic Growth and Public Policy, Washington, DC.

Wright, Vincent (1989),
The Government and Politics of France, Unwin Hyman, London.

BACKGROUND REPORT
ON THE ROLE OF COMPETITION POLICY
IN REGULATORY REFORM[*]

---

[*] This report was principally prepared by **Michael Wise** in the Directorate for Financial and Fiscal Affairs of the OECD. It has benefited from extensive comments provided by colleagues throughout the OECD Secretariat, by the Government of Japan, and by Member countries as part of the peer review process. This report was peer reviewed in October 1998 in the OECD's Competition Law and Policy Committee.

OECD 1999

TABLE OF CONTENTS

Executive Summary

Background Report on The Role of Competition Policy in Regulatory Reform

Competition policy should be integrated into the general policy framework for regulation. Its principles and analysis provide a benchmark for assessing the quality of economic and social regulations, as well as motivate the application of the laws that protect competition itself. Competition ideas are central to Japan's newest reform plans. Yet competition has historically played a subordinate role in Japan's regulatory policies, and aspects of Japan's traditional interventionist approach to regulation, such as controlling and guiding investment and permitting cartels, contradicted principles of modern competition policy. The attitude toward competition policy in Japan is changing. Reform steps and programs Japan has undertaken or announced would erode anti-competitive regulatory habits. Efficiency, investment, and innovation in the economy – as well as consumer welfare – will be boosted by measures such as eliminating supply-demand balancing as a justification for controlling entry, eliminating statutory exemptions from the general competition law, and eliminating implied exemptions accomplished by administrative guidance.

The need for strong competition policy in Japan will be even greater in future. As regulatory reform stimulates structural change, vigorous enforcement of competition policy is needed to prevent private market abuses from reversing the benefits of reform. Japan's Fair Trade Commission, one of the oldest and largest competition law agencies in the world, wields a wide array of substantive and procedural tools. But the FTC was relatively inactive for much of the period before the 1990s, although it was quite active in the 1970s. It was unable to prevent a generation of anti-competitive regulation that at one time explicitly exempted over a thousand cartel agreements from its jurisdiction. That situation has been changing since 1990, in part because concerns raised by trading partners have reduced resistance to the FTC's efforts. The FTC's resources have increased and competition enforcement has intensified, especially in traditional industrial and distribution sectors. In sectors that have been more directly regulated, such as transport and utilities, the FTC has employed study groups to develop policy ideas and recommendations. A test of the seriousness of competition policy will be whether the FTC can move into these areas, which have long been the preserve of specialised sectoral ministries, with effective law enforcement.

The conception of competition that the FTC is increasingly using to apply Japan's basic competition law is a radical change from the conception of managed, orderly accommodation that characterises much of Japanese business and the traditional government-business relationship in Japan. That dissonance implies that reform based on modern competition principles will be difficult. The FTC has adequate legal power, but at times it has been less than aggressive in using that power.

The success and sustainability of the current regulatory reform efforts depend strongly on better integration of broad-based competition principles into regulatory policies and on stronger application of competition principles through public and private enforcement action. FTC remedies should be supplemented by more effective and credible means for injured parties to obtain judicial relief directly. The FTC should be further strengthened, especially in legal and economic resources necessary to increase its enforcement activity, and other enforcement methods, including criminal sanctions against practices such as bid-rigging, should be pursued vigorously. Sectoral ministries should be responsible for helping to establish conditions for effective competition in the industries under their purview (perhaps through revision of the foundation laws), and for co-ordinating with the FTC to ensure effective enforcement (rather than protecting industries against enforcement action). And the government must follow through to eliminate exemptions from the general competition law, to eliminate administrative guidance that tolerates cartels, and to eliminate supply-demand balancing as an acceptable justification for controlling entry.

1. THE CONCEPTS OF COMPETITION POLICY IN JAPAN: FOUNDATIONS AND CONTEXT

For most of the post-war era, the principal goal of Japan's economic policy has been development and growth, and free competition has sometimes been seen as inconsistent with that goal.[1] Competition policy has been treated as a species of regulation, not an organising principle for the economy. Relative priorities are reflected in the prestige of the institutions responsible. Competition policy was assigned to a separate agency, independent of the government but politically not strong enough to promote its policies effectively, while the ministries that regulate industry and investment, and that have historically encouraged non-competitive practices, were more powerful. Japan's economic success now makes it possible, indeed imperative, to shift policy goals from "catch-up" development to consumer welfare. The competition agency is responding to this change by redirecting its own efforts, to concentrate on practices that impair efficient markets. The rest of the regulatory apparatus needs to follow that course too, as it is presented in the current deregulation programme, which recognises that growth can no longer come through direction from the centre, but must result from the self-reliant risk-taking of competitive enterprises.

The goals of the principal competition statute could serve as statements of purpose for regulations and policies about competition generally. The competition law's stated goals are "to promote free and fair competition, to stimulate the creative initiative of entrepreneurs, to encourage business activities of enterprises, to heighten the level of employment and people's real income, and thereby to promote the democratic and wholesome development of the national economy as well as to assure the interests of consumers in general".[2] Six goals or objects can be identified: free competitive processes, fair market outcomes, private innovation, economic growth (including business expansion, greater employment and higher incomes), political democracy, and consumer welfare. The statute itself offers little basis for balancing among them, but a leading judicial authority has said that the last two goals are the "ultimate purpose" of the law, implying that the others are subsidiary or supplemental.[3]

The formal deregulation program links competition policy to regulatory reform, without narrowing the selection of potential goals for competition policy. The 1998 Programme announces an overall purpose "to create a free and fair socio-economic system which is fully open to the world and based on the rules of accountability and market principles". Although the Programme's opening summary does not use the term "competition" the actual elements of the Programme include many that implement or rely on competition policies.

In Japan's traditional approach to market competition, fair treatment has been as important as free processes. In all settings, the term "competition" is typically accompanied by both "free" and "fair". The competition agency has considered fair competition to be as indispensable as free competition. Widespread public concern to protect the value of fairness thus supports this aspect of the competition agency's actions. The statutory definition of "competition" concentrates on process and immediate effects on particular businesses. "Competition" for most purposes, is a state in which firms can sell similar goods or services to the same consumers, or get similar products from the same supplier, "without undertaking any significant change in their business facilities or kinds of business activities".[4] Such a definition would encourage assessing competition in terms of how conduct diverges from "business as usual" rather than in terms of economic concepts such as excess profits, allocative efficiency, or innovation.

Preserving competitive industry structures by preventing high concentration has been a concern of competition policy, although the statutory purposes do not include it in those terms. At an operational level, many rules for assessing the competitive effects of conduct are structure-based. Until recently, the approach to mergers appeared to be basically structural. The most striking structural preoccupation was the ban on holding companies, which was only recently repealed. That ban, which followed the steps to break up the wartime *zaibatsu*, was probably also considered consistent with the goal of promoting "democratic and wholesome" development.

The goal of protecting consumer welfare appears increasingly. This goal may explain one aspect of traditional enforcement practice. Cartels that protect firms against losses in downturns have been tolerated,

---

Box 1.   Competition policy's roles in regulatory reform

In addition to the threshold, general issue, whether regulatory policy is **consistent** with the conception and purpose of competition policy, there are four particular ways in which competition policy and regulatory problems interact:

- Regulation can **contradict** competition policy. Regulations may have encouraged, or even required, conduct or conditions that would otherwise be in violation of the competition law. For example, regulations may have permitted price co-ordination, prevented advertising or other avenues of competition, or required territorial market division. Other examples include laws banning sales below costs, which purport to promote competition but are often interpreted in anti-competitive ways, and the very broad category of regulations that restrict competition more than is necessary to achieve the regulatory goals. When such regulations are changed or removed, firms affected must change their habits and expectations.

- Regulation can **replace** competition policy. Especially where monopoly has appeared inevitable, regulation may try to control market power directly, by setting prices and controlling entry and access. Changes in technology and other institutions may lead to reconsideration of the basic premise in support of regulation, that competition policy and institutions would be inadequate to the task of preventing monopoly and the exercise of market power.

- Regulation can **reproduce** competition policy. Rules and regulators may have tried to prevent co-ordination or abuse in an industry, just as competition policy does. For example, regulations may set standards of fair competition or tendering rules to ensure competitive bidding. Different regulators may apply different standards, though, and changes in regulatory institutions may reveal that seemingly duplicate policies may have led to different practical outcomes.

- Regulation can **use** competition policy methods. Instruments to achieve regulatory objectives can be designed to take advantage of market incentives and competitive dynamics. Co-ordination may be necessary, to ensure that these instruments work as intended in the context of competition law requirements.

---

while cartels that have tried to raise prices (or raise them too much) have been targeted, and not just by the FTC.[5] The FTC's efforts against resale price maintenance are also motivated by concerns about high consumer prices.

Economic growth has not, until recently, been recognised as a principal goal of competition policy, despite the statutory instruction. Instead, competition and growth were treated as inconsistent through much of the post-war period.[6] Principally because of concerns about growth, and secondarily because of concerns about fairness of market outcomes, other policies and interests have often trumped competition policy. This effect has not been confined to situations in which other social interests and values justify controls on business behaviour. Rather, competition policy has yielded to interests in ensuring stable supply or even protecting or promoting specific industries. The statute identifies developing the national economy and benefiting consumers as separate goals, implying that there might be trade-offs between them and that they might not always lead to the same policy decisions.[7] Promoting economic development is listed first.

Ambivalent views about the effects of competition are found in many countries. In Japan, scepticism may be reinforced by aspects of the culture and society. There is little reason to think that basic business incentives differ fundamentally between Japan and other market economies. Businesses everywhere need to make some profit (though the profit levels demanded in Japan may be lower than elsewhere), and businesses generally recognise that profits can be increased by collusion or exclusion.[8] But in Japan, cultural features such as emphasis on group cohesion, suspicion of individual difference, and concern to avoid personal embarrassment may further encourage collective action and help explain why the government has done so much to manage risk and suppress supposedly "excessive" competition throughout the economy.[9] Concerns about business and market stability, that more competition and less regulation will lead to job losses, are also commonly encountered in other market economies, but they seem unusually deep in Japan. Not only Japanese businesses, but Japanese consumers, are reportedly willing to pay higher prices, believing that the non-competitive system that produces them is somehow more stable, secure, and fair than a competitive market would be. Recognising Japanese cultural attitudes toward competition policy is important in assessing what direction policy and reform may take, because most of the formal structures implementing competition policy, as well as many proposals to reform those structures, were borrowed from, or imposed by, others. In the Japanese setting, those borrowed or imported forms may perform differently.

The idea of using cartels to manage investment, and to alleviate the pain of economic contraction, took hold in Japan during the post-war recession in 1905. Cartels had first appeared in the 1880s. There was no law against them, but they did not proliferate. The few formal cartels did include large export industries, though, such as spinning. When the Japanese government encouraged formal cartels in the 1920s, it followed the model of Germany. From 1920s through WWII, cartels were not only tolerated but officially sponsored and even required. Although there were some objections, most officials, businesses, and academics approved the idea of central direction. No foundation was laid for an anti-cartel competition policy.[10]

In the post-war US occupation, cartel policy reversed. The new antimonopoly act and the new legal structure against cartels, like the old laws that had promoted cartels, were largely imports from elsewhere. The substantive law was modelled closely on the US Sherman and Clayton Acts. The enforcement structure was modelled on the US FTC. The imported policy did not enjoy support in the business community, and it was politically vulnerable. When the occupation ended, the AMA was cut back in 1953, by eliminating the separate law controlling trade associations, eliminating the *per se* violations, and authorising relaxation of enforcement by permitting resale price maintenance and recession or rationalisation cartels. Aspects of that cutback followed a foreign model, too, namely a then-current proposal to allow depression cartels in the German competition law. But a further effort to vitiate the AMA almost completely in 1958 was defeated. Business and ministry interests in non-competitive solutions were countered then by support for the FTC from consumer, labour and agricultural groups.[11]

Although it did escape complete repeal, competition enforcement slept through most of the 1950s and 1960s, when the competition law went essentially unenforced.[12] "Competition" policy in many sectors became centrally guided investment and a proliferation of explicit exemptions and implicit guidance. Rivalry was controlled and focused on lowering costs and improving productivity in ways that stimulated export trade. Entry was subject to government supervision, as the government, not the market, took on the task of assessing the likely balance of supply and demand.

But the FTC continued to hold out the idea of promoting the competitive process. By the early 1960s, the law and the agency had enough of a record to begin to be taken more seriously as a Japanese institution, not an imported foreign one.[13] The FTC opposed some proposals to increase government direction and permit very large mergers, for example. But it was not until the end of the 1960s that the FTC tried to block a merger that another ministry promoted. It was not until the 1970s that the FTC used the law's criminal sanctions against price fixing, in response to the oil shocks. The FTC followed this increased enforcement effort with proposals for major amendments to strengthen the law. Most of these were adopted in 1977: surcharges from cartels, countermeasures against "monopolistic situations" reports on parallel pricing in oligopolies, stronger controls on aggregate concentration, and stronger remedies and fines generally. But other ministries also received new powers to guide industries through restructuring, and in the early 1980s the FTC's efforts to attack cartels were blunted by political pressures.[14] Despite the strengthened competition law, FTC enforcement retreated again. In the 1970s, the FTC took an average of 34 formal actions per year; in the 1980s, the average was 11. (Some observers believe that the stronger remedies actually led to the lower enforcement statistics, because businesses responded to the greater risk by destroying documents and thus making it harder for the FTC to prove violations.)[15]

Competition enforcement has revived again in the 1990s. The revival, like the original competition law itself, can be traced to pressure from abroad. This time, it was claims, in trade disputes with the US, that lax competition law enforcement gave Japanese firms unfair trading advantages while tolerat-

193

ing restraints on competitive imports. Whatever the merit of those claims, the response from Japan was a number of explicit commitments to increase the resources and the visibility of competition enforcement. Many of these represented changes that the FTC had long been advocating. The FTC was an object and active participant in the negotiations. At their conclusion, the Japanese government committed to increasing enforcement against exclusionary cartels, to greater reliance on more formal, public methods of enforcement and prosecutions, and to increasing attention to competition issues in the distribution system and in inter-corporate *keiretsu* groups. The FTC has increased its formal enforcement activity, strengthened its guidelines about horizontal and vertical issues, modernised its merger standards, added to its staff and budget, and raised its profile in advising about competition issues at other ministries.

Despite the recent successes, competition policy remains an awkward import into Japan's business and government culture, and its long-term status remains uncertain. A recent analysis by Japanese and British scholars describes the FTC as "a unique and vulnerable agency administering deeply unpopular laws based on a widely rejected model of market competition" playing an "ambiguous and difficult" role, with a "huge gap" between its theoretical powers and its actual practice. The gap is closing, but "the renaissance of competition policy in Japan is recent, partial, and far from fully secure".[16]

The evolution of Japan's notions about competition policy, the variations in the intensity and content of that policy, and even the uncertainty about the present level of commitment are paralleled in other OECD countries' experiences, of course. In the Netherlands, for example, a corporatist tradition encourages mutual support and co-operation, and for a long time maintaining small and medium sized businesses inhibited the development of strong competition policy, especially clear rules against cartels. There, too, cartels were not just tolerated, but encouraged, until recently when a major step in the regulatory reform process reversed that course. And the new emphasis on competition law enforcement there has yet to face the test of economic downturn and reaction. The US's history shows the same kind of alternations as Japan's, even though the US social and political culture supports the value of competition more strongly. In the US, too, the adoption of the original basic laws from 1890 to 1914 was followed by backlash and retreat in the 1920s. In the Great Depression, the first response of US competition policy was to emphasise competition as fairness, including co-ordination through industry-specific trade practice conferences and guides. These strategies, and regulatory structures with similar goals, overstayed into the post-war era, and their obsolescence helped spark the major regulatory reform movement of the 1970s. Now Japan too may be facing up to the obsolescence of its traditional conception of the relative roles of regulatory direction and competition policy.

The terms of the current debate about regulatory reform in Japan show the continued difficulty in accepting a conception of competition as self-generated rivalry, rather than something that is controlled and even created from the centre. The 1998 deregulation programme mixes competition and control. One of its general goals is creating conditions for effective, fair competition. The programme calls for abolishing rationalisation and recession cartels, and it implies that competition policy will now be included among the responsibilities of industry ministries. Entry restrictions, and particularly the concept of regulatory supply-demand balancing, are to be reviewed, and the programme states that the eventual goal is to ease and even abolish them. But the programme also includes sectoral emphasis and directed investment toward sectors that are believed likely to be the growth industries of the future or otherwise have feedback effects on economic performance generally. While more exemptions from the competition law will be eliminated, ministries will still have the power to help industries respond collectively to economic shocks and to guide restructuring. If the review is delayed or weakened, some of the controls on entry will remain in place, either indefinitely or on a timetable that will take another 15 years to complete.

Despite this transition difficulty, Japan's institutions and traditions can support stronger competition policy as a modern, internationally-endorsed alternative to inefficient and ultimately destructive coddling of non-competitive firms and industries. To do so, it is necessary, and fruitful, to expand the institutional basis for competition policy, by enabling private parties to take more effective independent actions and by giving other authorities in the government additional responsibilities to protect and promote competition. Regulatory practices reflect cultures, so they will not change quickly. But a broader and deeper commitment to competition policy could lead bodies that were once responsible for directing investment and avoiding failure to take on the new task of invigorating market institutions and enabling more efficient ways to cope with change.

2. THE SUBSTANTIVE TOOLKIT: CONTENT OF THE COMPETITION LAW

If regulatory reform is to yield its full benefits, the competition law must be effective in protecting the public interest in markets where regulatory reform enhances the scope for competition. Japan's general competition law provides a generally adequate substantive foundation for reform based on market principles. The complexity of the substantive law and the institutional relationships with other ministries afford many resources, but also many complications, for the reform process. The principal problem is not the content of the law, but its application, and especially the multitude of ways, official and covert, in which competition can be evaded.

The basic source of substantive Japanese competition law is the Antimonopoly Act of 1947, as amended. The AMA prohibits unreasonable restraints of trade, "private monopolisation" and "monopolist situations" as well as unfair practices and anti-competitive mergers. It is supplemented by numerous regulations and guidelines, as well as other laws dealing with aspects of unfair competition, notably concerning contracting and misleading marketing methods.[17] But competition policy in the broader sense has been fundamentally affected by a myriad of special laws and exemptions, formal and informal, that have encouraged or tolerated cartels, mergers, and distribution controls that would have contradicted the spirit, if not the letter, of the basic AMA prohibitions. In the last few years, steps have been taken to clear these away in order to move toward a generally applicable, consistent policy of competition as the rule for business behaviour.

2.1. Horizontal agreements: rules to prevent anti-competition co-ordination, including that fostered by regulation

Anti-competitive agreements among competitors are treated as "unreasonable restraints of trade" prohibited by Section 3 of the AMA. The statutory definition includes all forms of horizontal contract, agreement, or concerted action that control price or limit production, technology, products, facilities, or customers or suppliers.[18] The basic sanction is an order to cease the offending conduct or to take corrective action.

For violations related to prices, including those that affect prices by restricting output, the most important measure is a "surcharge". Conceived as a confiscation of the violators' improper profits, the surcharge is a percentage of the sales during the period of the agreement. The basic rate is six per cent. Lower amounts are assessed against cartels in wholesale or retail trade or those involving small firms. The rate is fixed by statute and must be assessed, regardless of any other factors in the case or of the actual excess profits, whenever the FTC finds a price-related violation. The rate was increased in the early 1990s, from 1.5 per cent, to bring it more in line with the rates applied in similar circumstances in the EU and the US. It is still somewhat below the basic rates applied in other jurisdictions, though; moreover, those jurisdictions also consider the actual level of excess profits in a particular case. The FTC's lack of discretion, both in collecting the surcharge and in setting the rate, is thought by some to be an advantage in the Japanese context, because it makes the process less controversial.

Criminal penalties are also available. Under the AMA, fines and imprisonment may be ordered against restraints of trade generally.[19] In addition, the Criminal Code includes a sanction against bid-rigging involving public projects.[20] The FTC has announced a policy of applying criminal sanctions in the most egregious cases, of price or output cartels, market allocation agreements, bid-rigging and boycotts, that are likely to have a widespread influence on society or that involve repeat offenders or firms that

Box 2.   **The competition policy toolkit**

General competition laws usually address the problems of monopoly power in three formal settings: relationships and agreements among otherwise independent firms, actions by a single firm, and structural combinations of independent firms. The first category, **agreements**, is often subdivided for analytic purposes into two groups: "horizontal" agreements among firms that do the same things, and "vertical" agreements among firms at different stages of production or distribution. The second category is termed "**monopolisation**" in some laws, and "**abuse of dominant position**" in others; the legal systems that use different labels have developed somewhat different approaches to the problem of single-firm economic power. The third category, often called "**mergers**" or "**concentrations**" usually includes other kinds of structural combination, such as share or asset acquisitions, joint ventures, cross-shareholdings and interlocking directorates.

Agreements may permit the group of firms acting together to achieve some of the attributes of monopoly, of raising prices, limiting output, and preventing entry or innovation. The most troublesome **horizontal** agreements are those that prevent rivalry about the fundamental dynamics of market competition, price and output. Most contemporary competition laws treat naked agreements to fix prices, limit output, rig bids, or divide markets very harshly. To enforce such agreements, competitors may also agree on tactics to prevent new competition or to discipline firms that do not go along; thus, the laws also try to prevent and punish boycotts. Horizontal co-operation on other issues, such as product standards, research, and quality, may also affect competition, but whether the effect is positive or negative can depend on market conditions. Thus, most laws deal with these other kinds of agreement by assessing a larger range of possible benefits and harms, or by trying to design more detailed rules to identify and exempt beneficial conduct.

Vertical agreements try to control aspects of distribution. The reasons for concern are the same – that the agreements might lead to increased prices, lower quantity (or poorer quality), or prevention of entry and innovation. Because the competitive effects of vertical agreements can be more complex than those of horizontal agreements, the legal treatment of different kinds of vertical agreements varies even more than for horizontal agreements. One basic type of agreement is resale price maintenance: vertical agreements can control minimum, or maximum, prices. In some settings, the result can be to curb market abuses by distributors. In others, though, it can be to duplicate or enforce a horizontal cartel. Agreements granting exclusive dealing rights or territories can encourage greater effort to sell the supplier's product, or they can protect distributors from competition or prevent entry by other suppliers. Depending on the circumstances, agreements about product combinations, such as requiring distributors to carry full lines or tying different products together, can either facilitate or discourage introduction of new products. Franchising often involves a complex of vertical agreements with potential competitive significance: a franchise agreement may contain provisions about competition within geographic territories, about exclusive dealing for supplies, and about rights to intellectual property such as trademarks.

Abuse of dominance or **monopolisation** are categories that are concerned principally with the conduct and circumstances of individual firms. A true monopoly, which faces no competition or threat of competition, will charge higher prices and produce less or lower quality output; it may also be less likely to introduce more efficient methods or innovative products. Laws against monopolisation are typically aimed at exclusionary tactics by which firms might try to obtain or protect monopoly positions. Laws against abuse of dominance address the same issues, and may also try to address the actual exercise of market power. For example under some abuse of dominance systems, charging unreasonably high prices can be a violation of the law.

Merger control tries to prevent the creation, through acquisitions or other structural combinations, of undertakings that will have the incentive and ability to exercise market power. In some cases, the test of legality is derived from the laws about dominance or restraints; in others, there is a separate test phrased in terms of likely effect on competition generally. The analytic process applied typically calls for characterising the products that compete, the firms that might offer competition, and the relative shares and strategic importance of those firms with respect to the product markets. An important factor is the likelihood of new entry and the existence of effective barriers to new entry. Most systems apply some form of market share test, either to guide further investigation or as a presumption about legality. Mergers in unusually concentrated markets, or that create firms with unusually high market shares, are thought more likely to affect competition. And most systems specify procedures for pre-notification to enforcement authorities in advance of larger, more important transactions, and special processes for expedited investigation, so problems can be identified and resolved before the restructuring is actually undertaken.

have not adequately remedied past violations. The public prosecutor handles criminal cases. Criminal actions under the AMA require a prior referral by the FTC. The prosecutor may bring an action against bid-rigging under the Criminal Code independently, without such a referral.

The balance between anti-competitive and pro-competitive effects is at issue, at least to some extent, in all cases under the AMA. At first, the law included *per se* violations, but those provisions were repealed in 1953. To find a violation of Section 3, the FTC must show that the conduct substantially restrained competition in a particular field and that it was contrary to the public interest. The "public interest" test is defined narrowly, though, in terms of consistency with the purposes of the AMA. And the implicit requirement to define a market and assess effects has not prevented the FTC from applying a presumption that agreements affecting price have the requisite effects. For example, in its Guidelines, such as those for trade associations, agreements that affect price or restrict entry are described as violations "in principle" implying that they violate the law even if, in a particular case, they are not shown to have substantially restrained competition in a particular market. These violations "in principle" are contrasted with other kinds of conduct, which might be defended on the grounds that, in the particular case, there is no anti-competitive effect. The FTC evidently uses a market share test to estimate competitive effects. Restraints that affect less than half of the market are not likely to be found illegal; those that affect more than 80 per cent are presumed to be illegal; those in between depend on other factors.[21] (One horizontal practice, boycotts, is also treated as an unfair trade practice under a different section of the law, where effects on competition need not be shown in particular cases.) The potential for balance in particular cases should make the law sensitive to economically important factors and avoid perverse applications. On the other hand, an enforcement agency's burden is greater where it is necessary to show effects and meet a public interest test, and this greater burden may make it more difficult to apply the law to non-competitive arrangements that have enjoyed tacit or explicit support from other parts of the government.

The widespread attention to fairness among competitors complicates developing clear rules against anti-competitive co-operation in an industry. It can seem natural to set a standard of fairness based on common industry practice. Indeed, guiding an industry to that consensus has long been perceived as a legitimate government role. Thus, a pervasive competition policy problem has been government sponsorship or toleration of horizontal industry co-ordination, either by promoting and defending explicit cartels and market divisions, or by less direct means, from using trade associations as surrogates or tools for government regulation, to encouraging tacit co-ordination in oligopolistic industries, to administrative guidance that confirms and polices non-competitive consensus.

Bid rigging, now an enforcement priority, is a prime example of government-tolerated collusion. Bid rigging often enjoyed the tacit or even explicit support of government agencies soliciting the bids. Most cases have been brought as standard administrative actions, but criminal actions are increasing. A 1997 AMA criminal case against the 25 designated vendors of water supply meters, for rigging bids to the Tokyo Metropolitan Government, led to convictions of 25 companies and 34 employees. Fines totalled ¥ 155 million, and the employees received prison sentences of six to nine months, suspended for two years.[22] A 1995 FTC criminal accusation led to a 1996 conviction against nine electrical equipment manufacturers for rigging bids to the Japan Sewage Works Agency, with fines totalling ¥ 460 million and (suspended) prison sentences. In addition, the FTC assessed surcharges of ¥ 1 036 million.[23]

Development of more vigorous enforcement against bid rigging in the construction industry, which has exposed the FTC to considerable domestic political risk,[24] was aided by prodding and example. In the late 1980s, complaints about bid rigging for projects at US military installations led to comparatively minor penalties under the AMA. The FTC, which may have been constrained by statutory technicalities, ended up sharing some of its investigatory material with the complainant.[25] The threats of independent lawsuits that followed led to settlements that were substantially larger. In the Yokosuka Naval Base case, the size of the settlement – ¥ 4 700 million – implied that the conspiracy was twice as large as the FTC had found and the actual anti-competitive effect was 20 times greater. Since then, the sanctions have been stiffened and the FTC has been more aggressive.

Bid rigging exemplifies the difficult position that the FTC has had to work in.[26] For a century, it was common for a ministry to designate which firms it would accept bids from, and for those firms then to agree among themselves which one would win it. Consumer groups have protested the high taxes that pay for this system, but the high profits have also underwritten support from powerful politicians. Actions against construction industry problems, even generic ones, could be construed as attacks on leading politicians. In 1984, political maneuvering forced the FTC to issue guidelines about the construction industry that allowed information exchanges to continue, even though they declared that bid-rigging practices were illegal.[27] But a consensus for reform, which developed after the Shin Kanemaru scandals in the early 1990s brought down the LDP government, now supports the FTC's concentration on this problem. A measure of the FTC's revival is that the 1984 guidelines were replaced in 1994.

Under the current guidelines, agreements about who will win a bid, what the minimum bid will be, or how to divide bids all violate Section 3 "in principle" that is, the parties cannot defend by claiming their conduct did not impair competition. Other kinds of conduct, including exchanges of information, are considered "highly suspect" if they appear to be elements of an explicit or tacit agreement to rig a bid. The guidelines educate as well as expound. They include detailed discussions of the basic laws and explanations of what kinds of conduct are likely to be permissible as well as illegal, along with summaries of the FTC decisions on the points discussed. Not only has the FTC been educating the industry about its potential liability, but it has also been educating the agencies that solicit bids about what they can do to protect themselves. Some successes are reported: the city of Zama adopted a policy to discipline suspected bid-riggers, and applied that policy in its latest tender to save ¥ 700 million on a road project.[28]

Trade associations are a common source of competition problems, in Japan as everywhere else. There are about 15 000 registered national and regional trade associations. In retail trade alone, there are about 4 000, many of them organised by product. Trade associations have facilitated long-standing anti-competitive relationships, both within and among industries. Associations of firms in related industries have reached and policed complex exclusive-dealing agreements to prevent new entry and stabilise customer relationships.[29] Correcting their anti-competitive behaviour is made more difficult where, as in Japan, associations have close relationships with related ministries, which use the associations to achieve administrative objectives. Thus an association may try to defend its action by claiming that it was doing what another ministry told it to do. The FTC has found that a high proportion of violations by trade associations have some connection with government regulations or administrative actions.[30] A 1998 FTC survey of non-profit entities, many of them trade associations under the statutory definition found cause for concern about preventing innovation or excluding competitors at five out of the 32 entities that were involved in setting and enforcing product standards and certifications (for water treatment, medical services, power plant equipment, LP gas equipment, and batteries).

A separate section of the AMA deals specifically with violations by trade associations. It prohibits a trade association from substantially restraining competition, limiting the number of firms in a field of business, "unjustly" restricting how member firms can do business, or causing firms, including those that are not members, to engage in unfair practices.[31] Trade associations must report to the FTC when they are formed and when there are important changes in their organisation. The special trade association provisions are potentially broader and more general than the AMA's other prohibitions, but the remedies available are narrower. At one time, enforcement against horizontal violations emphasised the special trade association provisions, with the result that individual companies avoided sanctions and publicity about their violations. The introduction of surcharges changed that treatment, because surcharges against a trade association are levied on its members. And trade association cases are now being brought more under the AMA's general sections, in order attach liability to the member companies and their officers.

Here, too, the FTC has relied strongly on guidelines and education as well as enforcement. The 1995 guidelines on the activities of trade associations set out the law and applicable penalties in detail. The guidelines also set out a procedure for trade associations to consult with the FTC in advance about whether their plans comply with the law. Much of the FTC's trade association-related work is advice in response to these applications. Even though it is thus regulatory guidance, rather than enforcement, it may be effective in heading off problems. About 30 per cent of these applications disclose potential violations. Because this advice does not appear in formal case statistics, the FTC may not be getting enough credit for its work on these issues.[32] Still, there is no doubt that the problems remain substantial.

Ministries' reliance on administrative guidance to help industries control or prevent competition has been a contentious and difficult problem. Informal guidance is officially banned. The 1993 Administrative Procedures Act specifies the formalities that are necessary for administrative action. Ministry instructions and advice are supposed to be developed and issued formally and publicly. And the FTC has announced, in its 1994 guideline about the treatment of administrative guidance, that even formal administrative guidance may not be a defence to conduct that otherwise violates the AMA. Under the guideline, a firm's compliance with an administrative instruction that is issued properly and pursuant to a specific law authorising it will not expose the firm to AMA liability. But the firm's agreement with its competitors to facilitate compliance could nonetheless violate the law. Following guidance that is not based on specific law or regulation exposes a firm to liability that depends on the purpose, content and method of the guidance. In determining the risk of liability from following this kind of administrative guidance, the criterion is whether the guidance has a direct impact on market mechanisms.

Some of the purposes of administrative guidance, such as protecting public health, safety, and the environment, are not very likely to affect the market mechanism directly in ways that could lead to violation of the AMA. Other purposes are more problematic, such as stabilising prices, ensuring fairness and transparency in business transactions, and protecting small business. And guidance for the purpose of preventing excessive competition, adjusting supply and demand, compensating for advantages or disadvantages among firms, maintaining order in an industry, or preventing prices from falling would obviously meet the "direct impact" criterion. Concerning content, guidance about business techniques, quality, standards, advertising, and representations may not necessarily have a direct impact on the market, even though these subjects are important means of competition. But guidance that could restrain firms' choices about entry, price, output, and investment is likely to have a direct and potentially problematic effect. Both concerning purposes and content, the FTC's guidelines about administrative guidance tolerate a good deal, perhaps to signal the agency's reasonableness and to emphasise its seriousness about the hard-core topics it wants to target. As for methods, these guidelines echo those about trade associations, in holding that guidance whose effectiveness depends on a trade association co-ordination or even on recognised tacit interdependence is also likely to have an impermissible effect. Significantly, a large proportion of the illustrative examples in these guidelines too are about trade associations.

Efforts to control anti-competitive administrative guidance point in the right direction, but it is not clear how much effect they are having. The FTC's guideline was issued in 1994, but there have only been two cases since then in which the FTC has found violations of the AMA where firms were evidently following informal administrative guidance. The 1998 deregulation programme instructs ministries to consult with the FTC in advance to ensure that removal of anti-competitive regulations is not thwarted by their replacement with the equivalent in the form of administrative guidance. This instruction would only deal with guidance achieved through explicit, overt regulation and decision. Covert, implicit guidance is also a serious concern. Despite the FTC's pronouncement that co-ordination sanctioned by informal instructions and advice violates the AMA, parties may be reluctant to call in enforcement action against it, for fear not only of their own exposure to liability, but more importantly of antagonising competitors, suppliers, or ministries with which they must maintain ongoing relationships. Covert, implicit guidance is more difficult to address than conduct pursuant to formal guidance. It is much more difficult to prove, and the relevant conduct may be difficult to attack legally. Anti-competitive effects might be achieved without culpable private action and without much ministry instruction. Relaxing a regulation in order to permit entry may be ineffective in promoting competition, if all potential entrants heed the informal warning of a powerful ministry to stay out. That appears to have happened in some transport and finance sectors. The result is equivalent to a boycott, yet there is no one to sue.

Despite these difficulties and complications, the fifty years of experience under the AMA has produced complex, flexible doctrines that appear capable of handling post-reform competition problems adequately. The absence of statutory authority for a strong presumptive rule against price fixing and bid rigging might make enforcement more difficult. The FTC has compensated, though, by developing and announcing such a rule *de* facto in its guidelines. This approach seems to enjoy judicial support, perhaps because of the locution, describing the forbidden conduct as anti-competitive "in principle" rather than illegal *per se*. In any event, enforcement actions proceed against bid rigging with evident success. Where the application of the law is mainly administrative, and administrative assessment of surcharges is the main remedy, the statute's requirement to show effect can be met without great procedural burden or cost.

The law is adequate, and the supplementary guidelines issued in the last few years are highly useful additions and supplements. The FTC has demonstrated it can do serious analysis of modern competition issues. But a good basic law and capacity for good analysis will not, by themselves, establish a good competition policy. Competition policy in Japan suffered from the appearance of political weakness, reflected in reluctance to take on such major and obvious competition problems as long-standing cartels in basic materials. There are very encouraging signs that this reluctance is being overcome. The FTC's renaissance was launched by extracting enormous financial sanctions from the cement industry in 1991, followed by challenging the cartels' enforcement mechanism of interlocking exclusive dealing agreements in 1995. But there is more to be done, for not every industry has received the message that the FTC is serious. A foreign academic reports that steel industry executives tell him that they are fixing prices, but that the industry does not expect the FTC to stop it.[33] The FTC has announced a policy of stronger action against the most serious cartel problems, but it has made only a few criminal referrals. What is needed now is more energy and focus on enforcement.

2.2. Vertical agreements: rules to prevent anti-competitive arrangements in supply and distribution, including those fostered by regulation

Japan's distribution sector is widely considered to be inefficient and non-competitive,[34] and anti-competitive distribution constraints have inhibited market access.[35] The body of laws and regulations governing distribution relationships are more than adequate to deal with competition problems. Again, the issue is not the quality of the competition law and regulations, but the strength of enforcement and of regulations or other practices that contradict them.

Several parts of the statute address distribution issues. The principal statutory foundation is the ban on unfair trade practices in Section 19. This provision is separate from the ban of unreasonable restraints on competition in Section 3, which has been limited almost entirely to horizontal relationships. (The FTC has taken the position that exclusionary group boycotts can be unreasonable restraints, as well as unfair practices.) The principal differences in the treatment of unfair practices, compared to unreasonable restraints, are that for unfair practices there is no "effects" test in particular cases, and the available sanctions do not include criminal penalties or surcharges. (Some vertical relationships might also be covered by Section 3's ban on "private monopolisation" if the party imposing a vertical restraint has market power; that would make criminal penalties available, but would require showing effects and meeting the "public interest" test.) The law about unfair practices is regulatory, set out in lists of specific practices in Section 2(9) of the AMA and a General Designation issued in 1982, as well as some industry-specific rules. These are supplemented by an extensive guideline about distribution systems and business practices issued in 1991. One practice, resale price maintenance, is considered an unfair practice and is also treated by a separate section of the law. The special provision serves mostly as a device under which the FTC may permit resale price maintenance for certain commodities. For all violations except those few that might be treated under Section 3 of the Act, the principal sanction is a cease and desist order.

The substantive standard for identifying a violation of section 19 is that the practice is "unjust" and that in turn is measured by its tendency to affect competition adversely. The FTC has tried to give the general term some content by distinguishing among different kinds of injustice and effects on different aspects of competition. The AMA describes six basic classes of unfair trade practice, each defined in terms of dealings between businesses: discrimination, pricing, inducing or coercing other businesses' customers, dealing on terms that restrict the others' business activities, using bargaining power, or interfering in another business's transactions or management. Some practices are presumptively illegal. To others, a broad rule of reason analysis applies. And for others, whether they are "unjust" is evaluated in the light of the industry's normal practices. Competition is said to be "fair" when three conditions are met. One is a free competitive process among competitors. Another, described as fairness of competitive method, is that competition is centred on price, quality and service. This condition is potentially problematic, for although it could be used to stop deception, it could also be used to stop innovation. Finally, the "basis" for free competition must be maintained, meaning that transactions are based on free and voluntary decisions.

These principles have been elaborated through complex rules – 16 in the basic 1982 General Designation, supplemented by dozens more in the 1991 distribution system guidelines that followed the SII negotiations. Treated most severely are collective refusals to deal, "unjust low price sales" and resale price maintenance, which are all considered presumptively unfair. Practices subject to a wider-ranging rule of reason analysis include individual refusals to deal, discrimination in price or terms, exclusion from a trade association, cornering a market (by paying too high a price), deception, tying, exclusive dealing, and inducing breach of contract or otherwise interfering with competitors' transactions or corporate governance. And practices whose fairness, and hence legality, is determined in light of normal business practice in the industry include inducing customers by offering benefits and using unequal bargaining power to compel favours from long-term suppliers or customers.

The FTC has tried to prevent distribution constraints from diminishing gains from reform. For example, the FTC took action against mobile phone companies' efforts to maintain retail prices through trademark-based marketing restrictions. The restraints included requiring agencies to sell trademarked phones at the same price that the supplier's own outlets charged, or simply at pre-set retail prices, and to include those pre-set retail prices in their advertisements and store displays.[36] These constraints may have been intended to prevent resellers from bundling the price of the phone in a service contract. Not only would that bundling make it more difficult to enforce a horizontal agreement about the price of the phones themselves, but also keeping the price of mobile phone service high would have made it the technology a less effective competitor to the traditional wire-line monopoly.

And the FTC has taken some actions to keep import markets open. In products from ice cream to pianos, distributors trying to control parallel imports of trademarked products have found themselves guilty of unfair practices under the AMA. Actions such as these have the short term effect of reducing the brand premium for some consumer products and reducing the effect of global price discrimination. But if they undermine efficient exclusive dealing arrangements that were entered to bring new products into a market, the long term effect may be to reduce, not expand, market openness. At least, these actions call for sensitivity to market effects, not formalism.

One aspect of the law about vertical relationships is being re-examined. The FTC continues to limit the exemptions from the ban on resale price maintenance. A few years ago, these included such things as non-prescription medicine for general use and 14 items of cosmetics with a price of lower than ¥ 1 030. Under the last deregulation plan, the FTC moved to abolish the exemptions on all of these items. As in other OECD countries, Japan confronts a particularly thorny problem in the treatment of resale price maintenance for copyrighted works. The FTC has held public meetings, collected comments from interested parties, and commissioned a report from a study group. The study group found few reasons supporting the continued exemption and recommended moving toward repealing this exemption, too.[37] The move to replace pervasive *ad hoc* exemptions with generally applicable rules is welcome. It may reinforce the move to eliminate similar *ad hoc* exemptions affecting horizontal conduct, where the anti-competitive effect is more serious. Some other OECD countries are re-examining the wisdom of *per se* treatment for vertical practices, and thus may be moving toward the kind of treatment Japan normally gives most such practices. As for resale price maintenance, in Japan's situation retaining a strong rule may be a necessary concomitant of strengthening horizontal competition and discouraging exclusionary boycotts.

2.3. Abuse of dominance: rules to prevent or remedy market power, especially arising from reform-related restructuring

The AMA contains three tools that can be applied to the problem of dominance, but they have not been applied effectively to restructuring network monopolies, nor to other commonly encountered competition problems that arise in the course of that restructuring. Along with unreasonable restraints, the law prohibits "private monopolisation".[38] This term refers to substantial restraints of competition accomplished by a single firm (or by firms acting together) through overtly exclusionary or controlling conduct. But the provision has almost never been used. More often, the FTC has taken action against abusive tactics and exclusionary practices by treating them as unfair practices, probably because the standards of proof are less demanding. Many unfair practices could also be treated as private monopolisation if dominance or market power were present. Indeed, for many unfair practices, liability depends on a rule of reason analysis. Finally, the law empowers the FTC to break up monopolies, without regard to whether they have engaged in monopolising practices.[39] In theory, this power might have been used to restructure network monopolies. But the process is subject to demanding requirements. The FTC must find that divestiture would not increase costs too much by undoing economies of scale, nor undermine the monopoly's financial position and thus impair its international competitiveness. And there must be no alternative sufficient to restore competition. The divestiture power was added in the 1970s, but it has never been used.

The FTC has not tried to apply the AMA's rules to the conduct of deregulating monopolies. The unfair practices rules about discriminatory pricing and refusal to deal might, in principle, address access problems that typically appear in the wake of deregulating network infrastructure industries. The FTC believes those rules would be applicable and vows that it will take necessary measures against private monopolising and unfair trade practices in deregulated sectors. But the FTC has not done so yet, and its view of the law's potential may be too sanguine. In utilities, sector regulators typically have competition-type powers, limiting the role of the AMA. These industry specific regulators will continue to supervise anti-competitive behaviour, especially concerning claims of discrimination and access. The FTC is likely to play a role only in the wholly deregulated parts, such as mobile telephones, and perhaps a limited, supplemental role about infringement of access rules that are set by others.

No use has been made of the AMA's existing tools to restructure monopolies in the course of deregulation. The AMA sets demanding hurdles, both to justify the use of structural remedies and to support a finding of a "monopolistic situation". One condition of the statutory definition is a market share over 50 per cent "in Japan".[40] The Guidelines applying this definition have interpreted it to provide only for national markets.[41] For purposes of the AMA, the Guidelines thus do not consider the possibility of monopolies at local scales. By contrast, the proposed guidelines for mergers, interpreting similar but not identical statutory language,[42] clearly recognise that markets can be local. In addition to the problems of doctrinal complications, though, political support for applying the AMA to restructuring is evidently lacking. As for dealing with access problems, some observers believe that the AMA will not be useful in network industries unless an explicit "essential facilities" rule is added to it, as Germany has recently done.

2.4. Mergers: rules to prevent competition problems arising from corporate restructuring, including responses to regulatory change

If cartel co-operation is prohibited more effectively, then even more mergers are likely. Thus, it is of highest importance that the substantive rules applied to mergers be up-to-date and transparent, and that they be applied sensitively yet firmly. The FTC has taken steps over the last few years to make more complete public explanations of the decisions it reaches and to bring its analytic methods up to date. Until recently, there were few cases or public explanations of how decisions have been reached, encouraging the conclusion that merger policy concentrated on structural issues. The law prohibits mergers whose effect may be substantially to restrain competition in any particular field of trade. (A merger could also be illegal, if unfair methods were used in effecting it.) The law covers complete and partial acquisitions of businesses and assets and other kinds of structural combination. Now, all such transactions are subject to pre-notification requirements, regardless of size. That will soon change, though. The FTC has also received annual reports on share ownership from all Japanese businesses with assets over ¥2 billion; that, too, is changing. Historically, the most important law about structure was the prohibition against holding companies. This complete ban has been eliminated as of the end of 1997.[43]

Merger enforcement procedures are unusual. Companies normally consult with FTC before even making a pre-merger filing. If the FTC advises, informally and non-publicly, that it has concerns, then the parties either correct the problem or abandon their plans. So the FTC has virtually never challenged a merger that was the subject of an actual filing. The FTC contends that problems are always resolved before the filing is even received.[44] There has been only one contested case in the FTC's history. In such a process, the FTC acts more like one of the sectoral ministries, as a regulator rather than a law enforcement body, exercising power through its discretion to grant or withhold permission according to standards that are matters for its own judgement.

The standards applied to merger decisions have emphasised structure, though they also include other factors for consideration. The 1980 guidelines identify the kinds of transactions that would get "closer examination". Under those guidelines, special scrutiny applied to a transaction if the merged firms would have a market share over 25 per cent or become the largest firm and have a market share over 15 per cent (or larger by more than a quarter of the market share of the second or third largest firm), or if it involved a top-three firm in an industry in which those top three firms had a share together over 50 per cent; or if there were only seven or fewer other competitors in the industry.[45] Reportedly, the FTC has typically examined closely transactions that would lead to firms with market shares much greater than 20 per cent. Much depends on how the markets are actually defined and on the application of more sensitive analysis of market conditions. The 1980 guidelines, which concentrate on market share, rank, and concentration, include no protocol for defining markets. They do list other factors to be considered when the FTC investigates more closely. But it has been difficult to understand how these criteria are applied in practice, because of the lack of public decisions.

New guidelines are being developed. The FTC requested public comments on proposed guidelines in 1998. These would move toward the position that the FTC has actually taken in some recent matters. Virtually all of the detailed structure-based criteria would be eliminated, except for some to characterise safe-harbours. Transactions would not be challenged if the resulting firm will rank below first in the market and its share would remain below 25 per cent, provided that the market is not oligopolistic (the guidelines' illustration is an industry where the top three firms' combined share remains below 70 per cent) and entry is easy.[46] And the revised guideline would explain analytic methods used to define markets or assess entry, tying them to descriptions of how the FTC has treated other merger cases. The new guidelines would also make clear that the FTC will be concerned about vertical effects such as foreclosure through exclusive or closed trading relationships.

The amended holding company law and the FTC's guidelines for applying it also now take a more modern approach to structural issues. A holding company can still be illegal if it is too large, if it combines large financial and non-financial enterprises, or if it includes large, highly interrelated firms in several industries. The rules for the first two types are based on total assets, and apply to combinations with assets over ¥15 trillion. Only the last type, which could apply to smaller groups, includes a criterion based on market definition or share (sales share over 10 per cent, or among top three in industry). But the legal standards include a test related to competitive effects, because a condition of "excessive concentration" is interference with the promotion of free and fair competition.[47]

The FTC has tried to respond to criticism, that its merger decisions offer no guidance, both through its proposed new guidelines and by issuing public statements describing its decisions. A recent description of a merger decision based principally on the potential competitive effects of imports shows the FTC's current approach. (This transaction is also used as an illustration in the new guidelines). The FTC did not challenge a petrochemical merger that produced market-leading shares in seven basic products. For most, the FTC found there was sufficient potential for import competition, although little actual imports, to dismiss the possibility of domestic effects. The FTC's summary of the case does not indicate what the FTC thought the world market shares or entry conditions were, but the "domestic" shares ranged as high as nearly 60 per cent. The reasons for finding no competitive concern varied for the different products, and included substitution potential, excess domestic production capacity, technological displacement, declining sales, internal consumption, and existence of another large firm as a competitive counterweight. The FTC concluded that overall, the proposed merger would not substantially restrain competition. Somewhat inconsistently, though, the FTC found that the potential for imports would discipline the market against competition problems, yet also called for a reduction in import duties to ensure a competitive environment.[48]

In banking, the FTC found that a merger would not impair competition, although it exceeded the 1980 guidelines' structural thresholds. In paper, a combination of a leading manufacturers and was approved, despite high market shares in some products, such as medium grade non-coated printing papers (about 35 per cent) and leading shareholdings in the top two distributors. The FTC accepted a settlement in which the parties agreed to shift capacity to other products to reduce their share of the paper market, and to reduce the shareholding in the distributors (leaving the combination as the largest shareholders, but with holdings equal to the next-largest one).[49]

The FTC's summaries do not describe any mergers or acquisitions in deregulated industries. Industry specific regulators still have power over transfers of licenses, and so *de facto* merger control authority. It would probably be difficult for the FTC to block an anti-competitive merger that a regulator wants to permit.

Economically sensitive merger policy could facilitate larger-scale reforms. One of the weaknesses of Japan's historic competition policy has been the tolerance of cartels as responses to depression or the need for rationalisation. Permitting mergers rather than cartels, especially when they involve financially weak firms, might be a faster and more efficient way to shift assets to more productive uses as economic and technical conditions change. Of course, these mergers, which are harder to undo than cartels, must not be allowed to create monopolies or erect barriers to new entry after conditions improve.

Until recently, lack of transparency has impaired the credibility and effectiveness of FTC merger enforcement. The process has not produced public explanations of how the law is being applied. Without that information, it is difficult to assess how well the FTC is doing it. Communications and decisions happen during purely informal contacts and negotiations. At that stage, there is no public, official proceeding of any kind, not even a pre-merger filing. Companies advise about their plans on the understanding that their communications are confidential. In those circumstances, the FTC would need their permission to disclose its action. The new guidelines, and the FTC's new practice of publishing summaries of some leading matters, should help. At least, companies are now on notice that their pre-filing contacts may eventually lead to some public disclosure. That might reduce the number of prior consultations and perhaps increase the number of filings that are publicly challenged. That could mean committing more resources to merger matters, but it could also lead to more public discussion of merger standards and perhaps even to judicial treatment of them. Those could both be significant benefits.

Several issues that arise in regulatory contexts would particularly benefit from clearer rules. One is the treatment of failing firms. The 1980 guidelines say that financial health and prospects will be taken into account, although they do not say how. A good explanation would encourage substituting sensitive merger control for the soon-to-be-eliminated recession cartels. The new guidelines would state that competition problems are likely to be limited, if the debt burden of one of the companies is too great, so that it can no longer finance operations and there is a high probability of bankruptcy and exit in the near future. Another issue where more explanation would be valuable is the treatment of efficiencies. The new guidelines would consider the positive impact on competition from improvements in efficiency, but they imply that these considerations will be given more weight when they help a lower-ranked company compete more effectively with a top-ranked one. And a third issue is the relationship between competition analysis and the policies and decisions of other, sectoral regulators. Some of those regulatory ministries have effective power to authorise or veto mergers in their industries, so the FTC's authority over those transactions under the AMA may not be practically significant. The FTC has evidently not used its consultation process to require changes in proposed mergers in regulated, or recently deregulated, sectors.

Some reforms of the AMA's other structural provisions have already been adopted or are underway. The change in the holding company law is perceived as a major reform. In addition, the investment and merger reporting systems are being revised. A 1998 bill, based on a 1997 FTC study group report, would change the scope of the obligation to report stockholdings, by raising the asset threshold from ¥ 2 billion to ¥ 10 billion (these thresholds, and those below, combine parents and subsidiaries), limiting the need to report changes, and eliminating reports about interlocking directorates and non-company holders. A modern merger notification system is also being adopted. Now, all mergers, regardless of size, must be notified. Under the new system, the requirement would apply only to mergers and acquisitions in which one party's total assets exceed ¥ 10 billion and another's exceed ¥ 1 billion. Other procedures would be spelled out, concerning deadlines and FTC requests for additional information. The merger reporting requirements could apply to transactions in foreign countries, but only if there is a subsidiary or business office in Japan with annual sales over ¥ 1 billion. The amendments, which also extend substantive jurisdiction to mergers involving foreign firms, became effective 1 January 1999.[50]

These reforms have been promoted as necessary for Japanese corporations to be able to restructure themselves flexibly and quickly and move into new businesses. These changes thus are seen as "deregulation" in the AMA itself. The holding company law was a symbolic battlefield for many years. The FTC endorsed the change after decades of bitter resistance. Now that the battle is over, it is difficult to understand what was really at stake. Changing the AMA may not have been the most critical factor in enabling holding company restructuring, as businesses are concerned about solving taxation and corporate law issues. The Ministry of Justice is working on amendments to the Commercial Code, to make holding company restructuring efficient. But the FTC's support signalled that it was no longer resisting the business community on this issue, and that it was itself willing to make accommodations of its traditional positions, in the interest of reform.

2.5. Competitor protection: relationship to rules of "unfair competition"

Much of Japanese's substantive competition law appears in the detailed rules about unfair trade practices. Some of the rules set out conventional competition law applications, while others, about deception, abuse of bargaining power, and interference with contract or other business relationships, are classic unfair competition issues. Here, as elsewhere, "free" is conjoined with "fair". All of the rules are, literally, about protecting competitors. The FTC contends that these rules protect the free competitive process and they are not applied to protect competitors, and its current applications appear consistent with sound competition analysis. The most common type of case appears to be against resale price maintenance, followed by refusals to deal in boycott situations.

The treatment of unfair practices represents a regulatory approach to competition policy, as contrasted to the law enforcement approach for restraints of trade and private monopolisation. When rules can be applied without a showing of economic or competitive harm in particular circumstances, then application can diverge from sound policy. Some old cases about "unfair" pricing suggest that happened at one time. The guidelines about unfair price cutting date from 1984. They prohibit pricing too far below cost for too long, if it might have a negative effect on other businesses. But actual effect need not be shown; the potential is enough and is nearly presumed. The relevant cost is the reseller's actual purchase price.

The fact that rules about practices in a specific industry must be adopted in consultation with the industry involved[51] implies that the process might be used to help industry co-ordinate, as well as to require it to compete. It reinforces the implication that the industry-specific rules are aimed first at achieving fairness among businesses, and second at preserving the competitive process for the benefit of the larger public. The FTC has tried in recent years to rely more on the general designations, but old "specific designations" still survive. Over the years, these have dealt with such topics as premium offers, labelling, wholesale-retail contract terms, newspaper pricing, textbook sales practices, competition and commercial terms in ocean shipping, and excessive lotteries.[52]

The "fair trade" tradition persists in the activities of the over 100 industry-based fair trade promotion associations. On the one hand, they serve to publicise the AMA and FTC policies. But they also provide forums for industry leaders and their legal experts to discuss guidelines about fair trade that some observers feel are not consistent with free trade. Discounters have complained that association activity has concentrated on preventing discounting and promotion, including violations of the special law about premiums that the FTC enforces.[53] Many of these organisations date from period in the 1950s and 1960s when the FTC was issuing industry-specific rules about fair competition.

In this area, the FTC itself is the principal regulator. The AMA's prohibition of unfair practices can be applied efficiently, for many of the rules do not require showing of particular effects, and businesses are less likely to resist enforcement because the sanction is limited to an order. This part of the law probably enjoys the strongest, widest support in the business community. It is thus unsurprising that the FTC has channelled most of its enforcement doctrine through this device (and the similarly efficient special provision about trade associations). And the efficiency and acceptance make it a plausible vehicle for consolidating the FTC's legitimacy and public image. Over the last several years the FTC has taken steps to reform its regulations about unfair practices. Its 1991 explanation of the rules covering distribution amounted to an effort to bring the regulations up to date and recognise how they should apply more sensitively to modern conditions, particularly market openness concerns that were raised in the SII negotiations. In 1996, the FTC revised the regulations applying the special law about the use of premiums and prizes as promotional devices, which is an instance of the "unfair practices" jurisdiction. The amendments permitted the use of somewhat larger prizes or lotteries, and eliminated some notification and administrative requirements.[54]

The FTC has not paid particular attention to unfair competition issues arising in deregulated sectors, except as these arise under more general competition rules. Business associations do not seem to be claiming any more that violations of their "codes of ethics" amount to unfair competition that the AMA should condemn.

2.6. Consumer protection: consistency with competition law and policy

Policy linkages between competition and consumer protection, although consistent and appropriate, are not institutionalised and hence are less effective than they could be as tools for reform. The FTC considers the AMA to be aimed at protecting consumer interests. And the basic consumer protection law, enacted in 1968, also mentions competition, calling for "necessary measures for regulating activities that unreasonably restrict fair and free competition concerning the prices of goods and services that are particularly important to the consumer life of the people".[55] In describing desirable competition as both free and fair, even the consumer protection law echoes the concern about fair play between businesses. The law goes on to provide for regulations indicating product quality and characteristics and for regulating "false and exaggerated indications". These dovetail well with the AMA's prohibitions of unfair practices, for one concern about misrepresentation is that it harms the honest seller as well as the misled buyer.

Institutional protections for consumers are weak, though. Consumer protection is under the aegis of the Economic Planning Agency, which is more of an advisory than an enforcement body. Consumer laws are being strengthened some. A new Product Liability Law took effect in 1995, and more protection for consumer contracts may be adopted. The "Consumer Protection Council" collecting many agencies with interests in these issues, has endorsed strict and impartial AMA enforcement as a means of creating conditions for helping consumers. Although this endorsement is certainly welcome, performance is more important. There seems to be no systematic co-ordination between consumer and competition issues and policies. The lack of clear co-ordination and mutual support mechanisms may represent a missed opportunity to promote an effective reform agenda. Consumer groups, although sometimes wary about how businesses might take advantage of consumer ignorance, and thus in some ways wary of regulatory reform, nonetheless recognise the benefits of greater choice and lower prices that come from more competition and market openness.

3. INSTITUTIONAL TOOLS: ENFORCEMENT IN SUPPORT OF REGULATORY REFORM

Reform of economic regulation can be less beneficial or even harmful if the competition authority does not act vigorously to prevent abuses in developing markets. In the 1990s, the FTC has re-emerged as an ambitious enforcer of competition-based policies. Whether it can maintain this role is the important question, and the timing is critical. On the one hand, the FTC can now show a record of vigorous enforcement as a tool for reform, to help the country emerge from its economic slump. On the other hand, the period of the FTC's revival corresponds to that same slump, and the FTC and the liberalising process may, fairly or not, end up being blamed for it.

3.1. Competition policy institutions

The FTC is a group of five commissioners, appointed by the Prime Minister subject to confirmation by the legislature. Administratively, it is attached to the Prime Minister's office. The FTC's work is done by a General Secretariat (upgraded from an Executive Office as part of a 1996 reorganisation), two staff bureaux and two departments.

The FTC was designed to act independently of the government or any ministry. Independence is reinforced by the Commissioners' tenure protections. They serve for five-year terms and may not be removed on the basis of policy disagreement. Independence is thus assured formally; however, the commissioners are not completely outside the political and government process. For one thing, commissioners and top staff are not outsiders. Rather, the choice of personnel shows that the FTC maintains long-term ties to the rest of the government. The Commissioners have traditionally been former officials from the Ministry of Finance (which was almost always the source of the Chairman), the central bank, MITI, and the Ministry of Justice, with one position also reserved for a senior career FTC official. These ministries, especially the Ministry of Finance, also supplied many of the senior staff, which has been the principal source of policy and enforcement initiative. Because of ties such as these, some observers believe that the FTC has not always been as independent in fact as it could be in principle.[56] These personnel patterns are changing, though, and these changes may portend greater independence and activity. The most recently appointed Chair was a prosecutor, not a MOF veteran.

Although the FTC need not consult any ministry before reaching a decision in an enforcement matter, ministries have not hesitated to give the FTC their views about how particular cases should be decided. In one well-publicised incident, in which the FTC did not take action in a construction industry case, the FTC denied that it declined to act because the construction ministry instructed it what to do. The FTC did not deny that the construction ministry had offered its views.[57]

Transparency supports independence. Conversely, the absence of public explanation may cast doubt on claims that decisions are reached independently. The FTC's tradition of acting informally has tended to undermine its ostensible independence. To be sure, informal methods can be efficient, and avoiding formal confrontation and public controversy is evidently an important cultural value. The FTC has responded to criticism about lack of transparency and over-reliance on informal methods. It has issued up-to-date, detailed guidelines, usually developed through a public consultation process. And it has begun to publicise regularly reports of its consultations and actions. These help to explain its approach to merger matters, for example, where the lack of formal decisions has left business in the dark about what the law means. Some observers credit the FTC with being both more transparent than before, and more transparent than most other parts of the Japanese government.

One reason advanced for maintaining independence is to separate competition policy under the AMA from industrial and trade policy. The final report of the Administrative Reform Committee in December 1997, which proposed to make the FTC an external bureau of a newly-created Ministry of General Affairs, emphasised the importance of maintaining its investigational and decisional independence, noting that because competition policy under the AMA sometimes works at cross purposes to industrial policy, the two should be kept clearly separate.[58] This recommendation is about keeping competition policy decisions under the AMA visibly distinct from industrial policy decisions. Whether competition enforcement decisions must be made by a body that is organically outside the government is a different issue. Independence from arbitrary political influence and clear separation of policy considerations can also be achieved by subjecting decisions to the discipline of a politically independent judiciary. And even a formally independent body can respond to implicit or explicit pressure to reach decisions that are consistent with other ministries' industrial and trade policy interests. Some observers believe that the FTC's studies about distribution practices are best explained as assistance to other ministries' arguments in trade negotiations.[59] On the other hand, the FTC has on occasion faced down another ministry in public, most famously in opposing the major steel merger that MITI had promoted in 1969. And some observers see the increase in FTC activity as a product of compromise with other forces.[60]

The FTC is the only independent agency in the Japanese government structure to survive from the occupation era. Other independent agencies were also created at that time, but all the rest were disbanded on the grounds that they were inefficient. That the FTC remains implies either that it alone was efficient, or that an inefficient agency was an acceptable tool for promoting an unpopular policy. Now, as controversy grows over past government economic policies, the FTC's separation from other government structures, which was once seen as a sign of weakness, may be seen as a strength. The model of independence is being tested again elsewhere, in the newly-created Financial Supervisory Agency.

A problem of institutional independence is that it tends to cut off access to the policy process within the government. The FTC has statutory responsibilities[61] for co-ordinating laws and orders that relate to the substantive concerns of the AMA. These consultation requirements give it the potential to become a core economic policy agency. Notice or consultation with other ministries are required if the FTC is going to take action under the AMA's special provision about "monopolistic situations"[62] or for approval of proposed exemptions, either under the AMA or particular ministry laws. The FTC has no authorization to participate in other ministries' regulatory processes, but some of the informal policy advice it has generated through study groups has earned it "increasing respect" in those ministries.[63] The consultations are typically relatively informal. In general, the FTC can affect the legislative process indirectly, by conveying its views through the Cabinet Secretary. It has reportedly done so only rarely, except for matters that directly affect its AMA responsibilities. The FTC in theory can exercise a veto over proposals for legislation that contradict the AMA, but in practice it has never done so. Instead, compromises have been reached. But FTC views have sometimes been effective. For example, on several occasions MITI has withheld administrative guidance at the FTC's request, particularly concerning the formation of joint sales agencies.

3.2. Competition law enforcement

Although policy is technically applied through law enforcement, the FTC's methods are more administrative and regulatory than litigious. Informal admonition has been more important than public prosecution. The FTC has been criticised for concluding too many cases with statements of "caution" or "warning" which carry little risk and cannot serve as predicate for private action. In 1990s, the FTC has greatly increased its reliance on stronger, more formal measures.

The FTC has complete power to initiate an investigation on its own authority. The FTC's principal investigative tools are powers to require testimony and to enter premises and inspect documents. An order to produce documents may follow the inspection. Testimony often takes the form of answers to an interrogatory questionnaire. The FTC exercises these powers on its own initiative, but it must go to court to obtain sanctions in the event of non-compliance. Those sanctions may not be serious enough to ensure full compliance: the maximum penalty for failure to respond to investigational process is a fine of ¥ 200 000.[64] Some other agencies, notably the tax authorities and the public prosecutor, have greater powers to obtain evidence. The most important kind of formal action at the FTC is a "recommendation" decision. After the investigation, the FTC may announce a recommended order. If the respondent accepts the recommendation, that becomes the final order, without a complaint or further proceedings. If the respondent rejects the recommendation, the FTC issues a complaint and the matter proceeds to an adversarial hearing and public record decision.

The AMA authorises the FTC to issue orders to cease and desist, to forbear from future violations, and to correct the effects of past violations. In practical terms, though, the most important administrative remedy is the assessment of surcharges against cartels and output constraints that affect price. The surcharge remedy was added to the law in 1977, as it became clear that non-pecuniary sanctions had no deterrent effect. The surcharge level was raised after experience showed that the initial level was still too low to deter. The amounts assessed in recent years are substantial, and in the aggregate they are roughly comparable with financial penalties assessed by EU and US enforcers. The total surcharges assessed in the most recent year were ¥ 5.9 billion.

Criminal enforcement has revived in the 1990s, but it is still rare. The context in which criminal enforcement is likely to be most significant is reform in public procurement, where prosecution may be the most effective weapon against pervasive bid-rigging. The FTC has announced a policy of increasing reliance on referrals for criminal prosecution in the most serious cartel cases. Despite the call for increased action, though, FTC referrals for prosecution average only about one cartel case per year.[65] Courts have assessed fines and imposed prison sentences, but no one has actually served any prison time yet as a result of a competition law conviction because the sentences have been suspended. The maximum criminal fine available under the AMA has been increased by a factor of 20, to ¥ 100 million.[66] Prosecutors are reportedly bringing Criminal Code actions against bid rigging on public projects, which do not require FTC referrals.[67] (The Criminal Code provision, which applies only to individuals and not to corporations, was originally interpreted narrowly, to prohibit only bid rigging that raised prices above a fair level. As late as 1968, courts ruled that bid rigging to prevent losses was legal.)[68] A liaison arrangement has been set up with the ministry of Justice to coordinate criminal actions. Now that the FTC and the prosecutor have brought exemplary actions to establish the principle, and the FTC leadership is better connected to the prosecutor's office, the use of criminal sanctions might increase.

The FTC's administrative law enforcement actions are subject to correction in court. Parties can appeal adverse decisions to the Tokyo High Court, and from there to the Supreme Court. On the one hand, the courts generally support the FTC's understanding of the law and policy. But on the other hand, practical outcomes show a tendency to split the difference. In the famous oil cartel case, the court ruled that adherence to administrative guidance did not make price-fixing legal, but then declined to find liability because the individuals probably felt justified in following the administrative guidance. In criminal cases, convictions have resulted in fines, but prison sentences have always been suspended. This decision pattern probably reflects accurately the legal culture's general tolerance of anti-competitive conditions and practices.

Box 3.   **Enforcement powers**

Does the agency have the power to take investigative action on its own initiative? Japan's FTC, like most Member country agencies (19), has some power to issue prohibitory orders on its own initiative. In one-quarter of the countries, even such "cease and desist" orders can only be issued by a court or separate decision-maker. About half of Member country agencies can impose financial penalties directly. Mandatory orders or criminal penalties can only be imposed by courts in most Member countries.

Does the agency publish its decisions and the reasons for them? Virtually all Member country enforcement agencies, including the FTC, publish their decisions and reasoning in some form. Where agencies do not do so themselves, effective decisions are made by courts that do.

Are the agency's decisions subject to substantive review and correction by a court? All Member country competition agencies must defend their actions in court if necessary.

Can private parties also bring their own suits about competition issues? Some kind of privately initiated suit about competition issues is possible in all but two or three jurisdictions. In a majority of countries, agencies explain the reasons why they do not take action in a particular case, and a party who is disappointed by the competition agency's inaction can challenge the agency in court.

Recognising perhaps that hard-nosed enforcement would be resisted strongly, the FTC relies heavily on guidelines and its own administrative guidance, that is, prior consultations and informal negative clearances and negotiated compliance. Guidelines are taken seriously and have become a major policy instrument.[69] Since its increased activism in the 1990s, the FTC has strengthened many of its old guidelines and issued some new ones. The subjects of AMA guidelines include trade association activities (1979, revised in 1994), mergers (1980, revised in 1994 and 1998), retail mergers (1981), stockholdings (1981, revised in 1994), unfair price-cutting (1984), unjust return of unsold goods (1987), patent and know-how licensing (1989), distribution systems and business practices (1991), joint research and development (1993), stockholding by financial companies (1994), administrative guidance (1981, revised in 1994), public bidding (1994), and holding companies (1997).

3.3. Other enforcement methods

Private parties who believe they have been victims of anti-competitive practices have some recourse to the FTC's process, but it is limited. The FTC receives many complaints. If the FTC receives a written complaint that specifies facts, the FTC is obligated to notify the complainant of its disposition of the matter.[70] But a disappointed complainant cannot take legal action to compel the FTC to act, or to appeal its refusal to pursue a case or finding of no violation.

Two kinds of private action are possible. Both are aimed at the recovery of damages for past violation; neither provides for supplementary or punitive damages or additional kinds of relief. Both types are used increasingly, but still infrequently. The private action provided in the AMA itself depends on a prior decision by the FTC. After the FTC finds that a party has violated the law, injured parties can sue to recover their damages. Defendants cannot defend on the grounds that they did not intend to cause damage; to that extent, collecting damages in a private action is supposed to be routine. In practice, it is not. The courts have not taken the FTC's "recommendation" decision as conclusive proof even of the underlying violation, but instead have re-examined the entire matter. In a few cases, plaintiffs have collected damages in actions under the AMA, but virtually always through settlements; the first successful damages action under the AMA, that is, a final judicial decision requiring indemnification, did not appear until 1993. In general, experience under the provision for private actions under the AMA has been disappointing. Moreover, because these actions depend on a prior FTC. finding, if the FTC does not pursue a case, the complainant cannot go to court under the AMA. Private actions under the AMA must be filed in the Tokyo High Court, which sits in a special panel to hear competition cases.

The second possibility, which does not depend on the FTC, is to seek damages under the Civil Code.[71] This is the only kind of action available to a disappointed complainant to the FTC. (Note that it is not necessary to go to the FTC first before filing suit.) Suits can be filed in local courts. The disadvantage of taking action under the Civil Code is that in actions under the Civil Code the complainant cannot usually obtain an injunction to stop harmful conduct. (This applies to Civil Code actions on nearly all kinds of legal theory, not just competition.) Although a prior FTC action would not by itself establish the basic violation in a Civil Code suit, the FTC's decision, or the evidence that supported it, can be filed with the court for its information, and it may help the plaintiff establish its case. And the substantive rules applied in these cases would be based on the FTC's AMA doctrines, such as the characterisation of price-fixing as a violation "in principle".

Stronger and more effective private relief has been a focus of trade negotiations and of study by the FTC and others. US and EU negotiators have urged that Japanese law and procedure be changed to make it easier for alleged victims to challenge anti-competitive conduct in court, without having to rely first on the FTC. The demands have concentrated on two issues: authorizing private parties to obtain injunctions under the AMA's substantive rules, and changing rules about proof of damages so plaintiffs could win more easily. A recent report by a MITI-sponsored study group on a related subject encouraged making some changes like these. The FTC's own views on this are guarded, neither endorsing nor rejecting the expansion of private rights of action. An FTC study group is reviewing whether new legislation should be introduced.

The FTC is concerned to be sure that the many related, complex issues are adequately addressed, so that remedies are consistent with other aspects of the civil justice system. In addition, the FTC's studied neutrality may reflect some concern that increased reliance on the courts will decrease the FTC's influence on competition policy. If parties could go directly to court to obtain orders about competition issues, then the courts would become alternative, and potentially more powerful, sources of competition policy. That, of course, is what some observers evidently want. Their concern is not that the FTC is over-worked, but that it is not showing enough initiative in its choice of targets. Third party injunction powers could be most useful for the kinds of constraints that impair market openness. Thus, trading partners have focused on this concern. The possibility of real relief from a court would mean that these problems would be taken to judicial decisionmakers instead of trade negotiators. The problems might thus be resolved more quickly and at a lower profile, and hence lower cost, as they could be treated simply as disputes between companies rather than between countries. Other laws provide potentially useful parallels; private parties can obtain injunctions in patent cases, for example. Although final rulings in such cases can take two years, it is possible to seek and obtain the equivalent of a preliminary injunction for immediate relief.

The problem of proving damages is a general one. In the heating oil cartel case, a consumer organisation sued for damages after the FTC found there was indeed a cartel, but the courts said the consumer organisation had to prove what the prices would have been without the cartel. The problem is not limited to competition cases, though. The usual rule in Japan's civil cases is that the claimant must prove causation and the amount of economic damages precisely. The FTC has promised to help plaintiffs develop their proof of this issue. (The AMA instructs that the courts are to ask for the FTC's opinion about damages, and the FTC is to respond. Since 1990, the FTC has responded to one request for advice about damages in a private case under the AMA,[72] and 14 requests about the existence of violations and damages in tax-payer cases concerning bid-rigging.) And the Code of Civil Procedure has recently been amended to permit the use of estimates. It is unclear whether this change would also apply to cases under the AMA. If the different treatment remains, that could encourage greater resort to the Civil Code alternative.

To rely on the courts very much, though, some other problems need attention. The court system is relatively small, so there are too few judges. And a judicial system in which the judge's principal role is analysing statutes may not be up to the task of deciding economically complex matters such as competition cases. Some have suggested creating an alternative institution for these kinds of cases, which could employ a wider range of expertise. Although the Tokyo High Court already specialises to some extent, in that it has exclusive jurisdiction over matters under the AMA, this court may be inconvenient for many claimants, and it may not have the capacity to handle these matters if they become numerous.

But the even greater practical impediment to expanded, effective independent private relief is that there are not enough lawyers, either. The reason is related to competition policy: the legal profession is, in practical terms, equivalent to a cartel that has effectively protected itself against competitive new entry. The number of new lawyers permitted to enter practice each year is tightly controlled. The bar exam passing grade is determined by the number of lawyers who will be admitted, rather than the other way around. The justification for this constraint is said to be the lack of sufficient opportunities for necessary on-the-job supervised training for new lawyers after they are formally admitted. This is, obviously, a "chicken and egg" problem. The three year programme calls for expanding the number of new lawyers. Proposals under consideration would increase the number from the current 700 per year to at least 1 000, if not 2 000. Even at the higher rate, it would take 10 years for the number of lawyers in Japan to double, and 50 years for the number of lawyers per capita to equal that in the EU. Another proposal under consideration is to permit people with several years of administrative legal experience to act as legal advisors, though not as barristers qualified to represent clients in court.

With too few judges and too few lawyers, litigation takes too long and costs too much. These hurdles would be of particular concern to private actions on behalf of ultimate consumers. In the pioneering, and ultimately unsuccessful, consumer action against the oil cartel, the time between filing and judgement was ten years. That experience has not been duplicated in any of the handful of later consumer actions, but it still affects the perceptions of how time-consuming the process can be. Even successful complainants have to pay their own attorneys' fees and costs. In the heating oil case, the consumer group relied on volunteer academic lawyers. These private actions on behalf of consumers

211

have been policy-oriented, and the plaintiffs probably did not expect to collect substantial damages. Such low expectations have not been disappointed. Even if a suit succeeds, it would be difficult to organise to collect in the typical consumer-injury case, where individual damage is likely to be small even though aggregate damage is huge.

An option would be to establish procedures for consumer class recoveries. Class action procedures for aggregating small claims efficiently could make consumer actions a more effective tool. In the SII talks, the US suggested this approach. The FTC responded by changing its previous policy of neutrality and promising to "affirmatively support" private actions as a policy device to supplement AMA enforcement, by providing plaintiffs with detailed opinions and allowing access to evidentiary materials. A side effect of this change in position was a change in the treatment of information companies had claimed was confidential. The FTC has made it clear that material will be disclosed if it would be useful and necessary to support the private suit. It will not be protected from disclosure simply because the company wants to protect it.

Although actions by consumers have been rare, actions by customers have increased and some have even succeeded. As might be expected, most of these have been brought over refusals to deal. Firms that are already parties to ongoing business relationships are probably reluctant to jeopardize them by suing. Toshiba paid damages for refusing to supply elevator repair parts, and discounters have won lower court rulings against brand name cosmetic and soap firms for refusals to deal. Cases like these "may offer up a wholly new and effective avenue in antitrust enforcement, not only through court action but also by obliging the JFTC to become more activist".[73]

One reason private actions have not been very successful may simply be their novelty and complexity. Time and trial are needed to identify and answer new substantive and procedural questions. But another reason for the lack of success, at least until recently, could be that the courts did not find a reason to accord priority to competition policy. Adding more formal and technical requirements and tools may not change outcomes, until there is also a change in the judges' priorities.

Despite the practical problems (and the likely objections from those in the business community who are most likely to be targets of lawsuits), expanding rights of private action could be valuable. It would bring in additional resources to competition policy enforcement. It would offer the prospect of tangible recoveries for victims of illegal practices. It would galvanise the FTC, too, by indirectly pressuring it to continue producing a high-quality product, namely effective, independent law enforcement. For if it did not, "customers" could shift their business to the competitive alternative.

3.4. International trade issues in competition policy and enforcement

The FTC's record concerning market openness issues is unclear. The FTC says it will deal fairly and strictly with problems of market access, applying the principle of non-discrimination, but it is difficult to identify law enforcement efforts with that focus. The adequacy of competition enforcement, including actions against impediments to market access, was major issue in SII talks with US, and has also been an issue in controversies with the EU. In response to claims that distribution restraints anti-competitively prevented trade, the FTC has done studies. The results of those studies tend to underscore the FTC's institutional ambivalence and to reinforce the impression of weakness in relation to other ministries. For although these studies appear to have found suspected practices that violated the law, they did not lead to law enforcement action, but only to admonitions, as the FTC concluded that a violation of the law was not proved. The 1997 report about distribution of photo film and paper concluded there was no evidence of possible violations, but the FTC made four specific "suggestions" about how the industry should improve competitively problematic aspects of its conduct and promised to apply the law in the future. Two other reports, on distribution practices and price disparities for medical supplies, produced similarly ambivalent results. Where manufacturer-supported closed trade relationships prevented entry and raised prices, the FTC's response was to ask the health ministry and other agencies to admonish buyers to do better. No action was recommended or taken against the suppliers who maintained the exclusive system, even though the

FTC pointed out that their practice of controlling their wholesalers' sales and prices, to police the exclusive arrangements, could be in violation of the AMA. The FTC simply requested that the manufacturers comply with the law. In contact lenses, manufacturers were trying to control retail prices, and practitioners were trying to reach agreements about discounts and pressuring large-volume competitors. Here, the FTC asked that all concerned familiarise themselves with the relevant distribution guidelines.[74]

The FTC's treatment of transnational effects appears tentative and perhaps inconsistent. In July, 1998, an FTC action against a Canadian company represented the first time it had asserted jurisdiction over a foreign firm based on a claim that its conduct had anti-competitive effects in Japan. This was a very small step, for the conduct at issue apparently took place in Japan. The FTC's delay in taking the step is probably due to uncertainty about its legal power, and not to uncertainty about the economic effects. On the issue of competitive effects from import trade, the petrochemical merger case described above shows some analytic inconsistency. The FTC permitted the merger because the threat of import competition would discipline market power, even while calling for reduced duties to ensure a competitive environment.

The business community is interested in greater international harmonisation in trade and competition issues, particularly concerning antidumping and merger decisions. The FTC's move to modernise the merger reporting rules and amend the guidelines may be seen as moves in the same direction. The FTC has long worked within organisations such as the OECD, but it has no special procedures for dealing with foreign entities or getting information from abroad. To make its rules and processes more comprehensible to foreign firms and governments, the FTC's International Affairs division has recently arranged for publication of a single-volume English translation of all the basic laws, guidelines, and reporting forms. The FTC has taken some advantage of informal agreements for the exchange of information and notifications with other OECD countries. Japan's Ministry of Justice has assisted foreign agencies in implementing international evidence-gathering processes. So far, the FTC is not a party to any formal enforcement or information sharing agreements, but in September, 1998 it announced the beginning of negotiations toward such an agreement with the US enforcement agencies.

Box 4. **International co-operation agreements**

Eight Member countries have entered one or more formal agreements to co-operate in competition enforcement matters: Australia, Canada, Czech Republic, Hungary, Korea, New Zealand, Poland and the US. And the EC has done so as well.

3.5. Agency resources, actions, and implied priorities

The higher priority now being given to competition policy is reflected in the resources devoted to it. The FTC one of the largest competition enforcement agencies in the OECD. And it has been growing, both in staff and in budget, despite the belt-tightening of the Japanese government. In FY1998, when overall government expenditures declined 1.3 per cent, the FTC's budget increased 1.1 per cent and 10 positions were added. Budget increases have generally kept pace with GDP, and personnel has increased at a faster rate than population or government employment generally.

As measured by the number of actions and decisions, the FTC is now placing the highest priority on horizontal violations, particularly bid rigging. In the most recent complete year (1997), the FTC took up 161 new matters, on top of the 66 that were carried over from before, and completed 136 of them, leaving 91 to be carried over into 1998. Those matters produced 27 final actions, of which 13 addressed bid-rigging. Other matters were concluded by administrative guidance measures, warnings of which are made public. The dispositions included 26 recommendation decisions, one surcharge order without a

Table 1.   **Trends in the FTC budget**

Fiscal year	1989	1990	1991	1992	1993	1994	1995	1996	1997	1998
FTC budget (¥100 million)	35.2	37.6	40.8	44.1	46.2	52.4[1]	52.4	53.8	55.6	56.2
Annual change (%)	8.4	6.7	8.6	7.9	4.9	13.4	−0.1	2.7	3.3	1.1
General budget[2] change (%)	3.3	3.8	4.7	4.5	3.1	2.3	3.1	2.4	1.5	−1.3

1. The FTC budget for FY1994 includes office relocation costs (¥230 million).
2. The total expenditure budget of the Japanese government, namely general account budget expenditures less national debt service and local allocation tax grants.
Source: FTC annual reports, questionnaire response.

Table 2.   **Trends in the FTC General Secretariat[1] staff**

Fiscal year	1989	1990	1991	1992	1993	1994	1995	1996	1997	1998
Total number of officials	461	474	478	484	493	506	520	534	545	552
Enforcement[2]	129	154	165	178	186	203	220	236	248	254
Merger review[3]	18	18	19	18	19	18	18	18	18	19
Advocacy[4]	16	16	15	15	15	15	14	23	23	23

1. Until FY 1995, the Secretariat office was the Executive Office.
2. Investigation Bureau (Investigation Department until FY1995) and Investigation Divisions of local offices.
3. Merger and Acquisitions Division (Enterprise Division until FY1995).
4. General Affairs Division of the Economics Affairs Bureau (Co-ordination Division until FY1995) and the Co-ordination Division.
Source: FTC annual reports, questionnaire response

recommendation decision, 13 warnings and 92 "cautions" (where violations were suspected but not substantiated). Over the last five years, horizontal violations have predominated, accounting for from two-thirds to nine-tenths of the orders issued each year. In 1997, about 19 of the orders involved either bid rigging or other horizontal practices, seven involved vertical agreements, and the others involved abuse of dominance or other unfair practices. Four involved trade associations. In 1997, the JFTC issued surcharge payment orders to 170 firms involved in 16 cases of price cartels and bid-rigging. The total amount of surcharges was ¥ 5.9 billion.[75]

Only about 30 staff are devoted to mergers and acquisitions. In 1997, when all such transactions had to be reported regardless of size, the JFTC received notifications for 3 596 planned mergers or acquisitions. This number was actually down slightly from previous years.[76] The FTC thus makes about the same resource commitment to this subject as the new Netherlands agency does, yet that agency is dealing with an economy one-tenth the size of Japan's, shares enforcement responsibility with the EU, and has already undertaken several major merger investigations. The FTC's extraordinarily low resource commitment[77] will have to change if the FTC is to play a significant role in ensuring post-reform competition as industries respond to changes in rules by trying to change their structures.

The FTC understands the importance of addressing AMA violations in those economic sectors where government regulations are still influential, because those violations could nullify the benefits of deregulation. It has taken some actions to that purpose. It probably could take even more. Some recent cases demonstrate this interest. One was against a trade group of insurers, whose premiums and conditions required approval from the Ministry of Finance. They acted together to decide on the rates and terms they would apply for, apparently prodded by informal guidance from the Ministry; the FTC successfully challenged this agreement as a violation of the AMA. Another case involved hospital food service. A public foundation designated by the government, which set standards, conspired with a major dealer about the content of those standards in order to exclude other firms from the food service business.[78] In telecommunications, when it became possible to buy (rather than rent) a cellular phone, some firms tried to control their distributors' resale prices and advertising; the FTC took action against this in 1997. And the FTC has taken action against efforts to return to price-fixing in trucking and taxis.

4. THE LIMITS OF COMPETITION POLICY FOR REGULATORY REFORM

4.1. Economy-wide exemptions or special treatments

The problem of government-sponsored anti-competitive behaviour is unusually great in Japan. It is broader than the familiar controversy over administrative guidance, extending to a wide range of actions that have historically protected non-competitive arrangements. Although there is no general exemption from the competition law for action mandated by a government authority, the law in fact cannot reach it because the AMA only deals with voluntary action. A provision of the AMA does make explicit that, where a specific statute governs an industry, conduct in accordance with that statute or an order properly issued under it does not violate the AMA.[79] As part of the deregulatory housecleaning, that provision is to be repealed.

Even where national government regulation has been reformed to promote competition, local government levels have sometimes interfered. The AMA applies to entrepreneurs, not to government officials, and thus the only recourse under the competition law is for the FTC to try to persuade the local governments not to do it. For example, after much effort the national laws that restricted large-scale retail stores are being relaxed. But local laws and processes, concerning land use and environmental impact, were quickly adapted to the same purpose, of permitting existing firms to exercise substantial veto power over the entry of potentially strong competitors. In 1998, the FTC surveyed pharmacies and found that some prefectural governments required potential new entrants to consult with the pharmacy association or even obtain a recommendation from the association before applying to go into business or to fill prescriptions.[80] But the only action the FTC could take against this means of preventing competitive entry was to ask the Ministry of Health and Welfare to inform prefectural governments about the purpose of the Antimonopoly Act.

Public entities are not completely immune from the law, though. A public entity that engages in economic activities from which it obtains an economic benefit could meet the statutory definition of a covered "entrepreneur".[81] In 1989, the Supreme Court found that a municipal slaughterhouse competing with a private one could be reached by the AMA. And a district court found that government-printed postcards that carried pictures or lottery data competed with privately printed ones and hence lost an otherwise-applicable immunity. Suits against government as such under the AMA are probably not possible.

Several aspects of the AMA may benefit small and medium sized entrepreneurs, who are in principle fully subject to the AMA. Legally-authorised, voluntary co-operative organisations of small entrepreneurs may be exempt from the prohibition against restraints of trade, as long as they do not restrain competition substantially or raise prices unjustly. The co-operative exemption does not extend to unfair trade practices.[82] Another benefit for small firms is that the surcharge rate applied to their price-related violations is generally half of what is applied to larger firms.

Box 5.   Scope of competition policy

Is there an exemption from liability under the general competition law for conduct that is required or authorised by other government authority? Like about half of the Member countries (15 out of the 27 reporting), Japan provides for some degree of exemption from the general competition law, for conduct that is clearly required by other regulation or government authority.

Does the general competition law apply to public enterprises? Japan, like every Member country except Portugal and the US, applies its general competition law to public enterprises.

Is there an exemption, in law or enforcement policy, for small and medium sized enterprises? Four Member countries reported some kind of exemption or difference in treatment for small and medium sized enterprises: Belgium, France, Germany and Japan.

4.2. Sector-specific exclusions, rules and exemptions

At one time, statutes and other decisions provided for more than a thousand explicit exemptions from the AMA. That number has been cut about 90 per cent, and steps are underway to reduce or eliminate still more. Those that remain are significant, although not remarkable. Many appear in areas where other OECD countries also have had some history of exemption or special treatment. The extraordinary number at the peak measures the historical lack of support for competition policy.

Exemptions came from several sources. Some were found in, or provided for in, the AMA itself. Many others are provided in the AMA Exemption Act. Most problematic are the multitude that were inserted into particular industrial laws. For several years, the FTC has been trying to get the number of exemptions down. After the SII talks, commitments were made to eliminate them by 1996; that target date has obviously been extended some. Plans are in place to eliminate nearly all of the exemptions that are still found in the AMA itself. An Omnibus Bill in 1997 eliminated many of the miscellaneous exemptions. The depression cartel system and the rationalisation cartel system based on the AMA, and the AMA Exemption Act itself, were set for repeal in the 1997 reform action plan.[83] Following up on that decision, the FTC held talks with the relevant ministries and agencies on the reform of all exemption systems. The three-year programme announced in 1998 included some fruits of those talks.

The table at the end of this section summarises the recent actions and plans for reducing the extent of exemptions. Of the approximately 90 listed there as of 1997, about one-third have been eliminated, there are plans to eliminate about another third, and about a third will be retained, in many cases with modifications to reduce their scope. The large number of individual items on the list does not necessarily correspond to economic or competitive importance, for some of the dozens that have already been removed appear to have been substantively minor. The fact that most items discussed in the 1998 plan will be retained indicates that the remaining exemptions will be harder to eliminate.

Eliminating a formal exemption will not always mean eliminating special competition-policy treatment for particular industries. Depression and rationalisation cartels will no longer be provided in the AMA itself, but other industry-specific laws should be monitored to ensure that they do not provide protection against competition law liability for firms that co-operate in restructuring under ministry guidance.

Similarly, it appears that changing certain exemptions for co-operatives may still leave sectoral ministries with responsibilities that might be exercised inconsistently with the AMA. The AMA contains a provision that should permit co-operatives and trade associations to engage in legitimate activities. Despite this continuing general protection, plans evidently call for several industrial laws to continue to provide specially for co-operatives and associations in those industries. Those laws are to be made substantively consistent with the related parts of the AMA. A purpose of retaining separate laws may be to remove the subjects from FTC oversight, though. If so, whether this change will actually lead to a reduction in anti-competitive ministry action will depend on how particular judgements are actually made. At a minimum, some form of strong co-ordination needs to be established, if not a clear FTC veto.

The problem that the exemptions represent will not be resolved completely just by the proposed changes in the laws, although those changes are certainly welcome. Much will depend on the sensitivity with which the no-longer exempted conduct is treated under the AMA. Conduct that is now formally exempted may be "exempted" *de facto* if the FTC finds it does not have an unacceptable effect on competition. Thus the proposed abolition of the AMA exemption for depression and rationalisation cartels does not necessarily mean that they will never again be permitted. Decisions not to sue in those conditions could well be defensible, under sound competition policy. Yet there may be some cause for concern that, in order to achieve the visible, tangible goal of eliminating exemptions, the FTC will compromise more than necessary in its own enforcement, by showing indulgence to ease the transition to real competition. Such a result would be entirely consistent with the Japanese process of policy development and consensus decision. But it would slow down the reform process by another half-generation.

The extent of formal exemptions does not by itself measure the extent of anti-competitive conditions that are either directed or protected by government action. Government bodies are deeply involved in managing one of the most critical competitive strategy variables, entry, by using judgements about the appropriate supply-demand balance as a criterion for issuing licenses or other necessary permits, or for informal or even indirect administrative guidance to the same effect. The 1998 deregulation programme sets out some principles for the next stage of reform, which if implemented could help eliminate some of these sectoral problems. It calls for the FTC to survey and make proposals about fields where entry is restricted, by supply-demand balancing or other regulations. And the FTC is to study fields where there has already been some relaxation, to report on the results and recommend further steps. The programme states that the eventual goal is to ease or abolish such regulations. Reaching that goal is critical to the success of reform based on competition principles. Thus, it is unfortunate that the programme calls only for further study and does not set clear, specific targets for eliminating the most important and well-known constraints by a date certain.

Airlines: The Ministry of Transport still controls entry and limits price competition. As a result, domestic airfares are about 20 per cent higher than in US. Some think real deregulation could save consumers about $2 billion per year. Even though new airlines are now permitted in theory, authorisation takes two years (four times longer than in other major jurisdictions), and the ministry insists on the entrant proving that it will break even. Plans contemplate that demand and supply adjustment clauses will be phased out FY 1999 and FY 2001. But at least until 1999, and perhaps much longer, the ministry will retain power to determine who can operate and what prices they can charge on particular routes.

Coastal shipping: There have been changes in the methods for industry restructuring. Technically, the "scrap and build" method for authorising new ship construction was eliminated. But that does not mean that entry is now free of control. To construct a new ship, a firm must get permission and pay a fee to cover the old ship's scrap value. According to some observers, the arrangements have the effect of limiting the tonnage available and increasing industry costs.[84] This "transition" measure will last until the funds balance; according to some observers, this could take 15 years.

Road transport: Entry costs are already lower in trucking, now that regulation has been relaxed some. But it has not been eliminated. The ministry imposes area control and requires a firm to have a minimum number of vehicles. Entry is thus still limited, despite the supposed repeal of the demand-supply adjustment clauses. Motor carriers must give advance notification of price changes, allegedly to prevent predation. This is likely to stifle effective price competition.[85]

Insurance: Some deregulation has happened here. For example, life insurance firms may now acquire casualty insurance firms, and vice versa. None have done so The FTC held a hearing but could find no "particular" anti-competitive administrative guidance from the Ministry of Finance discouraging mutual entry. It nonetheless asked the ministry to bear in mind the FTC's Guidelines about Administrative Guidance and enforce the revised Insurance Act to fulfil its promise of greater competition through mutual entry. There has now been some entry between these two sectors through the formation of subsidiary companies. Plans for the "big bang" include eliminating what was effectively a premium-fixing requirement. Formal rate setting agreements are evidently being eliminated, as they have been for interest rates on deposits at financial institutions. But it is not clear whether informal co-ordination has been eliminated.

Natural monopolies: The AMA now affords an exemption for the proper business operations of railroads, electric power, and gas, and other such industries to the extent they are inherently monopolies.[86] This exemption applies to production, sale, or supply in those industries. It is not clear whether it applies to all aspects of network function, including those that may have an impact on other, competitive industries and markets. This exemption will be retained. Although these industries are named in particular, their exemption evidently depends on the understanding that they are natural monopolies. If that changes as a matter of fact (or policy, in other laws), then this exemption might shrink. But the AMA's coverage of these network industries may still be displaced by sectoral regulation.

If, after abolition of supply-demand controls, utility regulation is redesigned on the basis of competition policy, the FTC's role should be more important, but it may still be indirect. Although responsibility for competition policy might be assumed by the FTC, regulators may also be involved, and their decisions

Table 3. **Summary of status of exemptions from Antimonopoly Action**

Description	Sector	Ministry	Legal basis	Status or plan
Intellectual property	General	FTC	AMA Sec. 23	To be retained
Cooperatives	General	FTC	AMA Sec. 24	To be retained, amended
Natural monopolies	General	FTC	AMA Sec. 21	Under review
Government authorization	General	FTC	AMA Sec. 22	To be repealed; bill in next session
Depression cartels	General	FTC	AMA Sec. 24-3	To be repealed; bill in next session
Rationalization cartels	General	FTC	AMA Sec. 24-4	To be repealed; bill in next session
Improvement projects	General	FTC	AMA Sec. 103	To be repealed; bill in next session
Agricultural cooperatives	Agriculture	Agriculture, Forestry and Fisheries	AMA Exemption Act, AMA Sec. 8; Agricultural Cooperative Association Law	Cooperatives exemption to be based on AMA Sec. 24; bill in next session
Agricultural disaster relief	Agriculture	Agriculture, Forestry and Fisheries	AMA Exemption Act, AMA Sec. 8; Agricultural Disaster Indemnity Law	To be abolished; bill in next session
Agriculture credit insurance	Agriculture	Agriculture, Forestry and Fisheries	AMA Exemption Act, AMA Sec. 8; Agriculture Credit Guarantee Insurance Law	To be abolished; bill in next session
Rural debt relief cooperatives	Agriculture, finance	Agriculture, Forestry and Fisheries	AMA Exemption Act, AMA Sec. 8; Rural Debt Liquidation Cooperative Law	To be abolished; bill in next session
Cartels for material purchase	Fishing	Agriculture, Forestry and Fisheries	Export Fisheries Development Law	Abolished
Cartels to prevent export competition	Fishing	Agriculture, Forestry and Fisheries	Export Fisheries Development Law	Abolished
Certain activities by designated organizations	Fishing	Agriculture, Forestry and Fisheries	Export Fisheries Development Law	Abolished
Cartels to adjust hauls of fish	Fishing	Agriculture, Forestry and Fisheries	Fisheries Production Adjustment Co-operatives Law	Abolished
Fisheries co-operative associations	Fishing	Agriculture, Forestry and Fisheries	AMA Exemption Act, AMA Sec. 8; Fisheries Co-operative Associations Law	Cooperatives exemption to be based on AMA Sec. 24; bill in next session
Plan to reduce number of fishing vessels	Fishing	Agriculture, Forestry and Fisheries	Special Measures Law for Fisheries Reconstruction	Exemption clause deleted
Compensation for fishing boat damage	Fishing	Agriculture, Forestry and Fisheries	AMA Exemption Act, and AMA Sec. 8; Fisheries Vessel Damage Compensation Law	To be abolished; bill in next session
Fishing, vessel damage	Fishing	Agriculture, Forestry and Fisheries	AMA Exemption Act, AMA Sec. 8; Fishing Vessel Damage Compensation Law	To be abolished; bill in next session
Fishing, loan guarantees for SMEs	Fishing	Agriculture, Forestry and Fisheries	AMA Exemption Act, AMA Sec. 8; Small and Medium Fisheries Loan Guarantee Law	To be abolished; bill in next session
Forestry cooperatives	Forestry	Agriculture, Forestry and Fisheries	AMA Exemption Act, AMA Sec. 8; Forest Cooperatives Law	Cooperatives exemption to be based on AMA Sec. 24; bill in next session

Table 3. **Summary of status of exemptions from Antimonopoly Action** (*cont.*)

Description	Sector	Ministry	Legal basis	Status or plan
Cartels in trading of materials for processed fruits	Fruit	Agriculture, Forestry and Fisheries	Law of Production of Fruit Agriculture	Abolished
Cartels to prevent excessive competition	Pearls	Agriculture, Forestry and Fisheries	Pearl Aquaculture Adjustment Provisional Measures Law	Abolished
Cartels to improve and maintain quality	Pearls	Agriculture, Forestry and Fisheries	Pearl Aquaculture Adjustment Provisional Measures Law	Abolished
Cartels to restrict production facilities	Pearls	Agriculture, Forestry and Fisheries	Pearl Aquaculture Adjustment Provisional Measures Law	Abolished
Price cartels for cocoons	Silk	Agriculture, Forestry and Fisheries	Sericultural Industry Law	Abolished
Designated cartels	Sugar	Agriculture, Forestry and Fisheries	Law relating to Stabilization of Sugar Price	Abolished
Mergers and acquisitions among wholesalers	Wholesale	Agriculture, Forestry and Fisheries	Wholesale Market Law	Abolished
Cartels to prevent excessive competition	Wholesale	Agriculture, Forestry and Fisheries	Wholesale Market Law	Abolished
Commodities exchanges	Commodities, agriculture	Agriculture, Forestry and Fisheries; MITI	AMA Exemption Act, AMA Sec. 8; Commodities Exchange Act	Review continues, aiming for abolition; bill in next session, perhaps
Cartels for fees for commercial usage of music records	Recorded music	Education	Copyright Law	Retained; procedures with FTC to be established; bill in next session
Credit associations	Credit	Finance	AMA Exemption Act, AMA Sec. 8; Credit Associations Law	Cooperatives exemption to be based on AMA Sec. 24; bill in next session
Credit guarantee associations	Credit	Finance	AMA Exemption Act, AMA Sec. 8; Credit Guarantee Association Law	To be abolished; bill in next session
Financial futures	Finance	Finance	AMA Exemption Act, AMA Sec. 8; Financial Futures Law	Review continues, aiming for abolition; bill in next session
Insurance cartels	Insurance	Finance	Law Concerning Foreign Insurance Groups	Abolished
Insurance cartels	Insurance	Finance	Insurance Business Law	Scope minimized, procedure with FTC
Rating organizations, non-life insurance	Insurance	Finance	AMA Exemption Act, and AMA Sec. 8; Law re Non-life Insurance Rating Organizations	To be abolished in principle; continued exemption re auto, earthquake; bill in Diet
Ship mutual insurance	Insurance, shipping	Finance	AMA Exemption Act, AMA Sec. 8; Shipowners' Mutual Insurance Association Law	To be abolished; bill in next session
Cartels to prevent excessive competition	Liquor	Finance	Law Concerning Liquor Business Associations and Measures for Securing Revenue from Liquor Tax	Abolished

Table 3. **Summary of status of exemptions from Antimonopoly Action** (*cont.*)

Description	Sector	Ministry	Legal basis	Status or plan
Resale price maintenance contracts	Liquor	Finance	Law Concerning Liquor Business Associations and Measures for Securing Revenue from Liquor Tax	Abolished
Rationalization cartels	Liquor	Finance	Law Concerning Liquor Business Associations and Measures for Securing Revenue from Liquor Tax	Reduced scope of exemption
Acquisition or possession of shares by companies with entrusted assets	Securities	Finance	Securities Investment Trust Law	Abolished
Securities associations	Securities	Finance	AMA Exemption Act, AMA Sec. 8; Securities Exchange Act	Review continues, aiming for abolition; bill in next session
Economic business by cooperatives	Tobacco	Finance	Tobacco Cultivators' Union Law	Cooperatives exemption based on AMA Sec. 24
Tobacco growers' union	Tobacco (growing)	Finance	AMA Exemption Act, AMA Sec. 8; Tobacco Cultivators' Union Law	Cooperatives exemption to be based on AMA Sec. 24; bill in next session
Employees' pension insurance	Pensions	Health and Welfare	AMA Exemption Act, AMA Sec. 8; Employees' Pension Insurance Law	To be abolished; bill in next session
Consumer cooperatives	General	Health and Welfare	AMA Exemption Act, AMA Sec. 8; Consumers' Livelihood Cooperative Association Law	Cooperatives exemption to be based on AMA Sec. 24; bill in next session
Health insurance	Health care	Health and Welfare	AMA Exemption Act, AMA Sec. 8; Health Insurance Law	To be abolished; bill in next session
Health insurance	Health care	Health and Welfare	AMA Exemption Act, AMA Sec. 8; National Health Insurance Law	To be abolished; bill in next session
Special contracts	Barbers, beauticians, laundries, and others	Health and Welfare	Law Concerning Coordination and Improvement of Hygienically Regulated Business	Abolished
Cartels to prevent excessive competition	Barbers, beauticians, laundries, and others	Health and Welfare	Law Concerning Coordination and Improvement of Hygienically Regulated Business	Exemption for unfair trade practices to be abolished; bill in next session. Cartels already abolished
Coal mining pension fund	Mining, pensions	Health and Welfare	AMA Exemption Act, AMA Sec. 8; Coal Mining Industry Pension Fund Law	To be abolished; bill in next session
Public employees insurance	Labor	Home Affairs	AMA Exemption Act, AMA Sec. 8; Local Public Service Personnel Mutual Aid Association law	To be abolished; bill in next session
Check clearinghouses	Finance	Justice	AMA Exemption Act, AMA Sec. 8; Bills of Exchange and Promissory Notes Act, Cheques Law	To be abolished; bill in next session
Acquisition of shares of companies under reorganization	General	Justice	Cooperation Reorganization Law	Retained
"Closed institutions"			AMA Exemption Act, AMA Sec. 8; Closed Institutions Ordinance	To be abolished; bill in next session
Workplace accidents	Labor	Labor	AMA Exemption Act, AMA Sec. 8; Industrial Injury Prevention Organizations Law	To be abolished; bill in next session

Table 3.   **Summary of status of exemptions from Antimonopoly Action** (*cont.*)

Description	Sector	Ministry	Legal basis	Status or plan
Cartels in domestic trading of exports by exporters and exporters' trade associations	Foreign trade	MITI	Export-Import Trading Law	Abolished
Cartels in domestic trading of exports by producers and distributors	Foreign trade	MITI	Export-Import Trading Law	Abolished
Cartels in import by importers and importers' trade associations	Foreign trade	MITI	Export-Import Trading Law	Abolished
Cartels in domestic trading by importers and importers' trade associations	Foreign trade	MITI	Export-Import Trading Law	Abolished
Cartels for adjustment of export and import by exporters, importers and export-import trade associations	Foreign trade	MITI	Export-Import Trading Law	Abolished
Cartels in exports by exporters and exporter trade associations	Foreign trade	MITI	Export-Import Trading Law	Managed in accord with treaties and international agreements
SME associations	General	MITI	AMA Exemption Act, AMA Sec. 8; Cooperative Societies of Minor Enterprises Act	Cooperatives exemption to be based on AMA Sec. 24; bill in next session
Economic business by cooperatives	General	MITI	Laws Relating to Organization of Small and Medium-Sized Business Associations	Limited the scope of exemptions
Business stability cartels	General	MITI	Laws Relating to Organization of Small and Medium-Sized Business Associations	Partially abolished
Rationalization cartels	General	MITI	Laws Relating to Organization of Small and Medium-Sized Business Associations	Partially abolished
Activities by designated organizations		MITI	Export-Import Trading Law	Abolished
Activities by trade unions	Labor	MITI	Export-Import Trading Law	Abolished
Economic business by cooperatives	Retail	MITI	Law on Cooperatives for the Promotion of Shopping Areas	Cooperatives exemption based on AMA Sec. 24
Small shopping district promoters	Retail trade, real estate	MITI	AMA Exemption Act, AMA Sec. 8	Cooperatives exemption to be based on AMA Sec. 24; bill in next session
Special contracts	SMEs	MITI	Laws Relating to Organization of Small and Medium-Sized Business Associations	Abolished
Underwriting and possession of shares of small and medium-sized companies	SMEs	MITI	Law on Investment Companies for the Development of Small and Medium-Sized Companies	Retained
SME Cooperatives	General	MITI; others	AMA Exemption Act, AMA Sec. 8; Cooperative Associations for Medium and Small-sized Enterprises	Cooperatives exemption to be based on AMA Sec. 24; bill in next session

Table 3. **Summary of status of exemptions from Antimonopoly Action** (*cont.*)

Description	Sector	Ministry	Legal basis	Status or plan
Aviation cartels (international)	Airlines	Transport	Civil Aeronautics Law	Retained; procedures to be established; bill in next session
Aviation cartels (domestic)	Airlines	Transport	Civil Aeronautics Law	Scope minimized, procedure with FTC
Transportation cartels	Auto transport	Transport	Freight Automobile Transportation Business Law	Abolished
Transportation cartels	Auto transport	Transport	Automobile Terminal Law	Abolished
Enterprise coordination	Land transport	Transport	AMA Exemption Act; Land Transport Enterprise Coordination Law	To be abolished; bill in next session
Coastal shipping cartels	Maritime	Transport	Coastal Shipping Association Law	Existing agreements to be abolished, but new system to be established, with procedures involving FTC; bill in next session
Joint shipping businesses	Maritime	Transport	Coastal Shipping Association Law	Retained for SMEs only; bill in next session
Maritime transport cartels (ocean shipping)	Maritime	Transport	Maritime Transportation Law	Retained; procedures to be established; bill in next session
Seamen's accidents	Maritime	Transport	AMA Exemption Act, AMA Sec. 8; Law re Promotion of Activities for Seamen's Accident Prevention	To be abolished; bill in next session
Coastal shipping cartels	Maritime	Transport	Maritime Transportation Law	To be limited to certain joint transport managements
Port-related cartels	Maritime, ports	Transport	Maritime Transportation Law	Abolished
Port-related cartels	Maritime, ports	Transport	Port Transportation Business Law	Abolished
Transportation cartels	Road transport	Transport	Road Transportation Law	Scope minimized, procedure with FTC
Warehousing cartels	Warehousing	Transport	Warehousing Business Law	Abolished
Small entrepreneurs' mutual aid groups	General		AMA Exemption Act, AMA Sec. 8	To be abolished; bill in next session
Potsdam Declaration directives			AMA Exemption Act; directives based on Potsdam Declaration	To be abolished; bill in next session

may be determinative, as a practical matter. In telecommunications, the Ministry of Post and Telecommunication will evidently apply competition principles indirectly. The FTC has tried to participate in decisions about reform in this sector, applying competition principles, but it is unclear that its contributions have had much influence. Technically, there is no formal exemption from the AMA, so the FTC and the ministry might share jurisdiction. But concerning mergers, for example, the ministry has statutory power to deny authorisation to acquisitions of major telecommunications businesses. The ministry thus has substantial influence concerning competition issues in this sector, although the FTC retains enforcement authority.

Similarly, important competition issues in electric power are likely to be decided by MITI, and in transport, by the Ministry of Transport. The ostensible reason is to take advantage of sectoral expertise, and to co-ordinate competition policy with legitimate elements of industrial policy. But this approach is also consistent with the traditional practice of vertically-segmented regulation.

Box 6. **Sectoral exemptions**

What is the extent of sectoral exclusions and exemptions? In 1995, the FTC estimated that about 40 per cent of the Japanese economy was in regulated sectors, and about 20 per cent in sectors with entry, price and output controls.[87] That figure has probably declined, as some formal exemptions have been eliminated.

---

5. COMPETITION ADVOCACY FOR REGULATORY REFORM

The FTC has a statutory responsibility to advise about laws and regulations that could affect competition.[88] It has fulfilled this function principally through the products of academic study groups. Over the last decade, these efforts have helped support significant changes. Much more could be done, though. Most importantly, as several speakers pointed out during the December 1996 seminar in Tokyo about the role of competition agencies in regulatory processes, a stronger enforcement record will lend authority and significance to the FTC's advice about regulatory policy.

When administrative bodies propose economic laws and ordinances, the FTC may consult at the planning and drafting stage if there is concern that they will include exemptions from the AMA or provisions which may restrict competition. In 1997, the FTC took part in discussions and consultations about the telecommunications laws and others.[89] Because the FTC is not in the cabinet, its views must be submitted through the Prime Minister's office, limiting the FTC's direct involvement. Organisations ordinarily have no authority to propose legislation outside their own jurisdiction. That is one reason to rely on study groups of outside experts to develop recommendations.

The principal method for analysing policy problems and proposing solutions throughout the Japanese government is by appointing a study group. Study groups may include representatives from business, labour, media, and consumer groups. Producer interests reportedly dominate these groups, directly or by proxy. The study group process is frequently criticised. Most groups include representatives of the industry or issue under review. Ministries appoint the members, based on expectations that they will direct the process towards what the ministries want. To reach a consensus report, it may be necessary to make compromises and to refrain from clear recommendations. The groups may take a long time on an issue, perhaps because those with an interest in maintaining the status quo can delay the process to resist recommendations for change. And many groups operate virtually in secret. The problems with study groups affect the FTC's own advocacy opportunities. At other ministries, it may be the study group, not the ministry itself, that must be addressed. Yet access to the study group process may be difficult. When the Ministry of Finance recently convened a study group about financial regulations, the FTC sent a representative to one meeting; this was the first time even that limited degree of participation had been possible. The process is becoming more open, in response to public pressures for transparency and accountability. Proposals are sometimes publicised in advance over the internet. Some meetings are now open to the public, and documents and materials for committee members are also available to the public.

The FTC has sponsored study groups on regulatory issues since 1985. The FTC's study groups do not seek to co-ordinate interests, but instead to gather expert advice. The fifteen members of its current study group on regulatory issues are mostly professors. The group's research work is done by the FTC staff. The group's current projects include trucking, airlines, electricity, gas, telecommunications, broadcasting, and resale price maintenance of copyright works.

Recommendations and reports by FTC study groups are credited with helping accomplish several major goals already. The single most significant project is probably the overhaul and repeal of the AMA exemptions. And the group played a role in changing the policy and the law about large scale stores. Detailed FTC research about regional enforcement pointed out problems due to local administrative guidance.

In 1997, three FTC study group reports were published: one on the domestic airline industry in March, and the others on the electric power industry and the gas industry, both in April. In airlines, the report found there had been some progress in domestic air passenger transport, and some effects could be seen, such as increased discounting. But the oligopolistic structure, of only three major airline companies, had not changed under partial deregulation, and competition in regular fares for competing routes has been limited since the introduction of the fare band system. The report concluded that more deregulation was necessary. Issues to be examined were the elimination of the supply and demand adjustment clause; the establishment of rules for reallocation of existing departure and arrival slots; the elimination of floor prices in the fare bands and the reconsideration of standard prices; and the elimination of the notification system for fares discounted by company policy.[90]

In the utility sectors, the report again emphasised the importance of eliminating the supply-demand balance power. Traditionally, utilities were categorised as concessions of public undertakings, for which balance of supply and demand were indispensable. Licensing, price control, and merger permission were all based on balance of supply and demand. The study group pointed out how the balancing clause blocked new services and was used as a shield to protect vested interests, distorting both the market and the regulatory process. Alternatives could achieve the same objectives more openly and objectively.

In electric power, the report called for deregulation, fostering of competitive conditions, and strict enforcement of the AMA. To introduce more competition in generation and retailing, the report proposed a bidding system, expanded retail supply, and self-generation in direct competition with the power companies. Issues identified for future discussion include liberalisation of retail supply, a review of the efficiency of vertically integrated systems of power generation, transmission, and distribution, development of competition between energy sectors, and the examination of the correct role of regulation through specific business laws. The responsible ministry has begun to undertake a reform program, but it is unclear to what extent the FTC study group recommendations are playing a role in it. In particular, it does not appear that strict enforcement of the AMA is part of the planned program.

In the gas industry, the report proposed reducing dependence on large-scale supply in city gas operations with the aim of deregulating entry and fostering competitive conditions. It also proposed that the consignment of city gas operations be legalised and that licensed gas operators be permitted to form small-scale networks within supply districts. Issues for future discussion include uniform regulations for the city gas industry, the framework for supply districts of city gas operators, vertical integration, and crossover entry between the electric and gas industries.

Despite a history of problems such as lack of transparency, the study group process is deeply entrenched in Japanese government practice. The FTC is thus likely to continue to rely on this method for much of its advocacy. FTC study group work has reportedly been influential on some matters, leading other ministries to treat the FTC as a more significant source of policy. More could be done to demonstrate the FTC's seriousness. In the current deregulation programme, the FTC may have an important new avenue for access and advocacy as part of the Secretariat to the Deregulation Committee. And the FTC's views would be taken even more seriously if the study group work was connected clearly to the FTC's main law enforcement responsibilities. The FTC staff who are already doing the background research for the study group could be a natural nucleus of expertise for bringing enforcement actions in these industries under study, where permitted by the AMA's jurisdictional constraints and other sources of exemption.

6. CONCLUSIONS AND POLICY OPTIONS FOR REFORM

6.1. General assessment of current strengths and weaknesses

The substantive legal basis for competition policy in Japan is sound. The competition law is essentially adequate to the task. Resources applied to enforcement, in budget and personnel, are increasing despite belt-tightening elsewhere in the government. The FTC has a record of more vigorous action over the last several years, and a reputation of some success in many manufacturing and distribution areas. Supporting the further extension of competition policy, a growing number in the government recognise the need for reform of regulatory systems that affect business initiative, for more competitive, self-reliant industry, and for less central direction.

But the countervailing weaknesses are troubling. There is pervasive scepticism, in the public and the government, about the process and benefits of competition, which supports a long-standing habit of relying on central direction and control. Support for, or even interest in, competition policy has been rare at the highest levels of the government. (Former Prime Minister Hashimoto, whose father was a principal author of the original AMA, was an exception to this history of indifference.) Even those who accept the need to move toward more competitive markets tend to see opportunities and needs for government direction, to facilitate the flow of capital and talent into new industries. That focus can obscure the more fundamental issue of ensuring that competitive decisions are made freely and independently by market actors as the basis for sustainable growth. Calls for stronger antitrust enforcement have traditionally come from labour and consumer groups, which are often somewhat suspicious of reform in other respects. Thus, it is not clear that the interests promoting reform understand the need for competition as part of that process. Meanwhile sectoral fiefdoms uniting industry and related ministries resist change and try to control competition, and the agency that represents competition policy has a reputation for weakness that it has not shaken. Because the recent strengthening of competition enforcement is a response to economic diplomacy, it is "more vulnerable, more superficial, and more eccentrically biased" than it would be if it sprang from a stronger domestic foundation.[91]

6.2. The dynamic view: the pace and direction of change

The present deregulation programme promises to continue in the right direction. But the pace has been slow, and the plans do not seem to call for speeding it up. Gradual introduction of competitive institutions permits inefficiency to survive for too long and thus delays potential gains in investment, innovation, and growth. Meanwhile, competition enforcement, though intensified, has not been strong enough to take a leading role. In other Member countries, antitrust challenge has opened up anti-competitive systems, such as exclusive distributorships that kept out new entrants. That is not happening yet in Japan. The objectives of the 1998 programme cannot be achieved without stronger competition policy enforcement, which can energise the process of regulatory reform by challenging existing structures that are no longer working. The programme implicitly recognises this by assigning an important role to the FTC.

6.3. Potential benefits and costs of further regulatory reform

The likely benefits of further competitive reform are incremental but significant. Consumer benefits, from lower prices, could be very large in many sectors. Synergies from increased competition and lower costs in business service sectors (such as telecommunications, transport, and finance) could be substantial and cross-cutting. Even if a major goal of Japan's reform process is improving its international competitiveness, rather than aiding consumers, greater reliance on competition should yield substantial benefits. Cross-country comparisons show that high productivity is best explained by the strength of competition.[92]

The costs due to transitional disruptions could also be large, though. The fear of those dislocations preserves the status quo and encourages rationalisations such as the belief that competitively efficient firms would not support local communities. There will certainly be tangible costs of restructuring, to move assets into more productive uses, and this risk should not be minimised. But a related cost, one that is difficult to quantify and address, will be psychological. Greater reliance on competitive processes will require changing expectations about the importance, and sources, of stability and security.

6.4. Policy options for consideration[93]

- *Strengthen rights of private action by providing for injunctions in independent private suits, easing the proof of damages in competition cases, and facilitating consumer and customer recoveries in price-fixing cases. The quota on new lawyers should be eliminated.*

These steps would apply more resources to competition policy issues, expand the base of support for it, and enlist other institutions in developing important policy principles. Broader rights of private

225

action, more effectively vindicated, would signify that competition policy creates basic legal rights for market actors and is not just a technical regulatory speciality. Other, related institutions may also need attention to make expanded private rights practically available. In addition to the obvious need to end the limit on the number of lawyers, it may also be necessary to add judges or establish a special court division, similar to the one that handles patent issues, to hear complex economic matters such as competition cases. Unless resources are added or streamlining procedures are developed, the promise of new avenues of relief may be disappointed by delays.

- *Increase the visibility and impact of FTC participation in policy-making.*

Establishing a forum for discussing and clearly deciding about matters that affect competition in the context of overall economic policy is critical for reform to succeed. The FTC should become in fact what it is in theory, the principal "horizontal" authority responsible for assessing as well as applying competition policy. This will require preserving the FTC's independence from political direction while permitting it to take a more central role in policy formation. Both directions will help it overcome overcoming its image as a weak agency. The FTC already has a new opportunity for substantial input into government-wide issues, through its assignments under the 1998 deregulation programme and its role on the secretariat to the Deregulation Council. It already has statutory responsibilities and opportunities for consultation, which it could and should exercise more vigorously. The plan for a Ministry of General Affairs, to which the FTC will be attached, may also promote a more visible and central policy role.

- *Explicitly include in the mandates of sectoral ministries and regulators the responsibility to support competition principles and enforcement.*

Making other ministries responsible for eliminating constraints on competition within their own jurisdiction would also extend the scope of competition policy and emphasise its broad, horizontal importance. To maintain the FTC's central responsibility, ministries should also be held responsible for co-ordinating with the FTC so that enforcement issues are referred there quickly. Major ministries might have antitrust bureaux (similar to MITI's Industrial Organisation section), to work with the FTC and to advise industries about their compliance obligations. These steps could be elements of the revisions of the ministries' foundation laws to clarify the relationship between the administration and the market, which are recommended in Chapter 2.

- *Establish a clear, public, effective relationship between consumer policy and competition policy.*

Another policy area to which competition policy should be better connected is consumer policy. A clearer institutional relationship should be developed between competition policy and consumer policy. This may require first the establishment of a stronger authority for consumer protection matters. Alternatively, the relationship might be underscored by assigning to the FTC the responsibility for implementing a market-oriented consumer protection policy complementary to the AMA. The FTC is already responsible for special statutes, such as those concerning premiums and representations, as well as provisions of the AMA that can be conceived in terms of consumer protection policy.

- *Complete the planned elimination and narrowing of sectoral and other exemptions from the AMA.*

These plans have been underway for several years, in several stages. It is imperative to follow through on the plans already announced for legislative action. For those items calling for further study, that process should be completed and legislation drafted to narrow any remaining exemptions as much as possible.

- *Improve the FTC's economic and legal resources, to enable it to undertake more sophisticated merger and monopoly enforcement, prepare more successful cartel cases and resolve market access problems.*

To demonstrate its seriousness and relevance, the FTC must not only maintain and even increase its attention to cartels and bid-rigging, but it should prepare to do more economically sophisticated cases as well, especially mergers, to deal with the restructurings that will inevitably follow more effective enforcement against cartels. This will call for continuing to deepen its expertise and improve the mix of skills, with greater emphasis on both economic analysis and on investigative and legal techniques. Continuing to bring in more persons with prosecutorial experience, in leadership positions, as permanent staff, and in personnel exchanges, should sharpen the FTC's enforcement capacities.

- *Target enforcement on practices that have been tolerated or promoted by informal administrative guidance, to reinforce the shift in regulatory philosophy away from central direction.*

Exemplary enforcement actions should vigorously implement the principles set out in the 1994 FTC guidelines about administrative guidance. Steps against co-ordination sponsored by other ministries are at the heart of the regulatory reform agenda. It will not be enough to consult with other ministries and ask them to stop encouraging or tolerating non-competitive behaviour. Rather, effective and visible sanctions must be applied to the private parties who use the cover of ministerial acceptance or instruction to prevent competition. The FTC faced up to some anti-competitive actions by other ministries even in the 1950s and 1960s. The FTC appears stronger now, and thus it should be able to do so with more confidence. FTC oversight of trade associations activities, where much of the impact of administrative guidance is felt, must be maintained and even intensified. The trend toward seeking stronger sanctions in trade association cases is right and should continue.

- *Publicise actions and reasoning, to educate the public and the business community about the effects and benefits of competition policy and law enforcement.*

The FTC has already taken many steps to correct historic problems of lack of transparency, by issuing detailed, updated guidelines based on its actual decisions, and by devising ways to explain to the public the cases it has disposed of without formal decisions, such as mergers. The FTC's efforts to explain its decisions and to open up its own regulatory process may be a model for other ministries to study. The FTC should continue to devise ways to explain its actions in as much detail as possible. This will not only assist business in understanding its obligations under the AMA, but it will develop public support for competition enforcement by demonstrating how it protects the public interest. And it will encourage the development of sound legal and economic policies, by making available more authoritative raw material for academic study and public debate.

- *Eliminate all "supply-demand balancing" aspects of permitting, licensing, and other forms of advice or intervention, formal or informal, within a fixed period, such as one year. Fix sunset dates of preferably less than two years on all such requirements that remain.*

The most important broad-ranging competition-based reform would be the elimination of all of these "supply-demand balancing" functions that serve to control and prevent pro-competitive entry. The current programme promises to move in the right direction, but the concrete content is disappointingly limited and the target dates are imprecise. Perhaps some further research would reveal obscure requirements that also deserve attention. But the major ones, such as those that still limit entry into transport sectors, are well known and need no further study. The action needed now is a firm, short deadline for their repeal.

- *Improve capacities to address international competition problems by reaching agreements with other countries on cooperation and enforcement.*

The FTC should enter bilateral co-operation agreements with other major international competition agencies. As the scope of its international jurisdiction expands, and as the market in Japan continues to open to more foreign trade and investment, the proportion of enforcement matters with significant international dimensions will only increase. Without clear arrangements with the enforcement authorities of its major trading partners, the FTC will be at an increasing disadvantage in taking accurate, timely action in these matters.

6.5. Managing regulatory reform

Many of these recommendations have been proposed by others, or are already under serious study in Japan. Thus, few would likely be considered too controversial. Planning and co-ordinating action to be sure that the public understands how it can benefit consumers and taxpayers should help overcome traditional scepticism. The current crisis presents the FTC with a great challenge, and a great opportunity. The policies of openness and market-driven competition that the FTC promotes increasingly represent the international standard. The FTC may thus become a leader, not a follower, if Japan chooses to work its way out of the economic slump by harmonising its regulatory policies with those of its major trading partners.

NOTES

1. See Iyori, H. and Uesugi, A. (1994), *The Antimonopoly Laws and Policies of Japan*, New York, pp. 30-52.

2. Act Concerning Prohibition of Private Monopolisation and Maintenance of Fair Trade (law No. 54 of 1947) ("AMA"), Sec. 1.

3. Oil cartel case, Supreme Court, 24 Feb. 1984. The Court said that the law's most important objective was to guarantee that price is determined freely in the market, but it also justified administrative intervention affecting price as long as the intervention was done by appropriate means that were not substantially incompatible with the law's "ultimate purpose" of promoting democratic and wholesome economic development and assuring the interest of consumers.

4. AMA, Sec. 2(4).

5. Tilton, M. (1996), *Restrained Trade: Cartels in Japan's Basic Materials Industries*, Ithaca, pp. 17-18.

6. See Iyori, H. and Uesugi, A. (1994), *The Antimonopoly Laws and Policies of Japan*, New York, pp. 41-48.

7. See First, H. (1995), "Antitrust Enforcement in Japan", Antitrust Law Journal, Vol. 64, p. 144.

8. First (1995), pp. 138-140.

9. See also Chapter 2 for additional discussion of the general style and purpose of regulation in Japan.

10. Iyori and Uesugi (1994), pp. 1-11.

11. Iyori and Uesugi (1994), pp. 11-20, 30-39.

12. Sanekata, K. and Wilks, S. (1996), "The Fair Trade Commission and the Enforcement of Competition Policy in Japan," in *Comparative Competition Policy: National Institutions in a Global Market*, G. B. Doern and S. Wilks, ed., pp. 102-138, Oxford.

13. See First (1995), p. 157.

14. Sanekata and Wilks (1996).

15. Iyori and Uesugi (1994), pp. 215-16.

16. Sanekata and Wilks (1996), p. 102.

17. Act Against Delay in Payment of Subcontract Proceeds, etc., to Subcontractors (law No. 120 of 1956); Act Against Unjustifiable Premiums and Misleading Representations (law No. 134 of 1962).

18. AMA, Sec. 2(6).

19. AMA, Secs. 89-100.

20. Criminal Code, Art. 96-3.

21. Iyori and Uesugi (1994), p. 73.

22. Fair Trade Commission (1998), Annual Report on Competition Policy in Japan, January-December 1997.

23. Fair Trade Commission (1997), Annual Report on Competition Policy Developments in Japan, 1996.

24. Sanekata and Wilks (1996), pp. 111-13; First (1995), pp. 174-75.

25. Iyori and Uesugi (1994), pp. 91-92.

26. Sanekata and Wilks (1996), refer to the FTC's political "tightrope," p. 112.

27. Sanekata and Wilks (1996), p. 113, argue that the permitted information exchanges "effectively perpetuated" the anti-competitive practices.

28. Asahi News (Internet), 9 September 1998.

29. Tilton (1996), pp. 13-14 and *passim*.

30. Fair Trade Commission (1997).

31. AMA, Sec. 8.

32. Sanekata and Wilks (1996), p. 133.

33. Tilton (1996); Tilton, M. (1998), "Regulatory Reform, Antitrust, and Market Opening in Japan", in Is Japan Really Changing Its Ways? *Regulatory Reform and the Japanese*, Lonny E. Carlile and Mark C. Tilton, ed., Washington.

34. *See* OECD (1997), *Report on Regulatory* Reform, Vol. 2, pp. 108-109; Iyori and Uesugi (1994), p. 293.

35. *See* Tilton (1998).

36. Fair Trade Commission (1998).

37. Fair Trade Commission (1998).

38. AMA, Sec. 3.

39. AMA, Sec. 8-4(1).

40. AMA, Sec. 2(7)(I). The standard is also met by a combined share of the top two firms over 75 per cent.

41. Guidelines Concerning "Specific Business Fields" as Defined in the Provisions of "Monopolistic Situations", November 29, 1977 (last revised June 1, 1997).

42. The Guidelines about monopolistic practices apply the terms of Sec. 2 of the AMA, which refer to goods of the "same description" or those "having strikingly similar function and utility" supplied in Japan. The proposed Guidelines for mergers interpret the terms of Sec. 15 of the AMA, "particular field of trade", to embrace goods or services that have "similar functions and uses". The merger statute addresses combinations of firms "in Japan", while the Sec. 2 defines "monopolistic situation" in terms of the share of sales or supply "in Japan".

43. Fair Trade Commission (1998).

44. Fair Trade Commission (1998).

45. The FTC guidelines thus do not use the Herfindahl index ("HHI"), an estimate of industry concentration used in several other Member states. The HHI is the sum of the squares of the individual market shares of all the firms in the industry. When these are expressed as percentages, the index ranges from zero, for atomistic competition, to 10 000, for pure monopoly. For comparison, the first and fourth tests in the FTC's guidelines would usually correspond to HHI levels of about 1 400 (although the first test could in theory be satisfied by an HHI as low as 700). The second and third tests do not clearly correspond to any particular HHI level; indeed, the second test could in theory be met at virtually any HHI level.

46. For purposes of comparison, this test of oligopoly structure implies an HHI of about 2 000. The lowest HHI that could theoretically meet this test is about 1 650.

47. Fair Trade Commission (1998).

48. Fair Trade Commission (1998).

49. Fair Trade Commission (1997).

50. Fair Trade Commission, 1998.

51. AMA, Sec. 71.

52. Iyori and Uesugi (1994), pp. 144-150.

53. Tilton (1998).

54. Fair Trade Commission (1997).

55. Consumer Protection Law, Art. 10.

56. Sanekata and Wilks (1996), pp. 123-24, contend that the FTC's "actual independence has been ambivalent and ambiguous", and its "denial that the Commissioners consider the interests of their parent ministries lacks plausibility. ... Thus, in practice, the constitution of the JFTC has been an actual impediment to the active enforcement of the Act".

57. First (1995), p. 175, citing news services and personal communications with FTC officials.

58. Fair Trade Commission (1998).

59. Sanekata and Wilks (1996), p. 106.

60. Sanekata and Wilks (1996), pp. 105-106; *cf.* (1995), p. 178.

61. AMA, Sec. 27-2.

62. AMA, Sec. 8-4.

63. Sanekata and Wilks (1996), p. 126-27.

64. AMA, Sec. 94-2.

65. First (1995), pp. 167-68; Fair Trade Commission (1998). The FTC's "continuing hesitancy" to bring criminal actions "has led observers to suggest that criminal sanctions against individuals have become an inherited treasure sword – used only for decoration". Sanekata and Wilks (1996), p. 119.

66. That is much lower than the ¥ 500 million that the FTC wanted, though. Resistance from the LDP construction *zoku* led to the lower figure. The largest fine collected so far is ¥ 60 million. Sanekata and Wilks (1996), pp. 113-17.

67. First (1995), p. 174.

68. Iyori and Uesugi (1994), p. 87.

69. Sanekata and Wilks (1996), p. 132; Iyori and Uesugi (1994), p. 67.

70. AMA, Section 45.

71. Civil Code, Section 709.

72. AMA, Section 84.

73. Sanekata and Wilks (1996), pp. 120-23, 130.

74. Sanekata and Wilks conclude that studies like these have been done in conjunction with MITI in order to develop "defences to criticism from overseas". Sanekata and Wilks (1996), pp. 106-7.

75. Fair Trade Commission (1998).

76. Fair Trade Commission (1998).

77. First (1995), p. 159.

78. Fair Trade Commission (1998).

79. AMA, Sec. 22. The specific statutes are listed in the Section 1 of the Act Concerning Exemptions from the Antimonopoly Act, which is to be repealed.

80. *Cf.* description of Kraft experience in Tilton (1998).

81. AMA, Sec. 2(1).

82. AMA, Sec. 24.

83. Fair Trade Commission (1998)

84. Prof. Ushio CHUJO, presentation to OECD mission seminar at EPA (July 1998).

85. Prof. Ushio CHUJO, presentation to OECD mission seminar at EPA (July 1998).

86. AMA, Sec. 21.

87. Fair Trade Commission, Annual report for FY1995, p. 132.

88. AMA, Sec. 27-2(v).

89. Fair Trade Commission (1998).

90. Fair Trade Commission (1998).

91. Sanekata and Wilks (1996), p. 134.

92. OECD (1997).

93. These options follow generally the relevant recommendations of OECD (1997):

   – *Review and strengthen where necessary the scope, effectiveness and enforcement of competition policy.*

   • Eliminate sectoral gaps in coverage of competition law, unless evidence suggests that compelling public interests cannot be served in better ways.
   • Enforce competition law vigorously where collusive behaviour, abuse of dominant position, or anticompetitive mergers risk frustrating reform.
   • Provide competition authorities with the authority and capacity to advocate reform.

   – *Reform economic regulations in all sectors to stimulate competition, and eliminate them except where clear evidence demonstrates that they are the best way to serve broad public interests.*

   • Review as a high priority those aspects of economic regulations that restrict entry, exit, pricing, output, normal commercial practices and forms of business organisation.
   • Promote efficiency and the transition to effective competition where economic regulations continue to be needed because of potential for abuse of market power. In particular: *i*) separate potentially competitive activities from regulated utility networks, and otherwise restructure as needed to reduce the market power of incumbents; *ii*) guarantee access to essential network facilities to all market entrants on a transparent and non-discriminatory basis; *iii*) use price caps and other mechanisms to encourage efficiency gains when price controls are needed during the transition to competition.

BACKGROUND REPORT
ON ENHANCING MARKET OPENNESS
THROUGH REGULATORY REFORM*

* This report was principally prepared by **DoHoon Kim** and **Akira Kawamoto**, Principal Administrators, of the Trade Directorate. It has benefited from extensive comments provided by colleagues throughout the OECD Secretariat, by the Government of Japan, and by Member countries as part of the peer review process. This report was peer reviewed in November 1998 in the Working Party of the OECD's Trade Committee.

TABLE OF CONTENTS

Executive Summary

Background Report on Enhancing Market Openness Through Regulatory Reform

Does the national regulatory system allow foreign and domestic enterprises to take full advantage of competitive global markets? Reducing regulatory barriers to trade and investment enables countries in an expanding global economy to benefit more fully from comparative advantage and innovation. This means that more market openness increases the benefits that consumers as well as producers can draw from regulatory reform. Maintaining an open world trading system requires regulatory styles and content that promote global competition and economic integration, avoid trade disputes, and improve trust and mutual confidence across borders.

Recognising the benefits from the integration in the open multilateral trading system, Japan has improved market access in the context of border measures to a level equal to or better than many other OECD countries. However, enhancing market openness by relaxing behind-the-border measures such as domestic regulations has been relatively slow in Japan. Japan has recently undertaken a number of promising deregulatory programmes such as the two Three year Programmes for the Promotion of Deregulation. Those Programmes clearly state *inter alia* that enhancing market openness is one of most important objectives. However, despite some progress made by these programmes, the Japanese regulatory system in many respects is still perceived as unfriendly to new competition, especially foreign competition. This may be due to the relatively poor extent to which six efficient regulation principles related to market openness identified by the OECD are integrated into the Japanese regulatory system.

Lack of transparency is one of main weaknesses of the Japanese regulatory system, because of both opaque administrative culture and lax implementation of laws. The weak enforcement of competition policy is another major weak point, because anti-competitive practices by private firms or semi-public organisations are seen to pose obstacles for market access in Japan. Major trading partners frequently express concerns about these two principles: transparency and application of competition policy. In addition, despite positive aspects such as the role of the Office of Trade and Investment Ombudsman (OTO), Japan is often criticised for acquiesing in many burdensome administrative procedures which are felt to unnecessarily hamper imports and inward investment.

Japanese regulatory reform programmes have closely reflected pressures from major trading partners to address the perceived causes of a wide range of trade friction. However, for reform to be truly effective more attention must be paid to the overall objective that is sought rather than particular problems that have arisen. Reform must thus move beyond being a reaction to foreign pressures and must instead be fully embraced by public authorities as being foremost in the interest of the national economy: to strengthen its competitiveness in an open global economy and to promote the welfare of its people. Japan needs to demonstrate clear commitment to its regulatory reform programmes through bold and coherent policies, linked with a strong commitment for rapid implementation.

1. MARKET OPENNESS AND REGULATION: THE POLICY ENVIRONMENT IN JAPAN

The Japanese government recognises explicitly the benefits that have accrued to the Japanese economy from the opportunities available today to globalise economic activities – opportunities which arise to an important extent from the open multilateral trading system.[1] Thanks to their participation in world competition, Japanese manufacturing industries have often succeeded in acquiring a high level of competitiveness and enhancing the national economic welfare.

The benefits of regulatory reform from the market openness perspective are still potentially very large in Japan. This has been shown by numerous studies on price differences between the Japanese domestic market and comparable foreign markets.[2] These price differences are persistently high despite the progress made in trade liberalisation, deregulation and structural reform, perhaps due to high trade protection for agriculture and some manufacturing sectors (according to Sazanami's work) or due to the inefficiency of highly regulated service sectors and utilities (according to Daiwa Economic Research Institute). The combined effects of both are probably responsible. The Japanese government, recognising the potential benefits, has also conducted surveys on price differences.[3] According to these surveys, citizens of Tokyo pay 8-30% more for their purchases than citizens in major other international cities and Japanese industries are paying almost twice as high for non-manufacturing intermediary inputs compared to their competitors of, and more than three or four times higher compared to those of other Asian emerging economies (see section 4.3 for detailed discussion).

Recognition of the benefits of globalisation and of further market opening reform have been reflected more and more in Japanese trade policy. In order to integrate its economy in the world trading system, Japan has continuously reduced its general tariff rates so that it now has one of the lowest average tariff rates within the OECD area, with 4.8% for all products and 2.5% for manufactured products.[4] The relative absence of formal non-tariff border measures in Japan is notable as well.[5] Japan has been also active in world-wide and regional trade talks/negotiations such as the WTO and the APEC.

Japan has also made clear that it intends to increasingly open its economy to global competition through deregulation. In its "Three-Year Programme for the Promotion of Deregulation" announced in March 1998, the Japanese government has committed to achieving "an open and fair *socio-economic system which is internationally open* and based on principles of self-responsibility and market mechanism". Some recent measures of regulatory reform have indeed resulted in visible improvement in Japanese market openness, such as oil import deregulation. Moreover, the Japanese government has shifted from its former export promotion policies to focus more and more on the promotion of imports and inward investment. For example, many supplementary incentives to imports and inward investments have been introduced, in addition to the ordinary financial and fiscal incentives for domestic activities. Japan has strengthened policy efforts on infrastructure for imports and inward investments, especially by expanding FAZs (Foreign Access Zones).[6] It also gives technical assistance for this purpose at the bilateral and/or regional level. In order to implement these measures vigorously, Japan adopted in 1992 a special law on Extraordinary Measures for the Promotion of Imports and the Facilitation of Inward Investment. In 1995, this law was prolonged for a further 10 years.[7]

However, against the background of the lingering large-scale Japanese surplus in trade, many trading partners have continuously raised concerns about the effective openness of the Japanese market. Compared to other OECD countries, Japan has been far below average in attracting foreign direct investment, despite the government's expressed policy stance to welcome it (see Figure 1). This has been seen by trading partners as a sign of the restrictive nature of the Japanese business environment, notably arising from domestic regulations. Indeed preliminary figures for 1997 suggest that despite recent market opening, FDI (foreign direct investment) inflows to Japan amounted to only US$ 3 224 million, it did not even place amongst the top 25 countries with respect to FDI inflows,[8] despite the fact that Japan's economy is the second largest in the world.

Figure 1. **Share of stocks of inward and outward direct investment in GDP in OECD countries in 1995**

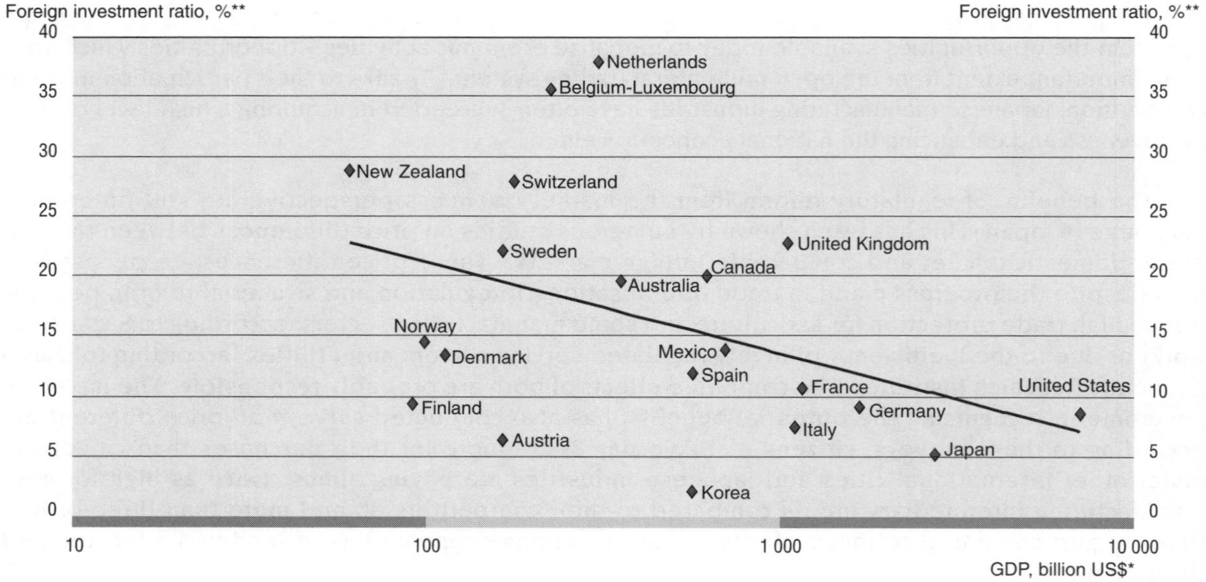

Foreign investment ratio, %**   Foreign investment ratio, %**

*   GDP measured at current prices and current PPPs in billion US dollars.
** Average of inward investment and outward investment relative to GDP (except for Mexico, inward only).
Source: OECD, *The Review of Regulatory Reform in the Netherlands,* calculated from AFA databases (DSTI, EAS Division) and DAFFE's Foreign Investment Database.

Since the 1980s, major trading partners have paid more attention to Japan's domestic regulations and its economic system, which they perceive as unfriendly to competition from foreign products and services. The US and EU have urged Japan to reform domestic regulations in order to enhance market access as well as domestic (behind the border) obstacles.[9] These trade talks have prompted Japan to take several deregulatory initiatives. *Recent Japanese deregulation programmes, especially those in the 1990s, therefore, cannot be dissociated from trade talks with major trading partners.*

Bilateral US-Japan consultations in several sectors began in the 1980s. Deregulation became an element of major trade debate in 1990 under the Japan-US Structural Impediment Initiative Talks, which targeted regulatory restrictions in sectors such as large-scale retail stores (see Box 1). The Japanese Cabinet stated in 1991 that one way of reducing trade impediments was to promote deregulation more strongly, and it recommended further measures in the telecommunication, financial services, and energy sectors. The Japan-US Framework for a New Economic Partnership, established in July 1993, centred on deregulation measures in eight areas related to international trade and investment. With the EU, Japan reached a bilateral agreement in the form of understandings in June 1995, to implement some deregulatory measures for automobiles and components.

International discussion has been increasingly focused on the public sector's regulatory requirements and processes. Trading partners have complained about complex rules, opaque decision-making, and non-transparent instructions from ministries and have urged Japanese government to make efforts to open government processes and simplify regulations. "Questions about the openness of the Japanese market have turned away from conventional trade policy issues towards differences in national business practices and regulations, which are not overtly protectionist..." the OECD Economic

---

Box 1. Japanese retail distribution and Large Scale Retail Stores Law

As an article of *International Economic Review* says, the Japanese system is characterised by large numbers of small retailers and few high-volume discount stores, The dominance of small retailers in Japan's distribution system has been attributed to traditional Japanese factors such as the importance of fresh food in the Japanese diet, which requires frequent shopping trips, and the role of offering employment opportunities for non-qualified or retired persons especially in relatively rural areas. This distribution system has been an unfavourable factor of market competition for foreign products, because incumbent producers have had dominant positions *vis-à-vis* wholesalers and retailers.

The Large Scale Retail Store Law has been pointed out by trading partners as another factor which has indirectly served as a market obstacle for foreign products. Under the Law, the shopping space size of a proposed large scale store has been subject to consultation with local small retail stores.[10] This, in turn, has hampered market access for new products and new competitors including foreign ones, as small retail stores tend to prefer long term relations with wholesalers or manufacturers.

Important changes in the law since the early 1990s have eased the opening of large stores. OECD, *Economic Survey*, 1995 states that liberalisation of Japan's Large Scale Retail Store Law has resulted in a sharp increase of applications to open large stores and overall gains are estimated at as much as US$ 45 billion.

Despite the recent decision to abolish the Law, foreign parties are still concerned that openings of large scale stores may be impeded. One reason is that regulating powers will be transferred to local authorities whose political leaders are likely to be influenced by the political power of regional co-operatives of small retail stores. Foreign parties are also concerned that the new law concerning the measures by large scale retail stores for preservation of living environment, could be used in a prohibitive way. On the other hand, some regional authorities which are less dependent on small retailers may try to attract large stores to stimulate the regional economy. In this case, abolishment of the Law can have a favourable effect on market competition.

Source: *International Economic Review*, Retail Distribution in Japan, September/October 1997, OECD *Economic Survey on Japan*, 1995.

Survey noted in 1991.[11] Besides, more attention is being given to harmonising procedures, standards, and rules with international norms.

While regulatory reform has been underway since the early 1980s to improve the competitiveness and efficiency of Japanese firms, economy-wide programmes of deregulation were initiated only in 1995, when the "Deregulation Action Programme" was launched. Those Programmes have clearly stated *inter alia* enhancing market openness as one of most important objectives. However, while trading partners have welcomed the progress to date, their requests for Japanese regulatory reform have persisted as well and the number of requests is increasing. It has been difficult to have a general picture of the current status of Japanese regulatory reform from market openness perspectives, due to the complexity, sheer size and coverage of regulatory questions as well as their continuous evolution. An overview of the reform and trade discussion will be useful at this juncture.

Bilateral trade talks, while addressing many concrete issues, have put relatively less priority on questions which tend to take longer to resolve. Trading partners have been keen to explain that their requests will not only serve foreign traders or investors but also benefit the Japanese economy, especially industrial competitiveness and consumer interests. However, bilateral trade discussions may have given the Japanese public the impression that reform, even if undertaken, has been imposed from the outside. Such impression may have diluted the effectiveness of market openness perspective in reform discussions. External pressures are sometimes discussed in Japan as useful and even necessary for meaningful reform. But there are also limits: if used excessively, the public image of such external pressures will deteriorate and negative views may be promoted by those who would like to maintain status quo of regulations.

Some observers hold the view that in the context of the Japanese political economy, the balance of power is advantageous for resisting reform.[12] Thus far, the business sector, especially the export oriented sector, has been the major promoter of regulatory reform in Japan. Its concerns over competitiveness in future have pressed government for deregulation initiatives, although there still remain strong sectoral reservations,

---

especially by regulated firms. Academics and media are sometimes strongly in favour of deregulation, but neither seek to be involved in detailed issues. Consumer voices have only been weakly heard in Japan, although they will stand greatly to benefit from reform. They have not come out strongly for government efforts toward deregulation and in some cases they have been hostile to further market openness.[13]

This image of strong external pressures and weak domestic support for reform suggest that clearer recognition in Japan of the economy-wide interests in both regulatory reform and market openness would be crucial in creating a firmer basis for future reform. When reform in a market openness perspective benefits foreign trade and investment, Japanese consumers and firms will benefit as well. Not only foreign voices, but also a growing number of surveys by Japanese institutions have found market openness perspectives are beneficial for the Japanese economy. Studies on price differentials between domestic and international markets have revealed that such differentials mainly reflect Japanese market access problems and that Japanese people are losing one of their main sources of welfare increase, in other words foreign sources, because of problems in the Japanese regulatory system. The Japan External Trade Organisation (JETRO) has published a number of sectoral studies from a market openness perspective. The 1997/1998 OECD Economic Survey also states the need to promote such a perspective: "While deregulation has been opening up new business opportunities and international competition has been exerting pressures on companies to remain competitive, changes in the Japanese business sector overall have not been sufficient to arrest the trend declines in profitability and the rates of new company formation".[14]

As seen in this section, market openness perspectives have been a strong driving force in past Japanese regulatory reform. They will continue to play an important role in the future. However, external pressure on specific issues is not a sufficient basis for bringing the sea-change in domestic regulation that is needed to achieve the benefits sought for the Japanese and world economies. On the one hand, more focus on domestic regulatory *systems* in trade talks will help to focus on more fundamental issues and thus resolve the trade debate more effectively. On the other hand, the reform discussion in the domestic context needs to be strengthened, linking recognition of the domestic benefits to greater market access. Japanese people may recognise that regulatory reform is not to simply reduce trade tension but also to reinvigorate the economic efficiency and to avoid welfare loss to Japanese economy.

2. THE POLICY FRAMEWORK FOR MARKET OPENNESS: THE SIX "EFFICIENT REGULATION" PRINCIPLES

An important step in ensuring that regulations do not unnecessarily reduce market openness is to build the "efficient regulation" principles into the domestic regulatory process for social and economic regulations, as well as for administrative practices. "Market openness" here refers to the ability of foreign suppliers to compete in a national market without encountering discriminatory or excessively burdensome or restrictive conditions. These principles, which have been described in the 1997 OECD *Report on Regulatory Reform* and developed further in the Trade Committee, are:

- *transparency and openness of decision making;*
- *non-discrimination;*
- *avoidance of unnecessary trade restrictiveness;*
- *use of internationally harmonised measures;*
- *recognition of equivalence of other countries' regulatory measures; and*
- *application of competition principles from an international perspective.*

They have been identified by trade policy makers as key to market-oriented and trade and investment-friendly regulation. They reflect the basic principles underpinning the multilateral trading system/ WTO in which many countries have undertaken certain obligations. The intention of the OECD country reviews on regulatory reform is not to judge the extent to which any country may have undertaken and lived up to international commitments relating directly or indirectly to these principles; but rather to assess whether and how domestic instruments, procedures and practices give effect to the principles and successfully contribute to market openness. Similarly, the OECD country reviews of regulatory reform are not concerned with an assessment of trade policies and practices in Member countries.

In sum, this report considers whether and how Japan's regulatory procedures and content affect the quality of market access and presence in Japan. An important reverse scenario – whether and how inward trade and investment affect the fulfilment of legitimate policy objectives reflected in social regulation – is beyond the scope of the present discussion. This latter issue has been extensively debated within and beyond the OECD from a range of policy perspectives. To date, however, OECD deliberations have found no evidence to suggest that trade and investment *per se* impact negatively on the pursuit and attainment of domestic policy goals through regulation or other means.[15]

2.1. Transparency, openness of decision making and of appeal procedures

To ensure international market openness, foreign firms and individuals seeking access to a market (or expanding activities in a given market) must have adequate information on new or revised regulations so that they can base their decisions on an accurate assessment of potential costs, risks, and market opportunities. Regulations need to be transparent to foreign traders and investors. Regulatory transparency at both domestic and international levels can be achieved through a variety of means, including systematic publication of proposed rules prior to entry into force, use of electronic means to share information (such as the Internet), well-timed opportunities for public comment, and rigorous mechanisms for ensuring that such comments are given due consideration prior to the adoption of a final regulation.[16] Market participants wishing to voice concerns about the application of existing regulations should have appropriate access to appeal procedures. This sub-section discusses the extent to which such objectives are met in Japan and how.

Lack of transparency in the Japanese regulatory system has been one of the major subjects of Japan's own regulatory reform efforts and important concern of major trading partners. Transparency is related with all the phases of the regulatory process: from the stage of formulating regulations to that of implementing them, including the stage of changing or reforming them. The Japanese government, recognising the importance and necessities to take actions to enhance transparency,[17] has undertaken various reform projects in this light in its administrative procedures. Despite these commitments and many attempts to improve the situation, there still remains the scope for further improvement.

Trading partners' concerns with regard to the non-transparency problem are consistent with Japan's own reform in this area and suggest the necessities to improve the situation. For example, the US has asked Japan to enhance transparency by improving use of the following strategies:[18]

- notice and comment procedures for regulations;
- information disclosure requirement for government entities;
- examination procedures for licences, permits and approvals;
- consultation process of advisory councils;
- private sector regulations; and
- information on administrative guidance.

The EU has also asked for improvements to transparency in several areas:[19]

- information disclosure;
- examination of all administrative guidance on competition policy principles;
- prior publication of and opportunity for comments on regulatory proposals;
- links and connections between industry associations and the administration; and
- publication of deliberations within advisory bodies.

According to major trading partners,[20] numerous non-transparency cases can be also found at the sectoral level, for example: implementation of the Building Standards Law for the housing sector; oppor-

241

tunity to comment on health care policies; the approval process of new products and services and regulations of private sector organisations in the financial services sector; the slot allocation system of international airports; the procurement process and review and comment procedures in the energy sector; consideration of a more cost-oriented interconnection accounting system for telecommunications; lack of comment opportunities before the advisory council on motor vehicle regulations; tariff review mechanisms;[21] and approval procedures for medical machines.

Concerning administrative culture, Japanese bureaucrats have often relied on "administrative guidance" rather than established laws and rules to enforce their policies. Trading partners have been concerned that this traditional administrative style may have reduced the level of transparency for outsiders, especially foreign ones (see background report on Government capacity to assure high quality regulation in Japan for more detailed discussion of administrative guidance).

The new Three year Programme has recommended that regulatory authorities ensure transparency when using administrative guidance, and many ministries and agencies seem to be following that recommendation. In June 1998, the Ministry of Finance announced that it had codified about 400 cases of guidance in a more formal form.[22] Even though this was well received by the financial sector, including foreign participants, an American firm in the sector still expressed concerns about non-transparent characters of Japanese administrative procedures.[23] According to it, despite the codification, the substance of most guidance has not changed much and some guidance still remains unwritten.

According to the Administrative Procedure Law, regulatory authorities should use guidance only based on the voluntary co-operation of subject parties and not treat them disadvantageously because of the non-compliance (Article 32). Therefore, administrative guidance seems to be officially no longer used in a binding manner. But, consultation continues to be used as a means to control the sectors, to co-ordinate their interests and even to disseminate regulatory information which may be used in the regulatory decision making process.[24]

Another issue is transparency of consulting procedures. Ministries and agencies rely on over 200 advisory councils (*shingikai*) to get broader general views on policies and policy directions. Advisory councils are composed of eminent scholars, journalists, and industry specialists including business leaders. Because of their composition, the advisory councils are considered to represent both general public opinion and specialist views. They are often called upon when ministries or agencies need to know public opinion before they make an important decision. However, because many members of advisory councils are involved in the sectors, and even come directly from incumbent business, they can be considered as "inner circle" members. In fact, advisory council members are usually selected by bureaucrats in a discretionary way. Moreover, the advisory councils' reports are usually (and always in the past) drafted by the bureaucrats who are supposed to consult them. Although there has been progress in terms of opening discussions by advisory councils to the public, further efforts are needed (see Box 2). The "public comment procedures" for regulatory decision making process that took effect in April 1999 are also promising.

Furthermore, many regulatory decisions are made without consulting advisory councils. Lower level regulations such as ministerial orders as well as other administrative conduct that may have regulatory effect[25] are not subject to advisory council discussions in most cases. Moreover, there is a risk that not all the advisory council members, because of their part-time status, may be able to spend much time discussing detailed issues in depth.

In the past, very few administrative procedures provided for comments and/or consultation by foreign parties on new or modified regulations before they were adopted. Inquiry commissions were sometimes convened and open public hearings were on occasions held for that purpose. Substantial progress has recently been made. Under the Three year Programme, as discussed in the background report on Government capacity to assure high quality regulation in Japan, the Cabinet recently adopted the proposal for the requirement of public comment procedures made by the Management and Co-ordination Agency. The requirement is applied to all governmental decision-making processes from April 1999. A standardised comment period is set at one month. This measure is expected to contribute to greater transparency in regulatory procedures in Japan. Furthermore, the "Central Government Restructuring

---

Box 2.   Shingikai (advisory councils): source or obstacle of transparency?

In Japanese policy processes including those concerning regulations, an important role is played by advisory councils (shingikai), or other forms of ad hoc meetings[26] for administrative operations under various names, such as discussion groups (*kondankai*) or study groups (*kenkyukai*). In most cases, competent government authorities serve as the active secretariat: identifying the issues to be discussed; proposing the candidates for such councils and ad hoc meetings; preparing for the discussion, such as providing issue papers and technical data; and drafting reports to be submitted by councils and ad hoc meetings. Use of such processes has been justified by 1) the fact that decisions often require technical expertise and practical knowledge; 2) the corporatist like rationale that consensus among relevant social interests should be achieved. Once the reports are published , their recommendations are regarded as more or less authorised and are likely to be translated into administrative actions, including regulations.

Although in principle those councils and ad hoc meetings have useful functions, criticism has been raised that they are vulnerable to abuse: they may be too susceptible to manipulation by the authorities that support them. The fact that fair and open discussion is not guaranteed has been seen as a weakness of the process: for example, who guarantees that all relevant interests are represented and their voices heard? Foreign trading partners have been among the first to complain that the process should be more open. They are systematically excluded from this policy making process even if they have crucial interests. They charge that regulations, as an overall result of the process, therefore operate in a sub-optimal manner. Foreign voices, when they have been included in those processes as reflected in the Final Report on US-Japan Structural Impediment Initiatives in 1990, have played a catalyst role for progress to date.

The Japanese Cabinet decided in September 1995 several measures to increase the transparency of councils and ad hoc meetings. It was agreed that advisory councils in principle should meet in open session and/or publish minutes. If these are impossible for good rationales which are announced to the public in advance, a summary of discussion at each session should be published. Those efforts across the government have been monitored by the Management and Co-ordination Agency. Its most recent report in March 1998 noted that 73% of advisory councils (*shingikai etc.*) have opened their discussions through open sessions and/or publication of minutes, up from 50% in 1996. The report states that 21.7% of advisory councils have received opinions from general public.

While the number of advisory councils opening the discussion to the public has recently increased, concerns, especially those by foreign trading partners, remain, since some advisory councils still only publish summaries of discussions, instead of full minutes. In addition, some ad hoc meetings do not publish anything at all.[27]

Furthermore, the goal of transparency may not be achieved if crucial deliberations, such as those on recommendations or interim reports, do not take account of a wide spectrum of views including those of foreign trading partners. In Japanese regulatory reforms, they have played an important role in promoting alternative ideas not heard in the "insider" discussions. Exposing crucial deliberations to public comments will safeguard the decision from being pressured by incumbent interests. Introduction of cross-cutting public notice and comment procedures as announced on October 20, 1998, will have a significant effect in opening regulatory procedures. Such an example is seen in regulatory reform discussions on telecommunications. The US, in its recent submission to the Japanese government on deregulation, has identified further areas that merit specific voluntary efforts in this regard, *i.e.* retail distribution, ports deregulation and construction.

Bill" stipulates that when an important bill is formulated, citizens' opinions including those of experts and interested parties, should be heard.

Information on established regulations (laws, cabinet orders and ministerial orders) is all published. Foreign parties can obtain that information. It is generally not translated into foreign languages except for a few areas. As Japan has notified the WTO, all of Japan's national legislative and regulatory measures are published in "Kanpo" (the official national gazette) and/or "Horeizensho" (Japan's Comprehensive Statute Book), and all of its prefectural regulatory measures are published in "Kenpo" (the prefectural gazette) or its equivalent.[28] Information on important regulations and policies can be found electronically on individual ministries' and agencies' Internet sites. But, in general the use of the Internet to disseminate regulatory information still lags well behind leading examples among OECD countries.

This openness does not apply to administrative conduct that may have regulatory effect, such as internal orders and communication notes.[29] Even though these regulations have as strong binding power as higher level regulations vis-à-vis bureaucrats in the regulatory decision making process, they are usually neither published nor communicated to the outside. It is sometimes difficult for foreign parties to know the reason why a certain administrative decision is made, especially when the decision is on the basis of these lower level regulations. This is one important source of the non-transparency of the Japanese regulatory system for foreign parties (see Box 3).

Concerning the openness of appeals procedures, foreign parties have three avenues to lodge appeals against administrative actions. The first is to address their appeals directly to the administrative bodies (superior bodies, if they exist) under the procedures established in the Administration Appeal Law. This should be the most streamlined and speedy procedure according to the Japanese government, because appeals are usually treated directly by administrative agencies. A drawback is that no time limit is defined in the Administration Appeal Law. In some cases, inquiry commissions can be convened to treat appeals in a neutral way, if special provisions are established in individual laws. In general, whether or not they address appeals, they can file a suit in the courts under the Administration Case Litigation Law. Even if in the cases where the Administrative Appeals are required by laws before suits, when no decision concerning an appeal is rendered within three months from initiation of the appeal, then foreign parties can file a suit in the courts under the Administration Case Litigation Law.

The second way to appeal is to file a suit in the courts against administrative actions for the purpose of cancelling them, as defined under the Administration Case Litigation Law. However, it may be time-consuming, especially considering the underdevelopment of Japanese legal services (see background report on Government capacity to assure high quality regulation in Japan about issues on Japanese legal services).

The third way is to lodge an appeal with the Office of Trade and Investment Ombudsman (OTO – see Box 5). The OTO is an independent government body which has the vocation to deal with market openness issues at the government-wide level. The appeals treated here tend to be limited to complaints within the existing regulatory system and OTO's authority has not been used to change the system itself. Among the three avenues of recourse, the most frequently used by foreign firms has been OTO. However, OTO cases have declined recently, too, possibly reflecting the disappointment by foreign parties about the limitation of its authority.[33] Foreign firms point out the risks arising from bringing issues publicly to the appeal procedures, because of the wide range of discretionary power of regulatory agencies. Foreign firms have to be concerned by possible retaliation by the agencies.

2.2. Measures to ensure non-discrimination

Application of the non-discrimination principle aims to provide effective equality of competitive opportunities between like products and services irrespective of country of origin. Thus, the extent to which respect for two core principles of the multilateral trading system – Most-Favoured-Nation (MFN) and National Treatment (NT) – s actively promoted when a country develops and applies regulations is a gauge of its overall efforts to promote trade and investment-friendly regulation.

Preferential agreements give more favourable treatment to specified countries and are thus inherent departures from the MFN principle. The extent of a country's participation in preferential agreements (which overall can be trade-creating or trade-diverting) is not in itself indicative of a lack of commitment to the principle of non-discrimination. However, in assessing such commitment it is relevant to consider the attitudes of participating countries towards non-members in respect of transparency and the potential for discriminatory effects. Third countries need access to information about the content and operation of preferential agreements in order to make informed assessments of any impact on their own commercial interests. In addition, substantive approaches to regulatory issues such as standards and conformity

Box 3. **Japanese regulatory system: different forms of regulations and administrative conduct that may have regulatory effect**

Type of regulation	Nature	Procedure	Remarks
Horitsu (laws)	Within the Constitution, any regulations can be set by laws.	1. Collect views from private sector through an informal or, if necessary, formal channel. 2. Exchange views with other ministries departments in an informal manner. 3. Start formal consultations with other ministries for agreements on draft. 4. Bring the draft to vice ministers meeting for approval. 5. Bring the draft to cabinet meeting for an approval. 6. Discussed and approved in the relevant Diet committee and in the Diet.	– An example of formal communication channel is *Shingikai* (advisory council). – Contacted ministries are those deemed relevant by the drafter. Cabinet Legislation Bureau must be always consulted. – Paper-based communication through minister's secretariats. – Members are senior civil servants. Unanimous approval is necessary. No records of discussion available. – Printed laws are available in the Gazette.
Seirei (cabinet orders)	Orders made by the cabinet in order to implement provisions of the Constitution or laws.	(same as 1. to 5. above)	– Printed cabinet orders are available in the Gazette.
Shorei (ministerial orders)	Orders made by a minister (1) in order to implement the relevant laws / cabinet orders, or (2) in case the laws / cabinet orders delegate authority to the minister.	– Only ministers can issue ministerial orders. – No binding procedure exists in government-wide level.	– Printed ministerial orders are available in the Gazette.

Type of administrative conduct	Nature	Procedure	Remarks
Tsutatsu (internal orders)	Communication tool from officials in higher positions to their subordinates, which may include unified interpretation of laws. Only valid and binding within government organisations.	– Although the National Government Organisation Law stipulates that only ministers and heads of commissions and agencies can issue internal orders, it is inherent for the heads of hierarchical organisations to issue them. – No binding procedure exists in national level.	Senior officials are usually entrusted by the minister to make internal orders. Consultation with other ministries is rare. Printed internal orders re available to the public on a request basis.
Jimu Renraku (communication notes)	Communication tool within bureaucrats, whose content can be anything such as report, interpretation of laws or factual notices. Only valid within bureaucrats.	– No binding procedure exists.	– Consultation with other ministries is rare. – Not available to the public
Gyosei Shido (administrative guidance)	"Administrative actions taken by administrative organs, although without legal binding force, that are intended to influence specific actions of other parties ... in order to realise an administrative aim". Internal orders and communication notes can be a basis of administrative guidance as bureaucrats follow them, and sometimes show them to "other parties" in order to make recommendations, suggestions, requests or warnings to "other parties".		

245

assessment can introduce potential for discriminatory treatment of third countries (if, for example, standards recognised by partners in a preferential agreement would be difficult to meet by third countries).

Japan is firmly committed to the MFN principle, although there are limited exceptions to this in the investment field (see below). The Japanese government has encouraged regulatory bodies to respect the non-discrimination principle, in their application of domestic regulations. Japan has adopted the MFN principle under the GATS with no exception. Furthermore, as Japan is not engaged in any kind of preferential trade agreement, it does not give more preferential treatment to some trading partners than to others under any regional framework. The only regional co-operation entity in which Japan takes part in is APEC. Since APEC has adopted "open regionalism", Japan respects the MFN principle in this regard.

Although the MFN principle is apparently well-respected in the Japanese regulatory system, some concerns have been assessed relating to Japan's commitments resulting from bilateral trade talks with major trading partners such as the United States, EU, and Canada. One concern is the risk of giving more priority to specific market openness issues raised by particular trading partners than to other issues.[34] The process may give those trading partners relatively large trade benefits, even though the issues are resolved without neglecting non-discriminatory principle.

With regard to the national treatment principle, there are several specific examples of formal exceptions for which trading partners have raised concerns: prohibition against partnerships between Japanese lawyers and foreign legal consultants and against the employment of Japanese lawyers by foreign legal consultants; and discrimination between foreign and domestic banks in funding mechanisms via the Bank of Japan. With regard to inward investment, Japan still maintains some notable exceptions to national treatment through regulations defined in the Foreign Exchange Law and other individual laws. Under the Foreign Exchange Law, a party desiring to acquire a certain percentage of shares in certain sectors through direct investment in Japan must first notify the Ministry of Finance. Affected sectors can be categorised into three groups. First, sectors which are liable to be detrimental to national security, to hinder the maintenance of public order, or to obstruct the protection of public safety. Telecommunications services (only NTT)[35] and electricity are notable examples of sectors that fall into this group. Second, sectors for which Japan has maintained reservations in the OECD code for the liberalisation of the movement of capital.[36] Third, Japan also maintains limited investment barriers based on reciprocity.[37]

Even though the Japanese regulatory system has evolved to reduce formal exceptions to the national treatment principle, many trading partners express their concerns about *de facto* discrimination in various fields. This *de facto* discrimination may be due to the fact that foreign firms, as newcomers, often lack the level of information that domestic incumbents have from their long-term relationship with regulators. When other administrative conduct that may have regulatory effects is applied, this scenario becomes particularly probable. Illustrative examples raised by trading partners are numerous. For example, the majority of domestically-produced fork-lift trucks and other industrial trucks (FLTs) are placed in the "small-sized special m.v." category whereas the great majority of imported FLTs are in the "large-special m.v." category, and the latter group is subject to stricter requirements. Foreign motorcycles tend to be large size which is more suitable for tandem ridings. Yet, the motorcycle market in Japan, in particular that for the large size motorcycle, is distorted due to the prohibition of tandem ridings on national expressways (see Section 3).

Moreover, foreign investors must wait for 30 days, counting from the date the Minister of Finance and the minister with jurisdiction over the sector receive the notification, before they can effectively start to materialise investment activities. Further, when it is deemed necessary to examine whether the notified direct investment 1) is liable to be detrimental to national security, to hinder the maintenance of public order, or to obstruct the protection of public safety; 2) causes a notable adverse effect on the smooth operation of the national economy, the Minister of Finance and the minister with jurisdiction over the sector are allowed to examine the case for a maximum of five months from the date of notification.[38]

Concerning non-discrimination, there seem to be more problems at the level of self-regulation of Japan's numerous industry associations and professional services associations than at the level of government regulations. Many Japanese ministries and agencies delegate technical regulations to these kinds of associations. Some associations, on occasion, apply self-regulation in a discriminatory way between their members and potential foreign competitors. Many concerns are expressed by trading partners about discriminatory practices of those associations.[39]

Japan is one of the most highly regulated countries in professional services, such as legal and accounting services.[40] The associations of these professional services apply many cases of exclusionary self-regulation, not allowing foreign counterparts the same opportunities to practice their professions in Japan as their own members. In addition, concerns are raised by trading partners about discriminatory practices on the part of Japanese manufacturers of flat glass: withholding of supply, use of restrictive trade associations, discriminatory pricing against customers who purchase foreign flat glass and the glass distribution network.[41]

Checking the drafting of regulations for their conformity with international treaties, *e.g.* those that include MFN treatment and national treatment, is the co-responsibility of the Cabinet Legislation Bureau and the Ministry of Foreign Affairs (MOFA). When higher level regulations (laws and cabinet orders) are discussed at the cabinet level, these two bodies should monitor whether they conform with Japanese international obligations and recommend any necessary changes. However, there is no central government body monitoring conformity with international treaties when ministries and agencies are implementing regulations, that is, at the level of administrative practices. Furthermore, as explained in the previous sub-section, since lower level regulations (ministerial orders, internal orders, and communication notes) are not subject to cabinet level discussions, they are not monitored by these two bodies.

2.3. Measures to avoid unnecessary trade restrictiveness

To attain a particular regulatory objective, policy makers should seek regulations that are not more trade restrictive than necessary to fulfil a legitimate objective, taking account of the risks that non-fulfilment would create. Examples of this approach would be to use performance-based rather than design standards as the basis of a technical regulation, or to consider taxes or tradable permits in lieu of regulations to achieve the same legitimate policy goal. At the procedural level, effective adherence to this principle entails consideration of the extent to which specific provisions require or encourage regulators to avoid unnecessary trade restrictiveness (and the rationale for any exceptions), how the impact of new regulations on international trade and investment is assessed, and the extent to which trade policy bodies as well as foreign traders and investors are consulted in the regulatory process.

Japan does not have explicit provisions requiring administrative procedures to be trade and investment friendly. Individual ministries and agencies are responsible for applying regulations and administrative procedures in ways that do not affect the free flow of trade and investment. They have often used their regulations in an "unnecessarily trade and investment restrictive" way in cases such as "demand-supply adjustment clauses" according to which they can prohibit new entry because of excess supply capacity (even when it is foreseen). and officially authorised cartel arrangements. Restrictive regulations have often been justified as to help achieve non-economic policy objectives such as safety. These regulations, while not explicitly discriminatory against foreign firms, have negative impact on trade and investment in many cases. Furthermore, these measures have been suspected to be used to protect vested interests of domestic firms.[42] As a result, with the notable exceptions of ministries overseeing sectors traditionally exposed to foreign competition, ministries and agencies tend to prefer regulations giving them close control of sectors rather than those enhancing market competition, economic efficiency and trade and investment.

One feature in Japanese administrative culture is that Japan tends to give regulators wide discretion in regulatory processes. Even though the Administrative Procedure Law obliges regulatory bodies to enhance administrative transparency and efficiency, it has not lived up to expectations. Predictability of processes can significantly reduce compliance burdens of regulated firms. Japanese bureaucrats should pay much attention to the effects of policy tools on the economy and on international trade and investment, while respecting proper administrative procedures defined at the Administrative Procedure Law when they choose their policy tools.

There is no provision which requires individual ministries and agencies to take account of the potential impact of their new or modified regulations on trade and investment. Moreover, contrary to most OECD countries, Japan does not have a well-established system of regulatory impact assessment for proposed regulations. Therefore, the choice of more trade and investment friendly regulations and/or administrative procedures relies upon the discretion of individual ministries and agencies (see the discussion on regulatory impact assessment in the background report on Government capacity to assure high quality regulation in Japan).

Trade restrictive administrative procedures are found in numerous fields. Regulations related to construction business and building materials have been frequently noted as unnecessarily burdensome and complicated by major trading partners such as the US, the EU, and Canada.[43] Japan has applied a complex regulatory system in this sector for reasons of Japanese cultural difference (preference for wooden houses and high risk of fire) and geographical/climatic difference (earthquake and typhoon). However, the complexity of the regulatory system of this sector has been pointed out as major trade restricting obstacle. Japanese quarantine and inspection procedures for fresh fruits and vegetables, flowers, frozen foods, and food supplements are also frequently criticised issues for unnecessary trade restrictiveness by many trading partners. Concerns expressed by trading partners are numerous in other sectors: burdensome regulations for electricity equipment (turbines and compressors, standby generator sets, power main signalling devices etc.) under the High Pressure Gas Law, the Electricity Utilities Industry Law and others (see Section 3). onerous tariff and licensing procedures, and burdensome certification procedures in the telecommunications sector; complicated examination procedures for telecommunications equipment; long customs clearance processing time, high user fees, short operation hours, and non-uniform application of customs regulations; excessively long and costly approval procedures for medical devices; costly and burdensome testing methods for pharmaceuticals; regulation allowing only paper-base invoice in spite of the Electronic Data Interchange (EDI) system; new vehicle registration process; licensing procedures for new entrants to the insurance market and restrictions on asset management; and application of unit testing rather than type approval for machinery.

Burdensome regulations have hampered inward investment as well. Complex legal provisions related to mergers and acquisitions have been pointed out as an important obstacle to direct foreign investment in Japan, though other cultural and institutional barriers such as a high level of cross-shareholding between allied companies; a low percentage of publicly-traded common stock; widespread mistrust of foreign ownership; reluctance of *keiretsu* members to see fellow members under foreign control; and non-transparent accountancy regulations are also noted.[44]

Despite the apparent lack of general provisions to avoid unnecessary trade restrictiveness in the Japanese regulatory system, some progress has been made in this regard. In fact, the Office of Market Access (OMA: cabinet level meeting in the context of OTO) adopted the "Policy Actions on Market Access Issues as Concerns Standards, Certification and Others" in July 1997. It stipulates that government bodies should avoid the use of standards, technical regulations and conformity assessment procedures including sanitary and phyto-sanitary regulations which are unnecessary obstacles to trade.[45]

Apart from legal provisions, MITI and MOFA play a role for this purpose in the Japanese administrative system. As MITI is mainly in charge of trade policy, it makes comments on regulations from the trade perspective through deliberations at the drafting stage, when new regulations are proposed for cabinet discussions. As MOFA verifies the changes in regulations from the point of view of conformity with international treaties, it should also check whether regulations have trade restrictive effects against those treaties. Hence, it is possible for newly proposed regulations to be checked from an international perspective. However, as some regulations contain specific technical elements related to specialised ministries and agencies, it can be very difficult for trade policy bodies to correctly assess the trade and investment impact. In addition, when regulations are established through ministerial orders, internal orders, or communication notes, they escape oversight by these trade policy bodies.

The lack of open consultation between government bodies (especially between trade policy officials and sectoral officials) makes serious regulatory reforms difficult, even if they are politically supported (even strongly pushed by prime ministers such as Hosokawa and Hashimoto) or if they are the subject of commitments at trade talks. Instead, sectoral regulatory authorities tend to prefer the "deregulation process" to organised consistent "regulatory reforms" at the government-wide level, because the former option implies that they can make relatively minor concessions and preserve their controlling power in the sector (see Box 4).

Box 4. **Lack of intra-governmental co-ordination impeding trade flows**
(An example of trade facilitation)

Japan introduced the Customs electronic data interchange (EDI) system in 1978. Today approximately 90% of import/export declarations are processed through the EDI system. With the EDI system, exporters, importers and their customs brokers can submit their declarations electronically from their offices. The EDI system improves the accuracy of declarations and speeds up customs procedures as a whole.

However, customs procedures are not the only regulations at the border. There are others such as quarantine, sanitary, phyto-sanitary, food security, and import/export licenses. Under the Japanese Customs law, merchandise not cleared by border controls of agencies other than Customs cannot obtain import permission from Customs. Among other agencies' regulations, until very recently, trade-related procedures were not computerised nor linked electronically to the Customs EDI system. The lack of electronic linkage among computer systems reduces the value of the Customs EDI system from the point of view of paperless and smooth information flow and avoidance of input duplication and error. That results in a delay to import clearance, raises storage costs, and reduces the competitiveness of foreign products. Since 1990, the US has complained about the lack of cooperation between Customs and other agencies, requesting Japan to establish an integrated import processing system. Other interested bodies have echoed these concerns.

In 1997, the sanitary and phyto-sanitary EDI system and the food security EDI system were linked electronically to the Customs EDI system. But, MITI's import/export license EDI system and the port authority's EDI system are under development and the possibility of their linkage to the Customs EDI system has just been taken into consideration.

In addition to the role of monitoring regulations from an international perspective, MITI operates a training program on the rules of the WTO and other international trade policies in order to enhance market openness. This program is for all government officials. It is deemed to improve public officials' perception of market openness. But as it is on voluntary basis, its impact to date has been limited.

One of the most important steps in favour of market openness which has been taken by Japan was the establishment of the Office of Trade and Investment Ombudsman (OTO)[46] in 1982. The OTO, a unique organisation, among OECD members, aims to reduce obstacles to market openness by receiving complaints on market access, relating to imports or inward investment, and by organising inter-ministerial co-ordinating efforts to deal with those complaints. The OTO has dealt with more than 500 complaints concerning market access. It has made several reports on major problems of market access and has taken government level policy actions to enhance market openness (see Box 5).

Box 5. OTO: the Japanese way to enhance market openness

Objective: The OTO (Office of Trade and Investment Ombudsman) was established on January 30, 1982 for the purpose of improving market access to Japan, through receipt and processing of complaints concerning market opening issues, including procedures for import of goods and services, direct investment in Japan, and government procurement.

Submission of complaints: Complaints are received mainly by the Secretariat of the OTO, established at the Co-ordination Bureau of the Economic Planning Agency. They can be brought to other relevant sections of the Japanese government, Japanese diplomatic missions and the JETRO. In the latter cases, they will be transferred to the OTO Secretariat. Complaints may take any form such as direct visit, mail, phone and/or e-mail (Internet), if they are clearly understandable and concern specific matters. As a general rule, they should be addressed directly by a complainant. However, proxy complaints will be accepted without the name of a complainant through foreign government organisations, foreign diplomatic missions, foreign government affiliated trade promotion organisations and/or other organisations approved by the OTO (*e.g.* foreign chambers of commerce and industry in Japan, major Japanese chambers of commerce and industry and other major business bodies).

Solving complaints: An (initial explanatory) answer will be delivered to the complainant within 10 days after the submission of the complaint to the OTO. If it takes more than one month to cope with the issue, the complainant will be kept informed by progress reports at least once every month. When the complainant does not agree with the explanation given by the relevant ministries or agencies, the issue will be deliberated by the Grievance Resolution Committee. Any issue which takes more than three months to cope with will also be deliberated by the committee. The final result will be reported to the complainant in written form.

Intra-government communication: In the best case, issues are resolved at the level of the OTO Co-ordination Meeting whose members are working level bureau directors. Otherwise, it can go up to the OTO Executive Meeting whose members are vice-ministers of ministries and agencies concerned. In extreme cases, the OMA (Office of Market Access: established on February 1, 1994 to reinforce the OTO), which is presided over by the Prime Minister and whose members are ministers, will decide. Apart from this administrative line of discussion, the MAOC (Market Access Ombudsman Council) is established to gather more neutral opinions and to give advice to the OMA. The MAOC is composed of distinguished scholars, business leaders and others. The Grievance Resolution Committee which is established under the MAOC will discuss any issue which cannot be resolved at the working level co-ordination meeting.

Accomplishments: As of February 25, 1998, the OTO has received a total of 568 complaints. 552 of those complaints have been processed. In 185 cases, Japanese procedures have been modified to facilitate imports. The OTO has given explanations on 209 other complaints judged to be based on misunderstandings.[47] Since FY 1992,[48] the MAOC has compiled yearly its "Recommendations on Market Access Issues as concerns the Standards, Certification and Others" concerning problems indicated by foreign and domestic businesses. Through this process, the MAOC has dealt with 293 cases, and has made 112 recommendations. Based on these recommendations, the OMA has taken "Policy Actions on Market Access Issues as concerns the Standards, Certification and Others" to implement them at the administrative level.

Source: EPA document.

Despite its positive role in enhancing market openness and reducing unnecessary trade restrictiveness of regulations, the OTO seems to be losing the initial positive view of some trading partners.[49] According to those trading partners, the OTO has become another example of the "Japanese way of enhancing market openness": the focus of activities is increasingly on border measures, shying away from issues behind the border. They evaluate the OTO as follows: its strengths are its policy objectives and its composition, which includes foreign representatives, and its weaknesses are its lack of authority *vis-à-vis* other ministries and agencies and the fact that most issues handled lead to minor improvements in implementation of regulations rather than more fundamental change in regimes. They believe that even if most activities of the OTO are helpful to solve specific minor market access problems, those are far from sufficient to effectively enhance market openness in Japan and to contribute to structural reforms of the Japanese economy.

2.4. Measures to encourage use of internationally harmonised measures

Compliance with different standards and regulations for like products often presents firms wishing to engage in international trade with significant and sometimes prohibitive costs. Thus, when appropriate and feasible, reliance on internationally harmonised measures (such as global standards) as the basis of domestic regulations can readily facilitate expanded trade flows. National efforts to encourage the adoption of regulations based on harmonised measures, procedures for monitoring progress in the development and adoption of international standards, and incentives for regulatory authorities to seek out and apply appropriate international standards are thus important indicators of a country's commitment to efficient regulation.

In Japan, government's involvement in standards and conformity assessment procedures is relatively active and Japanese consumers have a high level of confidence in the Japanese quality and safety systems. Some Japanese people have even expressed concerns that international alignment might degrade the quality and safety of products. Moreover, there is no general and standard provision which requires the use of internationally harmonised standards (see Box 6).

Trading partners are currently demanding the alignment of Japanese standards and certifications to international norms in numerous fields such as adoption of International Electrotechnical Committee standards for many electrical products; adoption of ISO standards and performance-based standards for various building materials and tank containers; NTT's adaptation of international standards with regard to line connectivity *i.e.*, standardised open interfaces; internationally-accepted labelling standards for processed foods and diary products; adoption of international regulatory framework for food additives; adoption of global standards of financial disclosure, supervision, accountancy rules and asset valuation; harmonisation of various regulations related to motor vehicle and component with UN-ECE and EU regulations; and recognition of ISO measurement criteria for recreational craft.

The WTO paid attention to this matter, too. It reports in the 1998 Trade Policy Review that "From Japan's perspective, 'Japanese standards and certification systems are now comparable with those of other countries in terms of transparency and conformity with international standards' From the perspective of some trading partners, however, 'access to the market continued to be hindered by exclusionary business practices and various non-tariff measures. These include burdensome testing, inspection and customs clearance procedures, the use of complex standards and difficulties of access to distribution networks."[50]

In spite of these limitations, Japan has recently announced several initiatives to make progress in this regard. The 1997 Policy Actions on Market Access Issues of the OMA states that ministries and agencies are encouraged to use internationally harmonised standards and certification procedures when they take the actions proposed in the grievance resolution process of the OTO. According to the Policy Actions, they are also encouraged to actively use foreign conformity assessment bodies, to promote mutual recognition and to simplify and speed up conformity assessment procedures.

The new Three year Programme also stresses international harmonisation of regulations in order to promote fundamental reforms of Japan's economy and society to attain internationally open, free, and fair systems. In addition, Japan has the role of APEC/PASC (Pacific Area Standards Congress) chair, and in this context, four case studies are being done on the issue of alignment of national standards with international ones. These studies are contributing to deepening understanding of the issue, including quality of international standards themselves.

Besides, there has also been progress made at the individual industry level. MITI has introduced 237 international standards in the list of technical standards requested under the Electrical Appliance and Material Control Law, instead of 120 aligned standards before. Through the first Three Year Programme (1995-1997), 1 700 JIS standards out of 8 000[51] have been aligned to international standards. Japan introduced the OECD principle of Good Laboratory Practice (GLP) into the Law concerning the Examination and Registration of Manufacture of Chemical Substances. In addition, Japan's accession to the revised

---

Box 6.   Japan's standards and conformity assessment systems

The standards and conformity assessment system in Japan has a dual structure. The government administers a variety of mandatory standards, and multiple public and private organisations manage a wide range of voluntary standards. The government is very actively involved in standards and conformity assessment.

Mandatory Standards

Mandatory standards are enforced through legislation, and compliance is governed by a certification system. Government-designated testing laboratories inspect for conformity. Compliance with mandatory standards is required before a product can be sold in, and imported to, Japan.

A partial list of legislation defining mandatory standards (numbers of standards in brackets): Consumer Product Safety Law (6), Electrical Appliance and Material Control Law (498), Pharmaceutical Affairs Law (2014), Food Sanitation Law (377), Fertiliser Control Law (126), High Pressure Gas Control Law (2), Safety Regulations for Road Vehicles (274), Law concerning the Safety Assurance and Quality Improvement of Food (150), Building Standards Law, Industrial Safety and Health Law, Telecommunications Enterprise Law, Plant Protection Law, Measurement Law, Law concerning Screening of Chemical Substances and Regulation of their Manufacture, and Radio Law.

Voluntary Standards

Voluntary standards are used for safety, compliance, and quality assurance. Voluntary marks are required *de facto* in many cases, because of their marketing leverage. Testing and certification bodies are designated by ministries which administer each voluntary standard.

The JIS Mark: a widely used quality mark applicable to over 1 000 different manufacturing products and encompassing 8 161 standards. MITI administers JIS and designates qualified Japanese and foreign testing organisations. Compliance with the JIS improves marketability and is also an important element in government procurement. MITI is planning to enlarge the list of accredited foreign testing organisations.

The JAS Mark: a quality assurance mark for beverages, processed foods, forest products, agricultural commodities, oils and fats, and processed goods made from livestock, fishing, and forestry raw materials. The Ministry of Agriculture, Forestry, and Fisheries administers 354 JAS marks.

Certification Marks: additional voluntary certification marks administered by various organisations. The "SG" mark is a quality mark administered by Japan's Consumer Product Safety Association. The "ST" mark is a safety mark administered by the Toy Safety Control Administration, a self-regulatory commission. In addition, the "ECO" mark is used for environmental standards and the "G" mark for design quality, etc.

Quality Control: Japan has developed a good quality control system, driven by the Japanese Industrial Standards Committee. This has made the introduction of internationally harmonised quality control standards such as ISO very slow. Now, Japan is actively introducing them and participating in international harmonisation activities.

Source: WTO, *Trade Policy Review of Japan*, January 1998 and John S. Wilson, *Standards and* APEC: *An Action Agenda*, October 1995.

1958 UN-ECE Agreement on automotive sector was submitted to the Diet on 3 March 1998. This is expected to have a positive impact on harmonisation in the sector (see Section 3).

There have been also recent moves towards performance-based standards, notably in areas such as building materials and electricity equipment. WTO Agreements, particularly TBT & SPS agreements, have played an important role in maintaining transparency and contributing to harmonisation in standards development. Japan recognises the importance of the obligations under those agreements, including notifications of draft technical regulations and standards. It has established practices aiming to ensure them. Ministries handling technical regulations and standards have familiarised themselves to the operation of the system.

Therefore, the picture is mixed, with continuous foreign complaints and ongoing initiatives towards harmonisation. One fundamental problem lies in the lack of data in assessing progress in harmonisation in various areas. This problem is not unique in Japan. Such data collection and assessment may be a useful step for Japan making further concrete progress in this field. Concerns are raised also about the effectiveness of cross-cutting commitment. This is because the Policy Actions and Three year Programme's statements have less binding power than individual laws on which individual ministries and agencies administering their standards and conformity assessment rely much more. Based on more precise assessment, Japan may consider strengthening such cross-cutting commitment of harmonisation.

2.5. Recognition of equivalence of other countries' regulatory measures

The pursuit of internationally harmonised measures may not always be possible, necessary or even desirable. In such cases, efforts should be made in order to ensure that cross-country disparities in regulatory measures and duplicative conformity assessment systems do not act as barriers to trade. Recognising the equivalence of trading partners' regulatory measures or the results of conformity assessment performed in other countries are two promising avenues for achieving this result. In practice, both avenues are being pursued in Japan in various ways. Recognising certification given to foreign products by foreign laboratories is one example. Such recognition can be accorded unilaterally, but also through the mechanism of a Mutual Recognition Agreement (MRA) between trading partners. Another example arises when certification operates through self-declaration of conformity by manufacturers; in this case, recognition of equivalence means that declarations of conformity by foreign manufacturers are also accepted: foreign (as well as domestic) producers can assess the conformity of their product with requirements set in a given market as they deem appropriate and will be treated the same way by regulatory authorities. The latter may then test products on the market under established procedures and take necessary measures as warranted, regardless of the origin of products.

In Japan, government's involvement in conformity assessment procedures has been considerable. Ministries often designate certification bodies for particular areas. Such bodies are often given de facto monopolistic function to certify designated products or services. These procedures are often criticised by trading partners on various accounts: lack of transparency in the procedures; high costs of certification; peculiarly burdensome procedures; and reluctance to accept the data obtained through internationally accepted methods.

Many trading partners as well as Japanese domestic businesses are demanding Japan to make further progress in various fields such as acceptance of foreign standards, foreign test data, foreign testing organisations and test laboratories for construction and building materials; acceptance of foreign clinical data in the acceptance of medical devices and pharmaceuticals; generalised recognition by Japanese standards related laws of European wide accreditation bodies (European Co-operation for Accreditation: EA) or of equivalent international bodies (ILAC for laboratory accreditation and IAF for accreditation of quality systems certification). recognition of motor vehicle test results from foreign testing institutes as part of completion inspection; recognition of Dutch inspection systems for cut flowers and flower bulbs; recognition of foreign test data obtained through good practice test methods for chemical residues in meat products; acceptance of all ingredients of cosmetics on EU lists; support for the efforts of private sectors with foreign parties to resurrect the ISO for boilers and pressure vessels; recognition of the validity of the physical inspection and certification of tank containers for the carriage of dangerous goods when this is authenticated and witnessed by agencies such as Lloyds Register, Bureau Veritas and Germanischer Lloyd; recognition of Canadian fumigation treatment for hay; recognition of inspections carried out by competent foreign bodies similar to NKK (Nippon Kaisi Kokkai: fire detection). wider recognition of foreign countries' investigation data pertaining to alcoholic beverages ingredient analysis; and no re-inspection if vessel was approved abroad.

However, some progress has recently been made through new cross-cutting initiatives such as:

– The Policy Actions of the OMA encourage regulators to actively use foreign conformity assessment bodies and to promote mutual recognition.

– The Social and Economic Plan Action Plan (adopted in 1997) stipulates that Japanese standards bodies should accept foreign data, introduce mutual recognition systems, and make the transition to self-certification for appropriate items.

_253_

– The OTO 1996 report states that some foreign inspection data are authorised and administrative discretion to assess conformity should be reduced.

Related progress has recently been made in telecommunication equipment. The MPT submitted a draft law to the Diet on March 16, 1998 for the establishment of a system allowing Japan to accept certifications and test results for telecommunications terminal equipment and radio equipment from conformity assessment organisations (domestic and foreign) recognised by MPT regardless of agreements for mutual recognition. The foreign organisations do not have to be recognised by foreign governments to be recognised by MPT. The draft law was approved on April 30, 1998. This is a first in allowing foreign bodies to conduct certifications in the Japanese system for mandatory standards area.

Japan introduced an accreditation system for testing laboratories in 1997. Accreditation bodies would assess and authorize testing competence of laboratories, based on internationally accepted guidelines. In October 1998, the Asia-Pacific Laboratory Accreditation Co-operation (APLAC) approved the participation of Japanese accreditation bodies. This opens the way in Japan for recognising equivalence of wide-ranging foreign testing results under APLAC umbrella with domestic testing results.

In addition, some trading partners positively appraise Japanese efforts to recognise regulatory measures and conformity assessment results performed in their countries. Examples of positive action include acceptance of EU official tests for frontal crash tests for automobiles; and commitment to incorporate the guidelines on acceptance of foreign clinical data into national regulations for pharmaceutical products. MITI has accepted 62 foreign testing bodies for technical regulations under 9 laws in its jurisdiction. Japan has recently amended the Industrial Standardisation Law so as to enable third-party certification bodies – domestic and foreign – to issue JIS mark. The number of accepted foreign inspection bodies are 142 at the moment. MITI has also transferred 126 items of government certification of 4 standard related laws under its jurisdiction to supplier's declaration scheme. Japan's accession to UN/ECE Agreement in automotive sector also has opened the way for more positive attitude towards accepting foreign certification on safety in the sector.

Japan has also engaged in various MRA negotiations with major trading partners, even if not many have yet been concluded (see table). In addition, Japan is asked by trading partners to engage in MRA negotiations in various fields such as: 1994 joint announcement on co-operation for mutual recognition in the field of building standards with Canada; test data and certification for medical devices by the EU and Taiwan; motorised agricultural and construction machinery[52] by the EU.

In sum, Japan's announced policy goal is supportive of recognition of equivalence of other countries' regulatory measures. Recent progress is consistent with such a goal and welcomed by trading partners as contributing to market openness. Considering wide-ranging complaints made by trading partners, however, the question is speed and momentum. Are current moves going to be extended to cover all the areas where trade concerns are arising? It is difficult to assess. However, in order to better achieve the policy goal of the Japanese government, a government-wide initiative to promote, wherever possible and appropriate, acceptance of foreign certifications and/or to introduce less burdensome conformity assessment procedures such as manufacturer's declaration of conformity looks promising.

2.6. Application of competition principles from an international perspective

Foreign trading partners have claimed that not only government regulatory actions, but also practices by private firms or semi-public organisations, have posed obstacles for market openness in Japan. The lack of adequate procedures to ensure transparency, pointed out in Section 2.1, may have contributed to these private practices. Such concerns have been widespread, and trading partners have recommended that Japan boost its efforts to vigorously implement the Anti-Monopoly Law.

The discussion has covered various aspects of the enforcement of competition laws and policy: strengthening the investigatory powers of the Japan Fair Trade Commission (JFTC)'s; strengthening penalties and sanctions; introducing a wider range of private remedies, including private injunctions and private damage relief; expanding the capacity of the JFTC. Complaints also point to the "grey" area where government functions, which are often regulatory, are delegated to private bodies or government regula-

Table 1. **Japan's participation in MRA negotiations**

Partner	Partner	Sector	Concluded	Effective Date	Type of Recognition
EU	Japan	Telecommunications equipment (including electromagnetic compatibility)	No		ACC CERT
		Electrical equipment (including electromagnetic compatibility)			
		Machinery			
		Pressure equipment			
		Medical devices			
		Pharmaceutical GMP			
		Chemicals GLP			
		Construction materials			
		Personal protective equipment			
APEC	APEC	Electrical and electronic equipment	No		ACC
		Food and food products	Yes	97.8	CERT
		Telecommunications equipment (including electromagnetic compatibility) and electrical safety)	No	99.7 (target)	
Australia	Japan	Low voltage equipment	No		
		Pharmaceuticals GMP			
		Medical devices			
		Pressure equipment			
		Housing and construction			
		Automotive products			

GMP: Good Manufacturing Practices
ACC: Conformity assessment dealing with the acceptance of data
CERT: Conformity assessment dealing with certification
GLP: Good laboratory practices
Source: Information provided by the government of Japan.

tion is seen to encourage anti-competitive behaviour by firms. In this regard, requests have arisen for more vigorous oversight by the JFTC of private practices relating to: administrative guidance; trade associations' activities, many of which are authorised by government regulation; and various "private" regulations. Trading partners have also urged further efforts to abolish exemptions to the Anti-Monopoly Law as well as more vigorous intervention by the JFTC in the regulatory decision making process primarily by strengthening its advocacy role.

The benefits of market access may be reduced by regulatory action condoning anti-competitive conduct or by failure to correct anti-competitive private actions that have the same effect. It is therefore important that regulatory institutions make it possible for both domestic and foreign firms affected by anti-competitive practices to present their positions effectively. The existence of procedures for hearing and deciding complaints about regulatory or private actions that impair market access and effective competition by foreign firms, the nature of the institutions that hear such complaints, and adherence to deadlines (if they exist) are thus key issues from an international market openness perspective.

If regulatory conduct affects the competition process impairing access to a particular Japanese market by foreign firms, the affected firms may file a complaint to the OTO. Even if the source of the market access problem arises from private conduct, then complaints may also be brought before the OTO.

Furthermore, anyone may report a suspected violation of the Anti-Monopoly Law to the JFTC and request an investigation be instituted pursuant to article 45 of the Anti-Monopoly Law. There is no discrimination on the treatment of complaints that either a foreign firm or domestic firm may raise. The JFTC has the duty to carry out a necessary investigation into relevant matters pertaining to the case in question. The JFTC does this in order to check whether the case may be relevant to the Anti-Monopoly Law or not and to determine whether there is violation or not. If the report above is done in writing and specifies concrete facts, the JFTC will send notification of the result to the person who made the report. The JFTC does not disclose any information concerning petitions because it is believed that the JFTC will face difficulty in obtaining co-operation from a complainant wishing to guard his or her identity secret. The JFTC gives explanations of its decisions to the complainant on demand, all the while taking business confidentiality into account. After a full investigation, decisions to order elimination measures are made in writing. They include a description of the facts found, the application of law made by the JFTC and the contents of the elimination measures. All the decisions to order elimination measures are made public. An appeal for the cancellation of the decision must be brought within thirty days (three months in case of decisions on monopolistic positions) from the date on which the decision becomes effective (*i.e.* the date of receipt by the parties of the decision, article 77). The delay between the issuance of decisions and their publication depends on the types of decisions. In the case of and hearing decisions, the delay is a few days, *i.e.* the time that is deemed necessary to reach the parties concerned. On the other hand, in the case of recommendation decisions, the decisions are published annually, since each recommendation itself is made public at the time of its issuance.

The JFTC may, even when an act in violation has already ceased to exist, order the entrepreneur to take necessary measures, if it is within one year (three years in case of surcharge payment orders) since the date of discontinuation of the act. The length of time period for reaching recommendation (starting from the initiation date of the formal investigation) is generally a half to one full year, although there are frequent exceptions to this time length. There is virtually no difference in time length for reaching the verdict with regard to complaints from foreign as compared to domestic firms.

Notwithstanding the formally equivalent treatment between foreign and domestic firms, a perception still exists on the part of many foreign firms that they do not, or would not, receive equivalent treatment. It may be the case that perceived differential treatment does not arise out of anything specific to the application of competition law and policy, but rather as a result of the interaction between other regulatory schemes and the competition law. For instance, it has been suggested that restrictions on the number of Japanese lawyers (*bengoshi*), the prohibition against partnerships between Japanese lawyers and foreign legal consultants (*gaikokuho-jimu-bengoshi*) or the hiring of Japanese lawyers by foreign legal consultants, restrictions on quasi-legal professionals, and the limitations on the ability of foreign legal consultants to confer with Japanese government agencies or authorities on behalf of clients may limit the effectiveness of foreign firms in giving adequate voice to their market access concerns. This problem may be exacerbated by continuing limitations on private injunctive relief and private damage actions for alleged violations of the Anti-Monopoly Law.

In addition to these procedural concerns, it is also possible that during the period of lax antitrust enforcement by the JFTC (which is changing as documented in the background report on The Role of competition policy and enforcement of regulatory reform) certain market access problems of foreign firms under Japanese antitrust laws were hidden or ignored because the lax enforcement could affect both foreign and domestic firms. As a consequence the past weak anti-cartel enforcement (particularly with respect to bid-rigging),[53] combined with past copious exemptions from the application of the Anti-Monopoly Law, and the past modest resources and prestige of the JFTC might still give rise to a lingering perception that an effective means of addressing market access concerns of foreign firms relating to regulatory or private conduct still needs further development in Japan. This might be particularly true with respect to distribution channels. Market access concerns with respect to distribution channels might also be remedied by continued efforts to increase transparency in the application of the Premiums and Misrepresentations Law.

Foreign firms also continue to complain about problems in gaining market access to Japan's distribution channels in sectors such as: autos and auto parts; paper and paperboard; flat glass; and photographic film. The JFTC might consider reviewing antitrust compliance programs of influential firms in these and other "highly-oligopolistic industries" to confirm that dominant Japanese firms are fully complying with the Anti-Monopoly Law and the JFTC's Distribution Guidelines. In this regard, the JFTC might also consider initiating a survey on the relationship between vertical *keiretsu* and certain perceived market access problems with respect to distribution. In particular, the JFTC might examine the extent and form of financial inter-relationships linking manufacturers and distributors in highly oligopolistic industries. Such a survey could, on an industry to industry basis, cover equity ties, provision of loans or other capital sources and the sharing of employees, facilities and equipment.

A particular setting for concern is the exertion or extension of market power by a regulated or protected monopolist into another market. The substantive problem, sometimes called "regulatory abuse", is addressed by laws about monopolisation, or by regulatory laws applied to particular markets. Foreign firms and traders could be implicated in two ways. First, an incumbent domestic regulated monopolist might gain an unfair advantage over foreign products or firms in an unregulated domestic market. Or, an incumbent foreign regulated monopolist might use the resources afforded by its protection at home to gain an unfair advantage in another country. These concerns might be brought to the attention of the JFTC using the procedures outlined above. The conduct of regulated firms in non-regulated market is subject to the Anti-Monopoly Law. There is no exemption in that regard. However, the JFTC is under no obligation to take any particular action beyond launching an investigation. There have been no cases of the JFTC taking action in the past three years relating to these regulatory abuse issues. One possible reason for the lack of these types of cases is that until recently, regulated monopolies in Japan required regulatory approval to engage in commerce outside of the scope of their specific grant of authority. The regulatory agency typically requires a separate accounting or the separation of companies when a regulated firm engages in unrelated business.

From the perspective of market access concerns of foreign firms, the telecommunications sector provides an interesting example of the potential for competition policy to be applied to address the anti-competitive exertion or extension of market power by a regulated monopolist. Foreign trading partners claim that the rates that telecommunications carriers must pay to connect to Japan's local telecommunications network are so high that they represent a barrier to entry for potential domestic and foreign entrants. Pursuant to the US-Japan Enhanced Initiative on Deregulation and Competition Policy, Japan has announced to submit a bill necessary to amend the Telecommunications Business Law at the Diet in the Spring of 2000 in order to implement a long run incremental cost methodology as early as possible, and to promote certain interim reductions in interconnection rates before then.

The application of competition principles is also important to determining other issues such as cross-subsidisation by the dominant carrier to other activities of its subsidiaries. In addition, delays in implementing interconnection with a dominant carrier might also serve as a significant barrier to entry. Interconnection is, however, only one side of the market access story. Another approach to facilitating new entry would be to allow competitors to establish their own networks themselves. This will require a more pro-competitive approach to rights of way such as: poles, ducts and conduits belonging to NTT or utilities; access to privately-owned buildings; and access to roads, highways, bridges, tunnels, subways and railroads. The JFTC could play a major role – if even only from competition advocacy – in establishing a more pro-competitive approach to telecommunications regulation and limiting the anti-competitive extension and exertion of market power by dominant carriers in this sector.

Other issues that could benefit from a competition policy oversight are barriers that increase switching costs for consumers such as restrictions on to local number portability and the absence of dialling parity. Finally, it is worth considering whether new entrants or non-dominant carriers (which in many cases will be foreign owned or controlled firms) should also be subjected to less onerous tariff and licensing approval processes than dominant carriers.

As Japan continues to implement regulatory reform, it is likely that the types of issues discussed in this section will only gain in prominence. In fact many of the reforms to the administration of the Anti-Monopoly Law, and much of the strengthening of the role of the JFTC in general, and in the particular context of regulatory reform (both documented in the background report on The Role of competition policy and enforcement of regulatory reform), are rooted in bilateral trade initiatives such as the Structural Impediments Initiative (SII) in the 1980s in addition to the US-Japan Framework Agreement for a New Economic Partnership (Framework Agreement) and US-Japan Enhanced Initiative on Deregulation and Competition Policy (Enhanced Initiative) in the 1990s. As more sectors of the Japanese economy are subjected to regulatory reform, the role of competition policy as a tool in addressing market access concerns can be expected to increase in importance.

257

3. ASSESSING RESULTS IN SELECTED SECTORS

This section examines the implications for international market openness arising from Japanese regulations currently in place for four sectors (two manufacturing and two service sectors): telecommunications equipment; telecommunications services; automobiles and components; and electricity. For each sector, an attempt has been made to draw out the effects of sector-specific regulations on international trade and investment and the extent to which the six efficient regulation principles are explicitly or implicitly applied. Particular attention is paid to product standards and conformity assessment procedures, where relevant. Other issues addressed here include efforts to adopt internationally harmonised product standards, use of voluntary product standards by regulatory authorities, and openness and flexibility of conformity assessment systems. In many respects, multilateral disciplines, notably the WTO TBT Agreement, provide a sound basis for reducing trade tensions by encouraging respect for fundamental principles of efficient regulation such as transparency, non-discrimination, and avoidance of unnecessary trade restrictiveness.

3.1. Automobiles and components

As highlighted by the process reaching to the 1995 US-Japan Automotive Agreement, the automobiles and parts sector has attracted considerable trade policy debate between Japan and its trading partners. The sector is characterised by dynamism. On the one hand, leading multinational firms have embarked on global market strategies, resulting in vigorous alliance formations involving different regions in recent years. Against this background, international trade and investment in the sector has been among the most visible and is bound to grow. Various types of trade and investment issues have been identified in the discussion among policy makers.[54]

On the other hand, due to high levels of safety and environment concerns relating to automobiles, regulations have been pervasive in this sector across countries. Those concerns are justified by risks arising from new technology as well as global environmental problems. Particular regulatory measures designed and implemented in order to address those concerns, however, have been often caused unnecessary burdens for business activities such as trade and investment. In some cases, they have been suspected as reflecting protectionist purposes, or as furthering national strategies for the industry. The efficiency of regulations in this sector has been examined and discussed from market openness perspectives in a number of trade fora.[55]

Foreign car manufactures exporting to a particular country must meet many kinds of regulations. Standards are often different among countries. Manufactures may have to adjust themselves to those standards by investing and operating different research, production and testing facilities. They also often have to present testing results for regulators in a number of countries. Differences in regulations may have arisen from natural conditions such as temperature or weather conditions. As historical development of regulations has been independent in each country, convergence is not ensured in principle. In addition, there may be different ideas among countries about how to address environmental concerns, or what level of risk is acceptable. However, there may be cases where different regulations involve unnecessary adjustment costs or duplicative costs.

Calls for regulatory systems in OECD economies to respond to globalisation have targeted this sector. The Geneva-based UN/ECE Working Party 29 has been the focus of international discussion in harmonising regulatory requirements in a number of European countries as well as promoting the reciprocal recognition of approvals granted on the basis of those prescriptions. Japan's move to enter this arrangement from November 1998 is a major development in this context. TABD (Trans-Atlantic Business Dialogue) has produced additional momentum for regulatory authorities across countries to pay explicit attention to the desirability of promoting the global harmonisation of vehicle standards.

3.1.1. *Standards and certification*

In Japan, the Road Vehicles Law stipulates that no motor vehicle may be operated on the road unless it conforms with relevant safety and environmental pollution control standards. Vehicles that have obtained type designation do not need to be individually inspected by the Ministry of Transport before they can be registered for use on the road.

The type designation system applies to mass-produced vehicles (Article 75, Road Vehicles Law). Under this system, a new car type is designated by the Ministry after it checks, *inter alia*, 1) whether the car meets regulatory specifications of the Ministry of Transport, 2) whether sufficient quality control in manufacturing process is in place and 3) whether a complete car inspection system is in place. For an imported car type of less than 2 000 in annual sales in Japan, simplified procedures for type designation called Preferential Handling Procedures (PHP) are applied: checks on 1) and 2) can be done by papers while complete car inspection is applied to each car. PHP is advantageous for the car type which is sold in small number.

There have been persistent external calls for efforts to harmonise Japanese automobile regulations, as well as to accept as equivalent, standards that are widely used in other countries, and for Japan to accept equivalence of foreign conformity assessment results such as test data. For example, the European Commission tabled in its proposals for the Deregulation Action Plan as many as 26 items in the automotive sector in October 1998 (In 1997, the number of items was 15). Among these broad range of issues raised by the EU, Japan is requested to: 1) bring Japanese regulations *e.g.* vehicle noise into line with international practice, and 2) recognise and accept test results from abroad. In addition, the EU requests improvements in type approval systems, such as extension of application of component type approval to more auto components, in order to reduce regulatory burdens for car makers.

The Japanese response has been rapid and encouraging. The Transportation Technology Council, advisory body to the Transport Minister, recommended that Japanese regulations be harmonised to international standards. The Japanese Diet has approved Japan's accession to the 1958 UN/ECE (United Nations Economic Commission for Europe) Agreement. This Agreement promotes harmonised technical specifications as well as reciprocal acceptance of conformity assessment in the auto sector with nearly 30 Contracting Parties, including 14 Member States of the EU as well as the European Community on its own right. Japan's entry will be in effect from November 24, 1998.

Japan has, as a first step to prepare for its accession, harmonised MOT technical regulations with UN/ECE regulations on the following 5 items:

- Reflectors (ECE Regulation No. 3).
- Lighting and signalling devices (ECE Regulation No. 7).
- Braking system (ECE Regulation No. 13H).
- Front fog lamps (ECE Regulation No. 19).
- Audible warning devices (ECE Regulation No. 28).

The Ministry of Transport is also proceeding with necessary changes to the type designation system for vehicles and vehicle equipment to accept certification by foreign bodies.[56]

In the medium term, Japan's entry to UN/ECE Agreement, which reflects more positive Japanese attitude towards harmonisation, will reduce technical barriers for global trade in the automobile sector. Rather than dealing with specific harmonisation/recognition issues item by item, the entry will establish a framework under which progress can be measured and remaining problems can be clarified quickly. By participating the discussion at international standardisation process, Japanese regulatory authority is going to pay explicit attention to the regulation's impact on trade, when formulating future technical regulations.

The question now is how fast and comprehensively the regulatory authority can move to achieve the announced policy goal. One European expert view holds that compared to the EU which has acceded to 78 UN/ECE regulations of the total of more than 100, Japan has still a long way to go. In considering the substantial work to be done to internationalise Japanese auto regulations, a systematic review of a broad range of current technical regulations will be needed for future regulatory reform. Such reform will bring about economic benefits, not only to exporters to Japanese market, but also to Japanese consumers who will gain from wider choice and less expensive prices without endangering safety or other social concerns.

3.1.2. *Avoidance of unnecessary trade restrictiveness in other areas of automobile regulation*

Another aspect of regulations in the automobile sector has attracted persistent attention by Japan's trading partners. Under the Road Vehicle Law, for the purpose of maintaining vehicle safety, only garages that are certified by the Ministry of Transport can conduct vehicle maintenance work (Article 77). Among the certified garages, only those that are designated by the Ministry of Transport can conduct vehicle inspections (Article 94-5). The United States has expressed concern that the requirements under this regulation, though applied on the basis of the non-discrimination principle, discourage establishment and operation of specialised garages more likely to deal with foreign-made automobile parts.

The response of the Ministry of Transport has been, *inter alia*, relaxation of requirements on certified garages. Reform has introduced, since February 1997, new categories of certified garages so that specialised garages can operate car maintenance services. While this reform has been welcomed as contributing to more openness in Japanese auto parts markets, the United States would like to promote further improvement by reforming qualification of mechanics: current qualification requirements for mechanics look too wide ranging while mechanics working for specialised garages may need expertise only in their specialised areas. Trading partners expect that such measures can facilitate establishment of new smaller car shops that have capacity for repair services and use more foreign-made auto parts than existing garages.

The Ministry has held public hearing in February in 1998, inviting interested parties including domestic and foreign businesses as well as foreign governments, but it is said to have been faced with difficulties to proceed due to opposition from existing garages and car makers, for the reason that the proposed change would reduce safety. The purpose of qualification system is to maintain safety quality of repair services and regulatory measures such as expertise requirement should not be more than necessary to achieve such purpose. Consideration of economic interests arising from safety regulations looks inappropriate to dominate the discussion of reform. Other concerns have been raised on unnecessary restrictiveness of existing inspection requirement. In Japan every car must be inspected by certified garages every two year. Trading partners have pointed out that the validity of inspection should be prolonged in light of technological development in the auto manufacturing since the time of the initiation of such requirement. The Japanese government promised to conclude its deliberations on this matter by March 1999. Foreign parties also claim that space and equipment requirements for garages are too restrictive.

Another example of regulations unnecessarily restricting trade are those affecting motorcycle use. Japan has a unique regulation (except for Korea) that prohibits tandem ridings on national expressways. Due to this prohibition, tandem motorcycles are unable to travel long distances in Japan. This has had a negative impact on the market for large size motorcycles which are likely to be more suitable for tandem ridings: the market volume of big bikes in Japan is only one third that in Germany and a quarter that in the US. Because foreign motorcycles exported to Japan tend to be large sizes, the prohibition of tandem ridings on national expressways has had the effect of preventing foreign motorcycles from penetrating to the Japanese market. Major trading partners have complained that the prohibition works as a barrier to market access.

The objective of the regulation is a reduction of traffic accidents of motorcycles. This explanation is not convincing since tandem ridings on normal roads are allowed, and the driving conditions are less favourable to motorcycles than on expressways. Some argue that the real regulatory objective is the prevention of joy riding on expressways. Yet, there are alternative ways to address such concerns, such as control at the toll gates of national expressways.

In both cases mentioned above, although regulatory objectives by themselves do not include trade restrictions and are justifiable, existing measures to achieve objectives are questioned from the perspective of market openness. This supports the argument for more open regulatory procedures to take into account of the concerns of a broad range of affected parties, including foreign businesses and consumers. Such mechanisms will help focus on appropriate regulatory measures to achieve the goal without causing unnecessary trade restrictiveness.

3.1.3. *Transparency in regulatory procedures*

Transparency in regulatory procedures is a high priority. For automobile regulation, MOT News, published in English by Office of International Affairs in Road Transport Bureau of the Ministry of Transport, has helped to inform foreign firms of important regulatory changes.[57] There has been more frequent use of public hearings for draft regulations, such as those held on the deregulation proposal for the mechanics system and proposed modifications to the type designation system.

Foreign firms operating in Japan, however, have had difficulty in consultations on new regulatory proposals. Consultation tends to take place at late stages, resulting in a lack of understanding by foreign manufactures and stronger reactions from them. One recent example is the proposal by the Ministry to introduce recall procedures and the new certification system. A foreign expert based in Japan observed that there may be no explicit intention to exclude foreign firms from consultation, and that going to domestic players first is often simply a matter of habit. Nonetheless, such habits support the case for procedural safeguards against exclusion. Trading partners have requested that the Japanese government allow foreign manufacturers, on an equal basis with Japanese manufactures, full and timely opportunities to comment on draft regulations and standards.

Japanese Ministries have started to use the Internet, as means of communication to the public. However, use of the Internet for dissemination of detailed regulatory information seems to lagwell behind the best practice countries such as the United States. In light of wide and non-discriminatory availability through information or the Internet as well as the need for more open practices by regulatory authorities, more use of the Internet is a promising avenue to impose transparency in sectors such as automobile, where regulations intervene with important business decisions. Recent use of the public comment procedures for new fuel efficiency standards is an encouraging example in this direction.

3.2. Telecommunication services

The telecommunications sector in Japan has been a major focus in trade discussions in recent years. The sector is a major part of foreign trading partners' recommendations submitted to the formulation and subsequent revisions of Deregulation Action Plan. Ongoing Japan-US trade discussions have spent considerable time and resources on the sector. In the context of multilateral trade relationships, Japan participated in the WTO negotiations on basic telecommunications services and joined in the agreement reached in February 1998. International discussions have had substantial impact on Japanese regulatory reform to date.

Although telecommunication services cross borders easily, the prevailing feature of the industry structure in OECD countries is the existence of dominant carriers who control the nation-wide network. Vigorous international competition, where firms from different countries compete effectively against each other in a particular national market, has not been common in this sector, although such competition has become the norm in many manufacturing sectors. Competition will produce benefits in terms of consumers choice, service quality, and price. The challenge for regulatory reform in each country is how to introduce and promote competition through the most efficient measures. Specific aspects of such measures may be different across countries, since countries differ in their tradition of regulatory rules and structures. Market openness, however, will contribute to development of efficient and competitive national telecom industries and deliver the most benefits to consumers.

A general overview and assessment of future policy options in Japan's telecommunications services sector is presented in the report on regulatory reform in the telecommunications industry in this volume. This section assesses particular aspects of regulatory reform from a market openness perspective. The major policy question is how more vigorous international competition can be ensured, so that Japanese consumers, and domestic and foreign businesses can maximise benefits from reform.

3.2.1. *Reform to date of particular interest to foreign competitors*

Since the privatisation of NTT in 1985 and subsequent liberalisation of the market, the Japanese telecommunications sector has progressively moved toward competition. A recent major step was the decision to restructure NTT under the control of a single holding company. The Deregulation Action Plan of 1998 includes the important decision to move toward introduction of interconnection rates based on LRIC (Long Run Incremental Costs) methodology (which is expected to facilitate entry of carriers by reducing the costs of interconnection to the dominant carrier NTT). This has been requested by foreign trading partners, and they are now paying careful attention to the progress.

The government has taken other steps on issues that have concerned foreign firms. For example, foreign ownership restriction of Type I carrier and KDD, as well as the "100 destination rule"[58] which imposed restriction on international transit services, have been abolished. International simple resale was also liberalised since the end of 1997. (On the other hand, foreign ownership restrictions on NTT and CATV still remain.) In addition, Japan's participation in the WTO agreement on basic telecommunications services, particularly its commitment with other countries to pro-competitive regulatory principles, will have positive impacts on the operation of the regulatory regime in Japan. These moves have been welcomed by trading partners.

3.2.2. *Foreign trading partners' concerns: uncertainty in pro-competitive approach*

While progress has been made in building a more market-based regulatory regime in this sector, observers, including foreign trading partners, see underlying and rather fundamental problems in the regulatory regime in this sector. Foreign firms in this sector are not confident that regulatory policies are committed to full-fledged competition. Foreign business operating in Japan point out that Japan's Telecommunication Business Law (TBL), and hence the market supervision by MPT, has weakness in commitment to the interests of competition and consumers in its regulating philosophy, compared to US, Germany and UK telecommunication laws: the Article 1 of the TBL states that the Law aims to protect interests of users, in parallel with other purposes including the general term of "promotion of public welfare"; it does not mention competition specifically. On the other hand, the Japanese government points out that its regulatory policies to date have been contributed to the interests of consumers through introduction of competition in the sector.

As mentioned, the key regulatory challenge is how to introduce effective competition in the market where a dominant carrier still exists. The task involves broad-range, technically complex issues such as establishing and monitoring interconnection rules, number portability and securing rights of way that are heavily controlled by incumbent interests. Without confidence that regulatory policy is aimed at resolving these issues over time in an open, non-discriminatory and pro-competitive way, incentives of firms to invest and innovate may be greatly reduced.

Such claims have been raised on: weakness in the TBL to take an explicit dominant carrier regulation approach; need of stronger competition policy; concerns on independence of the regulator. Furthermore, trading partners point out that discretionary power exercised by the regulatory authority is still too wide, giving a chilling effect to the market. Foreign firms may be the most sensitised to such risks because they know less about how discretion might work than domestic non-dominant firms including NCCs (New Common Carriers). For example, they claim that with respect to licensing of carriers, after abolition of demand-supply adjustment clauses, carriers still have to prove their business plans are "rational and certain", giving a wide range for discretion by authority. However, according to the government, the licensing procedures are based on examination standards that are clearly prescribed and publicly announced, and hence it believes that there is no room for exercising discretionary power.

As a result of the problems mentioned above, many foreign telecommunications firms believe that long-term investment has suffered in this sector in Japan. A pro-competitive regulatory regime, as recommended in the report on regulatory reform in telecommunications included in this volume, would greatly reduce uncertainty for future business activities by narrowing the scope of discretionary use of regulatory power. For example, in order to encourage innovative and vigorous business activities, positive and clear commitment by the regulatory authority to competition as well as its willingness to reduce regulations and implementation only to that purpose should be demonstrated. For this purpose, while recent revisions of TBL have been intended to increase competition, explicitly enshrined competition principles such as in 1996 US Act, or at least binding and clear statements on overall policy stance of regulation would be further useful.

3.2.3. *Transparency and openness of regulatory procedures*

Connection to the network and rights of way mentioned above is only a part of regulatory issues in telecommunication services which have a significant impact on competition, including international competition. There are a number of other issues that urge regulatory authorities to undertake study and to reach decisions on the daily basis. In the light of this situation as well as technical complexity and broad potential impact on the economy including its international aspects, regulatory decisions in this sector will particularly benefit from the openness and transparency of the procedures. As mentioned, authority's commitment to full competition has not enjoyed high level of confidence by foreign businesses. Recent announcement by the Ministry of Post and Telecommunications that it would implement a notice and comment process for major regulatory changes signifies the increasing recognition of this need. Positive attitude of the Ministry is welcomed all the more because such overall commitment for procedural transparency is still under consideration by government as a whole. One trading partner particularly appreciates its publication of manual for market entry to this sector, too. However, in order for the consultation process to really work – to contribute to the quality of regulatory decisions –, there is room for further improvement. Foreign telecommunications firms in Japan have complained that consultation periods for major regulatory changes are too short, and ask that the period be extended. They wish proceedings of the MPT's related Committee/Council/Study Group meetings to be published. Openness can be further promoted if written response is made to the comments, giving reasons for authority's actions.

In addition to a notice and comment system, the use of the Internet in disseminating detailed information on regulation would be a powerful tool to increase the level of transparency of regulations and the MPT has started to use its Home Page for the communication with the public. As described in the section on automobiles and parts, Japan can learn more from best practice countries such as the US in this context. Such reform will contribute to market openness of the sector too.

3.3. Telecommunication equipment

The size of Japanese telecommunication equipment market is the second largest in the world. It is also a rapidly growing market: domestic production of the equipment in FY 1996 was more than 4 trillion yen and it had grown by more than 36% compared to the previous year. Foreign manufactures have come to be greatly interested in Japanese market.

Regulatory systems relating to the equipment, while aiming inter alia at network compatibility, have been seen as affecting further expansion of trade. Conformity assessment procedures for telecommunication equipment, especially terminal equipment including mobile phones, have been cited as one example. Furthermore NTT, the biggest procurer of the equipment, has been said to be causing difficulties for more imports. NTT has made efforts to open up its procurement to foreign manufactures. Its procurement from foreign source has been increasing under the NTT Procurement Arrangement since 1981. However, a recent JETRO (Japan External Trade Organisation) survey[59] has pointed out possible NTT-related problems in the market. For example: *i)* Carriers, especially NTT, play major role in sales and marketing of terminal equipment and this relatively unique structure of distribution may prevent standardised and hence low cost products from entering Japanese market; *ii)* NTT-led R&D joint project with several makers has been dominant in the development of network equipment: such "carrier design" products may have nurtured close relationship between NTT and equipment manufactures and may have discouraged new comers to work

263

with NTT. On the other hand, the Japanese government holds the view that the procurement of NTT is a matter for the private sector and should not be regarded as government regulation. According to the government, NTT's practices, including its R&D activities, are open, fair, and non-discriminatory.

3.3.1. Conformity assessment procedures

Japan has two sets of technical standards and conformity assessment procedures accordingly for telecommunication equipment. Telecommunications Business Law mandates technical standards in order to secure connection of equipment to network. A public service corporation called JATE (Japan Approvals Institute for Telecommunications Equipment) has been authorised to certify its conformity. Radio Law mandates technical standards in order to ensure fair and efficient use of radio wave. A body called TELEC (Telecom Engineering Center, formerly called as MKK) has been designated by the Minister to certify products.

This regulatory system has been criticised as preventing optimal market competition that would finally result in wider choice and lower prices. According to the JETRO survey, the costs of certification are high in Japan, compared to some of the major OECD countries, while the MPT has pointed out that the costs in some European countries are higher than those in Japan. Several problems have been identified: i) Organisation that conducts certification has been a limited number, notably JATE and TELEC. These bodies can use data from testing laboratories or from the manufacturers themselves in their conformity assessment process, while some manufacturers have found it difficult to use such a system in practice. ii) Possible duplication arising from two types of regulations; when equipment is in both categories mentioned above, such as mobile telephone equipment, manufactures have to have their new products certified by the two bodies. iii) There has been no availability for manufactures' declaration of conformity which is less burdensome for manufactures.

The regulatory authority, Ministry of Posts and Telecommunications, has responded to question by introducing new legislation for rationalisation and more openness of current certification system. Passed by the Diet in April 1998, it allows foreign certification bodies (that are either foreign government bodies or those designated by the governments) can be recognised by the authority to certify products. It also allows data from testing institutions (foreign or domestic) recognised by the MPT to be used for obtaining certification. These measures, which came into force in March 1999, are to expand recognition of equivalence of foreign conformity assessment and are expected to contribute to market openness of telecommunication equipment market. In order to ensure such positive impact, the criteria to designate certification bodies and testing laboratories should be objective and according to international practice. The delegated rule-making on this should be subject to transparent and open public and notice procedures. Furthermore, the costs from complexity of the system would be reduced by the recent reform to receive "one-stop shopping" application.

Another notable development towards more open conformity assessment procedures is the ongoing negotiation on the Mutual Recognition Agreement (MRA) with the EU. Telecommunication terminal equipment is one of the items under negotiation. If successfully concluded, the MRA is expected to have a positive impact on further openness of the system. While progresses to date are encouraging, further reform efforts, such as further integrating the separate two systems as well as adoption of manufactures' declaration of conformity where possible and appropriate, will have promising benefits.

3.3.2. Standards and procurement practices of NTT

Substantial efforts have been made both by NTT and the Japanese government. The foreign products that NTT purchased amounted to 185 billion yen in FY 1997. NTT is providing the information of its procurement at its Home page of the Internet and has announced its fundamental procurement policy based on openness, fairness and non-discrimination. However, foreign trading partners still allege that the past measures have fallen short of truly open procurement.

They claim that NTT's procurement instructions are too complex and not well documented. As a result, the manufactures, who are familiar with these practices through a close relationship nurtured under the long-held monopoly position of NTT, are claimed to have advantage over foreign suppliers. The Ministry of Post and Telecommunications argues, on the other hand, that such an allegation is not factually correct.[60] It has been also pointed out that NTT-led research consortia may have discouraged entry of foreign firms. Furthermore, the JETRO report raised the view that rate of return regulation may be responsible for weak incentives for cost reduction by NTT and hence weakening its purchase of low cost products on which foreign manufactures have advantage. Due to technical and detailed nature of procurement practices, the policy judgement on these issues is bound to be complex. More vigorous competition in services market, however, will have positive impact on equipment market in the sense that the best quality and the least expensive products will be chosen to contribute to economic efficiency. In this sense, price-cap regulation introduced in 1998 (which will be implemented in 1999) is expected to shift the market towards this direction, by giving stronger incentives to NTT to seek more vigorously low-cost equipment.

It has been also pointed out that standards development of telecommunication equipment has often been heavily influenced by NTT. It has overwhelming technological advantage and has tended to produce Japan-specific standards. More open and internationally-oriented standards development, it is said, can enhance more vigorous competition, wider choice for consumers and innovation. NTT recognises that its technical specifications should be based on international standards, including *de facto* ones, where they exist. Again, this is not a simple question. Considering technology-driven nature of the telecommunication equipment, NTT's technological capacity can be seen as the assets for the future, not only in Japan. But at the same time, such potential benefits should be balanced by Japanese consumers' interests in having the least expensive equipment which has connection to the broadest part of the world.

3.4. Electricity

There are ten electricity utilities in Japan, who have enjoyed regional monopoly status for a long time. They are firms of large size and regarded as important representatives of Japanese business. During five decades in the post-war period, the electricity sector has been the major and stable establishment in Japanese industrial structure and its main concerns have been, understandable, domestically focused.

However, Japanese electricity prices, the highest in the OECD are affecting industrial competitiveness. Concerns about international competitiveness is the main driver of recent reform in this sector. The Ministry of International Trade and Industry (MITI) has established the target to reduce electricity price to "internationally comparable levels" by 2001. Recent reform introduced competition at the whole sale level from 1996 and made other several important changes (including easing some technical requirements for pre-inspection of new facilities). Further reforms, to introduce partial liberalisation of retail supply of electricity, are expected next year. The background report on Regulatory reform in the electricity industry makes the overview and assessment of this development.

The focus on international competitiveness in electricity prices, and the trend to market liberalisation, is putting pressure on the utilities to reduce costs. A focus on costs of investment in new electrical generating equipment, currently the highest in the OECD, is a logical starting point. The volume of annual investment by utilities in generation, transmission, transformation and distribution equipment of 4.4 trillion yen (this consists of approximately 1.6 trillion in generation, 1.5 trillion in networks (transmission transformation and distribution), and 1.3 trillion in plant improvements), makes a highly attractive market to foreign electrical equipment manufacturers. In recent years, as the share of foreign equipment sales in Japan has been at the level of around 9%, the potential for trade still looks significant.

Market openness perspectives can strengthen benefits from the ongoing reform in electricity. It would help to expand opportunities for less expensive input price, and hence can make a concrete contribution to the objective of reducing costs to internationally comparable levels. It may further bring benefits from innovative technology widely available in the world, such as that in metering. Such benefits would enhance broad consumer interests as well as the foreign trade and investment. The following analyses how market openness perspectives work to contribute to regulatory reform in Japan.

3.4.1. *Technical regulations and conformity assessment of electricity equipment*

MITI is mandated by the Electricity Utilities Industry Law (EUI Law) to set technical standards to ensure safety of electricity supply. Utility companies have to submit plan for construction work to MITI for its approval when they install or change electricity facilities such as turbines and boilers. MITI conduct mandatory inspection before the operation of the facilities (Article 48). Periodical inspection by MITI is also mandated for pressure-resistant facilities (Article 54).

Most of the technical standards set by MITI are said to have originated from ASME standards, which are used globally by electricity businesses. Until recently, technical safety standards by MITI were highly prescriptive, which left equipment manufacturers little flexibility in design of equipment. In reviewing electricity safety regulation, it was recommended that technical regulations should adopt performance-based standards that would provide performance needed to be achieved by equipment for safety purpose but allow manufactures flexibility in achieving it. Subsequently, in June 1997, performance standards was introduced by revision of related MITI internal order. Although some specifications remained in the form of "interpretation of technical standards", it was made clear that such interpretation is not mandatory.

This move reflects in part the concerns from trade perspectives that difference in standards across countries can become unnecessary trade obstacles. The current measure is expected to contribute to market openness in electricity equipment market and contribute to harmonisation process across countries. However, expert views are that there are obstacles in addition to technical regulations: for example, specifications set by utility companies may pose more serious difficulties (as discussed below). the upgrading of existing power generation facilities in Japan meets too burdensome procedures due to various regulatory restrictions.

Furthermore, they point out that there are unnecessary burdens in inspection procedures. Such burdens, while non-discriminatory in nature, may be excessive for the purpose of safety and they are likely to discourage trade in equipment in this area. While the periodical inspection has been recently prolonged from 24 months to 30 months, foreign businesses have seen this only marginal improvement.

Foreign trading partners have also expressed their concerns on the requirement from the High Pressure Gas Law (HPG Law) applied to electricity equipment. This regulation applies to the equipment that are not used directly for power generation, such as pollution control facilities. Inspection under the HPG Law is said to be complex and costly, imposing unnecessary burdens for foreign producers. Technical standards under the Law, it is said, should be brought in line with internationally accepted standards. According to MITI, the similar measure taken under the EIU Law, namely the reform of regulatory specifications towards performance-based standards, is under way to be implemented next March. Enforcers of the HPG Law regulations include 47 local prefectural governments and that has added to the complexity of regulations.

While MITI has addressed the particular concerns of exporters to Japanese market *i.e.* by lifting part of inspection requirement by the EUI Law or HPG Law for pressure-resistant facilities for imported equipment, more systematic review of safety regulations with a view to avoiding unnecessary trade restrictiveness would contribute to market openness: under such reform, economic gains can be shared with consumers without sacrificing safety concerns.

3.4.2. *Procurement practices by utilities*

Procurement of electricity equipment by utilities has been dominated by domestic manufactures. However, recent drive for lowering electricity price has given strong pressures to Japanese utility firms to change their practices, opening up their procurement process to wider range of businesses, including foreign ones. TEPCO (Tokyo Electricity Power Company) and other utilities have set up Internet sites to provide information on their procurement items and procedures, both in Japanese and in English. Utilities have shown increased interest for purchasing abroad by sending mission to foreign trade shows. These reflect utilities' growing concerns for cost saving as a result of introduction of competition to the sector. Foreign manufacturers clearly welcomed this move.

However, the specifications of utilities in procuring equipment have been frequently raised as fundamental problem. Technical specifications (standards) set by Japanese utilities are often said to be tailored to each company (ten "general" utilities exist in Japan), and too high for the purpose of maintaining an optimal level of safety or reliability. (An economist mentioned that Japanese electricity grid system is "Rolls Royce" among other countries.) Utilities also require stringent conditions for prompt deliveries and periodical inspection as well. While concerns for high quality is understandable and justified to some extent, the standards must be balanced against the impact on economic efficiency. If standards are set so high, the number of potential suppliers will be limited, reducing competition and raising costs.

More open equipment procurement practices will be encouraged by further promotion of competition in the electricity sector by future reform, through more pressures on electricity companies to search and purchase less expensive equipment. A central issue here is how quickly such reform will be implemented and its impact will be translated into equipment market. There may be a danger of a policy vacuum, since MITI has been reluctant to intervene directly in procurement practices of utilities. More focused attention on this issue, probably looking at the role of standardisation for example, will likely to contribute to consumer interests as well as to help ease potential trade tensions.

Furthermore, market liberalisation can be expected to affect only the cost for generation equipment, which is currently only about two-thirds of all utility investment. Investment in electrical networks (transmission, transformation and distribution) will not be subject to competition. Intensive policy efforts to ensure openness of procurement practices is even more necessary in this area. One possibility for the regulator to consider is to require utilities to tender for construction of major new network facilities (*e.g.*, transmission lines).

3.4.3. *Openness and transparency in the regulatory procedures*

Regulatory procedures in the electricity sector have been in the traditional style: the key discussion is based on informal consultation with major players; decisions are often formalised in advisory councils in closed session, while members of such councils have been selected from utilities, user industries, consumers and academics. Public comment and notice procedures has not been the norm. As foreign companies have not been very active in the Japanese electricity sector, their views have not been sought.

That attitude has to change in order to adapt to a more liberalised, and at the same time a more internationalised, electricity sector. Potential participants in the market may be more numerous than major players, including regulators, think. Exposing the discussion to public and even international view would increase confidence in decisions made and would ensure their quality. The current efforts to enhance openness are in the right direction and should be pursued further.

The commitment to a public notice and comment system in major regulatory decisions, made in telecommunication services area for example, is worthwhile to be pursued. MITI announced in August 1998 its intention to adopt public comment procedures to policy council deliberations. The coverage of such measure, however, has not been explicitly spelled out and the impact on significant regulatory decisions, which are expected to be made in electricity areas in future remains to be seen. If broadly and effectively implemented, it would ensure all the interested parties, including foreign firms, to make input to the decision making and help reach pro-competitive results. Publication of Study Group/Council proceedings are also useful for enhancing transparency. Furthermore, the use of the Internet would contribute to higher level of transparency as is seen in leading countries such as the US and should be pursued further.

4. CONCLUSIONS AND POLICY OPTIONS FOR REFORM

4.1. General assessment of current strengths and weaknesses

Recent Japanese regulatory reform programs have been launched to implement fundamental reforms in Japan's socio-economic structure and have also responded to concerns voiced by major trading partners (including foreign business communities) and suggestions made in international fora such as the WTO and the OECD. Even though the current programs have been largely based on Japan's own initiatives, the Japaness public still seems to relate them to foreign pressures. In fact, the image related with foreign pressures was one of main weaknesses of previous programs. While this image helped promote reform against strong domestic opposition, it also helped to make Japanese regulatory reform programs incremental, defensive and conservative. It did not helped the Japanese general public to accept reform and understand how reform was in its interests.

Japanese bureaucrats have had tendencies to keep regulated sectors at the close sight and to manage competition. Many trading partners have expressed their concerns about the demand supply adjustment clauses of individual sectors which give regulatory authorities the right to intervene, as this usually results in controlling the number of firms and limiting the entry of new competitors, domestic and foreign.[61]

Even when bureaucrats agree with the request to change the system i.e., to introduce more market mechanisms at the expense of direct control or regulations, they are usually reluctant to do so radically. This is partly due to their perception of responsibility with regard to specific sectors. But, it is also largely due to traditional inertia vis-à-vis change.[62] Sometimes, traditional values of regulations which have existed so long make bureaucrats hesitate to change. This stance of Japanese bureaucrats was one of the most important obstacles to the launching of government-wide regulatory reform. It has been continuously criticised by trading partners as a major obstacle to improving market openness. It has also been the main reason why Japanese deregulation measures have been incremental in nature. Despite requests from the prime minister's office and strong pressure from domestic and foreign businesses, bureaucrats still take the incremental approach by, for example, reducing some administrative procedures, or by allowing additional licences, (see the background report on Government capacity to assure high quality regulation for a more detailed discussion on "incrementalism" in Japanese deregulation programmes).

Although the Japanese government considers consultation with councils as a good method to hear public opinion and make administrative conduct more open and transparent, many trading partners have expressed their concerns about the council system. According to them, consultation with councils makes the decision making process more closed (in the sense that vested interests are reflected and not new competitors' views) and very slow.

One of the main strengths in the Japanese regulatory reform process is the desire of Japan to integrate in the globalised world.[63] Despite all the obstacles to enhancing market openness and to launching effective structural reforms, the efforts which have been made until now owe a lot to this desire. The Japanese general publicseems to accept the necessity of the integration of the Japanese economy in the globalised world. One of the Three year Programme's guidelines requires Japanese regulations to be aligned with international norms and is a notable example.

A second strength is closely related to the first one. The establishment of the OTO and the OMA is also perhaps the result of the desire of the integration in the world economy. The OTO has the right vocation to enhance market openness and consequently to contribute to regulatory reform in this regard. It has also a well established mechanism, multi-layer inter-ministerial co-ordinating meetings and special committee, to solve specific market access problems. In addition, the establishment of the OMA Cabinet level meeting has made the OTO more powerful at least at the institutional level. Japan may need, however, to reinforce its co-ordinating authorities over other ministries and agencies, since some trading partners seem to be losing interest in bringing complaints to OTO, due to disappointment with its lack of authority.

A third strength is the contribution made by foreign business communities. They are active in every phase of Japanese regulatory reforms. They are bringing forth the most current issues because they are very close to the market, playing the intermediary role between the Japanese government and governments of their home countries, and monitoring the implementation of Japan's commitments in deregulatory plans and in various level trade talks. However, their role is not very well received by the Japanese public. They may be playing a role which is missing but necessary in Japan, catalyst for change. However, their role is limited because they fragment reform, and focus change on trade disputes rather than deepen change.

Many weaknesses can be found in the Japanese regulatory reform process. First, one should mention the lack of serious support for regulatory reform and market openness. It is notable that supposed beneficiaries from reform, market openness and competition, consumers, are not very eager to support those initiatives but are sometimes opposed to so-called radical change. This is because consumers are not well informed about the potential benefits of reforms and market openness, and reforms have been often initiated to respond to the demand of producers, domestic and foreign. Political support seems to be not always strong enough to promote concrete regulatory reform programs in specific sectors especially when related to market openness. Consequently, the struggle is taking place among bureaucrats, between those who are convinced of the necessity of change and those who are eager to stick to their traditional way to govern. Since the actual power to decide something at the concrete level remains at the hand of the latter, it is still difficult to launch effective regulatory reform programmes, even if there are good guidelines for the programmes which are usually defined by the former. It seems essential for the former to develop a stronger constituency among the general public and politicians in order to effectively pursue further reform programmes.

Secondly, the distinction between the sectors traditionally open to international competition and the sectors protected from it is too prominent. The former sectors are generally competitive on the world market. Businesses active in these sectors are generally favourable to enhancing regulatory reform and market openness in the protected sectors, because they think that only further reforms in these sectors can help their own sectors to remain competitive. However, those protected sectors are still regulated and relatively well protected from foreign competition. Those involved in these sectors (regulators and regulated firms) even when conscious of the necessity to change, are eager to maintain the current situation. When sectors are represented by small business such as distribution firms, they are often politically strong enough to resist reform. Since ministries and agencies in charge of the two groups of sectors are well separated and independent from each other, effective government-wide initiatives for regulatory reform in view of enhancing market openness become difficult to launch.

Thirdly, the lack of strong competition policy enforcement is an important obstacle to market openness in the Japanese regulatory system. The JFTC seems to have difficulty taking vigorous enforcement actions against the sectors regulated by "major" ministries. In these sectors, anti-competitive business practices of either monopolising companies or exclusionary industry associations may not be appropriately treated by the competition policy authority (see the background report on The Role of competition policy and enforcement of regulatory reform for more detailed discussion). In addition, the Japanese business tradition of long-term close relationships between manufacturers and distributors remains a major obstacle to foreign access to the Japanese market.

Fourthly, there are no established methods to monitor adverse trade and investment effects of some administrative conduct. Informal communications such as administrative guidance still form a part of the "effective" regulatory structure in Japan. Government bodies in charge of monitoring regulatory processes do not have strong authority vis-à-vis individual ministries and agencies. Their monitoring role does not fully reach regulations such as ministerial orders or administrative conduct of other ministries and agencies, except at the inter-ministerial deliberation process of laws and cabinet orders. The advocacy role of MITI and MOFA for enhancing market openness (*e.g.* training) is also limited.

According to the self-assessed response by governments to the OECD indicators questionnaire on the six efficient regulatory principles with a market openness perspective, the Japanese regulatory system is relatively advanced in its application of the principles of non-discrimination and use of internationally harmonised regulations compared to OECD averages (see Figure 2). On the other hand, the Japanese regulatory system has a relatively wide scope for further imrpovement in the principles of transparency, openness of decision making and of appeals procedures; and application of competition principles from an international perspective. However, even regarding non-discrimination and international standards, more efforts are required, taking account of concerns of trading partners mentioned in Section 2.

269

Figure 2. **Japan's trade friendly index by principle**
OECD averages = 100

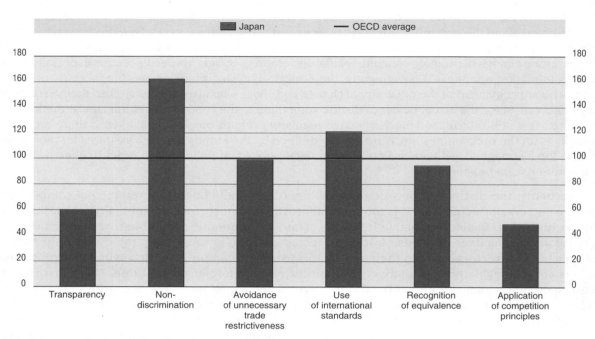

Source: Responses to the Indicator Questionnaire on Regulatory Reform, OECD, 1998.

4.2. The dynamic view: the pace and direction of change

Globalisation has dramatically altered the world paradigm for the conduct of international trade and investment, creating new competitive pressures in Japan and elsewhere. At the same time, the progressive dismantling or lowering of traditional barriers to trade and the increased relevance of "behind the border" measures to effective market access and presence has exposed national regulatory regimes to a degree of unprecedented international scrutiny by trade and investment partners, with the result that regulation is no longer (if ever it was) a purely "domestic" affair. Trade and investment policy communities have generally kept pace with these twin phenomena. However, a degree of regulatory catch-up is required. Concrete steps to increase awareness of and effective adherence to the efficient regulation principles and to deepen international co-operation on regulatory issues are encouraging trends in this context. Overcoming systemic intransigence and fostering a new regulatory culture will be pivotal to these efforts.

Currently, the US and the EU are engaged in dialogue with the Government of Japan on regulatory matters. These dialogues include the identification and canvassing of regulatory issues and suggestions for reform. Current reform policies emphasise the openness of reform authorities to external viewpoints, both domestic and foreign, suggesting that these dialogues will continue to be an important one for future regulatory reform. The quantity of international comments and requests has been large. The Commission of the European Communities provided, in August 1998, a 105 page List of EU Deregulation Proposals for Japan. Similarly, the United States government, in October 1998, submitted 52 pages of US proposals to the Japanese government for promoting further reform in the areas of telecommunications, housing, medical and pharmaceuticals, financial services, energy, legal services, and automotive and motorcycles as well as institutional reforms such as distribution, competition authority and Anti-Monopoly Law, and transparency and other government practices.

Some of the recent Japanese deregulation programmes such as the Big Bang in financial sectors and the abolishment of the LSRSL (Large Scale Retail Store Law), seem to be relatively well received by major trading partners.[64] Moreover, the "Three year Programme for the Promotion of Deregulation" decided by Cabinet on March 31, 1998 sets conformity to international standards as one of six main guiding principles of the Programme (see the background report on Government capacity to assure high quality regulation for more detailed discussion of the Programme). Trading partners recognise the progress achieved in many Japanese deregulation initiatives, although they are keeping pressure for further action.

However, Japan's reactions to direct bilateral trade pressures have been quite mixed. On the one hand, for the purpose of reducing trade conflicts, Japan appears to have taken a serious approach to those negotiations, but on the other hand, it has kept a somewhat defensive attitude regarding the requests of trading partners. As a result, deregulation and/or reforming programmes have been incremental in nature, giving away minimum concessions which touch on potentially vast areas but which result in very little change of the Japanese regulatory system. Their reforming efforts are generally neither adequate to efficiently enhance competition and market openness and to change the Japanese economic system nor sufficiently rapid to produce notable results.

Moreover, the deregulation initiatives reveal that the impediments to imports have not been well assessed. The measures have been concentrated on import procedures rather than the market structure. To date, promotion programmes have been more concerned about adjusting existing procedures than removing major obstacles of market access. The SEP, one of the Japanese economic reform initiatives, envisages the following steps "to promote imports and market opening measures: the creation of import-promotion zones, enhancement of import-related infrastructure, and provision of import incentives in taxation and financial assistance areas".[65] All the steps relate to border access. Hence, market openness at the border level has been enhanced. However, market openness obstacles include behind the border measures and conditions, such as distribution and access to consumers, where further progress is still needed (see Box 1).

4.3. Potential benefits and costs of further regulatory reform

Japanese consumers, who are not well informed by market information and are served by highly regulated service sectors and an inefficient distribution system, are losing substantial wealth because of the higher prices they pay compared to their counterparts in the OECD countries. In 1997 on the average, citizens of Tokyo pay 18% more for their purchases than citizens in New York, 8% than those in London, 23% than those in Paris, and 30% than those in Berlin. They also generally pay higher prices for most services. They also generally pay higher prices for most services. Because of protection and inefficiency in the distribution sector, they pay much higher prices for foods & beverages and clothes & footwear as well. As Kato said, "Japanese consumers are living miserably in spite of the abundant wealth they are creating".[66] According to Sazanami (1995), "Japanese tariff and non-tariff barriers inflicted a cost on Japanese consumers of 10 to 15 trillion yen in 1989 (75 to 110 billion US dollars at the 1989 exchange rate). At the expense of consumers, Japanese producers pocketed perhaps 7 to 9.6 trillion yen".[67]

Many Japanese manufacturing industries which used to be very competitive in the international markets seem to be suffering from declining competitiveness because of expensive domestic intermediary inputs in service sectors. According to MITI's survey report, Japanese industries are paying almost twice as high for non-manufacturing intermediary inputs compared to their competitors of Germany, almost three or four times higher compared to those of other Asian emerging economies, and more than eight times higher compared to their Chinese competitors. The price difference appears to be a bit moderated for manufacturing inputs.

The loss of consumer welfare and economic efficiency resulting from regulations not consistent with market openness principles has been very large in Japan. Potential benefits of further reform in this direction are very large as well. The gain which Japanese producers have pocketed thanks to the protection, will be lost if market opening reforms are fully implemented. However, Japanese producers can expect the sup-

Table 2. **Tokyo's price level compared to those of other international cities**

Products	New York	London	Paris	Berlin	Geneva
Total	*1.18*	*1.08*	*1.23*	*1.30*	*0.99*
Foods and beverages	**1.41**	**1.44**	**1.56**	**1.72**	**1.18**
Durable goods	**1.24**	0.78	0.85	0.86	0.85
Clothes and footwear	**1.33**	**1.37**	**1.36**	**1.16**	0.97
Energy	**1.54**	**1.41**	**1.15**	**1.12**	**1.01**
Water and sewage	**1.67**	0.78	0.61	0.33	0.87
Transport	**1.17**	0.94	**1.12**	**1.06**	0.96
Telecommunications	1.00	**1.16**	**1.03**	0.85	0.94
Health services	0.82	**1.55**	**1.72**	**4.02**	0.36
Education	0.55	0.56	**1.20**	**1.09**	0.51
Household services	**1.55**	**1.12**	**1.55**	**1.22**	**1.64**
Other services	0.90	0.87	0.93	**1.16**	0.83

Source: EPA, 1998 *Price Report*, October 1998.

Table 3. **International price difference for intermediary inputs**

	Japan	US	Germany	Korea	Taiwan	Hong Kong	Singapore	China
Total inputs	100	88	70	39	33	53	46	20
Manufacturing	100	91	101	55	65	67	66	45
Non-manufacturing	100	85	51	28	21	43	33	12

Source: MITI, *Survey on Price Differentials between Domestic and International Markets for Intermediary Inputs*, 1998.

plementary efficient gain in terms of competitiveness from those reforms, in exchange of the loss of "protection rent" which has been anyway smaller than consumers' welfare gain, as Sazanami estimated above.

4.4. Policy options for consideration

Considering the potential benefits of further regulatory reform from the market openness perspective, and the assessments of the Japanese regulatory system made above regarding its integration of the six efficient regulatory principles, the Japanese government is encouraged to consider the following six policy options and subsequent detailed recommendations in its further regulatory reform initiatives.

- Enhance transparency from the international perspective in the regulatory process through concrete and wide-ranging steps;

- heighten government capacity to promote market openness perspectives in regulatory reform;

- establish a systematic approach to cope with recurring themes in the trade debate, such as lack of openness of procedures, unnecessary trade restrictiveness as well as harmonisation of standards and recognition of foreign conformity assessment;

- engage pro-actively in public efforts to enlighten the Japanese public, including consumers, of the economy-wide benefits of regulatory reform;

- enhance regulatory co-operation with other countries; and

- strengthen competition policy enforcement recognising its increasing importance in promoting market openness.

Enhance transparency from the international perspective in the regulatory process through concrete and wide-ranging steps.

- Following on the announcement of October 1998 that so-called Public Comment Procedures will be adopted for new regulations, implement those procedures in a way that allows foreign firms to participate easily.

- Ensure that all regulations, including information relating to the decision making process, are accessible to foreign parties.

- Enhance the efforts to publish the proceedings (or video recordings) of deliberations or open sessions on regulatory decisions for all advisory council meetings.

- Enhance the efforts to include participants from variety of interests including foreign participants in all decision making process, including participation in advisory councils, that substantially affect the trade and investment openness of the Japanese regulatory system.

  Although Japan has made progress in exposing reform discussions more frequently to foreign trading partners, there are still concerns that proceedings are not transparent and vulnerable to bias in their operations. More cross-cutting commitment to open regulatory procedures will raise the level of reform discussions as well as reduce the risk of capture by incumbent interests. The benefits will be shared by consumers and new businesses, both domestic and foreign. Although initial progress was made in the early 1990s, the impact has been limited. A more open approach now seems to be emerging, as shown in the area of telecommunications, and it should be expanded.

- Expand the dissemination of detailed and updated regulatory information such as administrative conduct that may have regulatory effects, ongoing proposals put for comment procedures, and business formalities to ensure its maximum public availability, such as via the Internet.

  Considering the persistent concerns from abroad about lack of openness of regulatory procedures, the use of the Internet for dissemination of detailed and updated information has great potential. Although such use has started in Japan, it remains under-exploited, particularly when compared to practices in some other countries. The expansion of the Internet for this purpose will particularly benefit new or potential entrants for markets, especially foreign firms. This will go far toward strengthening confidence in Japanese regulation in the eyes of all the market players, domestic or foreign.

- Explicitly limit the discretionary power of ministries and agencies through concrete and effective measures such as limits provided by revised basic laws of ministries.

  A fundamental concern of trading partners is that Japanese regulations in practice allow too wide-ranging discretion for regulators in many areas, which results in general uncertainty for future business activities and investment. The limitation of such discretion is crucial not only for raising the growth potential of Japanese economy but also for achieving a clear policy statement favouring foreign direct investment. Transparent and effective remedies should be provided for those aggrieved by administrative actions under broad range of discretion, including foreign parties; explicit limits on discretionary power should be imposed through revision of the ministry's basic laws as well as well-defined and clear policy commitment made under laws delegating regulatory authorities.

Heighten government capacity to promote market openness perspectives in regulatory reform.

- Create a capacity in government, in co-ordination with the economy-wide regulatory reform programme 1) to recommend reform measures from a market openness perspective and 2) to monitor vigorously implementation of those reform measures through strengthened power *vis-à-vis* other ministries and agencies.

- Heighten the capacity of government officials to cope with the market openness issues by strengthening training programme on international rules for all regulatory officials.

  Domestic regulations will continue to be a focus of trade discussions concerning Japan. Foreign voices will have an important role in Japanese regulatory reform as in the past. The current link between market openness perspectives and regulations mainly comes from translating foreign complaints or requests for consideration by regulatory authorities on an item by item basis. There is no governmental function to work with regulators to systematically improve regulations for market openness, with a view to benefiting both Japanese consumers and foreign trading partners. In order to better achieve the announced Japanese policy stance in favour of international harmonisation of regulations, Japan needs to install a more effective mechanism as well as capacity to plan and implement reform from a market openness perspective. This would support Japan's own regulatory reform initiatives and reduce incremental approach that results in reactions to foreign pressures.

Establish a systematic approach to cope with recurring themes in the trade debate, such as lack of openness of procedures, unnecessary trade restrictiveness as well as harmonisation of standards and recognition of foreign conformity assessment.

- The RIA (regulatory impact analysis) programme recommended in the background report on Government capacity to assure high quality regulation should include assessment of trade and investment impacts. Individual ministries and agencies should be required to report this analysis to Cabinet meeting when they propose new regulations or modifications of existing regulations.

- Require that drafts or discussions of ministerial orders and administrative conduct having regulatory effect which are not scrutinised in Cabinet level meetings should be checked by trade policy bodies, through establishment of more effective consultation process between government bodies.

- Launch government-wide measures to accept the equivalence of foreign conformity assessment, and establish sectoral programmes of reviewing and harmonising technical regulations and standards.

  Japan's efforts to date on market openness aspects of regulations have centred on addressing specifically defined issues arising from the requests from its trading partners. This means that although concrete progress has been constantly made, similar concerns in different areas, have been repeated and fundamental problems have not been adequately addressed. By utilising the strengthened mechanisms recommended above, the Japanese government should take a more fundamental approach to address cross-cutting issues as well as establishing the framework under which future progress can be measured.

Engage pro-actively in public efforts to enlighten the Japanese public, including consumers, of the economy-wide benefits of regulatory reform and market openness.

- Promote current and future studies to identify the net benefits for Japan from regulatory reform and market openness.

- Disseminate the research findings widely to the public.

  Some of the Japanese public have had a negative impression of continuous external pressures on Japan to reform. In order to maximise benefits of regulatory reform from a market openness perspective in Japan, it would be useful to recognise its own interests in such reform with concrete evidence. Such studies have been undertaken more and more in Japan, at the OECD and elsewhere.

Enhance regulatory co-operation with other countries.

- Engage more vigorously in work with trading partners to promote harmonisation and recognition of foreign conformity assessment.

  Considering the weight it represents for the global economy, Japan's actions to harmonise regulations and promote recognition of conformity assessment across countries are increasingly crucial for the success of international co-operation. Japan's recent accession to international harmonisation agreement in automobile sector as well as its leadership in APEC standards area have been promising examples in this regard. Recent progress towards MRAs with the EU in several sectors is also a positive point for international regulatory co-operation. By engaging in such co-operation vigorously, Japanese regulators will have more chances to get acquainted with the impact of their regulations on international trade and investment. As regulators are involved more and more in international co-operation, they will face the new challenge to translate its implications to domestic regulatory measures more frequently and quickly. Current efforts should be strengthened and accelerated.

Strengthen competition policy enforcement recognising its increasing importance in promoting market openness.

– Reinforce the role of the JFTC in resolving market access problems.[68]

   Meaningful private injunctive relief and private damage actions, combined with reformed rules on Japanese lawyers and foreign legal consultants are important means of redressing some of these problems. Similarly, an expanded role for the JFTC in reviewing regulations that might pose market access concerns is also important.

– Apply competition policy more effectively to private anti-competitive practices by adopting the measures recommended in the background report on The Role of competition policy and enforcement of regulatory reform.

   In addition, many of the market access concerns directly related to regulation and regulatory reform appear to be linked, in part, to lingering perceptions about Japanese enforcement of competition policy applied to private anti-competitive practices. Accordingly, strengthened anti-cartel enforcement (particularly with respect to bid-rigging and other "hard core" cartels) and monitoring of potential anti-competitive abuses with respect to distribution channels are also important tools in redressing the market access concerns that arise in the particular context of regulatory reform.

NOTES

1. MITI (1998), *White Paper on Trade and Industry.*

2. See among others Sazanami, Yoko and others (1995), *Measuring Costs of Protection in Japan*, Institute for International Economics, January 1995; Daiwa Economic Research Institute (1994), *Deregulation Impact on Business*, (in Japanese) January; and Kato, Masashi (ed. 1995), *Economics of Deregulation*, (in Japanese) Toyokeizaishimbunsha, July.

3. EPA (1997), *1997 Price Report*, October 1997 and MITI (1996), *Survey on Price Differentials between Domestic and International Markets for Intermediary Inputs.*

4. Simple mean of post Uruguay Round Bound Tariffs. See OECD (1998), *Review of Tariffs and Non-Tariff Barriers, Tariff Regimes of the Quad Countries*, February.

5. For example, Japan currently does not apply any kind of quantitative trade restriction measures, except the import licencings applied to Chinese and Korean silk and silk products and MFA quotas for some textile products.

6. As one of the special measures to promote imports and inward investment, the Japanese government has established several special zones in the vicinity of main ports and airports. Those who want to establish infrastructure for the purpose of import facilitation in these zones can get various financial and tax incentives from the government.

7. Japanese Government (1998), *Measures for Promoting Foreign Direct Investment in Japan*, August.

8. OECD (1998), *Financial Market Trends* – 70, June, pp. 96-100.

9. In this process, foreign business associations are playing an important role in providing their negotiators with information about certain Japanese regulations which are considered to be major obstacles to effective market access in Japan.

10. One should not omit other important factors which have made the establishment of new large scale stores difficult in Japan. Apart from the Large Scale Retail Store Act, there are high land prices and an inadequate road system. *International Economic Review*, Retail Distribution in Japan, September/October 1997, p 9. See also Motoshige, Itoh, "Regulatory Reform: An Experience of the Japanese Distribution System" in *Regulatory Reform in International Market Openness*, 1996, OECD.

11. OECD (1991), *Economic Survey on Japan.*

12. Frank Gibney (ed., 1998), *Unlocking the Bureaucrat's Kingdom*, Brookings.

13. The Housewives Association was one of strong opponents to rice market liberalisation. The main reason cited for opposition was lack of confidence in the quality of foreign rice.

14. OECD (1998), *1997-1998 Annual Review – Japan*, ECO/EDR(98)14.

15. See, in particular OECD (1998), "*Open Markets Matter. The benefits of Trade and Investment Liberalisation*", Paris; OECD (1994), "*The environmental effects of Trade*", Paris; and the 1995 Report on Trade and Environment to the OECD Council at Ministerial level.

16. See related discussion in Chapter 2, "Regulatory Quality and Public Sector Reform", in *The OECD Report on Regulatory Reform, Volume II: Thematic Studies*, OECD, 1997, Paris.

17. According to the Japanese response to the indicators questionnaire on market openness, Japan showed a relatively low score for the questions related with transparency principle compared to OECD average. See the figure of comparative analysis among principles in Section 4.

18. US (1998), *Submission by the Government of the United States to the Government of Japan regarding Deregulation, Competition Policy, and Transparency and Other Government Practices in Japan*, October 7.

19. EU (1998), Commission of the European Communities, *Indicative list of EU Deregulation Proposals for Japan*, October 12, 1998.

20. US (1998), EU (1998), and Australian Government, *Submission of the Australian Government to the Japanese Government on the Deregulation Promotion Program*, November 6.

21. The problem is that firms often do not know which ministry requests should be submitted to and how these requests are handled.

22. MOF press release, June 8, 1998.

23. Interview by the OECD secretariat.

24. The JFTC has carried out a survey of foreign firms in Japan, asking these firms questions about Japanese industry associations. It shows that foreign firms believe that industry associations tend to be used for information dissemination and informal consultation by regulatory authorities. See JFTC (1996), *Report based on the survey on foreign fims about industry associations* (in Japanese).

25. In this report, the term "other administrative conduct" is used to designate such administrative conduct as internal orders and communications notes which does not bind the public directly but may have an indirect regulatory effect on the public through bureaucrats' administrative actions directed by that kind of conduct.

26. These ad hoc meetings are not limited to those specially convened for once in a purely ad hoc basis, but include those convened in a semi-regular basis, which can last for a certain period of time.

27. According to the Japanese government, all advisory councils (*shingikai*) are now publishing at least summaries of discussions. However, there are still many ad hoc meetings which do not publish anything at all.

28. WTO (1998), *Notifications under article 6.2 of the TRIMs Agreement on publications in which TRIMs may be found*, G/TRIMS/2/Rev. 4, 5 August.

29. According to the strict definition of the Japanese legal system, internal orders and communication notes are not defined as "types of regulations", because they are deemed to regulate not directly "private sectors" but "bureaucrats" themselves. However, as bureacrats administer policies and programs in accordance with them, sometimes with administrative guidance, they may have regulatory effect in the practical sense. Furthermore, regulated firms seem to usually consider internal orders and communication notes as another form of regulations, because these have regulatory effect on their relations with regulatory authorities by binding the decision of regulatory bureaucrats.

30. Unless entrusted by the relevant laws, it shall not have provisions creating penalties, imposing obligations or limiting nationals rights.

31. *Kokka Gyosei Soshiki Ho* (National Government Organisation Law), Art 12(1).

32. A definition is introduced in the background report on Government capacities to assure high quality regulation.

33. It seems that the OTO is recently receiving some collected packages of complaints directly from foreign chambers of commerce in Japan and foreign embassies, apart from the complaints directly addressed to the OTO at the individual company level. However, the fact that foreign companies are taking the option to pass through their representatives and not to lodge them directly to the OTO may show the disappointment of foreign companies on the effectiveness of the OTO.

34. The EU has continuously raised this kind of concern, when important trade talks have been held between the US and Japan. Some of market access improvements achieved by these talks seem to have benefited other trading partners. For example, Korea obtained more market access for Japan's semiconductor market after an accord to improve market openness in the sector had been reached between the US and Japan.

35. For telecommunications services, Japan has recently lifted restrictions for most of Type I carriers. It has also decided to abolish foreign ownership restrictions concerning KDD.

36. On the basis of reviews and submissions by member countries, the OECD maintains a list of reservations to the OECD *Code of Liberalisation of Capital Movements*, and OECD *Code of Liberalisation of Current Invisible Operations* (both of which are binding codes containing provisions on non-discrimination), as well as exceptions reported under the *National Treatment Instrument*. The Japanese reservations and exceptions to these instruments, last updated in January 1997, are available through: http://www.oecd.org/daf/cmis/country/japan.htm#n.

37. See Japan's Exceptions to National Treatment: http://www.oecd.org/daf/cmis/country/japan.htm#n.

38. Article 27 of the Foreign Exchange and Foreign Trade Law.

39. EU (1998).

40. See OECD (1997), OECD *Report on Regulatory Reform Volume* I : *Sectoral Studies*, Paris.

41. EU (1998).

42. See Frank Gibney (ed., 1998), U*nlocking the Bureaucrat's Kingdom*, pp. 2-3.

43. US (1998), EU (1998), and Web Site of Canadian Ministry of Foreign Affairs and Trade.

44. EU (1998).

45. EPA(1997), *Policy Actions on Market Access Issues as Concerns Standards, Certification and Others*, July.

46. The Japanese government gave priority to resolving trade obstacles over investment obstacles at the outset of the OTO. At that time, the OTO was called the Office of Trade Ombudsman. That is why the OTO omits the letter "I" even after it changed its name to include investment as well.

47. Remaining 158 cases are classified in the group for which the situation remains unchanged. In these cases, related ministries explained the reason why they do not change the current situation, and complainants understood the reason.

48. The Japanese Fiscal Year (FY) starts from the first April and ends in 31st March of the next year.

49. Meetings with the American Chamber of Commerce in Japan (ACCJ) and the European Business Council (EBC), July 23, 1998.

50. WTO (1998), *Trade Policy Review of Japan*, January.

51. According to the Japanese government, the number of JIS standards which can be aligned to international ones is limited to 3 000 out of total number of 8 000 and remaining 1 300 (3 000-1 700) JIS standards are already equivalent to international standards.

52. According to the Japanese classification, these machines are categorised into motor vehicles and regulated by Road Transportation Law.

53. Jiro Ushio (1996), chairman of the Japan Association of Corporate Executives, originally in the article "Spread the Gospel of the Market Economy", *Japan Times*, December 1996 1&4 and quoted in "Implications of Competition Policy for International Trade: How Different is Japan From Germany and Does it Matter? by Mark Tilton of Purdue University at http://www.nmjc.org/jiap/specrpts/reports/sp2_1998.htm, states, "Compared to [the] Anglo-Saxon model, the traditional market rules in Japan and Europe are closed by nature... Three Japanese practices go against [the liberal] Asia-Pacific model: market rigging within an industry, excessive government control, and a tendency not to throw bad eggs out of the market. Old-fashioned Japanese businesses tend to avoid competing in open markets. Some industries condone restrictive business practices and they gang up to shut out new entries. True, rigging the market is a highly efficient way to do business, no one gets hurt through government mediation, and everyone can keep the cost of sales low. The upshot is higher prices, and it is the consumer who ends up holding the bill. Compared to other countries (Germany 2.25%, US 6.96%, France 8.94%, and UK 20.65%)".

54. OECD (1997), *Market Access Issues in the Automobile Sector*, Paris.

55. See OECD (1997), "Product Standards, Conformity Assessment and Regulatory Reform", OECD *Report on Regulatory Reform Volume* I : *Sectoral Studies*, Paris.

56. MOT NEWS, May 20, 1998, Ministry of Transport.

57. For example, MOT *News* No. 88 published on May 20, 1998 explained on a number of revisions of the safety regulations for road vehicles, both for in accordance to Deregulation Action Plan as well as for responding to the need from Japan's entry into the UN/ECE 1958 Agreement.

58. The Ministry of Post and Telecommunications prohibits international Type I carriers from entering into agreements with foreign carriers to terminate international traffic until the Type I carrier has established one hundred or more destinations.

59. JETRO (1998), T*he Survey on Actual Conditions Regarding Market Access – Telecommunication Equipment*, Tokyo.

60. Ministry of Post and Telecommunications' Internet Home Page.

61. The current three-year deregulation programme plans to lift the demand supply adjustment clauses.

62. This inertia to change does not seem to be an unique phenomenon among Japanese bureaucrats. In fact, Japanese firms are very reluctant to shed their employees and/or to abandon their over-invested business, even when they are in great difficulty as they are now. See The Economist, "Corporate Japan goes to waste", August 29, 1998.

63. This desire can be found in various government documents. For example, the Maekawa Report (1986) which opened the avenue to of reform in Japan underlined the necessity of internationalisation of the Japanese economy. Various government White Papers have pronounced this desire as well.

64. Meetings with ACCJ and EBC, July 23, 1998.

65. WTO (1998), *Trade Policy Review of Japan*, January, p. 60.

66. Kato (1995).

67. Sazanami and others (1995), p. 2. Because they compared the level of CIF price of imported goods and the level of producer prices for similar goods, the welfare loss might have been underestimated. In fact, in their studies, the supplementary adverse effect of inefficient distribution system was ignored.

68. Many market access concerns reviewed in this report might be remedied to some extent by the general recommendations made in Chapter 3.

BACKGROUND REPORT
ON REGULATORY REFORM IN THE ELECTRICITY
SECTOR[*]

* This report was principally prepared by **Peter Fraser** of the International Energy and **Sally Van Siclen** of the OECD's Directorate for Financial, Fiscal, and Enterprise Affairs, in consultation with **John Cameron** of the IEA and **Bernard J. Phillips**, Division Head, of the Directorate for Financial, Fiscal, and Enterprise Affairs in the OECD. It has benefited from extensive comments provided by colleagues throughout the IEA and OECD Secretariats, by the Government of Japan, and by Member countries as part of the peer review process. This report was peer reviewed in December 1998 by the Standing Group on Long-Term Co-operation of the IEA and the Competition Law and Policy Committee of the OECD. The report has also been published by the International Energy Agency in its "Energy Policies of IEA Countries, Japan 1999 Review".

BACKGROUND REPORT
ON REGULATORY REFORM IN THE ELECTRICITY
SECTOR

TABLE OF CONTENTS

Executive Summary

Background Report on Regulatory Reform in the Electricity Sector

The Japanese electricity sector has been shaped by the Government's key policy goals and objectives of energy security, economic growth and environmental protection. The ten vertically integrated utilities that serve virtually all end-users of electricity in Japan have been responsible for enhancing energy security through diversification away from oil. Investment in nuclear power has been a major contributor to diversification and is expected to contribute to government efforts to limit carbon dioxide emissions from the energy sector.

Government concerns about high electricity prices (the highest in the OECD) have led to reforms of the sector of which the introduction of competition is seen as a key measure. Amendment of the Electric Utilities Industry law has required utilities to conduct tenders for independent power producers to supply short-term thermal power needs to the utilities. These tenders have been highly successful and demonstrate significant potential for other industrial companies to enter the power business. These tenders will be expanded beginning in 1999 (and overseen by a neutral agency) to compete to supply all future thermal power needs, unless a remarkable change in the situation occurs.

Proposals for reform of Japan's electricity sector have been introduced into the Diet. These proposals call for the liberalisation of the market for extra high voltage consumers (28 per cent of all supply) and introduce accounting measures to separate the activities of the incumbent utilities to ensure non-discrimination.

The decision to move forward with partial liberalisation of retail supply is an important, irreversible step for Japan to take towards its goal of internationally comparable electricity prices. In particular, the recognition of the need for equal conditions in competition between the utilities and new entrants, the need for fair and transparent rules on the use of power transmission lines, and the commitment to set a timetable for liberalisation are essential points in any liberalisation. Key recommendations for the first step of reform include:

- Adopt a comprehensive reform plan for the industry that lays out the time and criteria for evaluating progress with reform; monitor the progress of these reforms and, if there are problems with this progress, a timely adjustment towards other policies can be made.
- Strengthen competition principles in the overall policy framework and vigorously enforce the anti-monopoly law.
- Amend the Anti-monopoly Act to clarify that it also applies to the electricity sector.
- Ensure that regulation of the electricity sector is independent from policy functions and industry promotion functions, with transparent procedures and due process for the review of decisions.
- Separate accounts for natural monopoly activities and supply of electricity to captive customers from the potentially competitive activities.
- Reform standard electricity tariffs, and tariffs for networks and system services, to reflect costs by time of use.
- Revise the yardstick mechanism for regulating utilities to provide a greater incentive.

If after a reasonable period, such as by 2003, there is evidence of discriminatory behaviour, and the market is not sufficiently competitive, further changes will be necessary, taking into account the Government's policy goals and objectives. Recommendations for this second step are:

- Expand the set of eligible customers. If possible make all customers eligible.
- If difficulties with accounting separation are found, and not eliminated by measures to strengthen this separation, then require utilities to functionally separate their regulated activities from unregulated activities. The regulatory regime may need to be strengthened. Consider the full range of feasible separation options to promote competition in the industry.
- Develop electricity markets to manage short-term imbalances in supply and demand.

After the second step, under a review of the operation of the competitive electricity market in each utility service area in Japan. Depending on the outcome of this evaluation, consider what further practical regulatory and/or structural reforms should be introduced, consistent with the Government of Japan's reform objectives and overall energy policy goals and objectives. Among the options to be considered are:

- Measures to encourage further entry.
- Expansion of interconnections between regions.
- Modification of economic regulation of the utilities to provide them with greater incentives to operate and invest efficiently, as well as to compete.
- Measures to encourage the voluntary sale of utilities' generating capacity to multiple buyers.
- The full range of feasible horizontal and vertical separation options to promote further competition in the industry.

1. POLICY GOALS AND OBJECTIVES FOR THE SECTOR

The structure of the Japanese electricity sector has been shaped by the Government's key sectoral policy goals and objectives. Three of these are energy security, environmental protection, and economic growth. A recently emphasised policy objective contains an explicit target for economic performance in the sector.

Energy security has been the fundamental driver of the electricity policy for the past 25 years and is one of the "3Es" of Japanese energy policy. Japan has no economical natural energy resources of significance and the experience of dependence of imported oil during the oil crises of the 1970s has elevated security of supply to the main determinant of fuel supply mix. Policies toward this end have included strong government policy support for nuclear power, bans on new and replacement oil-fired power base-load capacity generation, low interest loans from the Japan Development Bank for utilities to invest in other power sources, and substantial research and development funding by government and by utilities. The policies have led to a much more diversified and less oil dependent power generation sector, as companies have moved to use more nuclear, coal and natural gas fired power generation and, to a much lesser extent, new renewable sources.

Environmental protection, focuses on the greenhouse gas emissions of the energy sector and particularly the government's commitments to stabilise carbon dioxide emissions at 1990 levels by the year 2000 and with the Kyoto agreement, to cut emissions of greenhouse gases by 6% below this level over the period 2008-2012.

Economic growth, or in other words, promoting economic efficiency of the energy industry is the second of the 3Es. The energy industry, and particularly the electricity sector, has been identified as inefficient and a potential damper on future economic growth due to relatively high prices.

Promotion of nuclear power: The three energy policy objectives – energy security, economic growth, and environmental protection – have led the government to conclude that additional use of nuclear energy is vital for Japan. The Japanese government will continue to promote nuclear power and more specifically the construction of 16-20 additional nuclear reactors by 2010.

The policy objective added most recently is for electricity prices to be at internationally comparable levels by 2001. Given current prices, this might only be achieved through reform that greatly increases economic efficiency in the sector. The government's Action Plan for Economic Structure Reform of May 1997 identified the pursuit of enhanced efficiency through competition as a basic principle for reform in the electric power sector. The government is committed to a fair allocation of the benefits of those efficiency gains.

1.1. Key features of the electricity sector

Ten heavily regulated investor-owned regional vertically integrated utilities (Hokkaido, Tohoku, Tokyo, Chubu, Hokuriku, Kansai, Chugoku, Shikoku, Kyushu and Okinawa Electric Power Companies) dominate the sector. While not monopolies in law, no new general electric utilities have been created since 1951. The utilities are vertically integrated and responsible for generation, transmission, distribution and retail supply. Three of the utilities (Tokyo, Kansai and Chubu) are very large by world standards, with Tokyo second in size only to Electricité de France. The sector is regulated by the Ministry of International Trade and Industry: MITI grants licenses to the utilities, regulates standard electricity rates and approves plans for expansion. MITI is also responsible for a large number of technical and safety regulations affecting the sector.

High costs lead to the highest electricity prices in the OECD. Electricity costs are high because a number of Japan-specific factors such as a lack of domestic energy resources for power generation, very high reliability and environmental operating standards, and large day/night and seasonal variations in demand. Costs of constructing new facilities are the highest in the OECD. One consequence of high prices has been the development of significant in-house generation of electricity in the industrial sector amounting to 28% of all industrial demand.

Initial reform efforts to address the problems of high costs have liberalised generation entry by allowing independent power producers to supply thermal[1] power to the utilities through a bidding process without requiring a permit from MITI, enabled customers to generate power at one site and "wheel" it for use at another site, allowed new networks to be established to supply specific customers, somewhat revised the rate-of-return regulation, and eased technical regulatory requirements. However, liberalisation of retail supply is still very limited (i.e., only self-wheeling). The government recognises that there continues to be a problem with the level of electricity prices in Japan. The Programme for Economic Structure Reform (December 1996) and the Action Plan for Economic Structure Reform (May 1997) aim, by 2001, to bring electricity costs to levels in line with those seen internationally.

2. INDUSTRY STRUCTURE

2.1. Participants

There are nine general electric utilities covering the four principal islands of Japan. A tenth company covers Okinawa. All of the utilities are privately owned and vertically integrated, from generation to retail supply, and they have mutually exclusive supply areas. There are no independent distributors of electricity. There is a small amount of inter-utility trade, amounting to about 55 TWh, or about 5% of total generation.

Table 1 shows sales of the general electric utilities. Tokyo has the largest sales, followed by Kansai, which covers Osaka, Kyoto and Kobe, and Chubu, which covers Nagoya.

Table 1. **General electric utility sales, 1997**

Company	Customers ('000)	Installed Capacity (MW)	Electricity Sales (GWh)		
			Residential	Commercial and Industrial	Total
Hokkaido	3 579	5 431	9 623	16 179	25 802
Tohoku	7 219	12 437	19 953	46 377	66 330
Tokyo	25 285	53 975	76 531	186 71.9	263 250
Chubu	9 525	29 274	28 360	87 211	115 580
Hokuriku	1 869	5 509	5 866	18 286	24 151
Kansai	12 157	37 051	40 574	97 273	137 847
Chugoku	4 869	10 936	14 623	42 230	56 853
Shikoku	2 690	6 314	7 809	17 152	24 961
Kyushu	7 700	16 983	22 534	51 003	73 537
Okinawa	688	1 434	2 358	3 648	6 006
Total	75 610	179 515	228 231	566 087	794 318

Source: Electric Power Industry in Japan, 1997/98, Japan Electric Power Information Center, Inc. Tokyo, 1997.

Electric Power Development Corporation (EPDC) owns and operates large-scale hydroelectric (mainly peaking) plants, coal-fired generating stations, geothermal generating stations and associated transmission assets. Its generating capacity amounts to 13 915 MW or about 6% of total capacity. EPDC sells power at cost to the ten utilities through long-term contracts. The government owns two-thirds of EPDC (the nine utilities i.e., excluding Okinawa own the other third) and had provided most of the financing. The government has announced plans to privatise EPDC by 2003. A broad privatisation is planned, including a listing on the Tokyo Stock Exchange. The company is currently restructuring its finances to become independent of the government.

The Japan Atomic Power Corporation (JAPC) was established in 1957 by the nine general utilities, EPDC and other nuclear enterprises to commercialise nuclear power development in Japan. Its three plants have a total capacity of 2 617 MW. JAPC sells power at cost to the nine utilities.

There are 34 public enterprises owned and operated by local governments which generate and sell power to the nine utilities. Their total capacity is about 2 492 MW (at the end of FY 1996) of mostly hydro-electric capacity.

Autoproduction by the industry sector accounts for 24 400 MW (at the end of FY 1996) of capacity, mostly from oil and coal cogeneration. Steel makers, chemical companies, oil refiners, cement producers and pulp and paper companies are all major producers of electricity for in-house consumption and/or sale to a utility through joint venture arrangements. Autoproduction supplies 28% of the total electricity used by industry.

2.2. Grid structure

The utilities serving the eastern part of Japan (Hokkaido, Tohuku and Tokyo) deliver electricity at a frequency of 50 Hz. Western Japan uses 60 Hz. All four main islands of Japan and the nine electricity generation regions have transmission links, making national inter-regional power exchange possible. Frequency converter stations are operated by EPDC at Sakuma and TEPCO at Shin Shinano, but total interconnection capacity between the two frequency areas is limited to 900 MW.[2] Transmission links have been upgraded to improve reliability, but are limited by the mountainous terrain and the elongated shape of Japan, which restricts opportunities for enhancing the networks through parallel transmission lines. Seven large transmission projects are under construction or have been planned to increase inter-regional linkages. Okinawa is not connected to the main grid. There is no grid connection with other countries.

Figure 1. **Electric utilities**

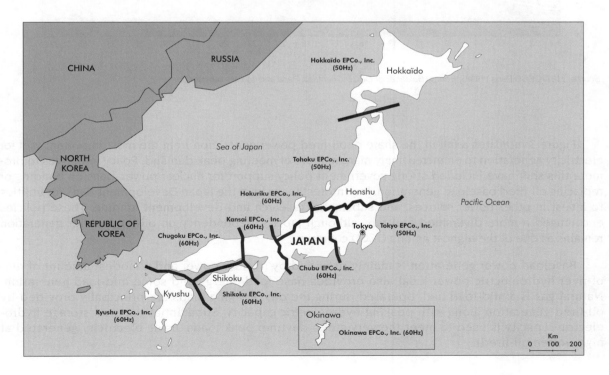

Source: MITI.

Supply and demand

Electricity consumption by sector is shown in Figure 2. Growth in demand has been rapid, especially in the residential/commercial sector. In recent years, air-conditioning demand has risen rapidly, sharpening the peak in demand on a hot mid-day in summer.

Figure 2. **Electricity consumption by sector**

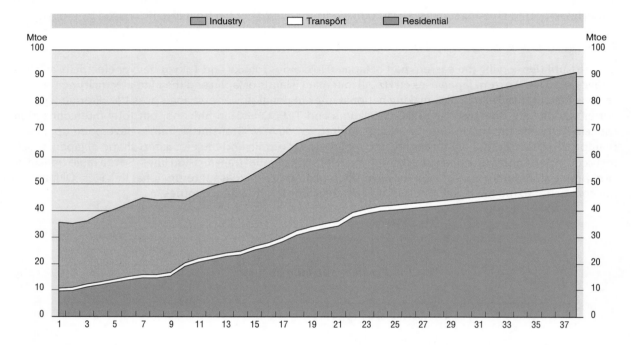

Source: IEA/OECD Paris (1998), *Energy Balances of OECD Countries,* Paris and country submission.

Figure 3 indicates a fall in the share of oil-fired power generation from the most important fuel for electricity generation to an increasingly marginal role of meeting peak demand. Policy initiatives to promote this shift have included strong government policy support for nuclear power, bans on building or replacing oil-fired baseload generation, low interest loans from the Japan Development Bank for utilities to invest in other power sources, and substantial research and development funding. These policies encouraged a more diversified fuel mix, although Japan's dependency on oil-fired power generation remains as one of the highest among OECD countries.

Baseload power generation is mainly provided by nuclear power and a modest amount of run-of-river hydroelectric power. Coal also provides base load energy and some mid-load generation. Natural gas is a mid-load fuel, operated during the day. Peaking loads are principally provided by oil-fired generation along with peaking hydroelectric capacity. Substantial pumped storage hydroelectric capacity is used to meet the very steep daytime peak loads, using electricity generated at night (often oil-fired).

Figure 3. **Electricity generation by fuel**

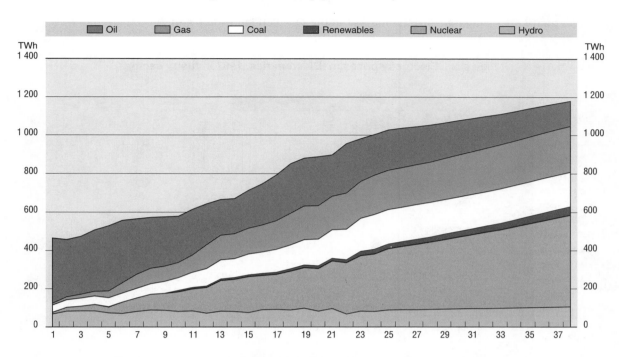

Source: IEA/OECD Paris (1998), *Energy Balances of OECD Countries,* Paris, and country submission.

Figure 4. **Daily load curve**

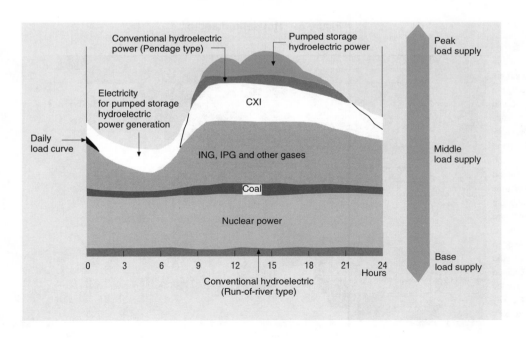

Source: Tokyo Electric Power Company (1998), *TEPCO Illustrated,* 1997, Tokyo.

3. PRICES AND COSTS

Electricity prices in Japan are the highest in the OECD (Figures 5, 6 and 7).

Figure 5. **Electricity prices in IEA countries, 1997 industry sector***

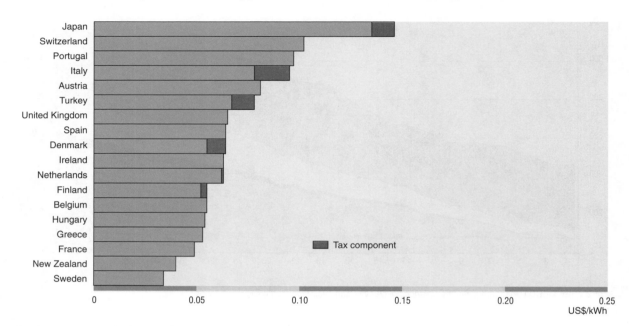

* Data not available for Australia, Canada, Germany, Luxembourg, Norway and the United States.
Source: Energy Prices and Taxes, IEA/OECD Paris, 1997.

Figure 6. **Household sector**

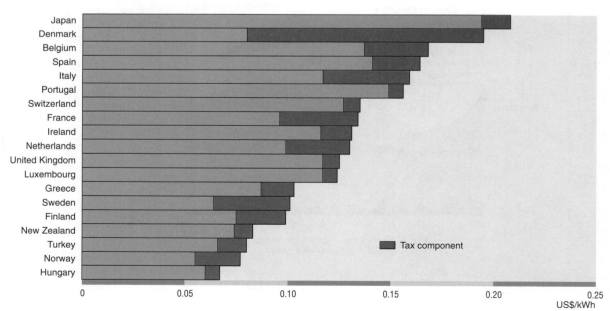

Source: IEA/OECD (1998), *Energy Prices and Taxes,* Paris.

Figure 7.   **Electricity prices in the industry sector, 1980-1997**

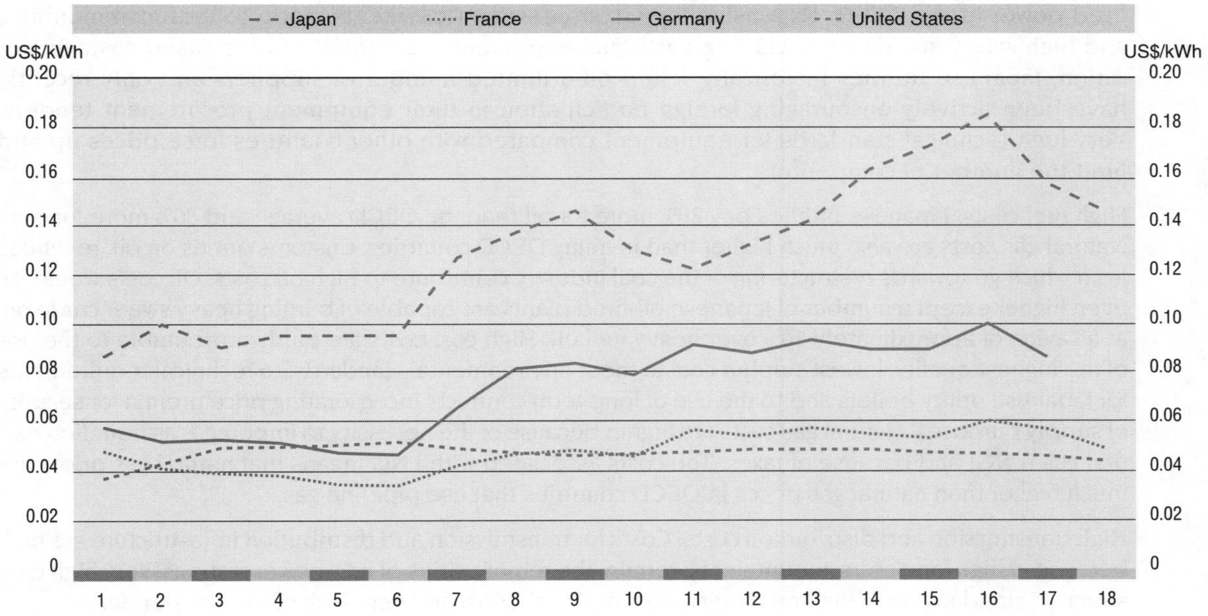

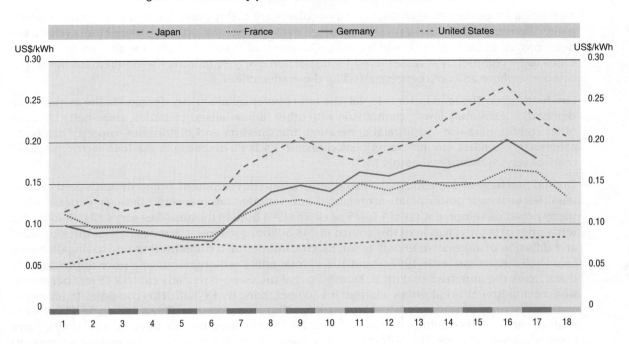

Source: IEA/OECD (1998), *Energy Prices and Taxes,* Paris.

Figure 8.   **Electricity prices in the household sector, 1980-1997**

Source: IEA/OECD (1998), *Energy Prices and Taxes,* Paris.

There are a number of reasons for these relatively high prices.

– High generation capital costs: Japan has the highest investment costs for nuclear, gas and coal-fired power in the OECD. Expensive land, compensation payments made to local communities, and high safety standards (including earthquake resistance) contribute to increased costs. In addition, Japanese utilities historically relied on a limited number of suppliers and only recently have been actively encouraging foreign participation in their equipment procurement tenders. Very high technical standards for equipment compared with other countries force prices up and limit the number of competitors.

– High fuel costs: Japanese utilities pay 20% more for oil than the OECD average and 80% more for coal. Natural gas costs are also much higher than in many OECD countries. Customs duties on oil, revenues from which go towards restructuring of the coal industry contribute to high oil costs. Oil costs would be even higher except a number of Japanese oil-fired plants are capable of burning heavy sweet crude oil, at a saving of approximately 50% over heavy fuel oil. High coal costs are partly attributable to the use of the highest quality, lowest sulphur coal to meet environmental standards, to technical requirements for Japanese utility boilers and to the use of long-term contracts incorporating price premia for security of supply purposes. Natural gas costs are higher because of the necessity to import gas as liquefied natural gas (LNG) and because of taxes. The costs associated with LNG means that natural gas prices are much higher than natural gas prices in OECD countries that use pipeline gas.

– High transmission and distribution costs: Costs for transmission and distribution infrastructure are high because of high land costs, mountainous terrain, the remote siting of new power stations, very high construction standards to withstand earthquakes and typhoons, and very high operating standards.

– Additional regulatory costs: Japanese environmental regulations are quite strict. As a result, nearly all coal-fired and most oil-fired power stations have equipment to greatly reduce SOx emissions (through flue gas desulphurisation). The majority of coal-fired plants also have advanced NOx removal technologies (principally selective catalytic reduction). The Air Pollution Control Law allows local government to set even stricter limits still, resulting in additional utility expenditures. For example, despite the use of advanced SOx emissions control equipment, utilities still use coal and oil with lower sulphur content.

– Regulations regarding maintenance of power plants are highly prescriptive. For example, nuclear plants are required to have a refuelling outage every 13 months, although longer fuel cycles have been proven to be both safe and feasible. Government regulations also require natural gas turbines to be completely disassembled for inspection every 30 months – a requirement not duplicated elsewhere and not recommended by the manufacturer.

– Low load factor: The load factor in Japan (the ratio of average electricity demand to the annual peak demand) is extremely low in comparison with other industrialised countries, principally because of air conditioning use. Additional generation, transmission and distribution capacity has been constructed to meet the increasing peak demand. Each 1% decrease in the load factor increases costs of service by approximately 1%.

– Tax and purchase of domestic coal: Subsidies for power development, primarily funds paid to communities near new power plants for regional development are recovered through a special electricity power development tax of ¥ 0.445 per kWh (1998 budget for subsidies was ¥ 224 billion). The remainder of tax revenue from this source (¥ 238 billion) goes towards measures for development and diffusion of alternative energy to oil. Electric utilities also committed to purchasing domestic coal (4.25 million tonnes in 1997, about 10% of total utility requirements) at a price approximately three times the imported coal price. Domestic coal prices were recently cut to ¥ 15 800 per tonne, with a commitment to cut prices a further ¥ 1 800 per tonne by FY 2001. This compares to imported coal prices of approximately ¥ 5 500 per tonne. The cost premium (¥69.8 billion in FY 1996) is shared among all the utilities, although the coal is actually used by only three general utilities and three wholesale utilities. The utilities also purchase power above cost from renewable sources, although the amounts involved here are quite small.

Figure 9. **Heavy fuel oil costs for power generation (Japan *vs* OECD)**

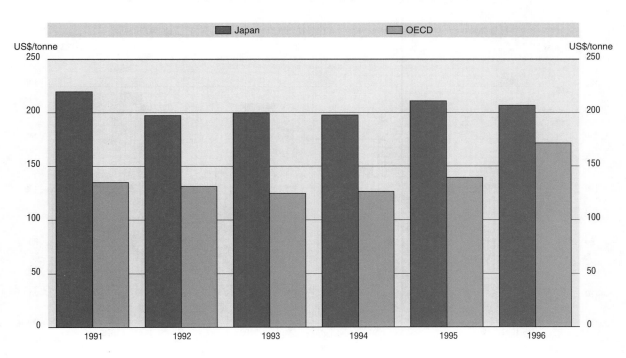

Figure 10. **Coal costs for power generation (Japan *vs* OECD)**

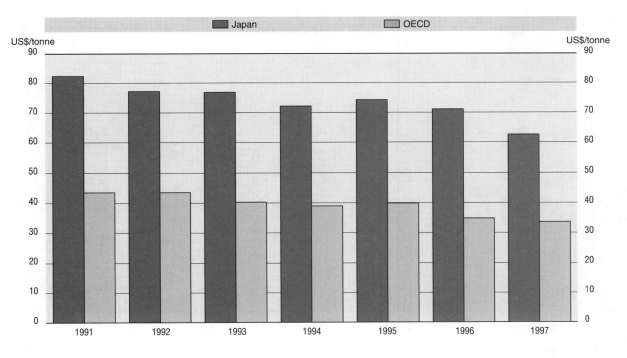

Source: IEA/OECD (1998), *Energy Prices and Taxes,* Paris.

293

Figure 11. **Natural gas costs for power generation (Japan *vs* selected countries)**

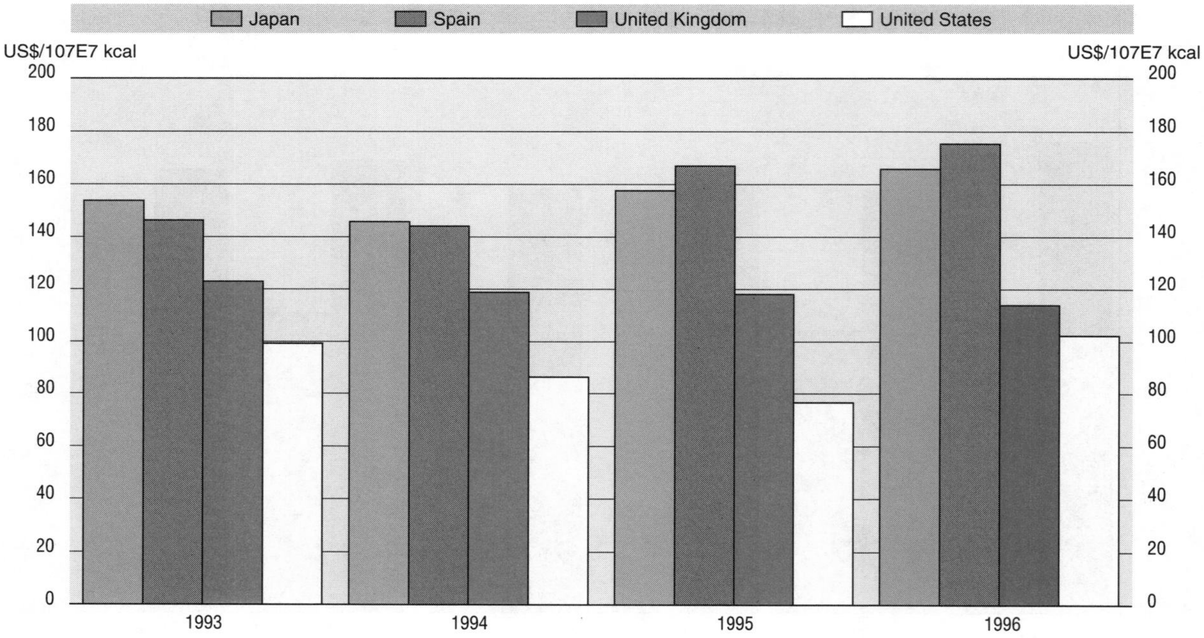

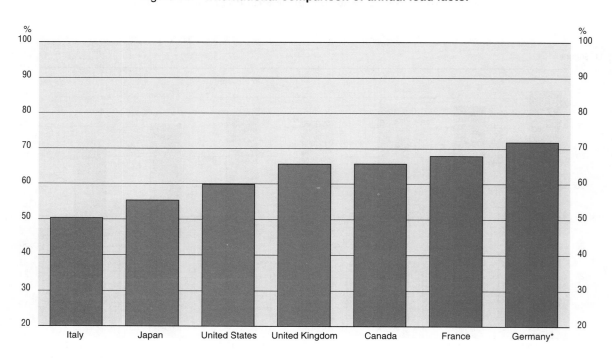

Source: IEA/OECD (1998), *Energy Prices and Taxes,* Paris.

Figure 12. **International comparison of annual load factor**

*   Former West Germany.
Source: Federation of Electric Power Companies.

Costs per kWh have changed little since 1990 despite significant growth in electricity demand, and reductions in interest rates and fuel costs. These factors have been nearly entirely offset by increases in personnel and maintenance costs as well as higher depreciation costs from new plants coming into service (Table 2).

Table 2. **Average costs per kilowatt-hour generated at 10 Japanese utilities 1990 vs 1996**

Average Costs (¥ per kWh)	1990	1996
Personnel	2.06	2.21
Fuel	3.83	2.58
Repair and Maintenance	2.11	2.40
Interest Charges	2.29	1.80
Depreciation	3.11	3.77
Taxes	1.69	1.72
Other (mainly power purchases)	4.45	4.93
Total	19.55	19.41

Source: Derived from information in *Electric Power Industry in Japan* 1997/98, Japan Electric Power Information Center, Tokyo, 1997.

4. REGULATION AND REGULATORY CHANGE

The electricity sector is regulated by the Ministry for International Trade and Industry (MITI). Within MITI, the Agency of Natural Resources and Energy oversees the sector.

4.1. Electric Utilities Industry Law and 1995 amendments

The Electric Utilities Industry Law is the main legislation governing the electricity industry. There are also a variety of MITI ordinances. The law makes clear the central role played by MITI in developing the structure of the industry (as regards entry, exit and expansion), the coordination of utilities, and the regulation of tariffs.

Regulation under the Electric Utilities Industry Law follows a form relatively common in Japan,[3] in which entry into a sector is restricted so that supply and demand are balanced. The law defines three main types of businesses in the electricity industry: the general electric utility supply business (general EUSB), the wholesale EUSB, and the special EUSB. MITI issues permits for these businesses. For MITI to issue a permit, there must be demand for the service; in the case of a general or a wholesale EUSB, the new business "must be necessary and appropriate for the comprehensive and rational development of the EUSB or otherwise for the promotion of the public interests"; in the case of a special EUSB, the new business must not harm the interests of electricity consumers in the general EUSB's service area and it must be "appropriate in view of the public interests". Permission from MITI is also needed to exit; permission is granted if the exit does not impair public interests. Entry into non-utility business activities by the utilities requires the permission of the MITI Minister.

No new general EUSB have been created since 1951 (with the exception of Okinawa). One special EUSB (which serves a few large customers within a general utility's area) has been created.

If a general EUSB wishes to supply outside its service area, it needs the permission of MITI. MITI will not grant permission unless *inter alia*, such supply would "not be easy to accomplish and not apposite to undertake" for the general EUSB in whose area the supply is to be made. Conversely, a general EUSB cannot, without good reason, refuse to supply electricity in its own service area.

A key part of the 1995 amendments to the Electric Utilities Industry Law was to liberalise entry rules for independent power producers (IPPs), *i.e.*, independent generators which sell power to the utilities. IPPs are no longer required to get a permit from MITI to enter the generating business (although they are expected to sign a contract of at least 10 years duration). Utilities have been required to conduct tenders to meet additional thermal power needs that would arise within a seven-year period. Two sets of tenders have been conducted to date (see section on the impact of the 1995 amendments).

MITI has decided to open the bidding system still wider in 1999, and plans to allow, barring a significant change, both utilities and IPPs to bid for thermal power plants coming on stream in 2008 and beyond. The amount of capacity to be tendered will be set by the utility as part of its normal planning process. The bidding process will be overseen by a neutral party. The utilities will be required to implement separate accounting for bidding on new plants.

In addition, the 1995 amendments simplified approvals for specified supply by the autoproducers.

Grid access regulation

The Electric Utility Industry Law requires designated utilities to notify tariffs to MITI. MITI can order transfer supply[4] if it is refused without good reason. MITI must approve tariffs and other conditions for back-up power supply to a special EUSB, and can impose tariffs and other conditions if a general EUSB and a special EUSB cannot negotiate an agreement.

Tariff and profit regulation

Standard tariffs and other conditions of supply must be approved by MITI. In order to be approved, the tariff "for supply of electricity shall be the sum of the fair and proper cost of electricity and the fair and proper profits under efficient management". Also, "there shall be no discrimination against specific persons". If, because of social or economic changes, the tariffs and conditions for the supply of electricity have become unfair and improper to the extent that advancement of public interests is thereby impeded, MITI may order the EUSB or wholesale supplier to submit an application for a change in the tariffs or conditions.

Utilities are permitted to offer optional tariffs to contribute to the efficient use of facilities. Interruptible supply contracts for large consumers and time of use rates have both been offered to contribute to load levelling.

The basic regulatory scheme for the Japanese electricity sector is rate of return. As of September 1998, the regulated rate of return on capital was set at 4.4%; by contrast, the rate of return on government debt at that time was under 1%. The asset price is based on a MITI assessment. MITI sets out the accounting system to be used by electric utilities.

The 1995 amendments adjusted the rate of return approach to allow slightly augmented incentives to reduce costs. These incentives are called "yardsticks" because they rely, in small part, on comparisons among the utilities. The current rate regulation process is summarised in the box below. The net impact of the latest yardstick assessment was to reduce utility revenues by 0.6% from what they would have been absent the yardstick aspect.

A fuel cost adjustment mechanism passes on most, but not all, changes in fuel costs to customers. Changes in average fuel costs exceeding 5% are reflected in prices. The mechanism ensures that customers benefit from falling fuel prices but, because it shifts the majority of the risk of changing fuel prices on to customers, it reduces direct incentives for utilities to manage their fuel costs.

System security regulation

Supply reliability is also regulated by MITI. Ministry ordinances set power quality standards (voltage and frequency). MITI can order utilities to improve facilities if service quality to customers is impaired.

Each utility submits an annual ten-year plan to MITI regarding electricity supply, and the installation and operation of facilities. MITI may, if the plan is "not proper and apposite for promoting rational and integral development of the electric utility supply business through... wide-area operations, recommend the designated electric utility supply business operator to change or alter the

---

Box 7.   Process of price regulation in Japan

Electric utilities file a rate application that sets out:

Costs (all operating and financial expenses) related to utility operations.

An estimate of a fair rate of return on capital.

Revenue requirement (the sum of the first two items less certain other revenues such as sales to other utilities).

An allocation of costs into rates which sets out rates according to voltage (and appears to show different costs attributed to different power facilities). Customer classes are:

- extra high voltage (> 20 kV);
- high voltage (6 to 20 kV);
- low voltage (under 6 kV *i.e.*, business);
- lighting (*i.e.*, residential demand for any use).

Standard consumer rates vary by voltage, but not by location. (Homogeneity across location is imposed to meet the policy objective of fairness.) Optional time-of- use rate packages are offered to customers but are not regulated *per se*.

MITI holds public hearings. The yardstick assessment involves comparing the utility to its own past performance and to the performance of the other utilities, on the basis of three categories (generation; transmission, transformation, and distribution; and general administration) where the costs compared are those over which the utility is considered to have control. For each category, the range of costs is calculated. For each category, the costs for each utility determine whether it is in the bottom third of the range, middle third, or upper third. Those utilities in the bottom third, *i.e.*, among the most efficient or most improved, are allowed to receive revenues equal to the value of their costs in that category. Those utilities in the middle third, are allowed to receive revenues equal to 99% of the value of their costs in that category. Those utilities in the top third, *i.e.*, among the least efficient or least improved, are allowed to receive revenues equal to 98% of the value of their costs in that category. Rankings are published.

---

plan". In the case of non-compliance with its recommendations, MITI may order utilities to supply, transfer, or receive electricity or to loan, borrow or share electrical facilities.

Technical regulation

MITI is also responsible for the safety and technical regulations of electrical appliances and facilities, nuclear fuel, boilers and pressure vessels. Delays arising from inspection of new generating plants before commencing operation have been a major concern of the utilities. The 1995 amendments reduced requirements for these inspections, but remain more strict than most other OECD countries, resulting in longer outages at power plants.

Impact of the 1995 amendments

The 1995 amendments to the Electric Utilities Industry Law have brought the entry of IPPs to supply the utilities. Two sets of tenders have been conducted to date. The average quantity of capacity bid exceeded the average quantity tendered at least fourfold. The prices of successful bidders were between 10 and 40% less than the "upper limit prices" calculated by the utilities, averaging almost 30% lower. The successful IPP bids total about 3% of all installed capacity and about 19% of all capacity outside the major utilities (including EPDC as described above). The summary of the IPP projects accepted by fuel is given in Table 3.

Average prices in the second set of tenders were 25 to 40% lower than upper limit prices.[5] According to MITI, there is a total 40-50 GW potential available, with the lower estimate taking into account environmental constraints and other constraints (water for generation and fuel supply). The upper estimate,

Table 3.   **IPPs by fuel**
Successful bids from 1996 and 1997 tenders

Fuel	Number of Projects	Capacity (MW)	Share (%)
Coal	13	2 844	46
Oil	17	2 425	39
Gas	5	842	14
Other	1	55	1
Total	**36**	**6 165**	**100**

Source: MITI.

about 25% of the existing capacity of the utilities, is large enough to account for most of the forecast increase in power demand between 1998 and 2010. The actual need for capacity could be considerably reduced if Japan is successful at increasing its load factor to a level comparable with other IEA countries.

The majority of capacity bid and the potential for new IPP capacity is coming from the steel industry (mostly coal-fired generation) and the petroleum refining industry (oil-fired generation). A number of these industrial companies are already autoproducers of electricity. Both industries have idle industrial land available and relatively easy access to fuel sources, allowing them to overcome two major hurdles with building new generating plants and bringing them online quickly. The lengthy time needed to obtain approval and construct coal-fired green-field plants (10 years or more) give these companies an advantage over utilities using greenfield sites.

Unlike most countries with IPPs, new gas-fired development plays a relatively limited role. Of the 36 successful IPP projects to date, only five use natural gas. The high cost of liquefied natural gas in Japan is a major factor. Also, at present, there is no third party access to LNG terminals in Japan. Furthermore, there is no instance to date of an electric utility, each of whom owns at least part of an LNG terminal, selling natural gas to an IPP.

The success of coal and oil-fired capacity in the bidding has raised concerns at the Environment Agency, who suggest that the IPP policy could raise Japan's CO_2 emissions by 1%. Emissions from IPPs are as high as 0.225 tonnes of carbon per MWh versus an average of 0.098 tonnes of carbon per MWh for utility plants (with the current fuel mix).[6] MITI plans to ask the utilities to treat lower CO_2 emitting plant more favourably than coal – perhaps by limiting the tender to certain kinds of fuels or requiring them to consider fuels in evaluating future bids.

Barring any remarkable changes, MITI is planning to allow both utilities and IPPs to bid, commencing in 1999, for all thermal power plants coming on stream in FY 2008 and beyond. The utilities believe that they can compete with IPPs partly through repowering existing plants *e.g.*, with combined cycle, to avoid the high costs of greenfield projects.

Another source of entry into generation is by industrial users, who build power plants either separately or as a joint venture with an electric utility.

Special electricity supply businesses are power utilities created to supply specified customers rather than offer general public service. In June 1997, Suwa Energy Service Company became the first firm to obtain a licence from MITI as a special electricity supplier. The company, was formed by Suwa Gas Company, a regional city gas company, to supply a hospital and retirement homes in a limited area with both electricity and heat produced by a cogeneration facility. The facility will open in February 1999 with a capacity of 3 MW. Other companies that plan to become special suppliers include East Japan Railway Co., Toyota Motor Corporation, and Tokyo Gas Co., Ltd.

4.2. Competition law

Competition law enforcement can protect competition in the new markets created by electricity sector liberalisation. The Japan Fair Trade Commission's (FTC) principal statute, the Anti-monopoly Act, prohibits unreasonable restraints of trade, "private monopolisation" and monopoly, as well as unfair practises and anti-competitive mergers. The FTC has substantial associated powers to enforce these prohibitions, including powers to investigate and prosecute violations, which can lead to fines or even imprisonment.

While the FTC might appear to have both the scope and the powers to police anti-competitive behaviour in the electricity sector, Section 21 of the Act appears to exempt electric utility services as an example of a natural monopoly. The FTC's involvement to date has been limited to the role of competition advocate, reviewing and commenting on electricity competition issues with the assistance of study groups, and generally favouring market reforms and particularly the amendment of Section 21.

Subsidies

The government is financially involved in the electricity sector in a number of ways. It is a direct owner of two-thirds of EPDC and of part of Japan Atomic Power Corporation (JAPC). The government is financially indirectly involved in the electricity sector through its involvement in fuels, notably in support of nuclear generation and coal-fired generation (through support of the domestic coal industry). The Japan Development Bank has historically provided utilities with low-interest loans for power generation, particularly from non-oil fuels; its loans total about 6% of power sector investment. The bank's policy to offer low-interest loans has now been extended to independent power producers, who can receive low-interest loans to cover up to 50% of their investment.

The Electric Power Development Company (EPDC), was created to assist in power development, and has since played a leading role in investment in leading edge power generation technologies such as "clean coal" generation facilities. Sixty per cent of EPDC's capacity is hydroelectric, of which 60% is pumped storage, but more than two-thirds of its energy sales come from coal-fired generation. The average capacity factor for hydroelectric (excluding pumped storage) was 30% in FY1997.[7] Since the price of electricity during peak times would be much higher than the average price, if peakload pricing were instituted, EPDC's hydroelectric facilities may be quite valuable. However, EPDC currently sells its hydroelectric energy at cost, which is less than ¥9 per kWh (excluding pumped storage), through long-term agreements with the nine utilities. This is far less than the estimated cost of new peaking facilities of ¥32 per kWh. Currently the excess rents of this low-cost high-value energy accrues to customers in the form of lower rates. However, if generation is liberalised, the utilities, rather than the customers, will enjoy these benefits.

5. ADVISORY BODIES

There are several advisory or policy institutions of interest. The Electric Utility Industry Council is a consultative body created by statute in MITI to "investigate and deliberate on important matters" relevant to the sector. The Council investigates and deliberates at the request of the MITI Minister, and sends recommendations to which he/she must to give due consideration. The recommendations of the Council usually become government policy. The Council is composed of presidents of the electric utilities, power equipment suppliers, large users of electric power, academics, journalists, small business owners and household consumers.

The Committee on Basic Policy, a body within the Electric Utility Industry Council, was established in response to the Government's Action Plan for Economic Structure Reform to deal specifically with current reforms. The Committee was established to advise on the following question: "How best should the electricity supply industry be organised in the future to realise internationally comparable levels in electricity prices by the year 2001, and to establish the foundation for reducing our country's electricity costs on a medium – to long term basis?". The Committee returned an interim report in May 1998 and made further recommendations in December 1998.

The Electric Power Development Coordination Council (EPDCC), chaired by the Prime Minister, settles annual electric power development plans, which identify planned facilities developments over the following 10 years. Utilities must also obtain agreement from the prefectoral governor before commencing construction. The Electric Power Source Siting Committee (composed of several ministers, academics, and representatives from industry) was formed in 1993 to advise the Prime Minister on the suitability of proposed sites.

The Administrative Reform Committee, reporting to Office of the Prime Minister, is responsible for developing policy recommendations and monitoring progress on broader structural reforms to the Japanese economy. The Committee is a driving force behind the government's program for structural reform: its recommendations have shaped the *Program on Economic Structure Reform* adopted by the Government in December 1996 and the *Action Plan for Economic Structure Reform* of May 1997. The Action Plan identified the pursuit of enhanced efficiency through competition as a basic principle for reform in the electric power sector. The Committee recently indicated that it will review reforms in the electric power sector with the intention of proposing more long-term reforms in March 1999.

6.   THE CURRENT STATUS OF REGULATORY REFORM

The interim report of May 1998 produced by the Committee on Basic Policy of the Electric Utility Industry Council recommended partial liberalisation of retail supply, which means allowing only some customers to choose suppliers while the rest would remain customers of their utilities exclusively (*i.e.*, captive customers). The report ruled out full liberalisation and the introduction of a pool market as inappropriate and premature for the time being. The Committee decided that it would further study a system of partial liberalisation with the objective of presenting recommendations to the full Council in December 1998. The study made recommendations on partial liberalisation, within the three constraints of:

– Ensuring maximum management autonomy and minimising administrative intervention.

– Guaranteeing equal and effective competition.

– Spreading the results of efficiency to all users and that partial liberalisation not adversely affect users to which such liberalisation does not apply.

The report of the Committee and of the Council in December 1998 is expected to form the basis of future amendments to the Electric Utilities Industry Law in 1999.

7.   CRITIQUE

The variety of policy goals and objectives in Japan with respect to the electricity sector present a challenge both for the traditional form of regulation in the sector and for reforming that regulation. One of these challenges is the harmonisation of the three goals of energy security, environmental protection and economic growth. An emphasised element in economic growth is the target of internationally comparable prices by 2001, which is very ambitious in light of the exogenous factors which contribute to high costs in Japan including high fuel and siting costs.

7.1. Tendering for IPPs

The 1995 amendments to the Electricity Utilities Law have begun a process of change in the Japanese electricity sector. The tendering for new "thermal" capacity, which the amendments enabled, was very important in revealing the extent of potential lower costs in generation.

The decision that tendering for new thermal capacity will be opened up to all bidders, including utilities, is a logical step forward. Care will need to be taken, however, to ensure that utilities do not subsidise this activity from their regulated activities. Where an IPP is selling only peaking energy to the utility, the IPP should be able to sell power at other times to other customers. Access to fuels, particularly to natural gas, is a vital factor in establishing IPPs. Third party access to the LNG terminals may be one way of introducing competition and may lower the cost of natural gas, thereby increasing the number of IPPs using natural gas.

Contracted IPP capacity represents only 10% of all new capacity scheduled to come into service over the next several years, and the tendering process, in and of itself, will not be enough to meet the Government's objective of reducing power costs to internationally competitive levels by 2001. Therefore moving beyond this tendering process to a partial retail liberalisation is a necessary step.

7.2. Price regulation

The present mechanism based on rate-of-return, even with a yardstick approach for setting the rate, gives utilities very limited incentives to reduce their costs, as nearly all cost savings are passed on to customers. While partial liberalisation of retail supply can be expected to provide some competitive pressure to reduce generation costs, there will be no corresponding pressure to reduce network costs. Furthermore, there are no competitive pressures on utilities to reduce supply costs for captive customers by purchasing power from other utilities or from IPPs.

Other forms of yardstick regulation do provide a stronger incentive for a utility to reduce costs, particularly regulation that makes a more direct link between one utility's regulated maximum price and other utilities' costs. This form of regulation allows more of a utility's cost savings to be retained in the form of greater profits and thus provides greater incentives for a utility to be cost efficient.

Similarly, the fuel-cost adjustment mechanism, while it ensures that customers obtain the benefits of a fall in fuel prices, reduces the incentive for the utility to reduce fuel costs, by changing fuel purchase strategies. The Government should consider whether to modify the mechanism to provide the utility with stronger incentives to reduce fuel costs.

7.3. Tariff reform reflecting time of use

Although the load factor continues to deteriorate, the high cost of producing electricity at peak periods has not been reflected in prices, except through a variety of optional programs. Over 170 optional programs have been developed, but they have affected less than 10% of contracted capacity. At the same time, substantial pumped-storage hydroelectric capability continues to be developed to increase capacity at peak periods. Peaking capacity for power generation is very costly. TEPCO estimates the avoided costs of peaking capacity at ¥ 32 per kWh or triple the cost of baseload power. Changing standard tariffs to reflect costs by time of use could reduce peak load significantly over time, saving Japanese electricity consumers billions of yen, and reducing the need for additional peak capacity. Implementation of this reform can be phased in, beginning with larger customers. As the cost of time-of-use metering is falling, it will become more economic for it to be used by smaller and less price sensitive customers.

A reform based on pricing by time- of-use is also needed for the utility services required by IPPs and liberalised customers. At present, back-up power is charged as a premium to ordinary rates, and wheeling (transfer supply) charges are a flat rate per kWh transmitted. These approaches are too simple to capture the costs which vary by time of use. Under partial liberalisation, large industrial customers purchasing power from IPPs, who have a flatter demand than commercial or residential customers, may actually be paying more for network services than the costs they are incurring. Tariffs for these services should also reflect time of use to ensure that the costs for transmission, distribution and ancillary services such as backup supply are fully recovered from each customer segment.

7.4. Partial liberalisation

It is expected that Japan will partially liberalise retail supply, while at the same time broadening tendering so that it includes not only IPPs but also utilities. Clearly, these changes will need to be accompanied by a variety of changes in regulation of the utilities in order to prevent cross-subsidies from regulated activities to competitive activities, and to ensure cost-reflective, non-discriminatory access by third parties to transmission and ancillary services.

The decision to move forward with partial liberalisation of retail supply shows that the Government recognises the need for reform. The move will provide valuable information about the ability to operate the Japanese network with an increased number of participants. It may bring the benefits of lower generating costs to major industrial consumers and may provide some information for further steps in liberalisation. This is an important step for Japan to take towards international comparability in electricity prices, consistent with its other major goals of energy security and environmental protection.

Partial liberalisation of retail supply means that certain customers may purchase power at a negotiated price from their local utility, from another utility or from an IPP. This means:

– such prices will no longer be set by regulated tariffs (except for network services) but through negotiation with the customer;

– these customers will have a choice of suppliers: their local utility, other neighbouring utilities and IPPs;

– these customers would, in principle, be able to contract for a variety of terms, not just 10-15 years as required by the current agreements between IPPs and utilities;

– the customers contracting with other suppliers could manage their risks with respect to their supplier (in effect managing their own security of supply) provided that they still have access to backup power at a cost-reflective price.

Partial liberalisation of retail supply requires a series of interlocking changes to ensure that the liberalisation has the intended effects:

– access to transmission and ancillary services (including backup) needs to be cost-reflective, economically efficient, and non-discriminatory in tariffs, terms and conditions;

– regulation is needed to avoid the cross-subsidisation of competitive activities of utilities by their regulated activities, and to encourage efficient use of system services;

– competition enforcement: is needed to curb anti-competitive behaviour;

– liberalisation of generation would mean that generators, including the utilities, IPPs and new entrants, are free to compete for liberalised customers.

Under partial retail liberalisation, utilities will continue to be responsible for the long-term security of supply of their captive customers. Customers in the liberalised market could become responsible for their own long-term supply security through contracts. Short-term supply security will be provided by the utilities through their network services.

Transmission and ancillary services

Transmission and ancillary services must be accessible at tariffs that reflect costs and that are non-discriminatory, in order to ensure that independent generators can compete with the utilities to supply to liberalised end-users. For liberalised customers and IPPs, efficient pricing of the use of network services is the key to ensuring efficient use and augmentation of the transmission network. The Japanese electricity system, despite its high reliability, is heavily constrained with respect to its transmission network. While a vertically integrated utility has no need to price transmission separately for its own use, IPPs and liberalised customers use only a part of the services provided by a vertically integrated utility, e.g., the transmission network, making such pricing necessary.[8]

Investments in nuclear plants

The Government of Japan has identified increased investment in nuclear power as important to meeting its energy security goals and greenhouse gas emission objectives. Utilities will continue to require assurances that they will be able to recover costs from investments in new nuclear plants. A cost recovery mechanism will continue to be required for any excess costs associated with renewable energy and, possibly, with nuclear power.

If economic incentives are insufficient in promoting investment, one option would be to guarantee that a share of the demand is met by nuclear-generated electricity. This could be accomplished by requiring all customers to purchase a portion of their supplies from nuclear-generated power. The nuclear share would be set by the government. It could be made consistent with the expected contribution by nuclear power to meeting the Kyoto target. In effect, this would create two markets, a market for non-nuclear power generation and a separate market for nuclear-generated power.

A market for nuclear-generated power, would assure utilities that there would be a market for the power generated from their nuclear power plant investments. In conjunction with the liberalisation of retail supply, this market would encourage utilities to compete with one another to supply this nuclear power in the most cost efficient way. For example, they could either increase output from existing plants, or build more efficient new plants. The Netherlands has recently passed legislation that introduces a system to guarantee that a specific share of total electricity is generated by renewable fuels. Such a system may be useful for Japan to study.[9]

Eligibility of consumers

The issue of customer eligibility is crucial to partial retail liberalisation. In Japan's case it would be administratively convenient if, at the first stage, liberalised customers were limited to "extra high voltage" customers, *i.e.*, industrial and commercial customers taking power at 20 kV or above. Delivery costs for these customers are already desegregated as part of the regulatory process. They would constitute a 28% share of energy sales of the utilities, already a significant step.

Alternatively, eligibility could be based on the equivalent annual consumption level. This consumption level could be set so that eligible customers included all customers in the extra high voltage category as well as customers with multiple sites whose aggregated annual consumption exceeds a certain level. It could also include groups of small and medium companies, if they decide to purchase electricity jointly. Allowing groups of customers to participate could provide valuable experience to both customers and utilities, despite being more demanding from an administrative point of view. Hence, the Government should encourage the utilities to implement, on a voluntary basis, a programme that would allow such aggregation.

Regulatory institutions

Changing the structure of a network-based industry such as electricity from a monopoly to a competitive market requires a sophisticated regulatory structure. A market environment requires regulatory institutions that make decisions that are neutral, transparent, and not subject to day-to-day political pressures. The new environment will increase the responsibilities of the regulator. In addition to regulation of tariffs to captive customers, the regulator will need to ensure non-discriminatory access conditions and economically rational pricing for those services (such as transmission and ancillary services) that are used by IPPs and large users. The regulator will need to ensure that there is not cross-subsidy from regulated to competitive businesses. Either the competition authority or the regulator will need to prevent anti-competitive behaviour.

In order to make fair and reasonably predictable decisions, the regulator must have analytical expertise and not rely on the expertise of the regulated utilities. The regulator must also be functionally separate from policy-making and from electricity industry promotion functions in order to maintain a neutral regulatory regime. To be seen to be fair, the regulator should have well-defined obligations for transparency, notably with respect to its decision-making processes and information on which the decisions are made. Further, the objectives of the regulator must be clearly stated, more specifically than, for example, "the public interest" and progress towards these objectives should be monitored. Finally, the powers of the regulator should be clearly stated. The combination of transparencies of objectives, powers, processes, decisions, and information, gives the public clear performance criteria to evaluate the extent to which the regulator is fulfilling its role.

The utilities' behaviour in a partially liberalised market should be made subject to the Anti-monopoly Act. This act should be amended to make it clear that it also applies to the electricity sector. The precise areas of joint or primary responsibility of the regulator and of the FTC should be specified, after due consideration of the institutions' legal bases, objectives, powers, degrees of transparency, and expertise. A possible division of responsibility is for areas where the FTC has expertise (such as with mergers and unfair practices, including market power abuse) to remain within its jurisdiction, while net-

303

work regulation, including prices and terms and conditions of access, would be the responsibility of the sector regulator. Each institution should exercise its powers in consultation with the other institution. The FTC thus would continue and increase its role as an independent institution.

To provide a solid basis for market regulation, many countries have established or are examining the establishment of "independent" regulatory bodies to regulate electricity after reform. For example, Australia, Finland, Italy, Norway, Netherlands, Spain, Sweden, United Kingdom and the United States use an independent electricity regulator. Germany and New Zealand use the competition authority to regulate electricity.[10] While specific arrangements differ in each country, to meet their specific situations, the essential features of independent regulation are: complete independence from the regulated companies; a legal mandate that provides for separating the regulators and the regulatory body from political control; a degree of organisational autonomy; well-defined obligations for transparency (e.g., publishing decisions) and for accountability (e.g., appealable decisions, public scrutiny of expenditures).

The current policy of the Japanese government is to have MITI remain the electricity sector regulator, with regulatory activities kept separate from the policy-making activities. However, at present, safeguards from political pressures that would instil market confidence are limited. Transparency needs to be ensured to regulate a competitive market in an open and fair manner. Significant reform of the institutional arrangements is needed to support partial liberalisation of retail supply.

The role of the Electric Power Development Coordination Council in deliberating fossil fuel utility generation projects should be reconsidered after the schemes of partial liberalisation and expansion of IPP bidding are established so that IPP and competitive utility projects are on equal footing.

Competition in generation

Reform in the electricity sector should enhance efficiency through competition in generation and retail supply. Developing competition in generation is the main purpose of reform of the sector.

Effective competition in generation requires several elements:

– non-discriminatory access, including economically rational pricing, to the transmission grid and provision of ancillary services;
– sufficient grid capacity to support trade;
– electricity industry law and competition law and policy that effectively prevent anti-competitive conduct;
– a sufficient number of generation market players to give rise to competitive rivalry.

Competition in generation is enhanced by:

– low barriers of entry into generation;
– a non-discriminatory efficient market mechanism for electricity trade;
– a stranded cost recovery mechanism, if necessary, that is non-distortionary and fair;
– greater elasticity of demand with respect to price changes; and
– end-user choice, with competition to supply end-users.

Discriminatory access to the transmission grid creates two types of inefficiencies: 1) higher-cost generators may be used instead of lower-cost generators, and 2) efficient entry by generators may be discouraged. Both of these effects increase costs which could be avoided with non-discriminatory access. However, a vertically integrated utility has strong incentives to discriminate in favour of its own generating assets, providing them with preferential access to its transmission grid.

Vertical separation

A combination of regulation and vertical separation of utilities can be used to counter discrimination in transmission access. There are tradeoffs between regulation and degree of vertical separation.

Where there is less vertical separation, there is a need for greater regulation, and vice versa. These two policy tools can be used to reduce the incentives and the ability to discriminate. Divestiture, that is, separation of ownership of generation from transmission, eliminates incentives to discriminate. Also, the ability to discriminate can be reduced in various ways and to varying degrees by the other types of separation (see box below).

Box 8. **Approaches to vertical separation between transmission and generation**

OECD countries are trying various approaches to vertical separation between generation and transmission. These approaches include (ordered by degree of separation):

- Accounting separation: keeping separate accounts of the generation and transmission activities within the same vertically integrated entity. In this case, a vertically integrated entity charges itself the same prices for transmission services, including ancillary services, as it does others and states separate prices for generation, transmission, and ancillary services.

- Functional separation: accounting separation, plus 1) relying on the same information about its transmission system as its customers when buying and selling power and 2) separating employees involved in transmission from those involved in power sales.

- Operational separation: operation of and decisions about investment in the transmission grid are the responsibility of an entity that is fully independent of the owner(s) of generation; ownership of the transmission grid remains with the owner(s) of generation.

- Divestiture or ownership separation: generation and transmission are separated into distinct legal entities without significant common ownership, management, control or operations.

Different strategies for vertical separation of generation and transmission are being employed in different countries. Japan has decided to implement accounting separation, and should carry this out as quickly as possible, making sure it is effectively implemented. In many OECD countries who have restructured their publicly-owned electricity systems, the transmission business has been made a separate company (United Kingdom (England and Wales), Norway, Sweden, Spain, Hungary, Finland, most states of Australia, New Zealand). However, other countries within publicly-owned utilities, such as France, Italy, and Austria, have opted for accounting separation, albeit with an independent network manager as required by the European Union Electricity Directive.

There are fewer examples of electricity reform in countries where utilities are predominantly privately owned, as in Japan. Accounting separation is used in both Germany and Scotland (United Kingdom). In the United States, federal regulators require functional separation of transmission and encourage operational separation. In certain US states that have implemented full liberalisation of retail supply, utilities have been encouraged (and in the case of Connecticut and Maine are legally required) to divest much or all of their generating capacity. As the utilities in Japan are privately owned, the Government of Japan considers that it has no legal authority to require private electric utilities operating in the ordinary circumstances to divest their property and assets. The box below discusses how accounting separation can be made to work.

Functional separation, *i.e.*, separate business units within the same corporate structure, reduces the ability to discriminate through the separation of personnel and of information systems. This should reduce the burden of regulation designed to control discrimination. For example, functional separation reduces the ability to misuse information in an anticompetitive way, because the information systems of the two parts of the companies are distinct.

Box 9. Making accounting separation work

Current proposals would make discrimination illegal in Japan under the Electric Utilities Industry Law. But beyond keeping separate accounts, no changes in the structure or operation of the electric utilities would be mandated in the current proposals.

Accounting separation does not require large changes in the structure of companies. Thus it can be implemented relatively quickly and, for privately owned firms, without intruding into private property issues. In order to be successful, accounting separation needs to be accompanied by appropriate regulation to ensure non-discrimination and cost-reflective pricing. The accounting information made available to the regulator must reliably detect anticompetitive or discriminatory behaviour that might occur.

Operational separation further reduces the ability to discriminate in grid operations and grid investments by creating an organisation responsible for independent management of the system known as an independent system operator (ISO). ISOs are new institutions, with a limited operational history in institutional and legal environments very different from those of Japan. There is not yet widespread agreement on key aspects of ISOs, notably with respect to forming a governance structure that ensures non-discrimination, and a management incentive system that leads the ISO to adopt correct transmission and ancillary services pricing policies. In Japan, there would also be the problem of ensuring sufficiently deconcentrated control of an ISO, and the limited interconnection between the 50 Hz and 60 Hz areas suggests that, if operational separation were implemented, at least two ISOs would be needed for the main islands. There can be no certainty that an ISO could be put into practice in Japan and the Government of Japan considers the concept inappropriate to Japanese circumstances.

Ownership separation, or divestiture, is intended to eliminate the incentive to discriminate, to reduce the need for regulatory oversight, and to deconcentrate markets when there are sales to multiple owners. Yet divestiture may raise issues of supply reliability because coordinated planning of generation and transmission investment is made more difficult. Divestiture can be either mandatory or voluntary.[11]

Competitive rivalry in generation

In addition to some degree of vertical separation, competitive rivalry among generators is a necessary condition for effective competition. Competitive rivalry is enhanced by the entry of IPPs selling to liberalised customers. It is also enhanced if many customers respond to liberalisation by installing their own generating capacity, using e.g. cogeneration or trigeneration,[12] to displace their use of utility electricity and generate surpluses that could be sold to other customers. This can also be done as part of a district heating and cooling business. Such action, or even the credible possibility of such action, would put competitive pressure on the utility to change its prices and reduce its costs to those customers who can credibly self generate.

An alternative means of increasing competitive rivalry is to enlarge the geographic scope of the electricity market to include several utilities. For example, if all six utilities in the 60 Hz frequency zone of Japan were in a single electricity trading region, no utility would have more than 35% of the generating capacity, much less concentrated than at present. The eastern 50 Hz zone has only three utilities, with the largest, Tokyo, possessing nearly 80% of the capacity. A nation-wide power market would, in principle, reduce the dominance of the large utilities further. However, interconnections between utilities are not strong (for seven out of nine utilities, interconnection capacity is less than 25% of peak load)[13] reducing the scope for power trading between service areas. Strengthening interconnections between utilities should be encouraged.

Figure 13. **Transmission interconnection capacities and peak loads for the nine utilities**

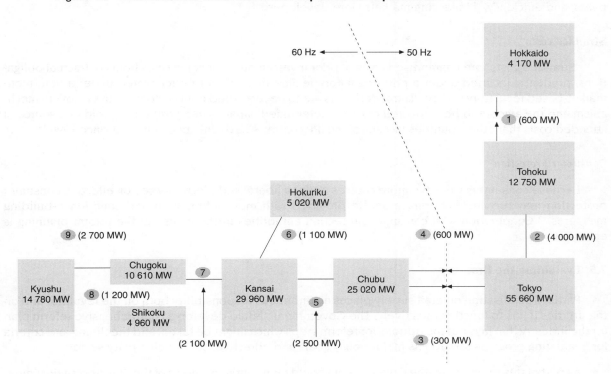

Source: Tokyo Electric Power Company.

Finally, a more severe approach is to create several competing generating companies by dividing the assets of an existing large utility. In some countries where the publicly-owned electricity systems (such as United Kingdom (England and Wales), Australia (most states), New Zealand) have been reformed, the decision has been made to divide the generating capacity of large publicly-owned utilities into several companies in order to create more effective competition. There are also instances (the United Kingdom and the United States) where privately-owned utilities have, in response to incentives, agreed to sell generating assets to address regulatory concerns about the effectiveness of competition in the electricity market. As noted above, the Government of Japan does not consider requiring such separation through divestiture to be an option for Japan.

Electricity markets

Open transparent markets for trading electricity, combined with a legal framework which facilitates direct bilateral contracting between customers and suppliers, forges a critical link between generation competition, competition in supply and end-user choice. Even under partial retail liberalisation, power generators and liberalised customers could encounter difficulties in ensuring that supply and demand are perfectly matched. This problem could be severe in a system such as Japan's, where transmission constraints can severely limit the physically possible trades of electricity during certain peak demand times. A limited spot "balancing" market could provide a practical means of managing such imbalances. Similarly, such balancing markets could be used to sell surplus IPP energy to utilities and liberalised customers and could be used to displace higher marginal cost resources. Appropriate governance (and, potentially, regulation) of the market would be important to ensure non-discrimination among participants, and efficiency, if balancing markets were developed.

Stranded costs

"Stranded costs" are unamortised costs of prior investments or ongoing costs from contractual obligations, prudently incurred under a prior regulatory regime that will not be recovered under a new, more market-based regulatory regime. If stranded costs are to be recovered from customers, the recovery mechanism and the amount to be recovered must be determined. Japan is in a position to avoid one source of stranded costs that other countries face, because IPP contracts have only been allowed since 1996.[14]

Consumer protection

Because consumers will have more choices under a liberalised electricity sector, effective consumer protection may require that consumers be provided with more information and confidence-building measures.[15] Cooperation with consumer protection authorities in the course of the reform planning is essential.

7.5. Evaluating the first step

Partial liberalisation of retail supply places an enormous responsibility both on the regulator and on the utilities if it is to function effectively. The Government should develop a comprehensive reform plan for the industry that lays out the options for reform steps which might be taken, and the timing and criteria for evaluating progress towards its major policy goals and objectives for the electricity sector.

As part of this reform plan, the Government should monitor the progress of the first step against measurable indicators and, if there are problems with this progress, the Government should take further steps.

If the following indicators are found, they probably show that sufficient competition has not been introduced:

- Limited switching by liberalised customers: The extent of customer activity, particularly by large industrial customers, is an indicator of the health of the market.

- Limited entry by IPPs: The extent of IPP activity is also an indicator of market health.

- Complaints by IPPs about discriminatory activity by utilities with respect to network services: Accounting separation does not affect the incentive for a utility to discriminate in favour of its own generating capacity and only slightly limits its ability to do so. Problems with discrimination would suggest that accounting separation is ineffective.

- Complaints by IPPs about abuse of market dominance: As utilities control most of the generating capacity, IPPs will be concerned about pricing practices by utilities that limit their ability to access liberalised customers, or the availability of backup power or ancillary services.

- Limited activities by utilities to compete with one another for customers: The utilities themselves are potential source of competition for liberalised customers. Limited utility activity may be an indication of either anti-competitive behaviour or limited transmission capacity.

- Regulatory difficulties with accounting separation: The regulator may well find it difficult to separate the various regulated activities of the utilities (e.g., supply to captive customers, competitive procurement, sales to liberalised customers) when the utility has not separated underlying functions. Inevitably, there is a degree of arbitrariness about how exactly costs are attributed to the liberalised customers and what is for captive customers. Therefore, the regulator cannot be expected to uncover all of the cross-subsidies with an aim of reducing discriminatory behaviour by the utility as much as possible. Utilities may also find such accounting cumbersome.

7.6. The second step

If the first step is experiencing several of the difficulties listed above, the government should be prepared to move quickly with other measures taking into consideration the policy goals and objectives such as economic growth, energy security, environmental protection, universal service and supply reliability:

The key elements of this second step are listed below:

– Additional liberalisation of supply by enlarging the number of eligible customers and, if possible, making all customers eligible.

– Strengthening protection against the cross-subsidisation of liberalised activity by regulated activity and of anticompetitive behaviour by strengthening of regulatory enforcement, by using a more strict application of accounting separation or by adopting other combinations of vertical separation and regulation. Functional separation or, if possible, operational separation of network services (transmission, distribution, and system operations) with appropriate regulation may bring more benefits of competition. All feasible forms of separation should be considered. Circumstances may arise where divestiture becomes feasible, for example, and this too should remain open for consideration.

– Regulation, independent of policy-making functions, designed to enhance the transparency and credibility of the regulator to all market participants.

– Promoting electric power trading by introducing, at least on a limited basis, a wholesale market, expanding interconnections and by requiring utilities to purchase power for captive consumers from the most economic source.

– Ancillary services which require the utility to offer, and the customer to purchase backup power and other system services.

– Nuclear power and renewables should continue to be supported by all customers.

The evolution from the current system to the second step is described in Table 4.

7.7. Further steps

Implementation of the measures proposed in the second step of reform should complete the process of liberalising retail supply and achieve functional separation of the competitive and monopoly activities. Subsequent evaluation of the performance of the electricity market would be needed to determine whether these measures have been effective in establishing competition in the electricity market in every utility service area throughout Japan. Among the performance indicators to evaluate are whether prices are approaching internationally comparable levels, whether independent generators experience discrimination, and whether there are difficulties in reaching environmental and energy security goals for the electricity sector. Depending on the outcome of such an evaluation, the Government should then determine whether further regulatory and structural measures might be necessary and practical in particular utility service areas including, for example:

– encouraging entry of new generating companies;

– expanding interconnections between regions to support greater trade;

– changing terms and conditions of access to networks;

– modifying economic regulation of the utilities to provide greater incentives to compete for customers;

– encouraging or requiring further vertical separation of network activities from competitive activities through strategies such as operational or ownership separation; and

– encouraging or requiring horizontal separation of the generating assets of utilities into a number of competing entities.

Table 4. **Evolution of the Japanese electricity sector**

Area	Current	Step 1	Step 2
Liberalisation of Retail Supply	No customer choice except for self wheeling and special retail supply.	Extra high voltage customers (average 28% of market) liberalised. Captive customers supplied by utility.	Expansion of eligible customers. If possible, extend to all customers.
Tariffs	Regulated standard tariffs. Optional time of use rates for all customers. Fixed tariff for self wheeling.	Regulated time-of-use tariffs for captive customers to manage peak loads. Time-of-use system tariffs for liberalised customers.	As in Step 1.
Network Access/ Separation	Vertically integrated with generation and retail supply.	Accounting separation of transmission, distribution and system operations. Regulated non-discriminatory terms of access to the grid (location-sensitive transmission and distribution and ancillary services tariffs).	Functional separation of transmission, distribution and system operations (or if possible, operational separation with oversight by a neutral national governing board).
Trading Electricity	Generation dispatched by each utility based on fuelling cost. Interutility trade to reduce costs. Optional time-of-use contracts to reduce peak load.	Time-of-use pricing for system services (liberalised customers) and retail electricity (captive customers). Liberalised customers negotiate contracts and purchase ancillary services as required. Inter-utility trade encouraged through expansion of interconnections.	Markets introduced by system operators to manage imbalances and cut utility generating costs. Time-of-use pricing for all customers. Inter-utility trade expanded through increased links and regulatory incentives to reduce costs.
Competition in Generation	IPP entry liberalised. Annual utility tender for 10% of system expansion needs through 2004. Beginning in 1999, barring a significant change in the situation, current plan is for utilities to compete with IPP for all thermal power needs through tender.	IPPs able to contract directly with liberalised customers. IPPs also compete with utilities to supply captive customers through competitive tender. Utilities sell to captive customers, compete for liberalised customers.	IPPs compete with utilities through sales in spot market as well as through contracts.
Economic Regulation	MITI regulation of retail prices through rate-of-return regulation with a yardstick mechanism. Notification of MITI for optional rates and wheeling charges. Competition authority (FTC) limited to comment role.	MITI regulates network prices, terms of access, transmission plans, and retail prices for captive customers. Improved yardstick regulation. FTC's authority clarified by amendment of Anti-monopoly Act.	Increased use of regulatory incentives to reduce network costs. Regulation of generation based on comparison with market prices. FTC regulates anti-competitive practises for liberalised customers. FTC consulted on amendments to access terms.
Security of Supply/Nuclear Power	Utilities have obligation to serve and plan for adequate supplies. Government policies support nuclear expansion and continued fuel diversification.	Utilities have obligation to serve and plan for adequate supplies for captive customers. Nuclear power development continues.	As in Step 1.
Renewable Energy	Utilities purchase renewable energy at special buyback rates. Government support for new energy through subsidies, low interest loans and tax privileges.	Utilities continue to purchase renewable energy. Existing commitments continued through subsidies, low interest loans and tax privileges.	As in Step 1.
Public Service Obligations	Obligation to serve all customers of utility (including, e.g., remote islands). "Postage stamp" pricing of electricity.	Captive customers served by utility at postage stamp prices. Utility sells ancillary services to liberalised customers.	As in Step 1.
Stranded Cost Recovery	Not applicable	Tax on electricity use or other mechanisms.	As in Step 1.

8. PERFORMANCE

As Japan is just beginning its market liberalisation, the performance measures below must be seen as benchmarks against which future performance can be measured. At this stage in international market reform of electricity, there is also little data for international comparison. It is not therefore clear how Japan compares with others.

8.1. Costs and productivity

Labour productivity: Market liberalisation should encourage electric utilities to make labour productivity gains. Japanese electric utility labour productivity, of 5.1 GWh generated per full-time employee, ranks among the better among OECD countries (OECD, 1997). These figures do not include the extent to which electric utilities outsource various tasks, which may in fact be more considerable in Japan than in other countries.

Fuel conversion efficiency: Efficiency of fossil fuel conversion to electricity at the utilities is average at 37% (net efficiency). This does not include power generation by large industry, which is more efficient through the use of cogeneration. The high cost and hence limited use of natural gas fuel, the fossil fuel that can be most readily used at very high efficiencies affect performance in this category. Market liberalisation may increase fuel conversion efficiency by encouraging use of cogeneration by liberalised customers.

Investment efficiency: Market liberalisation is expected to improve the productivity of utility assets. While there is very little surplus capacity in Japan compared to most other countries (about 9%), the load factor is very low. Pricing reforms that expose consumers to time of use prices are expected to provide the biggest gains in the productive use of assets.

The success of current IPP suggests that investment productivity will also improve under partial liberalisation of retail supply.

8.2. Prices and costs

IEA data rank Japanese electricity prices for both industrial and household consumers as the highest among OECD countries. Reasons for high prices have been documented in Section 1. It should be noted, however, that international price comparisons may be misleading, as we may not be comparing "like with like". For example, some countries' electricity prices may be distorted by subsidies and cross subsidies between consumer groups. Also, the financial position of companies across countries is not easily comparable and may lead to price differences that are unrelated to real efficiency and costs.

8.3. Reliability

Electricity supply reliability is very high, higher than most other OECD countries.

8.4. Environmental performance

Emissions of sulphur and nitrogen oxides from Japanese electric utilities are extremely low owing to very strict environmental standards at both the national and prefectural/municipal levels. Extensive emissions control investments (flue gas desulphurisation, selective catalytic reduction) have been added to coal-fired and most oil-fired generation. Emissions intensity from all plant of 0.17 g/kWh for sulphur oxides and 0.21g/kWh for nitrogen oxides in 1996 is bettered only by countries relying almost entirely on non-fossil generation. Carbon dioxide emissions from electricity production have increased 5% since 1990 – owing in large part to a rise in production of 7%. Carbon dioxide emissions intensity has fallen to 0.1 kg-C/kWh as there has been a substantial rise in nuclear generation and in new efficient combined cycle gas power generation.

9. CONCLUSIONS AND RECOMMENDATIONS

9.1. Conclusions

The 1995 amendments to the Electric Utility Industry Law have begun a process of change in the Japanese electricity sector. The tendering for new capacity by independent power producers, which the amendments enabled, revealed significant scope for cost savings in generation. A revised regulatory process has put greater emphasis on improving efficiency at the utilities.

The decision to move forward with partial liberalisation of retail supply is an important and irreversible step for Japan to take towards its goal of international comparability in electricity prices. The first step of partial liberalisation may bring benefits to both liberalised and non-liberalised customers; it may bring the significant benefit of information about potential efficiency gains, and make clearer the way forward. The principles guiding the discussion of the first step appear to be soundly based. In particular, the recognition of the need for equal conditions for competition between the utilities and new entrants, the need for fair and transparent rules on the use of power transmission lines, and the commitment to set a timetable for liberalisation highlight essential points of any successful market liberalisation in electricity. Furthermore, the Committee's recent decision to recommend that all extra high voltage industrial and commercial customers, representing 28% of total utilities' sales, is an important milestone.

However, this first step under consideration will need to be carefully monitored to assess whether partial liberalisation of retail supply meets all the energy policy goals of the Japanese government. To establish the foundation for reducing Japan's electricity costs on a medium- to long-term basis, and to meet all of Japan's policy goals, further liberalisation will be needed. Further liberalisation will enable markets to become established and to expand, which will induce more efficient ways of organising the sector, and ways of using existing assets in the sector. It is important that access to the transmission grid and ancillary services be non-discriminatory and cost-reflective. Both the demand and the supply sides of the markets for electricity should be sufficiently unconcentrated, and those parts of the sector remaining under economic regulation should be subject to credible, transparent regulation. Each of these conditions are part of the foundation upon which an efficient electricity sector is built. A more robust foundation would require additional conditions.

9.2. Recommendations

The government should adopt a comprehensive reform plan for the industry that lays out the timing and criteria for evaluating progress with reform of introducing effective competition for the electricity sector, taking into account its major policy goals (environmental protection, energy security and economic growth). It can be noted that development of such a comprehensive plan is consistent with the OECD report of Ministers on Regulatory Reform, which recommends a complete and transparent package of reforms designed to achieve specific goals on a well-defined timetable.

As part of this reform plan, *the government should define measurable indicators of these reforms so that progress toward their achievement can be monitored.* The Government should monitor the progress of these reforms and, and, if there are problems with this progress, the government can make a timely adjustment toward other policies.

Competition principles should be strengthened in the overall policy framework.

The following recommendations would apply particularly to the first step of reform.

Regulatory independence from day to day political pressures is essential to build confidence of all electricity market participants that government intervention in the electricity market will be neutral and transparent. Further, independence from the regulated companies, including but not limited to utilities, is needed to ensure transparent, fair, and reasonably predictable decisions. Therefore, *the regulation of the electricity sector should be independent from policy-making functions and electricity industry promotion functions, with trans-*

parent procedures and due process for the review of decisions. Transparency, expertise, independence and adequate legal pow- ers are particularly important. Co-ordination with the Fair Trade Commission should be clearly defined.

Non-discriminatory tariffs and terms of access to the networks and system services are cornerstones of electricity reform. Therefore, *the first step of reform should include the requirement for regulated terms and conditions of access to the network and provision of ancillary services. Separate accounts for natural monopoly activities and supply of electricity to captive customers are needed from the potentially competitive activities. Prices should reflect, to the extent possible, underlying costs to encourage efficient development and use of the networks.*

Standard customer tariffs do not reflect the high cost of peak power. Cost reflective pricing of energy would encourage those customers able to manage their load to use less energy on peak, thus reducing total electricity costs. *Therefore, standard electricity tariffs for captive customers, and network/ancillary service tariffs for liberalised customers, should reflect costs by time of use. Implementation of the time of use tariffs should be phased in, begin- ning with liberalised customers and the larger (power) captive customers.*

The current application of yardstick assessment to economic regulation provides only diffuse incen- tives for utilities to improve their efficiency. *Therefore, the yardstick assessment scheme should be revised to provide a greater incentive for utilities to improve their efficiency by providing a less direct link between prices a utility can charge and the corresponding cost, and providing a more direct link with the cost efficiency of other electric utilities, making suitable adjust- ments for utilities' unique physical situations.*

Competition law needs to be enforced vigorously where collusive behaviour, abuse of dominant position, or anti-competitive mergers risks frustrating reform. *The Anti-monopoly Act should be amended to clar- ify that it also applies to the electricity sector.*

If after a reasonable period, such as by 2003, there continues to be evidence of discriminatory behav- iour, and the market is not sufficiently competitive, despite accounting separation, further changes will be necessary:

The Government should expand the set of eligible customers. *If possible, make all customers eligible.*

If difficulties with accounting separation are found, and if measures to strengthen accounting sepa- ration have not eliminated these difficulties, then *utilities should be required to functionally separate their regulated activities from unregulated activities and the regulatory regime may need to be strengthened. The government should consider the full range of feasible separation options to promote competition in the industry.*

Increased activity in the trading of electricity will increase the need and the opportunity for a short- term electricity market to deal with imbalances between generation and loads. Therefore, *a short-term mar- ket for electricity sales should be created to optimise use of generating resources.*

Following the second step in the regulatory reform in the electricity sector, consistent with its reform objectives, the Government of Japan should undertake a review of the operation of the competitive elec- tricity market in each utility service area in Japan. Depending on the outcome of such an evaluation, the Government should consider what further practical regulatory and/or structural reforms should be intro- duced, consistent with Japan's overall energy policy goals and objectives. Among the options to be con- sidered are:

- *measures to encourage entry of new generating companies;*
- *the expansion of interconnections between regions in a way that supports greater competition as well as reliability of supply;*
- *modification of economic regulation applied to the utilities to provide them with greater incentives to operate and invest efficiently in monopoly activities of the sector, as well as to compete for customers in the competitive activities of the sector;*
- *measures to encourage the voluntary sale of utilities' generating capacity to multiple buyers; and*
- *the full range of feasible horizontal and vertical separation options to promote further competition in the industry.*

313

NOTES

1. That is, fossil-fired generation.

2. Electric Power in Japan 1997/98, Japan Electric Power Information Center, Inc., Tokyo, 1997.

3. See Chapter 3.

4. Transfer supply allows a customer who generates power at one site to use a utility's transmission lines to transfer the supply for use by the same customer at another site. Also known as self-wheeling.

5. Based on information provided by Nippon Steel.

6. Based on Environmental Agency information reported in International Environment Reporter, 154, Vol. 21, No. 4, 1998.

7. Implying that hydro facilities are used mainly for peaking or midload operation.

8. There are several transmission pricing schemes in use in various places outside Japan. Major schemes are as follows:

   – postage-stamp pricing: one price regardless of the locations of the buyer and seller;

   – contract-path pricing: summing prices of segments of transmission line between buyer and seller. For example, higher price if electricity is sent from Kyushu to Osaka, and lower price if electricity is sent from Kobe to Osaka.;

   – location-sensitive pricing: pricing that reflects the cost of location of generation relative to loads. IPPs willing to locate close to loads (e.g., in Tokyo) could have the effect of reducing transmission congestion, and hence would pay lower transmission costs than a new plant located remodely from users. Locational marginal pricing, a particular manifestation of location-sensitive pricing, prices transmission congestion dynamically to pass on the costs, and signal, of congestion when it occurs.

   Neither postage-stamp nor contract-path pricing is related to the actual flow of electricity, and hence the cost of the transaction, nor do they reflect the economic value of a part of the grid under a particular pattern of use. Thus, these pricing schemes do not provide incentives for efficient grid use or augmentation. Locational marginal pricing induces efficient grid operation and dispatch by reflecting congestion of each period of time.

   The adoption of an efficient transmission pricing scheme will likely have several positive effects. First, the changed economic incentives may cause utilities and customers to change how they use the transmission system; if they pay higher prices to use the system in a congestion-causing way, then they may change toward a pattern of use that causes less congestion. Second, the changed economic incentives may change the siting of new generation, so that it is closer to the load; where provision of "counter-flow" is rewarded, it is more likely to be provided. Combined with the liberalisation of generation entry, new generation can be sited where utilities would not otherwise be able. Third, the transmission prices will provide signals as to where reinforcement of the transmission network would have the greatest economic value.

9. Under the system of green certificates adopted in the Netherlands, renewable fuels generators are awarded tradable renewable fuels certificate by the government. Customers are required by the government to have a specific quantity of tradable renewable fuels certificates, depending on their total electricity usage. Customers can get these certificates only by buying electricity generated by renewable fuels, or buying a certificate stripped of its electricity. Hence, the certificates are a means of metering the generation of electricity by renewable fuels without forcing each customer, itself, to buy exactly the target average share of renewable fuels generated electricity. Thus, each renewable fuels electricity generator has incentives to generate electricity at lowest costs, since it competes with all other renewable fuels electricity generators in the Netherlands.

10. The purpose of independent regulation is to provide participants in the relevant sector, as well as potential investors, with confidence that regulatory decisions on, for example, the network tariffs, are fair, non-discriminatory, reasonably predictable, and not subject to political pressures. These require regulation to be regarded as

independent of both the regulated utilities and day-to-day political pressures. Over time, the regulatory decisions made in this way can help build the credibility and legitimacy of the regulatory regime, encourage investment, and help reforms to progress.

11. Divestiture raises important issues of property rights in Japan, where electricity companies are private entities. Under the current legal system, the Government states it has no legal authority to force the private utilities to divest their assets. Thus, if someday Japan were to turn to divestiture, changes in law would be required. Further, supply reliability is important in Japan, where customers place a high value on reliability. Given the large planned increase in the number of nuclear power reactors in Japan, it is possible that divestiture would affect the ability to make these long term investments. If divestiture causes coal and oil fired plants to shift to base load use, the Government of Japan is concerned that there would be environmental effects. Finally, the Government of Japan is concerned that voluntary divestiture based on economic incentives may increase the price of electricity. The Government of Japan states that it does not consider requiring separation through divestiture to be a feasible option.

12. Cogeneration refers to the simultaneous production of both electricity and useful heat. Trigeneration refers to the simultaneous production of electricity, useful heat, and cooling.

13. Based on interconnection capacity and peak load information provided by Tokyo Electric Power Company.

14. A major error in the IPP procurement process in other countries (*e.g.*, in the US in the 1980s or in the UK in the early 1990s) was for utilities to sign long-term contracts for IPPs at prices well above what could ultimately be sustained in the market. These IPP contracts became a source of "stranded costs" that needed to be dealt with in the transition to a fully liberalised market. Fortunately, the relatively low bids in the IPP offers to date make this risk in Japan smaller than was the case in other countries. However, contracts for future independent tenders could contain provisions that make allowance for further developments in fuel and electricity markets and allow contract prices and other contract conditions to evolve accordingly.

    Principles with respect to transparent, fair, and efficient stranded cost recovery include:
    – Transparency: The amount is determined in a transparent manner by the regulator for each utility.
    – Shared recovery: Cost recovery is to be shared equitably among different customer classes and with the utilities.
    – Non-distortionary recovery: Cost recovery does not induce excessive or insufficient entry, nor distort the marginal price of electricity.
    – Utilities have a responsibility to mitigate stranded costs: Full recovery of stranded costs is not normally guaranteed to the utilities, but utilities are given incentives to reduce the amount of their reported stranded costs.

15. In some countries, abuses against consumers have caused backlashes against reform itself. This is because many countries neglected to install consumer protection regimes that work well in new market conditions. This failure stems from the mistaken notion that market liberalisation means that all kinds of regulation will be reduced. On the countrary, in some areas it may mean more.

BACKGROUND REPORT
ON REGULATORY REFORM
IN THE TELECOMMUNICATIONS INDUSTRY*

* This report was principally prepared by **Wonki Min**, with the participation of **Dimitri Ypsilanti**, of the Directorate on Science, Technology, and Industry. It has benefited from extensive comments provided by colleagues throughout the OECD Secretariat, by the Government of Japan, and by Member countries as part of the peer review process. This report was peer reviewed in March 1999 by the OECD's Working Party on Telecommunication and Information Services Policies and by the Competition Law and Policy Committee.

TABLE OF CONTENTS

OECD 1999

Executive Summary

Background Report on Regulatory Reform in the Telecommunications Industry

The telecommunications industry has undergone significant regulatory reform over the last decade. By 1998, 23 OECD countries had liberalised their telecommunication markets, including voice telephony, infrastructure investment and investment by foreign enterprises. The success of this liberalisation process will depend on the presence of a transparent and effective regulatory regime that enables the development of full competition, while efficiently protecting the public interest. This report addresses whether Japan's regulatory regime makes possible a successful liberalisation process by assessing telecommunications regulations in Japan, recent regulatory reforms and their impacts on market performance.

Japan is one of the few countries to have introduced competition in the 1980s, along with the United States and the United Kingdom. Since market liberalisation began in 1985, Japan has introduced many liberalisation measures to encourage fair competition. In particular, following the February 1997 WTO agreement on basic telecommunications services, Japan made significant changes to its regulatory regime such as elimination of the article on the prevention of excessive facilities (so-called "supply-demand" standard for market entry) and foreign ownership restrictions on Type 1 carriers, except NTT. There are no longer any line-of-business restrictions in Japan and many major global companies are beginning to compete in the Japanese telecommunications market. As a result, there is strong competition in the national long distance market and the international market. In addition, the rapid growth of cellular mobile services and telephony services based on cable television (CATV) networks is raising the prospect that these can be an alternative to local fixed voice telephony service, which is currently dominated by NTT. The emergence of utility-based Type 1 carriers could also facilitate competition in the local voice telephony market.

However, in spite of the large number of market players, consumers have not yet benefited fully from liberalisation due to the tariff approval system which lasted until November 1998. Furthermore, many important regulatory safeguards, such as a LRIC (Long Run Incremental Cost) accounting system for interconnection, a universal service funding mechanism, number portability, carrier pre-selection and a method to select mobile licensees when the number of applicants is greater than what can be sustained by spectrum resources, are not in place yet.

In November 1998, the Ministry of Post and Telecommunications (MPT) introduced a tariff notification system, which allows companies to determine their own prices without obtaining approval from MPT except for NTT's local basic services. This decision is a milestone for the liberalisation of the telecommunications market since it finally makes effective price competition possible. However, the remaining regulatory issues should be addressed properly and promptly in order to ensure a fair and transparent competitive environment for all market players. In addition, there is a possibility that the proposed NTT break-up may not be effective to promote infrastructure competition because of the holding company structure. MPT should take necessary steps to establish a more effective regulatory framework in order to promote effective competition, increase consumer benefits and allow market-oriented business activities to develop.

1. JAPAN'S TELECOMMUNICATIONS SECTOR

1.1. The national context for telecommunications policies

As of 31 December 1997, with telecommunication revenues of $110.0 billion, Japan has the second largest telecommunications market in the world.[1] Its market size is less than half that of the United States ($256.8 billion) but twice that of Germany ($43.6 billion). The incumbent operator, NTT, is the world's largest telecommunications operator with $78.1 billion revenues.[2]

As of 31 December 1997, there were 47.9 telecommunication access lines (*i.e.* the total of fixed access lines and cellular mobile subscribers) per 100 inhabitants in Japan. This is just below the OECD average of 48.9.[3]

In Japan, the telecommunications industry is a core industry and has a significant impact on the entire Japanese economy (Tables 1 and 2). The telecommunications market is expanding rapidly and the level of investment by telecommunications Type 1 carriers[4] is the second largest across all industry sectors.

Table 1. **Market size by Type 1 telecommunications business**
(FY 1996 annual sales)
Trillion yen

	Electrical machinery	Auto-mobile	Electric power	Telecom (Type 1)	Iron and steel	Ship building	Gas
Market size	27.1	20.8	15.1	12.1	6.6	5.4	1.9
Growth rate[1] (%)	8.7	9.6	−0.1	21.0	1.5	5.6	5.3

1. Growth rate from previous fiscal year.
Source: "Outline of the Telecommunications Business in Japan", March 1998, MPT.

Table 2. **Facilities investment by Type 1 telecommunications business**
(FY 1997 plans)

	Electric power	Telecom (Type 1)	Electrical machinery	Services	Chemicals	Real estate	Auto-mobile
Investment	5.1	4.2	3.5	2.9	1.9	1.6	1.4
Growth rate[1] (%)	5.7	1.9	3.5	−12.0	3.3	2.2	7.2

1. Growth rate from previous fiscal year.
Source: "Outline of the Telecommunications Business in Japan", March 1998, MPT.

1.2. General features of the regulatory regime, telecommunications market and market participants

1.2.1. Brief history

Until 1952, Japan's telecommunication facilities and services were operated through a direct government monopoly by the Ministry of Telecommunications. In 1952, the Ministry of Telecommunications was transformed into a wholly state-owned corporation, Nippon Telegraph and Telephone Public Corporation (NTT), with a monopoly over domestic telecommunications. At the same time, Kokusai Denshin Denwa (KDD), a government-regulated corporation, became the monopoly provider of international telecommunications services. In line with the transformation of the Ministry of Telecommunications into NTT in 1952, the Ministry of Posts was reshaped as the Ministry of Posts and Telecommunications with supervisory responsibilities for NTT and KDD as well as direct responsibilities for postal services, postal savings and postal life insurance.

In the early 1980s, growing business pressure for reform and more flexibility in telecommunications policy resulted in 1982 in a recommendation by the Ad hoc Committee on Administrative Reform for full-scale divestiture and privatisation of NTT. Less drastic reforms were supported by business (*Keidanren*) and by NTT itself. Pressure from the Ministry of International Trade and Industry (with responsibility for the computer and computer services industry) to open value-added network service markets, as well as MPT's recognition that Japan's communication sector needed to respond to new demands for diversified communication needs, also fuelled the pressure for change.

In 1985, by enacting the Telecommunications Business Law (TBL), Japan introduced competition into its telecommunications market. Along with the enactment of the NTT Law, which aimed to give more autonomy to NTT, MPT implemented the so-called "First Reform of the Telecommunications System". Unlike many other countries, which liberalised their telecommunications equipment and services markets separately, under the TBL Japan simultaneously liberalised terminal equipment and introduced competition in telecommunications network infrastructure and services. The Law also made a clear distinction between market participants who own infrastructure and those whose activities are based on leased infrastructure. This distinction remains the basis of Japan's regulatory framework for the telecommunications sector.

With the enactment of the NTT Law in 1985, the process of privatising NTT began[5] and NTT was granted more autonomy in its management. Meanwhile, based on the NTT Law, MPT has the authority to supervise NTT when it carries out activities not stipulated in the NTT Law.

Box 1.   **Changes made by the enactment of the TBL (1985)**

- Introduction of competition in the telecommunications market.
- Liberalisation of value-added network service.
- Liberalisation of sales of telephone sets.

While "the first reform of the telecommunications system" in 1985 resulted in the introduction of competition in the Japanese telecommunications market, competition was far from effective. Since market entry and tariffs were subject to individual licensing or approval from the Minister, carriers were not able to make important business decisions without first obtaining permission from the Minister. Moreover, there was no competition in the local telecommunications market, and competition between NTT (or KDD) and the new entrants in long distance and international telecommunications markets was managed by MPT through the tariff approval system.

Although there are still some regulatory issues outstanding, MPT has also made significant efforts at further liberalisation of the telecommunications market since the first reform in 1985. In 1993, MPT decided to allow multi-station operators (MSOs) in the CATV market and, more importantly, to allow CATV companies to offer telecommunications services using CATV networks. In 1996, MPT announced "the second reform of the info-communications system in Japan"[6] which included many important policy changes, notably the break-up of NTT, the establishment of interconnection rules and the promotion of further deregulation such as the introduction of a tariff notification system for mobile companies.

As a result of commitments by Japan under the WTO agreement on basic telecommunications services and the second reform plan in 1996, a number of important changes have been made over the last several years. First, the TBL, NTT Law and KDD Law were amended in June 1997. In terms of the TBL, there were three important developments in favour of ensuring fair competition and enhancing the transparency of the regulatory regime. First, the so-called "supply and demand" provisions[7] used as basis for granting a license were abolished. These provisions, which allowed MPT to determine, on the basis of ensuring a balance between supply and demand, whether a Type I license should be provided, were regarded as a symbol of high entry barrier in Japan's licensing regime. Nevertheless, the remaining general public interest provisions in the TBL still give grounds for MPT to block new entry by companies if they cannot meet the examination standards (see Section 2.2.1). Second, a new interconnection scheme, including accounting separation and non-discriminatory interconnection for "designated facilities", was introduced to ensure transparent and fair interconnection conditions between the incumbent and new entrants (see Section 2.2.2). Third, new provisions for a numbering plan were added in the TBL in order to ensure equal access to numbers (see Section 2.2.5).

In May 1998, the TBL was amended to abolish the approval system for Type 1 carriers' retail prices and to replace it with a notification system from 1 November 1998. The amendment also made it possible to introduce price-cap regulation on NTT's local fixed basic service charges where competition is not fully developed (see Section 2.2.3). Together with the relaxation of restrictions on NTT's international telecommunications service, the amendment of the KDD Law allowed KDD to enter the domestic telecommunications market using its own domestic communications transmission lines and communications satellite. Furthermore, the KDD Law was abolished in July 1998.[8] The abolition of this law changes KDD from a special company to a private company and enables it to make autonomous business decisions. In addition, the 20% foreign ownership restriction on KDD has been lifted, in effect cancelling the reservation Japan had made at the WTO.

In the mobile market, NTT enjoyed a monopoly position until 1988. In December 1988, two companies entered the cellular market with analogue technology and in April 1994 MPT introduced competition by allowing four digital cellular mobile carriers to enter each of ten separate regional markets.[9] In April 1994, MPT also liberalised the mobile telephone equipment market by introducing COMA (Customer Owned and Maintained System) which allowed customers to buy their terminal equipment not only from mobile service companies but also from equipment retail shops. This led to significant price declines in terminal equipment and stimulated the growth of mobile services. In July 1995, further mobile market entry occurred when three PHS (Personal Handy-phone System) carriers were allowed to enter each regional market.

Box 2. Brief history of the Japanese telecommunications market

1952: Establishment of MPT

Establishment of NTT and KDD

1979: NTT starts mobile services

1985: Introduction of competition in the telecommunications market

- Granting Type 1 licenses to new common carriers (NCCs) (three national long distance carriers and two international carriers)

- Liberalisation of value-added network services

- Liberalisation of sales of telephone sets

1986: Privatisation of NTT

1988: NCCs enter the mobile market

1992: Separation of mobile business unit from NTT

1993: Division of the mobile business carrier separated from NTT into nine companies

1994: Introduction of competition by three or four carriers in each mobile market block

- Permission for three PHS carriers in each market block

- Liberalisation of the mobile telecommunications equipment market

1996: Announcement of NTT's break-up into one long distance company and two regional companies within a holding company structure

Introduction of tariff notification system for mobile operators

1997: Liberalisation of international simple resale (ISR) services including Internet telephony service

1998: Lifting of restrictions on foreign capital investment, except for NTT

Introduction of tariff notification system for all Type 1 Telecommunications services except NTT's local services

Abolition of KDD Law (Lifting foreign ownership restriction on KDD.

1.2.2. Break-up of NTT

Efforts to restructure NTT have been at the heart of Japanese telecommunications reform for a long time. The NTT divestiture debate began as early as 1981 when an MPT internal study group proposed the divestiture of NTT together with privatisation. Ever since, this issue has been under debate. However, it was not until 1990 that serious policy consideration was first given to the possibility of breaking up NTT. According to the NTT Law, the status of NTT was to be reviewed within five years after the enactment of the NTT Law in 1985. In 1990, at the time of review, the Telecommunications Council (the Council) recommended the break-up of NTT into one long distance company and a local company. While MPT supported the Council's recommendation as a means of promoting competition, it faced strong opposition from many other interested parties such as MITI, NTT, telecommunications equipment companies, *Keidanren* and the Ministry of Finance (MOF). Many argued that it was too early to decide and the MOF was afraid that a divestiture would adversely affect NTT's share price. By the end of March 1990 a compromise was reached: the NTT mobile business would be hived off into a separate company, and further efforts would be given to improving the efficiency of NTT's operation. In addition, it was agreed that NTT's status would be reviewed five years later.

In 1995, the debate was reopened and a range of proposals was made by government bodies. For instance, a sub-committee of the Prime Minister's Office filed a report which suggested that NTT should be split into one long distance company and four regional companies. The Fair Trade Commission (FTC) also submitted a report emphasising further deregulation rather than the break-up of NTT.[10] NTT's argument against any break-up stressed the importance of an integrated company in order to ensure NTT's R&D function, which was highly regarded as a national asset in Japan. The final report of Council was submitted in February 1996 with a proposal to break up NTT into one long distance company and two regional companies. However the government's final decision was delayed for one year because of political pressure.[11] Finally, the government announced its final decision in March 1997: it maintained the idea of dividing NTT into one long distance company and two regional companies, but also proposed a holding company to ensure unified R&D and manage the shares of the two regional companies.

Box 3.   1997 Changes in the NTT Law

- NTT will be restructured into one long distance company and two regional companies under a holding company which is not allowed to enter into any communications business.
- The holding company (Nippon Telegraph and Telephone Corp.) will be a special corporation that manages all shares of the two regional companies.
- The holding company is responsible for fundamental research.
- The regional companies (NTT East and NTT West) will be special corporations providing only regional communications services and obliged to provide universal service in their business areas.
- The long-distance company will be a private company that can enter the international telecommunications market.
- The holding company and the two regional companies will be regulated as special companies like the present NTT.
- NTT is allowed to enter the international telecommunications market through its affiliates even before the establishment of the long distance company.
- The changes should be implemented within two and a half years from the date of promulgation (that is, before the end of 1999).

There is a concern that the break-up would not be much effective in promoting local loop competition because of the holding company structure. It is unlikely that NTT East and West will be involved in infrastructure competition, given that it is not in the shareholders' interests for the holding company to allow NTT East and NTT West to enter each other's market. In addition, under the NTT Law, NTT East or NTT West cannot enter long distance markets.

1.2.3. *Major drivers of Japanese regulatory development in the telecommunications sector*

Five major elements have led Japanese regulatory developments in the telecommunications sector. Although at times one or another of these elements has overshadowed the others, all five have played an important role in moulding the current Japanese regulatory structure.

Catch-up

While Japan is one of the three countries that initiated liberalisation of the telecommunications market in the 1980s, it has never taken a leading role but has followed developments or positions elsewhere on many important regulatory issues. A long history of bilateral telecommunication meetings with the United States and the European Union has helped MPT officials to enlarge their knowledge of the US and the EU regulatory systems. In certain cases, Japan has tried to follow the US model, for example in the original proposals for divestiture of the incumbent. In other cases, such as market entry regulation, it has followed the UK model. Discussions on the divestiture of NTT began in 1981, just after the United States made public discussions on AT&T's divestiture. Although it took more than 14 years after AT&T's divestiture, Japan finally implemented a partial divestiture of NTT despite criticism about the effectiveness of the structure of the divestiture. The catch-up policy tended to result in an incremental approach to the liberalisation of telecommunications market through individual deregulation measures rather than a single comprehensive deregulation package underpinned by a clear goal of creating effective competition.

MPT vs. NTT

For a long time after 1985, one of the MPT's main policy goals has been the weakening of NTT's power by means of divestiture in order to promote competition in the telecommunications market. However, MPT has experienced difficulty in obtaining sufficient political and inter-ministerial support. Because of NTT's political strength, due to its more than 220 000 employees, and its economic power, based on its position as number one in purchasing power among all Japanese companies, NTT was able to resist MPT's attempt to break it up for 12 years. In the face of difficulties it faced for regulating NTT by divestiture, MPT started in the last several years to use regulatory safeguards as an alternative, and perhaps more effective, tool.

Unique market structure

Japan had a unique telecommunications market structure which was based on the line-of-business restrictions on NTT and KDD. From the outset, NTT could not enter the international market and KDD was limited to providing international telecommunication services. Therefore, unlike many other OECD countries, there have been two incumbents in the Japanese telecommunications market, one for domestic and one for international. Furthermore, for a long time there was no cross-competition between domestic long distance carriers and international carriers. In fact, there has been no company operating both domestic and international services until 1997. In addition, competition was developed differently in the long distance and the international markets. In the long distance market, new common carriers (NCCs)[12] have used least-cost routing chips (LCR) to entice customers from NTT, but in the long distance market, NCCs have made large investments to advertise their carrier identification codes to compete with KDD. As a result, consumers do not need to use carrier identification code for long distance services but need it for international services (see Section 2.2.5).

Consumer protection vs. industry promotion

MPT has authority both as a regulator and a policy maker in the telecommunications sector. As a result, unlike many other regulatory bodies in the OECD Member countries that solely aim to protect consumer benefits, MPT is responsible for consumer protection as well as industry promotion in the telecommunications sector. For instance, the "second info-communications reform" in 1995 had two goals: promotion *of users' benefits* and *revitalisation of industry.*[13] Considering the fact that the regulatory body's independence can be effectively ensured only when it distances itself from interested parties, there is concern that MPT's industry promotion function may have negative impacts on its regulatory function. In fact, it seems that previously MPT put more emphasis on the role of industry promotion by protecting carriers' interest through the recently abolished "supply-demand" provision and "tariff approval system".

NTT's R&D activities are one good example of the importance of industry promotion in Japan's telecommunications regime. The NTT Law stipulates that NTT should conduct research related to telecommunication technologies. Since its establishment in 1952, NTT's R&D has been regarded as a national asset and has played a vital role in the promotion of the competitiveness of the so-called NTT family companies, namely NEC, Hitachi, Oki and Fujitsu. However, NTT's role tends to be decreasing due to the rapid expansion of R&D activities on Internet and multimedia technologies in the telecommunications sector.

Foreign pressure

Since the early 1980s, Japan's trading partners, mainly the United States, have made the telecommunications sector the major target of pressure for open markets.[14] The annual Japan-US bilateral exchanges have increased pressure to liberalise Japan's telecommunications market. In 1998, when the United States submitted two proposals regarding deregulation to the Japanese government, telecommunications deregulation was the central issue. In recent years, the EU has also pushed for more open markets, and the deregulation proposal made to Japan in October 1998 also targets the telecommunications sector as the main area for deregulation. (See Section 2.2.7.)

It should be noted that foreign pressure does not necessarily only represent the interests of foreign companies, but may also include those of potential or new domestic carriers. Since it is uncommon in Japan for a single company to file a complaint to the government, many companies, including Japanese domestic companies, have tried to use the US Chamber of Commerce or the European Business Council, with *Keidanren*, to represent their interests to the government.

It is noteworthy that some significant changes in Japan's telecommunications regulatory regime resulted from their WTO commitments in the context of the agreement on basic telecommunications services, which was signed on 15 February 1997 and came into force on 5 February 1998. (See Section 2.2.7.) It seems that the role of multilateral negotiation as a force to push further reform in the Japanese telecommunications market will be strengthened as increased globalisation of telecommunications services occurs.

1.2.4. *Telecommunications market and participants*

Until recently, Japan had very distinctive telecommunications market structure based on line-of-business restrictions on NTT and KDD. After abolishing these restrictions by amending the NTT Law and abolishing the KDD Law, the market structure has significantly changed. Previously, in the national long distance market, there were NTT and three NCCs – DDI (Daini DenDen), Japan Telecom and Teleway Japan. In the international market, the participants were KDD and two NCCs, ITJ (International Telecom Japan) and IDC (International Digital Communications).

However, abandoning line-of-business restrictions not only allows NTT and KDD to expand their business coverage, but changes the whole competition environment by eliminating the separation between national long distance and international markets. In fact, the most significant change in the Japanese telecommunications market is the possibility for carriers to provide an integrated telecommunication service or a "one-stop service" to customers. In addition to NTT's entry into international markets and KDD's into national long distance market through its acquisition of Teleway Japan, other NCCs are improving their ability to provide one-stop service to customers through strategic alliances and mergers.

For instance, Japan Telecom has merged with ITJ, and DDI has decided to provide international services through a tie-up with the Canadian carrier Teleglobe.

In the mobile market, in addition to NTT DoCoMo, there are five or six cellular and PHS carriers in each market block.[15] Major players in the mobile market are DDI Cellular, IDO, TUKA, Digital Phone, Digital TUKA, DDI Pocket and ASTEL. Currently, cellular operators provide both analogue services based on TACS technology and digital service based on PDC technology. Since the PDC system was developed by NTT DoCoMo, some carriers are trying to use digital technologies such as CDMA (code division multiple access). In fact, DDI Cellular and IDO have entered into a strategic alliance to introduce a nation-wide "cdmaOne" service and three of their regional companies began services in July 1998. In the PHS market, although subscribers surpassed 7 million as of September 1997, the total number of subscribers has been declining since October 1997 as customers move from PHS to cellular networks. In addition, many PHS companies are losing money because of severe price competition. For example, liabilities of NTT Personal Group exceed its assets. As a result, NTT decided to transfer NTT Personal Group's PHS business to NTT DoCoMo in order to improve the PHS business operation.

In the market for local fixed telephony services, as of 31 March 1998, NTT had a 99.5% market share, as measured by the percentage of access lines (and 98% in terms of revenue). Because of NTT's dominance, other carriers have to use NTT's local loop to complete their services. Recent indications of potential changes may have implications for NTT's dominance in the local telecommunications market. For instance, local fixed optical fibre networks are being constructed by new entrants, such as electrical power companies, which can use their power cables as rights of way for optical fibre cables. Currently, ten electric utility companies are providing telecommunications services such as leased lines and integrated services digital network (ISDN). Among them, companies like TTNet in Tokyo and QTNet in Kyusyu have entered or plan to enter the local voice telephony market. In fact, TTNet is one of the local telecommunications companies offering cheaper local calls than NTT. Owing to its relatively cheaper price for local calls (9 yen for three minutes, or 1 yen cheaper than NTT), TTNet obtained 1.4 million subscribers in just six months after launching its business in January 1998. QTNet plans to offer local voice telephony services from April 1999.

As a result of earlier regulatory constraints on CATV, Japan's penetration rate for CATV service is very low (11.32% of households at the end of 1996) as compared with other OECD countries. However, the growth rate of CATV penetration (37.5% between 1995 and 1996) is much higher than the OECD average (7.8%).[16] In addition, while foreign ownership restrictions on CATV prevent foreign entities from owning more than 33% of CATV shares, since February 1998 these restrictions are not applied to CATV companies with Type 1 carrier licenses.[17] By October 1998, there were 48 CATV companies with a Type 1 carrier license. Although the number of CATV companies that hold a Type 1 license is increasing rapidly (Figure 1), only five companies currently have interconnection agreements with NTT and only two provide voice telephony services using their CATV networks. Titus Communications Inc. began to provide voice telephony services via cable used for television services in June 1997 and J-COM Tokyo Inc. began a similar service in July 1997. J-COM currently charges 8.5 yen per three minutes and its charges for calls within its network is 5 yen per 3 minutes. Despite the weak presence of CATV companies in the telecommunications market, their recent rapid growth rate suggests that they are likely to be a source of local loop competition against NTT East and West.

In the long-distance market, as of 31 March 1998, NTT had a 59.4% market share in terms of revenue. In the international market, as of 31 March 1998, KDD had a 63.7% market share in terms of revenue.

In the mobile market, as of March 31 1998, NTT DoCoMo had a 57% market share in cellular phone service and NTT Personal had a 28.3% market share of PHS in terms of subscriber numbers. Japan's mobile market is doubling in size each year, thanks to strong competition, which has led to significant price cuts. Since the introduction of the COMA system in 1994, the number of mobile subscribers has increased significantly. In 1993, mobile subscribers numbered 2.13 million; by 1998 there were 39.21 million. In 1995, Japan ranked eleventh in terms of mobile communication subscribers per 100 inhabitants in the OECD area, but by 1997 it had risen to fourth place. In terms of revenue, mobile services accounted for 11.46% of total telecommunications revenue in 1993; its share tripled in 1997 to 39.67%.

Figure 1. Number of CATV operators with a Type 1 carrier license

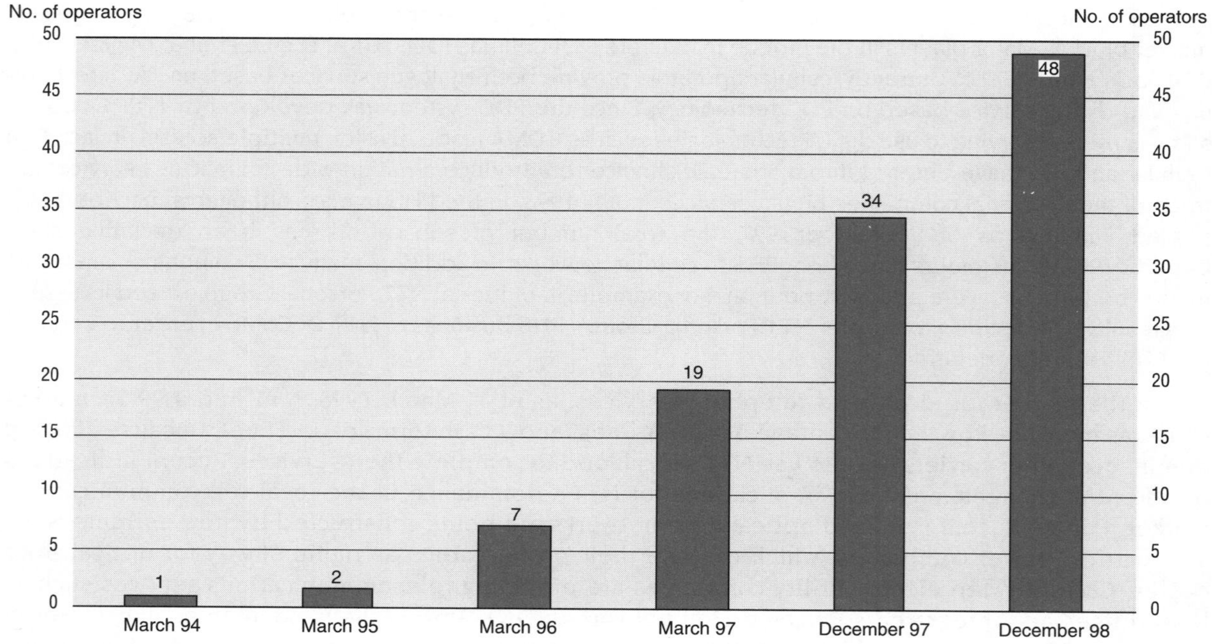

No. of operators

No. of operators

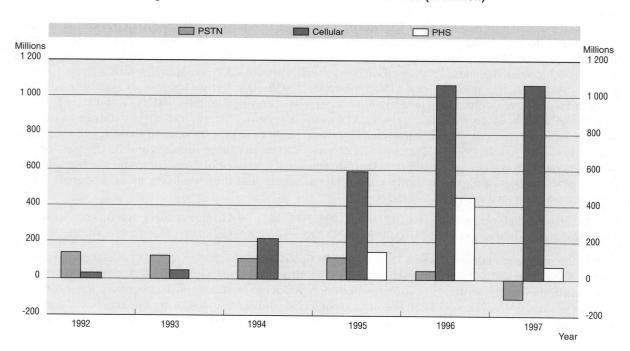

Source: MPT.

Figure 2. Number of customers for each service (in million)

Source: MPT and NTT.

Table 3. **Major participants in Japan's telecommunications market as of 31 March 1998**

Percentage share

	Local	Long distance	International	Cellular	PHS	Note
NTT/NTT DoCoMo	A 98.0	A 59.4	P	A 57.0	A 28.3	Cellular and PHS services are provided by NTT DoCoMo.
KDD/Teleway Japan	P	A 7.6	A 63.7			KDD plans to enter the mobile market through IMT 2000.
JT/Digital Phone		A 15.1	A	A 7.5		JT is a major shareholder of 3 Digital phone.
DDI/ DDI Cellular/ DDI Pocket		A 16.9	A	A 13.7	A 51.8	DDI entered into a strategic alliance with Teleglobe in order to provide international voice telephony services using ISR.
IDC			A			
Digital TUKA				A 5.6		JT is a major shareholder of 6 Digital TUKA companies.
TUKA				A 7.4		DDI is a major shareholder of TUKA Cellular Tokyo and Tokai which are in the Kanto and Tokai areas.
IDO				A 8.8		
TTNet	A	A 1.0				TTNet has a cross-investment alliance with KDD.
ASTEL					A 19.8	Regional NCCs, JT, Teleway and KDD are major shareholders of ASTEL

Notes: A = Currently active
P = Planning to enter.
All figures are based on the revenues as of 31 March 1998.
Source: MPT.

Table 4. **Number of Type 1 telecommunications carriers in Japan**

Fiscal year

	84	85	86	87	88	89	90	91	92	93	94	95	96	97
Type 1 carriers	2	7	12	36	44	62	68	70	80	86	111	126	138	153
NTT	1	1	1	1	1	1	1	1	1	1	1	1	1	1
NTT DoCoMo Companies										1	9	9	9	9
KDD	1	1	1	1	1	1	1	1	1	1	1	1	1	1
New Type 1 carriers		5	10	34	42	60	66	68	77	75	100	115	127	142
Long distance/International		3	3	5	5	5	5	5	5	5	5	5	5	6
Regional			3	4	4	7	7	7	8	10	11	16	28	47
Satellite		2	2	2	2	2	2	3	3	2	2	4	4	5
Mobile communications			2	23	31	46	52	53	61	58	82	90	90	84
Cellular phone			2	4	8	8	9	15	15	17	21	21	21	
Radio paging			2	20	26	33	36	36	36	31	31	31	31	31
PHS										23	28	28	28	
Convenience radio phone						2	4	4	7	7	7	6	6	
Ship telephone				1	1	2	3	3	2	2	1			
Airport radio telephone										2	2	2	2	2
Data communications						1	1	1	1	1	1	2	2	2

Source: MPT.

Table 5. **A Synopsis of telecommunication regulation in Japan**

Category	Regulatory restrictions	Notes
Entry regulations		
Type 1 carrier	Entry on the basis of permission	The mobile operator needs an individual license in addition to Type 1 permission.
Special Type 2 carrier	Entry on the basis of registration	Registration can be refused by the Minister in the light of a firm's lack of financial and technical capability.
General Type 2 Carrier	Entry on the basis of notification	
CATV	Entry on the basis of permission	Notification for less than 500 subscribers.
Broadcasting	Entry on the basis of individual licensing	
Line-of-business restrictions	No line-of-business restrictions but NTT is not allowed to enter into the CATV service market	
Foreign ownership restrictions	No foreign ownership restrictions except for NTT (less than 20%)	The foreign ownership restrictions on KDD were lifted after the KDD Law was abolished.
Price controls		
Type 1 carrier	Notification system and price-cap regulation	Price-cap regulation only applies to NTT local basic services.
Special Type 2 carrier	Notification system	
General Type 2 carrier	No regulation	
CATV operator	Notification system	
Interconnection controls		
Prices	Type 1 carriers with "designated facilities" need Minister's approval for terms and conditions	Separate accounting is required for "designated facilities".
Dispute resolution	Parties can ask for arbitration by the Minister	Parties can file a lawsuit within 3 months after Minister's decision when they are not satisfied with the result of arbitration.
Scope	All Type 1 carriers are required to provide interconnection.	
Spectrum allocation	Licensing is used for spectrum allocation	No specific spectrum allocation method such as auction or competitive test is adopted for spectrum allocation.
Numbering policy	Number portability and pre-carrier selection are not yet implemented	
Universal service	NTT is obliged to offer universal service without financial compensation from the government or any other carriers	

The explosive growth of mobile communication in Japan has had implications for fixed telecommunication services through substitution effects (Figure 2). The relatively high cost of joining the fixed network as compared to a mobile subscription seems to be attracting a growing number of users who only subscribe to mobile services. In Japan, subscribers to the fixed network buy a "right of connection" rather than a connection to a specific location. For this service they pay the highest initial connection fee (72 000 yen) in any OECD country. However, they can change location without paying a further connection fee, leave and rejoin the network, and resell their "right of connection". As a result of this high initial connection charge, the very low initial fee to join a mobile communication network, together with low user packages, is very attractive for users such as university students and new entrants to the labour market.[18] Since 1994, growth of numbers of mobile subscribers has surpassed that of PSTN (public switched telephone network) subscribers. More importantly, in 1997 the number of PSTN subscribers started to decrease.

At the same time as the number of PSTN subscribers are decreasing, a large number of existing PSTN customers are transferring to ISDN, largely due to the lack of initial connection charge, as well as the rapid growth of Internet use. As of end of October 1998, there were 3 250 535 basic interface circuits in use in Japan, up 79.3% from the previous year, and 40 707 primary rate interface circuits, up 40.0%.[19] In addition, three international carriers provide international ISDN services in Japan. As the end of fiscal 1996, there were 10 647 circuits; these are mostly used by businesses for international communications, such as video conferencing.

For high-speed digital transmission, NTT and 16 other long-distance and regional carriers offer leased line services. As of September 1997, 163 477 leased lined were in use, up 67.7% from the previous year. The market share (14.1%) of non-NTT carriers was down by 3.8% from the previous year. For international leased lines, at the end of fiscal 1996, three international carriers provided 1 771 lines, up 4.7% from the previous year.[20] It is expected that the demand for international leased lines will increase rapidly owing to the abolition of restrictions on international simple resale (ISR) services in December 1997.

As in many other OECD countries, use of the Internet has grown very rapidly in Japan. Between January 1998 and July 1998, Internet hosts per 1 000 inhabitants increased from 9.3 to 10.8 (by 15.7%).[21] The number of access points for Internet dial-up IP connections had reached about 4 600 at the end of January 1998. At of end of February 1998, Internet services were provided by 2 561 Type 2 carriers (*i.e.* approximately 40% of Type 2 carriers) and 15 Type 1 carriers.[22]

2. REGULATORY STRUCTURES AND THEIR REFORM

2.1. Regulatory institutions and processes

In Japan, the Ministry of Posts and Telecommunications is responsible for telecommunications policy and regulation. It is also responsible for broadcasting policy and for operating postal services, postal savings services and postal life insurance services. Unlike the situation in many other OECD countries, the same ministry has both a policy and a regulatory role. Within MPT, the Telecommunications Bureau is responsible for telecommunications regulation and the Broadcasting Bureau is responsible for broadcasting regulation. In addition, the Communications Bureau is responsible for longer-term policy-oriented issues such as the realisation of the info-communication society. MPT is one of the few regulators in OECD Member countries with the authority to supervise both the broadcasting (including content regulation) and telecommunications markets.

Like many other ministries in Japan, MPT has a policy council (*"shingikai"*), the Telecommunications Policy Council (the Council), which is in charge of developing telecommunications policy. Since the Council plays an advisory role, the Minister is not bound by the Council's decision. Nevertheless, in most cases the Council's recommendations have been adopted as MPT policy. While the Council has the authority to set its agenda freely without necessarily responding to the Minister's request, in practice, the Council set its agenda responding to the Minister's request. The members of the Council are appointed by the Minister from academia, industry, and consumer interest groups. As of October 1998, the Council had 22 members with a two-year term of service. In practice, before the Minister makes a policy decision, the Council discusses the issues (*e.g.* the break-up of NTT, an interconnection accounting system, etc.) and makes recommendations to the Minister.[23]

Although it is not a problem unique to MPT, the Council has been criticised for its compromising approach and rather lengthy procedures (see the background report on Enhancing market openness through regulatory reform, Box 2 for general information on advisory policy councils in Japan). Since the Council is composed of representatives of different interest groups, it is extremely difficult to obtain a clear-cut position on specific issues. The problem is exacerbated when the Council takes too much time to decide certain issues. The tendency to seek a compromise, combined with the tendency towards lengthy decision-making processes, tends to operate in favour of dominant market players who have an interest in maintaining the *status quo*.

In addition to the Council, study groups (*"kenkyukai"*) have played an important role in the policy-making process. MPT has many study groups composed of experts on specific issues, such as number

331

OECD Review of Regulatory Reform in Japan

portability, carrier pre-selection, interconnection accounting systems, etc. Study groups are set up by the Ministry or the Council in order to draft papers providing professional knowledge on specific policy issues to the Minister or the Council.

In Japan, the MPT is one of the leading ministries in the use of the so-called "green paper" approach in the policy-making process. This involves soliciting public comment when establishing new regulations that may have a significant influence on interested parties. For example, it asked for public comment on issues such as the interconnection accounting system and the break-up of NTT. MPT's green paper approach has generally been highly appreciated by many interested parties and clearly increases the transparency of the policy-making process.

In addition to MPT, the Fair Trade Commission (the FTC) has jurisdiction in the telecommunications sector. The FTC's authority is based on the Anti-monopoly Act (AMA). In telecommunications, there is no formal exemption from the AMA, so the FTC and the Ministry share jurisdiction. However, the FTC's involvement has been very limited (see Section 2.2.8).

In June 1998, 'the Basic Law for the Reorganisation of the Central Government Ministries and Agencies' was enacted. According to this law, MPT is to be integrated into a new Ministry of General Affairs along with the Ministry of General Affairs, the Ministry of Home Affairs and the FTC by 2003 (the target year for restructuring is, however, 2001). After the restructuring, although MPT will have to reduce the number of communications-related bureaux from the present three to two, it will retain all of its functions as regards telecommunications and broadcasting policy and regulation.

The restructuring plan has raised concerns relating to telecommunication policy and regulation (see the background report on Government capacities to ensure high quality regulation, for a general assessment of government downsizing in Japan). First, the number of different functions of the new Ministry of General Affairs will arguably be too large for a single ministry. This could result in delay on key issues, a problem of particular concern in a sector such as telecommunications where technology and services are changing rapidly. Moreover, given the wide range of areas under the responsibility of the ministry, some issues may receive insufficient attention at ministerial level.

Second, it does not seem that the integration of three ministries will facilitate the government's objective of building professional expertise within the Ministry, particularly in light of the fact that, in Japan, ministry personnel are shifted regularly every two years. In addition, rapid market and structural developments require expertise in handling the transition from monopolistic market structures to competition. Third, although the FTC is to implement the AMA independently regardless of the restructuring, the appearance of conflict because the FTC and MPT will be under the same Minister could introduce uncertainty in the market.

The rapidly changing communications market requires communications regulators to respond quickly to changes in order to take full advantage of technological developments and of creative business activities that benefit consumers. For this reason, the regulator needs to be equipped with professional knowledge and mechanisms that ensure timely action. The suggested institutional changes do not take account of this requirement. Therefore, the current restructuring plan should be reconsidered, so as to ensure an institutional structure which can provide an effective regulatory and policy regime for the Japanese communications market.

2.2. Regulations and related policy instruments in the telecommunications sector

2.2.1. Regulation of entry and service provision

Licensing regime

According to the TBL, telecommunications operators are classified as Type 1 telecommunications operators when they establish and operate network infrastructures, and as Type 2 telecommunications operators when they lease infrastructure resources. Type 2 telecommunications operators are further divided into special Type 2 and general Type 2 telecommunications operators (Table 6).

Table 6. **Classification of telecommunications services**

Type of business	Type 1	Special Type 2	General Type 2
Definition	Business that provides telecommunications services by establishing its own telecommunications circuits and facilities	Business that provides voice telephony services for an unspecified number of subscribers through the interconnection of both ends of leased circuits with public switched networks.	Business other than described for special Type 2 telecommunications business
Condition for entry	Permission	Registration	Notification

Source: MPT.

The amendments to the TBL in June 1997 resulted in several important competition-promoting changes in the licensing regime. Previously, the TBL's so-called "supply-demand" provision allowed MPT to prohibit, the entry of new companies if it thought that existing demand in the service areas did not warrant new suppliers. Although MPT still has authority to block market entry through the examination standard which is based on "general public interest" provisions[24] in the TBL (see box 4), the abolition of the "supply-demand" provisions has clearly increased transparency in Japan's licensing procedures. In addition, in June 1998, Japan abolished the so-called "100 destination rules", which prohibited international Type 1 carriers from entering into agreements with foreign carrier to terminate international traffic until a Type 1 carrier had established at least 100 correspondent agreements for its service.

While the abolition of the so-called "supply-demand" provisions has clearly enhanced transparency in the Japanese licensing regime, there is a need to revise regulations on licensing in order to obtain more transparency. MPT uses the examination standards[25] when it determines whether Type 1 business applicants meet the entry requirement standards in the TBL. These examination standards do not provide clear-cut information to applicants on the minimum requirements to receive licenses. In effect, this results in a consultation process whereby new entrants determine whether or not an application, once made, would be approved by MPT. There is a possibility that this unofficial consulting period can cause delays in launching a new business in spite of the standard processing period of 1-2 months guaranteed under the Administrative Law for handling applications. Such a process also tends to reduce transparency further. To avoid such problems, except in the case of spectrum allocation, which requires individual licensing system due to its scarcity, many OECD countries are lowering entry barriers to the telecommunications market. For example, the Netherlands has introduced a class licensing system whereby all applicants that meet clearly stated criteria attain market entry, and Denmark requires no official procedure to enter the market.

In the meantime, considering the large number of carriers in the Type 1 market, it seems that there is no more reason to maintain severe entry restriction in the marketplace.

In addition, Type 1 carrier applicants are required to specify in their application the category of telecommunications services (Table 7) and their proposed service coverage, to supply a business plan, and to provide information on progress on the implementation of the business plan supplied. Type 1 carriers are not allowed to change the category of telecommunications services and service coverage without the permission of the Minister. Thus, to expand network and service coverage from local to long distance services, a company is subject to MPT's approval.

Box 4. **Permission for a standard Type 1 carrier**

- A*dequate* financial basis and technical capability to undertake telecommunications business
- *Reliable* and *feasible* business plan
- Entry into the telecommunications business should be *appropriate* for the sound development of telecommunications

---

333

Table 7.   **Categories of telecommunications services offered by Type 1 carriers**

Type of service	Category
Voice transmission	A telecommunications service other than a data transmission service using telecommunications facilities with switching and transmission functions principally in the 4 Khz band (voice and other sounds); for communications with others
Data transmission	A telecommunications service solely for communicating using telecommunications facilities with switching and transmission functions for data and images; for communications with others
Leased circuit	A telecommunications service that allows a specific (legal or physical) person exclusive use of telecommunications facilities

Note: Type 1 applicants should provide the classification (*e.g.* domestic/international) and the service coverage for each type of service they apply for.
Source: MPT.

Based on the Radio Law, mobile operators with a Type 1 license also need separate licenses in order to launch their services (See Section 2.2.5).

In terms of special Type 2 carriers, even though companies can enter the market through registration, their registration can be refused if the Minister decides that the applicant does not have an adequate financial basis and the technical capability for undertaking a telecommunications business properly. These standards for refusal are very general. As a result, even special Type 2 carriers are subject to MPT's approval in spite of the term "registration" which, in other countries, normally means that companies can enter the market with very few formalities. However, in practice, no application has been rejected so far.

According to MPT, it is necessary to distinguish Type 1 and Type 2 carriers because the former has significant "public interest characteristics". However, the somewhat artificial separation between Type 1 and Type 2 carriers imposes a number of unnecessary burdens on carriers. The need for rights of way and huge up-front investment are the major reasons mentioned by MPT for regulating Type 1 carriers more heavily than Type 2 carriers. However, considering the fact that fragmented rights-of-way regulation restricts Type 1 carriers from accessing public and private lands even after possession of a Type 1 carrier license, and the fact that there are many different Type 1 operators whose initial investments vary significantly, such reasons provide few grounds for maintaining a distinction between Type 1 and Type 2 carriers. Furthermore, there is a possibility that heavy regulation on Type 1 carriers may hamper the development of infrastructure competition by discouraging possible new entrants to the telecommunications infrastructure market.

Because of the strict regulatory distinction between Type 1 and Type 2 business, it is not allowed to route both domestic and international traffic via combinations of owned and leased network facilities. Therefore, a single company cannot undertake both Type 1 and Type 2 business in an integrated way, even if the company holds both a Type 1 and a Type 2 permit. In practice, this causes a company to establish a different firm to provide each of the services. For example, Worldcom Japan has two different legal entities, one for Type 1 services and the other for Type 2 services. The need to establish a different entity to provide another type of service raises a couple of issues. First, it means an additional cost because the company will need to hire an additional chief telecommunications engineer (a requirement for Type 1 and special Type 2 carriers under Article 44 of the TBL). Second, establishing a new entity requires additional paperwork, including administrative and other company reporting requirements. It also disadvantages new entrants, as they often only construct parts of their infrastructure and relies for the remainder on leasing.

Since it is essential for telecommunications operators to use all possible means to provide a wide range of services to meet changing consumer demand, they should be allowed to provide all kinds of services without restrictions. Japan should abandon the current entry scheme and establish a simple and transparent scheme, preferably based on general authorisation, in order to ensure free and fair competition, which is essential to maximise consumer benefits.

Rights of way

According to the TBL, Type 1 carriers are entitled to rights of way to public water and private land. Nonetheless, due to the fragmented regulations on rights of way, new carriers have experienced difficulties in establishing their own networks even after receiving Type 1 carrier licenses. Since there are many laws (*e.g.* the Road Law, the National Asset Law and the Local Autonomy Law) with different jurisdiction over rights of way, carriers are required to receive separate permission from a number of government bodies. The number of government bodies which participated in the study group on rights of way clearly shows how much rights of way regulations are fragmented. In fact, 12 government bodies[26] were participating in the study group on rights of way. New Type 1 entrants have claimed that the current situation gives an unfair advantage to the incumbent and prevents them from infrastructure competition.

Since new entrants face difficulties in constructing new infrastructure, even after they have received Type 1 licenses, regulations on facility sharing (such as sharing of ducts) become even more important for ensuring that new entrants have fair access to end users. If facility sharing is effective, new entrants can construct new networks relatively cheaply and rapidly. According to the TBL, Type 1 carriers and special Type 2 carriers can request arbitration if they fail to reach an agreement for facility sharing. If a party is not satisfied with the result of the arbitration by the Minister, it can file a suit within three months of the decision. In principle, then, any Type 1 or special Type 2 carrier can request facility sharing with NTT and other utility-based Type 1 carriers[27] that own duct systems. In practice, when interconnection occurs at an NTT building, NTT should provide facility sharing for other carriers using NTT's conduits, ducts and poles from the point of interface to the first manhole, according to Article 14 of the "Agreement concerning Interconnection to Designated Telecommunications Facilities". This exception aside, the use of the facilities of NTT and other utility-based Type 1 carriers is subject to commercial negotiation and ultimately to ministerial authorisation.

However, many new entrants have difficulty reaching facility-sharing agreements with NTT and utility-based Type 1 carriers because of no standardised charges[28] and no limit on negotiation periods.[29] Because of these difficulties, some new entrants have argued for mandatory facility sharing, but the counter-argument made is that this would result in "free riding".

In the face of criticism about the fragmented regulations on rights of way, the Japanese government formed a study group under the Ministry of Foreign Affairs. It made a report on present conditions of access to poles, conduits, ducts and rights of way on 25 December 1998. Instead of providing new solutions on the rights-of-way problem, the report suggested improvement of current procedures to ensure timely, non-discriminatory and transparent access to the resources. Since there are so many regulations on rights of way, it is recommended that guidelines be published to access rights of way for new entrants in order to help them acquire the necessary information.

Line-of-business and ownership restrictions

All line-of-business restrictions in the telecommunications market have been removed as a result of the revision of the NTT Law in 1997 and the abolition of the KDD Law in 1998. The legal barrier preventing NTT and KDD from entering each other's market has been lifted. In addition, with the exception of NTT, companies can offer unrestricted telecommunications and CATV services.[30] However, in the case of the new IMT 2000 mobile services, "the basic guideline for introducing the third generation mobile communications systems", announced by MPT in July 1998, imposes line-of-business restrictions on operators who own local telecommunications networks by prohibiting them from providing IMT 2000 services by themselves.

With the exception of NTT, no ownership restrictions remain in the Japanese telecommunications market. As for NTT, foreigners (including foreign governments and their representative, and foreign judicial persons or associations) are not allowed, directly or indirectly, to hold 20% or more of its shares. In addition, the NTT Law mandates that the government must hold one-third or more of total outstanding shares, and NTT has to obtain authorisation from the Minister when it issues new shares, convertible debentures or debentures with pre-emptive rights on new shares. As a matter of principle, it would be better to remove

335

all ownership restrictions on NTT. The strong government ownership of NTT can raise problems of conflict of interest, as the government acts both as a shareholder and a regulator. In the longer term, as competition develops, MPT should abolish the NTT Law and treat NTT like any other company.

2.2.2. *Regulation of interconnection*

The most important regulatory safeguard to ensure fair competition is the establishment of a fair and transparent interconnection framework. Indeed, such a fair and transparent interconnection scheme is vital if there is no alternative local loop to that of the incumbent. Since NTT has a 99.5% market share, as measured by the percentage of access lines in the local market, it is essential for other carriers to inter-connect with NTT's local loop in order to terminate their calls. Thus, access to NTT's local loop is a corner-stone for the promotion of market competition.

According to the TBL, all Type I carriers are obliged to provide interconnection when there is a request from other carriers unless such provision is prevented by technical or significant economic obsta-cles.[31] In addition, carriers are expected to obtain the Minister's authorisation after reaching agreement. Considering that the TBL imposes special obligation on a "designated telecommunications facility" and ensures arbitration procedure when parties do not reach to agreement, such authorisation appears unnecessary. Indeed, many OECD countries regard an interconnection agreement as a purely commercial matter except in those cases where the incumbent is involved as an interested party.

To ensure interconnection to the incumbent's network, the Minister can determine that certain facil-ities of Type I carriers are treated as a "designated telecommunications facility". Such a designation is based on the number of telecommunications lines in each specific prefecture in which fair and transpar-ent interconnection needs to be assured in order to "promote benefits to users and rationally develop telecommunications". If the Minister designates a Type I carrier's facility, the Type I carrier must estab-lish a standard interconnection agreement, which is subject to authorisation by the Minister. A standard interconnection agreement should provide fair, transparent and non-discriminatory terms and conditions with fair cost-oriented rates for interconnection to all carriers.

In practice, NTT's local loop[32] is the only "designated telecommunications facility" in Japan and "NTT's Articles for Interconnection Agreements" for "designated telecommunications facilities" were approved by the Minister as a standard interconnection agreement in March 1998. In its standard inter-connection agreement, NTT provides six standard points of interconnection in its network architecture.[33] In addition, on the basis of the "Basic Rules for Interconnection", NTT provides unbundled network elements[34] to other carriers and charges separately for each. In practice, most interconnection has tradi-tionally been carried out with transit exchanges (ZC), because long-distance carriers had insufficiently developed facilities to set up POIs (points of interface) within the region. Since 1996, local exchange (GC) interconnection has been provided for regional and long distance carriers. This enables companies such as TTNet and Titus to enter the local residential market and to compete directly with NTT.

In order to ensure fair and transparent interconnection, the TBL also requires a Type I carrier with "designated telecommunications facilities" to publish the standard interconnection agreement and to maintain accounting separation relating to interconnection with "designated telecommunications facili-ties". In addition, the TBL requires an annual recalculation of interconnection charges based on the accounting result of the "designated telecommunications facilities".

A substitute for interconnection is the "consignment of business activities", which is based on an agreement between parties to handle their traffic. The major difference between interconnection and "consignment of business activities" is that in case of the latter carriers are not able to ask for arbitration when they cannot reach an agreement. Business practice has led some carriers to use "consignment of business activities" rather than interconnection; for example, international carriers are entering into "con-signment of business activities" with NTT DoCoMo in order to terminate incoming international phone calls. However, it seems that this "consignment of business activities" will soon be substituted by an interconnection agreement, because there is no incentive for international carriers to maintain "consignment of business activities" that do not provide the possibility to request arbitration.

Since 1994, the price of NTT's access charges has dropped significantly (Table 8). For example, from 1994 to 1998, charges for tandem switch interconnection have been reduced by 40%. In addition, a per second charge scheme was introduced in 1996.

Table 8.   **NTT's interconnection charge**

Type	FY 1998	FY 1997	Percentage change
GC connection: local exchange (telephone)	0.99 /call	0.99/call	0.0%
	0.0268/sec.	0.0289/sec.	−7.2%
	5.81/3minutes.	6.19/3minutes	−6.1%
ZC connection: transit exchange (telephone)	1.27/call	1.28/call	−0.8%
	0.0595/sec.	0.0647/sec.	−8.0%
	11.98/3 minutes	12.93/3minutes	−7.3%
GC connection: local exchange (ISDN)	2.31/call	3.38/ call	−31.6%
	0.052/sec.	0.086/sec.	−39.5%
	11.67/3 minutes	18.86/3 minutes	−38.1%
ZC connection: transit exchange (ISDN)	2.59/call	3.67/call	−29.4%
	0.0847/sec.	0.1218/sec.	−30.5%
	17.84/3 minutes	25.59/3 minutes	−30.3%

Note: The charge for three minutes is the charge that would be levied under a three-minute charging system and differs from the actual cost for a three-minute call. The three-minute charge system was introduced in fiscal 1996. Under this system a three-minute period is counted as a charge unit.
Source: MPT News, March 1998.

However, NTT's interconnection charge is still relatively high compared with other major carriers in the OECD region (Figure 3). Indeed, foreign trading partners, such as the European Union and the United States have raised high interconnection charges as a trade issue, arguing that high interconnection charges are a *de facto* market barrier that prevents foreign carriers from entering the Japanese market. In this regard, both the European Union and the United States have urged that Japan introduce an interconnection framework based on LRIC methodology, using forward-looking rather than historical costs. Currently, Japan is using an activity based cost accounting (ABC) system, essentially based on NTT's historical costs.[35] In its joint (with the United States) status report on deregulation, Japan announced that it would submit a bill to the Diet in 2000 in order to introduce the long-run incremental cost accounting (LRIC) methodology. It is recommended that efforts should be made to accelerate the implementation of LRIC to ensure more cost-oriented interconnection charges as soon as possible.

In principle, NTT's interconnection charges on "designated telecommunications facilities" are composed of access charges[36] and network modification charges[37] and both charges are standardised by "NTT's Articles for Interconnection Agreement". Therefore, carriers can access NTT's "designated telecommunications facilities" without the need for individual negotiations. However, charges on some unbundled elements are unreasonably high and need to be revised. For instance, despite the fact that NTT charges 50 to 120 yen per directory services inquiry to its customers, it charges new entrants 191 yen at the wholesale level. This implies either that the wholesale charges are much higher than costs or that NTT cross-subsidises its directory services from its other services. In any cases, this price structure virtually prevents new entrants from providing competitive service. Therefore, NTT's high prices for its unbundled elements should be adjusted in order to ensure fair competition in all possible service areas.

Another very important interconnection issue is the coverage of a "designated telecommunications facility". Currently, only NTT's local loop is a "designated telecommunications facility". However, considering the very fast growth rate for mobile services and the increasing percentage of calls between mobile and fixed telephones in Japan, MPT should consider designating NTT DoCoMo's network as a "designated telecommunications facility".

Figure 3. **Comparison of interconnection charges for call termination (as of July 1998)**

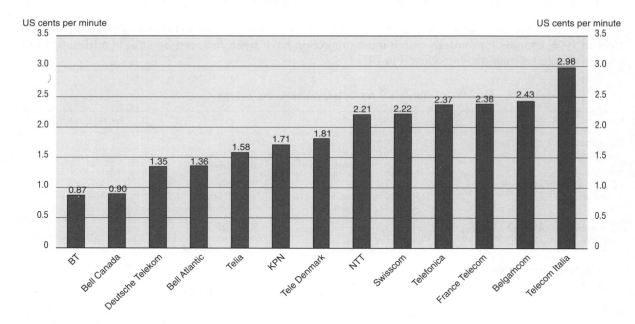

Note: NTT reduced its interconnection charges to 2.07 cents per minute following MPT's approval on 22 January 1999, which retroactively set new interconnection charges from April 1998.
Source: Ovum.

2.2.3. Pricing policy

In spite of its long history of telecommunication liberalisation, Japan's telecommunications prices have been high compared with those of other OECD countries (see Section 3.2), mainly because of the use of a tariff approval scheme for all Type 1 carriers' services until November 1998. Traditionally, NTT's local service charges were set well below cost, and NTT has used long distance service to subsidise losses on local service. This has meant that NTT's long-distance charges were much higher than costs. On the other hand, the prices charged by NCCs for their services had been set at a lower level compared to those of NTT and KDD. (See Figure 4 in Section 3.2.1.)

This process has favoured the NCCs by allowing them higher than normal profits that they could enjoy under the full price competition. Users, as a result, have not benefited from the full effects of competition. More price competition would have led to a faster decline in prices in long distance markets (and in other markets as well). A severe weakness of Japan's regulatory framework between 1985 and 1998 has been its inability to allow consumers to reap the full benefit of potential price competition.

As of 1 November 1998, while an approval system has been maintained for local basic telecommunications services, a price notification system is in place. According to the TBL, the Minister will determine whether a specific service is subject to price-cap regulation or the notification system. In practice, only NTT's local basic service will be subject to price-cap regulation. Such price-cap regulation is expected to be implemented after NTT's reorganisation. Until then NTT's local basic service charges are still subject to MPT's approval. All other service prices, including NTT's long distance service prices, will no longer need approval from the Minister. While no pricing regulation is imposed on general Type 2 carriers, special Type 2 carriers are required to submit prices for their services to the Minister before providing those services.

These changes are a significant development on the way to full-fledged competition in which Type 1 carriers can engage in full price competition in the retail market without MPT's supervision. It is expected that the abolition of the approval system will increase benefits to subscribers, both business and residential, by way of more intense price competition among Type 1 carriers. More importantly the change in the form of price regulation may be a turning point in Japan's move toward full-fledged competition. In addition, introducing a notification system and a price cap is a significant step in the right direction to ensure cost-based pricing in the marketplace.

As a result of recent changes, and even before the notification system was adopted, companies such as TTNet reduced local voice telephony prices to 9 yen for three minutes (the first time for over a decade that the local call charge has dropped below 10 yen) and acquired 1.4 million subscribers in only six months after launching its business in January 1998. To what extent the elimination of the price approval system will lead to significant price competition remains to be seen, but many market analysts are expecting significant changes.

While the decision to abolish the tariff approval system is highly commendable, the present regulatory structure still has some problems. First of all, the Minister still has authority to decide whether a specific service is subject to the notification system or price-cap regulation and can alter previous decisions at will. Second, under the new system, MPT still reserves the power to order carriers to revise their charges in certain cases, such as unfair discrimination and anti-competitive pricing. This, in turn, raises the issue of regulatory overlap between the MPT and the FTC, because unfair discrimination and anti-competitive pricing behaviour are in violation of the AMA. Moreover, under the new framework, users and carriers can file complaints and petitions to MPT regarding telecommunications service prices, other conditions, terms of service and their manner of operations. Thus, MPT's power to require price revision can constrict carriers in terms of price flexibility and impose a burdensome process to justify price changes.

In addition, on the basis of the AMA, regulations on anti-competitive behaviour should be undertaken on a more consistent basis across industries. If there is any need to increase capacity to deal with anti-competitive issues such as price fixing and predatory pricing in the telecommunications market, the solution should be to increase the regulatory capability of the FTC rather than to give new regulatory powers to the MPT.

For mobile services, a tariff notification system was introduced in December 1996. Consumers of mobile services have benefited from full-fledged competition. For example, following the introduction of the tariff notification system, NTT DoCoMo eliminated the connection fee (previously 6 000 yen), and reduced monthly subscription charges from 6 800 yen to 4 600 yen and three-minute call charges from 180 yen to 100 yen for digital cellular service. As a result of price competition, the number of mobile customers in Japan increased from 20.9 million in 1996 to 38.3 million by the end of 1997.

In Japan, unlike many other OECD countries, the incumbent is not required to charge uniform tariffs. Since Japan's universal service obligation covers only voice telephony services and does not require the application of a uniform tariff, NTT can differentiate its local service charges across regions if it obtains authorisation from the Minister. In fact, NTT's monthly subscription charges differ on the basis of the total number of access lines in a message area (Table 9). Allowing further geographical re-balancing will prevent a "cream-skimming" effect and will lead to more cost-oriented prices.

Table 9. **NTT's monthly subscription charges**

	400 000 or more access lines	50 000-399 000 access lines	Less than 50 000 access lines
Business	2 600	2 450	2 300
Residential	1 750	1 600	1 450

Source: InfoCom Research Inc., "Information and Communications in Japan 1997".

2.2.4. *Quality of service*

Although there are no regulations to ensure quality of service in telecommunications, Japan has in general performed well in this area. For example, in terms of faults per 100 lines per year Japan averaged 1.7 (end of 1995) compared to 5.5 for the United States during the same period.[38] As well, since 1992, waiting time for a new connection has been one day or less. In addition, NTT began nation-wide caller identification service in February 1998. To some extent, where price competition does not occur fully, companies use quality of service as a competitive tool. It would, however, be useful to users if carriers were required to publish regularly quality of service data on a comprehensive basis.

In Japan, there is no official institution with the authority to resolve disputes between carriers and consumers. Although 'the Telecommunications Consumer Affairs Office' of MPT is open for complaints on telecommunications services from consumers, it does not have the authority to resolve disputes between carriers and consumers. Considering the fact that consumers do not have the ability to compare many different carriers' quality of service, carriers should be required to publish the number of complaints and results of the resolution of those complaints.

2.2.5. *Resource issues*

Spectrum allocation

A mobile carrier needs two licenses to undertake its business: one for a Type I license based on the TBL and the other a license to establish a radio station based on the Radio Law.[39] According to the Radio Law, spectrum is allocated by first come first served basis. However, neither law has provisions on how to select licensees when there are many applicants for a limited number of potential licenses. In other words, no specific spectrum allocation method (*e.g.* auction or competitive test) has been in place in order to select mobile licensees when the number of applicants outnumbers the number of licences available.

The lack of an objective selection procedure for spectrum allocation has led to the practice of collective bargaining to formulate consortiums among possible applicants for spectrum acquisition. In reality, applications for spectrum have not outnumbered the number of licensees decided by MPT. Large companies have obviously benefited from this non-transparent procedure, because the TBL requires an "adequate financial basis" as one of the requirements for market entry. Furthermore, licensees have acquired spectrum without paying a fee. Thus, the companies that have been granted mobile licenses have enjoyed not only new business opportunities but also financial benefits.

Although *Keidanren* has recommended that an auction method[40] should be introduced so as to ensure more transparent and fairer spectrum allocation, the study group formed by MPT has argued that the adoption of an auction system may cause financial difficulties for mobile companies, hamper R&D ability, lower consumer benefits, and result in dominance by large companies.

The lack of a transparent and fair method to select licensees when applicants outnumber licences is a significant weakness of the Japanese telecommunications regulatory regime since it does not provide clear guidance for potential entrants on how to prepare to acquire a mobile license. According to MPT's spectrum allocation plan for IMT 2000,[41] if there are more applicants than the number of licenses available, MPT may select licensees by comparing aspects of individual applications or using a frequency auction method. It also points out that if an auction is introduced, it may take a reasonable time to prepare an appropriate regulatory framework. Although this shows that MPT is giving due consideration to establishing a new spectrum allocation method, it has not been decided which method would be introduced. Considering the rapid growth of mobile services in Japan and the need to allocate new spectrum for IMT 2000 services, it is vital that a transparent and fair spectrum allocation system be established as rapidly as possible.

Numbering issues

The accelerated development and modernisation of telecommunications infrastructure competition and the increasing number of new facility-based carriers in Japan have highlighted the importance of tele-communications numbering policy. In recognising the importance of numbering policy, MPT added relevant provisions for telecommunications numbers in the TBL when it was revised in 1997, in order to ensure fair and efficient use of number resources.

As in many other countries, "number portability"[42] is now recognised in Japan as an essential feature of a competitive telecommunications market. In a competitive market, telephone subscribers must be permitted to change telephone service providers without changing numbers, *i.e.* without taking on a new network identity. Recognising the importance of number portability, the Council recommended in its report, "Basic rules on interconnection", that it should be implemented as soon as possible and proposed FY 2000 as a target year for implementation. Based on the Council's proposal, MPT set up a "study group for the realisation methods of number portability" in August 1997. The study group has proposed the realisation method of number portability for fixed voice telephony service, ISDN and free-phone services.

Despite the lengthy period of study of number portability, MPT has not yet announced a concrete plan for implementation. This raises the question of whether implementation will be feasible in FY 2000. Considering the fact that NTT has virtually a 100% market share in local loop competition, number portability is essential for new entrants if they are to attract customers without imposing unnecessary costs or inconvenience. Since the implementation of number portability may take some time because of the need for technical changes once the plan is finalised, MPT should decide a concrete action plan to implement it rapidly. In addition, considering the rapid growth of mobile services in Japan, it is recommended to consider including mobile services in the number portability plan as well as geographic mobility where possible, as is being done in Denmark, the Netherlands and the United Kingdom in favour of the convenience of users.

Another important numbering issue is equal access to customers. Since carrier pre-selection has not been implemented yet, 13 years after competition was introduced, NCCs face unequal competitive conditions, which require customers to use additional prefix numbers to access NCC services. The "study group on dialling parity" submitted a report[43] on the implementation of carrier pre-selection in November 1998, which proposed to introduce carrier pre selection by the spring of 2001. Based on the report, it is planned that MPT will prepare legislation in April 1999, which is scheduled to come into force from 31 December 2000.

Perhaps the most significant factor hindering quick implementation of carrier pre-selection in Japan is the diversity of opinion among new carriers. While new entrants to the international market, such as Worldcom Japan, strongly support carrier pre-selection, many early NCCs are not enthusiastic. In spite of the four-digit carrier identification code (whereas KDD has only a three-digit code), the early international NCCs are opposed to a carrier pre-selection system because they have already invested heavily in advertising their current identification codes as a brand name, and have built up market share using the current system (Table 10).

Table 10.   **Carrier identification codes for international service**

	KDD	JT	IDC
Identification code	001	0041	0061

Source: MPT.

In terms of the national long-distance market, the original NCCs use LCR chips in their terminal equipment. Today, almost all telephone terminals sold in Japan have LCRs, except those sold by NTT shops. The original NCCs give commissions to retailers who sell telephones with their LCR chip, which enables subscribers to bypass the carrier identification code (Table 11) when using national long distance services. In addition to commissions to retailers, NCCs subsidise telephone terminal manufacturers who make terminal equipment with their LCR chips. Because NCCs have invested significantly in terminal equipment with LCR chips, they are also opposed to carrier pre-selection. NCCs insist that LCR chips should be allowed even if carrier pre-selection is introduced so as to protect consumers who already own terminal equipment with LCR chips. On the other hand, new entrants argue that the removal of LCR chips is essential to ensure fair access to customers. The interim report on the "study group on dialling parity" supported the position of the early NCCs.

Table 11.   **Carrier identification codes for national long distance service**

	NTT	DDI	JT	KDD
Identification code	None	0077	0088	0070

Source: MPT.

Given the various interests involved, MPT has not decided how many choices will be given to consumers, while it has proposed the date for implementation. As the incumbents (NTT and KDD) enjoy an advantage owing to the delay in implementing carrier pre-selection, MPT should promptly establish a concrete plan to introduce it. In addition, the carrier pre-selection mechanism should be decided so as to ensure fair competition between new entrants and current players (the incumbents and the early NCCs).

2.2.6. *Universal service obligation*

In Japan, the NTT Law specifies universal service as an obligation of NTT. According to Article 2 of the law, NTT should ensure appropriate, fair and stable provision of nation-wide telephone services, and these should be provided *impartially*. As a result, only NTT's fixed voice telephony service is regulated as a universal service. While the word "impartially" seems to suggest uniform tariffs nation-wide, NTT monthly subscription charges are different over regions based on the number of total access lines in a message area (See Table 9 in Section 2.2.3).

Compared with some other OECD countries,[44] universal service in Japan is limited, as it is focused on voice telephony. Because the funding of a broadly defined universal service requirement through levies on the telecommunications industry can reduce efficiency and undermine other policy goals, a limited universal service obligation helps to minimise any unnecessary economic burden on telecommunications operators. However, the report[45] from the study group for "Research into Universal Services and Rates in the Multimedia Age" recommended an expansion of the scope of universal service in order to avoid the development of a society of information "haves" and "have nots". If expanding the scope of universal service is deemed essential to meet this policy objective, it should be funded through general government revenues rather than license obligations or other forms of intervention in the telecommunications industry.

Currently, there is no funding mechanism for the provision of universal service, so NTT alone bears the burden of providing universal service. NTT has traditionally financed universal service through cross-subsidisation from low-cost to high-cost areas, or from long distance to local calls. As competition develops, it is increasingly difficult for NTT to use cross-subsidisation to provide universal service. Thus, the question of how to finance universal service is becoming a more important issue in Japan. There are two different opinions among carriers on whether to establish a funding mechanism for universal service. NTT argues that it is necessary to establish a mechanism to share the cost of universal service after its reorganisation since NTT East and NTT West will no longer be cross-subsidised by long distance services. On the other hand, companies such as KDD argue that establishing a universal service fund will prevent local markets from becoming more competitive and reduce incentives for NTT to increase its efficiency.

Any universal service funding mechanism[46] should be transparent and competition and technology neutral. It should also be held separate from interconnection payments. Some operators argue that since NTT interconnection charges are high, and not cost-based, they are obliged, under the current interconnection scheme, to subsidise part of the cost of universal service. When the LRIC methodology is introduced in 2001, interconnection charges should become cost-based. A universal service funding mechanism will then be needed to remove any unfair economic burden on NTT local companies.

2.2.7. International aspects

Japan's commitments in the context of the February 1997 WTO agreement on basic telecommunication services included national treatment of foreign companies (except for the 20% foreign ownership restriction on NTT and KDD (Table 12). Based on Japan's WTO commitment, MCI WorldCom Japan, became the first 100% foreign-owned entity to obtain Type 1 approval in March 1998. BT Communications Services also obtained a Type 1 license in July 1998. As of February 1999, there are six 100% foreign owned Type 1 carriers and 31 Special Type 2 carriers.

Table 12. **Japan's commitment to the WTO agreement on basic telecommunications services**

Range of services opened	Timing of liberalisation	Commitment to common set of regulatory principles	Foreign ownership restriction	Most favoured nation exemption
Full	As of enforcement of WTO agreement (5 February 1998)	Full	None except for NTT and KDD (less than 20%)	No

Note: The foreign ownership restriction on KDD was lifted after abolition of KDD Law.
Source: WTO.

In Japan's WTO schedule, there are two issues, which differ from those of other countries. First, unlike other signatory countries, which impose interconnection obligations on major carriers based on market power, Japan imposes interconnection obligations only on a major operator with control over essential facilities. This implies that Japan is not obliged to impose special interconnection obligation, which applies to a "designated telecommunications facility" such as NTT's local loop, on NTT DoCoMo or KDD, even though they have market power in their market segments. Second, the independence[47] of MPT can be put in jeopardy since the Japanese government owns a majority share of NTT. While MPT argues that NTT shares belong to the Ministry of Finance and not MPT, there is a possibility of a potential conflict of interest, since the government is at the same time an owner of NTT and a regulator of the telecommunication sector (both MPT and the Ministry of Finance are under the responsibility of the Prime Minister).

Trading partners like the United States and the European Commission complain that the Japanese regulatory framework is not transparent and prevents foreign companies from entering into fair competition. The background report on Enhancing market openness through regulatory reform analysed a number of concerns that Japan's trading partners have raised about the Japanese regulatory framework in the telecommunications sector. MPT has made significant changes to address concerns of foreign firms in particular. For example, along with lifting foreign ownership restriction on Type 1 carriers and KDD, the "100 destination rule" was abolished, and international simple resale has been also liberalised since the end of 1997.

Box 5. **Liberalisation policies in international telecommunication service**

Feb. 1996   Interconnection through a third country's switched transit is allowed
Dec. 1997   International simple resale is allowed
Feb. 1998   Elimination of foreign capital restrictions on Type 1 carriers (except NTT)
June 1998   Elimination of "100 destination rule"

As mentioned in the background report on Enhancing market openness through regulatory reform, major issues raised by the United States and the European Union relate to the licensing scheme, the interconnection charges framework, rights of way, scope of universal service, number portability, etc. Indeed, the issues cover virtually all the major regulatory safeguards in the telecommunications sector. Although Japan has no legal obligation to respond to demands from foreign trading partners, it has acceded to some requests such as the introduction of LRIC system in order to ease tensions with its trading partners. It needs, however, to be recognised that similar types of complaints, covering the same issues, are being made on a number of European Union member countries and the United States.

2.2.8. *Streamlining regulation and application of principles of competition*

The TBL has no specific provisions on regulatory forbearance, except as it relates to price regulation. Under the TBL, the Minister can decide whether a specific service is subject to price-cap regulation or the tariff notification system. As a matter of principle, as markets become more competitive, it will be necessary to reduce sector-specific regulation. Although it is very difficult to determine when there is sufficient self-sustaining competition, the decision to reduce sector-specific regulation should depend on the state of market competition rather than on general public interest criteria. In this regard, MPT should take into account the level of competition when determining which services will be subject to the tariff notification system.

In Japan, the AMA applies to the telecommunications sector. There are no exemptions. Therefore, the FTC can regulate any business activity that is in violation of the AMA. Since both the TBL and the AMA apply to the telecommunications sector, MPT and the FTC share, in principle, regulatory power in this industry. However, the FTC has sole responsibility for enforcing the AMA, while economic and technical regulations are implemented exclusively by MPT.

There are specific areas, such as price regulation and mergers, where both the MPT and the FTC have regulatory power. Regarding price regulation, the MPT has the authority to decide whether specific services are subject to the notification or to the approval system. When it is decided that a specific service (*i.e.* NTT local service) is to be subject to approval by the Minister, the Minister has the authority to impose price regulation on this service. On the other hand, under the AMA, the FTC has authority to regulate all forms of price-fixing activities and predatory pricing behaviour. Nonetheless, the FTC has never exercised its regulatory power on telecommunications pricing activities that have received approval from the MPT.

In the case of mergers between Type I carriers or a Type I carrier and other companies, both MPT and the FTC have independent regulatory powers under the TBL and the AMA. Article 16 of the TBL states that no transfer or take-over of the whole of a Type I telecommunications business shall take place unless it is authorised by MPT. While the FTC's decision on a merger case is based on whether there will be a substantial restraint on competition, MPT's decision is based on the same standards that apply to Type I license applicants. Since there are neither a formal consultation procedure between MPT and the FTC nor any concurrent jurisdiction requirements regarding merger decisions, each can block a merger with its own regulatory power. In the merger between KDD and Teleway Japan, the MPT and the FTC did not consult or share information. As a matter of principle, sharing information would help both bodies by allowing them to have a more comprehensive view of merger cases. In this regard, it is recommended that an information-sharing mechanism between the two bodies be established in order to increase the ability to deal with merger cases.

Until now, except for a very few FTC decisions[48] on mobile operators' anti-competitive behaviour such as fixing mobile phone handset prices, the FTC's involvement in the telecommunication sector has been extremely limited. However, as competition develops, the role of competition law in the telecommunications market should be strengthened and unnecessary sector specific regulation needs to be lifted by the regular review on sector specific regulation.[49] The effectiveness of forbearance reviews will be increased if interested parties such as carriers can have a right to request streamlining of specific regulations.

2.3. The dynamic view: convergence in communications markets

The rapid convergence-taking place between broadcasting, content and communications technology and services is bringing into focus the need for "next generation regulation". For regulators, the trend in technological and service convergence requires looking beyond current telecommunication regulatory frameworks to consider how to facilitate the process of convergence, maximise the benefits of competition among traditionally different sectors and ensure that their economies benefit from convergence through the development of new services, such as electronic commerce. Japan has an institutional advantage in meeting these challenges, since MPT is responsible for both telecommunications and broadcasting (and indirectly for content, since illegal and harmful content is managed through broadcasting licensing requirements) (Table 13).

Table 13. **Comparison of the regulatory frameworks of telecommunications and broadcasting**

	Telecommunications	Broadcasting
Regulatory regime	Telecommunications Business Law Radio Law NTT Law	Broadcast Law CATV Broadcast Law
Market entry	Permission: Type 1 Registration: special Type 2 Notification: general Type 2	Individual licensing: Broadcasting Permission: CATV
Regulatory institutions	MPT	MPT

Source: MPT.

MPT has made efforts to accelerate the process of convergence by allowing CATV operators to provide telecommunications services and lifting foreign ownership restrictions on CATV operators who have Type 1carrier licenses. In addition, "the study group for discussion on convergence and development of telecommunication and broadcasting" made a report on the policy issues of convergence in May 1998.

However, Japan, like most OECD countries, has maintained strong service-specific regulation in both markets and maintains a different regulatory framework for telecommunications and broadcasting. With the convergence of the two communications technologies and services, it will become increasingly difficult to designate individual operators and even services as falling into different service categories. The fragmented regulatory framework that presently exists in many OECD countries, which sharply distinguishes telecommunications and broadcasting, may hamper the future development of the communications sector. As for many OECD countries, a challenge for Japan will be to amend its regulations in order to take full advantage of the benefits flowing from convergence.

3. PERFORMANCE OF THE TELECOMMUNICATIONS INDUSTRY

3.1. Competition analysis

In order to promote fair market competition, all necessary regulatory safeguards should be in place so that new entrants have a level playing field with respect to firms with market power While many regulatory developments has been made in recent years, some essential regulatory safeguards such as forward looking interconnection accounting method, number portability, carrier pre-selection, spectrum allocation method for a limited number of licences, and universal service funding mechanism, are still not in place. As a result, in spite of quite a large number of market players, users have not benefited from competition as much as might be expected or compared with those of other OECD countries that liberalised their telecommunications market early such as the Untied States and the United Kingdom (see Section 3.2).

345

This regulatory problem should be kept in mind when assessing the level of competition in each telecommunication market segment.

In the fixed voice telephony market, the developments of the last several years would indicate that there has been good progress in the level of competition in the long distance and international markets. In particular, as of December 1997, 88 companies, including AT&T, provided call-back services in Japan. In addition to the current, relatively sound, market share of new common carriers in both markets (Tables 14 and 15), cross-entry by NTT and KDD into each other's market is expected to increase competition. Furthermore, new entrants such as WorldCom Japan and BT view these market segments as their strategic markets, so that competition will be strong.

Table 14. **National long distance market shares of new operators**
Share of switched minutes – per cent

	1984	1985	1986	1987	1988	1989	1990	1991	1992	1993	1994	1995	1996	1997
Australia								0	0.5	2	7.6	11.7		17.9
Canada							0	5	7	14	18			
Denmark													0	5
Finland										0	50	60	59	59
Japan[1]			0	3	6	10	15.9	22.4	26.8	29.1	31.3	31.9	35.7	40.6
Korea													9	8
Mexico													0	18.8
New Zealand								0	12	18	19	21	22	25
Sweden											0	5	10	17
United Kingdom		0	2	4	6	7	8	9	10.7	14	16.5	18.6	21	24
United States	19.8	20.2	23.2	28	31.5	35.1	37.4	37.8	39.5	39.8	41.5	44.5	47.8	48.6

1. Data for Japan are the combined share of NCCs inter-prefecture traffic as measured by number of calls.
Source: *Communications Outlook* 1999, OECD.

Table 15. **International market share of new market entrants**
Share of minutes of international traffic – per cent

	1986	1987	1988	1989	1990	1991	1992	1993	1994	1995	1996	1997
Australia						0	4.4	13	21	27.8	38	45
Canada[1]							0	7	20	37	43	44
Denmark										0	7.5	25
Finland								0	9	27	34	39
Ireland											0	9
Korea						0	20.1	25.5	31.3	27.4	26.5	32
Japan		0	3.1	6.7	18.3	26.7	30.4	33.1	33.7	33.8	35.1	40.6
Mexico											0	31.6
Netherlands											0	5
New Zealand					0	11	15	17.4	21	21	21.8	36
Sweden							0	7.4	15	21	25	32
United Kingdom	0	0.2	1.5	4.5	9	14	22.3	26.3	30.5	30.3	40	51
United States	5.7	7	10.9	16.7	21.6	25.2	29.7	37.8	41	44.2	50.1	54.7

1. Canada-United States route only.
Source: OECD, *Communications Outlook* 1999.

On the other hand, in the local-fixed voice telephony market, NTT's dominance can be expected to continue for some time. In most OECD countries, incumbents have strong market power in the local market even after liberalisation of the telecommunications market and Japan is no exception. As discussed before, NTT holds virtually a 100% market share in the local market. However, there are some signs of greater competition in this segment. For example, since January 1998, TTNet has successfully entered the residential voice telephony service market by providing telephone relay services linked to NTT's local exchange. A couple of cable companies also provide voice telephony services using their CATV networks. NTT will also face more competition from utility-based Type 1 carriers.

The mobile sector already has intense competition in Japan. There are five or six mobile operators in each market block. NTT DoCoMo has a dominant position (57% market share as of March 1998) in the lucrative cellular market, and DDI Pocket is the largest player in the PHS market. Mobile competition is already leading to structural change resulting, as mentioned previously, in the merger of PHS services and cellular mobile service companies. In addition, companies such as DDI Pocket are targeting data communication users to expand business opportunities and to try to reverse the flow of subscribers to cellular services. The adoption of the IMT 2000 standard in 2001 should intensify competition in this market segment.

Many major players like NTT, KDD and DDI aim to provide "one-stop shopping" for all telecommunications services to their customers. For instance, in October 1997, NTT established a subsidiary Type 1 international company, NTT Worldwide Network Corporation, in order to prepare for full-scale entry into the international service market after its reorganisation. In addition, NTT launched its "Arcstar" service that offers seamless, end-to-end international services to meet demand from multinational companies. In the longer term the provision of "one-stop shopping" will give customers more choice of telecommunications services.

The presence of major global telecommunications players in Japan will help to promote healthy and high-quality competition. Although entry into the Type 1 market had been restricted for a long time, many major global players are already in the Japanese market as investors in Type 1 carriers or as owner of Type 2 carriers. Besides MCI WorldCom Japan and BT which provides services as a Type 1 carrier, AT&T, C&W, Deutsche Telekom, Telstra, and many other international carriers have a presence in the Japanese telecommunications market. The elimination of the foreign ownership restriction on Type 1 licenses will increase the number of foreign carriers in the Type 1 market.

In summary, Japan has a very healthy competitive environment in terms of numbers and quality of players. The level of market competition will increase with the elimination of line-of-business and foreign ownership restrictions. Nonetheless, lacking some essential regulatory safeguard prevents Japanese consumers and telecommunications companies from taking full advantage of the benefits of competition.

3.2. International performance comparisons

3.2.1. *Price*

Among the many available performance indicators, price is arguably the most important in evaluating the success of liberalisation for users. According to MPT's "1998 White Paper Communications in Japan", in contrast to an average price rise of 4.7% in Japanese industry as a whole between 1990 and 1996, the telecommunications sector delivered reduced prices to consumers by an average 16.1%. The ripple effect is estimated to have accounted for a 0.39% fall in prices charged by industry as a whole, greater than the 0.32% due to lower charges in the gas and electricity industries and far outstripping the 0.09% contribution of the transport sector.

Since NTT's usage charges (10 yen for three minutes) for local fixed voice telephony service have not changed for decades, most reductions have occurred in national long distance and international fixed voice telephony services. The drop in long distance call charges between Tokyo and Osaka is often mentioned as an example of rapid rate reduction in Japan; it declined by 77.5% from 400 yen to 90 yen between April 1985 and February 1998.

Nevertheless, the benefits of competition have not been fully felt owing to heavy price regulation which was just removed in November 1998. Arguably, the benefits of competition can be most effectively compared across countries through changes in long distance call charges, since there has been no serious competition in the local market in most countries, and international call charges can be significantly affected by the calling pattern (i.e. the location of a country). Figure 4 shows long distance call charges over time in Japan and Figure 5 compares Japan's long distance charges with those of selected OECD countries. As Figure 4 indicates, all NCCs in the long distance market have had the same tariff structure (this is also true of the international market), and NTT's price and the NCCs' prices have been adjusted almost simultaneously under the tariff approval system.

Figure 4. **Rate reductions for long distance call charges**

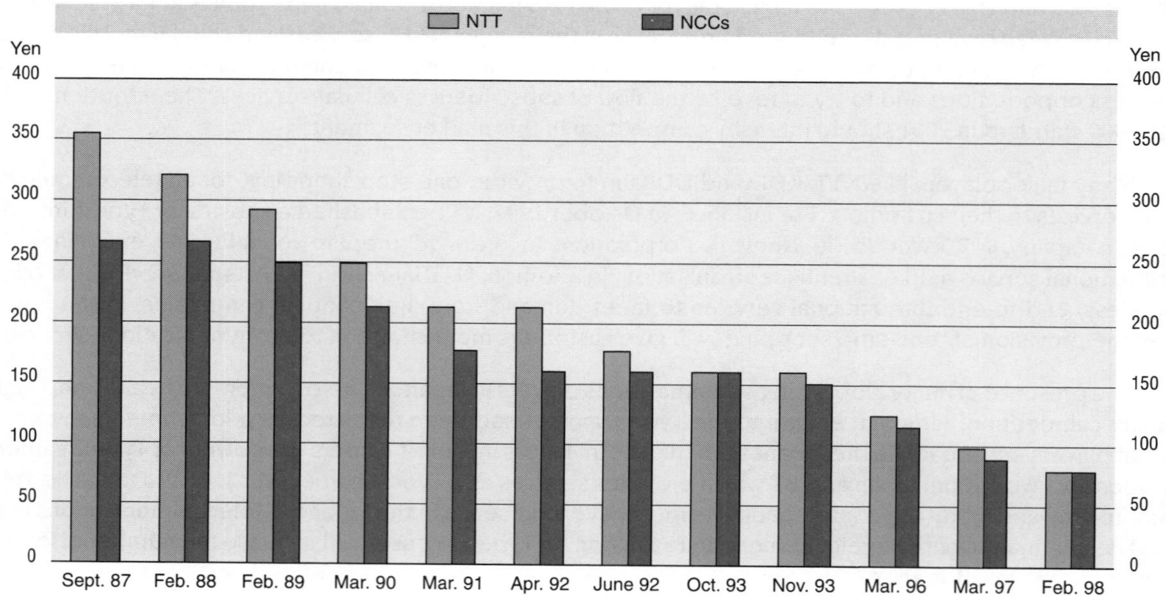

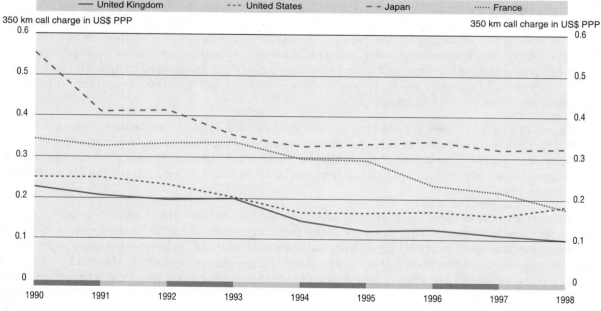

Note: A weekday, daytime, three-minute call for the maximum call distance. (Over 160 km for NTT and over 170 km for NCCs since March 1991. Previously, over 320 km for NTT and over 340 km for NCCs).
Source: 1998 NTT Annual Report, *Information and Communications in Japan 1997,* InfoCom Research Inc.

Figure 5. **Comparison of long distance call charges**

Note: Price of one minute, based on 4.5 minute call.
Source: OECD and EURODATA.

In spite of the massive price reductions in long distance call charges in Japan, Figure 5 shows that even France, which introduced competition only in 1998, has performed better than Japan over the period.

In terms of mobile services, current OECD comparative data are for analogue prices and are not appropriate to explain changes in cellular mobile tariffs in Japan. Since 1994, Japan has introduced digital mobile services and prices have been much lower than those for analogue services (Table16).

Table 16. **Comparison of mobile price charges in Japan**

	Analogue	Digital
Monthly subscription charge	6 600 yen	4 600 yen
Call charge (3 minutes)	150 yen	100 yen

Note: NTT DoCoMo's cellular phone rate (daytime during weekdays, intra-prefecture rates) as of February 1999.
Source: MPT.

In fact, there has been a series of price cuts in mobile services since the introduction of the tariff notification system in December 1996. From December 1996 to February 1999, in addition to the elimination of subscription charge, NTT DoCoMo has reduced its monthly subscription charges by about 32% (from 6 800 yen to 4 600 yen) and three-minute call charges by more than 44% (from 180 yen to 100 yen) for its digital cellular service. Other mobile carriers have also reduced their charges significantly during this period.

The mobile market shows the benefits that can be reaped from full price competition; changing price regulation for fixed voice telephony services may result in changes similar to those in cellular mobile prices.

3.2.2. Other indicators

As discussed in Section 2.2.4, the quality of Japan's telecommunications service is among the highest in the OECD. Carriers have invested significantly to upgrade their networks and adopt new technologies. In FY 1997, total investments by Type 1 carriers reached 4.2 trillion yen, representing over 9% of total investment (46.5 trillion yen) by all industries in Japan. As a result, much progress has been made in the telecommunications sector. For example, in 1993, only 72% of mainlines were digital; by 1997, 100% were digital (Table 17).

Table 17. **Digitalisation of fixed network**

	1993	1995	1997
Japan	72	90	100
United Kingdom	75	88	100
United States	82	90	94.5
OECD average	69.25	81.65	89.22

Source: OECD, Communications Outlook 1999.

In line with technological developments, many new services and discount schemes have been introduced since competition began in 1985. It is expected that this trend will be strengthened by the introduction of the tariff notification system in all telecommunications services. Between 1975 and 1985, there were only 13 new services and discount schemes, but since 1985 there have been 88 in all.

349

Figure 6. **The number of new services and discount services started in each fiscal year**

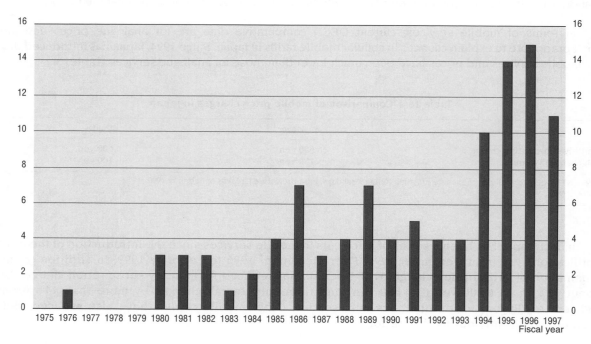

Note: For FY 1997, data from April to August 1996.
Source: MPT.

4. CONCLUSIONS AND RECOMMENDATIONS

4.1. General assessment of current strengths and weaknesses

Box 6. **Strengths**

- strength and high quality of new common carriers.
- No line-of-business restrictions.
- Fast development of alternative infrastructure.
- Recent acceleration of liberalisation efforts towards full fledged competition.

Japan has had 13 years of telecommunications liberalisation, with the result that it has a large number of carriers in each market segment. More importantly, except in the local market, the new common carriers have a relatively strong market share. It is expected that the level of competition will increase with the elimination of the tariff approval system and foreign ownership restrictions on Type 1 carriers. Furthermore, the presence of many major global telecommunications companies ensures high-quality competition among players.

Although carriers are experiencing difficulties to combine Type 1 and Type 2 services within a single company structure, there is no line-of business restrictions except those imposed on NTT. The revision of the NTT Law and the repeal of the KDD Law make it possible for all carriers to enter all telecommunications markets without restriction. In addition, CATV operators are allowed to provide their telephony services using their own networks. Together with the development of technologies which enable companies to provide less expensive local access through wireless local loops, the use of CATV networks for telecommunications will lead to increased network capacity, suitable for delivering multimedia and Internet services to end users.

There has been significant growth in mobile and CATV subscribers. Many young people choose a mobile phone not as a complement to a fixed telephone but as a substitute. CATV companies are attracting customers with new networks that can be used for telecommunication purposes. Furthermore, utility-based Type 1 carriers are beginning to compete in the local market. It is expected that the combination of these developments will enable users to enjoy more choice in all types of telecommunications services, including local voice telephony.

While Japan has liberalised its telecommunications market as early as 1985, most of the important liberalisation measures have been adopted very recently. In fact, the liberalisation has accelerated since the establishment of the second reform plan in 1996. Based on the second reform plan, many important liberalisation measures have been implemented in favour of full-fledged competition in the telecommunications market. Indeed, the recent introduction of tariff notification system is an important sign of changes moving toward full-fledged competition.

Box 7. **Weaknesses**

- Carrier classification system and market entry procedure.
- Difficulties in access to rights of way.
- Ownership and structure of NTT.
- No transparent spectrum allocation method for selecting licensees when the number of applicants exceed the available licenses.
- Lack of essential regulatory safeguards such as number portability and carrier pre-selection.
- No universal service funding mechanism.
- Combination of regulatory and industry promotion function.

Despite early liberalisation of the telecommunications market in 1985, there are still some regulatory problems. If not successfully addressed, they will impede the development of fair competition between the incumbents and new entrants. Consequently, users will not be fully benefited until these problems are resolved.

a) MPT has authority to grant Type 1 licences and to refuse Special Type 2 registrations by the examination standards that are based on the public interest provisions in the TBL. Furthermore, the regulatory distinction between Type 1 carriers and Type 2 carriers imposes many unnecessary burdens on carriers.

b) Fragmented regulations on rights of way prevent new entrants from constructing their own infrastructure and give an unfair advantage to the incumbents and utility-based Type 1 carriers.

c) Foreign ownership restriction on NTT still exists. In addition, mandatory minimum one-third government ownership of NTT raises a problem of conflict of interest, given that the government is both shareholder and regulator.

d) The holding company structure of NTT will restricts effective infrastructure competition between NTT East and NTT West.

e) The lack of a transparent and fair spectrum allocation method prevents companies from competing on a level playing field.

f) The lack of essential regulatory safeguards such as number portability and carrier pre-selection gives an unfair advantage to the incumbents and the early NCCs.

g) The lack of a universal service funding mechanism makes it difficult to prevent cross-subsidisation of NTT's services.

h) Since the regulatory body's independence can be effectively ensured only when it is separated from interested parties, MPT's responsibilities both on regulatory function and industry promotion function weaken the independence of regulatory function in the Japanese telecommunications sector.

4.2. Potential benefits and costs of further regulatory reform

In general, in spite of recent regulatory developments, Japan has yet to complete the reforms in its regulatory framework that would facilitate the transition from a monopoly to a competitive telecommunications market. As described in Section 4.1, outstanding regulatory issues need to be addressed appropriately and promptly if the benefits of competition are to be realised. While Japan has already taken a big step by abolishing the tariff approval system in favour of free price competition, many essential regulatory safeguards are not in place yet. Unless MPT makes swift actions to implement such safeguards, competition will continue to develop slowly.

However, if MPT makes the necessary changes, the impact could be significant thanks to an already developed market structure. It is important to ensure that market participants compete effectively in the market and that such competition is not constrained by MPT. It is suggested that Japan consider the following recommendations.

4.3. Policy recommendations

Ensure that regulations and regulatory processes are transparent and non-discriminatory and applied effectively

- *Establish effective government-wide measures, which resolve access to rights of way problems for new entrants in order to promote facility-based competition.*

The Japanese government should provide effective measures for resolving carriers' difficulties related to access to rights of way due to the fragmented responsibilities for rights of way. In particular, it would be recommended to enhance transparency of rights of way regulation by publishing a guideline to access rights of way just as market access. *Implement the LRIC methodology as soon as possible as a means of ensuring more cost-oriented interconnection pricing.*

Since the ABC accounting system is based on historical cost, new entrants face high interconnection charges. This prevents them from offering low-cost services to customers. Although MPT has already decided to submit the bill to the Diet in 2000 in order to introduce the LRIC method, the implementation timetable should be accelerated in order to ensure more cost-oriented pricing.

- *MPT should establish as rapidly as possible a transparent and fair spectrum allocation method to select licensees when applicants outnumber licenses in order to ensure that all applicants can compete fairly when applying for a mobile license.*

The lack of a transparent spectrum allocation method to select licensees when applicants outnumber licenses is a significant weakness of the Japanese telecommunications regulatory regime. Although MPT is considering introducing a new spectrum allocation method, it is not decided which method will be adopted and what the criteria will be for selecting new licensees. To ensure a fair chance to all potential entrants, the new spectrum allocation method should be in place in time for the allocation of spectrum for IMT 2000 services.

- *MPT should rapidly implement number portability and carrier pre-selection to ensure fair competition between current players and new entrants.*

The lack of number portability and carrier pre-selection gives an unfair advantage to the incumbent and to some extent to the early NCCs. MPT should promptly introduce these regulatory safeguards, which are essential to fair competition. Mobile services should be included in the number portability plan, and consumers should have sufficient carrier pre-selection choices to ensure fair competition between new entrants and current players.

Reform regulations to stimulate competition, and eliminate them except where clear evidence demonstrates that they are the best way to serve the broad public interest

- *To promote competition, the present carrier market entry requirements should be made simpler and more transparent.*

Under the TBL, the Minister has authority to grant Type 1 and to refuse Special Type 2 licenses using examination standards based on the public interest provisions in the TBL. Furthermore, carriers are not allowed to combine Type 1 business and Type 2 business. These regulations impose unnecessary economic burdens on carriers. MPT should abolish the current market entry scheme and establish a simple and transparent scheme such as 'class licence' system for all carriers.

- *The requirement of partial government ownership on NTT should be lifted so as to eliminate any conflict of interest by having the government as both a regulator and a shareholder.*

The NTT Law requires the government to hold one-third or more of NTT shares. As competition develops, the basis of regulation for NTT should move from treating it as a special company to using market power criteria and treating the company as a dominant player, which controls essential facilities. In this regard, ownership restrictions on NTT should be removed and it is also recommended that the Japanese government move faster towards full privatisation of NTT. In addition, current foreign ownership restriction also should be lifted.

- *A transparent universal service funding mechanism, that is competitive and technologically neutral, should be established.*

Current universal service obligations on NTT are implicitly funded through cross-subsidisation of NTT's services and make it difficult for NTT to establish cost-based charges for its services. Furthermore, the lack of an explicit universal service funding mechanism is one reason for high interconnection charges. Universal service cost should be transparent and clearly separated from interconnection charges. In this context, it is essential to establish a transparent and competitively and technologically neutral universal service funding mechanism in line with the break-up of NTT and the introduction of the LRIC system.

Review, and strengthen where necessary, the scope, effectiveness and enforcement of competition policy

- *As competition develops, the role of competition law in the telecommunications market should be strengthened, and sector specific regulation should be reviewed periodically in order to streamline the regulation.*

MPT should forebear from regulation in areas or for activities where sufficient competition has emerged and conditions will allow the development of effective and sustainable competition between carriers. Excessive sector-specific regulation on carriers may hamper development of the full benefits of competition. Periodic reviews of regulation to determine where streamlining can take place should be undertaken. It is recommended that all market players should be able to request streamlining reviews.

- *Options for making the NTT regional companies fully independent should be reviewed, because infrastructure competition between NTT regional companies appears unlikely develop under common ownership.*

The break-up of NTT is consistent with competition in the local market to the extent to that other competitors enter the market, but the holding company structure means that the NTT companies do not have strong incentives to compete against each other and have no incentive to enter into infrastructure competition. Thus, the benefits of divestiture may not be fully realised. The Japanese government should review the current holding company structure, making the NTT regional companies fully independent of each other, in order to realise the benefits of divestiture.

- *Regulatory functions should be independent from industry promotion functions, with transparent procedures and the process for the review of decisions.*

353

Both as a regulator and a policy maker, MPT is responsible for consumer protection as well as industry promotion in the telecommunications sector. Since the regulatory body's independence can be effectively ensured only when it is separated from interested parties, the Japanese government needs to ensure greater separation of regulatory functions from industry promotion functions.

NOTES

1. OECD, *Communications Outlook* 1999. The United States is the world's biggest market with total revenue of $254.6 billion.

2. NTT's revenue includes NTT DoCoMo's revenue.

3. OECD, *Communications Outlook* 1999.

4. Telecommunications operators which provide telecommunications services by establishing their own circuits and facilities.

5. The government issued the first block of 200 000 shares at 1 197 392 yen each in October 1986. It planned to sell one-half of the shares in four equal blocks annually beginning in 1986, but only sold part of the third block in 1988 due to the sharp drop in the stock price, and then postponed further sales. It is planned to sell 1 million shares in December 1998.

6. Deregulation, promotion of network interconnection and NTT's reorganisation are the three main goals of the "second info-communications reform".

7. The following provisions were deleted:
   − Article 10 (1): Telecommunications services shall be appropriate in the light of the demand.
   − Article 10 (2): Telecommunications circuit facilities shall not result in significant excess.

8. The abolition of the KDD Law was based on the "Emergency Economic Policy Package Reforming Japan for the 21st Century" which was adopted at a Cabinet Meeting on Economic Measures in November 1997. The package also included other telecommunications related issues such as:
   − reducing the scope of Special Type 2 carrier;
   − enabling Type 2 carrier to establish subscriber transmission circuit facilities which connect only one user;
   − reduction of Type 1 and Type 2 carrier categories to three (previously seven categories for Type 1 and four for Type 2);
   − abolition of the tariff approval system and introduction of the notification system.

9. There are ten market blocks: Hokkaido, Tohoku, Kanto, Tokai, Hokuriku, Kansai, Chugoku, Shikoku, Kyushu and Okinawa.

10. FTC pointed out that without further deregulation and equalisation of conditions for competition the break-up of NTT would not be effective in promoting competition in the entire telecommunications industry.

11. The NTT trade union intensely lobbied politicians against Council's break-up proposal. In fact, the Social Democratic Party took an official position against the break-up. It was very difficult for the Liberal Democratic Party to make a firm commitment due to the upcoming election.

12. Throughout the paper, the term NCCs stands for the original new common carriers in the long distance market (DDI, Japan Telecom and Teleway Japan) and in the international market (ITJ and IDC).

13. In addition, TBL Article 1 states that the purpose of the law is "… to ensure the proper and reasonable operation of telecommunications business, to secure the consistent provision of telecommunications services, and to protect the interests of its users, and thereby guarantee the sound development of telecommunications for the convenience of the public, and the promotion of public welfare."

14. In December 1980, the United States and Japan signed the first NTT Procurement Agreement.

15. There are ten market blocks (see note 10).

16. *Communications Outlook* 1999.

17. The Japanese Government announced the abolition of foreign ownership restriction on CATV companies by the end of 1998 based on the New Three-Year Deregulation Action Plan (March 1998).

18. Age distribution of cellular and PHS users.

Percentage, as of March 1997

	9	10-14	15-19	20-29	30-39	40-49	50-59	60	No response
Cellular	0.9	0.5	4.1	30.5	21.0	21.2	11.8	4.6	5.3
PHs	0.3	1.2	18.3	28.7	16.7	13.7	8.0	7.1	5.9

Source: MPT.

19. MPT, 1998 *White Paper Communications in Japan*.

20. MPT, 1998 *White Paper Communications in Japan*.

21. *Communications Outlook* 1999.

22. MPT, 1998 *White Paper Communications in Japan*.

23. Article 94 of TBL stipulates 21 specific cases in which the Minister should consult with Council before taking its decision.

24. MPT uses the examination standards when it decides whether applicants meet public interest provisions in the TBL.

25. Examination standards: 1. Regarding financial basis and technical capability to undertake telecommunications business, *a*) whether the fund raising plan for such telecommunications business by the applicant is drafted in a rational manner, *b*) whether the repayment plan for such telecommunications business by the applicant is drafted in a rational manner, *c*) whether necessary chief telecommunications engineer are supposed to be appointed in accordance with Article 3 of the "Regulations for Chief Telecommunications Engineer", by the commencement of telecommunications business. 2. Regarding reliable and feasible business plan, *a*) whether the applicant's estimated revenues and expenditure are calculated in a proper and clear-cut manner, and whether these estimates are drafted in a rational manner, *b*) whether the procurement of land sites, buildings and other plants for establishing telecommunications facilities can be expected, *c*) whether the applicant's plan for establishing telecommunications facilities and for delineating the area of operation are stipulated appropriately. 3. Regarding entry into the telecommunications business should be appropriate for the sound development of telecommunications, whether the applicant's commencement of telecommunications business impedes fair competition, and also whether the healthy development of telecommunications is promoted in line with the objectives of the law without detriment to the interests of the users and the benefit of the public.

26. They are Councillor's office on Internal Affairs of Cabinet Secretariat, Fair Trade Commission, National Police Agency, Economic Planning Agency, Ministry of Justice, Ministry of Foreign Affairs, Ministry of Finance, Ministry of Health and Welfare, Ministry of International Trade and Industry, Ministry of Transport, Ministry of Posts and Telecommunications and Ministry of Construction.

27. This refers to companies such as electricity companies, water companies, etc., that have ducts or rights of way owing to the nature of the services they provide.

28. While the fee for using one NTT pole is fixed at 1 600 yen per year, the fee for using NTT's conduits is calculated individually. In terms of electric utility companies, they calculate the fees individually.

29. There is no standard processing period for facility sharing.

30. The NTT Law prevents NTT from providing CATV service.

31. The interconnection obligation of Type 1 carriers can be exempted when:

– there is concern regarding the smooth delivery of telecommunications services;

– there is concern that the interconnection may materially impair the interest of Type 1 telecommunications carrier;

– legitimate reasons are provided by applicable MPT ordinances except for the cases specified in the preceding two cases.

32. More specifically, the scope of major designated facilities covers designated subscriber line transmission facilities, and intra-prefecture facilities for telephone, ISDN and leased lines (MPT notice No. 674, 24 December 1997).

33. Six standard points of interconnection are:

– subscriber line end;

– transmission equipment for access line;

- transmission equipment for local switch;
- transmission equipment for signalling tandem switch;
- transmission equipment for tandem switch;
- transmission equipment for tandem leased-line node equipment.

34. There are eleven unbundled functions:

- subscriber line transmission;
- local switching;
- ISM switching;
- local transmission;
- tandem switching;
- interoffice transmission;
- signal transmission;
- directory assistance service access;
- directory database access;
- operator assistance service;
- public telephone origination.

35. By the Interconnection Accounting Rules and Interconnection Cost Calculation Rules, the following costs are included in the interconnection charges:

- sales costs (interconnection-related only);
- operation costs;
- facility maintenance costs;
- common management costs;
- R&D costs (infrastructure-related only);
- fixed-asset retirement costs;
- depreciation costs;
- taxes and public dues;
- borrowed capital costs;
- equity capital costs;
- taxes related to profits.

36. Access charge = charge proportional to number of calls + charge proportional to time (cost of interconnection charges corresponding to traffic).

37. Network modification charge = annual charge (settled by calendar month).

38. *Communications Outlook* 1999.

39. According to the Radio Law, a license is given on a first-come first-served basis. After receiving an application, the Minister examines whether the application satisfies: 1) conformity of the construction design to the technical standards; 2) feasibility of frequencies being assigned; and 3) conformity of other particulars to the essential standards for the establishment of a radio station. When the application meets all requirements, the Minister gives the applicant a pre-permit. When a carrier with a pre-permit completes the construction of a radio station, the Minister grants a license based on its inspection of the radio equipment, the qualifications for radio operators as well as number of operators, timepieces and documents.

40. *Keidanren*, "Problems in Promoting Competition in the Information Communication Market", 1996.

41. According to "The Basic Guideline for Introducing the Third Generation Mobile Communications System (IMT 2000)", Japan will introduce IMT 2000 service in 2001. Three licenses will be granted based on applications from all interested parties. However, operators owning local telecommunications networks cannot provide IMT 2000 service by themselves.

42. Number portability is the term used to describe the ability of customers to retain their telephone number if they change service supplier.

43. Main points of the report:

- Coverage of carrier pre-selection: domestic and international calls originating from networks of regional NTT companies, except for those calls destined for cellular/PHS phones.

- Service categories: Local (intra-city) calls, inter-city calls within a prefecture, inter-prefecture calls and international calls.
- Registration method: It is required for users to register their carriers of choice to the regional NTT company. If not, they are regarded as having chosen NTT by default.

44. For example, the United States includes discounts to assist schools and libraries to connect to the "Information Superhighway" together with fixed voice telephony services.

45. The Study Group for Research into Universal Services and Rates in the Multimedia Age, chaired by professor Emeritus Yukihide Okano of the University of Tokyo, submitted its report to MPT on 31 May 1996. This study group was formed in October 1994.

46. The above-mentioned study group recommended a universal service fund as a mechanism to ensure access to multimedia services for Japanese society.

47. According to the definition of Japan's reference paper in the WTO agreement on basic telecommunication services, the regulatory body is separate from, and not accountable to, any supplier of basic telecommunications services. The decisions of and the procedures used by regulators shall be impartial with respect to all market participants.

48. In October 1997, FTC ordered Tohoku Cellular to remove restrictions on the indication of price on mobile phone handsets. In November 1997, FTC ordered mobile companies (NTT DoCoMo, Tokyo Digital Phone and TU-Ka Cellular Tokyo) to remove price restrictions on mobile phone handsets.

49. For example, the US Telecommunications Act requires FCC to have biannual review on its regulation.

OECD PUBLICATIONS, 2, rue André-Pascal, 75775 PARIS CEDEX 16
PRINTED IN FRANCE
(42 1999 01 1 P) ISBN 92-64-17061-8 — No. 50695 1999